Producing Indonesia

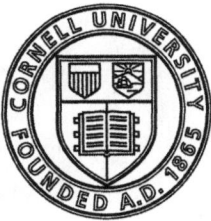

Cornell University

Eric Tagliacozzo, Editor

Producing Indonesia
The State of the
Field of Indonesian Studies

SOUTHEAST ASIA PROGRAM PUBLICATIONS
Southeast Asia Program
Cornell University
Ithaca, New York
2014

SEAP

Cornell Southeast Asia Program Publications
640 Stewart Avenue, Ithaca, NY 14850-3857

Cornell Modern Indonesia Project No. 76

ISBN: hc 978-0-87727-325-7
ISBN: pb 978-0-87727-302-8

Cover: designed by Kat Dalton

TABLE OF CONTENTS

ACKNOWLEDGMENTS

The title of "Producing Indonesia" for this volume is used with some trepidation. As a collective of some two dozen scholars of the country, spread across six disciplines, we know of course that we are not "producing" a nation that has (in fact) produced itself, through indigenous hands, over many years. In this sense, therefore, the title of our combined efforts in book form is meant in an ironic sense. But we do acknowledge that the production of knowledge about a place happens all the time, and that we as academic interpreters of the country play a part in that dialectic. In the pages that follow, a number of scholarly visions of the state of the field of Indonesian Studies are on view, as articulated by senior practitioners of this process. Many people need to be thanked for making this effort come to fruition. Thak Chaloemtiarana and Tamara Loos, former directors of Cornell's Southeast Asia Program, both helped make this volume and the conference that preceded it a reality, through their encouragement and their allocation of programmatic funds. Neither would have happened without their support. We are also very much indebted to the staff of SEAP, particularly Nancy Loncto and Wendy Treat, who aided enormously in the logistics for this project. In addition to the Cornell professors who served as discussants for the six sub-sections of the book here, our colleague Andrew Willford gave of his time and expertise at the conference, and through his careful critique of the papers on his panel. Deborah Homsher and Fred Conner at SEAP Publications helped usher the volume through the publication process, and were guardian angels in helping all appear in print. Fred Logevall and the Einaudi Center at Cornell also provided much needed financial support. Finally, Anto Mohsin, a graduate student in Science and Technology Studies at Cornell, kindly served as chronicler of the conference, and prepared an impressive sheaf of notes on the proceedings. We thank all of these people and institutions in helping us to realize this book project. We hope this volume will usher in a new stage in the evolution of Cornell's Modern Indonesia Project (CMIP), active since the 1950s in Ithaca, and will help launch a series of planned volumes on the breadth and depth of Indonesian Studies in the years to come.

— Eric Tagliacozzo

Introduction: The State of the Field of Indonesian Studies

Eric Tagliacozzo

In late April 2011 an extraordinary gathering was convened at Cornell University in Ithaca, New York. The meeting focused around the "State of Indonesian Studies" (the gathering's putative title), and eighteen senior scholars, scattered across six disciplinary fields and from literally all over the world, were flown in to spend a long weekend at the Kahin Center for Advanced Research on Southeast Asia. To our knowledge, a conference of this kind had never been attempted before—one that gathered many of the world's senior Indonesianists, representing many disciplines, into one room to talk with one another about the arc, breadth, and health of our common field. Cornell's Modern Indonesia Project faculty (CMIP[1]) hosted this event with humility, because it was really fortunate for us that so many top scholars took time out of their busy schedules, during the height of the teaching term, to come to Ithaca (as some say, the "most centrally isolated place in the United States") to be with us for those two days. Yet we also did this with pride, because Cornell has played a special role in building Indonesian Studies, not just in America, but in the world at large, a fact that comes out clearly from many of the papers assembled here.

This project of "building something sturdy in the field" was not accomplished by the generation of Cornell faculty members running the conference. Rather, it was done by an older generation (actually, several older generations now) of professors who have trained a large number of the specialists from around the world who continue to try to explain Indonesia as an entity across a large number of fields. So it seemed fitting that the meeting was held in Ithaca, and, at the same time, it was also fitting that when one looked out over the assembled audience, there were, in fact, a number of intellectual traditions representing various genealogies of knowledge on Indonesia. These were from Cornell, but also from Yale University (New Haven CT), Brown University (Providence, RI), the universities of Wisconsin (Madison, WI), Washington (Seattle, WA), and Michigan (Ann Arbor, MI), and the University of

[1] The Cornell Modern Indonesia Project was initiated in 1956 with translations of significant documents and literature concerned with (then) modern Indonesia. Over the years, the program resulted in translations of primary source materials as well as original studies of Indonesia's political events and the evolution of its history and government up through the end of the twentieth century.

California–Santa Cruz, for example. They were also from a number of traditions outside of the United States, including the Netherlands, the United Kingdom, Australia, and, perhaps most importantly of all, from Indonesia itself. And this, certainly, is a good thing. It leads one to suppose that the bloodlines have been mixing, and that the state of the organism, at least from a genetic point of view, is healthy in that our collective parentage is mixed, and will mix further in the future.

What we hope happened over the two days of the conference is that we received some ideas from all those assembled, individually and collectively, in answer to Gauguin's famous three questions: Who are we? Where do we come from? Where are we going? We feel this volume helps us to know something of the answers to those questions, and debates our gathered responses as much as we are able to do so several decades down the line from the initial founding of CMIP more than fifty years ago. This is important, perhaps especially now, as Indonesia is clearly "moving up in the world" and is becoming a place that seems more and more to be on the agendas of the wealthy, the powerful, and of influential states in global circles. We hope that these essays are able to tell us all something of the focus and direction of Indonesian Studies writ large, as well as from the perspectives of individual disciplines—anthropology, art, history, linguistics, government, and music. We are publishing here what we learned over the course of the conference so that not only those who took part in the meeting may benefit from the discussion, but also the wider public at large can benefit from this exercise in "taking stock." We hope that this first volume, a broad and diffuse attempt at measuring where we are, will be followed by others more closely focused on the individual academic disciplines represented below, so that we may extend this conversation to a larger group of scholars as finances and time commitments allow.

* * *

Anthropology. Marina Welker and Andrew Willford got us started by chairing the anthropology panel, which opened the proceedings. Welker is the author of several important articles on a US mining company in rural Indonesia that have been published in top-shelf ethnographic journals in the field over the past several years.[2] She was asked to introduce the papers of the assembled anthropologists and to provide some shape and context to their contributions as a whole. The first of these essays was by Danilyn Rutherford, the Chair of the Anthropology Department at the University of California, Santa Cruz. Rutherford's work has been focused mostly on the Indonesian province of West Papua, or what was formerly called Irian Jaya, the western half of the island of New Guinea. She has been concerned with both nationalism and the problem of audience in this unstable, often marginalized place.[3]

---

[2] For Marina Welker, see, for example, "The Green Revolution's Ghost: Unruly Subjects of Participatory Development in Rural Indonesia," *American Ethnologist* 39,2 (2012): 389–406; and "Corporate Security Begins in the Community: Mining, the Corporate Social Responsibility Industry, and Environmental Advocacy in Indonesia," *Cultural Anthropology* 24,1 (2009): 142–79. Andrew Willford, a Malaysianist by training, helped us enormously in co-chairing the panel, but, by agreement with Marina Welker, left the essay here for her to produce.

[3] See Danilyn Rutherford's two influential monographs, *Raiding the Land of the Foreigners: The Limits of the Nation on an Indonesian Frontier* (Princeton, NJ: Princeton University Press, 2003); and *Laughing at Leviathan: Sovereignty and Audience in West Papua* (Chicago, IL: University of Chicago Press, 2012).

Rutherford argues that the "mysterious" is a spectral presence in many of the best ethnographies about Indonesia; both strange, unexplained occurrences and people who seem to be beyond easy definition or definite placement in categories hover in standout ethnographies of this part of the world. This is important, because Indonesia during anthropology's coming-of-age period from the mid-1960s to nearly the end of the 1990s was ruled by the New Order state, a regime that had a real stake in the "mysterious" in certain ineffable ways. The New Order engaged in rigorous taxonomy and classification of its subjects to enforce its police-state structure. But, at the same time, it kept things "mysterious" and vague when it needed to, in order to deny Indonesians clarity in the processes that kept them as ruled subjects of a coercive apparatus. Rutherford explores this dichotomy in interesting and provocative ways in her contribution, maintaining this tension throughout the arc of her piece.

"A Dayak with Earrings and a Lance, SE Borneo, circa 1920," with permission

Ken George, formerly chair of the Anthropology Department at the University of Wisconsin, Madison, and since decamped to the Australian National University, writes about another form of the mysterious, that is, translation in its many forms. George has been instrumental in translating Indonesian life-ways, first with regard to headhunting in Sulawesi, and, more recently, with regard to Indonesian Islamic art through his study of an important modern painter in the archipelago.[4] George is interested in the ways that information on Indonesia is translated and packaged for the outside world—including by ethnographers. He laments in his essay the lack of

---

[4] See Kenneth M. George, *Showing Signs of Violence: The Cultural Politics of a Twentieth-Century Headhunting Ritual* (Berkeley, CA: University of California Press, 1996) and *Picturing Islam: Art and Ethics in a Muslim Lifeworld* (Malden, MA: Wiley-Blackwell, 2010).

specificity and locality that is often implied in this process, Indonesia being a place where "big concepts" have traveled well, but the actual lived realities—often very difficult ones—have not. George asks why this has been the case, when life on the ground in the country has often been so difficult, certainly in normative times, but particularly so in times of stress and upheaval. He asks for an anthropology of the archipelago that pays more attention to these local situations, and which doesn't only deal with big-picture issues that find eager audiences and welcome receptions when transmitted to the west. Toward this end he hopes for alliances to be forged among the various humanities and social-sciences disciplines, Indonesian subjects, and academic purveyors of knowledge who might be induced to report and translate on the realities for a large, global audience. Indonesians, he notes, deserve to have more known about the daily, lived realities of their struggle in the region.

Finally, Patricia Spyer, of Leiden University, presented a paper that was squared on how violence has been central to Indonesian society, both as a repeatedly recurring episode in various guises, but also in everyday life. Spyer's work is well-known in anthropological circles for its uses of history and circulation in thinking about transmission processes in the archipelago in a variety of ways.[5] Here Spyer explores how anthropologists in Indonesia can (and, she argues, should) use their profession to uncover modalities of violence, which have been nearly omnipresent in Indonesian life-ways for the past several decades. She argues for interrogating this state of affairs from both top-down and bottom-up perspectives. She sees the political history of the New Order as part and parcel of these equations, but she also asks that ethnographers approach the "violence of everyday life" in Indonesia from fieldwork vantages, not just from the realm of state policies and state changes that have riddled the modern history of the nation. As a witness to and interpreter of these processes, she sees symbols of violence in many places scattered across the country, and puts forward a plea that future ethnographers will work to identify and explain these iconographies as part of their work on the ground.

Taken as a set, then, the three anthropological contributions tease out and inform larger trends in the representation of Indonesia as a society ripe to be "known" in divergent ways. The essays have sound internal logics, but are also referential to each other in interesting and complex ways, and provide something of a blueprint for the future, as well as an explication of the past of ethnography in this nation.

* * *

Art History. Anthropology was followed by art history, chaired by Kaja McGowan, who is a specialist on Bali and well-published in this area.[6] Natasha Reichle, of the San Francisco Museum of Asian Art, got us all going with a broad and

---

[5] Three of the more important works in this vein include Patricia Spyer's monograph *The Memory of Trade: Modernity's Entanglements on an Eastern Indonesian Island* (Durham, NC: Duke University Press, 2000) and two edited volumes, *Border Fetishisms: Material Objects in Unstable Spaces* (New York, NY: Routledge, 1998) and *Handbook of Material Culture* (London: Sage, 2006).

[6] See Kaja McGowan's many articles and book chapters, but also *Ida Bagus Made: The Art of Devotion, a Volume Honoring the Fiftieth Anniversary of the Puri Lukisan Museum, Bali, Indonesia* (Denpassar: Yayasan Ratna Wartha [and Honolulu, HI: University of Hawaii Press], 2008).

interesting paper on Indonesian art history.[7] Reichle notes in her piece that Indonesian art history is not a crowded field, as she delicately puts it—there are few monograph-length studies on Indonesian Art when compared to other, more traveled parts of the world. Yet, she manages to ink quite an accomplished list of contributions nevertheless, precisely by opening up what is thought of as "art" and being very inclusive in her designations. So, while she certainly has something to say about the great temple structures of Java, which are recognizable icons of a tradition, she also brings forth the huge and bewilderingly complex category of "objects" as Indonesian art, too, significantly complicating matters. This is art history, but it's also archaeology, and it's anthropology to boot, so she speaks to a number of "allied disciplines." Reichle is nothing if not inclusive in describing what she sees as the "arc of the field," though she is careful to recategorize this definition in ways that suit her. The result is a well-drawn picture of what art not only is, but what it can be in the Indonesian context, across centuries, across geographies, and across disciplines, ultimately, as one tries to sketch a "field." Textiles, gold figurines, temple lintels, and even mundane objects all fall into her ambit, and to ours, to our great profit.

"Bas-Relief on the Borobodur, 1900–1940 Photo," with permission

Ed McKinnon, formerly with the Asia Research Institute in Singapore and also with the UNDP (United Nations Development Programme) in Aceh, delivered a very different kind of paper. McKinnon is one of the best-known archaeologists working on this part of the world. He has been in the field for decades, and has conducted some of the most cutting-edge research on classical-period digs in Indonesia, and

---

[7] Natasha Reichle's two most important contributions are: *Bali: Art, Ritual, Performance* (San Francisco, CA: Asian Art Museum, 2011) and *Violence and Serenity: Late Buddhist Sculpture from Indonesia* (Honolulu, HI: University of Hawaii Press, 2007).

particularly in Sumatra.[8] McKinnon gave a genealogy of archaeological management in Indonesia, parts of which (as a field) stretch back to the Dutch colonial period. He is explicitly interested in the notion of antiquities management as a subset of the larger issue of "cultural preservation," a rubric that is given government sanction in Indonesia and that encompasses, in fact, quite a lot of material on the ground to protect. He is interested in the ways that legal and administrative norms have come together both historically and in the present to create an extremely local–specific milieu for the preservation of archaeological and other monuments, scattered across the width and breadth of the Indonesian archipelago. Since McKinnon has had experience digging and prospecting in many places, he was able to give quite a detailed panorama of how these laws and regulations work in various parts of the archipelago, a subject that he has had to learn in some detail to be able to do what he does for a living. As was true in Reichle's case, there aren't a lot of people squarely situated in this field, but there are enough that the "rules and regs" matter, and their vagaries dictate the kinds of knowledge that can be produced. McKinnon showed this dialectic very clearly in his contribution, and showcased a sub-field of "art history" that often has been shunted to the side in Indonesian Studies, though doing so has been a loss for everyone involved.

Finally, the last art history presentation of the day was delivered by Astri Wright, of the University of Victoria. Wright is the author of noted studies on modern Indonesian art, and she provided a wonderfully different contribution and perspective relative to the more classically inspired Reichle and McKinnon essays.[9] And she did not disappoint on being different, in fact, wowing all present with her never-(ever)-to-be-plagiarized title, "The Arc of my Field is a Rainbow with an Expanding Twist and All Kinds of Creatures Dancing: The Growing Inclusivity of Indonesian Art History." All mirth (and post-modernism) aside, Wright provided an important essay that, in fact, echoed Reichle's in some respects, arguing for a wide interpretation of what Indonesian art history "is," and, perhaps more importantly, what it "can and should be." Crucial to her vision is modern Indonesian art—a notion so new, that it has not really been institutionalized yet in most places as a field of study in any recognizable way. Wright points to the trailblazing work of John Clark, who put modern Southeast Asian Art on the map in some respects, but she is also important in this initiative, and her books have helped pave the way toward new horizons. Wright talks about the place of architecture, the internet, and photography in her essay; this is not "your father's art history," not for this part of the world, to be sure. Yet she filled in a vital lacuna for all present in her analysis, as this newer work is for the most part material that not even most card-carrying Indonesianists know about, regardless of their specialties or disciplines. One can't say that of the Prambanan or of Borobodur, but it certainly seemed the case after we

---

[8] See, for example, two of his books: E. Edward McKinnon, *The Pulau Buaya Wreck: Finds from the Song Period* (Jakarta: Ceramic Society of Indonesia, 1998) and *Kota Cina: Its Context and Meaning in the Trade of Southeast Asia* (Ithaca, NY: Cornell University Southeast Asia Program Publications, 1984).

[9] The two most important works here are Astri Wright's *Soul, Spirit, and Mountain: Preoccupations of Contemporary Indonesian Painters* (Kuala Lumpur: Oxford University Press, 1994) and her coauthored text, with Agus Dermawan, *T. Hendra Gunawan: A Great Modern Indonesian Painter* (Jakarta and Singapore: The Ciputra Foundation and the Archipelago Press, Editions Didier Millet, 2001).

were enlightened about several decades' worth of developments on the newest directions of Indonesian "art."

* * *

History. The day ended not with the future, though, but with the past. Tagliacozzo chaired the history panel,[10] and Rudolf Mrázek, professor of history at the University of Michigan, was the first historian to present a paper to the group. A continuous theme in his essay was the notion of "returns"—he described this concept vis-à-vis several prominent practitioners in the field, who had started with a certain epoch in historical time and then moved outward from there, only to come back at a certain point, as if drawn back in. Cornell's George Kahin was among this group, Mrázek argued, and Kahin's work, particularly, "turned" on the year of 1945, a year that Mrázek calls a "chasm" in modern Indonesian historiography. For Jim Siegel and Ben Anderson, two more Indonesianists in the Cornell tradition who were referenced by Mrázek, neither of them card-carrying historians but both of them crucial for understanding the history of that same nation, 1965 was the "chasm" year, and they both returned to this year in their writings. Anderson had to turn literally away from this "tear" in history because he was banned from entering Indonesia as a result of his writings about 1965's events (Anderson et al., 1966, the so-called "Cornell White Paper"), but the "return" in his mind colored all of his later writing nonetheless. Yet Mrázek sees still other "returns" in the lineages of historical writing about Indonesia in its various schools: via Harry Benda (Yale), Herb Feith (in Australia), and others from various other traditions whom he mentions. These "returns," in fact, created schools to some extent, as temporal spaces were delineated into theaters of knowledge-production, and ultimately adapted conceptually by different lineages of historians of the nation.

Laurie Sears, professor of history at the University of Washington, delivered the next paper. Sears is the author of an oeuvre of work that combines history and the literary into one category; she is equally at home in both genres, and sees important convergences in how the two have mixed in modern Indonesian historiography.[11] In her contribution here, she argues that a circulation and recirculation of texts has been important to the making of modern Indonesian history, both as a field of inquiry and as the lived history of many millions of human beings. She is particularly interested in how Pramoedya—perhaps modern Indonesia's most notable author—fits into this process, through his writings about an important literary/historical figure (that is, an actual person) from the turn of the twentieth century in his fiction. This convergence, among others, serves to push Sears forward in looking at landmark works in the slipstream of Indonesian Studies, a process she describes in some detail in her essay. Edward Said, Benedict Anderson, and Don Emmerson are all identified here, but it is another, less-famous author, the modern feminist Ayu Utami, who emerges as

---

[10] My books encompass the history of smuggling in Indonesia, and also the history of the Hajj in the region. See Eric Tagliacozzo, *Secret Trades, Porous Borders: Smuggling and States Along a Southeast Asian Frontier, 1865–1915* (New Haven, CT: Yale University Press, 2005) and *The Longest Journey: Southeast Asians and the Pilgrimage to Mecca* (New York, NY: Oxford University Press, 2013).

[11] Two of Laurie Sears's most important books are *Shadows of Empire: Colonial Discourse and Javanese Tales* (Durham, NC: Duke University Press, 1996) and *Situated Testimonies: Dread and Enchantment in an Indonesian Literary Archive* (Honolulu, HI: University of Hawaii Press, 2013).

crucial in the unfolding of this discourse, due to the warnings she has bequeathed to the nation. Sears looks at the place of all of these figures in regards to 1965, the "tear" in history that Mrázek had also noted, a year that still haunts the intellectual life of the nation. Her contribution shows how literature and history sustain one another in the Indonesian context, and gives us a genealogy of knowledge with many of the field's major players being brought together in one, syncretic text.

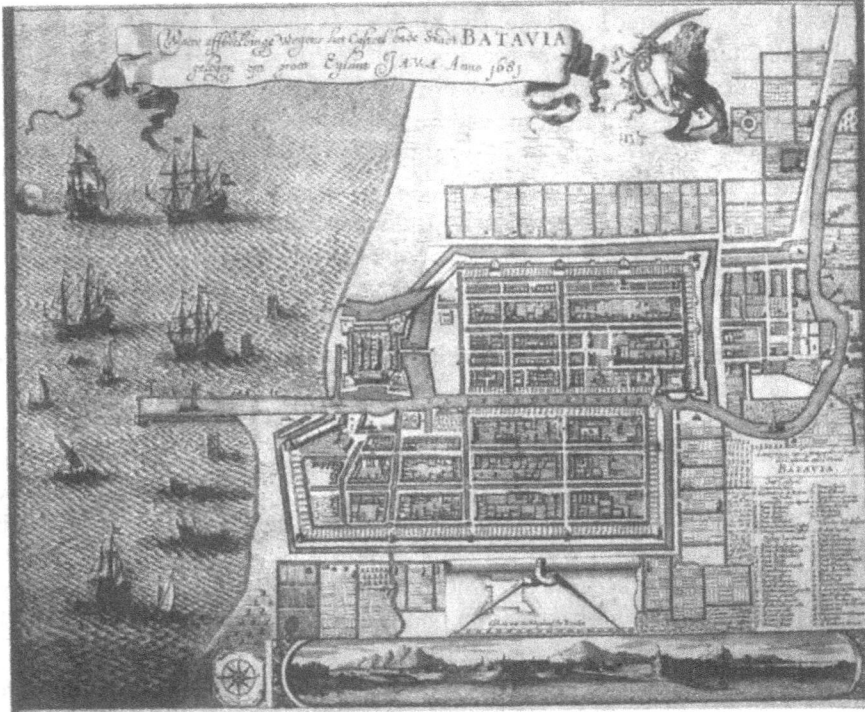

"Map of Batavia and its Citadel, 1681," with permission

Jean Gelman Taylor, of the University of New South Wales, who presented the history panel's last essay, perhaps traveled the farthest of all the participants to be part of the conference. Gelman Taylor is well-known for her early work on the social history of Batavia, but also for her overarching studies of Indonesian history.[12] Like Sears, she is also concerned in her contribution with genealogies, discussing the various *aliran* (or streams) of historical knowledge that came out of Indonesian history traditions in various places over time. Gelman Taylor speaks in depth about the Cornell model, and notes that the "house that Kahin built" from the mid-1950s into the mid-60s marked a time of incredible engagement with Indonesia, as fieldwork was accomplished in large quantities by those affiliated with the Cornell Modern Indonesia Project via the labor of many hands. After 1965, however, much of the CMIP analysis had to be conducted from farther away. Cornell's then-new journal *Indonesia* became one of the main ways to keep track of what was happening in the country and the intellectual trends therein. Gelman Taylor counterposes this

---

[12] See Jean Gelman Taylor, *The Social World of Batavia: European and Eurasian in Dutch Asia* (Madison, WI: University of Wisconsin Press, 1983) and *Indonesia: Peoples and Histories* (New Haven, CT: Yale University Press, 2003), in that order.

history of knowledge production with the "Leiden school" and the founding of the KITLV in 1851, as well as later developments with other knowledge-production sites in Amsterdam, and, ultimately, inside Indonesia itself. In total, she presents a story-arc of how thinking about Indonesia changed over a century and a half of colonialism, war, occupation, and independence, vis-à-vis a number of sites scattered across the world.

* * *

Language, literature. On the second day of the conference, "language and literature" took center-stage for the early morning session. This panel was chaired by Cornell's Abby Cohn (professor of linguistics) and Jolanda Pandin (Cornell lecturer in Indonesian). Both of these scholars have been important in thinking through the more technical aspects of language in Indonesia, though in very different ways.[13] The first presenter on this panel was Joseph Errington, a professor of linguistic anthropology at Yale University and the author of a number of books.[14] Errington argues that Indonesian has been inscribed with a history that seems to make the language the glue of New Order Indonesia. This is an assertion that proclaims Indonesian's institution as the lingua franca in the archipelago as a vital achievement of the Suharto regime. He argues against this vision and suggests, instead, that Indonesian was imposed coercively by Suharto during the New Order, and that it was used by the government to keep the masses pliable and responsive to its dictatorial programs. Rather than seeing the widespread use of Indonesian as something positive, Errington instead examines alternative histories, which challenge the usefulness of Indonesian across the entire archipelago in a post New Order world. He undertakes this examination both at the geographic level (setting trends in places like Java against those in Eastern Indonesia, for example), and on the demographic level (analyzing Indonesian's use in mid-size towns, large cities, and the countryside) to see how shifting the locus of inquiry changes the impressions of linguistic "facts" on the ground.

The second contribution on language is offered by Bambang Kaswanti Purwo, professor of linguistics at Atma Jaya University, Jakarta.[15] Purwo takes issue with the commonly held notion that Indonesian is an easy language to learn, one of the truisms one hears when one takes steps toward learning Bahasa Indonesia either for its own sake, or to do research in this sprawling country of more than seventeen thousand islands. Purwo refutes this notion, and offers instead an essay explaining

---

[13] While Jolanda Pandin attends to the teaching of the language in the classroom, Abigail C. Cohn is the author of many technical linguistic articles on the forms and function of Indonesian and Indonesian languages, linguistically, as well as co-editor (with Cécile Fougeron and Marie K. Huffman) of the *Oxford Handbook of Laboratory Phonology* (Oxford: Oxford University Press, 2012).

[14] See, for example, J. Joseph Errington, *Linguistics in a Colonial World: A Story of Language, Meaning, and Power* (Carlton, Victoria: Blackwell Publishing, 2007), *Shifting Languages: Interaction and Identity in Javanese Indonesia* (New York, NY: Cambridge University Press, 1998), and *Structure and Style in Javanese: A Semiotic View of Linguistic Etiquette* (Philadelphia, PA: University of Pennsylvania Press, 1988).

[15] Purwo is the author of, among other studies, *Panorama Bahasa Nusantara* (Masyarakat Linguistik Ind Rbit Referensia and *Pertemuan Linguistik Lembaga Bahasa Atma Jaya Keenam: Analisis Wacana, Pengajaran Bahasa* (Penerbit Kanisius).

how complex the language is in reality, especially when context and aspect are taken into consideration. A large part of his contribution has to do with "expectation" in Indonesian, and how expectation is built into the discourse of the language in interesting and often very delicate ways. One has to keep an ear finely attuned to these figments of language to really have a chance to grasp meaning across a wide spectrum of intended linguistic variance, he posits. This technical formation is useful in thinking through the basics of a language that is important in studying any and all of the other disciplines mentioned in this volume, from anthropology to history and from the fine arts through all of the social sciences. Students of Bahasa Indonesia will do well to realize that basic competence in this language is far different than actually "understanding Indonesian," a feat that is much more difficult to achieve.

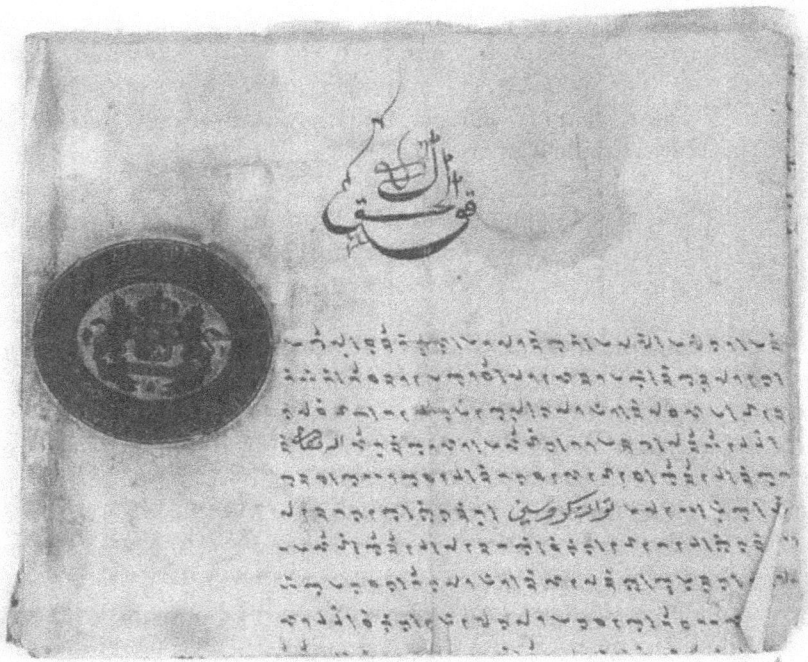

"Act with the Stamp of the Lord of Bone, Sulawesi, 1864," with permission

Tineke Hellwig, of the University of British Columbia, was the last scholar to present on the importance of language in the Indonesian case. Hellwig is a specialist on Indonesian literature, particularly from the colonial period and especially that literature having to do with gender.[16] Hellwig's contribution in this volume is the most encyclopedic of the language and literary offerings. She presents a full menu of attempts to categorize, classify, and explain the literature of the country over the past hundred-plus years, from Dutch colonial times stretching into the near-present. She is interested in showing how the philological origins of "studying Indonesian literature" were formed and developed over time, and how these moved from the colonial situation, where Indonesian literature was examined as a vestige of a

---

[16] See Tineke Hellwig, *Women and Malay Voices: Undercurrent Murmurings in Indonesia's Colonial Past* (New York, NY: Peter Lang, 2012) and *Asian Women: Interconnections* (Toronto: Women's Press, 2006).

classical past, to the post-colonial situation, where living traditions of Indonesian literature received much more attention. A linking theme through the two "fields" is the importance of gender and gendered writing, a string that Hellwig pulls through her analysis to connect the temporally separated fragments into a living whole. Hellwig is hopeful that Indonesian literature has a promising future, as new methodologies are being employed across disciplines now to say novel things about some of the old texts, which were previously thought to have already been adequately "explained." She argues, too, as a number of other authors here across the disciplinary rubrics have done, that translation will be crucial to finding new meanings. As more and more writing from the archipelago makes it out of *"tanah air"* and finds an appreciative and hungry-for-more global audience, this dialectic of translation will assume ever-more importance.

* * *

Government, political science. The Government and Political Science panel was chaired by Tom Pepinsky, who has been innovative in looking at new ways to examine the political economy of this huge, sprawling nation.[17] Edward Aspinall, professor in the Department of Political and Social Change at the Australian National University, kicked things off. His paper describes the tendency for Indonesia-watching political scientists to stick to the "center" in their analysis of changes in the body politic of Indonesia over the past several decades.[18] This cadence in vantage has been useful in some respects in saying "big things" about a big country, but, given the recent turn toward decentralization, this tried-and-true way of examining Indonesia has meant less and less to the ways in which politics affects the lives of most of Indonesia's 200-million-plus people. The genealogy of this sort of research was understandable for more than thirty years because of the ways that the Suharto dictatorship controlled access to the *desas* (villages) by foreign social scientists. That is, macro-approaches were, in many ways, the only game in town to be played, if one wanted to examine Indonesian politics. Yet the national political landscape has changed now in marked ways, and Aspinall argues that political-science research on Indonesia must change with the times, too. His intervention seems timely in that the discipline of political science now seems to be rediscovering the value of field research, sub-national comparisons, and careful data collection, so a re-emphasis on "dirt under the fingernails" research can only be a good thing. Certainly in a place like Indonesia, where model-building has often not worked, or worked very imperfectly, there was a general consensus at the workshop that other approaches need to be tried.

Bill Liddle, professor of politic science at the Ohio State University, took a very different tack in his own presentation. Liddle has been, perhaps, the most visible foreign political scientist in Indonesia itself for the past four decades, someone who

---

[17] See, for example, Thomas B. Pepinsky, *Economic Crises and the Breakdown of Authoritarian Regimes: Indonesia and Malaysia in Comparative Perspective* (Cambridge and New York, NY: Cambridge University Press, 2009), as well as, "Testing Islam's Political Advantage: Evidence from Indonesia," co-authored with R. William Liddle and Saiful Mujani, *American Journal of Political Science* 56, 3 (July 2012).

[18] See Edward Aspinall, *Islam and Nation: Separatist Rebellion in Aceh, Indonesia* (Stanford, CA: Stanford University Press, 2009) and *Opposing Suharto: Compromise, Resistance, and Regime Change in Indonesia* (Stanford, CA: Stanford University Press, 2005).

has been quoted and "made the rounds," so to speak, in Indonesian political circles as a popular and sought-after commentator.[19] Liddle argues here that mainstream methodologies for examining local politics in Indonesia can, in fact, be used to understand Indonesia, despite the distinctiveness of Indonesian politics. He sees structure as being important in any analysis of the Indonesian political scene, but he also sees a range of nonstructural factors as crucial in explaining how politics works on a day-to-day basis. Perhaps because of his extraordinary access over the past several decades, the individual decisions made by specific actors in the Indonesian political pantheon figure heavily in his worldview. Structure is fine, he suggests, and necessary for understanding Indonesian politics, but human choices are also vital in teasing out how and why political processes have unfolded as they have in the making of the Indonesian polity. Though Liddle has ample place in his reasoning for big-picture issues regarding how Indonesia works as a polity in the world, both globally and locally (through religion, trade, and other indices), his heart seems to suggest that individual decision-making counts for at least as much in shaping the politics of the everyday in Indonesian society, and interpretations must acknowledge those divisions.

"President Sukarno looks at the painting 'Sumilah' from the painter Sudibjo during a visit to a painting exhibition in Jakarta, 1945–1952," with permission

Don Emmerson, director of the Southeast Asia Forum at Stanford University and Emeritus Professor of Political Science at the University of Wisconsin, completes this troika of important political thinkers on how Indonesian society may be viewed and described over the past several decades. While both Aspinall and Liddle spend most of their time talking about approaches to Indonesian political science, Emmerson is more interested in delineating schools of specialty within the overall rubric, a useful

---

[19] R. William Liddle is the author of a huge body of articles published in political science and Asian studies journals, and also of *Ethnicity, Party, and National Integration: An Indonesian Case Study* (London and New Haven, CT: Yale University Press, 1970).

complement to the other two papers. Emmerson, like Liddle, has been an exhaustive commentator on the Indonesian political scene for many decades.[20] His contribution here asks whether, in the discipline-bound wars over methodological power and accuracy, political scientists of Indonesia have not lost sight of event-based issues that have been more important than grand theoretical narratives in the quest for explaining long-term processes. With a number of events on the table that can be seen as "seismic" in their relatively recent importance (e.g., the Indonesian Revolution of 1945–49, the 1965 coup that replaced Sukarno with Suharto, and the spectacular fall of the latter in 1998), there seems to be some weight to Emmerson's assertion. Models can often fall apart in the face of such sudden, drastic change; templates may, perhaps, become of less use than careful, on-the-ground study of "what is happening," rather than "what should be happening." Here again, though, the shift in the overall cadence of the discipline dogs the question: if political science is becoming more and more formal and quantitative, how can Indonesia be explained during its turbulent moments when most of the energy to interpret draws on larger theoretical projects? It is a conundrum that all three political scientists identify and grapple with here, with different answers emerging from each.

* * *

Ethnomusicology. The last panel of the workshop focused on ethnomusicology, and was cochaired by Cornell faculty members Marty Hatch and Chris Miller. Hatch has been renown as Cornell's Indonesia-centered ethnomusicologist for many decades, and Chris Miller, a performer of some distinction and an up-and-coming scholar of contemporary directions in Indonesian music, now runs Cornell's highly regarded world-class gamelan ensemble.[21] Marc Perlman, of Brown University, got us started on speaking about some of the traditional lines of Indonesian musicology, a tradition that he has published on in numerous journals, among many other topics.[22] Perlman notes that the study of Indonesian music has often formed along lines that have been well-accepted by the field, in a kind of formal obeisance to the great traditions of Javanese (and to some extent, Balinese) forms that are seen as "classical." These choices have delineated the outlines of the field in certain recognized shapes, and, in fact, are self-perpetuating in that successive generations of students follow, with little or no deviation, those well-worn circuits of study. Despite this tendency, Perlman notes, a number of new developments in Indonesia—most importantly the rise of "popular music," and the dissemination of media meant to distribute it in various forms—has opened the field in new and exciting ways, and in a manner that ethnomusicologists have had to acknowledge in the life-arcs of their

[20] Much of Don Emmerson's work has appeared in journals. See also Donald K. Emmerson, "Inclusive Islamism: The Utility of Diversity," in *Islamism: Contested Perspectives on Political Islam*, ed. Richard C. Martin and Abbas Barzegar (Stanford, CA: Stanford University Press, 2010).

[21] Martin Fellows Hatch was the editor of *Asian Music* from 1985 to 2004 and is on the board of its parent organization, the Society for Asian Music. He also founded the Cornell Gamelan Ensemble, which Christopher J. Miller now directs.

[22] Marc Perlman's scholarly writings have appeared in *Ethnomusicology, Asian Music, Musical Quarterly, Postmodern Culture, Music Perception, Indonesia,* and *Social Studies of Science.* He is also the author of *Unplayed Melodies: Javanese Gamelan and the Genesis of Music Theory* (Berkeley, CA: University of California Press, 2004), which won four prestigious awards.

own work. Perlman is sanguine about this process, even while never letting go of the more traditional forms of the discipline that are still important in studying what "Indonesian music is" in all of its history, diversity, and complexity.

"Bibi Radyah, the First Dancer of the Sultan of Jogja, 1921–26," with permission

One of the most important practitioners and theorists of this body of music has been Sumarsam, for many years resident director of the gamelan ensemble at Wesleyan University (Middletown, CT). Sumarasam is the author of a well-appreciated study on the development of gamelan in Javanese society, now a classic in the field.[23] If Perlman is interested in the effect of the "new music" on some of the classical traditions of Indonesian ethnomusicology, then Sumarsam is an advocate of the roots of the discipline, and he covers a great amount of detail as to how and why Javanese gamelan matters. Javanese gamelan is a field that very, very few know as well as he does, whether on the level of analysis or praxis. His exegesis on this topic goes back to some of the very beginnings of examination in "gamelan studies," indeed, back to colonial Dutch times, but it comes up very close to the present as well, so that the lifespan of the field is evident in his pages. An important current running through this work is the fact that, for the most part, Javanese gamelan has been a non-literate tradition—there are few sources to use in writing much of the history, despite its longevity. Sumarsam deals with this lacuna, and also includes a long explanation of a case that illustrates some of the divided parentage of this

---

[23] See Sumarsam, *Gamelan: Cultural Interaction and Musical Development in Central Java* (Chicago, IL: The University of Chicago Press, 1995).

supposedly epochal Central Javanese tradition, showing its roots in other Indonesian locales. His is an insider's knowledge not only of the history of the discipline, but also of its practice.

Finally, the last presenter was Andrew Weintraub, of the University of Pittsburgh, and author of two important books on popular culture forms in Indonesia.[24] Weintraub is the most prescriptive here of the ethnomusicologists; he not only took a snapshot of where the field has been, but also strongly advocated for the future directions of the collective, in a shape that he felt would benefit the field as a whole. Because Weintraub has been something of a trailblazer in Indonesian popular music studies, it should come as no surprise that he sees this sub-rubric—writ large of course, and inclusive of many genres and types of music—as being the most important vein to mine in the future study of Indonesian ethnomusicology. His is a populist message. It is difficult to argue with his assertion that the sheer numbers of people listening to Indonesian popular music make it important, and perhaps no less important than the more "refined" and "traditional" musical *aliran* outlined by Sumarsam and Perlman in their papers. Weintraub explicitly requires as part of his manifesto that Indonesian music must be taken seriously from outside of its canonical roots, and that this means being open to a wide menu and "playlist," as it were, of new forms. This was a wonderful, inclusive note on which to end. It was one that drew murmurs of agreement from most of those who were present, who clearly saw it as a useful last thought that went beyond ethnomusicology, pertinent and germane to the other disciplines presented at the workshop as well.

● ● ●

The essays in this volume catalogue, critique, and play with much of the humanities and social sciences disciplines that have been important in deconstructing Indonesian society over a long period, for at least the last 150 years. It was around this time, in the mid-nineteenth century or so, that "Indonesian Studies" become something of a nascent academic tradition, with its roots in Holland among the colonial elite, but spreading slowly to other students, outside of the colonizing regime. English, French, American, and Australian streams followed, among numerous others, but the most hopeful signal has been the emergence of critical Indonesian Studies conducted by Indonesians as well, though still in fewer numbers than everyone would like.

We are hopeful as a collective that the volumes that follow this one, each taking on one of the six disciplinary fields discussed here, will record this past and evaluate present trends, and will showcase the kinds of knowledge-production that have emerged across traditions in the deconstruction of this huge and fascinating country. Although we asked eighteen senior figures from six allied fields to come to this initial meeting and present an initial overview, later meetings and subsequent volumes will focus on one field at a time, thereby allowing us to deepen these initial bore-holes, and—we hope—will also include more Indonesian voices in this attempted archaeology as well. That is a project for future days, however. For now,

---

[24] See Andrew N. Weintraub, *Dangdut Stories: A Social and Musical History of Indonesia's Most Popular Music* (Oxford: Oxford University Press, 2010) and *Power Plays: The Wayang Golek Puppet Theater of West Java* (Athens, OH, and Singapore: Ohio University Press and Singapore University Press, 2004), book and CD-ROM.

we present these amended essays from the initial "State of Indonesian Studies" conference as a beginning, to outline what has been accomplished and what is still being attempted across the spectrum of the field. It was a great pleasure to host this first conference and we look forward to convening the next ones in the days to come.

Works Cited

Anderson, Benedict R. O'G. and Ruth T. McVey, with Frederick P. Bunnell. *A Preliminary Analysis of the October 1, 1965, Coup in Indonesia*. Ithaca, NY: Cornell Southeast Asia Program Publications, January 1966.

Aspinall, Edward. *Opposing Suharto: Compromise, Resistance, and Regime Change in Indonesia*. Stanford, CA: Stanford University Press, 2005.

——. *Islam and Nation: Separatist Rebellion in Aceh, Indonesia*. Stanford, CA: Stanford University Press, 2009.

Cohn, Abigail C., Cécile Fougeron, and Marie K. Huffman, eds. *Oxford Handbook of Laboratory Phonology*. Oxford: Oxford University Press, 2012.

Emmerson, Donald K. "Inclusive Islamism: The Utility of Diversity." *Islamism: Contested Perspectives on Political Islam*, ed. Richard C. Martin and Abbas Barzegar. Stanford, CA: Stanford University Press, 2010.

Errington, J. Joseph. *Structure and Style in Javanese: A Semiotic View of Linguistic Etiquette*. Philadelphia, PA: University of Pennsylvania Press, 1988.

——. *Shifting Languages: Interaction and Identity in Javanese Indonesia*. New York, NY: Cambridge University Press, 1998.

——. *Linguistics in a Colonial World: A Story of Language, Meaning, and Power*. Carlton, Victoria: Blackwell Publishing, 2007.

George, Kenneth M. *Showing Signs of Violence: The Cultural Politics of a Twentieth-Century Headhunting Ritual*. Berkeley, CA: University of California Press, 1996.

——. *Picturing Islam: Art and Ethics in a Muslim Lifeworld*. Malden, MA: Wiley-Blackwell, 2010.

Hellwig, Tineke. *Asian Women: Interconnections*. Toronto: Women's Press, 2006.

——. *Women and Malay Voices: Undercurrent Murmurings in Indonesia's Colonial Past*. New York, NY: Peter Lang, 2012.

Liddle, R. William. *Ethnicity, Party, and National Integration: An Indonesian Case Study*. London and New Haven, CT: Yale University Press, 1970.

McGowan, Kaja. *Ida Bagus Made: The Art of Devotion, a Volume Honoring the Fiftieth Anniversary of the Puri Lukisan Museum, Bali, Indonesia*. Denpassar: Yayasan Ratna Wartha [and Honolulu, HI: University of Hawaii Press], 2008.

McKinnon, E. Edward. *Kota Cina: Its Context and Meaning in the Trade of Southeast Asia*. Ithaca, NY: Cornell University Southeast Asia Program Publications, 1984.

——. *The Pulau Buaya Wreck: Finds from the Song Period*. Jakarta: Ceramic Society of Indonesia, 1998.

Pepinsky, Thomas B. *Economic Crises and the Breakdown of Authoritarian Regimes: Indonesia and Malaysia in Comparative Perspective*. Cambridge and New York, NY: Cambridge University Press, 2009.

Pepinsky, Thomas B., R. William Liddle, and Saiful Mujani. "Testing Islam's Political Advantage: Evidence from Indonesia. *American Journal of Political Science* 56.3 (July 2012).

Perlman, Marc. *Unplayed Melodies: Javanese Gamelan and the Genesis of Music Theory.* Berkeley, CA: University of California Press, 2004.

Purwo. *Panorama Bahasa Nusantara.* Masyarakat Linguistik Ind Rbit Referensia.

——. *Pertemuan Linguistik Lembaga Bahasa Atma Jaya Keenam: Analisis Wacana, Pengajaran Bahasa.* Penerbit Kanisius.

Reichle, Natasha. *Violence and Serenity: Late Buddhist Sculpture from Indonesia.* Honolulu, HI: University of Hawaii Press, 2007.

——. *Bali: Art, Ritual, Performance.* San Francisco, CA: Asian Art Museum, 2011.

Rutherford, Danilyn. *Raiding the Land of the Foreigners: The Limits of the Nation on an Indonesian Frontier.* Princeton, NJ: Princeton University Press, 2003.

——. *Laughing at Leviathan: Sovereignty and Audience in West Papua.* Chicago, IL: University of Chicago Press, 2012.

Sears, Laurie. *Shadows of Empire: Colonial Discourse and Javanese Tales.* Durham, NC: Duke University Press, 1996.

——. *Situated Testimonies: Dread and Enchantment in an Indonesian Literary Archive.* Honolulu, HI: University of Hawaii Press, 2013.

Spyer, Patricia. *Border Fetishisms: Material Objects in Unstable Spaces.* New York, NY: Routledge, 1998.

——. *The Memory of Trade: Modernity's Entanglements on an Eastern Indonesian Island.* Durham, NC: Duke University Press, 2000.

——. *Handbook of Material Culture.* London: Sage, 2006.

Sumarsam. *Gamelan: Cultural Interaction and Musical Development in Central Java.* Chicago, IL: The University of Chicago Press, 1995.

Tagliacozzo, Eric. *Secret Trades, Porous Borders: Smuggling and States Along a Southeast Asian Frontier, 1865–1915.* New Haven, CT: Yale University Press, 2005.

——. *The Longest Journey: Southeast Asians and the Pilgrimage to Mecca.* New York, NY: Oxford University Press, 2013.

Taylor, Jean Gelman. *The Social World of Batavia: European and Eurasian in Dutch Asia.* Madison, WI: University of Wisconsin Press, 1983.

——. *Indonesia: Peoples and Histories.* New Haven, CT: Yale University Press, 2003).

Weintraub, Andrew N. *Power Plays: The Wayang Golek Puppet Theater of West Java.* Athens, OH, and Singapore: Ohio University Press and Singapore University Press, 2004, book and CD-ROM.

——. *Dangdut Stories: A Social and Musical History of Indonesia's Most Popular Music.* Oxford: Oxford University Press, 2010.

Welker, Marina. "Corporate Security Begins in the Community: Mining, the Corporate Social Responsibility Industry, and Environmental Advocacy in Indonesia." *Cultural Anthropology* 24.1 (2009): 142–79.

——. "The Green Revolution's Ghost: Unruly Subjects of Participatory Development in Rural Indonesia." *American Ethnologist* 39.2 (2012): 389–406.

Wright, Astri. *Soul, Spirit, and Mountain: Preoccupations of Contemporary Indonesian Painters*. Kuala Lumpur: Oxford University Press, 1994.

Wright, Astri, and Agus Dermawan, eds. *T. Hendra Gunawan: A Great Modern Indonesian Painter*. Jakarta and Singapore: The Ciputra Foundation and the Archipelago Press, Editions Didier Millet, 2001.

ANTHROPOLOGY

ANTHROPOLOGY AFTER THE NEW ORDER

Marina Welker

The three reflections that follow on the state and future of anthropological scholarship on Indonesia share in common a commitment to place and particularity, although each figures the two in different ways.

Recalling that a fascination with the uncanny drew her to Indonesia in the first place, Danilyn Rutherford claims that the anthropology of Indonesia has remained on "the cutting edge of our discipline" because "we are drawn to things that we can't figure out."[1] In her account, place and particularity appear in the mysteries and ghosts that haunt our ethnographies. Addressing what makes ethnographic accounts of Indonesia both cutting edge and durable, Rutherford turns to an essay by James Siegel (1995) on Clifford Geertz's *The Religion of Java* (1960). Siegel highlights the moments in which Geertz observes the uncanny without subjecting it to analytic closure and academic understanding. Uncanny figures and occurrences remain alive in some of the best contemporary ethnographies, Rutherford reports, citing recent work by Karen Strassler, Daromir Rudnyckyj, and Jenny Munro. Rather than reducing Indonesia to one more token of a larger type (with globalization and neoliberalism, as the dominant types today, occupying some of the same semantic terrain once claimed by modernization and development), the mysterious (*ghaib*) preserves the possibility of things being heard but not understood, vanishing at the same time they come into view.

Rutherford's reflection moved me to read the essay by Jim Siegel she discusses. His tone, I find, is darker than hers. Whereas a couple decades before he might have said that people "fall in love" with Indonesia, in 1995 he remarks, "Indonesia is no longer attractive to me, but I cannot rid myself of it, even though I often would like to, and that is because I still cannot recognize this place." Malaysia, by contrast, "is ripe for comparison because it is recognizable" (93–94). Siegel's four-page piece appears, of course, in *Indonesia*, a less disciplined journal than most these days, one that allows for the possibility of posing questions without matching them with tidy answers, and hovering generatively between field notes and finished scholarly

---

[1] See Danilyn Rutherford's contribution in this volume.

argument.[2] The essay was published in a year that we might today periodize as "late New Order." But at the time, it surely felt more like high New Order, eternal New Order, to many citizens and foreign scholars alike.[3] This may have conferred a special appeal upon the notion that Indonesia eluded anthropological recognition and understanding; if anthropologists could not recognize and understand what they saw, then neither could the New Order state. As anthropologists increasingly responded to and criticized what Patricia Spyer describes as the "gravitational pull" of the New Order, they took heart in finding corners of life that had not yielded to the overreaching grasp of a state that was often depicted, from vantage points on the margins as much as within the centers, as leaving its fingerprints upon the most intimate realms of bodily life and subjective experience (Keane 1997; Steedly 1999). Although Suharto is gone now and the center seems more loose and disarrayed (Kusno 2010), unrecognizability may have retained its attractive qualities for anthropologists in the post-authoritarian era. Emerging scholarship on the post-New Order period, Rutherford points out, has illuminated fresh attempts to domesticate "formerly threatening forms of alterity" (e.g., Chinese Indonesians, West Papuans). New projects of rehabilitating "threatening others," in both their popular and state-supported guises, routinely fail, interrupted by the *ghaib* that eludes both scholarly understanding and multicultural domestication.

Where Rutherford embraces the intact alterity of the *ghaib*, Kenneth George draws on the late A. L. ("Pete") Becker to espouse translation, described as an act of apprenticing oneself to different ways of speaking. Translation is undertaken out of "intimacy, perseverance, and love," in spite of the knowledge that ultimately it is condemned to be "at once too exuberant, saying too much, and too deficient, not saying enough." Careful translation, George suggests, may help scholars to forge "imaginative solidarities around the particular ... solidarities of recognition, of thinking with, of learning from." Calling attention to the "urgent, critical, and ethical" problems faced in places like Indonesia where life is "precarious, vulnerable, and at risk," George's hope is for imaginative solidarities that not only link scholars and cross disciplines, but connect communities around religious, indigenous, and environmental concerns. George laments the fact that the scholarship on Indonesia that has traveled the best has tended to do so because it has "addressed 'big picture' issues ... with memorable analytic or conceptual terms ... that easily detach from the ethnographic or historical specifics in which they found formulation, and travel

[2] One example I have in mind here is an article by Marc Perlman ("The Traditional Javanese Performing Arts in the Twilight of the New Order: Two Letters from Solo," *Indonesia* 68 [October 1999]: 1–37), which meanders across conversations, hotel lobbies, musical performances, and the author's own thoughts and memories, conveying a vivid sense of what it was like to be in Solo as an ethnomusicologist in 1997, and then again in 1998, disoriented, after economic devastation had really taken hold, Chinese Indonesians had become the targets of systematic violence, and Suharto had fallen. Nuggets of interesting insight are loosely scattered throughout the article, but it lacks a conventional theoretical apparatus and argumentative structure. By contrast, see Jeremy Wallach's article ("Exploring Class, Nation, and Xenocentrism in Indonesian Cassette Retail Outlets," *Indonesia* 74 [October 2002]: 79–102), which is also excellent but much more disciplined and conventionally packaged and argued, leaving less room for reflection, speculation, imagination, and a raw sense of what it felt like to be in a certain place at a particular historical moment.

[3] I have in mind here Yurchak's reflection on how the Soviet Union felt like an eternal state, until it ended. See: Alexei Yurchak, *Everything Was Forever, Until It Was No More: The Last Soviet Generation* (Princeton, NJ: Princeton University Press, 2006.

through and across disciplines without them … Why don't the marvels—or the tragedies—of Indonesian lifeworlds travel as well as the concepts we harvest from them?"

Patricia Spyer's essay foregrounds the historical and ongoing role of violence in constituting Indonesia, arguing for an exploration of "how violence works through, informs, and destabilizes a variety of different historically specific social formations." Spyer understands violence broadly but insists upon careful investigation of its particular modalities in an effort to situate "violence in all its complex specificity within the production, structuring, and destructuring of social life rather than seeing it as somehow derivative" and assigning it an identity *a posteriori* (e.g., by describing and identifying violence as state, ethnic, religious, or communal). Spyer highlights the potential for anthropologists, in conversation with scholars from other disciplines and journalists, to shed light on violence in the overlooked, off-stage, marginal, fleeting, and banal textures and tempos of everyday life. In order to understand how headline-grabbing forms of violence seem to erupt out of nowhere, Spyer suggests, we must first understand the quiet violence that sustains the taken-for-granted shape of things and identities of selves and others in ordinary times, and how this order breaks down when dependable categories and distinctions lose their salience and "the world is experienced as out of joint." Since Suharto's fall, new media technologies and political reforms have saturated the public sphere with images of civil and state violence. The ways in which ordinary Indonesians produce and interpret these representations today, Spyer points out, may draw upon the New Order regime's visual iconographies of violence and its practice of using "forced witnessing" of violence to teach citizens lessons in national history and state power. As post-New Order projects and practices of remembering and forgetting are being consolidated in various attempts to straighten out history (*meluruskan sejarah*), Spyer asks how the creation of counter-archives might help keep history open.

To the long list of works on violence in Indonesia that Spyer cites, including multiple recent collections, I would only wish to add colonial scholar-official Christiaan Snouck Hurgronje's two-volume study, *The Acehnese* (1906). His preface to the English translation, which discusses how the Netherlands needed to better apply its military power to the task of subjugating the Acehnese, serves as a blunt reminder of the entanglement of knowledge and power when one turns to the rich ethnographic account that follows. Reading his detailed descriptions of how chicken thieves can quietly remove fowl from a coop by creating artificial rain, how burglars shake a house to check if its inmates are sound asleep before carrying out their nefarious purposes, and how murderers can kill a sleeping victim with a few quick spear thrusts through the floorboards of an elevated house, it is hard not to think of how such knowledge may have been mobilized in the guerrilla warfare strategies Snouck Hurgronje advocated for the Dutch (37; Mrázek 2010). This work, and Snouck Hurgronje's complicity in shaping violent forces that he could not control, speaks in important ways to contemporary debates over applied anthropology and counterinsurgency (Wertheim 1972).

"Only by being there," Siegel tells us (93), "only by hearing and by seeing can one find something one is not sure one is looking for." His words resonate with George's view that "the 'touch' of a place … ought to guide us in our particular intellectual ventures." This means that our works will not be narrowly local because world currents have continuously shaped Indonesia and are integral to its "touch." It also means that our inquiries will be oriented towards questions that ordinary

Indonesians find interesting or pressing. It makes sense that anthropologists today are preoccupied by the sorts of issues that Spyer and George cite and more: transnational forces including Islam and neoliberalism, the new middle classes, consumption, youth culture, urban life and the built environment, debt, media and technology, environmental crises, tourism, and cultural heritage industries. Yet new research objects may demand new methods that hinge less upon face-to-face interaction and are not confined within the container of the nation-state. As Rutherford and George point out, anthropologists increasingly rove across not just geographic but also disciplinary boundaries, drawing new questions and concepts from feminist theory, post-structuralism, subaltern studies and postcolonial theory, diaspora and border studies, political ecology, science studies, and the material and post-humanist turns. A commitment to place and particularity may serve as a useful guide as we consider how to engage with new trends on the academic scene.[4] We can pose the question: how will new theoretical concepts and methods serve and support, rather than diminish, our curiosity about and attentiveness to the particular wonders, surprises, ghosts, and forms of violence that make up Indonesia?

Works Cited

Cooper, Frederick. *Colonialism in Question: Theory, Knowledge, History*. Berkeley, CA: University of California Press, 2005.

Geertz, Clifford. *The Religion of Java*. Chicago, IL: University of Chicago Press, 1960.

Hurgronje, C. Snouck. *The Achehnese*. Trans. A. W. S. O'Sullivan. Leiden: E. J. Brill, 1906.

Keane, Webb. "Knowing One's Place: National Language and the Idea of the Local in Eastern Indonesia." *Cultural Anthropology* 12.1 (1997): 37–63.

Kusno, Abidin. *The Appearances of Memory: Mnemonic Practices of Architecture and Urban Form in Indonesia*. Durham, NC: Duke University Press, 2010.

Mrázek, Rudolf. *A Certain Age: Colonial Jakarta Through the Memories of its Intellectuals*. Durham, NC: Duke University Press, 2010.

Perlman, Marc. "The Traditional Javanese Performing Arts in the Twilight of the New Order: Two Letters from Solo." *Indonesia* 68 (October 1999): 1–37.

Siegel, James T. "In Place of an Interview." *Indonesia* 59 (April 1995): 93–96.

Steedly, Mary Margaret. "The State of Culture Theory in the Anthropology of Southeast Asia." *Annual Review of Anthropology* 28 (1999): 431–54.

Wallach, Jeremy. "Exploring Class, Nation, and Xenocentrism in Indonesian Cassette Retail Outlets." *Indonesia* 74 (October 2002): 79–102.

---

[4] Noting that the very expression of a "turn" tends to imply that scholars "take their intellectual curves together, and anyone who does not is off on a tangent or has entered a dead end," Fred Cooper argues that "Scholars' openness to new ideas and directions is one thing, taking 'turns' together another" (*Colonialism in Question: Theory, Knowledge, History* [Berkeley, CA: University of California Press, 2005], p. 5).

Wertheim, W. F. "Counter-Insurgency Research at the Turn of the Century: Snouck Hurgronje and the Acheh War." *Sociologische Gids* 19 (1972): 320–28.

Yurchak, Alexei. *Everything Was Forever, Until It Was No More: The Last Soviet Generation*. Princeton, NJ: Princeton University Press, 2006.

BOTH PLACES AT ONCE

Danilyn Rutherford

There is something about Indonesia that has gotten under my skin—something that made me want to become an anthropologist. The part of the world in which I specialize is only problematically Indonesian (we scholars of Indonesia's troubled eastern edge tend to call ourselves West Papuanists these days), and it's been decades since I visited Yogyakarta (where I taught English in the mid 1980s) or spent more than a few days west of the Wallace Line. Yet, despite my absences, even when I'm not paying attention, Indonesia still has its hooks in me. I don't think I'm alone in feeling this way.

James Siegel (1995) once wrote a short essay about Clifford Geertz, "In Place of an Interview," that touches on this phenomenon. Siegel begins by pointing out that the best books on Indonesia survive swings in intellectual fashion. Geertz's *The Religion of Java* (1960), for instance, has merited rereading over the years and decades, even among people who know nothing of Indonesia's "place in the world." Puzzled by this trait, Siegel longs to interview "the author [of *Religion of Java*] from inside the book"—not today's Geertz, but the Geertz who lives in the text—about his method. This is impossible, so instead Siegel analyzes the following passage (1995, 94), which recounts a street corner conversation between Geertz and someone named "Djojo" about the latter's "marvelous grandfather," who could "disappear magically" and "go great distances in a short time."

> His grandfather was arrested once by the Dutch and taken to Bragang and put into jail because of his *ilmu*—all his pupils walking along behind as he was led in. When they returned home, [they] found him there in the house ready to teach, and it turned out later that he was in both places at once: in jail and in his house teaching. He evidently applied his magical powers in the jail toward freeing the prisoners, and so the Dutch thought perhaps it would be better if they just let him go … Today the leading *dukuns* in Modjokerto are all at least middle-aged, but none is really old. Of the really well-known ones, three are *abangan*; one is *santri*; and one, the subdistrict officer, a *prijaji*. (Geertz 1960, 89.)

At the beginning of the passage, Siegel notes, "Geertz gives us an actuality": not an "informant," but "Djojo" and what Geertz recalls him recounting on an occasion that stands out as "a uniqueness, a coincidence of time, place, person, and speech"

(Siegel 1995, 94). This actuality recedes when we get to the final section of the quote, where Geertz deploys his now-disputed analytic categories (*abangan, santri, prijaji*) to speak with a neutrality that authenticates the tales of "miracles" that he has just passed along. "The observer makes me feel that I could listen myself. One need not be as knowledgeable about Java as he is in order to hear. Listening and understanding have become different activities. Achieving the latter does not satisfy the former" (Siegel 1995, 95). Siegel concludes: "The best books about Indonesia stimulate a desire for more that outweighs whatever they tell me ... But when what I hear is turned into understanding, it seems as though there is much more to know, but it has escaped me" (1995, 96). Much like Djojo's magical grandfather, "Indonesia vanishes the instant it comes into view" (1995, 96).

I couldn't help but keep Siegel's essay in mind as I turned to our task in this panel, which is to trace the arc of anthropological studies of Indonesia. I found myself thinking less about the field's arc than about its orbit—that is, about the puzzles that keep reappearing in widely divergent ethnographies. This was definitely the case as I attempted to catch up for this conference by reading two 2010 monographs and a 2009 dissertation by a new generation of ethnographers. Anyone who has stayed abreast of anthropological topics and trends will recognize the analytic categories deployed by these authors. In all these works, we find "conceptual terms detached from other contexts and applied to the Indonesian 'case,'" to recall a trend that Kenneth George describes later in this volume. Yet something far more enigmatic remains sheltered in these writings—a "quirk and murk" in excess of the understanding that they afford.

Take Daromir Rudnyckyj's *Spiritual Economies: Islam, Globalization, and the Afterlife of Development* (2010). Rudnyckyj, like so many anthropologists, is trying to make sense of neoliberalism, which he defines as "a relatively mundane but increasingly ubiquitous practice of making economic calculation a universal standard for the organization, management, and government of human life and conduct" (21). In the book's introduction, Rudnyckyj lays out Indonesia's recent history in terms that allow for broad comparisons. In Indonesia, as in "much of Asia, Africa, and Latin America," neoliberalism has taken the form of a transition from what Rudnyckyj calls "faith in development"—in the form of state-sponsored projects—to "developing faith"—initiatives designed to make individual citizens accountable for their own progress and prosperity. This new penchant for self-fashioning is ultimately traceable to the policies of international lenders, like the International Monetary Fund and World Bank, combined with the emergence of new "global assemblages," which integrate "production systems, financial activities, and labor markets across national borders" (5).

At Rudnyckyj's fieldsite, state-owned Krakatoa Steel, the barometer of this change is the adoption of Emotional Spiritual Quotient training, or ESQ, which is designed to prepare managers and employees to compete in an increasingly globalized—and privatized—industry. Taking the place of P4, a training package developed in the 1980s to inculcate the principles of the official state ideology, Pancasila, ESQ is a private operation, founded by Ary Ginanjar, a charismatic entrepreneur who has combined the principles of human-resources management and Islam to fashion a standardized program used in government agencies and private companies alike. Whereas P4 was dull and routinized, ESQ uses sound, images, and, most extravagantly, air conditioning to create an emotionally tumultuous experience for participants, who, at the climax, act out the drama of lying in their graves confronting the angels of death.

Although Rudnyckyj does much to make this situation recognizable as neoliberal, there are still signs in this ethnography of things heard but not understood if one focuses solely on global trends. Neoliberal reform takes an Indonesian twist. Drawing on Siegel's *Naming the Witch* (2006), Rudnyckyj describes ESQ as a "structure" that allows Krakatoa employees to avoid the fate of rural Javanese, who turned on each other in response to the loss of stable sources of recognition caused by the New Order's collapse. Through ESQ, "the resolution of this existential crisis entails not the killing of another but rather the simulation of the beginning of one's own afterlife" (Rudnyckyj, 209). ESQ invites participants to direct their violence inward in an effort to secure a sense of who they are.

In this post-New Order context, ESQ's mixture of Muslim piety and business self-help in many cases results in something other than the cultivation of a self-disciplined workforce invested in its industry's success. Founders of a new, independent labor union take the training and gain from it the determination to push for greater career mobility. Christians view the exercise as a barely veiled attempt to make them convert.

Some of Rudnyckyj's informants clearly have difficulty inhabiting the stable identity that ESQ promises to provide. Arfan, a Betawi man with Chinese ancestry, is not the only employee to respond to the most affectively loaded moments in the training by going into a trance, as the nurses walking the aisles with tanks of oxygen make clear. Arfan's trance takes the form of possession by a seemingly Chinese spirit. Rudnyckyj accounts for the spirit's appearance as a protest against New Order anti-Chinese policies and obliquely suggests that the spirit represents Arfan's sense of his own Chinese roots. But he also includes Arfan's account of how the "magical being" came to him by way of a neighbor, a maid whom Arfan helped when she became possessed after a trip to a beach next to a Chinese cemetery. "As I held her, it was like there was a movement or something mysterious [*ghaib*], and suddenly it entered inside of me" (Rudnyckyj, 204). It wasn't Arfan's heritage that possessed him—but something far more intractable, even alien to who he was.

Notwithstanding Rudnyckyj's more-or-less successful effort to make his findings appear as tokens of a neoliberal type, he is a good enough ethnographer to let us sense that there is more to the story. Although his coworkers at Krakatoa proclaimed that ESQ had exorcised the spirit, Arfan reported otherwise. After the fashion of spirit mediums depicted elsewhere in the region, the training helped Arfan arrive at a state where the "mysterious being's" visitations were no longer unpredictable and uncontrollable. Even as Rudnyckyj portrays ESQ as ushering Indonesians into the afterlife of development, his book also shows us shards of the past in the present, "magical beings" that precipitate, yet ultimately elude, the quest to contain the alterity that lurks within the history of a person, a family, or the nation. Individuals like Arfan are "both places at once"—the New Order and the post-New Order, not to mention post-colonial Banten and colonial Batavia. The effects are mysterious—*ghaib*. In the midst of neoliberal self-fashioning, something still vanishes the instant it comes into view.

The relationship among the histories of persons, families, and the nation lies at the heart of the second ethnography I want to consider, Karen Strassler's remarkable *Refracted Visions: Popular Photography and National Modernity in Java* (2010). Strassler wears her comparative touchstones more lightly than Rudnyckyj does—Benjamin,

Barth, and other thinkers make appearances, but only in order to help Strassler answer a peculiarly Indonesian question: what are some of the ways in which Indonesians have used photography to intertwine the national and the familial, grand narratives and the rhythm of everyday life? Strassler pursues this question by analyzing practices ranging from the use of blown-up identity photographs as family portraits to the staging of rituals in which guests at a children's birthday party pose for the camera while greeting their host after the fashion of visiting dignitaries.

Throughout the book, which runs from the colonial period to recent times, Strassler shows how the incorporation of photography and other imported technologies has been the work of Indonesia's most notable population of internal others: the Chinese. Sino-Indonesians have long dominated the ranks of 1) the amateur photographers who have captured the romanticized images of traditional life that adorn postcards and glossy coffee table books showcasing the nation; 2) the studio photographers who have created fantasy landscapes of modernity, exoticism, and rural beauty into which clients can transport themselves for the camera; and 3) the owners of photocopy shops and passport photograph booths that citizens of all walks of life must frequent to comply with the documentary demands of the Indonesian state. The book's final chapters focus on other internal aliens: student photographers, who documented police brutality during the mass demonstrations that marked the New Order's final days, and the documentarian-in-overdrive, Noorman, veteran of the revolution, former political prisoner, and mystic visionary who uses photographs, photocopies, and re-workings of official texts to prove that he is Sukarno's rightful heir.

Like Rudnyckyj, Strassler reveals the ways in which the transition to the post-New Order period has domesticated formerly threatening forms of alterity. In the case of student photographers, what were once potent and dangerous images hidden in personal collections now appear in exhibitions celebrating the nation's youth as the heroes who ushered in the new era of reform. Even Noorman's more radical counter-history seems tamer—less prone to evoke the powers and pleasures of transgression—now that Suharto is no longer in power. And yet, something heard but not understood remains evident in the magical—again, *ghaib*—flash of light in the photographs Noorman circulates showing himself wearing a white suit modeled on Sukarno's and surrounded by military officers at an official event. Between the lines of Strassler's ethnography, we see hints of a "world experienced, admittedly unevenly in some deep, far-going sense, as fundamentally disturbed."[1] At least one student photographer has died a death that did not make him into a national hero: Agus Muliawan, killed by a pro-Indonesia militia while documenting violence waged in East Timor on those who sought to leave Indonesia behind.

Which takes me to my final example, a moving dissertation by Jenny Munro, who studied at the Australian National University. Like Rudnyckyj's and Strassler's books, Munro's "Dreams Made Small: Humiliation and Education in a Dani Modernity" (2009) spans the New Order/post-New Order divide. Munro writes of university students from the Baliem Valley of West Papua who are pursuing degrees in North Sulawesi. Although Munro does not focus on West Papuan nationalism per se, she provides the most compelling account I have read of how Papuans' political aspirations—and, indeed, their very identity as Papuan—spring from their experience of everyday life. Where Strassler shows how everyday practices

---

[1] See Patricia Spyer's contribution in this volume.

reproduce selves, families, and the Indonesian nation all at once, Munro reveals an alternative. Everyday experiences of humiliation and education may reproduce Dani selves and family, but they drive them away from the Indonesian nation and into an imagining of politics that takes a different form.

Munro also doesn't write of neoliberalism per se, although her findings reveal processes that bear some resemblance to those described by Rudnyckyj. Munro writes of humiliation—and its deflection—in a setting where racist assumptions often come clothed in the technocratic language of development. She focuses on the effects of what she calls, borrowing from the anthropologist of Melanesia, Joel Robbins, "discourses of diminishment" that target the supposed "low quality" of the "human resources" of West Papuans (Munro 2009, 2). In reaction to these discourses, Dani students in North Sulawesi strive to improve themselves at the same time that their time abroad casts Indonesian accounts of modernity and multiculturalism into doubt. Instead of gaining the technical skills needed to "develop" their homeland, they quickly discover that they must navigate an arbitrary and often corrupt bureaucracy to schedule an exam or get their theses read. Eager to "experience the cultures and peoples of North Sulawesi," they soon come to realize that their stigmatization as "primitive" others thwarts their efforts to build relationships with non-Dani teachers, classmates, and neighbors. As a result, these students' quest for self-improvement leads them to turn inward towards their own group.

Living together in dormitories set aside for highlands students, *kakak*, or "older siblings," keep tabs on their *adik*, younger siblings, policing them for drunkenness or sexual dalliances. Student organizations hold elaborate, highly formal ceremonies and celebrations that give students a chance to display their organizational and rhetorical skill. In their interactions with one another, Dani students work against the racist stereotype of West Papuan highlanders as ignorant, promiscuous, drunken, and violent. In the course of doing so, they fashion an alternative image of what they call "quality," one in line with Dani conceptions of leaders as people with "good hearts, good hands, and a good voice" (Munro 2009, 66). This turn inward is accompanied by a turn away from Sulawesi and towards the students' Papuan homeland and the "sponsors" who are supporting their studies. Students expect to use what they have learned at the university to benefit their home communities, but the "results" of their studies rarely take the form that they tell themselves they will. Rather than bringing the benefits of development to Dani villages—building roads, supplying electricity, improving health care, opening schools—they end up serving their less educated friends, relatives, and neighbors in more subtle ways. Returned students act as mediators between local people and the Indonesian bureaucracy. By accompanying a mother to sign for her child's report card or an uncle to make an inquiry at a government office, they help villagers unschooled in the workings of the bureaucracy avoid the humiliation they themselves have suffered abroad.

Like Strassler and Rudnyckyj, Munro illuminates the post-New Order tendency to rehabilitate threatening others and the points at which this project fails. Perhaps the most vivid statement of Munro's argument comes in the conclusion, where she discusses the students' ambivalent perspective on the *koteka*, the penis sheath traditionally worn by Dani men. On the one hand, students react with embarrassment when watching Indonesian television programs showing highlanders wearing the garment. But those brave enough to don *koteka* in public for ceremonies and celebrations describe wearing one as a courageous, even thrilling, act. In the *koteka*, something is seen and felt in excess of the primitivizing stereotypes defining the Dani. At least on the face of it, Dani students' dreams are "made small" by their experience overseas. Yet the humiliation they suffer in Sulawesi still yields something significant: a tendency to turn the marks of stigma into a source of pride. If we want to understand Papuan nationalism—and other similar political movements—we must begin where Munro does: with the personal histories and life chances of stigmatized individuals, like the Dani students, and the politically consequential structures of feeling that these produce. But we also need to appreciate that these structures of feeling can lead us into realms where recognizable national categories don't apply.

In these excellent recent studies, the paradox described by Siegel still seems to hold. These are works embedded within different traditions of anthropology that render complicated situations understandable by deploying analytic terms with considerable comparative scope. These are works that bear the imprint of the teachers who trained their authors: Aihwa Ong (University of California, Berkeley) for Rudnyckyj; Ann Stoler, Webb Keane, and Rudolf Mrázek (University of Michigan) for Strassler; and the prominent historian of Melanesia, Chris Ballard (Australian National University), for Munro. Yet these are also studies that, by virtue both of their ethnographic method and what it reveals, showcase the limits of what comparison can reveal. In the 1990s, when I was writing my dissertation and beginning my first job, I played the same game of catch up. While reading recent books by anthropologists working in Indonesia, I found myself entertaining an irreverent thought: modernity, globalization, power, violence, resistance—these were all red herrings. The real topic of all these ethnographies? Ghosts. (*Hanging without a Rope*? *In the Realm of the Diamond Queen*? *Showing Signs of Violence*? *The Memory of Trade*? All full of ghosts. Not to mention *Wana Shamanship*. *Signs of Recognition*? It's full of ghosts, too. The ones that zap orators if they mess up the ancestors' words!) I'm not immune to this fascination with the uncanny. One of the main things that drew me to Indonesia when I joined Volunteers in Asia in the early 1980s was the fact that I had heard that there were people on Java who could fry eggs on their heads. Uncool, I know, but I don't think I'm beyond the pale. What has kept the anthropology of Indonesia on the cutting edge of our discipline is the fact that we are drawn to things that we can't figure out.

So much for the past in the present. What about the future? Science studies and the other fields listed by George (in this volume) have spawned new kinds of border crossing in anthropology that have led to an increased insistence on the materiality of social processes. Anthropologists are increasingly in dialogue with scholars from geography, environmental studies, and the natural and physical sciences. For the students I work with at the University of California, Santa Cruz, the agency of non-humans goes without saying, and humans themselves are but one of a multiplicity of species each with its own imperatives and traits. Just before beginning this commentary, I completed a reading course with two doctoral students who are going to work in or near Indonesia. For one of our meetings, we read James Scott's *The Art of Not Being Governed* (2009), a book that makes a bold argument, fueled by comparisons from across the world, on the origins of the so-called hill tribes of the Mainland Southeast Asian massif. Long depicted as holdovers from more primitive times, these groups are of relatively recent vintage. According to Scott, they were born of practices of evasion and appropriation among people seeking to avoid the exactions of lowland states. Notwithstanding the simplifications bemoaned by George, Scott's argument provides food for thought. "Being both places at once" was a stubborn, longstanding tendency for those on the edge of lowland polities, which appropriated labor and products often through violent means. This tendency was made possible not only by these erstwhile subjects' ingenuity in avoiding capture, but also by the landscape's material traits: the steep hillsides that no roads could reach, the soils that sustained swidden crops that ripened beneath the ground, hidden from the tax collectors' prying eyes. Or at least the landscape had this effect until the mid-1940s, when Scott ends his story: this was when airplanes, helicopters, radar, and other new technologies began to smooth the friction caused by this landscape, closing the gap between mountain villages and lowland states.

Scott mentions, but does not expand upon the resources afforded by Indonesia's rather different landscapes for people seeking to evade and appropriate state power. Nevertheless, I wonder whether a new generation of Indonesianists might find themselves emboldened to entertain an argument like Scott's in exploring why Indonesia's history often seems out of joint. In other words, they might be tempted to mobilize what Marina Welker described in her commentary on this session as the "power and salience of anthropology to render Indonesian lifeworlds at least partially recognizable" by tracing the deep histories that they "retranslate" and repeat (see Laurie Sears, this volume). In the early 1990s, my fieldwork in Biak exposed me to ways in which distant pasts of the sort that Scott refers to continued to haunt the present. Paying heed to this haunting helped me make sense of how Biaks managed to keep the New Order at bay even in a site where planeloads of tourists landed every day. I spilled a great deal of ink in my dissertation arguing against the premises of geographical determinism. I now wonder whether this was a mistake. Geography has surely played a role in shaping Biaks' ongoing relations with distant centers. So have social processes that are no less material—no less historical—than the landscapes in which Biaks have lived. The ethnographies I have discussed here reveal the continuing influence of the New Order on today's Indonesia. They also document ways in which the situation in Indonesia is truly new. And yet, their pages contain evidence of Indonesia's continuing susceptibility to specters that disrupt the smooth flow of history. Assumptions, urges, and fascinations of various vintages fly below the radar in many corners of Indonesia. The older models of regional politics proposed by Oliver Wolters (1982) and Ben Anderson (1972) might help us understand this disjuncture.[2] These assumptions, urges, and fascinations could be both signs and sources of the persistence of a notion of power as substantive even in "rationalized" settings where we might expect power to operate as a means to an end (see Weber 2009). Our willingness as anthropologists to think through such possibilities is no doubt to thank for our fruitful engagements with at least some sectors of the political science of Indonesia (see Edward Aspinall, elsewhere in this volume). Indonesia's present may well be just as much an afterlife as an era, as much a tissue of material traces as a now.

What evades recognition in the anthropology of Indonesia—what is heard but not understood—may in part mark the persistence of habits of thought and practice born of settings where contending regimes of value and authority came together. But only in part. Even the most savvy of analysts could never exorcise all of Indonesia's "magical beings." *Both places at once.* In area studies and anthropology. In Indonesia, the Netherlands, West Papua, and the United States. This is the difficult and

---

[2] I have Andrew Willford to thank for this insight.

seductive position I have come to occupy. It is hard to unhook oneself from things that vanish the instant they come into view.

Works Cited

Anderson, Benedict R. O'G. *Language and Power: Exploring Political Cultures in Indonesia*. Ithaca, NY: Cornell University Press, 1990 [1972]. 17–77.

Geertz, Clifford. *The Religion of Java* (Chicago, IL: University of Chicago Press, 1960.

Munro, Jenny. "Dreams Made Small: Humiliation and Education in a Dani Modernity." PhD dissertation, Australian National University, Canberra, 2009.

Rudnyckyj, Daromir. *Spiritual Economies: Islam, Globalization, and the Afterlife of Development*. Ithaca, NY: Cornell University Press, 2010.

Rutherford, Danilyn. *Raiding the Land of the Foreigners: The Limits of the Nation on an Indonesian Frontier*. Princeton, NJ: Princeton University Press, 2003.

Scott, James. *The Art of Not Being Governed*. New Haven, CT: Yale University Press, 2009.

Siegel, James. "In Place of an Interview." *Indonesia* 59 (April 1995): 93–96.

——. *Naming the Witch*. Stanford, CA: Stanford University Press, 2006.

Strassler, Karen. *Refracted Visions: Popular Photography and National Modernity in Java*. Durham, NC: Duke University Press, 2010.

Weber, Max. "Bureaucracy." *From Max Weber*. Ed. H. H. Gerth and C. Wright Mills. New York, NY: Routledge, 2009: 196–244.

Wolters, Oliver. *History, Culture, and Region in Southeast Asian Perspective*. Ithaca, NY: Cornell Southeast Asia Program Publications, 1999 [1982].

PUTTING THE QUIRKS AND MURK TO WORK: DISCIPLINARY REFLECTIONS ON THE STATE OF INDONESIAN STUDIES

Kenneth M. George

The letter of invitation to our conference expressed a longing for dialogue across disciplines, a dialogue that would help recuperate "the kind of interdisciplinary scholarship that Indonesian Studies has arguably lost in recent decades." I confess I didn't think things had come to that, and failed to pinpoint a moment of loss. Our interdisciplinary energies and engagements have seemed to me both lively and deep, and animate some of the best and most recent work on Indonesian religion, politics, environments, literature, music, violence, and visual culture. Speaking twelve years ago, Anna Tsing described the interdisciplinarity of Indonesian Studies, and Southeast Asian Studies more broadly, as a refreshing and inspiring site of innovation and "theoretically informed quirkiness" (1999, 15). Tsing attributed that quirky interdisciplinarity and promise to the marginal, odd-corner status of Indonesia and Southeast Asia in our disciplinary homes. Working interdisciplinarily and from the margins would give us room for what Tsing called a "creative refusal of orthodoxy."

Tsing gives us an appealing if romantic sketch of Indonesian Studies. Her sketch depicts disciplines as places of intellectual confinement and institutional entrenchment. Weary of being governed and stifled by these centers of orthodoxy, we turn to Indonesian Studies, a "contact zone" of liberating possibilities where we take up with roving bands of scholars who help us see and think otherwise. In time, disciplinary dispositions and desires pull us back, as do the enticements of disciplinary conversation, recognition, and address. We bring interdisciplinary sensibilities with us. We put the quirks (peculiar habits and strange occurrences) to work, transforming not only our home disciplines, but perhaps, too, the disciplinary sensibilities of those we met in the contact zone.

As much as I admire and take inspiration from Anna Tsing's account of what we do, I would like to work back through a few of its terms and prejudices with the aim of describing the arc of cultural anthropology in Indonesian Studies, and suggesting ways the next wave of anthropology might give Indonesian Studies fresh inspiration, direction, and reach. My first remark would be that cultural anthropology has always been a hybrid field, full of unruliness and surprise, especially the surprise that comes from ethnographic research. I like to think of ethnographic research as revisionary work that keeps our theoretical and conceptual accounts of the world plural, loose, and open to correction. Dwelling with the frictions, fictions, fantasies, and murk of a lived-in world is a way to allow the world to make a claim or a comeback against the theories that explain it. (See, in connection, Danilyn Rutherford's contribution to our conference [elsewhere in this volume], and her remarks about how ethnography [usefully, provocatively] shelters something that exceeds our understanding.) I am not suggesting that we do away with theory, but, rather, that we not so deeply succumb to it, or to the often-suffocating reading formations and discipleships that authorize it. Ethnographic research does not stand in for the whole of anthropology, of course, but it is essential to the comparative analysis of cultural concepts, "the forms of life that articulate them, [and] the powers they release or disable" (Asad 2003, 17). It does not have to hew closely to a Malinowskian, long-term immersion "in the field." In fact, many working in anthropology and Indonesian Studies have found revealing and crucially needed new ways of ethnographic contact in mediascapes, virtual worlds, and short-term fieldwork.

For me, Indonesian Studies is, before all else, about the worldly murk that is Indonesia, and only then about the quirky company of anthropologists, historians, political scientists, literary and art historians, linguists, musicologists, artists, and scientists who are trying to make sense of it. "Indonesian Studies" in this sense is a name for the multidisciplinary scrutiny and vulnerability that comes from dwelling in a place in the world called "Indonesia." It is the collaborative interdisciplinary zone that Tsing describes, I agree. And yet the picture she paints obscures something of importance to us: "Indonesian Studies" is not a contact zone alternative to or outside of a discipline—especially the discipline of anthropology—but a meeting ground where anthropologists, historians, musicologists—pick your field—convene to assert, discover, or renew their own disciplinarity in the exploration of Indonesian lifeworlds, in all their quirkiness and murkiness. Nor should we forget that the disciplinary and multidisciplinary trajectories in Indonesian Studies have their own histories, stretching back into the colonial era.

Cultural anthropology is generally acknowledged as the discipline that played most prominently in defining and peopling "Indonesian Studies" (and much of Southeast Asian Studies) in the United States from 1950 through 2000. Its heyday has passed. History and political science now match it in disciplinary prominence or influence. Consider the disciplinary background of the winners of the Harry J. Benda Prize in Southeast Asian Studies over the past twenty years, as just one measure of anthropology's diminished shadow. Between 1991 and 2001, anthropologists specializing in Indonesia won six of ten awards. Among award-winners since 2001, we find but one anthropologist who specializes in Indonesia; and the winning work was an archival, rather than a field-based, study.

During this period of preeminence, cultural anthropology was instrumental in helping promulgate the idea of Indonesia as a place of "traditions," "peasantries," "simple societies," and "cultures" that were passing through the threshold of modernization and finding transformative incorporation within the ·nation-state. Although some of the major works of the period, including Clifford Geertz's *The Religion of Java* (1960) and *Peddlers and Princes* (1968) and James Peacock's *Rites of*

Modernization: Symbolic and Social Aspects of Indonesian Proletarian Drama (1968) are works of urban anthropology based on fieldwork in Javanese cities and towns, I believe the preponderant number of US anthropologists were drawn to rural villages and precincts to find "culture" and "traditional order."[1] Cultural portraiture and an emphasis on cultural "coherence" (e.g., Becker and Yengoyan 1979) pushed economic and political anthropological studies of Indonesia to the margins, a trend that mirrored the thematic changes in Geertz's scholarship as he shifted his fieldwork from Java to Bali (see Yengoyan 2009).[2]

My sense is that up until around 1980, anthropologists of Indonesia—in contrast to historians like Oliver Wolters and a few political scientists like Benedict Anderson—did not draw deeply from sources outside their discipline. Thick-description, particularism, emphasis on the local, and the bounded comparative scope of Leiden school structuralism and the Comparative Austronesian Project (at the Australian National University) did not spark interdisciplinary engagements of broad or lasting significance. A loosening occurs in the 1980s, as feminist studies, post-structuralism, cultural studies, and postcolonial studies (all deeply shaped by Foucauldian understandings of power and knowledge) brought broad changes to the academy. Geertz's discussions of culture-as-text by then, too, had found congenial and/or critical reception among historians and scholars of literature, and this opened a way for anthropologists to see how their work, their discipline, and their ideas about "culture" were being viewed. "Culture" and "ethnography" had caught on, or were caught up in disciplinary critiques. I think these changes gave cultural anthropologists a sense that we might have an interdisciplinary audience from whom we wanted to learn, to whom we needed to appeal, and to whom we might give account of ourselves.[3]

Despite all the rich and fascinating research we have brought into print since 1980, I would be hard-pressed to say that the anthropology of Indonesia has produced many break-out, must-read works that have shaped the horizons or direction of these enriching ventures across the discipline and the academy more broadly. Subaltern studies, border studies, diaspora studies, postcolonial studies, transnational studies, political ecology, practice theory, science studies, actor-network theory, and early work on globalization found their principal formulation in other ethnographic sites. Indonesian exemplars went unnoticed or were eclipsed by studies conducted elsewhere. Works on Indonesia that did find legs, irrespective of discipline—Benedict Anderson's *Imagined Communities*, Anna Tsing's *Friction*, or Robert W. Hefner's *Civil Islam*—did so because they addressed "big picture" issues

---

[1] The works by Geertz and Peacock that I mention were Sukarno-era studies conducted in urban East Java, and focused on Javanese rather than Indonesian national culture. The subsequent era of work on culture and traditional order did little to admit or call attention to the coercion and quietude that were so basic to Suharto's authoritarian rule. Analytic interest in nationalism and state power takes off in the mid- and late-1980s as anthropologists begin to work the ideas of Benedict Anderson, Michel Foucault, and James Scott into their studies. Feminist anthropology makes inroads about the same time, in the late 1980s and early 1990s.

[2] My views on the period no doubt owe much to my own graduate training on the anthropology of Southeast Asia, first with James L. Peacock, and, subsequently, with Alton L. Becker and Aram A. Yengoyan.

[3] We should not overlook the impact of Clifford Geertz's call for interdisciplinarity in his essay "Blurred Genres: The Refiguration of Social Thought" (*American Scholar* 49,2 [1980]: 165–79). The essay also reawakened hopes that work done in Indonesia might have appeal to the broader academy.

(nationalism, globalization, and "political" Islam) with memorable analytic or conceptual terms that they coined and used as book titles.[4] All of the books I have mentioned touch on politics or the global order, and perhaps that is what gives them cross-disciplinary traction. Works on literature, art, music, law, translation, media, public culture, or religion (as such, not as politics)—call them the humanities—don't do as well at finding readerships beyond the orbit of Indonesian Studies or Southeast Asian Studies.[5]

But something else is going on, too: "imagined communities" and "friction"— like "flexible citizenship" and "weapons of the weak"—are conceptual terms that easily detach from the ethnographic or historical specifics in which they found formulation, and travel through and across disciplines without them. This is no doubt a strength of the works that produced the terms, and yet it unsettles me from time to time. Indonesia and Indonesian Studies are places of such wonder and concrete attachment for me, especially the wonder and attachments that come through ethnographic fieldwork or ethnographic reading. Why don't the marvels— or the tragedies—of Indonesian lifeworlds travel as well as the concepts we harvest from them? Forging imaginative solidarities around the particular seems to me work that is every bit as important and as useful as forging conceptual tools for work in other places. Solidarities of recognition, of thinking with, of learning from.

Ethnographic work on Indonesia often comes across as minor key, paling beside the images that establish Indonesia in the popular or student imagination. The tsunami of 2004, and before it, the Kuta bombing of 2002, show the power of spectacle and the circulation of images and journalistic stories to bring Indonesia to the attention of Americans and to draw them into communities of compassion, fear, or grief.[6] The pace, focus, and reach of global media surely surpass Indonesian Studies—wed as we are to the slow-time of fieldwork, books, classrooms, conferences, performance spaces, and galleries—in giving Indonesia recognition. As what? A place of terror and cataclysm? These can fuse together very dangerously in the popular American imagination. Take, for example, Richard Ellis's enthusiastic review of Simon Winchester's *Krakatoa—The Day the World Exploded: August 27, 1883,* which appeared in the *New York Times,* April 20, 2003. Picking up on passages by Winchester, Ellis writes that "Islamic militants" (that is a quote) took advantage of a post-Krakatoan spiritual panic to Islamize Java. Here we see Ellis repeating the familiar prejudices of the colonial era: Natives are superstitious, and Muslims are

---

[4] Looking toward work done in Malaysia that also "found legs," we could point to James Scott's *Weapons of the Weak* and Aihwa Ong's *Flexible Citizenship.* See James C. Scott, *Weapons of the Weak: Everyday Forms of Peasant Resistance* (New Haven, CT: Yale University Press, 1987); and Aihwa Ong, *Flexible Citizenship: The Cultural Logics of Transnationality* (Durham, NC: Duke University Press, 1999).

[5] Webb Keane's *Christian Moderns* is an important exception. Its discussion of religion, modernity, and semiosis has found a growing audience in anthropology and religious studies. See: Webb Keane, *Christian Moderns: Freedom and Fetish in the Mission Encounter* (Berkeley, CA: University of California Press, 2007). I note, too, that Daromir Rudnyckyj's *Spiritual Economies: Islam, Globalization, and the Afterlife of Development* (Ithaca, NY: Cornell University Press, 2010) and Karen Strassler's *Refracted Visions: Popular Photography and National Modernity in Java* (Durham, NC: Duke University Press, 2010), both won major disciplinary prizes in 2011: the Sharon Stephen Prize (Rudnyckyj), awarded by the American Ethnological Society; and the Gregory Bateson Prize (Strassler), awarded by the Society for Cultural Anthropology.

[6] The Kuta bombing and the 2004 tsunami have also refigured our ethnographic frames. See George 2004.

armed and dangerous outsiders. He does this in the same sentence in which he likens Krakatoa to "weapons of mass destruction." The shock-and-awe war in Iraq had begun only a month before, and Ellis's review reads to me as an effort to open a front of the war on Islam in the popular understanding of Indonesia (and its vulcanology).

I am not sure how far others would agree with me, but I think disciplinary trends and popular media accounts of the sort I have described have worked to diminish student interest in the anthropology of Indonesia since 2001. I don't know what will renew curiosity. Campaign and post-election press stories about US President Obama's childhood in Jakarta didn't really take in the imagination; our students are from all over the world now, and Obama's years in Indonesia do not appear exceptional. Fanfare from the American Anthropological Association notwithstanding, the release of *Surviving against the Odds: Village Industry in Indonesia,* by Obama's mother, Stanley Ann Dunham, did not seem to ignite student imagination, either. (See my review of the book, 2010b.) Like hope, curiosity is a disposition, a "structure of feeling" toward the world that is contingent upon, and inflected by, historical forces largely external to (but always penetrating) the academy—class, capital, gender, age. Let me make it a lifeworld concern: One's place in the global (dis)order.

What's a discipline to do? One answer is to keep doing what we anthropologists do best—bringing our ethnographic, comparative, and critical sensibilities into our conversation with others. For cultural anthropologists working on Indonesia, it means attending to the murkiness and quirkiness of the everyday and to the environmental and societal degradation that my colleague Rob Nixon (2011) calls "slow violence." Having questioned narratives of modernization, the status and future of the nation-state, and Geertzian notions of cultural system and interpretation, anthropologists have been refiguring—implicitly and explicitly—the parameters of Indonesian Studies. It may be that the turn to the idea of "nature–culture" that has taken hold in some precincts of what is now an increasingly or broadly post-culturalist cultural anthropology may count importantly to what Indonesian Studies will become, or will house. This merger of geography, political ecology, environmental anthropology, resource management, development, health, and science studies may go a long way toward recapturing student interest in Indonesia and taking some fields in Indonesian Studies in a post-humanist direction.

I also anticipate vibrant anthropological and historical discussion from Indonesianists about how states and state power are imagined and put into practice, both in theory and on the ground. A bigger challenge perhaps comes from James C. Scott's *The Art of Not Being Governed: An Anarchist History of Upland Southeast Asia* (2010), for it is making a considerable splash (see, for example, Hammond 2011; Krasner et al. 2011; Lieberman 2010), and may be on its way to becoming the key work that will introduce a generation of students to Southeast Asia. The sweep of ethnographic and historical material in the book is dazzling, as are the implications of its arguments for political theory. Indonesian materials do not figure significantly in this deeply romantic and utopian work, but it is from our position in this exclusionary zone that an ethnographically and theoretically informed critique of the work should be possible. Scott's study of deliberate and reactive statelessness, however compelling, imposes a stubbornly deterministic, political logic on upland peoples—state evasion—to explain all facets of upland life. Upland lifeworlds and politics are far more complex than Scott's stated simplifications would admit.

The state-of-the-field essays prepared well over a decade ago by John Bowen (1995) and Mary Steedly (1999) did a superb job of capturing the disciplinary energies of anthropologists prior to Suharto's fall in 1998, and called special attention to work that explored public culture, religion, gender, or violence. From what I can see, studies of public culture and violence have been pretty steady, the latter relating especially to the political turmoil after Suharto's fall, but also reaching back to the murky violence basic to his regime and the operations of the Indonesian nation-state (Rutherford 1998, 2003; Siegel 2000, 2006, 2010). (For more on the ethnography of violence in Indonesia, see Patricia Spyer's contribution in this volume). Islam, meanwhile, has come to occupy the forefront of anthropological studies in Indonesia. Though most American anthropologists presently working on Indonesian Islam lack a command of Arabic, they nonetheless have aimed at grasping the ethics of self-fashioning during a time of deepening popular piety, a theme in some of my own recent work (George 2008, 2010a), but a topic that reaches back to James T. Siegel's classic work, *The Rope of God* (1969) and James Peacock's *Muslim Puritans* (1978). I would point, in particular, to work by Suzanne Brenner, Carla Jones, Daromir Rudnyckyj, and James B. Hoesterey, who have looked at Islam and self-fashioning in urban Java and West Java with respect to gender and class (Brenner 1996, 2011; Jones 2010), neoliberal "spiritual economies" (Rudnyckyj 2010), and media, civic virtue, and moral reform movements (Hoesterey 2008, 2012). I am aware of research being done, too, on NGOs, corporations (Welker 2009, 2011), health, environment, and development (such Tanya Li's *The Will to Improve* [2007]), but confess I hardly keep up.

Indonesia has yet to grab much attention in the field of Southeast Asian art history. In the meantime, the field of visual cultural studies has sparked new ethnographic ventures in Indonesian Studies. Karen Strassler's *Refracted Visions: Popular Photography and National Modernity in Java* (2010); Kathleen Adams' work on Toraja material culture (2006); ruminations by James Siegel on cameras and Aceh (2010); and essays by Patricia Spyer on photography in Aru (2009), on media and murals in Ambon (2008), and her edited volume with Mary Steedly (*Images that Move* 2013) have been pioneering the ethnographic study of visual culture in Indonesia. For my own part, I have been pushing for an interdisciplinary "ethnographic art history" in my work on contemporary Indonesian Islamic art (2010a; 2012a; 2012b). Within Indonesian Studies, there has been little precedent for art historical investigation and analysis beyond the fine surveys provided by Claire Holt (1967) and Asti Wright (1994), or for explorations in visual culture, and so it comes as no surprise that anthropologists pursuing this work on the visual find themselves having to improvise investigative protocols or to borrow them from studies unrelated to Indonesian particulars.

Helping to shift and refigure the ethnographic field of "Indonesian Studies" are the efforts of historians and literary historians working on the Indian Ocean region. I have in mind not only the work of our host, Eric Tagliacozzo (2009), and Michael Laffan (2007, 2011), but also the striking social, religious, and literary connections painstakingly detailed in Sheldon Pollock's work on what he calls the "Sanskrit cosmopolis" and the "cosmopolitan vernacular" (2009); Ronit Ricci's (2010, 2011) fascinating and revealing portrait of Islamic literary networks and the "Arabic cosmopolis" linking Arabic, Tamil, Malay, and Javanese versions of *The Book of One Thousand Questions*; and Engseng Ho's extensive project on the Hadramawt Arab diaspora that sprawls across the Indian Ocean from Yemen to Indonesia (2004, 2006).

These works give us imaginative lift and leverage, and open "Indonesian Studies" to potentially broader audiences. Their emphasis on diaspora and networks, on people, things, and ideas in motion, works fruitfully to keep us from sequestering our analyses within states and tightly bound locales. Above all, I think these studies can help us provincialize the Middle East within a history of Islam, and remind audiences (and deans with faculty lines) that Islam is produced transnationally and should not be equated with the Middle East.

Prospects for interdisciplinary discussions with specialists on South Asia and the Middle East seem to me especially promising. Much of what I read in visual culture and art history comes out of ethnographic and art historical work in India, Pakistan, and South Asian diasporic networks (e.g., Dadi 2010; Ramaswamy 2010), and a recent symposium convened in Doha, Qatar, to discuss the cultural politics of national and religious iconographies in the work of (formerly Indian, and now late Qatari) painter M. F. Husain allowed several of us to find resonant comparisons with work that has been done in Southeast Asian art and art history. As but one further and wonderful example of cross-regional exchange: In 2008, Sri Lanka specialists Charles Hallisey (Religious/Buddhist Studies, Harvard) and Deborah Winslow (Anthropology, National Science Foundation) convened a day-long pre-conference event at the Annual South Asia Meeting in Madison, Wisconsin, on J. Stephen Lansing's *Perfect Order: Recognizing Complexity in Bali* (2006). The goal was to "stimulate new questions and investigations that went beyond [the book's] geographic focus on Bali and its special interpretive concerns." Participants included specialists on Southeast Asia and Sri Lanka, as well as Lansing himself, who participated via a video feed from Bali.

Our interdisciplinary work does not have to be confined to academic constituencies. And it does not have to traffic in traveling theories or concepts. Unexpected solidarities can form around the concrete marvels of Indonesian life. In March 2010, Kirin Narayan and I traveled to Baroda, India, to meet with activist–scholar Ganesh Devy. Professor Devy has been a leading voice in defending and preserving aboriginal, or adivasi, languages and cultures across India, politically delicate work in that many adivasi peoples are locked in, or subject to, armed conflict with the government as their land and resources have been usurped by predatory corporations and state agencies. After meeting with him, we had a chance to go to the Bhasha Adivasi Academy at Tejgadh, Gujarat, founded by Devy, but now administered and staffed by Rathwa adivasi, who are famous for their wall painting, a practice deeply entwined with shamanism.

During the drive to the academy and then later, as we were escorted through a museum of adivasi folk arts, my fieldwork with the mappurondo religious enclave in South Sulawesi's hill country became a source of curiosity. The staff members who were showing us around peppered me with questions about mappurondo women's rituals and trance. I found myself explaining and even acting out portions of women's rituals recalled from over two decades earlier—material that was extraneous to my first and only book of mappurondo ritual life (1996). I had gone to this adivasi academy to learn more about indigenous communities in India, and yet the force of my interlocutors' curiosity turned me back to contemplating hard-won materials from field research in Indonesia, and how they might find an appreciative audience in the transnational networks linking indigenous peoples.

At the beginning of this paper I mentioned how Tsing attributed the innovativeness of Indonesian Studies simultaneously to the marginal status of

Indonesia in our home disciplines and to our inclination toward interdisciplinary conversation. All the same, I am convinced that the "touch" of a place—Indonesia—guides or ought to guide us in our particular intellectual ventures. This touch does not have to incline us toward narrow localisms and particularisms, but should instead open us to understanding the world currents that make Indonesia the place it is, even as it leaves us vulnerable to the phantasms, compulsions, and wonders conjured by Indonesian cultures.

It was the distinct feeling of being "out of touch" with Indonesia that prompted me to travel there again in June and July 2011, not long after the Cornell conference. It had been roughly nine years since I had done sustained fieldwork in Indonesia. So much was changing there, and I was unnerved by doubt. I no longer knew if I had sufficient resilience or imagination to reinvent myself, or to readjust my ethnographic dispositions, groomed as they were for so long in the fields of folklore, the ethnography of speaking, and the cultural anthropology of the Geertzian epoch. What gave me special pause was a news item mentioning that, sometime in the previous two years, Indonesia had passed a demographic threshold: More Indonesians now live in cities than in rural or non-urban settings. All my fieldwork since 1995 had been in Bandung, and a quick look through online databases suggested that the majority of the US dissertation projects on Indonesia in the discipline of cultural anthropology over the past ten years have been based on urban field research. Another challenge to my habits of thinking came from Sam Campbell-Nelson, a son of good friends, now in his mid-twenties, who grew up in Kupang and the upland village of Lelobatan, in West Timor. His stories about predatory marble mining, environmental damage, and various NGO counter-initiatives earlier in the decade disturbed me, but did not surprise. This did: In 2010, there was still no electricity in Lelobatan. Part of the week's routine for the upland farming families in Lelobatan is to send someone to walk for several hours to the town of Kapan to recharge the family cell phone(s) for Rp2000 per charge per phone. The phones are used to SMS/text-message networks of kin and friends scattered in Kupang and throughout Indonesia. What should we make of this?

In June I traveled in the Sulawesi highlands to the headwaters of the Salu Mambi, the site of my fieldwork in the early to mid-1980s and a place I had not seen in sixteen years. Once a remote part of South Sulawesi, the region (refigured as part of Kabupaten Mamasa) now belonged to the new province of West Sulawesi, whose governor hailed from the headwater settlement of Aralle. The dirt roadway opened by the Dutch in the 1930s between Polewali and Mambi—rutted, muddy, incessantly under collapse, and only occasionally in repair—was still the main artery in and out of the region, and kept upland communities economically and socially harnessed to Makassar and the province of South Sulawesi. Fearing continued deforestation and large swaths of resource extraction, I instead saw what appeared to me as better forest cover than I had known in the 1980s. Smallholder farmers had abandoned shade-grown robusta coffee for cocoa, and signs of the material prosperity attributed to the chocolate boom—buildings, clothes, electricity, foods, fuels, motorbikes, televisions, cellphones, obesity—were abundant in both hamlets and marketplaces. Muslim townsfolk in Mambi were far more observant than they had been sixteen years before, consonant with the rise of popular piety throughout Indonesia and efforts to promulgate and constrain sensibilities and conduct in line with shari'a law. Upland Christians seemed factionalized, and preoccupied with efforts to establish kin-based congregations under the aegis of the Protestant Gereja Toraja Mamasa. The divisive politics that accompanied decentralization and the partition and reorganization of highland administration in 2003–04 had lost their rawness, but was reprised in partisan debate over the decision of the Menteri Dalam Negeri in late June to unseat the Bupati of Mamasa following the latter's conviction on corruption charges.

I might linger on any number of changes, such as all-season motorbike trails, and the boom in cellular (mobile) phones, which caught on only after the first cell tower was erected in the valley in 2010. Now that there is "signal" (*sinyal*), people are scrambling to purchase cell phones to maintain family and trade contacts through voice and text-messaging. Yet the most stunning change, in my view, has been the scale of indebtedness in the highlands, prompted by the proliferation of banks and credit schemes. Civil servants seemed most active (but hardly alone) in this regard, borrowing to build and furnish middle-class homes, to purchase motorbikes and phones, to fund schooling, to pay for weddings and the hajj, or to meet health care costs associated with major operations and catastrophic illnesses. Corruption and rising prices on goods are also creating a demand for money. The rapidly expanding economy is surely luring people to borrow for business or trade ventures, too. (Tending rice fields and gardens—the mainstays of the 1980s—does not figure strongly in the new economic thinking of upland townsfolk, and fields are now rented out or put up as collateral on loans.) The levels of debt described to me strike me as disproportionate to people's incomes and capacity to pay off their loans. My hunch is that the debt levels mentioned to me may be attributed to the financialization of Indonesia's economy, and its penetration into everyday life. Travel in July to Rantepao (Tana Toraja), Kupang, Bandung, and Jakarta, only deepened my apprehensions about the place of household debt in everyday life. Urban roads choked with motorbikes and autos, lurid accounts of debt collectors intimidating or murdering borrowers, and the frenzy of shopping malls all attest to the life and afterlife of credit in Indonesia. One can find online reports that suggest that household debt is not a threat to Indonesia's financial sector, but seldom does one spot a report that assesses how the financial sector's credit instruments may be a threat to households.

It is hard for me to be upbeat about Indonesia. From the environmental and health risks posed by the predatory mining of manganese in Nusa Tenggara Timor, to the persecution of Ahmadiyya in West Java, and all the money-politics in between, I come away with exceptionally bleak feelings. As I write this in early 2012, I have been mourning, too, the passing of my teacher, A. L. ("Pete") Becker, just a short six weeks ago. Among the best of Pete's lessons about perspective and perspectivism were his insights about translation. All translation (Pete would say, quoting or paraphrasing José Ortega y Gasset) is at once too exuberant, saying too much, and too deficient, not saying enough. Yet one did not stop translating. What perhaps has to drive translation—though Pete never said so, to my recollection—is the intimacy, perseverance, and love needed to apprentice oneself to different ways of speaking. Living with a Javanese shadow play, a Burmese proverb, or a Malay sentence, Pete reminded us, meant knowing the wonders of what to say and what not to say, when, how, and to whom. Life in Indonesia today seems, to me, so precarious, vulnerable, and at risk that Pete's lessons about the said and unsaid ought to be pushed into more urgent, critical, and ethical register. To quote Elizabeth Povinelli (2011, 191) from her work on "economies of abandonment," anthropologists need to "rigorously demonstrate the noncorrespondence between what is claimed and what is, and the techniques of power that allow the claimed world to appear not merely the actual world but the best of all actual worlds."

Works Cited

Adams, Kathleen M. *Art as Politics: Recrafting Identities, Tourism, and Power in Tana Toraja, Indonesia*. Honolulu, HI: University of Hawaii Press, 2006.

Anderson, Benedict O'G. *Imagined Communities: Reflections on the Origin and Spread of Nationalism*. New York, NY: Verso, 1983.

Asad, Talal. *Formations of the Secular: Christianity, Islam, Modernity*. Stanford, CA: Stanford University Press, 2003.

Becker, Alton L. *Beyond Translation: Essays toward a Modern Philology*. Ann Arbor, MI: University of Michigan Press, 1995.

Becker, Alton L. and Aram Yengoyan, eds. *The Imagination of Reality: Essays in Southeast Asian Coherence Systems*. New York, NY: Ablex, 1979.

Bowen, John. "The Forms Culture Takes: A State of the Field Essay on the Anthropology of Southeast Asia." *Journal of Asian Studies* 54.4 (1995): 1047–78.

Brenner, Suzanne. "Reconstructing Self and Society: Javanese Muslim Women and 'the Veil.'" *American Ethnologist* 23.4 (1996): 673–97.

——. "Private Moralities in the Public Sphere: Democratization, Islam, and Gender in Indonesia." *American Anthropologist* 113.3 (2011): 478–90.

Dadi, Iftikar. *Modernism and the Art of Muslim South Asia*. Chapel Hill, NC: University of North Carolina Press, 2010.

Dunham, Stanley Ann. "Surviving against the Odds: Village Industry in Indonesia." *Museum Anthropology Review* 4.2 (2009): 255–57. Online open journal.

Geertz, Clifford. *The Religion of Java*. Chicago, IL: University of Chicago Press, 1960.

——. *Peddlers and Princes: Social Development and Economic Change in Two Indonesian Towns*. Chicago, IL: University of Chicago Press, 1968.

——. "Blurred Genres: The Refiguration of Social Thought." *American Scholar* 49.2 (1980): 165–79.

George, Kenneth M. *Showing Signs of Violence: The Cultural Politics of a Twentieth-Century Headhunting Ritual*. Berkeley, CA: University of California Press, 1996.

——. "Violence, Culture, and the Indonesian Public Sphere: Reworking the Geertzian Legacy." *Violence: Culture, Performance and Expression*. Ed. Neil L. Whitehead. Santa Fe, NM: SAR Press, 2004. 25–54.

——. "Ethical Pleasure, Visual Dzikir, and Artistic Subjectivity in Contemporary Indonesia." *Material Religion* 4.2 (2008): 172–93.

——. "Ethics, Iconoclasm, and Qur'anic Art in Indonesia." *Cultural Anthropology* 24.4 (2009): 589–621.

——. *Picturing Islam: Art and Ethics in a Muslim Lifeworld*. Malden, MA: Wiley-Blackwell, 2010.

——. Review of S. Ann Dunham, *Surviving against the Odds: Village Industry in Indonesia. Museum Anthropology Review* 4.2 (2010): 255–57. Online open journal.

——. "Lifewriting and the Making of Companionable Objects: Reflections on Sunaryo's *Titik Nadir." Locating Life Stories: Beyond East-West Binaries in (Auto)Biographical Studies.* Ed. Maureen Perkins. Honolulu: University of Hawaii Press, 2012a. 35–54.

——. "The Cultural Politics of Modern and Contemporary Islamic Art in Southeast Asia." *Modern and Contemporary Southeast Asian Art.* Ed. Nora A. Taylor and Boreth Ly. Ithaca, NY: Cornell Southeast Asia Program Publications, 2012b.

Hammond, Ruth. "The Battle over Zomia." *Chronicle of Higher Education.* http://chronicle.com/article/The-Battle-Over-Zomia/128845/. Accessed December 26, 2011.

Hefner, Robert W. *Civil Islam: Muslims and Democratization in Indonesia.* Princeton, NJ: Princeton University Press, 2000.

Ho, Engseng. "Empire through Diasporic Eyes: A View from the Other Boat." *Comparative Studies in Society and History* 46.2 (2004): 210–46.

——. *The Graves of Tarim: Genealogy and Mobility across the Indian Ocean.* Berkeley, CA: University of California Press, 2006.

Hoesterey, James B. "Marketing Morality: The Rise, Fall, and Rebranding of AA Gym." *Expressing Islam: Religious Life and Politics in Indonesia.* Ed. Greg Fealy and Sally White. Singapore: Institute of Southeast Asian Studies, 2008. 90–107.

——. "Prophetic Cosmopolitanism: Islam, Pop Psychology, and Civic Virtue in Indonesia." *City & Society* special issue, "Muslim Cosmopolitanism: Movement, Identity, and Contemporary Reconfigurations." Ed. Mara A. Leichtman and Dorothea Schulz. 24.1 (April 2012): 38–61.

Holt, Claire. *Art in Indonesia: Continuities and Change.* Ithaca, NY: Cornell University Press, 1967.

Jones, Carla. "Materializing Piety: Gendered Anxieties about Faithful Consumption in Contemporary Urban Indonesia." *American Ethnologist* 73.4 (2010): 617–37.

Keane, Webb. *Christian Moderns: Freedom and Fetish in the Mission Encounter.* Berkeley, CA: University of California Press, 2007.

Krasner, Stephen D., et al. "State, Power, Anarchism." *Perspectives in Politics* 9.1 (2011): 79–102.

Laffan, Michael F. *Islamic Nationhood and Colonial Indonesia: The Umma Below the Winds.* London: Routledge, 2007.

——. *The Makings of Indonesian Islam: Orientalism and the Narration of a Sufi Past.* Princeton, NJ: Princeton University Press, 2011.

Lansing, Stephen J. *Perfect Order: Recognizing Complexity in Bali.* Princeton, NJ: Princeton University Press, 2006.

Li, Tania Murray. *The Will to Improve: Governmentality, Development, and the Practice of Politics.* Durham, NC: Duke University Press, 2007.

Lieberman, Victor B. "A Zone of Refuge in Southeast Asia? Reconceptualizing Interior Spaces." Review of James C. Scott, *The Art of Not Being Governed: An Anarchist History of Upland Southeast Asia. Journal of Global History* 5 (2010): 333–46.

Nixon, Rob. *Slow Violence and the Environmentalism of the Poor.* Cambridge, MA: Harvard University Press, 2011.

Ong, Aihwa. *Flexible Citizenship: The Cultural Logics of Transnationality.* Durham, NC: Duke University Press, 1999.

Peacock, James L. *Rites of Modernization: Symbolic and Social Aspects of Indonesian Proletarian Drama.* Chicago, IL: University of Chicago Press, 1968.

——. *Muslim Puritans: Reformist Psychology in Southeast Asian Islam.* Berkeley, CA: University of California Press, 1978.

Pollock, Sheldon. *The Language of the Gods in the World of Men: Sanskrit, Culture, and Power in Premodern India.* Berkeley, CA: University of California Press, 2009.

Povinelli, Elizabeth A. *Economies of Abandonment: Social Belonging and Endurance in Late Liberalism.* Durham, NC: Duke University Press, 2011.

Ramaswamy, Sumathi, ed. *Barefoot across the Nation: M. F. Husain and the Idea of India.* Oxford: Routledge, 2010.

Ricci, Ronit. *Islam Translated: Literature, Conversion, and the Arabic Cosmopolis of South and Southeast Asia.* Chicago, IL: University of Chicago Press, 2011.

Rudnyckyj, Daromir. *Spiritual Economies: Islam, Globalization, and the Afterlife of Development.* Ithaca, NY: Cornell University Press, 2010.

Rutherford, Danilyn. "Waiting for the End in Biak: Violence, Order, and a Flag-Raising." *Indonesia* 67 (April 1998): 39–59.

——. *Raiding the Land of Foreigners: The Limits of the Nation on an Indonesian Frontier.* Princeton, NJ: Princeton University Press, 2003.

Scott, James C. *Weapons of the Weak: Everyday Forms of Peasant Resistance.* New Haven, CT: Yale University Press, 1987.

——. *The Art of Not Being Governed: An Anarchist History of Upland Southeast Asia.* New Haven, CT: Yale University Press, 2010.

Siegel, James T. *The Rope of God.* Berkeley, CA: University of California Press, 1969.

——. *A New Criminal Type in Jakarta: Counter-Revolution Today.* Durham, NC: Duke University Press, 2000.

——. *Naming the Witch.* Stanford, CA: Stanford University Press, 2006.

——. *Objects and Objections of Ethnography.* New York, NY: Fordham University Press, 2010.

Spyer, Patricia. "In and Out of the Picture: Photography, Ritual, and Modernity in Aru, Indonesia." *Photographies East: The Camera and its Histories in East and Southeast Asia.* Ed. R. C. Morris. Durham, NC: Duke University Press, 2009. 161–82.

——. "Blind Faith: Painting Christianity in Post-Conflict Ambon, Indonesia." *Social Text* 26.3 (2008): 11–37.

Steedly, Mary. "The State of Culture Theory in the Anthropology of Southeast Asia." *Annual Review of Anthropology* 28 (1999): 431–54.

Steedly, Mary, and Patricia Spyer, eds. *Images that Move*. Santa Fe, NM: SAR Press, 2013.

Strassler, Karen. *Refracted Visions: Popular Photography and National Modernity in Java*. Durham, NC: Duke University Press, 2010.

Tagliacozzo, Eric. *Southeast Asia and the Middle East: Islam, Movement, and the Long Duree*. Stanford, CA: Stanford University Press, 2009.

Tsing, Anna Lowenhaupt, contributor. *Weighing the Balance: Southeast Asian Studies Ten Years After*. Proceedings of two SSRC meetings, November 15 and December 10, 1999. New York, NY: Southeast Asia Program, Social Science Research Council, 2000.

——. *Friction: An Ethnography of Global Connection*. Princeton, NJ: Princeton University Press, 2004.

Welker, Marina A. "Corporate Security Begins in the Community: Mining, the Corporate Social Responsibility Industry, and Environmental Advocacy in Indonesia." *Cultural Anthropology* 24.1 (2009): 142–79.

——. "Corporate Lives: New Perspectives on the Social Life of the Corporate Form." Introduction to Special Issue in *Current Anthropology* 52.S3 (2011): 3–16.

Wright, Astri. *Soul, Spirit, and Mountain: Preoccupations of Contemporary Indonesian Painters*. Oxford: Oxford University Press, 1994.

Yengoyan, Aram A. "Clifford Geertz, Cultural Portraits, and Southeast Asia." *Journal of Asian Studies* 68.4 (2009): 1215–30.

AFTER VIOLENCE—A DISCUSSION

Patricia Spyer[1]

Who does not recall the scene of animal fury and unleashed bestiality, the explosion of chicken blood, feathers, and dust, the glint of razor-sharp spurs slicing the air, and the ragged blood-drenched remains of the defeated cock at the center of Clifford Geertz's *Balinese Cockfight*? "Deep play" was his term for this dramatic combination of status warfare, emotional excess, and displaced or sublimated violence of central significance to Balinese society of the time (1973). I begin with this privileged disciplinary trope of anthropology—and not just the anthropology of Indonesia—because, like Geertz, I am interested in the variety of forms that violence may assume, within particular circumstances and locations, and the complex ways in which violence inflects, molds, and suffuses the social—quite spectacularly at times though more often in subtle, oblique ways.

Invited to consider the arc of Indonesian studies from the perspective of my own discipline, anthropology, I might have chosen any number of topics to address. Looking back, say, from the mid-nineties on, most salient for me is the move away from scholarly work beholden in one or another fashion to the New Order's gravitational pull—of which the almost perfunctory invocation then of Jakarta's Indonesia-in-Miniature park with its odd semblance of order and undisturbed diversity seems especially emblematic (Acciaioli 1985; Pemberton 1994; Rutherford 1996; Spyer 1996). The belated recognition of Islam's central if previously too often disavowed place in Indonesia's making, and the understanding of Indonesia as shot through and contoured by larger transnational forces and flows, have been the sources of much excellent work in recent times, as has, more generally, the analysis of religion's many complicated lifeworlds across the archipelago (Aragon 2000; Beatty 1999; Bowen 1993; George 2010; George and Wilford 2005; Ho 2006; Keane 2007; Laffan 2003; Tagliacozzo 2009). Apart from the focus on Indonesia's new middle classes—their aspirations, fashions, and "air-conditioned lifestyles" (Brenner 1999; Jones 2007; van Leeuwen 1997)—together with the neo-liberal environment that

[1] I would like to thank Erik Tagliacozzo for inviting me to the "State of Indonesian Studies" conference, as well as the two respondents on the Anthropology panel—Marina Welker and Andrew Wilford—my co-panelists, Ken George and Danilyn Rutherford, and the larger audience of Indonesianists for their generous discussion and questions. I would also like to acknowledge Rafael Sánchez's helpful comments on an early version of this essay and Karen Strassler's on a much later one.

shapes these (Rudnyckyi 2010; Welker 2011), the increasing attention to cities, the built environment, and urban and youth culture offer exciting perspectives on both the everyday and the more extraordinary challenges and concerns that confront the country's citizens (Baulch 2007; Mrázek 2010; Simone and Rao 2012). Another topic that stands out is the mounting awareness of the extent to which media and technology inform the constitution of subjectivity as well as their larger role in the formation of "Indonesia"—from the pleasures of listening to the radio and the smoothness of asphalt roads in the late colonial Netherlands East Indies, as described in Rudolf Mrázek's *Engineers of Happy Land* and the celebrated contribution of print capitalism to Indonesia's "imagined community," recognized by Benedict Anderson, to Karen Strassler's recent compelling analysis of the "refracted visions" and visual technologies through which that same community has come to know and recognize itself over time (Mrázek 2002; Anderson 1991; Strassler 2010). Religion and the state, along with culture theory and other topics dealt with, respectively, in John Bowen and Mary Steedly's fine state-of-the field reviews from the 1990s, also warrant revisiting in the wake of the New Order's demise (Bowen 1995; Steedly 1999). While my contribution here touches variously on some of the above, I focus especially on violence. This essay is therefore not only highly circumscribed but necessarily partial, shaped as it is by my own research interests and sense of what, broadly speaking, animates the more recent and ongoing anthropological and related scholarly work on Indonesia.

Specifically, I consider themes of violence and its varied formation that tend to be overlooked or not always recognized as such, being resistant, perhaps, to more conventional ways of understanding what constitutes violence. The kinds of violence whose operation and modalities I consider here—culled widely from the rich body of ethnographic and historical work on Indonesia—tend to be located off-stage or at the margins of what is sometimes narrowly circumscribed as "real" violence or violence that is characteristically spectacular and "eventful," of the kind that the mass media often identify with "hot spots." For those familiar with the innovative ethnographies on Indonesia that take marginality as a central problematic, it should come as no surprise that there is much to be gained by looking *there* and, perspectively, *from there* (Steedly 1993; Tsing 1993).[2] It is also "the so-called margins," as Jean and John Comaroff insist, "that often experience tectonic shifts in the order of things first, most visibly, most horrifically—and most energetically, creatively, ambiguously" (2006, 41). In Jemma Purdey's "Describing *kekerasan*," a thoughtful overview of writing about violence in Indonesia after the New Order (2004), she raises the issue of violence on the margins, identifying it primarily with particular kinds of violence— violence against women, violence against migrants, domestic violence, and then violence that for a variety of reasons appears especially difficult to access or gauge, including what Purdey terms "psychological" violence and violence that would be "unsayable," or only narratable with considerable difficulty (207). Invoking Achille Mmembe on the postcolony, she recognizes how state or authoritarian violence may

---

[2] Mary Steedly notes how the idea of marginality offered an important corrective to anthropological studies that took a bounded, autonomous place for culture as their point of departure while also recognizing that "even the most isolated locales were those through which ... power and influence emanating from dominant centers located elsewhere." Mary Steedly, "The State of Culture Theory in the Anthropology of Southeast Asia," *Annual Review of Anthropology* 28 (1999): 443.

penetrate and suffuse every space from the economy and domestic life to language and consciousness—even after it is gone.

Rather than violence that simply has been "overlooked," it is more precisely the latter "spirit of violence," in Mmembe's formulation, which I am most interested in pursuing here (Mmembe 2001, 175). In my work on Ambon, for instance, I do so by foregrounding and problematizing the idea of postviolence, exploring theoretically how this concept acknowledges the fraught temporalities, displacements, and often contradictory regimes of change entailed in violence's production and its complicated afterlives (unpublished manuscript, 2006). In pursuing the spirit of violence, I also heed Mary Steedly's call in her 1999 review article "The State of Culture Theory in the Anthropology of Southeast Asia" to not only localize violence—something that much recent work on violence in Indonesia does a very good job of—but to keep "the landscape of the banal" in view (1999, 445–46). To the crucial temporality of, in her words, the "things that don't fall apart" and "the ordinary routines of everyday life ... when expectations hold," I would add the way in which the banal is itself rearranged by violence as the investment and trust in everyday appearances wane and the taken-for-granted shape of things—foremost, perhaps, that of others and selves—and the circumstances in which these conventionally manifest themselves shift, morph, and may become unmoored, often in highly disturbing and startling ways (ibid). Relevant also to grasping the relationship between violence and the everyday is what Gyanendra Pandey has called "routine violence," or the violence that is part and parcel of the production and continuity of contemporary political arrangements, or, put otherwise, the enabling conditions of what commonly counts as violence (2006).

A few caveats are in place. I do not mean to suggest that Indonesia is an especially or unusually violent country. A number of scholars have expressed concern about the centrality of violence as a topic of study following Suharto's fall, although this would seem to overlook how all the writing about violence represents an attempt to come to grips with the legacy of a regime that was itself inaugurated by extreme violence and deployed violence strategically and deviously in the process of developing its own particular brand of governmentality.[3] Some also venture that writing about violence is itself laden with risk; one Indonesian colleague even condemned the publications appearing on the Ambon conflict while it was still underway as unequivocally "written in blood" (personal communication). Other authors hasten to underscore how Indonesia's violence is neither novel nor recent but longstanding as they marshal such glaring examples of New Order brutality— beyond its "foundation" on "a mountain of skeletons" (Anderson 2008)—as the invasion and occupation of East Timor, the devastating military actions in Aceh and Papua, and the so-called Petrus murders of the 1980s (Pannell 2003, 1; Schulte Nordholt and van Klinken 2010, 6). Somewhat differently, Pemberton's groundbreaking book *On the Subject of "Java"* shows how the unruffled "appearance of order" that characterized the Suharto regime hinged on a discourse of culture that was itself violently repressive and authoritarian (1994).

---

[3] As Purdey observes, "some would argue that the recent interest in violence among scholars has placed violence at the centre of Indonesia's history" prompting "some to ask, is there anything else but violence in Indonesia?" Jemma Purdey, "Describing Kekerasan; Some Observations on Writing about Violence in Indonesia after the New Order," *Bijdragen tot de Taal-, Land en Volkenkunde* 160, 2/3 (2004): 196.

Focusing on violence more broadly does not mean glossing over the crucial differences between such distinct events and processes as the violence that overtook a young Kodinese girl hit by a Japanese truck whose sudden death due to novel, outside forces became commemorated in the "metaphoric fragility" of a foreign green bottle (Hoskins 1998, 178); or the complicated "acting out of violence"— physical as well as symbolic—on the built environment, whether in the failure of the new architecture that has arisen in Jakarta's Chinese district of Glodok in the aftermath of the May 1998 anti-Chinese gang rapes and riots to acknowledge and enable a working through of the trauma (Kusno 2010, 9), or the way in which martyrs' graves and other monuments erected post-conflict in North Maluku treacherously commemorate the religious aspects of the conflict there (Duncan 2009). Or, for that matter, the differences between traditional forms of violence like headhunting (Hoskins 1996), their newer "sublimated" versions (George 1996), the frequent exoticization of such practices in the media, or the way in which memories of oppression and violence at the hands of former Dutch colonizers, Indonesian state representatives, or in response to the New Order's development policies have spawned a generation of "new headhunters" (Pannell 2003, 80–82; Tsing 1996, 189–201). Meriting close attention is the violence intrinsic to representation from atrocity's reckoning in numbers or the ways in which the value of an art object, itself possibly acquired by force or as a result of war's displacements, becomes enhanced through its provenance from an allegedly "ferocious tribe," to the example of a Chinese-Indonesian photographer who confided to the anthropologist, "Look for yourself ... no matter how good the photograph, if it has a Chinese face, it won't win a contest ... I have to know my place. I am a minority here. How could a Chinese face represent Indonesia?" (Cribb 2001; Forshee 2003; Strassler 2010, 66).[4] Nor is the breakdown of trust in a community and the violence that may ensue the same as violence propagated by the state, its agents, or policies. One effect of the New Order's demise has been to reduce the tendency to think of the state as transcendent, Oz-like, and unified in its intentionality and will (Steedly 1999, 443), thereby opening up the possibility of recognizing the many agencies and agendas of which it is composed, as well as "the absence of a full state monopoly of legitimate violence" in twentieth-century Indonesia (Anderson 2001, 18). More insidious forms of violence include the way in which rumors and media reports feed on and foster violence, including crime, the specters that haunt Indonesian massacres refracted, following Siegel, through communists in 1965 and '66 and criminals in the so-called "mysterious killings" of 1983 and '84, and the threat of violence that keeps rape victims from going public and away from courts, keeps a debt system in place, or that underwrites self-censorship among journalists, politicians, artists, and ordinary citizens (Aragon 2005; Bubandt 2008; George 2010; Heryanto 1990, 1999; Keane 2009; Sen and Hill 2000; Siegel 1998, 211; Spyer 2005, 2000).

---

[4] Karen Strassler, *Refracted Visions: Popular Photography and National Modernity in Java* (Durham, NC: Duke University Press, 2010), p. 66. See also James T. Siegel on violence against the "Chinese" in Indonesia, a referent that he puts in quotes because "aggression against them is inextricably bound up with the definition of their citizenship, their loyalty to the nation, and their participation in the revolution. The insistence that they are not Indonesian, determined with regards to citizenship or sentiment, is, of course, always set against the possibility that they are members of the nation, just like 'us' from an Indonesian point of view." James T. Siegel, *A New Criminal Type in Jakarta: Counter-revolution Today* (Durham, NC: Duke University Press, 1998), p. 211.

Notwithstanding this enumeration of select violent events and processes, my aim in honing in on these other modalities of violence is not cumulative in the sense of adding more kinds of violence to the ones we already know. I aim instead to bring into sharper focus a problematic that has been emerging in some of the recent work on Indonesia—one that situates violence in all its complex specificity within the production, structuring, and destructuring of social life rather than seeing it as somehow derivative, one that tracks violence at the myriad sites of its production as opposed to an approach that assigns an identity to violence *a posteriori*, so that violence remains beholden to that identity, a mere byproduct thereof. This means understanding violence as a verb rather than a predicate or as something not merely expressive of the subject at hand in the sense of designating a property thereof, as is often the case in discussions of so-called ethnic violence, religious violence, communal violence, state violence, and the like. Rather than assuming types of violence, horizontal or vertical, or violence appended to sociological categories— ethnicity, religion, community—which violence then both depends on and disturbs, I join other scholars of Indonesia in exploring how violence works through, informs, and destabilizes a variety of different historically specific social formations.

Notable are some especially insightful analyses of the roots, genealogies, dynamics, effects, and figures that are key to, or a result of, violence, or that haunt violence's myriad operations—from the *jago, preman, dalang, cakalele* warrior, *witch, provokator,* and *massa* to the *pengungsi* or Internally Displaced Person (IDP), the latter a "new kind of person," following Hedman, "emblematic of the reordering of state processes through democratization (2008, 3)."[5] One of the most promising of the analytical possibilities entailed in this recent work is the sustained exploration and questioning of the nature of identity itself, recognizing that while identity is always necessarily fraught and internally divided, there is also much under ordinary conditions to keep it familiar, recognizable, and unremarkably in place. When, by contrast, the world is experienced as somehow out of joint—then things look different. A series of cascading events, all tellingly bearing their own name, made such an awareness inescapable in Indonesia—among these *Krismon,* the 1998 monetary crisis, then *Kristal,* or total crisis, through the heady spring of protests inaugurating *Reformasi,* Suharto's dramatic May 1998 step-down, and, following on its heels, the poetically named *pemekaran* or exuberant administrative "flowering" that has accompanied national decentralization. Even if all of this is reassuringly

---

[5] On these various figures see Kees van Dijk, *A Country in Despair: Indonesia between 1997 and 2000* (Leiden: KITLV Press, 2001); Henk Schulte Nordholt, "The Jago in the Shadow: Crime and 'Order' in the Colonial State in Java," *Review of Indonesian and Malaysian Affairs* 25,1 (1991): 74–91; Loren Ryter, "Pemuda Pancasila: The Last Loyalist Free Men of Suharto's New Order?" in *Violence and the State in Suharto's Indonesia,* ed. Benedict R. O'G. Anderson (Ithaca, NY: Cornell Southeast Asia Program Publications, 2001); Siegel, *A New Criminal Type in Jakarta;* Patricia Spyer, "Some Notes on Disorder in the Indonesian Postcolony," in *Law and Disorder in the Postcolony,* ed. Jean Comaroff and John L. Comaroff (Chicago, IL: University of Chicago Press, 2006), pp. 188–218; Phillip Winn, "Sovereign Violence, Moral Authority, and the Maluku Cakalele," in *A State of Emergency: Violence, Society, and the State in Eastern Indonesia,* ed. Sandra Pannell (Darwin: Northern Territory Press, 2003). Recent collections on violence in Indonesia include Benedict R. O'G. Anderson, "Introduction," in *Violence and the State in Suharto's Indonesia;* Dewi Fortuna Anwar, Hélène Bouvier, Glenn Smith, and Roger Tol, eds., *Violent Internal Conflicts in Asia Pacific: Histories, Political Economies and Policies* (Jakarta: Yayasan Obor, 2005); Freek Columbijn and Thomas Lindblad, eds., *Roots of Violence in Indonesia: Contemporary Violence in Historical Perspective* (Singapore: ISEAS, 2001); and Ingrid Wessel and Georgia Wimhöfer, eds., *Violence in Indonesia* (Hamburg: Abera Verlag, 2001).

designated a "period of transition" or cast, in other words, as a sort of "awkward moment of still-youthful legitimacy" (Morris 2013), such formulation glosses over the many alternations and adjustments—including the pervasive violence—of a world experienced, admittedly unevenly, in some deep, far-going sense as fundamentally disturbed.

Writing of urban space and architecture in the Indonesian capital, for instance, Abidin Kusno locates the unprecedented politics of memory and its articulation in Jakarta's built environment in direct relation to a sense of "looseness" at the center following the Suharto regime's collapse. "It is as if a central support that had stabilized the island of Java for ages has been removed," Kusno observes, "a sense of restlessness prevails among the inhabitants. There is a sense among the population that the center is no longer there, fixing, watching, and ordering their conduct" (2010). A number of consequences of this sense that the center is falling apart—a condition issuing in what in my own work I call "orphaned landscapes" (work in process)—include the creation of various civilian groups in Jakarta formed either loosely or tightly around identities "below" as well as "above" the nation, with familiar groupings those of class, professional, religious, ethnic, political, and moral affiliations and the increasing tendency of citizens to act on their own, with everyone safeguarding his or her own space and with little sense or obligation to a larger public (Kusno 2010).[6]

In his nuanced study of the patterning and unfolding of religious violence in Indonesia, John Sidel, citing René Girard, notes, more generally, how, "it is not the differences but the loss of them that gives rise to violence" (Sidel 2006, 13). Sidel's book *Riots, Pogroms, Jihad* on religious violence in Indonesia and his article on "The Manifold Meanings of Displacement" in Hedman's volume on *Conflict, Violence, and Displacement in Indonesia* is exemplary of the kind of analysis that I highlight here (Sidel 2006, 2008). While Hedman's introduction brings to the fore how displacement in conflict and violence has long been an integral if overlooked dynamic in the making of the Indonesian nation-state—or, at one and the same time, both a crucial structuring and destructuring dimension *within* violence's operation rather than beyond or *after* it—Sidel attends not only to the forced migration brought about by the inter-religious pogroms of 1999 and 2001 in Central Sulawesi, Maluku, and North Maluku, but also how these displacements were indebted, in turn, to the process of displacing internal anxieties regarding religious identities onto "others" that prefigured and animated the more identifiable physical violence (Hedman 2008, Sidel 2008). Crucial, again, here is a sense of the state's perceived withdrawal as the privileged arbiter of difference or a "loosening" at the center. Extreme manifestations of the loss of difference that gives rise to violence and must form part of its understanding are the incapacity to figure oneself at the heart of the brutal witch killings in East Java, analyzed by Siegel, or, somewhat differently, the unprecedented

---

[6] The important issue here is the imagination or "sense" of a loosening and withdrawal of the center that has had crucial effects in Jakarta as well as across the archipelago post-Suharto. I agree, however, with Henk Schulte Nordholt and Gerry van Klinken, who claim that it would be too simplistic to assume that the state has actually weakened. From a narrow and institutional perspective, the central state may *seem* to be weakened but they argue that quite a different picture emerges if one takes into account power structures across the country, both formal institutions and informal networks. See Henk Schulte Nordholt and Gerry van Klinken, "Introduction," in *Renegotiating Boundaries: Local Politics in Post-Suharto Indonesia*, ed. Henk Schulte Nordholt and Gerry van Klinken (Leiden: KITLV Press, 2010), p. 8.

spate of possessions in the context of Ambon's war when, in an urban environment carved into Muslim versus Christian territories, a number of Christians were possessed by Muslim spirits (Siegel 2006; Spyer forthcoming a). More revealing, though, was the identity of the key protagonist of these events—a Javanese convert to Christianity or prior "Muslim" and migrant "outsider," and, thus, a multiply split subject from the start. Along with a more in-depth consideration of these and other analyses, which situate violence's production in the uncertainties, realignments, and desperate work of constituting and refiguring identities in extraordinary circumstances, a longer discussion than is possible here, would review the body of work on the genealogies, roots, patterns, agencies, and temporalities informing Indonesia's recent violence.

In an article titled "Questions on Witnessing Violence," published in *The Jakarta Post* in April 2011, Intan Paramaditha, the Indonesian filmmaker, writer, and doctoral student at New York University's Cinema Studies Department, writes how

> ... violence is ... neither new nor exotic for us Indonesians. We have been trained to see it, even live with it, since [an] early age. For some of us, watching *Pengkhianatan G30S/PKI* [The September 30, 1965, Movement/Communist Treason film] was an initiation to adulthood; we were suddenly forced to learn that we had a history, the one built upon eye-gouging women and decomposed tortured bodies. This was the form of violence legitimized and endorsed for public viewing to suit the interest of the Suharto regime. But later we knew we should look for what was not supposed to be seen. We engaged in the long project of unearthing the New Order crimes to make hidden violence visible. Like information, most violence during those times was spectral. The ability to see was a luxury. What is "new" since *Reformasi*, with thanks to the internet technology, is that we have passed the crisis of visibility. Before our eyes, everything is laid bare. Or is it? (Paramaditha 2011)

If I cite Paramaditha at some length, it is because she introduces so lucidly a number of important issues such as the pedagogical use of violence and violent images by the Suharto regime, the strategic pernicious play of visibility and invisibility, the redistribution of visuality and transformation of visual regimes in and in response to violence and political upheaval, and the role of mediation, technology, and spectrality. Ample evidence in the ethnographic and historical work on Indonesia attests to the importance of these themes and dynamics from the "forced witnessing as New Order pedagogy," including images of privileged violent incidents like the "disinterring of the bodies of six murdered generals from a well in 1965" featured in school textbooks, the ritualized annual screening of the New Order docudrama about the coup attempt, the highly tutored children's drawings of codified images of, say, the Indonesian Revolution or the crude cement statues of policemen overseeing traffic, to the "shock therapy" deployed in the "Mysterious Killings" of the early 1980s.[7]

---

[7] On the New Order pedagogy of forced witnessing and children's drawing contests, see Strassler's "*Reformasi* Through Our Eyes: Children as Witnesses of History in Post-Suharto Indonesia," *Visual Anthropology Review* 22,2 (2006): 53–70. Curtis Levy's film trilogy *Riding the Tiger* (1993) on Indonesia's authoritarian history with a particular focus on Suharto's New Order includes a scene depicting the production of the cement policemen. On the logic of shock therapy, see Joshua Barker, "State of Fear: Controlling the Criminal Contagion in

In the context of Indonesia's *Reformasi,* the "forced witnessing" of the New Order seems to have given way to other understandings of witnessing, though some of these—notably those involving children—remain indebted to the earlier pedagogical tradition in terms of strictly demarcating what should be seen and/or envisioned from what decidedly should not. New concerns about subjecting children to violent images on television surfaced alongside the figure of the child witness whose alleged unmediated innocence justified her recurrent appearance in anti-violence Public Service Announcements on radio and TV, while a limited repertoire of acceptable visions emerged in the pro-peace children's drawing contests that were ubiquitous across the archipelago (Spyer 2006; Strassler 2006). Among the many images exemplifying tutored vision are pictures of smiling mosques flanking smiling churches produced in refugee camps in North Sulawesi, a handshake conjoining a Muslim *imam* and a Protestant minister hovering like huge heroic busts over a cityscape that evokes the mass media images of the 2002 Malino II Peace Agreement and received first prize in an Ambon contest, and images of smiling soldiers pointing guns at smiling demonstrators, which together with similar images in other media not only recall New Order iconography of 1965–66 student demonstrations, but, characteristically, "'screened' out more disturbing memories of looting, military and police violence, and attacks on Chinese-Indonesians" (Spyer 2004a, 2004b; Strassler 2006, 63). Besides the child witness, photographs of student activists in 1998–99 enjoyed a special status as both witnesses of and documents of "history-in-the-making," while the moral agency attributed to their student makers meant that such photographs were seen as capable of extending the original act of witnessing beyond this charged if singular moment, thereby collectivizing the experience and historical potency of Indonesia's dramatic Reform (Strassler 2010).

Generally, what Paramaditha also invites us to consider is the larger connection between aesthetic-epistemological transformation and the post-New Order project of political reform—how practices and formations of visuality, witnessing, publicity, spectacle, and the like have been affected and altered by the collapse of the regime, the serial crises surrounding it, and the everyday complexities confronting the post-authoritarian fledgling democracy. Notable during *Reformasi* and its aftermath has been the acute awareness of visibility and, correspondingly, the proliferation of visual metaphors (Siegel 1998, 75, n1). Let me simply mention a few examples— Strassler's characterization of *Reformasi* as a time when many Indonesians felt that the eye of the international community was upon them (*di mata internasional*) and the possible implications thereof (Strassler 2004, 705); and Steedly's analysis of how highly popular forms of supernatural entertainment appropriate and remediate urban legends, moral panics, and familiar ghost stories in the process of transmuting a political desire for openness or "transparency" among members of the post-*Reformasi* generation, into the deeply ambivalent wish/dread for ordinarily invisible occult powers to "make an appearance" in everyday life (Steedly 2013). Less than six months after the May 1998 riots, Siegel observed how the term "transparency," hijacked from IMF (International Monetary Fund) discourse, had come to describe "the desirability of political events also being open to view" (1998, 75, n1). To cite Paramaditha, the desire to "unearth New Order crimes" and make "hidden violence visible" clearly inspired, among other initiatives in the immediate post-Suharto

Suharto's New Order," *Indonesia* 66 (October 1998): 7-42; and James T. Siegel, "Early Thoughts on the Violence of May 13 and 14, 1998, in Jakarta," *Indonesia* 66 (October 1998): 75–108.

period, a number of films, including documentary filmmaker Lexy Junior Rambadeta's *Mass Grave* (2001), featuring the exhumation of a mass grave and dramatically contested reburial of twenty-six victims of the 1965–66 killings, and, somewhat differently, Garin Nugroho's moving reenactment *Puisi Tak Terkuburkan* (2000)—literally, *Poetry Cannot Be Buried*—in which the Acehnese *didong* poet Ibrahim Kadir, who was imprisoned during these times, plays himself as color gradually seeps into the dark enclosure of the prison and displaces the black and white of the film.[8] Much as hidden violence conjures that which cannot be "buried" or concealed, so, too, inversely, do structures of visibility produce their own invisibilities as Strassler shows in her sensitive analysis of the gendered visibilities that showcase male-on-male violence while the "sexualized nature of the violence against Chinese-Indonesian women" prevented them from submitting themselves to "a public eye whose demand for transparent revelation could not be disentangled from pornographic probings and the threatening scrutiny of the military-state apparatus" (Strassler 2004, 716). At the other end of the archipelago, a situation of general blindness that I identify with Ambon's war produced forms of extreme perception, including the emergence of what I call anticipatory practices and hyper-hermeneutics as attempts to foresee and see through the shape-shifting, potentially treacherous appearances of a situation in which people often felt they could see nothing at all (Spyer 2006, 206).

Of interest also are the many representations of violence, traces of violence, and attempts to come to grips with violence in contemporary Indonesian art. Kenneth George discerns in some of the artist A. D. Pirous's paintings from 1998 "signs of anguish and troubled subjectivity"—a blackened, seemingly burnt surface "with a lurid and rounded red 'wound' of modeling paste and paint at its heart" and two Qu'ranic paintings featuring Pirous's novel depiction of the mysterious three-syllabic *Alif Lam Mim* that opens several sura and intimates for George a "crisis or collapse of legibility" registered in this work made in *Reformasi's* unfolding context (2010, 111). Another powerful example of the often intimate relay between the aesthetico-epistemological and political transformation is Nancy Florida's subtle tracking of the morphing werepig and monstrous specters in the Yogyakartan artist Djokopekik's three-painting series done in the final years of Suharto's regime (Florida 2008). Or consider Mary-Jo Delvecchio Good and Byron Good's analysis of the images of Indonesia as a nation "run amok" or "sick" in a number of artworks of the time (2008), or the careful scrutiny of the 50,000 rupiah bill bearing Suharto's face in the immediate aftermath of the regime's fall. An artist in Yogyakarta, a major site of anti-Suharto student protests, displayed an enlarged image of the bill with a hole where the "smiling general's" face normally would have been (Strassler 2009). The installation's title, "Anybody Can Be President," registers the ludic euphoria following the dictator's fall as it also highlights the privileged role of the streets and the performances taking place there, especially the ubiquitous *demo,* or demonstration. Such a close consideration of money as a material artifact is itself, more generally, a sign of crisis—one that in rapid succession was both financial and political in Indonesia—since under ordinary conditions money's materiality remains largely ignored (Foster 1998).

Especially these last examples draw attention to the many ways in which objects, object worlds, the natural and the built environment are implicated in violence—

---

[8] The English title is *A Poet: Unconcealed Poetry.*

unmoored, displaced, revalued, disfigured, destroyed, or redrawn by its traces, signs, or denial. Violence often compels a turn to or the creation of novel forms of expression and media. George was "floored" by a painting by Pirous featuring for the first time in his long artistic career a human figure, tellingly, Teuku Oemar, a martyr from the Dutch–Acehnese war (1873–1914), wielding a sword (George 2010, 112). I was similarly dumbfounded by the sight of huge Jesus faces on hijacked billboards and murals with Christian themes towering over passers-by in Ambon's postwar streets—even more so when I discovered that the painters and their young male supporters identified with the traditionally aniconic, Dutch colonial-derived Calvinist church (2008).

Thinking about the possibilities of violence's representation post-Suharto means taking into account the impact of media's liberalization during the late New Order and how the spread nationally of cell phone and video technologies, especially in areas at a remove from the capital, often received an added impulse from conflict. Such disturbances also, of course, provided new subject matter and, over time, a novel commodified value attached to the audiovisual testimony of violence and to the documentation of human suffering and urban destruction. The events also provided new experiences for many Indonesians, such as seeing one's own locality relayed back in the form of national and international news or via the more locally produced video CDs that spun off of various conflicts. In terms of further assessing the relationship between locality and violence's representation it might also be instructive, along the lines of Barker and Lindquist's article on "Figures of Indonesia Modernity," to gather together "figures of Indonesian violence"—the *provocator* and *preman*, to be sure, but also, say, the figure of the child mentioned above as both an uncontaminated, often clairvoyant, and privileged witness to violence and an embodiment of the future—in order to see what kind of larger landscape might emerge around them. (Barker, Lindquist, et al. 2009). Indeed, a brutal example of one such "gathering" provides the narrative scaffolding of *Jakarta 2039: 40 tahun, 9 bulan setelah 13–14 Mei 1998* based on a short story by Seno Gumira Ajidarma, with illustrations by Aznar Zacky. As the story is set in the Indonesian capital Jakarta forty years and nine months after the May 1998 rapes, the reader becomes gradually aware of the fraught kinship linking a former rapist, a Chinese-Indonesian victim of the rapes, and a forty-year old woman who was born nine months after these events and given up for adoption.

In terms of the future of the anthropology of Indonesia, I hope to see several things—further investigation of the complex relations among distinct forms and processes of violence—and let us not forget that even if we tend to recall Geertz's cockfight for its spectacular reading of sublimated violence, cockfighting was illegal at the time and this particular fight saw the arrival of police on the scene. I would also welcome more exploration of how transformations of an aesthetic-epistemological nature correspond, however complexly, to social and political change in Indonesia. Such exploration would necessarily entail an explicit engagement with how the process of "straightening history," called for under the sign of *Reformasi*, has subtly redrawn the horizons of our own and our students' research—the "archive" of 1965 and '66 has come into view, there is a renewed interest in the Netherlands, at least, in the "neglected" 1950s, and a remarkable Dutch–Indonesian *Recording the Future* project underway focused on post-Suharto

Indonesia.[9] Begun in 2003 and focused on documenting "daily life" in eight different locations across Indonesia, the project envisions a massive archive under construction for one hundred years and is animated by a nostalgia for a fleeting, impossible-to-capture "everyday," as such projects always are, and the sense of not knowing what the future holds or from where or how it will arrive. Yet *Recording the Future* might also be seen as a kind of counter-archive, offering perhaps the possibility of going against the grain of Indonesia's new "straightened history." From this perspective and in some unknowable future, it might even provide an alternative take on "the state of Indonesian studies."

Works Cited

Acciaioli, Greg. "Culture as Art: From Practice to Spectacle in Indonesia." *Canberra Anthropology* 8 (1985): 148–74.

Ajidarma, Seno Gumira and Aznar Jacky. *Jakarta 2039: 40 Tahun 9 Bulan Setelah 13–14 Mei 1998*. Jakarta: Galang Press, 2001.

Anderson, Benedict. "Obituary for a Mediocre Tyrant." *New Left Review* 50 (2008): 27–59.

——. "Introduction." *Violence and the State in Suharto's Indonesia*. Ed. Benedict R. O'G. Anderson. Ithaca, NY: Cornell Southeast Asia Program Publications, 2001.

——. *Imagined Communities: Reflections on the Origin and Spread of Nationalism*. London: Verso, 1991.

Anwar, Dewi Fortuna, Hélène Bouview, Glenn Smith, and Roger Tol, eds. *Violent Internal Conflicts in Asia Pacific: Histories, Political Economies, and Policies*. Jakarta: Yayasan Obor, 2005.

Aragon, Lorraine. "Mass Media Fragmentation and Narratives of Violent Action in Sulawesi's Poso Conflict." *Indonesia* 79 (April 2005): 1–55.

——. *Fields of the Lord: Animism, Christian Minorities, and State Development in Indonesia*. Honolulu: University of Hawaii Press, 2000.

Barker, Joshua. "State of Fear: Controlling the Criminal Contagion in Suharto's New Order." *Indonesia* 66 (October 1998): 7–42.

Barker, Joshua, and Johan Lindquist, and others. "Figures of Indonesian Modernity." *Indonesia* 87 (April 2009): 35–72.

Baulch, Emma. *Making Scenes: Reggae, Punk, and Death Metal in 1990s Bali*. Durham, NC: Duke University Press, 2007.

Beatty, Andrew. *Varieties of Javanese Religion: An Anthropological Account*. Cambridge: Cambridge University Press, 1999.

Bowen, John. "The Forms Culture Takes: A State-of-the-field Essay on the Anthropology of Southeast Asia." *Journal of Asian Studies* 54 (1995): 1047–78.

---

[9] *Recording the Future: An Audiovisual Archive of Everyday Life in Indonesia in the 21st Century*. A collaboration of the Royal Netherlands Institute for Southeast Asian and Caribbean Studies (KITLV), Offstream Film, and the Indonesian Institute of Sciences (LIPI). 2003 ff.

——. *Muslims through Discourse*. Princeton, NJ: Princeton University Press, 1993.

Brenner, Suzanne. "On the Public Intimacy of the New Order: Images of Women in the Popular Indonesian Print Media." *Indonesia* 67 (April 1999): 13–37.

Bubandt, Nils. "Rumors, Pamphlets and the Politics of Paranoia in Indonesia." *Journal of Asian Studies* 67 (2008): 789–817.

Columbijn, Freek, and Thomas Lindblad, eds. *Roots of Violence in Indonesia: Contemporary Violence in Historical Perspective*. Singapore: ISEAS, 2001.

Comaroff, Jean, and John L. Comaroff. "Law and Disorder in the Postcolony: An Introduction." *Law and Disorder in the Postcolony*. Ed. Jean Comaroff and John L. Comaroff. Chicago, IL: University of Chicago, 2006.

Cribb, Robert. "How Many Deaths? Problems in the Statistics of Massacre in Indonesia (1965–66) and East Timor (1975–1980)." *Violence in Indonesia*. Ed. Ingrid Wessel and Georgia Wimhöfer. Hamburg: Abera Verlag, 2001.

DelVecchio Good, Mary-Jo, and Byron Good. "Indonesia Sakit: Indonesian Disorders and the Subjective Experience and Interpretive Politics of Contemporary Indonesian Artists. *Postcolonial Disorders*. Ed. Mary-Jo DelVecchio Good, Sandra Teresa Hyde, Sarah Pinto, and Byron Good. Berkeley, CA: University of California Press, 2008.

Dijk, Kees van. *A Country in Despair: Indonesia between 1997 and 2000*. Leiden: KITLV Press, 2001.

Duncan, Christopher R. "Reconciliation and Revitalization: The Resurgence of Tradition in Postconflict Tobelo, North Maluku, Eastern Indonesia." *Bijdragen tot de Taal-, Land- en Volkenkunde* 165.4 (2009): 429–58.

Florida, Nancy. "A Proliferation of Pigs: Specters of Monstrosity in Reformation Indonesia." *Public Culture* 20.3 (2008): 497–530.

Forshee, Jill. "Traces of Theft and Loss: Arts, Provenance, and Violence in Sumba and Timor, or Can Anyone Own Anything from Anywhere?" *A State of Emergency: Violence, Society, and the State in Eastern Indonesia*. Ed. Sandra Pannell. Darwin: Northern Territory Press, 2003.

Foster, Robert J. "Your Money, Our Money, the Government's Money: Finance and Fetishism in Melanesia." *Border Fetishisms: Material Objects in Unstable Places*. Ed. Patricia Spyer. New York, NY, and London: Routledge, 1998.

Geertz, Clifford. "Deep Play: Notes on the Balinese Cockfight." *The Interpretation of Cultures*. New York, NY: Basic Books, 1973.

George, Kenneth M. *Picturing Islam: Art and Ethics in a Muslim Lifeworld*. Chichester: Wiley-Blackwell, 2010.

——. *Headhunting Ritual*. Berkeley, CA: University of California Press, 1996.

George, Kenneth M., and Andrew C. Wilford. *Spirited Politics: Religion and Public Life in Contemporary Southeast Asia*. Ithaca, NY: Cornell Southeast Asia Program Publications, 2005.

Hedman, Eva-Lotta E. "Introduction: Dynamics of Displacement in Indonesia." *Conflict, Violence, and Displacement in Indonesia*. Ed. Eva-Lotta E. Hedman. Ithaca, NY: Cornell Southeast Asia Program Publications, 2008. 3–27.

Heryanto, Ariel. "State Ideology and Civil Discourse." *State and Civil Society in Indonesia*. Ed. Arief Budiman. Center of Southeast Asian Studies, Monash Papers on Southeast Asia, No. 22, 1990.

——. "Rape, Race, and Reporting." *Reformasi: Crisis and Change in Indonesia*. Ed. Arief Budiman, Damien Kingsbury, and Barbara Hatley. Clayton: Monah Asia Institute (Monash Papers on Southeast Asia 50), 1999. 99–134.

Ho, Engseng. *The Graves of Tarim: Genealogy and Mobility across the Indian Ocean*. Berkeley, CA: University of California Press, 2006.

Hoskins, Janet. *Biographical Objects: How Things Tell Stories of People's Lives*. London: Routledge, 1998.

——.*Headhunting and the Social Imagination in Southeast Asia*. Stanford, CA: Stanford University Press, 1996.

Jones, Carla. "Fashion and Faith in Urban Indonesia." *Fashion Theory: The Journal of Dress, Body, and Culture* 11.203 (2007): 211–31.

Keane, Webb. "Freedom and Blasphemy: On Indonesian Press Bans and Danish Cartoons." *Public Culture* 21 (2009): 47–66.

——. *Christian Moderns: Freedom and Fetish in the Mission Encounter*. Berkeley, CA: University of California Press, 2007.

Kusno, Abidin. *The Appearances of Memory: Mnemonic Practices of Architecture and Urban Form in Indonesia*. Durham, NC: Duke University Press, 2010.

Laffan, Michael. *Islamic Nationhood and Colonial Indonesia: The Umma Below the Winds*. London: RoutledgeCurzon, 2003.

Leeuwen, Lizzy van. *Airconditioned Lifestyles: Nieuwe Rijken in Jakarta*. Amsterdam: Amsterdam University Press, 1997.

Mmembe, Achille. *On the Postcolony*. Berkeley, CA: University of California Press, 2001.

Morris, Rosalind C. "Images of Future History and the Posthuman in Postapartheid South Africa." *Images That Move*. Ed. Patricia Spyer and Mary Margaret Steedly. Santa Fe, NM: School of Advanced Research Press, 2013.

Mrázek, Rudolf. *A Certain Age: Colonial Jakarta Through the Memories of its Intellectuals*. Durham, NC: Duke University Press, 2010.

——. *Engineers of Happy Land: Technology and Nationalism in a Colony*. Princeton, NJ: Princeton University Press, 2002.

Pandey, Gyanendra. *Routine Violence: Nations, Fragments, Histories*. Stanford, CA: Stanford University Press, 2006.

Pannell, Sandra, ed. *A State of Emergency: Violence, Society and the State in Eastern Indonesia*. Darwin: Northern Territory Press, 2003.

Paramaditha, Intan. "Questions on Witnessing Violence." *The Jakarta Post*, April 4, 2011.

Pemberton, John. "Recollections from "Beautiful Indonesia" (Somewhere Beyond the Postmodern). *Public Culture* 6 (1994a): 241–62.

——. *On the Subject of "Java."* Ithaca, NY: Cornell University Press, 1994b.

Purdey, Jemma. "Describing Kekerasan: Some Observations on Writing about Violence in Indonesia after the New Order." *Bijdragen tot de Taal-, Land en Volkenkunde* 160.2/3 (2004): 189–225.

Rudnyckyi, Daromir. *Spiritual Economies: Islam, Globalization, and the Afterlife of Development.* Ithaca, NY: Cornell University Press, 2010.

Rutherford, Danilyn. "Of Birds and Gifts: Reviving Tradition on an Indonesian Frontier." *Cultural Anthropology* 11.4 (1996): 577–616.

Ryter, Loren. "Pemuda Pancasila: The Last Loyalist Free Men of Suharto's New Order?" *Violence and the State in Suharto's Indonesia.* Ed. Benedict R. O'G. Anderson. Ithaca, NY: Cornell Southeast Asia Program Publications, 2001.

Schulte Nordholt, Henk. "The Jago in the Shadow: Crime and 'Order' in the Colonial State in Java." *Review of Indonesian and Malaysian Affairs* 25.1 (1991): 74–91.

Schulte Nordholt, Henk, and Gerry van Klinken. "Introduction." In *Renegotiating Boundaries: Local Politics in Post-Suharto Indonesia,* eds. Henk Schulte Nordholt and Gerry Van Klinken. Leiden: KITLV Press, 2010.

Sen, Krishna, and David T. Hill. *Media, Culture, and Politics in Indonesia.* Melbourne: Oxford University Press, 2000.

Sidel, John T. "The Manifold Meanings of Displacement." *Conflict, Violence, and Displacement in Indonesia.* Ed. Eva-Lotta E. Hedman. Ithaca, NY: Cornell Southeast Asia Program Publications, 2008.

——. *Riots, Pogroms, Jihad: Religious Violence in Indonesia.* Ithaca, NY: Cornell University Press, 2006, esp. 13.

Siegel, James T. *Naming the Witch.* Stanford, CA: Stanford University Press, 2006.

——. *A New Criminal Type in Jakarta: Counter-revolution Today.* Durham, NC: Duke University Press, 1998a.

——. "Early Thoughts on the Violence of May 13 and 14, 1998, in Jakarta." *Indonesia* 66 (1998b): 75–108.

Simone, Abdoumaliq, and Vyjayanthi Rao. "Securing the Majority: Living through Uncertainty in Jakarta." *International Journal of Urban and Regional Research* 32.2 (2012): 315–35.

Spyer, Patricia. *Orphaned Landscapes: Religion, Violence, and Visuality in Post-Suharto Indonesia.* Unpublished.

——. "Treacherous Matters or Some Notes towards a Symptomatology of Crisis." *Material Religion: The Journal of Objects, Art, and Belief.* Special Issue. "Matter of Contention: Relics and Other Sacred Objects at the Crossroads of Religious Tradition." Guest ed. Ra'anan Boustan and Adam Becker, forthcoming a.

——. "Streetwise Masculinity and Other Urban Performances of Postwar Ambon: A Photo-Essay." *Growing Up in Indonesia: Experiences and Diversity in Youth*

Transitions. Ed. Kathryn Robison. London and New York, NY: Routledge, forthcoming b.

——. "Images Without Borders: Violence, Visuality, and Landscape in Postwar Ambon, Indonesia." *Images That Move.* Ed. Patricia Spyer and Mary Margaret Steedly. Santa Fe: School of Advanced Research, 2013.

——. "Blind Faith: Painting Christianity in Post-conflict Ambon, Indonesia." *Social Text* 96 26.3 (2008): 11–37.

——. "Some Notes on Disorder in the Indonesian Postcolony." *Law and Disorder in the Postcolony.* Ed. Jean Comaroff and John L. Comaroff. Chicago, IL: University of Chicago Press, 2006. 188–218.

——. "Media and Violence in an Age of Transparency: Journalistic Writing on War-Torn Maluku." *Religion, Media, and the Public Sphere.* Ed. Birgit Meyer and Annelies Moors. Bloomington, IN: Indiana University Press, 2005.

____. "Why Can't We Be Like Storybook Children? Media of Violence and Peace in Maluku, Indonesia." *KITLV Press-Jakarta,* 2004a.

____. "*Belum Stabil* and Other Signs of the Times in Post-Suharto Indonesia." *Indonesia in Transition: Rethinking "Civil Society," "Region," and "Crisis."* Ed. Rochman Achwan, Hanneman Samuel, and Henk Schulte Nordholt. Yogyakarta,: Pustaka Pelajar, 2004b.

____. *The Memory of Trade: Modernity's Entanglements on an Eastern Indonesian Island.* Durham, NC: Duke University Press, 2000.

——. "Diversity with a Difference: Adat and the New Order in Aru (Eastern Indonesia)." *Cultural Anthropology* 11.1 (1996): 25–50.

Steedly, Mary Margaret. "Transparency and Apparition: Media Ghosts of Post-New Order Indonesia." *Images That Move.* Ed. Patricia Spyer and Mary Margaret Steedly. Santa Fe, NM: School of Advanced Research Press, 2013.

——. "The State of Culture Theory in the Anthropology of Southeast Asia." *Annual Review of Anthropology* 28 (1999): 431-54.

——. *Hanging Without a Rope: Narrative Experience in Colonial and Postcolonial Karoland.* Princeton, NJ: Princeton University Press, 1993.

Strassler. Karen. *Refracted Visions: Popular Photography and National Modernity in Java.* Durham, NC: Duke University Press, 2010.

——. "The Face of Money: Currency, Crisis, and Remediation in Post-Suharto Indonesia." *Cultural Anthropology* 24.1 (2009): 63–103.

——. "*Reformasi* through Our Eyes: Children as Witnesses of History in Post-Suharto Indonesia." *Visual Anthropology Review* 22.2 (2006): 53–70.

——. "Gendered Visibilities and the Dream of Transparency: The Chinese-Indonesian Rape Debate in Post-Suharto Indonesia." *Gender and History* 16 (2004): 689–725.

Tagliacozzo, Eric, ed. *Southeast Asia and the Middle East: Islam, Movement, and the Longue Duree.* Stanford, CA: Stanford University Press, 2009.

Tsing, Anna Lowenhaupt. *In the Realm of the Diamond Queen: Marginality in an Out-of-the-Way Place.* Princeton, NJ: Princeton University Press, 1993.

Welker, Marina. "Corporate Lives: New Perspectives on the Social Life of the Corporate Form." *Current Anthropology* (Supplement to April 2011): S3. Ed. Damani J. Partridge, Marina Welker, and Rebecca Hardin.

Wessel, Ingrid, and Georgia Wimhöfer, eds. *Violence in Indonesia.* Hamburg: Abera Verlag, 2001.

Winn, Phillip. "Sovereign Violence, Moral Authority, and the Maluku Cakalele." *A State of Emergency: Violence, Society and the State in Eastern Indonesia.* Ed. Sandra Pannell. Darwin: Northern Territory Press, 2003.

Films and Videos Consulted

Levy, Curtis. *Riding the Tiger.* A three-part documentary TV series. Olsen Levy Productions, 1992.

Nugroho, Garin. *Puisi Tak Terkuburkan* (A Poet: Unconcealed Poetry). S.E.T. Audiovisual Workshop and Garin Nugroho, 2000.

Rambadeta, Lexy Junior. *Mass Grave.* Off Stream Productions, 2001.

ART HISTORY

"To Look for Water with Water": Toward Collaborative Global Conversations on the State of Indonesian Studies

Kaja M. McGowan

In 1962, renowned Indonesian historian Soedjatmoko (in collaboration with Mohammad Ali, G. J. Resink and George McT. Kahin) edited and conceived the introduction for the 1965 manuscript on a collection of studies on Indonesian history and historiography. This first Cornell Modern Indonesia Project (CMIP) initiative was responsive in large part to the demand from Indonesian scholars for an autonomous Indonesian history. Soedjatmoko's reflections continued to resonate as we convened a second CMIP conference in April 2011, almost fifty years later, on "the State of Indonesian Studies."[1] A brief look at his reflections will set the stage for my own. First, we are still grappling with the fact that Indonesian historiography is notoriously full of gaps, and our knowledge of its periods is still woefully uneven. There is no continuous historical narrative, and, as E. Edwards McKinnon experienced with his paper on Indonesian archaeology and cultural heritage management (in this volume), the entire political terrain and cast of characters may shift dramatically from the time of presentation to publication. Secondly, Soedjatmoko took time to mention an important new addition in the 1960s that allowed, in part, for a less Java-centric approach to the region—namely, the discovery of Buginese–Makassarese indigenous historical sources. And today, I can likewise applaud, as one of several scholarly endeavors, the recent, and, I might add, sumptuous publication of *Philippine Ancestral Gold*, written and edited by Florina H. Capistrano-Baker (2011), a text that promises a wholly new kind of comparative "decentering" aimed at placing the Philippines in relation to premodern developments, not only in Indonesia, but in a broader Southeast Asian context. With important essays by co-editors John Guy and John Miksic, this book documenting the Ayala Museum's Gold Collection makes an invaluable contribution to the study

---

[1] Conference on "The State of Indonesian Studies," held at the George McT. Kahin Center for Advanced Southeast Asian Research at Cornell University, in Ithaca, New York, April 28–30, 2011.

of Indonesian (and more broadly Southeast Asian) art and maritime history of the period before intensive European contact and cultural dislocation. Finally, Soedjatmoko mentions the fruitfulness of "the application of social science methods to Indonesian historiography" as leading to "the development of interdisciplinary approaches" and to a "recent trend toward the consideration of theoretical problems involved in modern Indonesian historiography" (Soedjatmoko 1965, xii). With regard to these collaborative conversations, Soedjatmoko observes that "we have barely scratched the surface" (1965, xii). As surfaces go, I find myself wondering how he would have received our attempts at collaborative conversations almost fifty years later?

To propose collaboration across established boundaries of practice is always a risky business. More often than not, it provokes anxiety and considerable professional skepticism. Such was the case in part at the April 2011 CMIP Conference, where internationally renowned scholars convened to present papers on the "arc" of their separate disciplines. The morning began with anthropology, followed in quick succession by art history, history, language, government, and ethnomusicology. As the Cornell discussant for the art history panel, I had the great pleasure of introducing, in the order of their appearance, the three presenters: Natasha Reichle, Associate Curator at the San Francisco Asian Art Museum; E. Edwards McKinnon, most recently with ARI (Asia Research Institute) in Singapore and UNDP (United Nations Development Program) in Aceh; and Astri Wright, Professor of Art History at the University of Victoria. The "arc" or (as Danilyn Rutherford suggested) the "orbit" of their divergent work engages simultaneously the fields of History of Art, Archaeology, Artistic and Performance Practice, Museum Studies, and Visual Studies, while spanning premodern and contemporary periods at the interstices of professorial, curatorial, and cultural heritage management venues. That the state of Indonesian studies (like many other area studies programs) exists at the moment in mere survival mode came as no surprise to the participants. Indeed, one real impetus for our gathering was to encourage the comparatively beleaguered arts and humanities to establish common ground with the sciences. Not least was the recurring question of how to evaluate properly the "objects" that might result once such common ground is painstakingly (or haphazardly) and objectively (or subjectively) established. Would such collaborative results constitute art or anthropology, history or political science, language or music? And what about those disciplines that were not represented by the conference?

Throughout the proceedings, I was struck by a certain amount of persistent (perhaps playful?) crossfire among the participants from the separate panels. Playful, maybe, for even in humor, as we know from our various encounters with the faithful *punakawan* clowns in the wayang, the source of laughter is often where our most serious ideas can be formulated. So, when encouraged to collaborate in conference settings, why do academics for the most part persist in setting up the sciences and the humanities as if they are at odds with one another, when a potentially more fruitful response might be to ask if science and art are inherently at odds at all? And the resonant image that seemed unobtrusively to bear this out for me during the conference was ethnomusicologist and composer Chris Miller performing his own composition, entitled "three blue lotus," during a perceived "break" in the seriousness of the proceedings. Composed in 1994 to accompany choreography by the legendary Indonesian dancer Bambang Mbesur, "three blue lotus" must have mesmerized audiences in Java as a group of dancing women reportedly moved elegantly in a tight cluster across the stage to the silvery, aquatic sheen sustained by Chris playing the bowed *gender*. I say "silvery sheen" because the effect was hypnotic as Chris, poised gracefully in space, held two bows in either hand, and, leaning down, repeatedly, aligned and re-aligned the hairs on the bows to the edges of the metal leaves (*daun*) on a giant handmade *gender*-like metallophone. His body in motion reminded me of men in Indonesia, timelessly, descending the banks of streams and rivers, and dredging up from the depths two buckets of water at a time to be carried (*mamikul*), balanced on either end of a stick on strong shoulders, over the land.

"To look for water with water" (*nggolek banyu pepikulan warih*) is one of two Old Javanese proverbs, stitched into the footnotes of Soedjatmoko's essay, "The Indonesian Historian and His Time," that speak volumes in relation to Chris Miller's composition, as I will argue momentarily. On one level, "three blue lotus" seems to explore the balanced phrasing and slow pace of traditional Javanese *karawitan*, while the combination of Javanese *pelog* and *slendro* scales on another level allows for voice-leading that almost hints at the kind of movement between dissonance and consonance found in Western polyphony. As the haunting composition was performed at Cornell's Kahin Center *sans* dancers, I found myself remembering Rabindranath Tagore's supposed statement when first he experienced Java: "I see India everywhere, but do not recognize her!" This is where contemporary art and performance pieces like "three blue lotus" can provide access to knowledge and power that, in the words of Stanley J. O'Connor, serve as "centers of experience" (1992, 150). How do we restore works of art to life as it is (or was) lived, recognizing in the process the possibility for diverse subjectivities and interpretational strategies?

I began over the summer to see those two bows in Chris's performance as the overlooked, but ultimately overarching metaphor, for the entire CMIP proceedings. Indeed, "three blue lotus" can serve as a powerful, performative "center of experience" like none other, an invitation, if you will, to enact collaborative global conversations across the scholarly disciplines. Not a conversation that reduces to sameness, but one that gains working ground through its momentum, counterpoint, and its celebration of sustainable difference. What if, instead of two violin bows, for example, Chris—like a *dalang*—could "hold" a political scientist by the feet, and bring his (or her) "field" into dialogic sound with an anthropologist's or an art historian's? I can imagine a certain amount of kicking and screaming, as was evident at the conference, but, in the end, in Chris's capable hands, the resonators would force an engagement. Certainly, Chris Miller's research and his compositions as an innovative ethnomusicologist, integrating arts and sciences in a way that is both theoretically and technically sustained, points us powerfully in that direction.

One of the most rewarding and conceptually significant areas of scholarly practice in the last two decades has been the increased insistence on a multi-vocal approach to historical interpretation that recognizes this complexity. The emphasis more recently on globalization as a process has enlivened all the disciplines. Of course, globalization is not new, as some scholars and cultural theorists might think, but an historical process with deep roots, especially in an area of the world like Indonesia with such an ancient, cosmopolitan maritime history. Significantly, a global analysis shifts the conversation away from simple polarities like center-periphery to a "multi-dimensional global space with unbounded, often discontinuous and interpenetrating subspaces" (Kearney 1995, 549) or boundaries that, in the groundbreaking analysis of Eric Tagliacozzo, are more "porous" in nature

(2005). In taking examples of shared practice as the starting point for a different kind of intellectual exchange, I am not advocating the collapse of one discipline into another, but rather what soon became apparent from closer readings of virtually all the papers presented at the CMIP conference in April 2011: that those involved make use of an area studies model while engaging an increasingly more interdisciplinary and historically situated globalism.

Certainly the field of Islamic art history, to offer one salient example, can benefit from this new situated globalism. Most historians of Islamic art incline the field toward Arab centrism, and pay little to no attention to Southeast Asia. Instead, they devote their studies to works found in the Middle East, South Asia, and North Africa, or to the contemporary projects emerging from the diasporic and transnational networks of Muslim artists who come from those regions. Even academic legacies of European colonialism play a part in the discipline's marginalization of countries like Indonesia. Kenneth George (2009) is playing a prominent role in encouraging this project of recognition and recuperation. As the papers from the art history panel will attest, scholars are increasingly experimenting in exciting new ways with collaborative practices for an exploded art history without borders. It is a new art history that acknowledges and works with what are often deeply conflicted concepts, narratives, and methodologies that interrogate the very notion of art history as a unified field.

"To look for water with water" is, according to Soedjatmoko (1965, 410), one of two favorite expressions in Javanese mysticism in connection with the concept of knowledge through self-identification. The second one is "to look for fire with light" (*nggolek geni dedamaran*). These references to proverbs in the footnotes help Soedjatmoko sketch the outline of what he refers to as "the ahistorical view of life," an outlook, or "tendency to mythologize" that he argues constitutes in large measure "the cultural subsoil throughout Indonesia, which such later cultural influences as Islam, Christianity, and modern secular education have not been able entirely to destroy or replace. In short, the fact that the ahistorical view of life in Indonesia is nowhere systematically formulated, and has not yet been adequately described or studied, does not in any way diminish its reality and pervasiveness in Indonesian society today." (2005, 410–11). The quest for water in the present (*banyu*) is carried on the shoulders of Indonesian contemporary artists as a continuing revision of older and perhaps once more sacred aquatic vestiges (*warih*) found in forms, formats, and iconography. This semantic transcendence does not translate effectively into English, where water is water is water … but this marked Indonesian tendency to mythologize can be seen to inhere best in objects and performances like Miller's "three blue lotus," for example. Objects and performances, of course, tie historical inquiry to specific moments and contexts; analyzing these is still in many ways what art historians do best.

In conclusion, I am reminded of historian Rudolf Mrázek's frequent references throughout the conference to the cemetery on Pleasant Grove Road, where many of the founding fathers of Cornell's Southeast Asia Program have come to reside. On the rare occasions when the sun shines in Ithaca, New York, I have taken my young son, Surya, there. One day, while he was still in preschool, and still enamored with building skyscrapers out of wooden blocks, we stopped to have a picnic on the grass near the now familiar graves. Suddenly, surrounded by ornately carved standing stones, he piped up, and said with enthusiastic reverence: "Mommy, this is a whole city!" I was reminded of a quote by O'Connor, one that I use often in my classes:

Our visual realm is an ancient city. Each new structure is constrained by the foundations of the past, by the labyrinthine lines of its streets and alleys, by its accommodation or disjunction with the broken facades and ruined walls of earlier ages. Each new building revises the framework by which the city is apprehended as a totality.[2]

Each new building, each grave, is not only constrained by the foundations of the past, but its base connects earth and sky. There is a Balinese saying with transcendent qualities similar to those of Soedjatmoko's Old Javanese proverbs: *Ngelidin sema, tepuk setra* ("avoid the cemetery, find the cemetery"). *Sema* and *setra* both mean "cemetery," the first in Low Balinese, the second in High Balinese. This expression has been compared to our, perhaps more familiar, "out of the frying pan and into the fire," but what a different trajectory is implied. These subtle Javanese and Balinese semantic ascensions are simply lost in translation. These slippages argue forcefully in the wake of our "global turn" for the profound importance of being able to establish rootedness to local places and languages, those quintessential moments that resist translation. When walking amidst these rivers of stone, and visiting the graves of remarkable men like George Kahin and Oliver Wolters, I do not see them as absent in any final sense of the word. Rather, as in the great ancestral realm of fluid things (*warih*), they continue to move in quiet streams through each of us, buoying us up if we let them (*banyu*).

Works Cited

Capistrano-Baker, Florina H., John Guy, and John Miksic, eds. *Philippine Ancestral Gold.* Makati City: Ayala Foundation, Inc., 2011 (2012).

George, Kenneth. "Ethics, Iconoclasm, and Qur'anic Art in Indonesia." *Cultural Anthropology* 24.4 (2009): 589–622.

Kearney, Michael. "The Local and the Global: The Anthropology of Globalization and Transnationalism." *Annual Review of Anthropology* 24 (1995): 547–65.

O'Connor, Stanley J. "Humane Literacy and Southeast Asian Art." *Journal of Southeast Asian Studies* 26, 1(1995).

——. "Memory and Discovery in Southeast Asian Art." *Asian Art & Culture: Southeast Asia Today.* Arthur M. Sackler Gallery, Smithsonian Institution (Winter 1995): 2-6.

Soedjatmoko, Mohammad Ali, G. J. Resink, and George McT. Kahin, eds. *An Introduction to Indonesian Historiography.* Ithaca, NY: Cornell University Press, 1965.

Soedjatmoko, "The Indonesian Historian and His Time." *An Introduction to Indonesian Historiography.* Ed. Mohammad Ali, G. J. Resink, and George McT. Kahin. Ithaca, NY: Cornell University Press, 1965: 404–15.

Tagliacozzo, Eric. *Secret Trades, Porous Borders: Smuggling and States Along a Southeast Asian Frontier, 1865–1915.* New Haven, CT: Yale University Press, 2005.

---

[2] Stanley J. O'Connor, "Memory and Discovery in Southeast Asian Art," *Asian Art & Culture: Southeast Asia Today* (Winter 1995): 5.

CONTINUITIES AND CHANGE: SHIFTING BOUNDARIES IN INDONESIAN ART HISTORY

Natasha Reichle

The letter of invitation to this conference suggested we review the arc of the field of art historical studies over the past two or three decades, and also look to the future of the discipline. But "arc" may not be the best word to describe the path of the study of Indonesian art history. The trajectory of the field seems more to me like one that moves outward, but constantly circles back; spreading, but interlacing, more like the threads of a textile than the curve of a ball thrown to the sky. Our work is deeply indebted to the research of earlier generations of scholars, who studied many aspects of the material culture of the archipelago in the late 1800s and early 1900s. But equally important is the recent work of those international archaeologists, philologists, and historians whose research helps situate works of art in the times and places of their creation.

Although I have been looking closely at Indonesian art for almost twenty years, I still feel like a student in the field, and it was tempting to make this essay into a list of people whom I admire and from whom I have learned. That said, scholars of Indonesian art make up a fairly small lot. The number of art historians in the United States and Canada teaching Southeast Asian art history are perhaps a dozen at most, and those who may specialize in the arts of Indonesia could probably be counted on one hand. The field is made larger if you consider scholars working in Europe, Australia, and Asia; but it is not a crowded discipline.

Indonesia is vastly under-represented in art historical studies. A quick online search of the University of California–Berkeley library brought up dozens of volumes on the Cathedral of Notre Dame in Paris, but only one book on the Central Javanese temple of Candi Sewu. Little has been published on major monuments like those comprising the ancient temple complex at Prambanan. From a curatorial perspective, we might note that it has been twenty years since the "Festival of Indonesia," the last large international exhibitions in the United States focusing on Indonesian art. The 2011 exhibition on the arts of Bali at the Asian Art Museum in

San Francisco was the first major exhibition on the subject ever presented in the United States.[1]

The field of art history broadens a bit if we lay claim to scholars of other disciplines whose work focuses in some way on Indonesia's material and visual culture: archaeologists, visual anthropologists, and historians of the performing arts. This very freedom—to explore related areas, from literature and literary theory to history, anthropology, archaeology, and religion—is what has attracted many to the field. During the colonial era, scholars often had a remarkable breadth of knowledge; J. G. de Casparis was a historian, archaeologist, epigrapher, and Sanskritist. Today, few scholars possess such varied skills; thus, interdisciplinary interaction is all the more vital. Our pursuits are interrelated and interdependent. An art historian is not only interested in the form of a sculpture, but also the translation and dating of its inscription, the iconography and religious tradition it may represent, and the type of stone from which it is carved.

For many years, Indonesian art history, if taught at all, was part of a survey course covering all of Asia or South and Southeast Asia (often spanning this entire region in fifteen weeks). A frequently used textbook was Philip Rawson's *Art of Southeast Asia*, the only compact, inexpensive, illustrated volume available for teaching. This book, originally published in 1967, is now woefully dated, but still in print (1990) and used in classrooms today.[2] Years ago, syllabi in History of Art departments were full of such survey courses, which looked chronologically at the art of Southeast Asia as divided into their modern nation states of origin. In the week or two of lectures devoted to Indonesian art, the major focus would have been on the "classical" Central Javanese Hindu and Buddhist temples, with perhaps a mention of later developments in East Java. Art of the outer islands, modern and contemporary works, and the performing arts had little place in the curriculum.

While general art history surveys have their uses, today many educators have shifted and focused their methods of teaching Southeast Asian art. While still presenting surveys, scholars also address subjects and issues of interest that are not linked solely by chronology or geography. Classes may delve into themes of narration, the importance of water, networks of trade, conceptions of sacred space, or the transmissions of religion.

These subjects are not entirely new, but were ushered in by a generation of scholars who sought to broaden and deepen the field by both looking to the peripheries and reexamining the centers. Reviewing the history of the field of Indonesian art history, I have also been struck by the strength, even predominance, of women's voices in the discipline, from Claire Holt, Satyawati Suleiman, Hariani Santiko, and Endang Sri Hardiati to many in today's younger generation of scholars.

---

[1] Fortunately, museums outside of the United States, especially those in Europe, Singapore, and Australia, have explored the arts of Indonesia. Recent examples include *Indonesia: Discovery of the Past*, organized by the Museum Nasional, Indonesia, and the Rijksmuseum voor Volkenkunde, Leiden (2005); *In Northern Sumatra: The Batak*, at the Musée du Quai Branly (2007); and *Sumatra: Crossroads of Cultures*, at the Rijksmuseum voor Volkenkunde (2009). Many smaller university museums have also mounted excellent exhibitions covering a wide range of material.

[2] Other publications from the 1960s, like A. J. Bernet Kempers's *Ancient Indonesian Art* (Cambridge, MA: Harvard University Press, 1959), or Claire Holt's *Art in Indonesia: Continuities and Change* (Ithaca, NY: Cornell University Press, 1967) are certainly better works on Indonesia, but are both out of print.

OBJECTS AS EVIDENCE

Initial Western research on Indonesian art can be credited to pioneering Dutch scholars, often astoundingly erudite men, trained in classical philology and deeply knowledgeable about literature, archaeology, religion, and epigraphy.[3] In the late nineteenth and early twentieth century, these men were responsible for archaeological studies of ancient sites in Java, Sumatra, and Bali. Some, coming from a background in South Asian literature and religion, focused on finding Indian precedents for Javanese sculpture or on discovering texts that could explicate narrative reliefs on temple walls. Scholars who followed looked more closely at local contexts and indigenous literature in their examination of this material.[4] While the study of religious texts is often necessary for the identification of deities, motifs, and narratives on Hindu and Buddhist temples, today it is acknowledged that art objects should not be read only in relation to texts.

In a tribute written upon the retirement of the South Asian art historian Walter Spink, Janice Leoshko wrote:

> Certainly categorizing images from a relevant textual source is an important aspect of the pursuit of understanding art objects, but too many studies chart the history of ... art solely in this manner. Ironically such studies, which purport to be about the development of imagery, often provide simply a succession of one type replacing another with little or no reflection upon the ways in which such imagery emerged, changed, circulated, interacted, or developed, perhaps independently from texts. Texts can be useful for understanding themes encountered in art (and may even have inspired such presentations), but images present such themes in an entirely different manner, in virtually a different language. What is still lacking in many studies of Buddhist art is not only a more thorough consideration of the complex relationships between texts and images but a more direct confrontation and consideration of the nature of art objects (Leoshko n.d.).

Visual imagery has its own unique constraints and possibilities, which often rise out of spatial concerns. Leoshko goes on to comment on the need to acknowledge the agency of artists in the production of works of art and to realize that human actors struggled with real materials as well as complex religious ideas when producing these objects.

Still, there is resistance to the idea that works of art are valuable primary sources of information about culture. Just this year (2011), at the Association for Asian Studies conference, during a panel discussing the field of art history, a scholar from another discipline asked, "But where is the evidence in art history?" The question points to the biases still present in the minds of some that reject material culture as worthy evidence—as valuable as inscriptions, texts, and interviews, which are the more traditional types of evidence used by the historian. Yet can one find any textual source that could tell us as much about the social and religious practices,

---

[3] The list of these scholars is long: N. J. Krom, Th. van Erp, J. L. A. Brandes, W. F. Stutterheim, F. D. K. Bosch, and J. G. de Casparis, to name just a few.

[4] An incomplete list would include Boechari, R. Soekmono, Satyawati Suleiman, Jan Fontein, Claire Holt, A. J. Bernet Kempers, Jacques Dumarcay, O. W. Wolters, and Stanley J. O'Connor.

architecture, and performing arts of the Central Javanese period than the over three miles of reliefs at Borobudur?

Some thirty years ago a generation of scholars, like Stanley J. O'Connor (at Cornell University) and Joanna Williams (at University of California–Berkeley), encouraged students to look at Southeast Asian art in new ways, to question the traditional boundaries that defined the field. Today, I'd like to focus on a few of these new directions of art historical study. They involve exploring different ways of conceiving of artworks, including examining their changing meanings over time; new ways of looking at geography, borders, and the exchange of art across them; and a broadening of the types of art we study, the subjects of the discipline.

THE LIVES OF OBJECTS

Is Borobudur a mountain, stupa, or mandala, or can it be all three? It may have been conceived of one way by a sculptor, another by a patron, and a third way by a priest. It continues to be a center for Buddhist pilgrimage, but also has been a site of political protest, as well as a national (and nationalist) monument (Errington 1998). In recent years, several art historical studies have followed the biographies of objects, showing the complex interactions between visual imagery and changing societies, and tracing the mutating meanings of works of art as they move through time and across cultures. Ritual tool, household decoration, colonial booty, art object, collector's item, *pusaka*, national treasure—objects constantly accumulate new significations and new audiences.

One aspect of this type of study is the history of collecting and collections. In two recent publications, the history of the Netherlands' exhibitions of Indonesian objects in the world fairs of the late nineteenth and early twentieth centuries is examined by Marieke Bloembergen (2006) and Frances Gouda (1995). Their work considers, among other things, the display of Indonesian art in these expositions as part of a larger effort of the Netherlands to represent and promote itself as a colonial power. The meanings of Indonesian art acquired by museums during the colonial period have also been reconsidered over the last decade by several Indonesian and Dutch curators in publications and joint exhibitions organized by the Rijksmuseum voor Volkenkunde, Leiden, and Museum Nasional, Indonesia (Ter Keurs and Hardiati 2006; Ter Keurs 2007).

DIFFERENT NOTIONS OF REGION

Just as in wider studies of Southeast Asia, recent scholarship on Indonesia has focused on breaking through the restrictions of national boundaries, whether by studying the movement of ideas and objects across the Indian Ocean and South China Sea or by acknowledging the truly cosmopolitan nature of cities in early times. Tracing the movement of objects and ideas through maritime trade routes, religious networks, colonial conquest, or modern paths of tourism are all intriguing directions of study.

Initiatives like the Nalanda–Sriwijaya Center encourage scholars to share their knowledge of the cultural links between regions of Asia, and the religious and economic networks that facilitated the movement of new ideas, technologies, and belief systems. The role of networks of trade informs Jan Wisseman Christie's work on textiles in ancient Java (1993), and Elizabeth Lambourn's studies on early Islamic tombstones of Indonesia (2004, 2008). Much more recent cross-cultural interactions have been explored by Kathleen Adams (2006), Andrew Causey (2003), and Jill Forshee (2000) in their works on the impact of tourism on artists from Sulawesi, Sumatra, and Sumba.

FROM THE CENTER TO THE PERIPHERY

In the festschrift to Stanley J. O'Connor published in 2000, Nora Taylor commented on how many of O'Connor's students moved away from the study of monuments and ancient sculpture toward visual engagement with a wide range of non-traditional subjects (2000, 12). Kaja McGowan's challenging and multi-layered readings of objects, texts, voices, and performances, and the interweaving narratives permeating them, is but one example.[5]

A theme in some recent studies of Indonesian art suggests a movement away from the arts of the court and toward an examination of objects made in and often for a domestic or village environment. Recent works include studies of domestic architecture and terracotta traditions, as well as Balinese offerings. Publications on textiles of the archipelago have been particularly strong. Both elite and everyday, but rarely accorded the stature of sculpture or architecture, weaving traditions are being documented and even revitalized with the help of scholars. At the Fowler Museum at the University of California–Los Angeles (UCLA), Roy Hamilton's contributions are especially notable. Large and important monographs have recently been published on Minangkabau, Iban, and Batak weaving (Summerfield 1999; Gavin 2004; Niessen 2009), as well as Ruth Barnes and Mary Hunt Kahlenberg's masterful survey of Indonesian textiles (2010). For years, most Indonesian textiles were assumed to be not much older than a century, but Kahlenberg's carbon-14 dating of textiles, and discovery of some that were over five hundred years old, has challenged notions of the antiquity of cloth in Indonesia.

ART OF TODAY

Another subject of art historical research that has vastly expanded over the past three decades is the study of modern and contemporary arts. Claire Holt's pioneering book, *Indonesia, Continuities and Change* (1967), was the first to give the modern arts of the region equal footing with ancient architecture and sculpture. Continuing in this line, Astri Wright's *Soul, Spirit, and Mountain* (1994) explored Indonesian contemporary art, drawing on the voices of living artists and exploring local inspirations and cultural contexts. In recent years, perhaps more than any other subject, art historians have turned to examining modern and contemporary artists, particularly in Bali.[6]

---

[5] Kaja McGowan, "Maritime Travelers and Tillers of the Soil: Reading the Landscape(s) of Batur," in *Studies on Southeast Asian Art: Essays in Honor of Stanley J. O'Connor*, ed. Nora A. Taylor (Ithaca, NY: Cornell Southeast Asia Program Publications, 2000), pp. 32–48.

[6] See, for example, Kaja McGowan, *Ida Bagus Made: The Art of Devotion* (Ubud, Bali: Museum Puri Lukisan, 2008); Hildred Geertz and Ida Bagus Madé Togog, *Tales from a Charmed Life: A Balinese Painter Reminisces* (Honolulu, HI: University of Hawaii Press, 2005); Christopher Hill, *Survival and Change: Three Generations of Balinese Painters* (Canberra: Pandanus Books, Research School of Pacific and Asian Studies, Australian National University, 2006); Helena Spanjaard, *Pioneers of Balinese Painting: The Rudolf Bonnet Collection* (Amsterdam: KIT Publishers, 2007);

The burgeoning international market for contemporary Asian art has increased interest in Indonesian artists and led to numerous gallery exhibitions, catalogues, and monographs. It has also encouraged graduate students to enter the field, allowing them to see possibilities in the job market beyond the limited number of teaching or curatorial positions. Yet Holland Cotter's recent *New York Times* article, "Under Threat: The Shock of the Old," decries the pull toward the new at the expense of the old. He writes:

> Lack of visibility tends to lead to lack of financing, which translates into slow, halting research, leaving vast amounts of foundational field work barely started. All the while, time is taking its toll. Cultures are vanishing and changing form in urbanizing Africa. Ancient monuments are crumbling in India. Vital aesthetic traditions in China are fading fast. As an additional handicap, again, contrary to multiculturalist expectations, the numbers of new graduate students in most non-Western fields have not grown significantly in decades. The bottom line is plain: unless some of those few scholars stay on the case, we risk losing both the art and the history in "art history," particularly where conservational safeguards are fragile or difficult to maintain (Cotter 2011).

Cotter's lament echoes that voiced by a fourteenth century Javanese poet, who describes in the *Siwaratrikalpa* the decrepit temple ruins of Java: "Heart-rending was the spectacle of the reliefs; young maidens were standing gazing skywards, as if proclaiming their grief at being abandoned and no more visited by wandering poets" (Teeuw 1969). Ideally, the ancient and the contemporary can both be showcased, and in ways that can draw connections between the past and the present.

MINDING THE GAP

We need to study modern and contemporary artworks and to continue to examine the peripheries, the overlooked, the porous borders and new movements in Indonesian art. But as someone who came to the field because of a love of the great stone temples and statues of ancient Indonesia, I feel there is so very much material from the early historical period through early Islamic times that remains to be explored. Work produced by Indonesian archaeologists is not widely distributed, and their important research deserves greater recognition. Especially fascinating are new discoveries and excavations in West Java that provide some of the earliest evidence of Indic religions on Java. This new information is sometimes mentioned briefly in Indonesian newspapers, and reported in Indonesian archaeological reports and conference papers, but not broadly known or circulated (Manguin and Indrajaja, 2011).

Michele Stephen, *Desire, Divine and Demonic: Balinese Mysticism in the Paintings of I Ketut Budiana and I Gusti Nyoman Mirdiana* (Honolulu, HI: University of Hawaii Press, 2005); and Adrian Vickers et al., *Crossing Boundaries: Bali—A Window to Twentieth Century Indonesian Art* [Melintas Batasan: Bali—jendela seni Indonesia abad kedua puluh] (Melbourne: Asia Society AustralAsia Centre, 2002); Nora A. Taylor and Boreth Ly, eds., *Modern and Contemporary Southeast Asian Art: An Anthology* (Ithaca, NY: Cornell Southeast Asia Program Publications, 2012); and Adrian Vickers, *Balinese Art: Painting and Drawing of Bali: 1800–2013* (Tokyo and Rutland, VT: Tuttle Publishing, 2011).

With some exceptions, it is mostly scholars in Asia, Europe, and Australia who are on the forefront of reexamining ancient Hindu and Buddhist material. Endang Sri Hardiati has published widely on sites in Sumatra, Java, and Bali. Veronique Degroot's recent study of Central Javanese temples is the first in a century to inventory the region looking at both major structures and the remains of more peripheral temples (Degroot 2010).[7] Likewise, Marijke Klokke and Pauline Lunsingh Scheurleer have reexamined sculpture and temples in Central Java, looking closely at objects and moving beyond the early scholarship on this region. John Miksic's prolific publications on a wide range of subjects, including ceramics, earthenware, and gold, are valuable sources providing new archaeological research to English-speaking audiences.

Of the many subjects of study for future scholars of visual culture, a particularly fruitful period may be the years after the fall of the Majapahit. Early Islamic architecture, manuscripts, and other artworks have received limited scholarly attention. Two recent museum exhibitions on the art of Islamic Southeast Asia began to fill some gaps in knowledge (Bennett 2005; De Guise 2005), but what do we know about artistic production in the sixteenth, seventeenth, and eighteenth centuries?

THE LURE OF TECHNOLOGY

A major change in the field over the past twenty years, and especially the last decade, has been the impact of new technology on art historical research. Access to databases of articles allows researchers instantly to find information that could otherwise have taken weeks to retrieve. Bibliographical databases likewise serve to help scholars find sources. The move from individual or institutional slide libraries to vast collections of photographs available online has enabled some scholars to have almost instantaneous access to a wide range of images. With digital photography and email, these images can be quickly shared, exchanged, and discussed with other scholars around the world. GPS technology can now pinpoint remote archaeological sites and record the coordinates on a photograph even as it is taken.

The access to information and images is not yet universal, and many scholars are affiliated with institutions without the funds to subscribe to these services, or cannot afford the technology necessary to use these resources. We also always need to bear in mind that these modes of technology are tools and not answers. No photograph can substitute for visiting sites in person. No GPS can provide you with the dozens of conversations you might have while slowly making your way through the countryside—talk that might reveal local recollections of the past or reframe the site's meaning and context. Photographs of an image might not show the inscription on its back; they cannot illustrate how or when the sunlight strikes a monument, or indicate how an object interacts with its geographical surroundings.

Other technological developments that are bound to influence the field are advances in archaeological science. Thermoluminescence and radiocarbon testing as well as dendrochronology may help provide methods of dating objects. Other techniques can help determine ancient methods of artistic production, the composition of alloys, or patterns of corrosion.

---

[7] Kathleen O'Brien, Mary-Louise Totten, Lydia Kieven, and Julie Gifford are other scholars whose doctoral research focused on ancient material.

With advances in technology come opportunities for furthering the exchange of knowledge, especially across international borders. The field would do well if there were the means of providing Indonesian students access to recent Western research and expensive academic publications, as well as providing scholars outside of Indonesia easier access to difficult-to-find Indonesian publications, excavation reports, and theses.

Indonesian art history remains a very young field, with vast areas of study left to explore. What limits the field are the practical concerns of money and jobs. The lack of financial resources and job opportunities leaves the handful of professors who teach Indonesian art history with difficult decisions. With so few positions available in either academia or outside of it, should professors only encourage dissertation research on topics that are likely to lead to publication? Can museums only afford shows with enough "mass appeal" to draw in large crowds? Although it is not fun to discuss, money plays a real role in the future of the field. At this moment of devastating budget cuts across the United States and elsewhere, especially at public universities, the academic discipline is getting even smaller with no money available to replace retiring scholars at major institutions.

As many new paths open up in the field of Indonesian art history, other sites of study (as evidenced in this volume by Edward McKinnon's essay on antiquities in Aceh) are in danger of being lost forever. Art serves as an important tool in cross-cultural and cross-religious education for people of all ages. At a time when these issues are as important as ever, a great challenge is how we can continue to support the discipline—the revitalization of the Cornell Modern Indonesia Project is certainly a step in the right direction.

Works Cited

Adams, Kathleen M. *Art As Politics: Re-Crafting Identities, Tourism, and Power in Tana Toraja, Indonesia.* Honolulu, HI: University of Hawaii Press, 2006.

Asia Society. *Crossing Boundaries: Bali—A Window to Twentieth Century Indonesian Art (Melintas Batasan: Bali—jendela seni Indonesia abad kedua puluh).* Melbourne: Asia Society AustralAsia Centre, 2002.

Barnes, Ruth and Mary Hunt Kahlenberg, eds. *Five Centuries of Indonesian Textiles.* Munich and New York, NY: Prestel Verlag, 2010.

Bennett, James Stevenson, and National Gallery of Australia. *Crescent moon: Islamic Art and Civilisation in Southeast Asia.* Adelaide: Art Gallery of South Australia, 2005.

Bernet Kempers, A. J. *Ancient Indonesian Art.* Cambridge, MA: Harvard University Press, 1959.

Bloembergen, Marieke, and Beverley Jackson. *Colonial Spectacles: The Netherlands and the Dutch East Indies at the World Exhibitions, 1880–1931.* Singapore: NUS Press, 2006.

Brinkgreve, Francine, and David J. Stuart-Fox. *Offerings: The Ritual Art of Bali.* Sanur, Bali: Image Network Indonesia, 1992.

Brinkgreve, Francine, and Retno Sulistianingsih. *Sumatra: Crossroads of Cultures.* Leiden: KITLV Press, 2009.

Causey, Andrew. *Hard Bargaining in Sumatra: Western Travelers and Toba Bataks in the Marketplace of Souvenirs.* Honolulu, HI: University of Hawaii Press, 2003.

Cotter, Holland. "Under Threat: The Shock of the New." *New York Times*, April 14, 2011, sec. Arts/Art & Design. http://www.nytimes.com/2011/04/17/arts/design/non-western-art-history-bypasses-the-ancient.html?pagewanted=all&_r=0, accessed June 13, 2013.

Davis, Richard H. *Lives of Indian Images.* Princeton, NJ: Princeton University Press, 1999.

De Guise, Lucien, ed. *The Message and the Monsoon: Islamic Art of Southeast Asia—From the Collection of the Islamic Arts Museum Malaysia.* Kuala Lumpur: Islamic Arts Museum Malaysia, 2005.

Degroot, Véronique. *Candi, Space, and Landscape: A Study on the Distribution, Orientation, and Spatial Organization of Central Javanese Temple Remains.* Leiden: Sidestone Press, 2010.

Errington, Shelly. *The Death of Authentic Primitive Art: And Other Tales of Progress.* 1st ed. Berkeley, CA: University of California Press, 1998.

Fontein, Jan. *The Sculpture of Indonesia.* Washington, DC: National Gallery of Art, with New York, NY: Harry N. Abrams, Inc., 1990.

Forshee, Jill. *Between the Folds: Stories of Cloth, Lives, and Travels from Sumba.* Honolulu, HI: University of Hawaii Press, 2000.

Gavin, Traude. *Iban Ritual Textiles.* Singapore: Singapore University Press, 2004.

Geertz, Hildred. *Images of Power: Balinese Paintings Made for Gregory Bateson and Margaret Mead.* Honolulu, HI: University of Hawaii Press, 1994.

Geertz, Hildred, and Ida Bagus Madé Togog. *Tales from a Charmed Life: A Balinese Painter Reminisces.* Honolulu, HI: University of Hawaii Press, 2005.

George, Kenneth M. "Designs on Indonesia's Muslim Communities." *Journal of Asian Studies* 57.3 (1998): 693–713.

——. "Ethics, Iconoclasm, and Qur'anic Art in Indonesia." *Cultural Anthropology* 24.4 (November 2009): 589–621.

——. "Some Things That Have Happened to the Sun after September 1965: Politics and the Interpretation of an Indonesian Painting." *Comparative Studies in Society and History* 39.4 (October 1, 1997): 603–34.

Gifford, Julie. *Buddhist Practice and Visual Culture: The Visual Rhetoric of Borobudur.* London: Routledge, 2011.

Gouda, Frances. *Dutch Culture Overseas: Colonial Practice in the Netherlands Indies 1900–1942.* Amsterdam: Amsterdam University Press, 1995.

Hamilton, Roy W. et al., *Gift of the Cotton Maiden: Textiles of Flores and the Solor Islands.* Los Angeles, CA: Fowler Museum at UCLA, 1994.

Hamilton, Roy W. et al., *Material Choices: Refashioning Bast and Leaf Fibers in Asia and the Pacific.* Los Angeles, CA: Fowler Museum at UCLA, 2007.

Hill, Christopher. *Survival and Change: Three Generations of Balinese Painters.* Canberra: Pandanus Books, Research School of Pacific and Asian Studies, Australian National University, 2006.

Holt, Claire. *Art in Indonesia: Continuities and Change.* Ithaca, NY: Cornell University Press, 1967.

Hoskins, Janet. *Biographical Objects: How Things Tell the Stories of Peoples' Lives.* New York, NY: Routledge, 1998.

Keurs, Pieter ter, ed. *Colonial Collections Revisited.* Leiden: CNWS Publications, 2007.

Keurs, Pieter ter, and Endang Sri Hardiati. *Indonesia: Discovery of the Past.* Amsterdam: KIT Publishers, 2006.

Kieven, Lydia. *Following the Figure with the Cap: A New Look at the Religious Function of East Javanese Temples (Fourteenth to Fifteenth Centuries).* Leiden: KITLV, 2012. Sydney: University of Sydney, 2012.

Klokke, Marijke J. "Indonesian Art." *Art of Southeast Asia.* Ed. M. Girard-Geslan, M. J. Klokke, A. Le Bonheur, D. M. Stadtner. New York, NY: Abrams, 1998: 333–417.

Klokke, Marijke J., and Pauline Lunsingh Scheurleer, eds. *Ancient Indonesian Sculpture.* Leiden: KITLV, 1994.

Lambourn, Elizabeth. "The Formation of the Batu Aceh Tradition In Fifteenth-Century Samudera-Pasai." *Indonesia and the Malay World* 32.93 (2004): 211–48.

——. "Tombstones, Texts, and Typologies: Seeing Sources for the Early History of Islam in Southeast Asia." *Journal of the Economic and Social History of the Orient* 51.2 (2008).

Leoshko, Janice. "The Importance of Questions." http://walterspink.com/the-importance-of-questions, undated. Accessed March 24, 2011.

Lunsingh Scheerleer, Pauline. *Goud uit Java* [Gold from Java] Zwolle: W Books, 2012.

Lunsingh Scheurleer, Pauline, and Marijke J. Klokke. *Ancient Indonesian Bronzes: Catalogue of the Exhibition in the Rijksmuseum Amsterdam with a General Introduction.* Leiden: E. J. Brill, 1988.

Manguin, Pierre-Yves, and Agustijanto Indrajaja. "The Batujaya Site: New Evidence of Early Indian Influence in West Java." *Early Interactions between South and Southeast Asia.* Ed. Pierre-Yves Manguin, A. Mani, and Geoff Wade. Singapore: ISEAS, 2011.

McGowan, Kaja. "Maritime Travelers and Tillers of the Soil: Reading the Landscape(s) of Batur." *Studies on Southeast Asian Art: Essays in Honor of Stanley J. O'Connor.* Ed. Nora A. Taylor. Ithaca, NY: Cornell University Southeast Asia Program Publications, 2000: 32–48.

——. *Ida Bagus Made: The Art of Devotion.* Ubud, Bali: Museum Puri Lukisan, 2008.

Miksic, John N. *Earthenware in Southeast Asia: Proceedings of the Singapore Symposium on Premodern Southeast Asian Earthenwares.* Singapore: NUS Press, 2003.

Niessen, Sandra Ann. *Legacy in Cloth: Batak Textiles of Indonesia.* Leiden: KITLV Press, 2009.

O'Brien, Kathleen. "Means and Wisdom in Tantric Buddhist Rulership of the East Javanese Period." Sydney: University of Sydney, 1995.

Rawson, Philip S. *The Art of Southeast Asia: Cambodia, Vietnam, Thailand, Laos, Burma, Java, Bali.* London: Thames & Hudson, 1990.

Reichle, Natasha. *Violence and Serenity: Late Buddhist Sculpture from Indonesia.* Honolulu, HI: University of Hawaii Press, 2007.

Spanjaard, Helena. *Pioneers of Balinese Painting: The Rudolf Bonnet Collection.* Amsterdam: KIT Publishers, 2007.

Stephen, Michele. *Desire Divine and Demonic: Balinese Mysticism in the Paintings of I Ketut Budiana and I Gusti Nyoman Mirdiana.* Honolulu, HI: University of Hawaii Press, 2005.

Summerfield, Anne, et al. *Walk in Splendor: Ceremonial Dress and the Minangkabau.* Los Angeles, CA: Fowler Museum at UCLA, 1999.

Taylor, Nora A., ed. *Studies on Southeast Asian Art: Essays in Honor of Stanley J. O'Connor.* Ithaca, NY: Cornell Southeast Asia Program Publications, 2000.

Teeuw, A. et al. *Siwatrikalpa of Mpu Tanakung.* Bibliotheca Indonesia, 3. The Hague: Martinus Nijhoff, 1969.

Totton, Mary-Louise. "Weaving Flesh and Blood into Sacred Architecture: Ornamental Stories of Candi Loro Jonggrang." Ann Arbor, MI: University of Michigan Press, 2002.

Vickers, Adrian. *Balinese Art: Painting and Drawing of Bali: 1800-2010.* Tokyo and Rutland, VT: Tuttle Publishing, 2011.

Vickers, Adrian, and Robert Cribb. *Crossing Boundaries: Bali—A Window to Twentieth Century Indonesian Art* [Melintas Batasan: Bali—jendela seni Indonesia abad kedua puluh]. Melbourne: Asia Society AustralAsia Centre, 2002.

Waterson, Roxana. *The Living House: An Anthropology of Architecture in South-East Asia.* Hong Kong: Periplus Editions (HK), 2010.

Welling, Wouter, and Helena Spanjaard. *The Dono Code: Installations, Sculptures, Paintings.* Amsterdam: KIT Publishers, 2010.

Wisseman Christie, J. "Texts and Textiles in 'Medieval' Java." *Bulletin de l'Ecole Française d'Extrême-Orient* 80.I (1993): 193–95.

Wright, Astri. *Soul, Spirit, and Mountain: Preoccupations of Contemporary Indonesian Painters.* Kuala Lumpur: Oxford University Press, 1994.

ARCHAEOLOGY AND CULTURAL HERITAGE MANAGEMENT: A PERSONAL REVIEW, 1970–2011

E. Edwards McKinnon

Having had an interest in the history of Sumatra since arriving in Indonesia in 1960, my personal exposure has been primarily to Sumatran sites but, over time, during several years as a development consultant, I have accrued a familiarity with a wide range of remains throughout Java, parts of Kalimanatan, Sulawesi, Bali, Lombok, and Flores, and with the archaeologists who work on them.

BACKGROUND TO THE CURRENT SITUATION

The former Dutch colonial Antiquities Service (Oudheidkindige Dienst) was essentially Java-centric and concerned mainly with the conservation and rehabilitation of architectural remains such as colonial fortifications and temple sites. It undertook some very creditable work at sites such as Borobudur and Prambanan in Central Java, published comprehensive annual reports, and made extensive collections of photographs that are now extremely useful—the core collection is in Leiden, with copies available in Jakarta. The first "Inventory of Antiquities" for sites in Sumatra was published in 1912.[1] Some records have inevitably been lost— especially as over the years following Independence the institutions concerned have moved offices on several occasions.

The present development has grown from very small beginnings. When A. J. Bernet Kempers, the last Dutch head of the Antiquities Department, left Indonesia in 1954, there were only two qualified degree holders, Satywati Suleiman and Soekmono. By the 1960s, the staff of this small office, based in Jalan Kimia, Jakarta, had grown to include R. P. Soejono, the prehistorian; Boechari, the epigrapher; Uka Tjandrasasmita, the Islamic scholar; and Sri Soejatmi Satari, together with Sri Woerjani Kami and Roendarwati.

Following Independence, the former Antiquities Service was split into two—one branch to undertake field research (which became the National Research Centre for Archaeology), and the second, the Directorate of Conservation of Antiquities, to

---

[1] Nicolaas Johannes Krom, "Inventaris der Oudheiden," *Oudheidkundig Verslag*, Bijlage G (1912): 32–51. Inventories of sites in Java had been published earlier.

undertake preservation and conservation work. Resources were very limited. The split was, one suspects, for financial reasons. This dualist approach to what is essentially a single focus has created problems regarding both administration and efficiency, although cooperation between the two parts is now better than it was in the past.

Archaeology is perhaps best established in Java, where architectural work has long-established roots under the Dutch colonial Antiquities Service, especially in Central Java, with its many temple remains. Borobudur, unique throughout the Buddhist world, and Prambanan, which was damaged in the recent Yogya earthquake (2006), are both located in Central Java. Elsewhere, with limited resources and weak management capability, results have been mixed, the more so with the delegation of authority to regional administrations following the fall of Suharto in 1998. Indeed, having a dual system—with the relevant institutions for archaeological research and site conservation managed from Jakarta, and responsibility for relevant legislation delegated to regency governments—has given rise to a whole host of new problems. This situation has been exacerbated by the political decision to split off cultural affairs from the Department of Tourism and Culture and return "culture" to the Ministry of Education, where it long suffered almost orphan status.

Indonesian archaeology has tended to be boxed into discrete chronological categories: Prehistory, the so-called classical Hindu–Buddhist period, Islamic, and Colonial. The present field now also subsumes work in Paleogeography, Paleoenvironment, Paleoanthropology, Ethnography, Epigraphy, and Cultural Resource Management (CRM).

Over the years, conservation efforts have been undertaken at numerous sites in Sumatra. These include the masonry forts on the coast of Aceh Besar, work on the brick-built temples (biaro) of the Padang Lawas in North Sumatra, the rebuilding of the brick-built temples at Muara Takus in Riau, the reconstruction at Muara Jambi, and the establishment of parks at Bukit Seguntang and Karanganyar in Palembang. At the two latter sites, following the uninformed influence of local government, there is now a kind of local Disneyland.

Considering the vast distances involved (Sumatra is some 1,200 kilometers in length), and the difficulties posed by a relatively weak infrastructure and supervision from a centralized institution, much of the restoration and construction work has been reasonably well done, though not perhaps always to "Western" taste. In Jambi, the impact of having a building supervisor (mandor) from Trowulan, in East Java, for example, may have had an influence on the reconstructed brick-built architecture of ancient Muara Jambi. In Aceh, by comparison, what had been a series of sixteenth-century lime-plastered forts have been, in part, turned into cemented buildings that have lost some of their original character.

The main complaint about most, if not almost all, ancient remains officially listed as heritage sites was, and is, the lack of meaningful site management—coupled with a dearth of background information for visitors. Far too many sites remain unlisted, and, consequently, unprotected. A few sites now have information boards, but for a long time the only notices to be seen were those informing the visitor that the site was protected under the legislation of the former colonial Monumenten Ordinantie of 1931 and Law No. 5 of 1992, and that penalties were to be imposed for any destructive act. Given jurisdictions' very limited budgets, no money was allocated for putting up informative notice boards or kiosks. Even the prohibition notices were merely painted on metal sheeting, and peeled off after a relatively short period.

Aceh, Pancu Bay. A sultanate-period burial ground at Lampageu almost inundated by the tide due to ongoing subsidence. (photo: Linda North, 2011)

NATIONAL LEGISLATION: LAW NO. 11/2010 ON CULTURAL HERITAGE

New legislation for improved cultural heritage management was introduced in 2010. The concepts introduced under the law are positive and a great improvement on earlier legislation. Responsibility for conservation, however, now rests with regency (*kabupaten*) governments that have little or no appreciation of the value of cultural heritage and, consequently, afford it little priority for attention or finance.

The key points in the new law, which replaces the largely ineffective law No. 5 of 1992, are:

> More attention is to be paid to the roles of regional governments and communities (following the devolution of administrative power to regional administrations after the fall of the New Order in 1998).
> Provides regulations for the listing of cultural remains that are now the responsibility of Regency- and Municipal-level governments.
> Imposes a prohibition on the sale and export of cultural materials out of Indonesia.
> Includes the concept of a "cultural landscape" in regulations
> Defines the meanings of the term *cagar budaya* (cultural remains) into objects (*artefacts*), buildings, structures, sites, and specifically defined areas (*kawasan*).

Provides governmental support for conservation efforts—for the protection, development, and utilization of cultural remains; and the provision of incentives, such as a reduction in land taxes and income tax.

Provides higher penalties than before for infringements of the law, for example, by stipulating a minimum sentence of three months (in prison), so that a judge cannot give a sentence of less than three months. For government employees, the term of imprisonment would be an additional one-third of the term of imprisonment compared to what would have been imposed on an ordinary member of the public for the same infringement.

COMMENT

The challenges that must be met in order to implement the above legislation, challenges similar to those posed by the previous law No. 5 of 1992, are, of course, (1) having the basic knowledge and management capability in place to ensure that work is done properly and (2) finding the political will to enforce the regulations and being able to mobilize effective law enforcement at all levels. There are hundreds, if not thousands, of regulations on the statute books at both national and lower levels that are not enforced, and which are, often, for all practical purposes, unenforceable. There are also many governmental regulations that inhibit effective management. For example, a major problem affecting the implementation of annual programs is the inability of the government at various levels to have funds released in good time to achieve the given objectives. Consequently, planned activities may be telescoped into very brief periods rather than spread out evenly over the financial year.

In its country paper relating to heritage management in Indonesia, UNESCO (United Nations Educational, Scientific, and Cultural Organization) has inferred a seemingly very low level of awareness of the value of cultural heritage amongst all levels of officialdom in Indonesia.[2] This is a major impediment in achieving the aims of the new legislation. The abject lack of appreciation of awareness of cultural materials is due, in part, to established perceptions left over from the past. Indeed, in many instances, such failings can be traced back to the declaration of Independence in 1945 and to the centrist and educational policies of the New Order government of the late Haji Mohammad Suharto. With little or no allowance for initiatives at a local level, and the perceived need for a unifying system of administration, the earlier, individual, and traditional forms of government that had survived Dutch colonialism were swept aside. At the same time, the imposition of "approved" forms of religion for use on personal identify cards has also caused great changes in the way different ethnic groups perceive their past: now, everyone must belong to one of the "approved" religious categories.

In practical terms, law enforcement requires the support and approval of local, district-level regulations by local administrations, but, above all, more competent and better educated officials than is typical, and an improved awareness and recognition of the value of heritage remains at all levels of the bureaucracy. For the present, the theory on which the new law is based is very different from reality. Over the past two years, the destruction of numerous archaeological sites or the threat of destruction due to development and other factors has given rise to the realization that the present bureaucratic system is hopelessly inadequate to manage the nation's

---

[2] UNESCO Indonesia Country Paper, 2007 (partial download in author's possession).

cultural heritage. Cultural development policy has tended to focus upon grandiose cultural festivals and similar prestige projects, while valuable archaeological sites have been damaged or destroyed. Cases in point are the transformation of various parts of the extensive medieval Muara Jambi site into coal dumps; the destruction of the southeast and northern ramparts and ditches of the Benteng Puteri Hijau site at Namorambe, south of Medan; and the transformation of part of the Namorambe site into an area of cheap and poorly built housing units.

FORMAL ADMINISTRATIVE STRUCTURE
Ministry of Education (formerly Culture and Tourism)

The following institutions formerly formed part of the Ministry of Culture and Tourism,[3] but are now under the umbrella of the Ministry of Education, Directorate General of Antiquities. The archaeological research and conservation units are funded by the central government, whereas museums are now funded through local provincial budgets. Most institutions and museums are overstaffed with administrative personnel. The majority of officially listed sites under the supervision of the various BP3 (Balai Pelestarian Peninggalan Purbakala, Archaeological Heritage Conservation Center) now have paid caretakers who receive honoraria to keep an eye on the site concerned, but field inventories, it seems, are often incomplete.

National Research Institute for Archaeology (Pusat Penelitian dan Pengembangan Arkeologi Nasional, P3N)
Jakarta: Jl. Raya Condet Pejaten No. 4, Jakarta Selatan 12510
Regional Archaeological Institutes, Regional Antiquities Offices, and Provincial Museums

1. *Regional Archaeological Institutes (Balai Arkeologi: BALAR)*

There are eleven regional archaeological research institutes that are each responsible for various aspects of archaeological research.

Balai Arkeologi Aceh & Sumatera Utara, Medan
Balai Arkeologi Sumatera Barat & Riau, Pagaruyung
Balai Arkeologi Sumatera Selatan, Palembang
Balai Arkeologi Jawa Barat & Lampung, Bandung
Balai Arkeologi Jawa Tengah & Jawa Timur, Yogyakarta
Balai Arkeologi Bali, NTB (Nusa Tenggara Barat) & NTT (Nusa Tenggara Timur) Denpasar
Balai Arkeologi Kalimantan, Banjarmasin
Balai Arkeologi Sulawesi Selatan & Sulawesi Tengah, Makassar
Balai Arkeologi Sulawesi Utara, Manado
Balai Arkeologi Ambon, Siwalima, Ambon
Balai Arkeologi Irian, Jayapura

---

[3] www.budpar.go.id/userfiles/file/strukturorganisasi.pdf, accessed in 2011. Due to the reorganization, this source has now disappeared from the Internet.

With the best will in the world, it is unlikely that those institutions have the resources, either in financial support or manpower capability, to deal with the ever-increasing destruction of antiquities by land development due to population expansion and an official lack of awareness of the cultural value of such remains. Restrictive financial regulations work against introducing and using innovative approaches that are needed to incorporate non-governmental bodies and individuals. Moreover, there is little or no effort to educate the younger generation and rising middle class to the economic value of cultural remains and how these treasures might be better exploited.

2. Regional Antiquities Conservation Offices (BP3)

There are ten regional conservation offices with management capabilities. They are listed here based on their recent achievements or failures, ranging from very poor to reasonably good.

Balai Pelestarian Peninggalan Purbakala, Aceh & Sumatera Utara. Banda Aceh, NAD
Balai Pelestarian Peninggalan Purbakala, Sumatera Barat & Riau, Batusangkar
Balai Pelestarian Peninggalan Purbakala, Sumatera Selatan & Bengkulu, Jambi
Balai Pelestarian Peninggalan Purbakala DKI Jakarta, Jawa Barat & Lampung, Serang
Balai Pelestarian Peninggalan Purbakala Borobudur, Borubudur, Jawa Tengah
Balai Pelestarian Peninggalan Purbakala Jawa Tengah, Prambanan, Klaten, Jawa Tengah
Balai Pelestarian Peninggalan D.I. Yogyakarta, D.I. Sleman, D.I. Yogyakarta
Balai Pelestarian Peninggalan Purbakala Jawa Timur, Mojokerto, Jawa Timur
Balai Pelestarian Peninggalan Purbakala, Bali, NTB & NTT, Bedulu, Bali
Balai Pelestarian Peninggalan Purbakala Sulawesi Selatan & Sulawesi Tengah, Makassar

I am most familiar with the capabilities of the Aceh and Sumatera Utara office, based in Banda Aceh. The management capability of this unit must be among the poorest in Indonesia. It has failed miserably to undertake meaningful conservation or restoration at numerous sites in the region, and, since the major tsunami of December 2004, allowed several coastal sites in Aceh Besar regency, such as Banda Aceh's Gampong Pande, simply to disappear in the gradually subsiding inter-tidal zones.

It has also failed to take any meaningful action with relation to the protection or conservation of sites such as Kuta Po Daniet at Neuheun, now almost totally destroyed; or Kuta Lubhok in Lamreh, Aceh Besar, or the severely damaged Benteng Puteri Hijau at Namorambe, south of Medan.

Again, innovative, effective approaches to cultural management are now needed. In all likelihood, non-governmental institutions might do a far better job of conservation management than the often dysfunctional governmental institutions officially tasked to undertake such work. Legislation would, however, have to be introduced at the regency level to allow such measures.

Aceh, Gampong Pande, sultanate-period tombstones at Cot Makam gradually disappearing due to ongoing subsidence in the inter-tidal zone. (Author's photo)

3. National and Regional Provincial Museums

Apart from the National Museum in Jakarta, which, since 2007, has new buildings and greatly improved exhibitions, responsibility for these institutions is now with regional administrations.

Museum Nasional, Jakarta
Museum Negeri Aceh, Banda Aceh, NAD
Museum Negeri Propinsi Sumatera Utara, Medan
Museum Negeri Propinsi Sumatera Barat, Padang
Museum Negeri Propinsi Riau, Pekanbaru
Museum Negeri Propinsi Yogyakarta, Yogyakarta
Museum Pusaka Nias, Gunung Sitoli, Nias

Some museums with meaningful local support, such as the Museum Negeri Sumatera Utara, have vigorous extension programs and lively interaction with schools and other educational institutions. Others are less fortunate and have become victims of local political maneuvering. The director of the Museum Negeri Aceh was moved to an administrative advisory position in the provincial cultural agency and for two years literally sat behind an empty desk while the museum stagnated. He has now been reinstated.

The background to museum development in Indonesia and the many factors—political, social, and economic—affecting this has been discussed in depth by Rath (1997). Much of what she says in this detailed analysis is, of course, also relevant to the field of cultural resource management.

Up until now almost all Indonesian archeologists have been public servants. There are, however, an increasing number of young, independent individuals who are beginning to show direct interest in the field and concern for the conservation of cultural remains generally. This private interest is reflected in the appearance of a number of non-governmental organizations (NGOs) active in the cultural heritage sphere. The basic management capability of the above-mentioned governmental institutions requires to be reviewed and upgraded. Generally, the bureaucratic system in Indonesia is essentially weak, self-serving, and often of little support to the general public. This is certainly true of many of the cultural agencies and the antiquities services, although there are signs that, with local government support, some institutions are beginning to make efforts to establish meaningful outreach programs and to raise awareness of the value of cultural heritage.

PUBLICATIONS, WEBSITES, AND BLOGS

There is now a remarkable range of publications on archaeology available in Bahasa Indonesia. A limited number of English texts, such as the *Bulletin of the Research Centre of Archaeology of Indonesia* (Bulletin Pusat Penelitian Arkeologi Nasional) and a number of translations are also available from P3N Jakarta. The Indonesian publications usually appear as small booklets or periodicals, although there are now some much more substantial publications put out by LIPI (Lembaga Ilmu Penelitian Indonesia, Indonesian Institute of Sciences) and a limited number of private publishers.

Each institution also now has its own website, with some being much more active than others. The Balai Bandung, for example, has arkeologisunda. blogspot.com, which has a range of up-to-date information in Bahasa Indonesia on sites in West Java. The website arkeologi.web.id gives a wide range of data in Bahasa Indonesia.[4]

Periodicals registered with ISSN numbers appear on a fairly regular basis. These include *Kalpataru*, from P3N; *Arabesk*, published by BP3 Aceh & Sumatera Utara, in Banda Aceh; *Berita Peneitian Arkeologi* and the *Berkala Arkeologi Sangkhakala*, published by the Balai Arkeologi Medan; as well as *Amoghapasa*, published by BP3 Batusangkar, in West Sumatra. Elsewhere, there are also institutional periodicals such as the *WalennaE* from the Balai Makassar.

Although these publications are available free of charge, getting them into the hands of the general public is a challenge. Distribution is made to related institutions, universities, and others on a mailing list. Private individuals normally have to request such publications, and they are freely given on request.

The quality of writing varies, as one might expect. Some articles are very good, but others—being esoteric or technical excavation reports—are not likely to be popular with the general public. There are also regular reports on archaeological finds in both national and regional newspapers. *Kompas* (Jakarta), for example, regularly carries archaeological news. In places where archaeologists and historians

---

[4] Both websites mentioned here were accessible in July 2013.

take an active interest in local culture, as is true in areas such as Aceh and north Sumatra, local newspapers are quite good at reporting recoveries—although it has to be said that the coverage and accuracy, due to the poor understanding of the subject, sometimes leaves something to be desired.

Recently the EFEO (Ecole Français d'Extrême-Orient) has begun to produce a range of excellent Bahasa Indonesia publications. *Lobu Tua, Sejarah Awal Barus* (2002) and *Barus Seribu Tahun Yang Lalu* (2008)—originally published in French by Archipel—are two prime examples that appear to have circulated well. Mention should also be made of Jaques Dumarcay's bilingual edition—English and Bahasa Indonesia—of *Candi Sewu and the Buddhist Architecture of Central Java*, published in 2007. Some editions are first-time publications, such as Hasan Djafar's *Kompleks Percandian Batujaya, Rekonsruksi Sejaraj Kebudayaan Daerah Pantai Utara Jawa Barat* (2010), which complements Pierre-Yves Manguin and Agustijanto Indrajaya's writings (e.g., 2006) on the subject.[5]

In 2006, LIPI published a festschrift for R. P. Soejono, which is a mixture of articles in English and Bahasa Indonesia.[6] Uka Tjandrasasmita's *Arkeologi Islam Nusantara*, published in 2009, may, however, now require revision.[7]

Harry Widianto and Truman Simanjuntak's impressive presentation book, *Sangiran Answering the World* (2009), and, more recently, Harry Widianto's *Human Path After Sangiran Era* (2011), give good coverage of the Sangiran site.

Cooperation between Malaysian and Indonesian archaeologists has also resulted in the publication of *Zaman Klasik di Nusantara, Tumpuan Kajian di Sumatra.*[8] More recently, in 2012, the Medan Municipal Agency for Planning and Development (Badan Perencana Pembangunan Daerah, BAPPEDA,) produced a *History of the City of Medan* (Sejarah Kota Medan) in Bahasa Indonesia as well as explanatory leaflets relating to the Kota Cina site at Medan Marelan.

Blogs with archaeological information would appear to be quite popular, although the usefulness of content appears to vary considerably.

The greatly improved access to archaeological information is encouraging and should generate new public interest in the field. Raising awareness of the value of cultural heritage, however, will be a long, slow, and uphill task. Getting school children to visit museums to undertake cultural projects is a major step forward.

---

[5] Manguin Pierre-Yves and Agustijanto Indrajaya, "The Archaeology of Batujaya (West Java, Indonesia): An Interim Report," in *Uncovering Southeast Asia's Past: Selected Papers from the 10th International Conference of the European Association of Southeast Asian Archaeologists*, ed. Elisabeth A. Bacus, Ian C. Glover, and Vincent Piggott (Singapore: NUS Press, 2006), pp. 245–57.

[6] Hubert Forestier, Dubel Driwantoro, Dominique Guillard, Budiman, and Darwin Siregar, "New Data for the Prehistoric Chronology of South Sumatra," *Archaeology: Indonesian Perspective—R. P. Soejono's Festscrift*, ed. Truman Simanjuntak, M. Hisyam, Bagyo Prasetyo, and Titi Surti Nastiti (Jakarta: LIPI, 2006), pp. 177–92.

[7] Uka Tjandrasasmita. *Arkeologi Islam Nusantara* (Jakarta: Kepustakaan Populer Gramedia, EFEO, Direktorat Jenderal Sejarah dan Purbakala, Departemen Kebudayaan dan Parawisata, Fakultas Adab dan Humaniora Universitas Islam Nasional Syarif Hidayatullah, 2009).

[8] Bambang Budi Utomo (P3N) and Nik Hassan Shuhaimi Nik Abd. Rahman, *Zaman Klasik di Nusantara, Tumpuan Kajian di Sumatra* (Kuala Lumpur: Dewan Bahasa & Pusaka, 2008).

NGO Activity in Archaeology and Cultural Heritage Management

There has been relatively little non-governmental involvement until fairly recently. The New Order government was extremely suspicious of any kind of non-governmental institutional activity, as this was usually seen as seditious. Non-governmental bodies were thus relatively weak under Suharto's regime. This said, progress is being made, as may be seen with the formation of the Indonesian Heritage Trust (Badan Pelestarian Pusaka Indonesia, BPPI) in Jakarta, which is mainly concerned with the conservation of architectural remains and which has been active since 2004; the Sumatra Heritage Trust (Badan Warisan Sumatra, BWS) in Medan, formed in 1998; and the Aceh Heritage Trust, formed in Banda Aceh in 2005.

Indonesian Heritage Trust

BPPI meets on a regular basis, with meetings held at its offices in Jakarta or nearby. It has held seminars and exhibitions to promote better understanding of conservation and undertaken a survey of fortifications throughout Indonesia. Its three basic objectives include:

Advise government on essential inputs relating to conservation regulations, policy strategy, and development programs and management of institutions at both the central and regional levels;
Assist and strengthen communities in conservation efforts; and
Develop a system for funding conservation.

Eight programs have been undertaken to date, which include the following:

Discussions and accompanying exhibition regarding Heritage Awareness, a program for raising awareness of the value of "Heritage";
Emergency response for heritage conservation, in light of natural disasters;
Establishment of a National Heritage Cities Network, "Heritage Action" (in Nias and West Sumatra);
Playing an active role in the compilation of new heritage legislation; and
Establishment of a comprehensive database of cultural heritage remains and networking with international and regional institutions, including ICOMOS (International Council on Monuments and Sites) and UNESCO.

Four programs were implemented during 2011 and are ongoing in 2013 according to BPPI:

Collect inputs for a national conservation strategy;
Undertake a program for education, capacity building, and conservation; a pilot project run with Dutch assistance to introduce archaeology and cultural heritage to school children is currently underway in Yogyakarta.
Develop a funding program for conservation; and
Undertake a special, quick-action conservation program.

The BPPI boasts linkages to some fifty-two conservation institutions throughout Indonesia, and central government officials are often in attendance at meetings. Despite a general lack of philanthropic funding in Indonesia, the BPPI has been relatively successful in raising money for conservation and heritage training work. The clock tower in Bukit Tinggi, West Sumatra, was renovated largely with funds raised by the BPPI. Its horizons are, however, heavily blinkered, as it lost the opportunity to raise the issue of the wanton destruction of the Benteng Puteri Hijau site with the Regent of Deli Serdang district when it held its annual meeting in Medan in 2011.

Sumatra Heritage Trust

The Sumatra Heritage Trust (SHT, or Badan Warisan Sumatera, BWS) was established to try to protect colonial-period buildings in the city of Medan. It has active links to other heritage conservation societies in Sumatra. Its basic objectives are to influence regional heritage capability by preparing and recommending heritage policy and heritage management guidelines; ensuring the survival of heritage initiatives; and creating and developing awareness of the value of cultural heritage.

Kota Cina: despite being declared as a protected archaeological site, several areas are now divided up into "kaplingan," for sale as housing plots. (Author's photo)

The SHT has had varying success, as valuable colonial-period buildings are still disappearing in Medan. Few public servants in the Medan municipality or neighboring regencies have any perception of the value of cultural heritage or how it might be used to develop tourism and boost the local economy. Legislation to assist in the protection or conservation of old buildings and archaeological sites in the municipality of Medan was finally enacted in 2012.

The Aceh Heritage Community

The Aceh Heritage Community was created following the disastrous earthquake and tsunami of December 26, 2004. Its purposes are to:

Record the heritage damaged or destroyed by the tsunami;
Raise support for repairing damaged and preserving endangered heritage;
Identify and safeguard the surviving heritage, so that more will not be lost during the rebuilding process; and
Create and maintain a database on Acehnese heritage, especially since the key archival and cultural institutions, the Pusat Dokumentasi Aceh (Aceh Documentation Center) and The Lembaga Kebudayan Aceh (LAKA, Aceh Cultural Foundation), were destroyed during the tsunami.

Other similar, non-governmental institutions exist in Pangkalpinang, Bangka; Palembang, South Sumatra; Belitung; Bengkulu; Nias; Padang, West Sumatra; Denpasar, Bali; Bandung, West Java; Yogyakarta, D.I.Y.; Cirebon; Malang; Semarang; Solo, Central Java; and Surabaya, East Java.

UNIVERSITY OF MEDAN CENTRE FOR HISTORY AND SOCIAL STUDIES (PUSSIS UNIMED).

The University of Medan's Centre for History and Social Studies (PUSSIS UniMed, Pusat Studi Sejarah dan Ilmu-Ilmu Sosial UniMed), headed by Ichwan Azhari since 2007, has organized field visits for students to several historical sites around Medan, built a modest field museum at Kota Cina (which is also used as a kindergarten for young mothers in the village during morning hours), and taken positive action to canvass governmental interest to try to preserve remains at Kota Cina and the Benteng Puteri Hijau earthwork complex at Namorambe, in Deli Serdang regency, south of Medan.

PUSSIS was granted municipal funding to purchase two key areas of land at the site in 2011, but at the last minute the owners refused to settle for the agreed price and the funds were returned to the government. Sadly, despite the site being listed as a *Cagar Budaya* by the Medan Municipal government, much of the area has already been divided up into building lots by developers, both at Kota Cina and within the earthwork area at Benteng Puteri Hijau.

At the behest of PUSSIS, the Medan Municipal Agency for Planning and Development produced colored leaflets in Bahasa Indonesia and English describing the historical significance of the Kota Cina site and its context in medieval trade.

This goes to show that with the right approach and goodwill, some progress may be made in this sphere. It has certainly taken time. Support from the local press goes a long way in promoting an improved awareness of the value of cultural heritage,

Kota Cina, small carved stone pegs probably used as gaming pieces. These are also known from Kedah and Singapore (center). (Author's photo)

Benteng Puteri Hijau, the southeastern rampart before destruction by a national housing development ministry project in 2008. (Author's photo)

but whether any meaningful action will be taken actually to preserve undisturbed and interesting features in various parts of the Kota Cina site still remains to be seen.

Pressure by non-governmental institutions can, however, have an impact on the bureaucracy, as protests raised by BPPI in relation to a scandal about the location and construction of a field museum at Trowulan, in East Java, cost the then director general of antiquities his job. With an ongoing debate about the Gunung Padang site near Cianjur, in West Java, one wonders, however, whether many of the so-called experts in this field are, indeed, properly qualified.

EDUCATION, COOPERATION, AND TRAINING

The Indonesian Institute of Sciences has, of course, played a major role in the development of archaeological work in Indonesia. LIPI authorizes what cooperative research may or may not take place.

International Cooperation, 1970–2010

Counterpart	Research	Social	Education	Equipment	Period and Location
UCFS	*				1977; Sumatra
MNHN	*	*	*	*	1984–present
EFEO	*	*	*	*	1976–present; Java, Sumatra, Bangka
ORSTOM	*	*		*	1993–1997; Java, Sumatra
Ford Foundation			*		1991–1993; Field School, Trowulan
ANU	*			*	1997–1999
James Cook-ANU	*	*		*	1995–1998
UW–M	*				1997
UNE–P3G	*				1997–1999; Flores
ARI–NUS	*				2005, 2010; Jambi survey
ARI–NUS/ EOS–NTU	*		*		2010–2011; Aceh
Frei Universiteit Berlin	*		*	*	2006–present; West Sumatra, Korinci

Key:
ANU: Australian National University, Canberra
ARI-NUS: Asia Research Institute, National University of Singapore
EFEO: Ecole Français d'Éxtreme Orient, Paris
EOS-NTU: Earth Observatory of Singapore, Nanyang Technical University, Singapore
MNHN: Museum National d'Histoire Naturelle, France
ORSTOM: Office de la Recherche Scientifique et Technologie d'Outre-Mer
UNE: University of New England, Armidale, New South Wales, Australia
UCFS: University of Chicago (IL) Field School, USA
UW–M: University of Wisconsin–Madison, USA

Source: Adapted from Truman Simanjuntak, "Kerjasama Internasional Sebuah Refleksi," in *25 Tahun Kerjasama Pusat Penelitian Arkeologi dan École Française d'Extrême-Orient* (Jakarta: Pusat Penelitian Arkeologi, École Française d'Extrême-Orient, 2002), pp. 41–57.

Two universities have faculties of archaeology that currently offer degree courses in archaeology: Universitas Indonesia at Depok, Jakarta, and Universitas Gaja Mada at Yogyakarta. The Jurusan Arkeologi at Universitas Udayana, Denpasar, Bali, and Universitas Hasanuddin in Makasar also offer a degree. Field schools for young archaeologists at Trowulan were funded by the Ford Foundation in 1991–93, and a small field school was undertaken in Central Java in 2010, funded by ISEAS Singapore (Institute of Southeast Asian Studies).

Various overseas universities have funded tertiary degree courses for Indonesian archaeologists, such as Australian National University, but the main, consistent support over the years has come from the bilateral assistance program of the Ecole Français d'Extrême-Orient, which funded both an entire series of important excavation projects and numerous degree and other courses in France. Only the EFEO, supported by the French Foreign Ministry, has a permanent office in Jakarta. Moreover, in recent years, the EFEO has funded the translation and publication of books on history and archaeology in Bahasa Indonesia (as noted earlier), fulfilling a need in this sphere.

Such cooperation benefits both parties, especially where foreign institutions bring much needed funding to undertake work that might not otherwise get done. Until 2011, a Memorandum of Understanding with the National Research Centre of Archaeology in Indonesia was sufficient to initiate cooperation. Research visa applications now require the approval of LIPI, which may mean that approval becomes somewhat more complicated and difficult. How things work out in the future remains to be seen.

RECENT DEVELOPMENTS IN ARCHAEOLOGY THROUGHOUT THE ARCHIPELAGO

Pre- and Protohistory

Two recent developments at different ends of the archipelago have captured considerable interest. First is the discovery of the 20,000-year-old, so-called "Hobbit" humanoid (*Homo floresiensis*) by a joint Australian–Indonesian team in 2003, in the Gua Buah, a limestone cave in Flores. There has been some considerable dispute as to whether this specimen really represents a separate species. Second is the confirmation of Hoabhinian remains in a cave on the island of Nias, off the west coast of northern Sumatra (Forestier et al. 2005). Of lesser international note are the surveys undertaken by the P3N and an EFEO team in 2001, which put South Sumatra in the news.

In 1996, an early first millennium (c. 300 CE) settlement site was discovered at Karangagung, Kecamatan Lalan, Kabupaten Musi Banyusin, west of the Musi estuary in south Sumatra (Soeroso 2002), and warrants a mention as well—this is the area identified by O. W. Wolters as "Salty Face," or Mukha Asin in early Chinese texts. An extended program of excavation work is ongoing at this and neighboring sites where organic remains are well preserved. The Karangagung site would appear to have links with Oc-Eo in southern Vietnam.

A cave, the Gua Pawon in the karst west of Bandung, was initially excavated by a group of amateurs some years ago. Their results have recently been followed up by the Balai Arkeologi Bandung with some success.

Classical (Hindu Buddhist) Archaeology

Excavations undertaken in Palembang have affirmed Srivijaya period (c. 600 CE) settlement along the banks of the Musi river (Manguin 2004). It seems, however, that the Pertamina fertilizer plant built at Sabokingking may have destroyed whatever traces of earlier settlement remained in this area. Cornellians were actively involved in the field survey work in the search for Srivijaya.

Archaeological surveying in the swamps of Sumatra can be both exhausting and dirty work. O. W. Wolters and A. C. Milner in Palembang, 1978. (Author's photo)

In the Kerinci region, new work has been undertaken on megalithic sites (Bonatz 2006). In west Sumatra, new discoveries have come to light along the upper reaches of the Batang Hari river in the area known as Dharmasraya.

In west Java, work on the Batujaya site, near Krawang, on the north bank of the Citarum river site, has revealed tangible evidence for continuity between pre- and proto-historical settlement and an extensive complex of brick-built *candi*, or temples, some showing traces of stucco work (Manguin and Agustijanto Indrajaya 2006) . This area has also yielded remains of early mitred Visnu images—one of which was also recovered at Kota Kapur, on the island of Bangka (Manguin 2004). Manguin's work has resulted in the recognition of two early trade networks—one Vaisnavite, one Buddhist—linking Java to the north and to the west, and provided evidence of the continuity of settlement with changes in this region over a millennium.

Some interest was shown in the badly disturbed Muara Kaman site in Kutei in 2006, where the local regency government is belatedly showing some interest in taking steps to preserve the architectural and cultural remains. A hoard of late first millennium Buddhist bronzes was discovered at Muara Kaman in about 2004. A descriptive inventory of some badly corroded imagery also found at the site is in press (Edwards McKinnon in press).

Excavation and conservation work has continued at the Trowulan site in East Java, where construction of a new site museum planned to be built over valuable cultural remains led to controversy and upsets in the erstwhile Ministry of Tourism and Culture. The museum site was relocated.

Islamic Archaeology

Excavation and conservation work in Banten has continued at Banten Lama, where Japanese work has recorded much in the way of Japanese ceramic imports. Excavations at Banten Girang has been described in detail by Guillot (1994). The Banten Girang site is now inaccessible, however, due to being totally occupied by housing.

Work in Aceh and on the west and east coasts of Sumatra has begun to reveal traces of early Islam along the coast of Aceh Besar (Suwedi 1996; Edwards McKinnon [in press], 2006; Guillot and Kalus 2008); Barus (Perret and Surachman 2009) and the possibility of earlier, pre-Islamic settlement at Pase.[9] Medieval Indian involvement in Sumatra and inter-regional maritime trade networks is now beginning to be much better understood.

Colonial Archaeology

The VOC (Vereenigde Oostindische Compagnie, Dutch East India) fort, Fort Rotterdam in Makassar, has been renovated and the fortifications at Somba Opu, under threat of being turned into a theme park, are belatedly to be taken in hand by the BP3.

Excavation work on the former Honourable East India Company settlement at York fort at Bengkulu (Bencoolen) was undertaken under the direction of John Miksic in the early 1990s, but, unfortunately, reports of this work remain largely unpublished. Fort Marlborough at Bengkulu is maintained in a good state of repair, and the former British cemetery in Bengkulu was saved from destruction by the efforts of Janet Donald, wife of the then British Ambassador.

RECENT EXPERIENCE—AND PITFALLS FOR THE UNWARY

In 2006, the Asia Research Institute (ARI) at National University of Singapore (NUS) submitted a modest but somewhat underfunded project proposal (US$300,000) to the post-tsunami Badan Rehabilitasi dan Rekonstruksi (BRR, Reconstruction Body) for Nanggroe Aceh Darussalam (NAD) to undertake a survey of archaeological sites that had been damaged, destroyed, or endangered by the December 2004 earthquake and tsunami. After months of negotiations, this proposal was seemingly rejected by the BRR. No reasons were given.

In the meantime, the BP3 for NAD had been spending not inconsiderable funds on the so-called rehabilitation of the BP3 office in Banda Aceh and on a limited number of damaged coastal burial complexes and masonry-built forts at Ladong (Indrapatra) and Meunasah Keude, at the Krueng Raya. Apart from some ill-informed

---

[9] Personal communication, Heddy Surachman, 2011.

Jambi Kota. Remnants of stucco work from a colonial-period building.
(Author's photo)

and very poorly organized work at the damaged Syiah Kuala complex, and the repair of a wall of the fort opposite Meunasah Keude, the other work was seemingly limited to erecting walls and fences around the burial complexes in Gampung Pande, Kecamatan Kota Raja, Banda Aceh, and the fort complex at Ladong. The fencing at Ladong was particularly badly done, as it obscured the view of the Ladong River—the existence of the river being the very reason for the erection of the forts in the first place. That fencing has since been damaged by coastal erosion. At the Tengku di Kandang complex in Gampong Pande, the fencing was erected prior to new road construction with the consequence that the access gate to the burial ground could not be opened further than about twenty centimeters, making entry to the complex almost impossible. Two nearby burial complexes, that of the Puteri Hijau and Raja-Raja, were also fenced at the same time.

In early 2007, encouraged by favorable noises from the World Bank office in Banda Aceh, I prepared an alternative proposal to undertake the inventory work required to compile a comprehensive list of all known damaged burials sites on the coastline of Aceh Besar; create a community-managed heritage park at Ujung Batee Kapal, Lamreh (the site of an ancient settlement related to Lamri or Lamuri); and initiate community-based site management with small grants for local community heritage initiatives. When nothing more was heard from the World Bank, this proposal was then submitted to the Governor's Office, which was purportedly supporting measures to promote tourism for Aceh—but, once again, there was no response. Cultural Heritage Management (CHM) was obviously not on the horizons of either the BRR or the provincial administration.

Having completed my work in Aceh, I then submitted the proposal to the UNESCO office in Jakarta in 2007, as it had an ongoing CHM rehabilitation project in Nias. The UNESCO officials appeared interested, and I understood they rewrote the proposal to fit their project proposal guidelines. Since then, however, nothing more has ever been heard! When the deputy director of the Nias Museum asked me to donate a number of ceramic reference books for the museum library, I was told there were no funds to purchase books.

Benteng Puteri Hijau, bulldozer damage to the northwestern earthen rampart inflicted by a second housing project (2011). (Author's photo)

The experience in Aceh was again reflected by unnecessary, wanton damage inflicted in 2008 to the ramparts of the Benteng Puteri Hijau (the fort of the Green Princess) site at Deli Tua/Namorambe, south of Medan, by a government-sponsored housing project, the Perumahan Taman Puteri Deli complex. Some hundreds of meters of earthwork were bulldozed for the erection of housing, and structures were built within the site in close proximity to the spring known as the Pancuran Puteri Hijau—long regarded in local lore as a *keramat,* or shrine, as the place where the princess came to bathe. It is a sacred spot, visited by many Malays and other locals. Whether the proximity of the housing violates the environmental regulations that relate to construction in the proximity of springs of fresh water, I have not yet been able to ascertain.

When questioned about the permit that was issued in 2004 for the construction project, the officials of the Cultural Agency of Deli Serdang regency said that they knew nothing of the existence of an ancient site at Deli Tua/Namorambe. Seemingly, no one had told them of its existence or submitted an official report stating that there was an archaeological site at Deli Tua Lama—although John Anderson had reported on it in his *Mission to the East Coast of Sumatra in 1823* (1826, 1971) and various local historians, such as Tengku Lah Husny (n.d.) and Tengku Luckman Sinar (1991), had discussed the site and its history in their writings. Indeed, in 2007, a former Regent of Tanah Karo had written personally to the Regent of Deli Serdang expressing his concern about the site. The local Archaeological Institute had never undertaken any survey of the area—like Kota Cina and Kota Rentang, it was too close to Medan to incur travel payments and subsistence honoraria, and thus, despite its cultural and historical importance to both the Malay and Karo elements of the population, had been ignored.

When I learned of the imminent threat to the site at Namorambe, I wrote directly to the Director of Antiquities in Jakarta, who initiated a survey visit but then delegated responsibility to the BP3 based in Banda Aceh. A cursory excavation was undertaken, which concluded that the earthwork was indeed "man-made." A small number of Hoabinhian Sumatraliths were recovered, suggesting that the area had been inhabited much earlier than was suspected from surface recoveries alone, which indicated a 1400–1500s CE settlement. But once again, despite a visit by the Indonesian Human Rights Institute, nothing has been done to advance discovery and exploration at this site.

THE ASSOCIATION OF INDONESIAN ARCHAEOLOGISTS

Ikatan Ahli Arkeologi Indonesia (IAAI, Association of Indonesian Archaeologists) was founded by R. P. Soejono in 1973, and has been an activating force among archaeologists by holding congresses and meetings, and publishing papers from proceedings.

Mention should be made, however, of the attrition that has occurred among the new generation of archaeologists over the years. Several promising young people have met untimely ends due to accidents or illness. Sadly, both Lukman Nurhakim, former head of the Islamic Section at P3N, and Halwany Michrob, of the BP3 in Banten, died of cancer. Several other relatively young colleagues have also died from heart attacks and other illnesses.

SUMMARY

Although there is a spark of hope for the future of archaeology and cultural heritage management in Indonesia, much remains to be done at all levels—from improving government policy downward to increasing local respect and care for these sites, both to improve direction and management capability and to open the door for greater involvement of the private sector. Under the direction of Tony Djubiantono at the P3N, the situation was briefly much more open to international, cooperative work. The realization that government alone cannot adequately handle the preservation of cultural remains would be a big step forward. The active involvement of non-governmental groups and local communities in assisting conservation and site management would move preservation forward. Also, the process of raising awareness of the value of cultural heritage remains must begin with children in schools across the archipelago. There is a lot of useful local knowledge that has been under-utilized or is being rapidly forgotten. The conservation of cultural heritage can in some instances be combined with improved environmental conservation, and management and interest from a rising middle class may eventually promote change. The fact remains that an unresponsive bureaucracy, institutional weakness, and cumbersome and inappropriate financial regulations do more harm than good.

Now that there is freedom of speech in Indonesia, individuals are beginning to speak out about issues that were previously swept under the carpet. Thus, more concerns are being brought to the public's attention, including the importance of and threats to cultural heritage. The access afforded by websites can also go a long way to promote a better awareness of the economic potential for well-informed tourism, and to encourage local administrations to put into place effective local legislation for improved cultural heritage management. Issues of responsibility and accountability are gradually being brought forward so that, in time, change will inevitably occur, and—I hope—for the better.

Works Cited

Anderson, John. *Mission to the East Coast of Sumatra in 1823*. Kuala Lumpur: Oxford University Press Reprints, 1826, 1971.

Bambang Budi Utomo and Nik Hassan Shuhaimi Nik Abd. Rahman. *Zaman Klasik di Nusantara, Tumpuan Kajian di Sumatra*. Kuala Lumpur: Dewan Bahasa & Pusaka, 2008.

Bloembergen, Marieke, and Martin Eickhoff. "Conserving the Past, Mobilizing the Indonesian Future. Archaeological Sites, Regime Change, and Heritage Politics in Indonesia in the 1950s." *BKI*, Journal of the Humanities and Social Sciences of Southeast Asia and Oceania 167 (2011): 405–36.

Bonatz, Dominik. "Kerinci – Archaeological Research in the Highlands of Jambi on Sumatra." *Uncovering Southeast Asia's Past—Selected Papers from the 10th International Conference of the European Association of Southeast Asian Archaeologists*. Ed. Elisabeth A. Bacus, Ian C. Glover, and Vincent Piggott. Singapore: NUS Press, 2006: 310–24.

Bonatz, Dominik, John Miksic, J. David Neidel, and Mai Lin Tjoa Bonatz, eds. *From Distant Tales: Archaeology and Ethnohistory in the Highlands of Sumatra*. Newcastle upon Tyne: Cambridge Scholars Publishing, 2009.

Djafar, Hasan. *Kompleks Percandian Batujaya, Rekonsruksi Sejaraj Kebudayaan Daerah Pantai Utara Jawa Barat*. Bandung École française d'Extrême-Orient, Pusat Penelitian dan Pengembangan Arkeologi Nasional. Jakarta: KITLV, 2010.

Dumarcay, Jacques. *Candi Sewu and Buddhist Architecture of Central Java*. Jakarta: Forum Jakarta-Paris Kepustakaan Populer Gramedia, Pusat Penelitian dan Pengembangan Arkeologi Nasional, and École française d'Extrême-Orient, 2007.

École française d'Extreme-Orient dan Pusat Penelitian Arkeolgi. *25 Tahun Kerjasama Pusat Penelitian Arkeologi dan École française d'Extreme-Orient*. Jakarta: École française d'Extreme-Orient dan Pusat Penelitian Arkeolgi, 2002. Proceedings of a seminar held in Palembang, July 16–18, 2001.

Edwards McKinnon, Edmund. "Mediaeval Landfall Sites in Aceh." *Uncovering Southeast Asia's Past — Selected Papers from the 10th International Conference of the European Association of Southeast Asian Archaeologists*. Ed. Elisabeth A. Bacus, Ian C. Glover, and Vincent Piggott. Singapore: NUS Press, 2006: 325–34.

——. "A Hoard of Ancient Buddhist Bronze Scrap from Kutei, East Kalimantan." Paper presented at the conference "Buddhist Dynamics in Premodern Southeast Asia." March 10–11, 2011. Singapore: ISEAS, in press.

Forestier, Hubert, Dubel Driwantoro, Dominique Guillard, Budiman, and Darwin Siregar. "New Data for the Prehistoric Chronology of South Sumatra." *Archaeology: Indonesian Perspective — R. P. Soejono's Festscrift*. Ed. Truman Simanjuntak, M. Hisyam, Bagyo Prasetyo, and Titi Surti Nastiti. Jakarta: LIPI, 2006: 177–92.

Forestier, Hubert, Truman Simanjuntak, Dominique Guillaud, Dubel Driwantoro, Ketut Wiradnyana, Darwin Siregar, Rokus Dua Awe, and Budiman. "Le Site de Tögi Ndrawa, Ile de Nias, Sumatra nord : les prèmieres traces d'une occupation hoabinhienne en grotte en Indonesie." *PALEVOL Science Direct* 4 (2005): 727–33.

Guillot, Claude. *Banten avant l'Islam*. Paris: EFEO, 1994.

Guillot, Claude, ed. *Lobu Tua, Sejarah Awal Barus*. Jakarta: École française d'Extrême-Orient, Association Archipel, Pusat Penelitisn Arkeologi, and Yayasan Obor Indonesia, 2002.

Guillot, Claude, Marie-France Dupoizat, Daniel Perret, Untung Sunaryo, and Heddy Surachman. *Barus Seribu Tahun Yang Lalu*. Jakarta: Archipel, Jakarta KPG (Kepustakaan Populer Gramedia), École française d'Extrême-Orient, Association Archipel, Pusat Penelitian dan Pengembangan Arkeologi Nasional, Forum Jakarta–Paris, 2008.

Guillot, Claude, and Ludvig Kalus. *Les Monuments funéraires et l'histoire du sultanat de Pasai à Sumatra (XIIIe-XVIe siècles)*. Paris: Cahier d'Archipel 37, 2008.

Krahl, Regina, John Guy, J. Keith Watson, and Julian Raby. *Shipwrecked: Tang Treasures and Monsoon Winds*. Singapore: Smithsonian Institution, National Heritage Board, and Singapore Tourism Board, 2010.

Krom, Nicolaas Johannes. "Inventaris der Oudheden" (An Inventory of Antiquities) *Oudheidkundig Verslag* (O.V.), Bijlage G. (1912): 32–51.

Manguin, Pierre-Yves. "The Archaeology of the Early Maritime Polities of Southeast Asia." *Southeast Asia from Prehistory to History*. Ed. Peter Bellwood and Ian Glover.London: Routledge Curzon, 2004: 282–313.

Manguin, Pierre-Yves, and Agustijanto Indrajaya. "The Archaeology of Batujaya (West Java, Indonesia): An Interim Report." *Uncovering Southeast Asia's Past — Selected Papers from the 10th International Conference of the European Association of Southeast Asian Archaeologists*. Ed. Elisabeth A. Bacus, Ian C. Glover, and Vincent Piggott. Singapore: NUS Press, 2006: 245–57.

Perret, Daniel, and Heddy Surachman. *Histoire de Barus III. Regards sur une place marchande de l'océan Indien (XIIe-milieu du XVIIe s)*. Paris: Cahier d'Archipel 38, 2009.

Pusat Penelitian Arkeologi Nasional. *Rapat Evaluasi Hasil Peneitian Arkeologi III*. Jakarta: Departemen Pendidikan and Kebudayaan, 1988.

Rath, Amanda. "Cultural Sublimation: The Museumizing of Indonesia." *Explorations in Southeast Asian Studies* 1.1 (1997), www2.hawaii.edu/~seassa/explorations/v1n1/art2/v1n1-art2.html, accessed September 16, 2013.

Republik Indonesia: Kementerian Kebudayaan dan Pariwisata, Direktorat Jenderal Sejarah dan Purbakala. Jakarta. *Undang-Undang No. 11, Tahun 2010 Tentang Cagar Budaya*. (Republic of Indonesia Law No. 11, 2010, relating to Cultural Heritage. Jakarta: Ministry of Culture and Tourism, Directorate General of History and Archaeology.)

Soeroso, M. P. "Pesisir Timur Sumatra Selatan Masa Proto Sejarah: Kajian Pemukiman Skala Makro." Paper presented at the Pertemuan Ilmiah Arkeologi IX dan Kongres IAAI (*Ikatan Ahli Arkeologi Indonesia*, Association of Archaeology Experts of Indonesia), Kediri, July 22–28, 2002.

Suwedi, Montana. *"Pandangan Lain Tentang Letak Lamuri dan Barat (Batu Nisan Abad KeVII-VIII Hijriyah di Lamreh dan Lamno, Aceh)*. (A Differing Viewpoint Relating to the Position of Lamuri and Barat [Seventh and Eighth Century Hijrah Datings for Grave Markers at Lamreh and Lamno, Aceh]). *Kebudayaan* 6 (1996–97): 83–93.

———. "Nouvelles données sur les royumes de Lamuri et Barat." *Archipel* 53 (1997): 85–95.

Tengku Lah Husny. *Sejarah Melayu Pesisir*. Medan: printed privately, undated.

Tengku Luckman Sinar. *Sejarah Medan Tempo Doeloe*. Medan: Lembaga Penelitian dan Pengembangan Budaya Melayu, 1991.

Truman Simanjuntak. "Kerjasama Internasional Sebuah Refleksi." *25 Tahun Kerjasama Pusat Penelitian Arkeologi dan École française d'Extrême-Orient*. Jakarta: Pusat Penelitian Arkeologi, École française d'Extrême-Orient, and Kedutaan Besar Prancis di Indonesia, 2002: 41–57. (From the proceedings of a seminar held in Palembang, July 16–18, 2001.)

Truman Simanjuntak, M. Hisyam, Bagyo Prasetyo, and Titi Surti Nastiti, eds. *Archaeology: Indonesian Perspective—R. P. Soejono's Festscrift*. Jakarta: LIPI, 2006.

Uka Tjandrasasmita. *Arkeologi Islam Nusantara*. Jakarta: Kepustakaan Populer Gramedia, EFEO, Direktorat Jenderal Sejarah dan Purbakala, Departemen Kebudayaan dan Parawisata, and Fakultas Adab dan Humaniora Universitas Islam Nasional Syarif Hidayatullah, 2009.

Widianto, Harry, and Truman Simanjuntak. *Sangiran Answering the World*. Sangiran: Conservation Office of Sangiran Early Man Site, 2009.

Widianto, Harry. *Human Path after Sangiran Era*. Sangiran: Conservation Office of Sangiran Early Man Site, 2011.

THE ARC OF MY FIELD IS A RAINBOW WITH AN EXPANDING TWIST AND ALL KINDS OF CREATURES DANCING: THE GROWING INCLUSIVITY OF INDONESIAN ART HISTORY

Astri Wright

PREAMBLE

When Eric Tagliacozzo and Kaja McGowan invited me to this conference featuring senior Indonesian Studies scholars who would reflect on how their fields have developed over the last thirty years, I wrote back to ask if I was senior enough for this honor. Kaja responded that I should be there because I am "a pioneer." At first, I thought, "uff da": pioneers usually claim to discover new territory and phenomena perfectly "old hat" to "the natives." From the Indonesian perspective, modern Indonesian art certainly did not need to be discovered: it developed and struggled and flourished (and, at times, floundered) in certain places and social groups, completely independently of any external (or, indeed, internal) scholarship around it.

And maybe that's the way it always is: reality is primary, scholarship secondary. Because, in terms of the discipline of art history in Western(-style) universities, Indonesian studies curricula, and Western-based/-driven curatorial practices, it *was* (with one luminous, foundational exception) "undiscovered" until the early 1990s. In the academic research and teaching curriculum of the early 1980s when I entered grad school, the subfield I today work within only had one source written in English,[1] the work of Claire Holt. Not trained as an art historian specifically, but a dance historian, dancer, writer, and cultural observer,[2] Holt was well before her time

---

[1] Or, for that matter, in Dutch, French, or other European languages.

[2] I believe Holt's book achieved its remarkable quality and relevance to Indonesian contexts and its varied definitions of "art" largely because of her extensive Indonesian fieldwork from 1930 to the late 1960s. Her close connections with other scholars and experts in the field, both Indonesian and European, solidified her interdisciplinary arts background, which liberated her from the limitations of classical European definitions of "art" and "history," even as she

when she, as a matter of course, and based on her long periods of firsthand exposure to the many aspects of creativity in different parts of Indonesia, not only focused on Java and not only included the living arts (dance, wayang, multimedia performance in ritual and community celebratory contexts), but also the modern period, discussed in Part III of her 1967 book, *Art in Indonesia*.[3]

Fortuitously for me, the time frame set by the organizers of this conference coincided with the duration of my own direct involvement in the field. I came to Cornell's Southeast Asia Program (SEAP) and the art history department in 1982 to study Southeast Asian art history with Stan O'Connor after earning a BA in Asian Studies and Chinese art history, followed by two years' independent study and freelance cultural journalism in China. The awareness of modern Asian artists' existence, struggles around, and commitment to local and global modernist genres of creativity that I had gained in China now deepened, as I immersed myself in Southeast Asian area studies, particularly Indonesian Studies, as I read and reread Holt, attended the weekly SEAP film series, and talked with Cornell's graduate students, including many Indonesians. Above all, my first trip to Indonesia for language studies in Salatiga in 1984, which offered first encounters with Indonesian artists and the discovery of an art world a generation or two younger than what Holt had described, was what inspired my choice of a PhD topic, which picked up the torch of Holt's work that had begun three decades earlier.

But I am getting ahead of myself. Moving along from the invitation to the time frame, I now turn to the word "arc" used by the organizers when they asked us to speak to the arc of our field. I like the word. It's both vague and vivid. It is open-ended even as it stands in danger of being too simple a metaphor for the subject. Like others writing in this volume, I also felt the need, at the outset of writing my paper, to come up with an evocative word, image, or metaphor; I needed one that was both performatively alive *and* representative of the field(s) I navigate. This is how the complex, animate image in my title was born. Indeed, the fields of study that compose and bracket Indonesian arts are full of color and chaos. And, speaking for myself, they trigger my imagination as well as my analytical brain, my inner artist as well as the scholar. I see some of this in my Indonesianist colleagues active in the contemporary cultural arena, as well—the commitment and willingness to: keep joining a dance into new terrain with a beginner's and even a literary-poetic mind wide open (and that openness keeps us very much in the student mode); to build trails for our non-specialist students to follow yet not impose excessive order where there is none, even when one's bent is more theoretical; to strive to see the whole picture in all its components and nuances even as we know we will fail to see it all; and to continue to report back to our various Europe-originated institutions, audiences, and increasingly multicultural but mostly non-Indonesian worlds.

Before I proceed, some caveats need to be in place. First, the absence of images in this essay is a handicap. In a field where the primary data consist of visual imagery (nature-based, human-made, or a combination—primary data that are unusually

---

held the classically trained art historians and their work in the highest esteem. Claire Holt, *Art in Indonesia: Continuities and Change* (Ithaca, NY: Cornell University Press, 1967).

[3] For an excellent discussion of Southeast Asian art history textbooks, and the general myopia of academic art history as a field, see Jan Mrázek, "Ways of Experiencing Art: Art History, Television, and Javanese Wayang," in *What's the Use of Art? Asian Visual and Material Culture in Context,* ed. Jan Mrázek and Morgan Pitelka (Honolulu, HI: University of Hawaii Press, 2008), pp. 287–94.

open-ended because they are non-verbal, and while often embedded in concrete materials, always subject to a broad continuum of interpretations, whether emic or etic), not to have any representations even as we are discussing their study is unfortunate. Even speaking to ideas (here, the intellectual developments of the field) rather than imagery (the products of artistic imaginings and adherences), it is intriguing to postulate that the images on book covers designed and published over the last three decades in themselves might communicate insights in ways either complementary to or incrementally beyond the words.

Another caveat is that, being by nature oriented towards edges, fringes, and challenges to conventionally inscribed presences and absences, and having been trained in area/interdisciplinary studies to be attentive to a broad spectrum of scholarship, I find the most bare-bones story I wish to tell goes far beyond the scope of the space allotted each chapter in this volume. Thus, I have only been able to draw the tail of the lemur (see footnote 11), and I must apologize, up front, for all the names, titles, and ideas missing in the following pages.

THE ARC OF THE FIELD OVER THE LAST THIRTY YEARS

Thirty years is a long time to assess developments in a relatively young field that has seen such a lot of growth, on four continents, by insider, outsider, and border-crosser scholars, along lines of consolidating older research subjects as well as expanding into newer areas. How does one build a meaningful and representative narrative in a few pages? A panel of eight to ten specialists would be the dream scenario here. My discussion will hopefully complement, but not overlap with, the papers by colleagues in Indonesian art history and visual aspects of anthropology, with all of our interlinking research areas and different points of departure One way of telling this story is to look at the flow of subject areas in the subfields, which I define as part of Indonesian art history, decade by decade.

In the late 1970s and early 1980s, the European paradigm of "art history" began to expand to include a broader "visual field." In beyond-European art histories, this was largely a result of greater sensitivity to local contexts in the wake of the emergence of an anthropology of art and growing postcolonial and post-structuralist critiques of power structures, political and intellectual. This tempered the dominance of classical[4] stone monuments and sculpture as the only themes in the field of Indonesian art history (though these continued to have the highest status with journals, publishers, and academic institutions). This trend grew stronger throughout the next ten years as new areas of Indonesian art history continued to emerge, while the number of conventional studies decreased, and as interdisciplinary cross-talk expanded and deepened.

The most radical expansion in Indonesian art history is linked to the late 1980s and early 1990s explosion of curatorial, art market, and publishing interest in the modern and contemporary arts of Asia as a whole, beyond India, China and Japan.[5]

---

[4] By "classical" I mean Hindu or Buddhist art genres known from India- and Sanskrit-based studies of archaeology, as founded by the British in the Royal Archaeological Service of India and their Dutch colleagues in the Netherlands East Indies.

[5] In our corner of the academic world, this happened simultaneously with the launching of a handful of research initiatives, many of them by Cornell SEAP graduate students focused on the modern arts of Southeast Asia (chronologically, Apinan Poshyananda for modern Thai art, myself for modern Indonesian art, and Nora Taylor for modern Vietnamese art).

Alongside this expansion, art historical and anthropological studies of indigenous and popular media arts converged with ideas from visual- and popular-culture studies to create a much more inclusive and regionally representative approach to researching, teaching, and representing Indonesian art worlds at a distance from the source. The breadth of data and approaches within today's field of contemporary Indonesian art studies (studies that go beyond "history") offer more creative leeway to the individual researcher and university instructor than ever before, with all the potential for pitfalls and brilliance this entails. I date the "birth" of this international and more inclusive field of modern arts in Asia to 1991, when John Clark and the Humanities Research Center at the Australian National University in Canberra convened "Modernism and Postmodernism in Asian Art"—the first international conference on the subject (Clark 1993).[6] Indonesia was represented there by Jim Supangkat, Helena Spanjaard, and myself. Other parts of Southeast Asia represented were Malaysia, by two Malaysian scholars (arguably ahead of the Indonesians in the English-language academic world due to historical circumstances, though, in fact, not, given the blind spot towards beyond-Western modernisms till now), and Thailand, by Apinan Poshyananda. Of course, the three heavyweights in Asian art—India, Japan, and China—were represented as well. John Clark himself, with his primary background in Japanese art, and a secondary background in Chinese art, launched his more comparative involvement with Asia as a region at this conference, a new direction that led to his seminal work, *Modern Asian Art* (1998). Following close on the heals of Canberra, the Asia Society in New York convened the First Roundtable Discussion on Modern Asian Art in 1992, and the Second Roundtable was held in Bombay (organized by The Asia Society and the Bombay National Centre for the Performing Arts) in 1994. And it was already in 1993 that the Queensland Art Gallery in Brisbane, Australia, launched the first grand-spectacle exhibition event for contemporary Asian art: the Asia–Pacific Triennial of Contemporary Art. New York followed in 1996 with the exhibition and catalogue "Contemporary Art in Asia: Traditions, Tensions."

Because of the contemporary nature of this research area and related curatorial initiatives (in tandem with the political upheavals that kept Indonesia in the news and the activist artists passionately and visibly engaged), audiences well beyond the academic world became involved with some of the subjects of our research (see Wright 1994; Turner 1980; Clark 1993; Queensland Art Gallery 1993, 1996, 1999; Asia Society in New York 1996).[7] Because of the necessity of fieldwork, due to the lack of

---

[6] 1991 was also the year I finished my PhD and took my Cornell training and Indonesia research with me as an immigrant to yet a new country for me—Canada. Thus, 2011 also marks the beginning in Canada of a regularly taught undergraduate/graduate curriculum in modern and contemporary Southeast Asian art, with a particular focus on Indonesia. The year 2011 also marks twenty years since the first large exhibition of modern and contemporary Indonesian art in the United States, in connection with the Festival of Indonesia (1990–91). Preparation for the exhibition was itself a fascinating story of collaborative (insider and outsider) scholarly and curatorial efforts coming together, on the cusp of the old and new. The exhibition found great support in political and business circles and passionate support in some parts of the art world in Indonesia, while it met with great resistance from the established art world institutions in the United States, even the ones dedicated to Asia.

[7] The first three Asia-Pacific Triennials of Contemporary Art (1993, 1996, 1999) attracted, quite remarkably, 60,000, 120,000, and 155,000 visitors, respectively. The Australian scholars, less fettered by classical concerns and more directly affected by their nation's proximity to Indonesia as a living political, economic, and touristic reality (and in some quarters, a

significant documentation, contemporary Asian art became a subfield where outsider scholars liaise and often collaborate with insider colleagues (whether academics or experts within their own non-institutionalized knowledge cultures). This signifies an important departure from earlier and other modes of scholarship.

Other new subfields within Indonesian art history came into focus in the 1990s. The general field of architecture began to expand beyond the century-long focus on temple architecture in stone to include: indigenous vernacular architecture, with systematic studies conducted from eastern to western Indonesia;[8] urban architecture;[9] Islamic architecture, mainly religious;[10] residential and expatriate architecture; luxury resort architecture;[11] and, finally, the newest edge: eco-architecture.[12] Indonesian architectural research has traveled quite a distance from studies on the Borobudur or the candi of the Dieng Plateau; yet new studies within these areas are also gracing the expansion and deepening of our field.

At the same time as the new arena for modern art was being developed, new, comparative, and theoretical perspectives generated innovations and refinements within the classical subject areas: archaeology, early architectural monuments, iconography, and so on. A tenuous dialogue between historical and contemporary analyses begins to surface in some scholars' work, a trend that also can be seen elsewhere in Southeast Asia, notably Thailand, Vietnam, and the Philippines.

---

perceived security threat), were among the first to engage with the modern Indonesian (and other Asian) art worlds, even when trained in other areas of Asian art; see online scholarly profiles and publications listed in the bibliography by John Clark and Caroline Turner.

[8] This expansion was carried out mostly by Dutch symbolic anthropologists. Some of the names noted here are Reimar Schefold, Peter J. M. Nas, Gaudenz Domenig, and Marcel Vellinga.

[9] Here Abidin Kusno's work on architecture, space, and memory in Jakarta stands out. See Abidin Kusno, *Behind the Postcolonial: Architecture, Urban Space, and Political Cultures in Indonesia* (London and New York, NY: Routledge, 2000); and *The Appearances of Memory: Mnemonic Practices of Architecture and Urban Form in Indonesia* (Durham, NC: Duke University Press, 2010).

[10] For some examples, see Hasan Muarif Ambary, *Some Aspects of Islamic Architecture in Indonesia* (Jakarta: Pusat Penelitian Arkeologi Nasional, 1994); Agus S. Ekomadyo, "Architectural Representation of Islamic Modernism and Neo-Modernism in Indonesia: Between Internationalism and Regionalism—Case Study: Architecture of Achmad Noe'man," paper submitted to Regional Architecture and Identity in the Age of Globalization, The Center for the Study of Architecture in the Arab Region (CSAAR) 2007; and Wilhelmina Bouwsema-Raap, *The Great Mosque of Banda Aceh: Its History, Architecture, and Relationship to the Development of Islam in Sumatra* (Bangkok: White Lotus Press, 2009).

[11] The majority of the publications in the last two categories are well-researched, exquisitely documented books for the general public, hence a hybrid category bridging university and community readerships, and mostly focusing on Bali. Some are corporate advertising, offering a new genre of writing to often underemployed academics. For examples, see Gianni Francione, *Bali Modern: The Art of Tropical Living*, photography by Luca Invernizzi Tettoni (Hong Kong: Periplus; and North Clarendon, VT, Tuttle Publishing, 2000); Rio Helmi and Barbara Walker, *Bali Style* (New York, NY: Vendome Press, 2003); and the article on the Amanwana, on Moyo Island on the Flores Sea in West Nusa Tenggara, in a globe-spanning volume entitled *Jungle Luxe*. See Justin Henderson, *Jungle Luxe: Indigenous-style Hotel and Remote Resort Design around the World* (New York, NY: Rockport Publishers, 2000), pp. 108–111.

[12] In the first decade of the twenty-first century, one particularly compelling example in this category is the Green School in Bali. See www.greenschool.org. It is compelling to me because it is a school, not a luxury residence, and it is not exclusively used by non-Indonesian expatriates.

Meanwhile, perhaps the most significant shift that began in the 1990s, which has continued at an always accelerating pace, is the presence and expansion of the Internet. Since its wobbly beginnings, the Internet has evolved to become a vital place for both historical and contemporary research. For contemporary art and culture, due to its rapidly shifting nature, the Internet is sometimes the only source available and as such is a tool of inestimable value with its potential for instant global reach and research. For historical subjects, the Internet offers a lot for Indonesian studies; for Indonesian art history, it is still a significant tool for measuring the absent and progressing visibilities, particularly in the large art history databases and encyclopedia.[13]

Apart from having spawned a new kind and site for publishing, the Internet offers new kinds of work for scholar-editors and -curators, as well. From 2000–03, I had the good fortune to be asked by American Bandung- and Germany-based expatriate Gary Crabb to curate "Javafred," a website he has dedicated to contemporary Indonesian art and artists (http://www.javafred.net/). Javafred has an extensive list of Indonesian (and a few Indonesia-involved) artists (approximately seventy) and a large number of readings in English available here (more than 130 readings, mostly in English but some Indonesian), plus it provides a page of links to twenty-three other sites relevant to contemporary Indonesian art. Here, the most abundant one, for our purposes, is "Universes in Universe," dedicated to "Visual arts from Africa, Asia, the Americas in the international art context," run by a Berlin-based organization.[14] Other sites of use to my field are the online visual and textual materials of the Singapore Art Museum, the Fukuoka Art Museum, and the Asian Art Archive out of Hong Kong.

In the 2000s, we saw an increase in architecture-related publications and also significant developments related to photography, developed as a field of study particularly by anthropologists since the early 1990s (Reed 1991; Knaap 1999; essays by Pemberton, Siegel, and Spyer in Morris 2009; Candra Naya 2010; Haryanto 2010; Strassler 2010). The current discourse is less about photography as either documentary or art form and more about it as a new area of everyday performance and public visual culture to theorize; yet the areas of shared concern with contemporary art are salient, and Strassler's contribution, in particular, is inspiring also in the art history context.[15]

This past decade has also seen the discussion around world/global/globalizing art history come to the fore at the center of the discipline of art history (see below). In addition, indigenous-with-settler or border-crosser artistic conversations and collaborations are more apparent. Now the indigenous or aboriginal artists are

---

[13] The BBC's "A History of the World in One Hundred Objects"—a fantastic series, in itself, with creative reformulations of history and "art" (though only a small fraction of the objects are presented as "art")—maintains the old lack of awareness of geography. Among the relatively few objects listed under "Southeast Asia," a large percentage are from India, Japan, China, or Tibet, or are stories telling war memories of Western soldiers who fought there during WWII.

[14] The Indonesian art section can be found at: http://universes-in-universe.org/eng/art/asia/indonesia

[15] Always looking for intelligent, creatively framed introductions to areas of Indonesians' visual culture, which can inform both teaching and research, and with a decades-long interest in (and practice of) photography worldwide, my visceral response when I first perused this book was: "Yes! Finally!"

speaking for themselves and taking part in the discussion of appropriation, authenticity, identity, and repatriation, and artists and art historians are increasingly conversing, their discourses at times overlapping within the same person— sometimes among outsider scholars, as so often are found in Indonesia since the beginning of modern art there. Also, indigenous dimensions in the modern and contemporary arts are becoming more evident, from vantage points that are no longer attempting to "otherize" or ghettoize indigenous artists and their work (Wright 2007 b, Wright forthcoming).

Now, I want to shift gears to another way of telling the story of notable developments in the arc of the field over the last three decades, which is to examine a few over-arching categories or branches within Indonesian art history.[16] I call the first category "Indigenizing Archaeology" (for more details, see Edward McKinnon's chapter in this volume). In addition to Dutch- or Cornell-trained archaeologists (some of whom have made Indonesia and Singapore their homes), leading Indonesian archaeologists like Soekmono, R. P. Soejono, and Edi Sediawati have come to the fore. Several revisions of Dutch-colonial and subsequent outsider-archaeologist interpretations have been made (e.g., concerning the theory that candi were most likely, according to the evidence, purely commemorative structures rather than sites where royalty's ashes were actually interred; see McGowan 2008, 243). In Australia, Ian Glover started his career as an expert on the archaeology of prehistoric East Timor before moving on to mainland Southeast Asia (Bellina et al. 2010). David Bulbeck, one of the twenty-one archaeologists who contributed research papers to the volume honoring Glover, has worked on megaliths and pottery in Sulawesi. Archaeobotany and bioarchaeology, emerging over the last few decades (Oxenham 2006), may provide interesting information relevant to indigenous arts. I found a recent publication on the prehistory of Papua of interest: Juliette Pasveer's *The Djief Hunters* (2004) focuses on flora and fauna and includes examples of early use of animal parts for body decoration.[17]

The second category I call "Consolidating the Classical" (for more details, see Natasha Reichle's paper in this volume). Classical here refers to a framework developed around the study of Indian art and religious concepts, which require of

---

[16] The caveat here is, of course, that many studies cross and combine categories in various ways, from the conventionally interdisciplinary to the nearly literary; never has the academic writer had more freedom to choose her or his modalities than now.

[17] Examples from prehistoric archaeology, which partners nicely with the branch of symbolic anthropology concerned with the signification of animals, as well as with the study of indigenous arts' formal/aesthetic inspirations from natural and animal forms, are found in Juliette M. Pasveer, *The Djief Hunters: 26,000 Years of Rainforest Exploitation on the Bird's Head of Papua, Indonesia* (Leiden: A. A. Balkema Publishers, 2004). The author documents the prehistoric evidence of "the Spilocuscus Maculates, the common spotted cuscus (named Swi in Meybrat language), a lemur-like animal" whose tail creates a perfect spiral (p. 410). Art historians of Indonesia and Oceania know that the spiral is a common form found throughout many of the archipelago's cultures, from wall painting to carving and hand-movements in dance, but the prehistoric peoples referred to as the Djief hunters get a step more literal than that: the "tail of the dead Swi is used as decoration on the hand of the people, as a bracelet" (p. 410). This recalls the use of "found (natural) objects" that McGowan calls the "raw ingredients." Kaja M. McGowan, "Raw Ingredients and Deposit Boxes in Balinese Sanctuaries," in *What's the Use of Art? Asian Visual and Material Culture in Context*, ed. Jan Mrázek and Morgan Pitelka (Honolulu, HI: University of Hawaii Press, 2008), pp. 238–71.

the scholar a detailed knowledge of Sanskrit and South Asian art, and iconographic and textual studies. The older methods and topics in these classical, historical subject areas build our understanding of transregional and crosscultural exchanges resulting in mostly stone monuments and sculpture created during the fashionably intercultural periods of Indian influence (some Buddhist, but mostly Hindu). Among the publications that span the academic and the curatorial worlds, and thus reach a larger audience than most academic publications, is Jan Fontein's *The Sculpture in Indonesia*, the scholarly exhibition catalogue commissioned for this high-visibility Festival of Indonesia-sponsored exhibition (1990).[18]

Scanning the field of Indonesian art history, we generally see a major difference in approaches between colleagues in the older schools of the discipline, as practiced in Europe—in particular, the Netherlands—and the more interdisciplinary and contemporary approaches practiced in North America and Australia. This "divide" between Dutch and "new world" scholarship pertaining to Indonesia is evident in a publication on the classical arts of Java, *Worshiping Siva and Buddha: The Temple Art of East Java*, by Kinney, Klokke, and Kieven (2003).[19] This book exemplifies how less-known material is still to be found in the older grooves of Indonesian art history. In her review of this book in the *Journal of Asian Studies* (McGowan 2005), Kaja McGowan, after commending it highly as an introductory survey, calls for future researchers to take the methodology a step further and link the classical story sought in stone monuments with the living, local interpretations and webs of meaning the temples embody, which lend to the stone edifice a life quite apart from its dependency on indic models.

The third category I call "Expanding the Classical." In addition to consolidation, in the classical areas, I see expansion in the types of sites, artworks, methods, and monuments researched; new ones have come to light and been analyzed using the classic tools of iconographic, architectural, spatial, religious, and textual analysis, and more. Hilda Soemantri's important work on Majapahit terracottas (1997) represents an expansion of the range of arts studied in the classical period: conventional classical art history considers clay and objects in more-ephemeral-than-stone materials to be less important, all the more so if their usage is in vernacular settings.

One of the subject areas that has taken off from the 1990s onwards is Balinese arts, within the general expansion of Bali studies as well as generalist publishing on the island.[20] Hildred Geertz's *Life of a Balinese Temple* takes us into the fabric within

---

[18] This consisted of several paradigmatic exhibitions, which pronounced Indonesian art history to consist not only of classical art but also court arts and island/indigenous arts. See Helen Ibbitson Jessup, *Court Arts of Indonesia* (New York, NY: Asia Society Galleries, 1990); and Paul Michael Taylor and Lorraine V. Aragon, with assistance from Annamarie L. Rice, *Beyond the Java Sea: Art of Indonesia's Outer Islands* (Washington, DC: National Museum of Natural History, Smithsonian Institution, and New York, NY: H. N. Abrams, 1991).

[19] In Kinney et al., one of the bylines read: "This richly illustrated volume is a study of the temples created in East Java between the tenth and sixteenth centuries, filling an important scholarly lacuna." See Ann R. Kinney, Marijke J. Klokke, and Lydia Kieven, *Worshiping Siva and Buddha: The Temple Art of East Java* (Honolulu, HI: University of Hawaii Press, 2003).

[20] In scholarship on Balinese arts, the last two decades have had brilliant additions to the classical as well as new areas of scholarship, from textiles, offerings, the storytelling of Kamasan painting at Klungkung, as well as numerous monographs and gallery catalogues on modern and contemporary arts, both urban and village-based. We also see publications in arts and religion by dedicated non-academic writers such as Fred Eiseman and Jean Couteau. An

and around the temple in a way that goes beyond the study of the stones and architectural forms, their ties to Indian prototypes, and any potential texts associated with the structure (2004). We should also note Kaja McGowan's historical/ contemporary, lateral/linear, incisive reflections written as a serious/humorous dialectic, in "Raw Ingredients and Deposit Boxes in Balinese Sanctuaries" (2008a). Both of the above categories point to a study of monumental architecture in stone; historically, only religious (and, as such, "Indic") architecture seemed to warrant serious study; we shall see how the idea of architecture and space has expanded in the last decade plus. Natasha Reichle's work on late Buddhist sculpture from Indonesia is a contribution in this category (2007).

Another aspect of expansion in this subfield of Indonesian art history, which a number of pioneering scholars of Indian and Indonesian art brought into their methodologies (notably Stella Kramrisch and Claire Holt), is that, over the last thirty years, Indonesian art scholars have begun to pay more attention to the artists themselves and (also inspired by the anthropologists) their material and imaginative lifeworlds. In Indonesia, except for the literary arts, the visual artists are for the most part anonymous to outsiders at a distance,[21] until the mid-nineteenth century, and only then begin to become noted by name increasingly in the realm of modern, European-inspired arts.

My fourth category is "Textiles and Heritage Objects." Forerunners (1960s, 1970s) to the later establishment of textiles as a field of scholarly inquiry lie in the brochure- or pamphlet-size publications produced on the occasion of small-scale exhibitions organized by or around the collections of Americans who had lived and collected in Indonesia. One early exception is Monni Adams's work on textiles of East Sumba. Indonesian textile studies began in earnest with Mattiebelle Gittinger's *Splendid Symbols* in 1979 and subsequent conferences and editions of essays (1979, 1989). Among the many important names in Indonesian textile studies since then are Sandra A. Niessen, Ruth Barnes, Mary Hunt Kahlenberg, Mary-Louise Totton, Roy Hamilton, and a number of others.[22] Here Jessup's *Court Arts of Indonesia* (1990) offers

---

in-between level of publishing is one I have encouraged three of my MA students to pursue, since even at the MA thesis level in this young field of ours, original contributions and syntheses of scattered older research can be made that are worthy of an intelligent, interested academic and general readership. See Claire Fossey, *Rangda, Bali's Queen of the Witches* (Bangkok: White Lotus Press, 2008); Beth Fouser, *King Prasat Thong and the Building of Wat Chaiwatthanaram* (Bangkok: White Lotus Press, 1996); and Wilhelmina Bouwsema-Raap, *The Great Mosque of Banda Aceh: Its History, Architecture, and Relationship to the Development of Islam in Sumatra* (Bangkok: White Lotus Press, 2009).

[21] Labeling artists in Western art history curriculum as "anonymous" is another Europe-centric fallacy. All artists are, of course, known within their own societies and circles, often well beyond their own life-span, through the oral tradition, a form of record keeping only beginning to be understood in some areas of the academic world.

[22] I can still taste the excitement I felt after Stanley O'Connor guided me to reading *Splendid Symbols* and remember well the awe I felt at the cross-disciplinary tools, the imagination, and the ability to move between vastly disparate worlds and practices evident in the work of people like Tom Harrison, and, of course, Stan himself. It is a cycle of return to be working on aspects of modern–contemporary and contemporary–indigenous art in my current research. See Astri Wright, "*Titik Pertama, Titik Utama*—First Dot, Main Dot: Creating and Connecting in Modern/Indigenous Javanese/Global Batik Art," in *Modern and Contemporary Southeast Asian Art: An Anthology*, ed. Nora Taylor and Boreth Ly (Ithaca, NY: Cornell Southeast Asia Program Publications, 2012), pp. 131–70. Given the ways that the artist partners I discuss in this article span ancient, indigenous, modern, and contemporary practices, it seems fitting that they,

a whole body of arts not yet in focus within the Western discipline of art history even though objects such as those presented, above all the textiles and the keris (daggers), are very much at the heart of indigenous appreciation and collecting of "empowered objects" in Indonesia.

Another volume coauthored by Indonesian and outsider-scholars, which considers "heirloom" arts (*pusaka*) as a natural part of Indonesia's art history, is *Art of Indonesia*, edited by Haryati Soebadio and John Miksic (1993). A hybrid body of contemporary art that combines the old Javanese practices of meditative production of *pusaka* arts, respect for their inheritance of empowered symbols, and the creative freedom and functions of modern art, is the collaborative batik-art of American-and-Javanese artist partners, Nia Fliam and Agus Ismoyo (Wright 1994; Totton 2008). Innovations in the study of the multimedia visual art of vic can also fit in this category, though some of these works slide into the modern/contemporary category, too. Studies of note in the research on wayang's modern forms, both in Indonesia and increasingly globally and transculturally, are Jan Mrázek (2002, 2005) and Matthew Isaac Cohen (2007, 2010).

The fifth category, "Embracing the Indigenous," can be seen as linked to the preceding one, as it captures another aspect of the expansion beyond the Indic-local artistic conversations, into new subfields that highlight arts in the non-India-interested (or less-interested) small-scale societies, many of them arts that have been labeled tribal, indigenous, and mostly studied by anthropologists of art, who have been producing materials some of us art historians consider central to an Indonesian art history. Important names linked to publications in the 1980s are Jean Paul Barbier, publications from the Barbier-Müller Museum, Jerome Feldman, and many others. Two examples in the field that first engaged me as a potential research field are works by Bernard Sellato and Michael Heppell, Limbang Anak Melaka, and Enyan Anak Usen. *Naga and Hornbill* (Sellato 1989), is an early coffee-table book with short text, in both English and Indonesian, funded by an oil company active in both the Malaysian and Indonesian parts of Borneo (and presumably engaged in the larger processes of destroying the habitat of the peoples celebrated in the book). The text and bibliography are introductory level, and the photos, which show people at work and rest, in everyday and ritual situations, as well as a rich range of artifacts, are excellent. More important from a scholarly perspective is *Iban Art*, the first book I have come across devoted exclusively to Iban art rather than the broader category of Dayak. This book grew from an exemplary collaboration between one outsider-scholar with easier access to the research and publishing apparatus and two insider-experts with easier access to local knowledge (Heppell et al., 2005).

My final, sixth category presents the newest addition to the subject areas in Indonesian art history discussed here, and, it would seem, the one that has caught the strongest wind in its sails over the last twenty years: "Modern and Contemporary [Asian/South Asian/Southeast Asian] Indonesian Art." The emergence of this field marks the moment when European, American, and Australian scholars stop, take off their academically trained lenses, look around in the field, and discover that there are modern artists at work all around them, creating

---

along with historical and contemporary Southeast Asian Textiles, were centrally featured in "Out of Asia: Art that Sustains," the last exhibition to be held at the Textile. The elegant old mansion was closed in October 2013, and the museum moved its collections and operations to new quarters at George Washington University, Washington, DC. See http://textilemuseum. org/exhibitions/OutofSoutheastAsia.html.

art beyond touristic souvenirs, in familiar media, art that at first glance looks like copies of, or homages to, modern Western art, and, at second glance, begins to echo themes and forms familiar from Indonesian arts beyond the classical. This is when our discipline stops being Euro-blind to the modern: I see a more abrupt and less-heralded expansion into modern and contemporary visual discourses, with Holt as the lone forerunner researching in the 1950s and 1960s, but no one picking up her thread until the mid-1980s. Here we can mention: modern and contemporary Indonesian art (painting, sculpture, installation art, performance art); architecture (residential and public, religious and secular); the bourgeoning film industry; hybridized, transnational forms of older arts like wayang; dance; and performance.

BRIDGES IN MODERN AND CONTEMPORARY INDONESIAN ART HISTORY

It is here, in Indonesia's modern and contemporary art history, that we see a bridging of the gap between Dutch and other scholarship. This is also where we see a vibrant field of local discourses, practiced by a wide variety of people (from the self-taught to university-degree holders), in local media, symposia, and informal discussions. While Indonesians have been active participants in their own cultural debates from the early twentieth century onwards, and in my research field from the 1930s onwards, the last thirty years have seen an explosion of interest in modern Indonesian art within Indonesia and in contemporary art, in particular. Some of this has to do with the relationship between the commercial art market and critical and art historical discourses. Due to language gaps and the absence of effective book marketing between art worlds and across oceans, the Indonesian side of the discourse can be hard for outside students to grasp.

The first accredited Indonesian scholar to research modern art in Indonesia was Sanento Yuliman, who wrote his doctoral dissertation on nineteenth-century Raden Saleh at the Sorbonne, in Paris. People who conducted systematic research into twentieth-century modern and contemporary Indonesian art were outsider scholars Holt, Wright, and Spanjaard, as a group spanning fieldwork from the 1950s to today. Helena Spanjaard arrived in the field a year before I did, however, due to her "unusual" choice of topic for her doctorate ("unusual" as judged from a Dutch art history perspective, which typically saw Asian art history topics as archaeological, classical, and historical), and the subsequent institutional lag, it was not until 1998 that she was able to finish her dissertation (2003). Praising Holt's (1967) approach to Indonesian art, Spanjaard writes: "Dutch art historians usually considered changes in the direction of the west and modernity as a threat to the traditional Indonesian culture. It is no coincidence, therefore, that the pioneering work in the area of modern Indonesian art was done by Americans and Australians" (2003, 9). During the past decade, Spanjaard, who is an independent researcher not attached to a university, has been a very prolific freelance art historian, writing beautifully produced and well-funded books for Indonesian patrons and art foundations (2004, 2007, 2008).

Today we see a lot of overlap of roles among scholars and lay people writing about art; here, as elsewhere in the post-post-modern era, categories are fluid. Indonesian art writers have always played numerous roles simultaneously, if they were so inclined: artist, curator, critic, general writer, art historian; many Indonesian artists are also active as authors who write about art (e.g., Pirous 1995).

The two most established modern art experts I met in the field when I arrived in the late 1980s were Kusnadi, active from the 1950s on as an artist and photographer as well as a government official in various branches of the Ministry of Culture's bureaucracies, and Drs. Sudarmadji, who worked in Jakarta's municipal art museum Balai Seni Rupa, and was active as a regularly contributing art writer and curator in the 1960s through 1980s. Their writing focused mostly on artist biographies and art world connections, allegiances to teachers and other artist groups, and they became known in the art community as art critics (*kritik/kritikus seni*). This period saw little analysis of or close engagement with the work of art.

In the mid-1970s, a group of new voices began to be heard in Indonesian art circles, a transition that marks the shift from "modern" to "contemporary" and from more insular to more internationally engaged work. One of the seminal artists in the New Art Movement (Gerakan Seni Rupa Baru), Jim Supangkat (trained at Institut Teknologi Bandung [ITB]), worked closely with Sanento Yuliman (also out of ITB), who was, as far as I have been able to find out, the first Indonesian with a doctorate in art history and who became the spokesman for the Gerakan Seni Rupa Baru in the mid-1970s. He was positioned as the father of an academically informed modern art history discipline in Indonesia when he passed away suddenly in 1991.[23]

Jim Supangkat picked up the torch and gave up his art career to deepen his involvement with art criticism. He has since become Indonesia's most internationally active art writer, curator, and critic, self-taught in art history, with a leaning towards theory (Supangkat 1996, 2010). In a climate where art history is not taught as a university subject, he gradually acquired what I see as a vital balance between local and foreign knowledge, frameworks, and ideas. By the mid-1990s, Jim had formulated the term "multi-modernisms" in a climate where a few scholars are casting around for useful terminology (local-, glocal-, multicentered modernisms) central to discussions of modern art worldwide, terminology that restores agency to all participants.

The most productive art writer in Indonesia since the mid-1980s is Agus Dermawan T., who has also been active as curator and often works closely with the commercial art world establishment. Cornell's library holdings have no less than thirty-nine titles by him, writing solo or as a coauthor.

Another Indonesian who held a PhD in art history but focused on the historical period is the late Hilda Soemantri, who wrote her dissertation under Stanley O'Connor on Modjopahit terracottas. Hilda was herself a modern artist and an accomplished ceramic sculptor (Wright 1994). M. Dwi Marianto obtained his PhD in the mid-1990s under Adrian Vickers at Wollongong University in Australia. He has been active as both scholar and curator over the last two decades, at times in collaboration with Cemeti (Marianto 1999–2006).[24] Younger generation Indonesian

---

[23] In September 2000, Sanento Yuliman was posthumously awarded the first Indonesian art critic's award. See "Darga Gallery Awards Indonesia's Foremost Art Critic," *The Jakarta Post*, September 28, 2000, http://www.thejakartapost.com/news/2000/09/28/darga-gallery-awards-indonesia039s-foremost-art-critic.html, accessed July 14, 2011.

[24] This picture is not completely up-to-date. I would think there are several younger scholars who have earned their doctoral degrees in art history, possibly from Australian universities. Several are progressing on their dissertations with Kaja McGowan at Cornell. One candidate is currently working on his interdisciplinary PhD on the globalization of wayang as a contemporary multimedia art form under my co-supervision (with Michael Bodden as the other co-supervisor) at the University of Victoria.

art writers without academic degrees who have nonetheless been very actively engaged in the art world include Suwarno Wisetrotomo, often working with Agus Dermawan T. and others; Rizki A. Zaelani, often working in tandem with Jim Supangkat; Hendro Wiyanto; Asmudjo Jono Irianto; and others.

Now, one can ask: where are the women's voices? While early writings by outsider-scholars Wright and Spanjaard were available, it did take a while before the work of female Indonesian art-writers began to be seen in book form. Arahmaiani, who plays many roles, should be mentioned: an internationally well-known and provocative performance artist, she is also a poet, essayist, and speaker who has engaged with a broad spectrum of cultural identity issues (Arahmaiani 2003, 2004). With her powerful independent, non-conformist voice, she also engages in humanitarian work, including mediation between polarized groups in the community. Outsider-turned-Indonesian Mella Jaarsma has since the mid-1990s become a voice heard. Jaarsma does not focus on women's issues per se in the art world. Carla Bianpoen, in contrast, does. Bianpoen, a journalist who has written for Jakarta's English-language newspapers about a range of topics from the 1980s onwards, increasingly in the 1990s focused on gender and development and eventually on women artists (Bianpoen et al. 2007).

Finally, within a modern-contemporary Indonesian art world that has by now become well known through scholarly monographs, journal articles, and myriad popular media articles, where is the current "edge"? While tattoo-art could be called the fastest internationalizing art form of the 1990s and early 2000s, much of it with inspirations in Indonesian and Oceanic traditions, I would choose Street Art as the new edge in the 2000s and 2010s. In the late 1980s, Heri Dono and Eddie Hara started a new style in Indonesian painting when they drew on their individual blends of Western-modernist, comic book, and street-art/graffiti forms and applied these forms to their painted canvases (Wright 1994). In the late 1990s, Apotik Komik, a group of artists who work with comic book images, took some of these conventions to the streets, as public art, to critique and counterbalance the growing commercialization of art in Indonesian and regional galleries and auction houses. Members of Apotik Komic have become increasingly active internationally over recent years (Chin 2002; Olympia-Rafah Mural Project 2006). In the twenty-first century, street artists have emerged all over Indonesia, where artist groups such as "PLSCK Clan" have been working in South Jakarta since 2004 and "Squadcore" has been painting graffiti in Yogyakarta since 2006. Among the many solo artists, Crazy Zamtwo has been producing graffiti in Bandung since 2006 (Fraser 2011, 7). One international website has a rich array of 491 pictures of street art done in twenty-eight Indonesian cities, from Aceh to Ujungpandang (FATCAP, 1998–2011). Here is a dissertation and full-color book waiting to be written.

GLOBALIZING THE FIELD

The new buzzwords in art history studies of modern and contemporary work are "globalization," "global art history," "world art history," and "cross-/trans-cultural," and a key topic is the death of the relevance of the nation as a meaningful category. It's as if the issues pondered, researched, analyzed, and hypothesized by those of us who started researching modern Asian art movements that and artists who developed as a result of interregional conversations between parties with their own agency and intentions, have finally taken off in the global arena. The paradigm-shifting explorations under way, here, in the discussions about the possible anatomies of a global art history came together at the Thirty-Second Conference of CIHA (Comité International d'Histoire de l'Art) in Melbourne, in January 2008. The title of the conference was "Crossing Cultures: Conflict, Migration and Convergence."[25] A staggering 1,108 page volume, which included 224 of the papers presented, was published a year later (Anderson 2009).[26]

Committed to qualitative research, I also like to play with what numbers can show whenever possible. So, as an experiment, I counted how many papers from this conference were found in the respective, relevant categories, judging by their titles. I used national and regional classifications (labels proclaimed outdated in some of the very papers I was classifying accordingly), except for two categories, which I called the "Islamic world" and "aboriginal/indigenous." While many of the papers naturally spanned two or more of the categories, making simple counting hard, the clusterings still provide a fair sketch of where we are to date in the discipline if we accept that these conference papers make up a representative sample. The dominance of Eurocentric papers, or papers focused on artists of European descent practicing in the Western world, was clear since these constituted half or more of the number; this was by far the largest clustering (eighty-six titles, by my quick count).[27]

---

[25] For a quick glimpse into the anatomy and importance of this conference, see the online review by one of the pioneers of modern and contemporary art in Australia, Caroline Turner. Caroline Turner, "A New Global Art history: CIHA 2008 (Congress of the International Committee of the History of Art), *Artlink* 28,2 (2008), www.artlink.com.au/articles/3118/a-new-global-art-history-ciha-2008-28congress-of-th/, accessed July 1, 2011.

[26] This conference series originated at the Vienna World Fair in 1871, and art historians in Australia have held conferences on a regular basis around the world since 1891. Thus, this theme seemed both timely and historically representative. The next CIHA, however, held in Nuremberg, Germany, titled "The Challenge of the Object," was extremely Europe-centric, with some limited attention devoted to Brazilian and Hispanic art. Historical Asian art was featured in relation to religion and regional exchange; the word used about planet-wide issues was "world" rather than "global," and there was hardly anything on modern or contemporary Asian art. Caroline Turner's paper offered an exception to this, as it discussed a Chinese artist living in diaspora. The Australian academics seem to be doing the best job of keeping their finger on this hotspot in art history. The conference "The World and World-Making in Art: Connectivities and Differences," hosted by the Australian National University August 11–13, 2011, co-convened by Caroline Turner, Michelle Antoinette, Zara Stanhope, and Jacqueline Menzies, is one example of this. For the purposes of Asian and specifically Southeast Asian art history, and within that, Indonesian art history of the modern and contemporary era, in global perspective, publications forthcoming from this conference (including a book with the working title, *Asian Connectivities*), is eagerly awaited. As for the CAA (College Art Association), Asian artists active in America receive some attention from the association (for example, the resurgence of interest in Yayoi Kusuma), but most years, Southeast Asia and Indonesia, whether viewed from local or global perspectives, occupy marginal to invisible positions. Most of the conferences where Asian Art History is featured in depth are discipline- and geographical area specific, such as, primarily in North America, ACSAA (The American Committee for Southern Asian Art, which covers South and Southeast Asia and the Himalayan region); art history panels are also featured at the AAS (the Association for Asian Studies). Even in these venues, while film is a hot contemporary topic, modern and contemporary art is less so. The curatorial field has a somewhat different profile, which I haven't touched on here, but here again, for instance, New York's featuring of Southeast Asian contemporary artists at a high-profile institution like the Guggenheim in 2013 (the "No Country" exhibition) lags behind Australia's high-profile Queensland Art Gallery's regular featuring of these local-to-global, interlinked art worlds.

[27] Caveat: in this count, I did not distinguish between European and European-descent Americans, Australians, New Zealanders, et cetera, since these do not constitute a more

The second largest category was papers with the terms "global," "world," or "cross-cultural" in the title (forty-nine found—and here, many of the comparisons were between one Euro/-pean/-origin culture and another, rather than between cultures located further afield in the global). Aboriginal/indigenous art was the third largest category, with about thirty-two papers on that topic. For South America, there were roughly six titles; for the Islamic world (mostly Turkey, Iran, and India), about nine.

For titles focusing specifically on some aspect of "Asia," I found six (and for "East Asia," one); for China, eight; for Tibet, one; for Central Asia (Kazakstan, Uzbekhistan), one; for India, seven; for Japan, eleven; for Southeast Asia, one; Indonesia, one (on gamelan); the Philippines, one; Vietnam, one; Korea, one; and Africa, one. About half the Asia-related papers were among the eighteen papers in Panel 17, titled "Parallel Conversions: Asian Art Histories, Twentieth to Twenty-First Centuries."

A more recent publication that features many of the best-known players in Southeast Asian art discourses employs three focii (pan-Asia, geographical subregions, and nations) as frames of reference (Chiu and Genocchio 2011). Of the twenty-four articles, at least nine are devoted to "Asian" art and another four specifically to Chinese art. Only two articles are devoted to "Southeast Asian" art; meanwhile, Indian, Indonesian, Japanese, and Korean art are represented by one article each. While Thailand and the Philippines and Singapore are mentioned in various essays, they are not represented in separate articles.

Despite the fuzziness of the quantitative methodology, above, I think the clusterings illustrate how we are just at the beginning of the conversation about an art history we can call global in a balanced manner. Yet at this juncture, as evidenced by the last fifteen or more years of innovative contributions from non-specialist art-writers, and some scholars and curators with no area studies training who have moved into the center of the global art history debate, I see a certain crisis looming for scholars trained in regional art histories (other than Western, particularly modernist ones, of course).

I still believe the pros in area studies outweigh the cons, for both outsider and insider scholars.[28] But one real danger with area studies is the isolation of people into geo-ghettos. People focused on specific geographical areas of study (and most often such specialization tends to be within the scholars' own cultures) generally pay less or even no attention to other regions or cultures. This situation is not necessarily rooted in each individual's world view but may often be a default strategy for those who lead extremely busy lives, as well as a result of funding structures, curriculum design, departmental nomenclature, and so forth. But the end result is that Asianists tend to speak to Asianists, Latin Americanists to Latin Americanists, Indonesianists to Indonesianists. Furthermore, each circle has its emphases or dominant actors: when the focus is Asianist, we see China dominating the picture.

James Elkins (an American art historian not, it seems, formally trained in any of the Asian/African/indigenous modernisms, but a remarkably productive and

complex picture in terms of ethnicity, religions, cultures, and so on than do the different peoples and languages in regions like "South Asia" or "Southeast Asia."

[28] One of the cons is the isolation of art history within area studies, where the art historians tend to spend far more time attending other disciplines' colleagues' panels than vice versa. Whether within Asian studies, or Southeast Asian studies, or Indonesian studies, books with an interdisciplinary Indonesian studies focus rarely include an art historical chapter; if art is discussed, it is far more likely to be by an anthropologist.

insightful scholar leading the global art history discourse in North America) eloquently describes the white-Western-centric stranglehold still exerted by publications on the global modern, giving limited space to beyond-European or European-derived cultures. While Elkins subscribes to the necessity of a Western master discourse of modernist painting as a benchmark (I disagree that this is a necessity, in the long term), even as he invites its interrogation, he documents how publications on global modern and contemporary art fail to include artists from nations like Chile, Indonesia, Kenya, Panama, and Tibet (Elkins 2010).

Yet, a major theme among many of the presenters at the 2008 CIHA conference in Melbourne was the obsoleteness of the nation and region as categories. I think it of vital importance that we resist this general trend towards dismissing national and regional specialization in these areas "beyond Europe." We do not need to keep focusing on the nation as primary signifier, "site of pleasure," and so on, but we do not have to cast it out, for it is one among several useful containers. In fact, we have an opportunity here to model an approach for the rest of art history, demonstrating how Indonesianist, Southeastasianist, Southasianist (et cetera) art historians can contribute in important ways both to the methodologies and to subject areas in the global art history discussions.

In this globalizing era, then, we are still somehow ghettoized within our geographical classifications, and our in-depth area expertise is somehow seen as irrelevant to or hampering the theorizing of the global. Meanwhile, the result is myriad conference papers and articles so involved with theorizing the global that actual data—primary (visual) and secondary (written, interpretive, art analytical)— are absent, and artists not of European descent are rendered invisible—once again. Hence, I do not at this time in the development of our fields embrace the idea of dispensing with the region or the nation or the culture group altogether; this seems to be currently the only system of classification in which Indonesian art gains any visibility.

My answer to the current dilemma, then, is: area studies needs to stand on more than one leg. I propose *three* legs. It needs to be area-focused as well as whole-world or globally focused, and it needs to be non-centric or non-elitist. Area studies are the perfect stepping stone from local to global. And we world-minded people of today need to be able to hold more than one category in mind at any given time more than ever before in history; modern Indonesian artists do this with ease.[29]

As John Clark writes in his CIHA essay (2009, 59):

... art history as a knowledge field will also meet its own dead end if it declines to allow the opportunity provided by the generation of new concepts and research strategies from other than Euramerican sites. These produce the crucial notions for understanding a newly globalised art of interstitiality, cross culturality, hybridity, and diaspora. It is the Asian (and Latin American and

---

[29] For reflections on their multiple layers of geo-ethnic identity relevant to the local/national/regional/global layers that must be part of a world art history, see my work with and on Sudjana Kerton, Affandi, Abdul Aziz, and others: "Body Abroad, Soul at Home, and the Heart in Both Worlds (Sudjana Kerton in America)," *Sudjana Kerton: Changing Nationalisms*, Retrospective Exhibition Catalog (in Indonesian and English), Jakarta: Sanggar Luhur, National Gallery, November 22–December 12, 1996, pp. 162–85. For similar reflections by A. D. Pirous, see Kenneth George, *Picturing Islam: Art and Ethics in a Muslim Lifeworld* (Oxford: Wiley-Blackwell, 2010), pp. 42–43.

African, and, interior to these, Indigenous) contexts of art production that are peculiarly suited to provide instances of these positions, in a network of art practice and art knowledge that has overwhelmed early categorical distinctions in art history but has thereby enriched it with new fields to aesthetically explore and conceptually understand.

The danger as far as I can see is that the local will disappear in a mishmash of global perspectives where once again the European(-derived) ones remain dominant.[30] The "glocal" of a decade or more ago easily gets lost. Outside of the "global art/-history" debate, at the level of artists engaging, I found the following phrase written at the bottom of an international graffiti and street-art site: "All our content is geo-localized, so you can quickly discover main artistic trends from all over the world" (FATCAP, 1998–2011). Let's hear it for geo-localized scholarship that perhaps starts in the streets and in nonscholarly conversations, inside and out of clouds of clove-scented smoke. In fact, isn't this to a large extent what colleagues in my research field (cultural anthropologists and art historians alike) have been doing for the last three decades, each in our own way?

CHALLENGES FOR INDONESIAN ART HISTORY

Indonesian art history still has a distance to go before it is decolonized and can stand as more representative of indigenous views of art and its histories and contemporary avatars and offshoots. The biggest task that remains for Indonesian art historians is to keep on pushing our research and teaching frameworks to become even more region-relevant and –representative, and to show the links and exchanges across regions and cultures. I think this is a post-colonial task of continued urgency: that we not ditch the local perspectives in favor of, or to privilege, a new generation of Western-driven global ones. The main themes that can be identified as relevant to an Indonesian art history would be inclusive of the concerns, stories, and image cultures and material cultures of the archipelago, and representative of its many histories of both internal and external connections. While these can be studied within this highly multidisciplinary field, one challenge is for art historians to keep in sight and be able to define what we can offer that is complementary to, and less often found in, the often theory heavy writings on visual culture by anthropologists and others. If we are truly going to be regionally relevant, an Indonesian art history would want to include everything that has received the attention of creative image making, and been subject to the skillful manipulation of materials, whether aural, oral, visual, or other-sensory, whether performative, concrete static, in lasting or in ephemeral materials. In the end, we might place everyday and ritual/ceremonial/art world performances at the center and examine the arts that surround and support

---

[30] In my graduate seminars, which are devoted to Indonesian, Southeast Asian, and South Asian mo-co arts, several students over the last couple of years have become so excited at the discussions of what constitutes a global art history that they completely ignored the "local" part of the issue and failed to acquire or reflect Indonesian (et cetera) expertise in their research papers. This happened despite the repeated emphasis in class readings and discussions of the importance of a multipronged knowledge base in any true "global" venture. It is a matter of continuous amazement to me how quickly and easily the dial defaults back to the familiar paradigm of Eurocentrism, even in the case of students with non-European ethnic roots.

these, in a multimedia fashion, rather than focusing so squarely on the material object.

Thus, the curriculum on Indonesian art would include a much broadened definition of art and would feature what the European (or Euro-style/-trained) art historians were quite happy to leave to the anthropologists: art in small-scale societies, tribal or otherwise, and the courtly arts; village arts; throughout the archipelago as a whole, art fashioned from wood, bamboo, fronds, flowers, grains, and grasses; textiles, jewelry; metalwork; and, of course, art made from the post-industrial modern materials of concrete, steel, even petrol products, found objects, and garbage. In the discipline of art history, literacy in the visual-creative would remain central, but cross references to other creative arenas would be a necessary secondary literacy to enrich and ground observations made in the visual field (the lilt or twist of a melody; the texture of a tuning in an instrumental harmony; the spacing of dancers at a funeral; the choice of time of day for a particularly charged event). In this respect, I think art historians trained in Indonesian studies and Southeast Asian studies are well ahead of the game of European-style art history, which still dominates or underpins the study of various periods as well as modern and contemporary art. But this does not mean that we cannot do better in relation to what region-relevant and localized art histories of Indonesia's many different cultures should strive to be. This will be an ongoing dialogue with our work-institutions, publishers, and curriculum committees.

Stanley O'Connor inspired us all to rethink ways of speaking and conceptualizing about art (O'Connor 1983). Among others, Jan Mrázek frames the issues from our current perspective in his usual creative and incisive ways in the concluding essay in *What's the Use of Art?* (Mrázek and Pitelka 2008). Reichle's research and curating work presenting the first major (and monumental) exhibition of Balinese art in the United States, "Bali: Art, Ritual, Performance," represented an unprecedented visual presentation of an art world that captured much of its multidimensionality. Rather than specializing, as most exhibitions do, in sculpture or textiles or modern art, "Bali" pushed towards a holistic art history of Bali, particularly as installed and, to a lesser degree, as collapsed into two dimensions when documented in print and photos (Reichle 2010).

Another challenge for Indonesian studies and for all academics, for that matter, though particularly for outsider-scholars working across geo-cultural boundaries, is how to share our work with the people about whom we write. The answer may vary between individual scholars and fields but it is not a question that should remain unaddressed. Let me reflect, from my own vantage point, on where I see public and postcolonial publishing strategies intersecting since the 1990s, when publishing about Indonesian art of all periods, from classical to indigenous to modern and contemporary, surged. The latter arena has seen an eruption of publications in the general readership and coffee-table category. This represents an unprecedented, extensive wave of private publishing initiatives by a variety of persons and organizations. Indeed, individual artists, art foundations, small galleries in Indonesia, and individual collectors publish more books on Indonesian art than do universities or government art organizations.[31] Among such players, the collector-as-

---

[31] Here the Cemeti Gallery, now the Cemeti Art House (Rumah Seni) and the Cemeti Art Foundation (Yayasan Seni Cemeti) in Yogyakarta, founded in 1988 by Dutch-born artist Mella Jaarsma and Central Javanese artist Nindityo Adipurnama, must be mentioned as having the longest and most notable track record of research, publishing, international and local artist

publisher constitutes the most notable category in terms of quality publications, since this group generally has the most funds to put into their projects. These collectors, who are often educated abroad, are generally able to afford to hire national and international art researchers and writers, and are willing to include a large number of high-quality color reproductions in their publications.[32] All of these categories produce data that belong in research libraries accessible to scholars in the field.[33] Some of these publications can be considered repositories of modern and contemporary Indonesian art history in the making. Here we also see both outsider and insider writers represented, side by side and in dialogue.

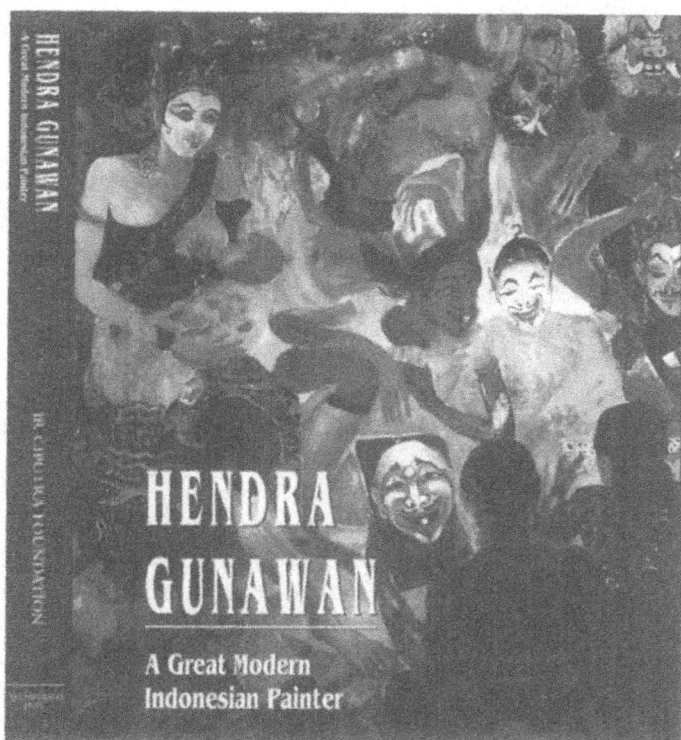

Book cover, *Hendra Gunawan: A Great Modern Indonesian Painter*

It is within this perspective that I, like Helena Spanjaard a few years later, decided in the mid-1990s to, on occasion, become an art historian for "hire" ("have art history, will travel") in Indonesia, where art history is (still) not developed as an

exchanges, and exhibitions, both group and solo. In 2007, the CAF was renamed the Indonesian Visual Art Archive (IVAA; see http://www.ivaa-online.org/).

[32] In fact, one could argue that these publications in one manner are closer to the life of visual arts in the sense that the proportion of visual to verbal is far greater than in academic publishing, where the expense and legalities restricting the reproduction of each image usually prohibit the inclusion of more than a small number of plates. This, of course, does not account for the distancing that takes place when experiencing the living arts through the flattened, shrunk, and de-energized medium of photography. See Mrázek and Pitelka, *What's the Use of Art?*

[33] An academic pioneer's dilemma is how the absence of accessible data triggers the need to produce data to excite other scholars and draw them into the new field, and to provide material and ideas for others to work with, even at a distance.

academic field and is not (to my knowledge) taught at the university level. To me, this was one response to being a postcolonial scholar that presented itself, though it was not without its ethical conundrums. But it did allow me to concentrate a significant amount of my academic writing in bilingual (Indonesian–English) publications accessible in Indonesia. This did mean that, given the time restraints of full-time teaching and family raising, my choice caused me to publish less extensively in academic journals that used to be (and for the most part still are) unavailable to people outside of university cultures, particularly in Asia and certainly among most Indonesians interested in the art world.[34] Since my work coincided with an era during which collectors and artists in Indonesia began to take publishing art books seriously, this choice served several needs, including allowing me to address the pressing ethical issue that confronts the academic in cross-cultural research who fails to share her knowledge with the majority of her informants and bring it back to the actual physical domain of the research field.

SUGGESTIONS FOR THE CMIP

In the invitation to the "State of Indonesian Studies" conference, we were also asked to reflect on possible future projects for the CMIP (Cornell Modern Indonesia Project). Speaking for the Indonesian art history side of Indonesian studies, I would suggest in general that future conferences and publications take care not to focus only on the new, but also on foundational works in which the new developments have taken root. For my corner of the field, my specific recommendation is to get Claire Holt's book, *Art in Indonesia: Continuities and Change* (1967), back into print.[35] I have argued for over two decades that Holt's *Art in Indonesia* is the single best introductory level textbook available on Indonesian art history and still way ahead of other available textbooks on Indonesia or even Southeast Asia as a region. In a globalizing era, quality culture-specific textbooks are of paramount importance so that we avoid yet another round of centric discourses.[36]

This time, why not publish a paperback edition of the book so it is affordable and accessible to students and can be used as a textbook throughout the English speaking world? Also, in this new edition, include Claire Holt's article published in *Indonesia* in 1970 (Holt 1970) as an appendix or postscript chapter. Alternatively, as explored with Marty Hatch during our postpanel discussion, in which there seemed to be support from those Indonesianists involved in the arts, have a group of current Indonesianist art historians provide commentary or updates after each of Holt's

---

[34] Ironically, or perhaps humorously, choosing to publish in venues that were more accessible to the Indonesian art world has made my work far less available in the academic sphere. This illustrates the absence of bridges between the two worlds, where on-the-ground library purchasers are not employed. The exception here are Cornell's Kroch library and the Library of Congress. Of the "obscure" publications I have contributed to over the last two decades, Cornell seems to have most of them, with twice as many titles as the Library of Congress.

[35] *Art in Indonesia* has been out of print since at least 1982, when I first started searching for it and came by an affordable copy only with great good luck in a used bookstore in Amsterdam. The one copy I've seen available on Amazon since then was listed at over US$300.

[36] For a sensitive analysis of the merits of Holt, *Art in Indonesia*, see Mrázek and Pitelka, *What is the Use of Art?*, p. 293.

chapters. Finally, why not go a step further and publish an affordable Indonesian translation of this wonderful monograph?[37]

Taking my cue from that, another recommendation to the CMIP is to revive the idea of translation programs and funding, such as those that existed in the 1950s. I am not the only one calling for translations: Soelebar Soekarman of the Jakarta Art Institute has been wanting to translate both Holt, *Art in Indonesia*, and Wright, *Soul, Spirit, and Mountain* (1994), for fifteen years now. John Clark, at the Thirty-Second CIHA conference in Melbourne in 2008, in his call for strategies of inclusion, envisioned a journal of translation in art history and future CIHA conferences that would involve a rich array of translators so we can move beyond the dominance of English-based discourses (Clark 2009, 58).

CONCLUSION

As someone who chose to work in the contemporary art history field, I find the various conversations taking place very exciting. I celebrate the paradigm shift reflected in terminology, where "borderline" artists and art historians become "border-crosser" artists and art historians, and the "mestizo" (the neither-here-nor-there) art, artist, scholar, or idea may be reframed as integrative, hybrid, fusion, cool, hip (both-here-and-there) so that such practitioners are seen gelling into a new tribe of sizeable, free eccentrics and new thinkers rather than outcasts, where the old does not disappear but in turn does not resist the new. I celebrate us becoming as creative in embracing the kaleidoscopic differences within and without, individually and socially, like the cyber-punk poem by Guillermo Gomez Pena and like the choreography in Garin Nugroho's 2006 film *Opera Jawa—Requiem from Java*, which draw on Javanese, Latino, Hawaiian, and other global aesthetics to produce something that tickles one's senses down to the marrow.

At the same time, I insist that we have to be vigilant against the current widespread trends to privilege only the modern and contemporary. To limit myself here to speaking of our discipline, we need the classically and the conventionally trained scholars who know their complex set of tools and are able to use them to expand the current discourses in both historical and contemporary subject areas. Interpretation and elucidation each have their creative sides, and the more tools at our fingertips, the greater the scope of the knowledge that we can explore. Contemporary theory has its own fashion life; visual arts that persist beyond dozens of human lifetimes outlast intellectual and economic fashions and therefore offer richer narratives when investigators approach them from many angles.

We need both the depth-divers and the horizon-walkers, the elaborators and the pioneers. Research areas exist and swell, decline and morph, always signifying, whether or not Western-trained scholars notice. But when we do take notice, we

---

[37] My own book, *Soul, Spirit, and Mountain: Preoccupations of Contemporary Indonesian Painters*, fell out of print soon after its publication by Oxford University Press's branch in Selangor, Malaysia, in 1994. If I won the lottery, I would buy back the rights from OUP and do a new, bilingual edition of it in paperback. And again, sell it at an affordable price. At the time of its publication, I had such a long list of people to whom I had acquired *hutang budi* in Indonesia, particularly in Java and Bali, above all the around seventy artists who had shared information and images with me, that it was a travesty to discover the OUP's pricing, which made it impossible for Indonesian artists, let alone art students and art lovers, to buy it and impossible for me to offer the book as a gift to most of my deserving collaborators.

enrich our knowledge base, our curriculum, and our abilities to conceptualize, yea, even relate to our world, their world, *the* world, in new ways. And in the end, there is pioneering in the older modes of scholarship and there is the grounding in standing on our elders'/mentors' shoulders, massaging them into renewal yet always with respect.

For our discipline of Indonesian art history, I say to present and future practitioners: honor and learn at least the basics of the older tools (archaeology; study of classical monuments, reliefs, and sculpture; iconography; inter-textual analysis; formal analysis; and so on). Also learn ethnographic, biographical, and sociopolitical analysis and, above all, good oral history research practices. Pursue these subjects and methodologies even as we develop new ones. Do learn the language, Bahasa at the very least, and do not remain content to join the new generation of arm-chair art historians who do *no* fieldwork around the world, even as they theorize global art history. Meanwhile, so many areas I wanted to mention, which have broadened or deepened Indonesian art history, have not been explored here—film, tattoos, ceramics, cartoons, numismatics, multimedia performance arts (both traditional-contemporary and modern-contemporary), and much more.

While the story of the field of Indonesian art studies does not end, this paper has to. The conversation is far larger than this part of it. I see our discipline working at its best when we recognize it as a collective and collaborative process, each of us working on the subjects and in the ways that suit our particular constellations of talents the best, and putting our ideas out there into the larger conversation. And above all not forgetting that primary partners in this conversation are Indonesians and their spectacular and endangered slice of the world's flora and fauna. May we continue to model and teach the versions of postcolonial world-mindedness to which we are each best suited.

The desire to learn, to grow, and to connect know no geographical or ethnic boundaries. To all budding "pioneers" out there who are not yet sure how to rationalize your crazy hunches towards things your own group does not yet know, I offer the words of Jean-Luc Godard: "[S/He] who jumps into the void owes no explanation to those who stand and watch." You just might land in a dynamic place on some pulsing rainbow, surrounded by creative and fascinating cohorts, and both create a new home and return to enrich those parts of the world still ignorant about it, with your stories. *Terima Kasih dan Selamat untuk semua.*

Works Cited

Ambary, Hasan Muarif. *Some Aspects of Islamic Architecture in Indonesia.* Jakarta: Pusat Penelitian Arkeologi Nasional, 1994.

Anderson, Jaynie, ed. *Crossing Cultures: Conflict, Migration, and Convergence: The Proceedings of the Thirty-Second International Congress in the History of Art.* Carlton, Victoria: Miegunyah Press, Melbourne University Publishing, 2009.

Arahmaiani, *Roh Terasing* [Poems]. Jogjakarta: Bentang Budaya, 2004.

Arahmaiani and A. Anzieb, eds. *Petruk Dadi Guru.* Magelang, Jawa Tengah: Studio Budaya and Galeri Langgeng, 2003.

Asia Society AustralAsia Centre. *Crossing Boundaries, Bali: A Window to Twentieth Century Indonesian Art. Melintas Batasan, Bali:* Jendela Seni Indonesia Abad Kedua Puluh; and Melbourne: Asia Society AustralAsia Centre, 2002.

Asia Society, New York. "Multiculturalism/Multimodernism." *Contemporary Art in Asia: Traditions/Tensions.* Ed. Apinan Poshyananda. New York, NY: New York Asia Society Galleries, exhibition catalogue, 1996.

Bellina, Berenice, Elisabeth A. Bacus, Thomas Oliver Pryce, and Jan Wisseman Christie, eds. *Fifty Years of Archaeology in Southeast Asia: Essays in Honour of Ian Glover.* Bangkok: River Books, 2010.

Bianpoen, Carla, Farah Wardani, Wulan Dirgantoro. *Indonesian Women Artists: The Curtain Opens.* Jakarta: Yayasan Senirupa Indonesia, 2007.

Bouwsema-Raap, Wilhelmina. *The Great Mosque of Banda Aceh: Its History, Architecture, and Relationship to the Development of Islam in Sumatra.* Bangkok: White Lotus Press, 2009.

Candra Naya. *First Indonesia Salon of Art Photography, 2010.* Jakarta: Candra Naya Photographic Society, 2010.

Chin, Michelle. "Apotik Komik Are Going to Paint the Town Red." *Latitudes* 20 (September 2002), http://www.michellechin.net/writings/12.html. July 10, 2011.

Chiu, Melissa, and Benjamin Genocchio, eds. *Contemporary Art in Asia: A Critical Reader.* Cambridge, MA: MIT Press, 2011, unfinished (no images) manuscript. PDF file found (March 7, 2011) at: ftp://ftp.mitpress.mit.edu/DESIGN/Emily/8430_ms.pdf

Clark, John, ed. *Modernity in Asian Art.* University of Sydney East Asian Series Number Seven. New South Wales: Wild Peony Press, 1993.

Clark, John. *Modern Asian Art.* Honolulu, HI: University of Hawaii Press, 1998.

——. "Beyond the National, Inside the Global: New Identity Strategies in Asian Art in the Twenty-First Century." *Crossing Cultures: Conflict, Migration, and Convergence: The Proceedings of the Thirty-Second International Congress in the History of Art.* Carlton, Victoria: Miegunyah Press, Melbourne University Publishing, 2009. 58–59.

Cohen, Matthew Isaac. "Contemporary Wayang in Global Contexts," *Asian Theatre Journal* 24.2 (Fall 2007).

——. *Performing Otherness: Java and Bali on International Stages, 1905–1952.* Houndsmill, Basingstoke, Hampshire: Palgrave Macmillan, 2010.

Coomaraswamy, Ananda K. "*Samvega:* Aesthetic Shock." *Coomaraswamy: Selected Papers: Traditional Art and Symbolism.* Vol. 1. Ed. Roger Lipsey. Princeton, NJ: Princeton University Press, 1977 (1943). 179–85.

Ekomadyo, Agus S. (ITB Bandung), "Architectural Representation of Islamic Modernism and Neo-Modernism in Indonesia: Between Internationalism and Regionalism—Case Study: Architecture of Achmad Noe'man." Paper submitted to *Regional Architecture and Identity in the Age of Globalization,* Center for the Study of Architecture in the Arab Region (CSAAR) 2007. http://www.ar.itb.ac.id/

ekomadyo/index.php?option=com_content&task=view&id=5&Itemid=6, accessed March 3, 2011. See item 2, here.

Elkins, James. "Writing about Modernist Painting Outside Western Europe and North America." *Transcultural Studies* 1 (2010). http://archiv.ub.uni-heidelberg.de/ojs/index.php/transcultural/article/view/1928/1782.

FATCAP. "Street-Art in Indonesia." FATCAP, the graffiti and street-art resource, at www.fatcap.com/country/indonesia.html, accessed March 3, 2011.

Fraser, Alison. "Bombing Java: Contemporary Street Art Subculture." Seminar paper written in HA430 for Prof. Astri Wright, University of Victoria, Department of History in Art, March 2011.

Fontein, Jan, ed. *The Sculpture of Indonesia*. Washington, DC: National Gallery of Art, 1990.

Fossey, Claire. *Rangda, Bali's Queen of the Witches*. Bangkok: White Lotus Press, 2008.

Fouser, Beth. *King Prasat Thong and the Building of Wat Chaiwatthanaram*. Bangkok: White Lotus Press, 1996.

Francione, Gianni. *Bali Modern: The Art of Tropical Living*. Photography by Luca Invernizzi Tettoni. Hong Kong: Periplus; and North Clarendon, VT: Tuttle Publishing, 2000

Geertz, Hildred. *Images of Power: Balinese Paintings Made for Gregory Bateson and Margaret Mead*. Honolulu, HI: University of Hawaii Press, 1995.

——. *The Life of a Balinese Temple: Artistry, Imagination, and History in a Peasant Village*. Honolulu, HI: University of Hawaii Press 2004.

George, Kenneth. *Picturing Islam: Art and Ethics in a Muslim Lifeworld*. Oxford: Wiley-Blackwell, 2010.

Gittinger, Mattiebelle. *Splendid Symbols: Textiles and Tradition in Indonesia*. Singapore: Oxford University Press, 1979 (1990).

Gittinger, Mattiebelle, ed. *To Speak with Cloth: Studies in Indonesian Textiles*. Los Angeles, CA: Museum of Cultural History, University of California, 1989.

Greenschool. Green School Bali Indonesia. www.greenschool.org/. May 2013.

Haryanto, Goenadi. *Buku fotografi 64*. Jakarta: Indomultimedia Communications Group, 2010.

Helmi, Rio, and Barbara Walker. *Bali Style*. New York, NY: Vendome Press, 2003.

Henderson, Justin. *Jungle Luxe: Indigenous-style Hotel and Remote Resort Design around the World*. New York, NY: Rockport Publishers, 2000.

Heppell, Michael, Limbang Anak Melaka, and Enyan Anak Usen. *Iban Art: Sexual Selection and Severed Heads*. Amsterdam: KIT Publishers, with Leiden: C. Zwartenkot Art Books, 2005.

Holt, Claire. *Art in Indonesia: Continuities and Change*. Ithaca, NY: Cornell University Press, 1967.

——. "Indonesia Revisited." *Indonesia* 9 (April 1970): 163–88.

Irianto, Asmudjo Jono. *1001 Doors: Reinterpreting Traditions.* Exhibition, January 26–February 6, 2011. Ciputra Marketing Gallery. Catalogue in Indonesian and English. Jakarta: Jakarta Contemporary, 2011.

Ismoyo, Agus, and Nia Fliam, "Fiber Face: Cross-Cultural Batik Collaborations. In Indonesian and English. Ed. and curated Mary-Louise Totton. Kalamazoo, MI, and Yogyakarta: University of Western Michigan/Rumah Budaya Babaran Segaragunung, 2008.

Jessup, Helen Ibbitson. *Court Arts of Indonesia.* New York, NY: Asia Society Galleries, H. N. Abrams, 1990.

Kinney, Ann R., Marijke J. Klokke, and Lydia Kieven. *Worshiping Siva and Buddha: The Temple Art of East Java.* Honolulu, HI: University of Hawaii Press, 2003.

Knaap, G. J. *Cephas, Yogyakarta: Photography in the Service of the Sultan.* With a contribution by Yudhi Soerjoatmodjo. Leiden: KITLV Press, 1999.

Kraus, Werner. *Raden Saleh: Ein Malerleben Zwischen Zwei Welten.* Maxen: Verlag Niggemann and Simon, 2004.

Kusno, Abidin. *Behind the Postcolonial: Architecture, Urban Space, and Political Cultures in Indonesia.* London and New York, NY: Routledge, 2000.

——. *The Appearances of Memory: Mnemonic Practices of Architecture and Urban Form in Indonesia.* Durham, NC: Duke University Press, 2010.

Marianto, M. Dwi, Astri Wright, and Hilda Soemantri. *Revolusi & Evolusi Sudjana Kerton/The Revolution and Evolution of Sudjana Kerton.* In Indonesian and English. Bandung: Sanggar Luhur, 1999.

Marianto, M. Dwi. *Surealisme Yogyakarta.* Yogyakarta: Rumah Penerbitan Merapi, 2001.

——. *Seni Kritik Seni.* Yogyakarta: Lembaga Penelitian, Institut Seni Indonesia Yogyakarta, 2002.

——. *Quantum Seni.* Semarang: Dahara Prize, 2006.

McGowan, Kaja M. Review of Ann R. Kinney, Marijke J. Klokke, and Lydia Kieven. *Worshiping Siva and Buddha: The Temple Art of East Java. Journal of Asian Studies* 64.1 (February 2005).

McGowan, Kaja M. "Raw Ingredients and Deposit Boxes in Balinese Sanctuaries." *What's the Use of Art? Asian Visual and Material Culture in Context.* Ed. Jan Mrázek and Morgan Pitelka. Honolulu, HI: University of Hawaii Press, 2008a. 238–71.

——. "Ida Bagus Made: The Art of Devotion—In Celebration of the Fiftieth Anniversary of the Puri Lukisan Museum, Bali, Indonesia." Ubud, Bali: Yayasan Ratna Wartha, 2008b.

Morris, Rosalind C., ed. *Photographies East: The Camera and Its Histories in East and Southeast Asia.* Durham, NC: Duke University Press, 2009.

Mrázek, Jan and Morgan Pitelka, eds. *What's the Use of Art? Asian Visual and Material Culture in Context.* Honolulu, HI: University of Hawaii Press, 2008.

Mrázek, Jan, ed. *Puppet Theater in Contemporary Indonesia: New Approaches to Performance Events*. Ann Arbor, MI: University of Michigan Center for South and Southeast Asian Studies, 2002.

Mrázek, Jan. *Phenomenology of a Puppet Theatre: Contemplations on the Art of Javanese Wayang Kulit*. Leiden: KITLV, 2005.

——. "Ways of Experiencing Art: Art History, Television, and Javanese Wayang." *What's the Use of Art? Asian Visual and Material Culture in Context*. Ed. Jan Mrázek and Morgan Pitelka. Honolulu, HI: University of Hawaii Press, 2008. 238–71.

Olympia–Rafah Mural Project. "Sama Sama/Together." Collaboration with Apotik Komik, Yogyakarta, Indonesia, and Clarion Alley Mural Project, San Francisco, CA, and Olympia, WA, USA, 2006. http://olympiarafahmural.org/who%E2%80%99s-on-the-wall/national-participants/sama-samatogether/. July 11, 2011.

Oxenham, Marc, and Nancy Tayles, eds. *Bioarchaeology of Southeast Asia*. Cambridge: Cambridge University Press, 2006.

O'Connor, Stanley J. "Art Critics, Connoisseurs, and Collectors in the Southeast Asian Rain Forest: A Study in Cross-Cultural Art Theory." *Journal of Southeast Asian Studies* 14.2 (September 1983): 400–408.

Pasveer, Juliette M. *The Djief Hunters: 26,000 Years of Rainforest Exploitation on the Bird's Head of Papua, Indonesia*. Leiden: A. A. Balkema Publishers, 2004.

Pirous, A. D., and Setiawan Sabana. "Developments and Current Issues in Contemporary Indonesian Art." Network Indonesia, 1995. http://users.skynet.be/network.indonesia/ni3001a32.htm, accessed July 4, 2011.

Queensland Art Gallery. *Asia-Pacific Triennial of Contemporary Art*. Brisbane: Queensland Art Gallery, 1993.

——. *The Second Asia-Pacific Triennial of Contemporary Art*. Brisbane: Queensland Art Gallery, 1996.

Reed, Jane Levy, ed. *Toward Independence: A Century of Indonesia Photographed*. San Francisco, CA: Friends of Photography, 1991.

Reichle, Natasha. *Violence and Serenity: Late Buddhist Sculpture from Indonesia*. Honolulu, HI: University of Hawaii Press, 2007.

Reichle, Natasha, ed. *Bali: Art, Ritual, Performance*. San Francisco, CA: Asian Art Museum, Chong-Moon Lee Center for Asian Art and Culture, 2010.

Schefold, Reimar, Peter J. M. Nas, and Gaudenz Domenig, eds. *Indonesian Houses*. Vol. 1: *Tradition and Transformation in Vernacular Architecture*. Leiden: KITLV Press, 2003; Vol. 2: *Survey of Vernacular Architecture in Western Indonesia*. Leiden: KITLV Press, 2008

Sellato, Bernard. *Hornbill and Dragon/Naga dan Burung Enggang. Kalimantan, Sarawak, Sabah, Brunei*. In Indonesian and English. Jakarta: Elf Aquitaine Indonésie, 1989.

Soebadio, Haryati, ed. *Art of Indonesia*. Ed. and trans. John Miksic. Photography by Tara Sosrowardoyo. London: Tauris Parke Books, 1993.

Soemantri, Hilda (Hildawati Soemantri Siddhartha). *Majapahit Terracotta Art*. Jakarta: Ceramic Society of Indonesia, 1997.

Soetriyono, Edy, and Ipong Purnama Sidhi, eds. *Sanento Yuliman dan Kritik Seni*. Sanur, Bali: Darga Gallery, 2000.

Spanjaard, Helena. *Modern Indonesian Painting*. Tran. S. Wessing. Sotheby's, 2003. [A revision of Spanjaard's 1998 dissertation, "Het ideaal van een moderne Indonesische schilderkunst, 1900–1995, de creatie van een nationale culturele identiteit."]

——. *Exploring Modern Indonesian Art: The Collection of Dr. Oei Hong Djien*. Singapore: SNP Editions, 2004.

——. *Pioneers of Balinese Painting: The Rudolf Bonnet Collection*. Amsterdam: KIT Publishers, in cooperation with the Rudolf Bonnet Foundation, 2007.

——. *Indonesian Odyssey: A Private Journey through Indonesia's Most Renowned Fine Art Collections*. Photographs by Kurniawan Wigena. Jakarta: Equinox Asia, 2008.

Spanjaard, Helena, and Wouter Welling. *The Dono Code: Installations, Sculptures, Paintings*. Amsterdam: KIT Publishers, 2010.

Strassler, Karen. *Refracted Visions: Popular Photography and National Modernity in Java*. Durham, NC: Duke University Press, 2010.

Supangkat, Jim. "Multiculturalism/Multimodernism." *Contemporary Art in Asia: Traditions/Tensions*. Ed. Apinan Poshyananda. New York, NY: New York Asia Society Galleries, exhibition catalogue, 1996. 70–81.

——. *Pleasures of Chaos: Inside New Indonesian Art: A Project by Primo Giovanni Marella*. Bologna: Damiani, 2010.

Taylor, Nora, and Boreth Ly, eds. *Modern and Contemporary Southeast Asian Art: A Critical Anthology*. Ithaca, NY: Cornell Southeast Asia Program Publications, 2012.

Taylor, Paul Michael, and Lorraine V. Aragon, with Annamarie L. Rice. "Beyond the Java Sea: Art of Indonesia's Outer Islands. Washington, DC: National Museum of Natural History, Smithsonian Institution, and New York, NY: H. N. Abrams, 1991.

Turner, Caroline. *Tradition and Change: Contemporary Art of Asia and the Pacific*. Queensland: University of Queensland Press, 1993.

——. *Art and Social Change: Contemporary Art of Asia and the Pacific*. Canberra: Pandanus Books, Research School of Pacific and Asian Studies, Australian National University, 2005.

Turner, Caroline. "A New Global Art History: CIHA 2008 (Congress of the International Committee of the History of Art), *Artlink* 28.2 (2008). http://www.artlink.com.au/articles/3118/a-new-global-art-history-ciha-2008-28congress-of-th/. July 1, 2011.

Vellinga, Marcel. *Constituting Unity and Difference: Vernacular Architecture in a Minangkabau Village*. Leiden: KITLV Press, 2004.

Webb, Jennifer, ed. *Beyond the Future: The Third Asia-Pacific Triennial of Contemporary Art*. Brisbane: Queensland Art Gallery, 1999.

Wiyanto, Hendro. *Paradigma dan Pasar: Aspek-Aspek Seni Visual Indonesia*. Yogyakarta: Yayasan Seni Cemeti, 2003.

——. *Gambar alam niskala Made Wianta*. In Indonesian and English. Jakarta: Galeri Canna, with Denpasar: Wianta Foundation, 2004.

——. *Heri Dono*. In Indonesian and English. Jakarta: Nadi Gallery, 2004.

Wright, Astri. *Soul, Spirit, and Mountain: Preoccupations of Contemporary Indonesian Painters*. Kuala Lumpur: Oxford University Press, 1994.

——. "Body Abroad, Soul at Home, and the Heart in Both Worlds (Sudjana Kerton in America)." *Sudjana Kerton: Changing Nationalisms*. Retrospective Exhibition Catalog. In Indonesian and English. Bandung: Sanggar Luhur; Jakarta: National Gallery, November 22–December 12, 1996. 162–85.

——. "Worlds Apart and Gently, Intently, Meeting: Reflections on Abdul Aziz's Art." *Abdul Aziz: The Artist and His Art*. Ed. Mary Northmore-Aziz. In Indonesian and English. Bali: Mariz Foundation, 2005. 128–45.

——. "Affandi in the Americas: Bridging the Gaps with Paint and Personality." *Affandi 2007*. Vol. 1. Ed. Sardjana Sumicha. In Indonesian and English. Jakarta and Singapore: Bina Lestari Foundation and the Singapore Art Museum, 2007a. 134–99.

——. "Archive, Market, and Parade: The Making of an Ancestor in Modern Indonesian Art." Paper presented at "ENCOUNTERS," Department of History in Art Annual Faculty Symposium, University of Victoria, September 22, 2007b.

——. "Titik Pertama, Titik Utama—First Dot, Main Dot: Creating and Connecting in Modern/Indigenous Javanese/Global Batik Art." *Modern and Contemporary Southeast Asian Art: A Critical Anthology*. Ed. Nora Taylor and Boreth Ly. Ithaca, NY: Cornell Southeast Asia Program Publications, 2012. 131–69.

Wright, Astri, Dwi Marianto, and Hilda Soemantri. *Revolusi & Evolusi Sudjana Kerton/The Revolution and Evolution of Sudjana Kerton*. In Indonesian and English. Bandung: Sanggar Luhur, 1999.

Wright, Astri, and Agus Dermawan T. *Hendra Gunawan: A Great Modern Indonesian Painter*. In Indonesian and English. Jakarta and Singapore: The Ciputra Foundation; the Archipelago Press, Editions Didier Millet, 2001.

Yuliman, Sanento. *Seni Lukis Indonesia Baru: Sebuah Pengantar*. Jakarta: Dewan Kesenian Jakarta, 1976.

——. "Modern Art in Indonesia." *Contemporary Indonesian Art: Painting and Print*. Exhibition Catalogue on the Occasion of an Exhibition of Fourteen Indonesian Artists from Bandung in Kuala Lumpur, Malaysia, December 15, 1990–January 6, 1991. http://www.javafred.net/rd_sanento_1.htm. May 2013.

——. *Dua Seni Rupa: Sepilihan Tulisan Sanento Yuliman*. Jakarta: Yayasan Kalam, 2001.

HISTORY

TRIANGULATING HISTORIES OF HISTORY IN INDONESIA

Eric Tagliacozzo

The history panel for this book is made up of three distinguished practitioners of the discipline: Rudolf Mrázek, of the University of Michigan; Laurie Sears, of the University of Washington; and Jean Gelman-Taylor, of the University of New South Wales. Each has been important in sketching out new directions for the discipline of Indonesian History, though each has done this in very particular and individual ways. Despite their varied approaches, one can discern certain common themes in their essays here, in looking at the arc of the field as a whole: a concern with memory (with a capital "M"); a common identification of streams (or *aliran*, in Bahasa Indonesia), that is to say, genealogies of knowledge; and a tendency to look for fissures, or breaks, in the historical terrain, with each author identifying a number of those here. There are also some important differences among the three: differences in emphases; differences in geographies of the production of knowledge; and differences in their interpretations of meaning of what is being produced. Taken together, however, these three essays provide a very exciting overview, I think, of many of the main currents of historical thinking about Indonesia over the past half-century or so.

Rudolf Mrázek got us started by telling us that he visited George Kahin's and Oliver Wolters's graves when he returned to Ithaca, New York. This was a kind of homage, and he noted Harry Benda's grave is in nearby New Haven, Connecticut, citing Benda as another example from the first generation of master historians of Indonesia who are now all gone. We all refer back to these founders of our craft, Mrázek told us. Those who have departed are remembered even now, and ritualized to some extent in the writings of their disciples of several generations. George Kahin's last book (2002), *A Testament*, was a kind of circling back to Indonesia, "as he encountered it for the first and for the last time," Mrázek argued, and, therefore, "time is thus folded in the book." Kahin was with the young Indonesian revolutionaries in 1948 and 1949; there were smiles of "welcome back" to his doctoral student, and then, later, to the student-turned-professor, Rudolf Mrázek, in 1989 and 1990. Mrázek noticed the same dynamic for Oliver Wolters; he also left a testament in his last book (Wolters, 1999). This was the idea of return—of scholars going back at the end of their careers to moments and ideas and notions where they had once started. If I can embellish here on Mrázek's observation, I think we can certainly find this dynamic existing beyond the Indonesian Studies fold; the pattern he describes was true for Kahin, certainly, but it was also true for Tony Reid (with Aceh, 2005); for Jim Scott (with Burma, 2009); and for Jonathan Spence (for the late Ming period as a temporal preference, 2007). Perhaps there really is something to be said for scholars returning to their "first intellectual loves" at the end of their scholarly lives—a kind of call back to the center of what got them interested in their fields, before a quiet slip into retirement.

Cornell and the origins or streams (again, *aliran*) is a common theme in a number of these papers. For Mrázek, he sees provenance in the three S's: Sukarno, Suharto, and Jim Siegel. Mrázek says that Kahin's intellectual life for a long time turned around the chasm of 1945; this was also true for Siegel in the tear of history manifested by 1965. Ben Anderson's tear was also 1965, but he moved outside of this tear, too (by necessity, being banned from Indonesia after the coup), toward translation, toward Thailand, and toward the Philippines and even Latin America (1983). And there were parallel streams, too: Benda at Yale, and Onghokam, his student; Herb Feith, and his Cornell–Indonesian–Australian school. There was also the commonality of Benda and Wolters in the Japanese camps: a kind of cross-fertilization borne of violence and repression. And in identifying streams of Indonesian Studies, one must also not forget the "originals": Kees van Dijk, for example, and his magisterial work on the Dutch Indies in World War I (2007); and another Dutchman, Harry Poeze, on the great radical Tan Malaka (1976). Poeze's volume one of this work appeared in 1972, and then nothing further came out until—almost miraculously—two more huge volumes appeared just a few years ago, in 2007, a monumental achievement in Indonesian history. So there has been space, too, for "originals" outside of the streams, figures who have worked outside of the main currents to some extent, though they are also implicated in the slip-streams of such flows.

For Laurie Sears, the energy of history writing also strays into the political, as well as the literary. She starts out with Indonesia's greatest modern writer, Pramoedya, whose masterpiece, *The Buru Quartet*, written in Buru from 1966–79, when Pram was a political prisoner along with twelve thousand other dissenters there, is a kind of locus-classicus of modern Indonesian historiography. She sees Pramoedya's hero, Minke, as Tirto, the great *fin de siècle* Indies writer, and the first to conceptualize the nation as a mix of all of its component racial parts: Balinese, Ambonese, Sumatran, Chinese, and Eurasian. In this history, through Minke/Tirto, Sears asks: who is the narrator of modern Indonesian history? She sees a constant recirculation and reediting of books, of the story of the nation, a kind of circuit that (in fact) "makes" the nation through the written word. And she also sees certain texts as pivotal in this process, with three being more important than others in her estimation. In 1978, Edward Said's *Orientalism* deconstructed the philological foundations of Asia; in 1983, Ben Anderson's *Imagined Communities* appeared to near universal acclaim; and in 1984, Don Emmerson's seminal article, "Southeast Asia: What's in a Name?" was printed, relegating "nations and whole regions" to "becoming imaginary overnight." All were watersheds in marking new currents, new possibilities for writing an Indonesian history, she argues. All (with Pramoedya in an allied track along literary lines) made possible configurations of Indonesian historiography that we see before us today.

Yet just as with Mrázek's template of possibilities, one suspects Sears's sympathies rest most with one last publishing event described in her essay. This was Ayu Utami's feminist critique (1988), coming just as the New Order was falling in the last years of the twentieth century; Sears calls this the failure of the New Order's "masculinist activism." The ramifications on history and history writing were manifest. All Indonesians are orphans of 1965/66, Sears says, and must regain their memories—if Ayu Utami taught us anything, it is that Indonesians must learn to think critically again, and realize that under New Order politics, words and images were used to keep Indonesians from learning about their history. Sears tells us that Indonesians must undo "the phantasms of the past"—and that this will take a long time. She circles back to Pramoedya then, and observes that Pram made a list after Buru of all who died there, to preserve their memory. New research shows that Pram relied on his fellow inmates to reassemble the destroyed archive of these people's stories, letters, and memories of the Indonesian past. History and fiction come together, she tells us; they translate each other. They change each other. Sears elucidates in her essay the possibilities of this marriage, refracted through politics and memory and the possibilities of feminism, but also serving as an avenue of rescuing lost histories. Hers is an activist vision of Indonesian history under construction; a kind of evolving project of resuscitation that must continually breathe life into itself, and into its Indonesian subjects, both living and dead.

Jean Gelman Taylor, the final component of this troika of important thinkers, goes back to the beginning, in a way, in tracing an arc of the practice of modern Indonesian history. She starts her narrative by recounting the founding of Cornell's Modern Indonesia Project in 1954, and George Kahin's research agenda of the time, in the new nation of Indonesia, which had just been born. She also identifies the founding of Cornell's journal *Indonesia* in 1966 as seminal to this process, and the appearance of the Cornell White Paper in that same year as foundational to this process (Anderson et al., 1966). Taylor says that these two events of 1966 ended an admirable cycle of fieldwork and academic collaboration between Indonesia and the outside world that had been so productive for the previous ten-plus years. Yet, of course, this was only just one of several possible "beginnings"; far older trajectories can be found, too, in these genealogies. In Holland, the KITLV (Koninklijk Instituut voor Taal-, Land- en Volkenkunde, Royal Netherlands Institute of Southeast Asian and Caribbean Studies) was founded in 1851, and by the next year, the *Bijdragen* (BKI, or *Bijdragen tot de Taal-, Land- en Volkenkunde*, Journal of the Humanities and Social Sciences of Southeast Asia and Oceania) was first published. This program-and-journal arrangement happened in the heyday of colonial times (*tempoe doeloe*)—a full century earlier than Cornell's program's founding. Indonesian authors made up only 1 percent of all articles appearing in the BKI during the colonial era, but in 1969 the KITLV opened an office in Jakarta for collecting Indonesian-language books, a move applauded by some and seen as neo-colonial by others. Recently, this venerable institution of knowledge production on the history of Indonesia has been under threat of dismantlement because it is seen as too antiquated a model by some in the Dutch government, which controls the funding for such institutions. Thankfully, that eventuality now seems to have been avoided, but this threat to the KITLV is a clear signal that some paradigms of the recording and writing of history back in the old colonial metropole will be forced to adapt and change.

Taylor sees other possibilities manifesting themselves. In Amsterdam, the HSN (Historical Sample of the Netherlands) audiovisual archive, "Recording the Future," in operation from 2003 onward, has been documenting Indonesian life under the catchphrase that "everyday life, once forgotten, is lost forever." Heather Sutherland (formerly of the Vrije Universiteit), was asked to take stock on the 150th anniversary of the *Bijdragen,* and she—and others, together whom might be called part of the "Amsterdam School"—have shown that even in a small country like Holland, there are radically different ways of viewing Indonesian history. (Those with a memory of debates between Amsterdam's Jan Breman and Leiden's Vincent Houben will no doubt agree with this sentiment. The "heat and light" from those disagreements on how to view Indonesian colonial history are only just now dissipating, fifteen years later.) Yet it may be appropriate to end with an Indonesian stream in studying Indonesia, after all, and here Taylor touches on UGM (Universitas Gadjah Mada) in Jogjakarta, and Bambang Purwanto's provocative 2006 book, *Gagalnya Historiografi Indonesiasentris* ("Has Indonesian-centric Historiography Failed?"), in particular. Taylor critiques what she calls the "fuzzy thinking" of lumping together the historical personage of Gadja Madah himself (from Majapahit times), Diponegoro (from the Java War, in 1825), and Cut Nyak Din (from the Aceh War, in the 1870s through the 1890s), all as "Indonesians," but she is also sympathetic to the overall project. You don't allot 350 years to Dutch colonial history *en toto,* she argues; this is just part of a larger Indonesian history, one that is still being fashioned and told. Yet it is instructive that so few non-Indonesian scholars actually show up in person in the main centers of academic learning in Indonesia to write their histories of the country. This sort of dialectic would never be tolerated in the production of historiography on China, Japan, or India, for example. This is part of a pattern that should still change, one can argue, and in fact must change if Indonesia is to take more of a part in writing its own history among the historians hailing from other nations. This is certainly a worthy goal. The essays here describe how the intellectual journey of writing an Indonesian history has happened, both through the various *aliran* and through the people who have made this an often coherent (and at other times, a very fractured) endeavor. They are instructive in this sense, and are inspirational as a set, but they are also cautionary tales in a way, alluding to the many complex elements that go into fashioning any history of a nation.

Works Cited

Anderson, Benedict. *Imagined Communities.* New York, NY: Verso, 1983.

Anderson, Benedict R. O'G., and Ruth T. McVey, with Frederick P. Bunnell. *A Preliminary Analysis of the October 1, 1965, Coup in Indonesia.* Ithaca, NY: Cornell Southeast Asia Program Publications, January 1966.

Dijk, Kees van. *The Netherlands Indies and the Great War, 1914–1918.* Leiden: KITLV, 2007.

Emmerson, Donald K. "Southeast Asia: What's in a Name?" *Journal of Southeast Asian Studies* 15 (March 1984): 1–21.

Kahin, George McT. *Southeast Asia: A Testament.* Abingdon: Routledge, 2002.

Poeze, Harry. *Tan Malaka: Strijder voor Indonesie's Vrijheid: Levensloop van 1897 tot 1945.* 's-Gravenhage: Martinus Nijhoff, 1976.

——. *Verguisd en Vergeten: Tan Malaka, de Linkse Beweging en de Indonesische Revolutie, 1945–1949,* Vol. 1–3. Leiden: KITLV, 2007.

Pramoedya Ananta Toer. *The Buru Quartet* (comprising these four books: *This Earth of Mankind, Child of All Nations, Footsteps,* and *House of Glass*). New York, NY: Penguin Books, 1982 passim.

Purwanto, Bambang. *Gagalnya Historiografi Indonesiasentris.* Jogjakarta: Ombak, 2006.

Reid, Tony. *An Indonesian Frontier: Acehnese and Other Histories of Sumatra.* Singapore: Singapore University Press, 2005.

Said, Edward. *Orientalism.* New York, NY: Vintage Books, 1978.

Scott, James. *The Art of Not Being Governed.* New Haven, CT: Yale University Press, 2009.

Spence, Jonathan. *Return to Dragon Mountain: Memories of a Late Ming Man.* New York, NY: Viking, 2007.

Utami Ayu. *Saman.* Jakarta: Gramedia, 1998.

Wolters, Oliver W. *History, Culture, and Region in Southeast Asian Perspectives.* Ithaca, NY: Cornell Southeast Asia Program Publications, 1999.

THE LAST THIRTY YEARS: IN SEARCH OF GMIP

Rudolf Mrázek

We met at a site of memory and, like sites of memory are, this one sits a bit awkwardly in its place. Many of the things memorable actually did not happen here, but about a ten-minute walk away, at 102 West Avenue, where the Cornell Modern Indonesian Project offices and lecture room had been located since the 1950s and through the 1970s. There is a parking lot at that site now.

I had been very eager to attend this conference since I got Eric Tagliacozzo's invitation. I thought about what I might say, but much more about the pleasure of being here again, a "coming home" of sorts (which student of Indonesia does not think about Ithaca as a sort of home?), like being at a family reunion (most of the time, admittedly, such a reunion ends with me grumbling to myself). In my excited mood, as I thought about this paper, I heard my mother: "Rudo"—she called me Rudo—"there is no fun anymore down here." She looked disconcertedly around herself, at me, and then up, whereto most of the people she loved had already departed. She was beginning to say this when she reached the age I am now. Indeed, getting ready for this meeting, I thought of a cemetery, the one in Ithaca, up there behind Hasbrouck, across the way from the golf course. This is where George Kahin's grave is, and Oliver Wolters's grave is just a few steps away.

I.

The organizers suggested to the conference participants that we take a look at what has been published about modern Indonesia in the last thirty years or so (about modern Indonesian history in the case of Laurie Sears, Jean Taylor, and me) and say what we think has been the best, freshly young, attractive, and inspiring—what has the greatest capacity to keep the Cornell Modern Indonesia Project going? Which means, to rejuvenate it.

Thinking of "young, attractive, and inspiring," instantly George Kahin's name came to my mind. His last book, *Southeast Asia: A Testament*, was published in 2002, and so it qualifies for the in-the-last-thirty-years category. First and foremost, the way it was written is most appealing. Some parts of the manuscript Kahin evidently still typed and retyped, as we all do. However, so I imagine, more of it he scribbled as notes and then dictated them to Audrey, as he already had become quite ill and had to know that not much time was left. The book is like that. It is about childhood and youth, about Indonesia, Vietnam, Cambodia, Ho Chi Minh, John Foster Dulles, Cornell and Cornell again, and Indonesia and Indonesia again. There is a sense of the urgency of life getting short and of history catching up with the life of a scholar.

There is not much of a line between life and scholarship in the book; there is one flow and one kind of milestones. What might have happened is often as important as what actually did. At the outset of World War II, Kahin volunteered for the US Army and was rigorously trained for an engagement in Italy—which did not happen. Then he was reassigned and trained for the US invasion of Western Indonesia—which did not happen, either. Underneath, since before the time he volunteered (and this might have been the most important motivation), there was Kahin's experience working for the Japanese Americans interned in camps. There was no distinguishing between this and Kahin's unshakeable conviction about the truth of FDR's ideals about how the United States, as the upcoming world superpower, should behave in the war and after the war.

Kahin's *Testament*, when I read it for the first time in 2002, made me clearly aware of what I had felt but vaguely before—what to me had been the most captivating in Kahin's writing since I first read (decades ago, in Prague) his *Nationalism and Revolution* (1952).

Much of Kahin's biography had been well known before *Testament*. Kahin got his academic education at Johns Hopkins University, the best of schools, the ultimate in sophistication and rigor, with the best and most engaged teachers of the time and country. Much of what happened next has become legend. Kahin arrived in Indonesia in 1948 to do the research for his dissertation. The revolution was raging, negotiations were going on, and people (by the thousands) were dying in battle, of hunger, and of exhaustion. It has equally become lore—that an American graduate student driving his Lend-Lease Jeep across the battle lines with a US flag and an Indonesian flag on the hull of the car. That I knew. But only after reading *Testament* did I learn how much George Kahin was in trouble at the time.

Kahin made some very deep and warm friendships across the lines—mostly with Indonesians and mostly Indonesians who spoke English, people of the same age or a little older than he was—Suripno, later executed as a communist and a rebel against the republic; Natsir; Hatta; Subandrio; and Sukarno, the president. In Yogyakarta, the center of the republic and a city under siege, Kahin was explaining (much of it also to himself) what the upcoming US elections might mean for the world and Indonesia. People asked him questions of beliefs and ideology as a matter of life and death—of death, in fact, in the cases like Suripno. Kahin, as seriously as that, gathered all his youthful convictions to remain true to himself in the maddening place, even to remain optimistic—to see the Indonesian revolution as ultimately victorious.

This was how the 1952 book, *Nationalism and Revolution*, was structured and why it is so moving. Kahin's GI and FDR vigor, his Johns Hopkins learning, permitted him to frame the Indonesian revolution and modern history, to explain it, to arrange its pieces together——in this way, *Nationalism and Revolution* and indeed, under the book's impact, the Cornell Modern Indonesia Project came into being. Indonesia remained—stretching and kicking in the frame, under this structure and these explanations. What is momentous about this, what George Kahin accomplished through his life and what he is conveying to us so powerfully in his *Testament*, is a description of (however strong a word this may be) a failure. This is what only a scholar who is best schooled and is most true to the truth of scholarship can do.

Kahin's writing and teaching—and this is why he became so important to me and, I am sure, to others—for the rest of his life remained suspended at the moment of his first encounter with Indonesia and its (also unfinished) revolution. His Indonesian friendships lasted equally until the end of his or their lives, and the friendships, too, have remained suspended at the same moment. Smiles with which historical figures in Indonesia received a student coming to them with a letter from Kahin or just a mention of Kahin's name, were smiles of that moment, too. The years that passed were telescoped into the smiles—a gift to every historian, but also moments of sadness. "Suspended" and "telescoped" suggest the kind of history Kahin wrote—acquiring its fullness as the time passed. The friends aged, some died, and some others did things unexpected and unwanted. Indonesia's unfinished revolution became increasingly a matter of remembrance at the same time as FDR ideals were becoming those of an American lefty and Sukarno was caving in to Suharto.

Kahin's remaining at that moment of his first encounter with Indonesia made his scholarship powerful. Kahin's *Testament*, I suspect, did not bring CMIP the kind of money and grants that Kahin's *Nationalism and Revolution* did. But there is magic in *Testament* that can do much to keep CMIP as alive as it should be. It can help to keep this building still a home for Kahin, sort of, with George still present, sort of, a young man, still volunteering for war, still crossing the lines, with the best schooling that had (not) prepared him for what he was given to crash against—(un)prepared and surprised by it for the rest of his life, to quote another true explorer: "That which is new, the discovery, obviously does not depend on chance, but on *surprise*."[1]

* * *

I do not have to leave the Cornell cemetery yet. Oliver Wolters's grave is there, not too far from Kahin's, and Wolters qualifies, too, for a top slot in my last-thirty-years-young-and-beautiful contest. Wolters's *History, Culture, and Region in Southeast Asian Perspectives* (1982) was published only twenty-nine years ago, and its second, updated edition as recently as 2001! There is a wealth of knowledge, to be sure, on Indonesia in that book, but, more importantly for me, on historians of modern Indonesia, how they are made, and what can future ones learn from them. Like Kahin, Wolters was best prepared to do his scholarship, and, like Kahin, he wrote his ultimate book and spent his ultimate years thinking about "surprise."

Oliver Wolters was a student of D. G. E. Hall at the University of London (I was looking at a framed photograph of Hall on a fireplace mantle as I was giving the oral version of this talk). Several super-excellent scholars who call Wolters their teacher attest to Wolters's academic credentials. Yet, Wolters's reputation seemed to live by this as much as by stories. And he enjoyed the stories being suspect. I have never really known for sure whether, as a British civil servant during the Malayan Emergency, he indeed "hunted the communists." I know that he spent much of World War II in a Japanese concentration camp, but he never wrote nor talked (as far as I know) about it. He wrote and talked, and very much so (as we all know), about

---

[1] Pierre Joliot, quoted in Paul Virilio, *The Aesthetics of Disappearance*, trans. Philip Beitchman (Cambridge and New York, NY: Semiotext(e), 2009), p. 46. Emphasis mine.

his "hunt" for where the center of Sriwijaya might have been. It was a lost city, and it might have never existed, as he, of course, knew better than anybody else. But as his time was getting short, he might say, with that little smile of his, now he simply had to find it.

There is nothing very explicit in Wolters's *Southeast Asia* about World War II, or about the Indonesian revolution; neither is there much explicit about the bloody and murderous mid-1960s. Yet Wolters was passionately and youthfully curious about people like Pramoedya Ananta Toer as they emerged from the camp and began to publish their histories. This had been underneath but very close to the surface in his writing—very near in character, in fact, to his search for the empty center of Sriwijaya, and also to his adventurous sorties into Vietnamese studies, truly adventurous for his age, as well as, on a more theoretical level, to his critique of national-cum-regional assertiveness, his presenting a naïveté of a place as a conviction, to his fascination, very close to the end of his life, with one particular sentence in, of all people, Henry James, to his youthfully anti-categorical notion of Southeast Asia as "*mandala*" (with the lost city of Sriwijaya, I am sure, in the center of it).

Oliver Wolters loved Cornell in a British way that I could never really understand. He might sometimes look cold, even sarcastic. I am not sure where he ever felt at home, certainly not at the cemetery. His "stuff" (his famous word) and his scholarship (one and the same thing in his case, as in Kahin's) were made of tangents: almost touching, reader as well as history.

* * *

I would very much like to smuggle Harry Benda into this thirty-years-young-and-inspiring company, but it does not work. Benda died young, in 1971, just short of the age of fifty-two; most importantly, he is not published any more (I move that the next Harry Benda Prize for Southeast Asian Studies by the American Association of Asian Scholars be given to someone who proves that he or she has read some pages, say one hundred, of Benda). There is also no grave for Harry Benda at the Cornell cemetery; he is buried in New Haven, Connecticut, where he had been on the Yale faculty at the time. It is not easy to argue that, with George Kahin and Oliver Wolters, Harry Benda belongs to the great, the still young, and the momentous.

Like Kahin and Wolters, Benda got the best academic education he could at the place and time and for his age. The school of his life, I think, was the Gymnasium, an eight-year school for students between ten and eighteen, most wonderful and stiffest among the institutes of learning, and since the eighteenth century designed to produce an enlightened and loyal citizenry of, first, the Prussian and Austrian empires and, then, of the nation states of Central Europe. The sciences were taught at the Gymnasium (in the most constructive sense); languages, dead as much as alive; and authors, like Herodotus or Plutarch, as well as the most solid classics among the moderns. Benda, like Kahin and Wolters in their own time and place, could not have been more intensely (un)prepared for what had been lying in wait for him—to put it simply, for modern Indonesia.

World War II touched Benda's life as much as it touched the lives of Kahin and Wolters, only in a much harsher way. Much of Benda's life was crushed and—no metaphor this—burned into ashes. Benda, a Czech Jew, was born in the Sudetenland, the northwestern part of Czechoslovakia, on the German border. Just out of

Gymnasium, in his late teens, he was sent by his parents in haste to the Netherlands to save him from the Nazis. Hitler invaded Czechoslovakia, moved against Western Europe, and Benda moved, too, on the run, as far as he could, to the Netherlands East Indies. People who came to know him there described him as moving up, on his way, toward a truly bright career in business (Wertheim and Wertheim-Gijs Weenink 1991, 162 *passim*).

Since childhood, Benda was bilingual in Czech and German (and there was the Gymnasium's Latin, Greek, and French); in Batavia and Semarang, he learned to speak Dutch fluently and flawlessly in a few months (his Czech remained rich and extraordinarily beautiful; I can attest to this). He seemed well on his way, but then the war caught up with him anyway, and he was interned in Java, in a Japanese camp. In the camp, among many new people, with the Dutch colonials behind the wire, he met Wim Wertheim, a Dutch Jew, and a future father of the Dutch radical sociology of Indonesia. As one story goes, Wertheim told Benda, "After all this is over, why do textiles? Why not history?"[2]

The whole Benda family back home (except a brother and one aunt, I believe) perished in the Nazi camps (this much for the ashes). Given that fact and given the way the Czechs behaved to the Jewish returnees after the war, it clearly made no sense for Harry Banda to come back. Equipped with experience like this, on a foundation like this, into a matrix like this, Benda built his scholarship.

His going to study Indonesia looked much like deciding to go on running. From the camp in Java, Benda got to New Zealand, where he asked for but was not given citizenship. Then and therefore he applied (yes, you guessed it) to Cornell and to George Kahin (Kahin 1972, 211–12). Benda got his Cornell PhD and then taught, first in Rochester, and then at Yale. As yet another story goes, at Yale, with quite some accent (Czech? German? Jewish?), impatiently, he corrected the English grammar of his Anglo-Saxon students. He became a very popular teacher: standing room only. One student of his, now a distinguished scholar, who talked to me recently did not recall Benda ever mentioning camps or whatever had happened to him personally. He was "apolitical," exactly like Wolters. When I insisted, the former Benda student began to wonder whether the camps and all the rest might not, perhaps, be beneath Benda's "extreme sensitivity" to the matters of freedom and justice—and, yes, beneath those unexpected and sudden attacks of the blues, of bitterness and, evidently, helplessness, especially in the last years of his life, at the turn of the 1960s and 1970s, when he watched the democracies launching the Vietnam war. An effete snob no, an egghead yes.

It can be only in part correctly said about Benda (what had been only in part correctly said about other Jews from that part of the world) that he wrote "for another society" (Bloch 2000, 41). Benda remained a foreigner, but intimately belonged to Liberec, to Prague, to Batavia, to Ithaca, to Jakarta (to Tel Aviv), and, finally, to New Haven. Distance was in his nature, and it *was* the method and strength of his scholarship. He wrote history of modern Indonesia from the point of view of the Gymnasium, the roads of exile, and the camps, but this was for him the only engaged way of looking. As Wertheim suggested to him in the camp, Benda "did history," and, in a sense, indeed, in a sophisticated businesslike manner. He did

---

[2] Personal communication, Wim Wertheim. For Wertheim on Benda, see Wim Wertheim, "Harry Benda (1919–1971)," *Bijdragen tot de Taal-, Land- en Volkenkunde* 128,2/3 (1972): 214–18.

the themes that he knew were needed. The work he left us is frustrating by how flatly it is displayed, by how it is fragmented and unfinished.

Benda "did" editions and readers, mainly for the purpose of teaching. He published mostly in a format of short papers: tradition and trade, on patterns of administration, on peasant movements (this he knew was what was "really badly needed"; I am not sure to what extent, if any, James Scott's institute at Yale has a connection with it), on elites and on intellectuals, Western and non-Western, on communism and the communist elites, on the structure of history, on the Samin movement (with Lance Castles), and on democracy (Benda 1972). Most significant of all, he wrote on Islam, a theme that most of all was as if "for another society," that only now, forty years after Benda's death, is in "high demand." Benda's major published work on Islam (1958), the *Crescent and the Rising Sun*, resembled a finished and definitive, polished, and, as much as it could be, closed study. Before anybody else could even think of it, almost instantly after the book came out, Harry Benda, wittily, sharply (and then repeatedly) criticized his own book for all its possible failings, mercilessly, almost tearing it to pieces.

Kahin kept thinking the FDR way, long after FDR was left by the wayside, out of most mainstreams. Wolters kept on his trail toward the center of Sriwijaya, which he knew best might have never existed. The core of their importance has been in their being different. But hardly anyone would say that they wrote in accents. Harry Benda, however, kept to his Gymnasium codex of style. He also kept on speaking and writing like one of the Sudetenland, of that Europe, and like a Jew of that time. My true excitement in reading Benda comes from his language. Accented, and with the accent(s) so difficult to trace, Benda's perfectly correct English texts can still make American students uneasy when assigned. The students, *surprised*, can be wonderfully woken out of any stupor in which, in other classrooms, they may find themselves to be. But, as already noted, Benda's texts are assigned rarely.

II.

Mother, of course, was not completely serious. There can still be some pleasure, not only at the cemetery. Ben Anderson and Jim Siegel, for instance. Only, why were they missing from the conference? I was surprised. "*Si je savais ...,* " as a boy Aztec (or was it a boy Tintin?) grumbled to himself on an occasion like this in *La Guerre des Boutons*.

Jim Siegel, probably, would not like to be included among historians, and Ben Anderson likewise. Still, and for the last thirty years that we are talking about, I can see these two along with Kahin, Wolters, and Benda, as momentous for writing history. I also so very much want to believe that the good of scholarship in the next thirty years will happen through the two of them.

Since it was published in 1969, Siegel's *Rope of God* has been my treasured book on modern Indonesian history—yes, history. But, what he wrote after this was still unexpected. To me, the truly crashing moment came in 1993 in his *Solo in the New Order*, when the author walks through a Surakarta alley (I write this from memory, it had to be something like that), he is too tall for the place (you know him), and he bumps his head against some shop awning or whatever. A Chicago-trained anthropologist (and what more can be said?), in search of knowledge, at that instant, all of a sudden, could not be more awkward. He reached the apex of the search, and it could not have happened at another place. This is the naïveté of a place I mentioned when talking about Wolters, a funny moment, and a good joke (everybody was laughing on that street). Inevitably, at that moment, on that street, in the author, in the book, in the reader, in that historical place, the "new order," everything begins to move and sound, everything, including an analytical framework that might have been brought in, in the first place, including Siegel's and his reader's *concept* of modern Indonesia. The author and the concept stumble, the historical time collapses at the edge of coherence. Indonesia appears! (I am proud to add that another head-on, awning-bashing moment in the book comes when a man in Solo, to general mirth, is hopelessly trying to pronounce "*Cékoslowakia*.")

After *Solo in the New Order* came Siegel's *Fetish and Recognition* (1997), *The New Criminal Type* (1998), *Naming the Witch* (2006), and *Objects and Objections* (2011). Even Siegel's devoted readers (who had believed they knew) were taken by a surprise that is not always easy to deal with. (We may be crashing against books.) Siegel's new discoveries are not easy to place. Each next book of Siegel's is one too many. One feels like one is at a corner of a big and unknown street with three guidebooks (or more) in hand, looking for a way to go. This is how Siegel may guide you through a city, and how he can make Indonesian history for you (uncannily) familiar.

As in Wolters or Benda, politics in Siegel might not be readily apparent. But, and very much so, Siegel's scholarship also grew out of an encounter with a chasm, a surprise, a sense of being unprepared for it by academic training, however tip-top. Since his earliest writings, and with an increasing clarity, especially since *Solo in the New Order*, Siegel's urge to know and tell grows out of his encounter with the madness, the cunning, and the murders of the mid-1965 and 1966. As had been the case in Kahin, Wolters, and Benda, and there might be very little in common between him and them besides this, Siegel's merit and obsession are in submitting a report on a jolt by which history and writing of history moves.

The shock of 1965, and perhaps even more its aftermath, the slow and often shameful demise of the 1945 generation of the Indonesian nationalism, the dictatorship of the next thirty years, Indonesian aggression against East Timor, rapes of Chinese Indonesians by other Indonesians, have made Cornell even more Cornell than it had been before. George Kahin, directing the Cornell Modern Indonesia Project, tried to understand and help his junior colleagues and students as fathers do—with deep compassion but limited powers of persuasion. People now looked at the revolution of 1945 from a substantially greater distance. Claire Holt emerged as the most beloved presence at that difficult moment. A dancer (although she could not really dance any more at her age), she took it on her to chart the steps, set the pace, and lead.[3] Her exquisite ways, and I will never forget them, are clearly to be recognized in Jim Siegel and in others who passed through Cornell during that time. Ben Anderson has taken on Claire Holt's testament most intensely, provocatively, and politically.

Ben Anderson's *Java in a Time of Revolution* (1972) must always be read together with Kahin's *Nationalism and Revolution*, even though the latter came out (exactly)

---

[3] Claire Holt, ed., with the assistance of Benedict R. O'G. Anderson and James Siegel, *Culture and Politics in Indonesia* (Ithaca, NY: Cornell University Press, 1972). Jim Siegel and Ben Anderson were also contributors together with, among others, Taufik Abdullah, Sartono, Dan Lev, and Clifford Geertz (who wrote the postscript). Claire Holt died in 1970. Of the authors of the volume, only Bill Liddle was present at the conference at Cornell.

twenty years earlier. In these two books, the time, again, is telescoped in a single moment. Since 1972, neither of these two books is complete without the other.[4]

As in the case of Jim Siegel, in Ben Anderson's case all had been signaled already in his earliest writings and, of course, in *Java in a Time of Revolution*. Yet the Anderson that I propose as one of the last-thirty-year-bests has appeared fully only as his *externation*[5] from Suharto's Indonesia starting in 1966 began to look endless, and as it clearly became unbearable. That Anderson survived the 1970s, 1980s, and Suharto, too. He is getting younger as we speak. What happened in his writing during the last thirty years or so was not a radical break. It all was being done in small steps and could be overlooked at the time (merely building an uncomfortable feeling, tension, and energy) and still remains in the mold of Kahin's or Kahinian ethics of writing history.

A Siegel-like, head-against-the-awning moment probably came (or it rather was when I got it) with Ben Anderson publishing his two-part translation of the Javanese *Suluk Gatoloco* (1981, 1982) exactly thirty years ago. Since then, it has been for me as a reader, and I guess for him as an author, a continual adventure. Anderson's *translations* (for lack of a better word) from Javanese, Indonesian, Thai, Tagalog, Spanish, again Indonesian, and, most recently, Dutch,[6] have become the most exciting body of writing on modern Indonesian history, yes, history. These translations (and sometimes his editing of translations by others)[7] are rigorously correct, and what seems to matter most for Anderson is caring about the details. At the same time, less and less are they renditions of established works of canon, both literary and historical. One is made *uncomfortable* (again this word!) about Anderson's choice. One is made to wonder, and question the canon—so disquietingly appealing is the "waste" (as people of the canon would have us call it) that Anderson now chooses to bring to us. And, as in the cases of Kahin, Wolters, Benda, or Siegel, the mold in its entirety, the modern Indonesia project, is never cast away. Anderson is the one next in the line.

Ben Anderson translates into English, into his English—some may say "Eaton English" (and what more can be said). The untamed Javanese, Thai, or Indonesian (so gently Anderson works with them) is pushed against a template of English "perfection." Anderson translates modern Indonesian, Javanese, Thai, Tagalog, or Spanish as much as he translates modern English. Very much like his and Siegel's "discovery," the late Pramoedya Ananta Toer, Anderson (also a prisoner of the New Order) engages in an endeavor to dislodge the language (and culture) from and into

---

[4] See also George Kahin's introduction to the second edition of *Nationalism and Revolution* (Ithaca, NY: Cornell Southeast Asia Program Publications, 2003).

[5] I use a non-existing English word, "externation." *Externeering* was the term the Dutch authorities used for banning their political opponents from the colony.

[6] See, for instance, Benedict Anderson, *The Spectre of Comparison* (London: Verso, 1998). So far unpublished, as far as I know, Anderson's translation of Tessel Pollmann's "'Men is fascist of men is het niet': De Indische NSB als imperiale droom en koloniale melkkoe," in *Het koloniale beschavingsoffensie: Wegen naa het nieuwe Indië, 1890-1950*, ed. Marieke Bloembergen and Remco Raben (Leiden: KITLV Uitgeverij, 2009).

[7] Arief W. Djati and Ben Anderson, eds., *Menjadi Tjamboek Berdoeri: Memoar Kwee Thiam Tjing*, trans. James Siegel (Jakarta: Komunitas Bambu, 2010); and Tan Swie Ling, *G30S 1965: Perang Dingin dan Kehancuran Nasionalisme: Pemikiran Cina Jelata Korban Orba*, trans. Ben Anderson (Jakarta: Komunitas Bambu, 2010).

which he translates; even, in critical moments, to "put it into deadlock."[8] Anderson has made Cornell, during the last thirty years especially, more than Cornell had ever been by studying the vulgarity, assertiveness, and dullness (the same things) of *Suhartese*, of post-*Suhartese*, of *motherese*, and, not in the least, of *Cornellese*,[9] languages which we speak, write, and think—tongues of banality, of dictatorships, and, too often, also of disciplines. (If only Ben one day would "do Czech," too!)

III.

The Indonesian revolution of 1945 and the cruel event of 1965 formed two generations of scholars. The next historical watershed that is still with us has been no less formative. It is a surge rather than a watershed—as big and overwhelming, however slow, extended over a long time and thus much less perceptible in its working and impact. To find a name for it, I call it a surge of liberalism, and I see it flooding equally the world, academia, and studies of modern Indonesia. If we wished to find a spokesperson for it, Hannah Arendt may do. When she was asked, more than thirty years ago, "Politics of left and right?" she answered:

> I really don't know and I've never known. And I suppose I never had any position … I don't think that the real question of this century will get any kind of illumination by this kind of thing.[10]

What mattered, Arendt explained, was "the right to have a political home."[11]

This surge has been difficult to deal with for a scholar and especially for a historian, more difficult than to deal with the revolutions and the mass murders. The liberalism is even more dangerous to encounter than is its "neo" mode, because it is "so calm, so soft" (to quote a TV cigarette advertisement of the 1960s). Softly and calmly it overflows all liveliness, including the professional one—not really right, not really left, not really East and not really West, not really colonial, and not really free; instead, multi-cultural, ethno-musical, and global.

So many scholars now are eagerly receiving the waters, pushing ahead even, to become an avant-garde of it. They *are* by being the surge, with their unshakeable confidence in learning, academic freedom, sophistication, and brilliance. Their projects *are* by being analytical frameworks, to guarantee that no one, a young scholar especially, stumbles in the field. All awkwardness is dealt with swiftly, heights of awnings are carefully measured before anyone starts marching, and the chasms are surfed over. The truth of discipline (and a discipline) is to keep to a

---

[8] "One of the phenomena by which one recognizes an event is that it is like a point of the real that puts language into deadlock." Alain Badiou, as quoted in *León Ferrari and Mira Schendel: Tangled Alphabets*, ed. Luis Pérez-Oramas (New York, NY: Museum of Modern Art, 2009), p. 41. Should we call it *latah*?

[9] "Motherese" is a sociolinguistic term describing a parent or a person of authority speaking or writing over-distinctly and over-simply to a child or anyone without authority to convey how things are to be done. *Suhartese* and *Cornellese* are my inventions, offered in the same vein.

[10] Heonik Kwon, *Ghosts of War in Vietnam* (Cambridge: Cambridge University Press, 2008), p. 157. Kwon with this book became the first laureate of the Kahin Prize in Southeast Asian Studies (2008).

[11] Ibid, p. 159.

genre. "Methodologically closed systems" become "unhypothetical imperatives";[12] scholars become like the tough men of Mahogany: they "exchange glances before they express opinion" (Benjamin 2003, 22)[13] It is not (only) that I do not want to name names. We all are affected.

Both a consequence and a cause of the surge may be a progressive disappearance of drama in history. In Indonesia, namely, the figures are long gone, like Charles O. Van der Plas of 1945, with his flying beard, beating down on Sukarno's just-born republic. Gone are the figures of naked violence. I have above my desk (on loan from Ruth McVey) a wayang puppet from about 1948, a Dutch soldier in a green uniform, fat and with a crude face, a bulging eye, and a Rudolf-like red nose, all the signs that could make the work of a historian so easy. Gone are the martyrs of the revolution, with long hair, bamboo spears, and scared eyes of a child; no more Bandung, the city in flames, no more, even, General Suharto practicing pistol shooting. Instead, the gray Singapore-like or Freeport-like landscapes, Habibies, SBYs, and even NGOs—so well meaning. Only a brilliant scholar may be able to deal with it—brilliantly.

* * *

The impact of John Roosa, a young Canadian scholar, on current scholarship is not in brilliance. His book *Pretext for Mass Murder: The September 30th Movement and Suharto's Coup d'État in Indonesia* (2006) moves slowly from fact to fact, and it does not make for easy reading. Yet, the book's Indonesian edition was banned, and it remained so until recently. Judging from reviews and from how people talk about it, the book has become an inspiration for many and an irritation for perhaps as many as that.

I like to think of John Roosa as of "my" Cornell. Like the scholarship of Kahin, Benda, Siegel, or Anderson, *Pretext for Mass Murder* is made of one historical moment, and it remains in that moment. John Roosa's "Kahinian moment" is the bloodshed and "the mystery" of 1965, and—as in the case of Kahin and the others who followed him—it has been equally made and remained in what happened afterward, or, more precisely, what did not happen, what has failed to follow. This is a chivalry in the face of a surge for you! Left and right still matter. No, this cannot become a political home for modern Indonesia, surely not forever. This has to be merely a protracted morning-after, following what began with the fall of Suharto and still lasts—these hopes sinking into dullness (and petit-bourgeois ambitions), this liberal brilliance à la Indonesia—that which has been called by the condom word *reformasi*.

IV.

Last year, John Roosa and friends suggested that I give a paper to the Indonesian Institute of Social History in Jakarta. John was the only Westerner among the fellows as far as I knew. I had been taken somewhere in Jakarta. There was a large,

---

[12] The terms in quotation marks are from "The Shape of the Inconstruable Question," in Ernst Bloch, *The Spirit of Utopia*, trans. Anthony A. Nassar (Stanford, CA: Stanford University Press, 2000), pp. 177, 184.

[13] See "Commentary on Poems by Brecht" in Walter Benjamin, *Selected Writings 4 (1938–40)* (Cambridge, MA: Harvard University and Belknap Press, 2003), p. 22.

nondescript house (as one might say in a novel) in a side alley. It certainly was at the outskirts. The house looked deserted, and it seemed to me to be made of just one very large room. There were books along all the walls and boxes with photocopies; I found later that many of Pramoedya's papers were in some of the boxes. After some time, people began to come, mostly with their hands full of plates with food, and they all smiled and some kissed me by way of introduction. There were children, of course, and it was never clear who was a fellow, who a family member, and who was just passing by.

I would very much like to believe that this is the modern Indonesia, as it is becoming to be. When the hour arrived (two hours later), they did not let me talk much; the whole discourse became, sort of, one interruption that extended into the very late afternoon. All of them were intensely concerned with the topic I brought in, something about the 1930s (!), and, in a flash (of laughter most often), they made it into a topic of theirs. They had just come from a demonstration (it turned quite violent, this one), and, for tomorrow, they were planning to go to another one. Discussion of the 1930s raged exactly like the planning of the demonstration. Each of them (I dare say, including the children, relatives, and passersby) had been writing one thesis or another, and all of them were theses on history. There were good jokes, and it was astonishing fun, why not say it, like at a cemetery.

John Roosa (and hopefully he also represents a generation[14]) in one particular way goes further than Kahin, Wolters, Benda, or even Anderson and Siegel. More of John Roosa's "full time" is spent in Indonesia. His family, in its core members, is Indonesian. Naturally, most of his intimate friends and trusted colleagues seem to be Indonesians. Roosa appears to be more substantially of Indonesia or, to use a Gymnasium term, of the "Orient." Still, without a doubt, he is the next in the distinguished line of scholarship that we can still hardly imagine otherwise—Western, American, and, yes, White. Roosa, to use a postmodern term for change, is still "dis-oriented."[15] The tension, the trauma, that kind of engagement and dedication that have been so powerful and inspiring in the writing on modern Indonesian history in the last thirty years and beyond, are still in Roosa's writing.

Reading John Roosa and seeing him in Indonesia, I think more than ever of what might have happened if Taufik Abdullah, for instance, remained at Cornell beyond his time as a graduate student there—what would have happened to Taufik, and what would have happened to Cornell? Indeed, what would happen if more than thirty years later more than just one Indonesian scholar were invited to this present conference? Perhaps we might then get into some very new yet equally wonderful Kahinian trouble. For instance, we might then get some sort of GMIP, *Gatoloco Modern Indonesia Project*, on our hands.

---

[14] Other key members of this generation may be Eric Tagliacozzo, *Secret Trades, Porous Borders: Smuggling and States along a Southeast Asian Frontier, 1865–1915* (New Haven, CT: Yale University Press, 2005); Karen Strassler, *Refracted Visions: Popular Photography and National Modernity in Java* (Durham, NC: Duke University Press, 2010); and Andrew Goss, *Floracrats: State-Sponsored Science and the Failure of Enlightenment in Indonesia* (Madison, WI: University of Wisconsin Press, 2011).

[15] "This situation is the same as that which sends us from the nondetermined cardinal points (from a dis-oriented world) to a sense of orientation that is supposed to sense in the absence of any sensible Orient ..." Nancy Jean-Luc, *The Sense of the World*, trans. Jeffrey S. Librett (Minneapolis, MN: University of Minnesota Press, 1997), p. 79.

Works Cited

Anderson, Benedict R. O'G. *Java in a Time of Revolution*. Ithaca, NY: Cornell University Press, 1972. Second edition. Jakarta: Equinox, 2006.

Anderson, Benedict, trans. "The *Suluk* Gatoloco I." *Indonesia* 32 (October 1981): 109–150.

——. "The *Suluk* Gatoloco II." *Indonesia* 33 (April 1982): 31–88.

——. *The Spectre of Comparisons*. London: Verso, 1998.

Benda, Harry J. *Continuity and Change in Southeast Asia: Collected Journal Articles*. New Haven, CT: Yale University Press, 1972.

——. *The Crescent and the Rising Sun*. The Hague: W. van Hoeve, 1958.

Benjamin, Walter. *Selected Writings 4 (1938–40)*. Cambridge, MA: Harvard University and Belknap Press, 2003.

Bloch, Ernst. "The Philosophy of Music." *The Spirit of Utopia*. Trans. Anthony A. Nassar. Stanford, CA: Stanford University Press, 2000.

Djati, Arief W., and Ben Anderson, eds. *Menjadi Tjamboek Berdoeri: Memoar Kwee Thiam Tjing*. Intro. James Siegel. Jakarta: Komunitas Bambu, 2010.

Goss, Andrew. *Floracrats: State-Sponsored Science and the Failure of Enlightenment in Indonesia*. Madison, WI: University of Wisconsin Press, 2011.

Holt, Claire, ed., assisted by Benedict R. O'G. Anderson and James Siegel. *Culture and Politics in Indonesia*. Ithaca, NY: Cornell University Press, 1972.

Jean-Luc, Nancy. *The Sense of the World*. Trans. Jeffrey S. Librett. Minneapolis, MN: University of Minnesota Press, 1997.

Kahin, George. *Southeast Asia: A Testament*. New York, NY: Routledge, 2002.

——. *Nationalism and Revolution in Indonesia*. Ithaca, NY: Cornell University Press, 1952. Second edition. Ithaca, NY: Southeast Asia Program Publications, 2003.

——. "In Memoriam. Harry J. Benda." *Indonesia* 13 (April 1972): 211–12.

Kwon, Heonik. *Ghosts of War in Vietnam*. Cambridge: Cambridge University Press, 2008.

Pérez-Oramas, Luis, ed. *León Ferrari and Mira Schendel: Tangled Alphabets*. New York, NY: Museum of Modern Art, 2009.

Pollmann, Tessel. "'Men is fascist of men is het niet': De Indische NSB als imperiale droom en koloniale melkkoe." *Het koloniale beschavingsoffensie: Wegen naa het nieuwe Indië, 1890-1950*. Ed. Marieke Bloembergen and Remco Raben. Leiden: KITLV Uitgeverij, 2009.

Roosa, John. *Pretext for Mass Murder: The September 30th Movement and Suharto's Coup d'État in Indonesia*. Madison, WI: University of Wisconsin Press, 2006.

Siegel, James T. *Rope of God*. Berkeley, CA: University of California Press, 1969. Second edition. Ann Arbor, MI: University of Michigan Press, 2000.

——. *Solo in the New Order: Language and Hierarchy in an Indonesian City.* Princeton, NJ: Princeton University Press, 1993.

——. *Fetish, Recognition, Revolution.* Princeton, NJ: Princeton University Press, 1997.

——. *A New Criminal Type in Jakarta: Counter-revolution Today.* Durham, NC: Duke University Press, 1998.

——. *Naming the Witch.* Stanford, CA: Stanford University Press, 2006.

——. *Objects and Objections of Ethnography.* New York, NY: Fordham University Press, 2011.

Strassler, Karen. *Refracted Visions: Popular Photography and National Modernity in Java.* Durham, NC: Duke University Press, 2010.

Tagliacozzo, Eric. *Secret Trades, Porous Borders: Smuggling and States along a Southeast Asian Frontier, 1865–1915.* New Haven, CT: Yale University Press, 2005.

Tan, Swie Ling. *G30S 1965: Perang Dingin dan Kehancuran Nasionalisme: Pemikiran Cina Jelata Korban Orba.* Intro. Ben Anderson. Jakarta: Komunitas Bambu, 2010.

Wertheim, Wim, and Hetty Wertheim-Gijs Weenink. *Vier Wendingen in Ons Bestaan: Indië verloren-Indonesië geboren.* Breda: De Geus, 1991. 162 *passim.*

Wertheim, Wim. "Harry Benda (1919–1971)." *Bijdragen tot de Taal-, Land- en Volkenkunde* 128.2/3 (1972): 214–18.

Wolters, O. W. *History, Culture, and Region in Southeast Asian Perspectives.* Revised edition. Ithaca, NY: Cornell Southeast Asia Program Publications, 1999.

——. *History, Culture, and Region in Southeast Asian Perspectives.* Singapore: Institute of Southeast Asian Studies, 1982.

THE AFTERWARDSNESS OF INDONESIAN STUDIES

Laurie J. Sears[1]

I began with the tetralogy *Bumi manusia* (This Human Earth), particularly working on the currents that ebbed and flowed during the period of Indonesia's National Awakening. And so there came to be a new reality, a literary reality, a downstream reality whose origin was an upstream reality, that is, a historical reality. A literary reality that contains within it a reorientation and evaluation of civilization and culture, precisely what is not contained in the historical reality. So it is that the literary work is a sort of thesis, an infant that on its own begins to grow in the superstructure of the reader's society. (Pramoedya 1992)

To conclude, I would like to say that Freud's concept of afterwardsness (*Nachträglichkeit*) contains both great richness and a certain ambiguity, combining a retrogressive and a progressive direction. I want to account for this problem of the different directions, to and fro, by arguing that, right at the start, there is something that goes in the direction of the past to the future, from the other to the individual in question, that is in the direction of the adult to the baby, which I call the implantation of the enigmatic message. This message is then retranslated, following a temporal direction which is, in an alternating fashion, by turns retrogressive and progressive (according to my general model of translation-detranslation-retranslation). (Laplanche 1999)

Many non-historians criticize historians and their work, embracing the ideas of writers on history like Hayden White, Michel de Certeau, or Michel Foucault. Non-historians sometimes think historians are not aware of the limits of historiography.[2]

---

[1] Parts of this essay first appeared in the Afterword of my book *Situated Testimonies: Dread and Enchantment in an Indonesian Literary Archive* (Honolulu, HI: University of Hawaii Press, 2013).

[2] For a recent discussion of historical writing on Southeast Asia, see Rosalind C. Morris, "Remembering Asian Anticolonialism, Again," *Journal of Asian Studies* 69,2 (2010): 347–69, where she considers the work of two historians, two political scientists, and one scholar of English literature. Anthropologists have been at work deconstructing historical narratives for some time. For a useful selection see Brian Keith Axel, ed., *From the Margins: Historical Anthropology and Its Futures* (Durham, NC: Duke University Press, 2002), especially the essays by Nicholas B. Dirks and Ann L. Stoler.

Many historians, as well as other social scientists, use literature in their work, usually without a critical methodology, to give their work color and emotion. I suggest that we need a way of reading literary works as both history and literature that does not ignore the formal, aesthetic aspects of literary sources. I see this as a useful concept for the past and future of Indonesian studies. This is what I address in this essay through my use of the Freudian concept of Afterwardsness (*Nachträglichkeit*). I draw on my conception of literary works as "situated testimonies" in literary and historical archives (Sears 2007, 2010, 2013). The idea of situated testimonies is inspired by Donna Haraway's (1988) idea of situated knowledges—knowledge that is positioned ideologically and through its politics of location. But it also draws upon the work of Gayatri Spivak and others who have criticized the field of comparative literature for its failure to engage seriously with non-European works. In her book *Death of a Discipline* (2003), Spivak suggests that one must take time to give the literatures of the global south the same close readings as those of Europe. I believe that giving the literatures of Indonesia and other countries of the global south theoretically informed postcolonial close readings is a way to invigorate the study of Indonesian histories.

NACHTRÄGLICHKEIT, OR AFTERWARDSNESS

Nachträglichkeit is a word popularized by Freud in the late nineteenth century in connection with sex, trauma, seduction, and time. It refers to how an adult, who might see an event as sexual years after it occurred, would not have seen it as sexual, or traumatic, before adolescence. (I provide an example on the next page.) I am interested in the transnational discourse of psychoanalysis that was coming into focus in Europe at the turn of the last century. By the second decade of the twentieth century, psychoanalysis had entered the vocabulary of Indies intellectuals. Psychoanalysis has been important for historiography and literary studies, and especially for Indonesian historiography. It has been incorporated in the literary works of both Dutch and Indonesian authors. The idea has been used to explain the origins of traumas, especially those arising from sexual experiences. For most of the twentieth century, the term has been translated as "deferred action" by James and Alix Strachey, the official translators of the twenty-four volumes of the Standard Edition of Freud's work. The French psychoanalyst Jean Laplanche, best known for his co-authored *The Language of Psychoanalysis* (1967), offered a new translation of *Nachträglichkeit* in the 1990s: *après coup* in French, or "afterwardsness" in English. But Laplanche did not just retranslate the word, he also retranslated the idea.

In his reworking (1999), Laplanche argues that messages given in early childhood by caregivers/mothers/punishers leave traces—what Lacan called enigmatic signifiers.[3] These enigmatic signifiers implant ideas, and these ideas, called "intrusive intimacies" by Laplanche, must be retranslated to work through traumatic memories. Thus, Laplanche, going beyond Walter Benjamin's well-known ideas of translation,[4] gives a broad theory of translation as well as one that involves time, desire, intimacy, and signification. This resignification of the idea of *Nachträglichkeit*

---

[3] See Jacques Lacan, *Ecrits: A Selection*, trans. Bruce Fink (New York, NY: W. W. Norton, 2002), p. 15.

[4] Walter Benjamin, "The Task of the Translator," in *Illuminations*, ed. and intro. Hannah Arendt (New York, NY: Schocken Books, 1968), pp. 69–82.

has influenced my thinking about the field of Indonesian studies and my ideas for rewriting and rethinking Indonesian histories.

Laplanche (1999) gives an example to illustrate his rethinking of afterwardsness. He says that Freud used to tell an anecdote to illustrate his use of the idea *Nachträglichkeit*. It concerned a young man who saw a picture of himself being suckled as a baby by an attractive young woman. The young man was regretful that he did not realize the attractiveness of the woman at the time. Freud focuses on two different moments in the life of the young man to illustrate the change in sexual awareness after puberty. But Laplanche argues that what Freud left out was the third person: the young wet-nurse and her bodily pleasures and enigmatic messages. This subaltern figure, and her desires, were left out of Indonesian histories written by Dutch and other non-Indonesian scholars for most of the twentieth century.

As an example of the workings of afterwardsness for historical writing, I want to take Indonesia's most famous author, Pramoedya Ananta Toer, and his Buru Quartet. Pramoedya wrote the Buru Quartet when he was imprisoned and "thrown away" by the oppressive Indonesian New Order government, from 1966–79. He spent ten of those years in the gulag of Buru Island with thousands of others (ca. 12,000). After the overthrow of the Sukarno government, the New Order government embraced capitalist development and the anticommunism of the Cold War era. While he was in the Buru gulag, Pramoedya first told the story and then wrote the story of Tirto Adhi Soerjo, a man whose life Pramoedya had been researching in the 1950s and 1960s for a history book. Why is Tirto so important for Pramoedya and for Indonesian studies? Tirto Adhi Soerjo, 1875(?)–1918, was one of the first Native writers, newspaper editors, and newspaper owners in the Dutch East Indies at the turn of the last century. Tirto was the first Native to publish in what is variously called low Malay, market Malay, servant Malay, or the command Malay of the Dutch. Whatever it was called, it was the language of the Chinese Malay press in the Indies and of the many hundreds of Chinese Malay novels that had been appearing since the mid-nineteenth century.

Due to the tragic events in Indonesia during the mid 1960s, instead of writing Tirto's story as "history," Pramoedya wrote the story as fiction. He used the story to keep up the hopes of his fellow male prisoners on Buru Island. He embellished Tirto's tale with beautiful *Njai* characters, beautiful Eurasian women, and beautiful Chinese and Japanese women who appeared in the archive of newspapers Pramoedya had been reading with his students in Jakarta in the 1950s and 1960s. Pramoedya winds up writing the story of Tirto in the popular Indonesian language of the people, just as his hero, Tirto, had done. Pramoedya (1985) creates Tirto as Indonesia's first national hero because Tirto was the first Native, possibly because of his periods of exile, to conceptualize the nation as a mixture of all the peoples of the Indies, not just the Javanese. He saw Malay, Javanese, Balinese, Ambonese, Sumatran, Chinese, and Eurasian peoples as part of an Indies state of "subjected peoples" (*bangsa-bangsa yang terperintah*). Tirto was the first non-Chinese Native to write fiction in Malay. He was one of the first Natives to challenge Dutch power in print through his mastery of Dutch.

Pramoedya rewrites the history of Indonesia through his stories of Minke, the fictional Tirto. Pramoedya rewrites the history of the Indonesian National Awakening, as he calls it. Before the publication of the Buru Quartet, "Indonesian" history had been told by the Dutch and other Euro-Americans. Pramoedya changes the history of Indonesia through fiction; he believed that fiction could change history. If we reread Pramoedya's quote on the opening page and then go back to Laplanche's example of Freudian afterwardsness, we can begin to re-identify the characters in Freud's story: the baby is the doubled real-life and fictional Tirto/Pram being suckled by the wet-nurse; the grown-up man is the doubled Tirto/Pram again; and the wet-nurse is the subaltern woman/*rakyat*/*njai* who nurtures the hero and helps him to retranslate her enigmatic messages and intrusive intimacies into a vision of the nation-in-waiting. The hero comes to consciousness through this nurturing and turns the people into the nation. Pramoedya, like Tirto, is traumatized by the possibility of his erasure from history. Tirto died in ignominy after his third exile from Java, and he was lost to history until the work of Pramoedya brought him back to life. Pramoedya identified with Tirto, his exile, and his wrongful persecution by the state. Little is known of the circumstances of Tirto's death in 1918, but Pramoedya writes about Tirto's death in detail through his narrative of Minke in the Buru quartet.

Through Pramoedya's rescue and retranslation of Tirto's story, he reinvigorates his own literary career. Pramoedya also rewrites the history of the Indonesian National Awakening, as he calls it, rescuing Indonesian history from the hands of Dutch and other Euro-American scholars. It is Pramoedya's rewriting of Indonesian history that is accepted and taught today in many US classes of Indonesian studies. Tirto plays a large role in this rewriting of Indonesian history. Tirto was unable to narrate his own story after his exile in 1913 to an eastern island of the Dutch Indies. Pramoedya was unable to invent and narrate the story of Minke's exile before his own exile to Buru. This is a story of afterwardsness. Although Tirto/Minke's story came first, it cannot be narrated until after Pramoedya's exile, until Pramoedya lived through what Minke, and perhaps Tirto, lived through. We have the vision of Tirto and Pramoedya forever retranslating the messages of their youth, trying to get the nation—and their role in it—right. In the last book of the Buru Quartet, Pramoedya (1988) introduces a new narrator, a colonial collaborator raised to the level of the Algemeene Secretariat (Algemeene being the highest body of colonial advisors to the governor-general). This character is Pramoedya's vision of the Dutch scholar and Advisor for Native Affairs R. A. Rinkes who, some scholars today argue, brought Tirto down. But Pramoedya makes this character a Native, a French-educated police commissioner from Manado, with European status like Minke.

The question Pramoedya leaves hanging for his readers is one of authorship. Who is the narrator of the Quartet: Minke/Tirto, the Manadonese policeman, Nyai Ontosoroh—who supposedly takes the manuscripts to France—Pramoedya himself, or, as Hilmar Farid (2007) and Max Lane (2008) have recently argued, the community of prisoners on Buru Island? There is no answer to this question other than the continuing circulation and editing of the books. Does this allow for any Indonesian to become an author of the nation? Or does it suggest that, like Pramoedya on Buru, the books are authored, edited, and reedited by many people? This, again, recapitulates Laplanche's notion of rewriting/retranslating the intrusive intimacies/messages of the past.

WRITING HISTORIES OF INDONESIA

In 1978, Edward Said published *Orientalism*; in 1983, Benedict Anderson published *Imagined Communities*; and in 1984, Donald Emmerson published his essay "'Southeast Asia': What's in a Name?" Nations and whole regions became imaginary overnight as ideas of autonomous history—Jacob van Leur and John Smail's histories written from the point of view of Southeast Asia rather than Europe—were beginning to fade under the shadow of Indonesia's New Order regime and the New Order's narration of history. *Orientalism* had revealed the implication of area studies in imperial and orientalist thinking, changing the field of Indonesian studies, and area studies in general, forever.[5] By the 1990s, in the wake of the linguistic turn and the currency of poststructuralist and postcolonial theories, there was nostalgia for the work of the old orientalists who actually knew things, although they were romantics, as area studies scholars were fleeing from the empiricists and rational-choice people. By reviving Tirto, Pramoedya was able to incorporate the missing "native" into the picture, fulfilling Jacob van Leur's and John Smail's dream of writing history from the perspective of the "native." But this could only be done through literature. The New Order government shut down the writing of history in Indonesia, allowing the field to be dominated by outsiders from the United States, Australia, and Europe. Indonesian literatures and performances of the middle New Order period were isolated, a shriek, or a silence in the theater of people, like Putu Wijaya and Rachman Sabur, both for those who did and those who did not write engaged literature. The engaged literature of Pramoedya or Rendra was banned, and the literature by authors like Putu Wijaya was considered isolated. By the 1980s and 1990s, Pramoedya was read outside of Indonesia, and by the late 1990s, the *sastra wangi* (fragrant literature, seen as a pejorative term by women) writers used sex to cover up their critiques of politics, power, and patriarchy. Ayu Utami's work is the most interesting of this group. Her critique came before the New Order fell. Her work is dark and tortured, showing the damage the New Order wrought and the failures of the Indonesian nation's masculinist activism.

AYU UTAMI AND THE UNDOING OF THE MASCULINIST VISION OF THE NATION

Ayu killed the dream of Pramoedya and Tirto, as the failures of Gus Dur and *Reformasi* may have killed the dreams of Cornell scholars, such as the late and sorely missed Daniel Lev. As Pramoedya said in his blurb on the cover of the 1998 Indonesian printing of Ayu's *Saman*, if he tried to understand what Ayu was saying, he would feel like he was a *tapol* (*tahanan politik*, political prisoner) again.[6] Presumably, Pramoedya did not want to be under house arrest in Ayu's feminist world. Ayu's newest work (2010) offers a complex answer for Indonesia's many problems that echoes the intentions of Pramoedya's work: teach critical thinking to the masses. This message is more radical than that of the Dutch ethicists, the revolutionary fighters, or the parliamentarians. Ayu uses feminist, poststructuralist, and psychoanalytical criticism to formulate her ideas of critical spiritualism and

---

[5] See Jean Taylor's essay in this book, in which she argues that Said's book set the field of Indonesian studies back many decades. This would make a fascinating subject for a conference. As I see it, Said offered a necessary corrective to previous work on the colonial period.

[6] Pramoedya Ananta Toer, "Integritas penulisnya tinggi ... Saya tidak kuat melanjutkannya. Melanjutkan membaca ini rasanya saya jadi tapol lagi" ["The integrity of the author is high ... I am not strong enough to continue. To continue to read this would make me feel like a political prisoner again"], in Ayu Utami, *Saman*, 2nd Edition (Jakarta: Kapustakaan Populer Gramedia, 1998), back cover. Ellipsis in original.

critical thinking. Thus, the subaltern woman—not Ayu herself, but those she writes about—whose voice was missing from the picture of afterwardsness is being filled in, albeit slowly.

In her ambitious 530-page novel *Bilangan Fu* (2008), Ayu makes a departure from her first two novels: the setting is rural rather than urban, the novel ambles through Java's past, rock climbing is a major focus (as is making fun of political correctness), and Ayu appears committed to teaching those who read her books how to think and act critically. If Freudian discourse was evident in her first novels, *Saman* (1998) and *Larung* (2001), Freudian words and ideas are of major importance in this book. The Oedipus complex is explored at great length through Javanese and Sundanese tellings of incest myths: the stories of Watugunung and Sangkuriang. How does the Oedipus story, an ancient Greek myth given new meanings by Freud in the fin-de-siècle period, translate into Indonesian stories today? Watugunung and Sangkuriang are "Oedipal" stories, but they have very different resonances in Java and Sunda, where Greek tragic flaws or Freudian Oedipal complexes were rarely the point of the tales. Ayu does introduce a Freudian Oedipus story in which a father threatens to castrate his adopted son to test the son's loyalty, but it is not the point. In Ayu's novel, the son appears willing to surrender to his father's will because the son does not believe an adoptive son has a right to go against his father's wishes. An adopted son owes his father everything. The Oedipal is deferred, but returns later when the son sleeps with his adoptive father's young wife in response to his repressed anger at his father, his budding sexuality, and the willingness of the wife, who is also repressed and angry, and mute. The husband forces his mute wife and his twelve-fingered and twelve-toed adopted son to act out the Sangkuriang characters as part of a "freak show" that they, and ten other so-called physically deformed characters, must perform for village audiences. Words that have become associated with Freudian discourse, like "libido," "phantasy," "melancholy," "trauma," "hysteria," "schizophrenia," "sublimation," and "the unconscious," regularly appear in the book.

The detranslation and retranslation of Indonesian Oedipal stories through their interactions with Freudian ideas also carry out the work of afterwardsness. Freud's ideas can change the ways in which Indonesian readers understand their myths, and Javanese and Sundanese incest stories can change the way in which Indonesians and Indonesianists understand Freud. Ayu presents twists on the stories that make them her own: Parang Jati, the adopted son, interprets the Oedipus story—and Ayu equates Watugunung, Sangkuriang, and Oedipus—as a story of men trying to get back into their mothers' wombs; the adoptive father *asks* his son if he can castrate him, and the son is too stunned by the request even to reply; and, in the quasi-incest scene, there is a voyeur, a third person. This voyeur is of particular interest because, in Laplanche's reinterpretation and retranslation of *Nachträglichkeit* mentioned above, he focuses on a third person, in his example a wet-nurse, who shifts the attention away from what had been a story of two moments in the life of one person. Through her retranslations of Indonesian myths, Ayu gives feminist retranslations of masculinist Freudian discourse.[7]

---

[7] See Ayu Utami, *Bilangan Fu* (Jakarta: Kapustakaan Populer Gramedia, 2008), "Selected Index," pp. 532–33, where Ayu offers help to the reader and has one entry "Sangkuriang—Watugunung—Oedipus, 533. See also 37–62 for more on this theme. For Laplanche's comment on the third person in his reinterpretation of *Nachträglichkeit*, see Jean Laplanche, *Essays on Otherness*, ed. and trans. John Fletcher (New York, NY: Routledge, 1999), pp. 264–65.

This Freudian discourse is also part of Ayu's attempt to enrich the Indonesian language by circulating foreign ideas and giving them Indonesian translations. Ayu points to the ways in which Freud's ideas continue to serve as a transnational discourse of desire. Ayu's style of writing has always emphasized a search for the right word, and readers—Indonesian and foreign—find her vocabulary challenging. *Bilangan Fu* is more accessible than *Larung*, in fact, and perhaps the success of her earlier work has freed her to reach out to broader audiences. The large novel, in both length and thematic richness, is spawning twelve shorter novels—a so-called mystery series—one of which has already been published: *Manjali dan Cakrabirawa* (2010). The *Bilangan Fu* series, based on the characters from the large first volume, targets a wider audience than its source novel. There is no lack of sex, one of Ayu's trademarks, in *Bilangan Fu*, but, even more than sex, a theme of voyeurism permeates the novel, perhaps part of Ayu's strong critique of Indonesia's relatively new anti-pornography laws by which the State is always watching. A harsh version of this law passed in 2006 and was followed by a modified but still harsh version in 2008.

Ayu introduces phantoms and phantasies in *Saman* and *Larung*, but, in *Bilangan Fu* and *Manjali dan Cakrabirawa*, she differentiates more clearly between the two. In these newer novels, she offers a methodology of critical spirituality to articulate how the New Order, the military, or power (*kekuasaan*) in general, used phantasies and the phantasmatic scenes they enable to scare the people, intimidate them, and, when necessary, incite them to violence.[8] Yet Ayu does not want to ignore or erase the phantoms of the past that haunt the archives: the phantoms and traumas of 1965–66 and 1998. In *Manjali dan Cakrabirawa*, Ayu introduces First Lieutenant Musa Wanara, a military man and an orphan who does not know that his father was a member of Sukarno's Cakrabirawa elite military guard, or that his mother was a member of Gerwani, the pre-1965 women's organization associated with the Communist party. Musa Wanara befriends one of the book's heroes, Yuda (think Judas), who, without telling his politically correct best friend Parang Jati, teaches groups of elite military men the skills of rock climbing. Musa has some remnants from his unknown father, one being a piece of paper with "Cakrabirawa" written on it. Musa knows that Lieutenant Colonel Untung, the instigator of the first military coup in 1965 where six generals and one adjutant were rounded up and killed, was a member of the Cakrabirawa guard.[9] But Musa confuses the Cakrabirawa guard, rightly or wrongly associated with the Indonesian Communist party, and the mystical knowledge of Cakrabirawa or *Bhairawa Cakra* that is supposed to confer occult power on the person who possesses the mantra.[10]

---

[8] See Laurie J. Sears, *Situated Testimonies: Dread and Enchantment in Indonesian Literary Archives*, 2013, for a detailed discussion of this subject.

[9] The *Bhairawa Cakra* is part of an oral tradition of powerful black magic known in Javanese mysticism. It is believed to confer power on its user to defeat one's enemies. See also Ayu Utami, *Manjali dan Cakrabirawa* (Jakarta: Kepustakaan Populer Gramedia, 2010), pp. 33–36.

[10] The military coups of September 30th and early October 1965 are divided now by scholars into two parts: the first coup was partly an internal military coup led by Lieutenant Colonel Untung, the commander of the Cakrabirawa presidential guard. Untung and a few other military men were misled by the mysterious Indonesian agent Kamaruzaman, known as Sjam. At least a few of the coup leaders, including the communist leader Aidit, were members of the PKI (Partai Komunis Indonesia, Indonesian Communist Party), although the PKI central command and the PKI's millions of followers were not aware of the plans for the coup. The second coup was lead by General Suharto and brought to power the New Order government that lasted thirty-two years. See John Roosa, *Pretext for Mass Murder: The September 30th*

Cakrabirawa has many resonances in Indonesia today. It may have become tainted by its association with Untung and the September 30th Movement, but a famous statue of the Hindu–Buddhist Bhairava (I/J Bhairawa) is the centerpiece of the National Museum in Jakarta. The statue, which dates from the fourteenth century, is over twelve feet tall and could stand as a symbol of the religious syncretism that Pramoedya and many orientalist scholars saw as the source of Java's weakness and Ayu sees as the source of Java's strength. In Musa Wanara's attempt to steal the *Bhairawa Cakra* artifact that has been uncovered by Parang Jati and an archaeological team in the novel, Musa is injured and falls into a coma. The *Bhairawa Cakra* artifact falls deep into a hole as if lost forever. As he regains his memory, Musa Wanara will also gain the knowledge of his parentage. In what is presented as a meaningful coincidence, Parang Jati and Marja, the book's young heroine, find Ibu Murni, a former Gerwani woman, and Musa Wanara turns out to be her long lost son. Ayu suggests that all Indonesians are the orphans of 1965–66, of Cakrabirawa and Gerwani, and they, too, must participate in a long process of regaining their memories and acknowledging themselves as children of their newly recognized and damaged parents. This, perhaps, is Ayu's version of Freud's neurotic family romance.

Ayu develops "critical spirituality" to prevent the people, both university students like her three heroes and ordinary folk, from being mystified and duped by superstition and ghosts—like the *Bhairawa Cakra* mantra—while allowing them to continue to follow local beliefs that respect nature and Java's spirit guardians. As Ayu explains critical spirituality (I *spiritualisme kritis*), she has to explain what it is not.

> It is not a spiritual belief [*aliran kepercayaan*]. It's actually a critical path [*laku kritik*]. It's an attitude of critical spirituality. It's critical of truth that is offered by every religion. This critical attitude is not necessarily skeptical. A person with critical spirituality does not have to doubt truth. S/he can have faith. But such a person is also aware that truth is always postponed. God always appears as a mystery.[11]

Ayu also explains, through the politically correct Parang Jati in a conversation with the cynic Yuda, why truth must always be postponed.

> Kindness alone can be realized today. Truth you must bear on your shoulders so that it doesn't fall to earth and touch the ground, show itself, today. If truth incarnates today, it becomes power.

Movement and Suharto's Coup d'État in Indonesia (Madison, WI: University of Wisconsin Press, 2006) for the most thorough research on this topic. See also Robert Cribb, "Problems in the Historiography of the Killings in Indonesia," in *The Indonesian Killings 1965–1966*, ed. Robert Cribb (Clayton, Victoria: Centre of Southeast Asian Studies, Monash University, 1997).

[11] "Aliran ini sesungguhnya bukan aliran kepercayaan. Melainkan sebuah 'laku kritik'. Yaitu sikap spiritual-kritis. Ialah sejenis sikap kritis terhadap kebenaran yang debawakan setiap agama. Sikap kritis di sini tidak selalu datang dengan sikap skeptis. Seorang yang spiritualis-kritis tidak harus meragukan kebenaran. Ia bisa saja beriman. Tapi seorang spiritualis-kritis adalah orang yang sadar bahwa kebenaran selalu tertunda. Tuhan selalu merupakan misteri." See Ayu Utami, *Bilangan Fu* (The Fu Numeral) (Jakarta: Kapustakaan Populer Gramedia, 2008), p. 452.

But you can't just throw truth away like something without value. If you do that, you will become an arrogant person and stubborn, too.

You, one more time, must bear truth so that it doesn't touch the ground and become power.

Do you understand? I don't think so.[12]

Ayu's conceptions of critical spirituality and postponed truth are complex processes that unfold, and continue to unfold in her *Bilangan Fu* series. Not only is there critical thinking and a critical path involved, but also a need to separate many dichotomies that Ayu believes became confused due to the lack of critical thinking in education during the New Order period. Through her work, Ayu, like Pramoedya before her, has taken upon herself a major task: reacquainting Indonesians with their history, teaching them to think critically, and, for Ayu in particular, enriching Indonesian as a literary language. During the New Order, words and images were designified and resignified in order to keep Indonesians from learning about their past. Ayu explains this process clearly in *Manjali dan Cakrabirawa*:

After thirty years where slander and fantasies were spun in blood, it definitely won't be easy for Musa Wanara to accept that his father was Cakrabirawa and his mother was Gerwani. To be able to accept this deep within, he would have to change his view of Indonesian history. He would have to free himself from the prison of state indoctrination which has said that this is a war between hallowed Pancasila and despicable communism. It's a war between good and evil even though neither has a clear form. Everything with form also has original sin. Because of that no one is innocent. The PKI is not innocent. The military regime is not innocent either. Let us not see history as a struggle between the armies of satan and the angels. *Let us see human beings.*[13]

The New Order spun its version of history through the schools, the media, and through its bloody wars against its own people in Aceh and East Timor after the 1965–67 violence. Ayu recognizes the difficulty of undoing and the necessity to undo these phantasies and phantoms of the Indonesian past. She also recognizes that it will take a very long time.

---

[12] *"Hanya kebaikan yang boleh mewujud hari ini. Kebenaran harus kau pikul agar jangan jatuh ke tanah dan menyentuh bumi, menjelma, hari ini. Sebab, jika kebenaran menjelma hari ini, ia menjelma kekuasaan.*

"Tapi kau juga tak boleh membuang kebenaran dari pundakmu seperti benda yang tak berharga. Sebab, jika demikian, maka engkaulah si congkak berhati degil itu.

"Kau, sekali lagi, harus memikulnya, agar jangan ia menyentuh tanah dan menjelma kekuasaan.

"Mengertikan kau? Kukira tidak." Ibid., p. 408. Italics in original.

[13] *"Setelah tiga puluh tahun fitnah dan fantasi berkelindan dalam darah, sungguh tak akan mudah bagi Musa Wanara untuk menerima bahwa dia berayah Cakrabirawa dan beribu Gerwani. Untuk bisa menerima itu dengan lapang dada, ia harus mengubah pandangannya mengenai sejarah Indonesia. Ia harus membebaskan di dari sandera indoktrinasi negara, yang mengatakan bahwa ini adalah perang antara Pancasila yang suci dan kommunisme yang keji. Perang antara kebaikan dan kejahatan hanyalah sesuatu yang tak bertubuh. Tapi segala yang memiliki tubuh memiliki pula dosa asal. Karenanya tak ada yang suci. PKI tidak suci. Rezim militer pun tidak suci. Maka, marilah, jangan kita melihat sejarah ini sebagai pertarungan bala tentara setan dan malaikat. Lihatlah pada si manusia."* Ayu Utami, *Manjali dan Cakrabirawa* (Jakarta: Kepustakaan Populer Gramedia, 2010), p. 240. Emphasis in original.

THE FUTURE OF INDONESIAN STUDIES

After he is released from Buru in 1979, with the last group of detainees, Pramoedya was put under house arrest in Jakarta. He then published a biography of Tirto along with many of Tirto's essays and some of his extant fiction. In his publishing of Tirto's work, Pramoedya (1985) retranslated Tirto's writings to make them more acceptable, he says, to today's readers. Pramoedya makes an archive, collects stories, and struggles to separate history from fiction. While in the prison camp, Pramoedya made a list of all those who died there to preserve their memory. New research by Indonesian scholars tells us that Pramoedya relied on his fellow prisoners in the camp to reassemble his destroyed archive of stories, letters, and memories of the "Indonesian" past. Max Lane (2008) has suggested that this is why Pramoedya blurred the author/narrator of the Quartet, to acknowledge the help he received from others. We may learn more about this in the near future. Pramoedya continually worked to preserve the memories of the past, to teach the people through his work. But his experiences in Buru changed him. They made him both tougher and more compassionate. They enabled him to write and rewrite Tirto's story and thus his own. He wrote about the upstream/downstream "realities" of history and fiction, each one changing the other. As Pramoedya says in the quotation that opened this essay: "A literary reality that contains within it a reorientation and evaluation of civilization and culture, precisely what is not contained in the historical reality." The violence and killings of the 1960s caused Pramoedya to write the story of the nation's birth the way he did. According to Pramoedya's stories, the nation's birth comes after the nation's death.

In *Naming the Witch* (2005), his remarkable book on another period of change marked by regime violence in postcolonial Indonesia, James Siegel writes about the killing of witches in East Java after the fall of the Suharto government in 1998–99. He expands some of his insights from his earlier work on violence in Indonesia and moves toward a very specific study of how and why witches were identified and killed in one area of Indonesia during a time when centralized state power had weakened. He suggests, "Witchcraft makes comprehensible what is beyond reason."[14]

If this essay argues that novels can be seen as situated testimonies of the past, ethnography is also a form of situated testimony. Although ethnography is now practiced in the United States with elite subjects as well as non-elite ones, and in other parts of the world, it has often been undertaken by outsiders who present an outsider's view of another culture. Today, members of mixed or non-mixed ethnic groups carry out research within their own families or communities, but the premise is often that the researcher is not quite a primary part of the community. It is through ethnographic practice, often "participant observation" both qualitative and quantitative, that the researcher hopes to gain insights. When community members are identifiable, ethnographic practice encourages a blurring of several community

---

[14] James Siegel also distinguishes the experience of witchcraft from that of trauma in the case of a man's death from voodoo or witchcraft in Australia. "Belief causes his death. Belief and not trauma. The person who suffers from trauma repeats the traumatic event in his dreams or in his speech precisely because he cannot believe it. He cannot understand what happened to him, even though he can say what it is that occurred." See James Siegel, *Naming the Witch* (Stanford, CA: Stanford University Press, 2005), p. 48.

members to protect individual identities within specific communities. Socio-cultural anthropologists value vivid descriptive writing, first-person narratives, and anecdotal information. These are exactly the qualities that make anthropological writing accessible and engaging. In addition to being a type of situated testimony, ethnography is also a method of secondary revision or elaboration, a stage of Freud's theory of "Dreamwork." There is a series of events and characters observed by an ethnographer, like the events in a dream, and the ethnographer must then find a narrative or theoretical line through which to interpret these events. An ethnographer has a connection and perhaps a responsibility to the rules of the discipline to provide his/her testimony of events and people in such a way as to ring true to readers of the work.

A novelist does not operate under the same constraints as an ethnographer, but novelists have their own attachments to forms of truth-telling. In the wake of the anthropological critiques that started in the mid 1980s with the publication of James Clifford and George E. Marcus's edited volume *Writing Culture* (1986), ethnography has been seen, at least within certain groups of socio-cultural anthropologists, as a poetic form of writing about the Other. Novelists like Ayu Utami and Pramoedya have a commitment to what Anne Anlin Cheng calls a "desire for history" or "documentary desires."[15] Ayu, in particular, sees her work as a form of testimony that mixes historical events with phantasies, psychic life with sexual mores, biblical tales with electronic love letters. Historians, in contrast, are urged to adopt "neutral" and "objective" stances in their work and to hide any ideological attachments they may have. They are taught to avoid "I-statements"; they are taught to erase themselves from their stories, producing what Donna Haraway (1988) has called "the view from nowhere," the opposite of her idea of situated knowledge. This does not mean, in my opinion, that the work of historians is more committed to truth-telling than that of novelists or ethnographers, but that some historians may be more naïve about their ideological relationship to the stories they tell. Today many ethnographers, literary critics, and historians want to make their readers aware of their ideological commitments.

Similar to Siegel's analysis of witchcraft discussed above, Ayu's novels also offer critical interpretations of how phantoms and witches might link to Freudian notions of trauma, melancholia, sadomasochism, and *Nachträglichkeit*. In Ayu's first two novels, *Saman* and *Larung*, Ayu's twinned heroes are both wounded, and one is psychotic. The characters Saman and Larung are both witches who haunt the present in uncanny ways: Saman is a sympathetic witch and Larung is not. It is Ayu's intention to help translate the traumas these men have experienced through the form of the novel. I am suggesting that translation is a larger process than movement between two languages or even two cultures. As Jean Laplanche (1999) says, "In my view, afterwardsness is inconceivable without a model of translation: that is, it presupposes that something is proffered by the other, and this is then afterwards retranslated and reinterpreted." I see this as the work of future historians of and from Indonesia.

---

[15] Anne Anlin Cheng, *The Melancholy of Race* (New York, NY: Oxford University Press, 2001, 143ff.), suggests that this is mainly true of minority writers in the United States, but I am suggesting it is true of many novelists who seek to provide an experience of a past they have witnessed or a future that they imagine.

Works Cited

Adhi Soerjo, Tirto. "Busono." Trans. Joost Coté, Elizabeth Riharti, and Markus Soema. *RIMA* 32.2 (Summer 1998).

Anderson, Benedict O'G. *Imagined Communities: Reflections on the Origin and Spread of Nationalism*. Rev. ed. London: Verso, 1991.

Antze, Paul, and Michael Lambek, eds. *Tense Past: Cultural Essays in Trauma and Memory*. New York, NY: Routledge, 1996.

Antze, Paul. "The Other Inside: Memory as Metaphor in Psychoanalysis." *Regimes of Memory*. Ed. Susannah Radstone and Katharine Hodgkin. London: Routledge, 2003: 98–99.

Axel, Brian Keith, ed. *From the Margins: Historical Anthropology and Its Futures*. Durham, NC: Duke University Press, 2002.

Benitez, Francisco, and Laurie J. Sears. "Passionate Attachments to Area Studies and Asian American Studies: Subjectivity and Diaspora in the Transpacific." *Transpacific Studies: Culture and Capital between Asia and the United States*. Ed. Janet Hoskins and Viet Nguyen. Forthcoming.

Breuer, Josef, and Sigmund Freud. *Studies on Hysteria*. Ed. and trans. James Strachey, with Anna Freud. New York, NY: Basic Books, 1957 [1895], reprinted 2000.

Cheng, Anne Anlin. *The Melancholy of Race*. New York, NY: Oxford University Press, 2001.

Clifford, James, and George E. Marcus, eds. *Writing Culture: The Poetics and Politics of Ethnography*. Berkeley, CA: University of California Press, 1986.

Cribb, Robert. "Problems in the Historiography of the Killings in Indonesia." *The Indonesian Killings 1965–1966*. Ed. Robert Cribb. Clayton, Victoria: Centre of Southeast Asian Studies, Monash University, 1997.

Emmerson, Donald K. "'Southeast Asia': What's in a Name?" *Journal of Southeast Asian Studies* 15.1 (March 1984): 1–21.

Farid, Hilmar. "Indonesia's Original Sin: Mass Killings and Capitalist Expansion, 1965–66." *Inter-Asia Cultural Studies* 6.1 (2005): 3–16.

Farid, Hilmar. "Pramoedya's Buru Quartet." Presentation at the Fifth Annual Meeting of the International Convention of Asia Scholars. Kuala Lumpur, August 1–4, 2007.

Felman, Shoshana, and Dori Laub. *Testimony: Crises of Witnessing in Literature, Psychoanalysis, and History*. New York, NY: Routledge, 1992.

Haraway, Donna. "Situated Knowledges: The Science Question in Feminism and the Privilege of Partial Perspective." *Feminist Studies* 14.3 (Autumn 1988): 575–99.

Klinken, Gerry Van. "The Battle for History After Suharto." *Beginning to Remember*. Ed. Mary S. Zurbuchen. Singapore: Singapore University Press and Seattle, WA: University of Washington Press, 2005.

Lane, Max. *Unfinished Nation: Indonesia Before and After Suharto*. London: Verso, 2008.

Laplanche, Jean, and Jean-Bertrand Pontalis. "Fantasy and the Origins of Sexuality." *International Journal of Psycho-Analysis* 49.1 (1968). Originally published in French as "Fantasme originaire, fantasmes des origines, origine du fantasme," in *Les Temps Modernes* 19.215 (1964).

Laplanche, Jean, and Jean-Bertrand Pontalis. *The Language of Psychoanalysis*. New York, NY: W. W. Norton, 1967.

Laplanche, Jean. *Essays on Otherness*. Ed. and trans. John Fletcher. New York, NY: Routledge, 1999.

Laub, Dori. "Bearing Witness, or the Vicissitudes of Listening." *Testimony: Crises of Witnessing in Literature, Psychoanalysis, and History*. Ed. Shoshana Felman and Dori Laub. New York, NY: Routledge, 1992.

——. "On Holocaust Testimony and Its 'Reception' within Its Own Frame, as a Process in Its Own Right: A Response to 'Between History and Psychoanalysis' by Thomas Trezise." *History and Memory* 21.1 (Spring 2009): 127–50.

Leys, Ruth. *Trauma: A Genealogy*. Chicago, IL: University of Chicago Press, 2000.

Maier, Hendrik M. J. "Flying a Kite: The Crimes of Pramoedya Ananta Toer." *Figures of Criminality in Indonesia, the Philippines, and Colonial Vietnam*. Ed. Vicente L. Rafael. Ithaca, NY: Cornell Southeast Asia Program Publications, 1999.

Morris, Rosalind C. "Remembering Asian Anticolonialism, Again." *Journal of Asian Studies* 69.2 (2010): 347–69.

Pramoedya Ananta Toer (see Toer, Pramoedya Ananta)

Roosa, John. *Pretext for Mass Murder: The September 30th Movement and Suharto's Coup d État in Indonesia*. Madison, WI: University of Wisconsin Press, 2006.

Said, Edward. *Orientalism*. New York, NY: Vintage Books, 1979.

Sears, Laurie J. "Reading Ayu Utami: Notes toward a Study of Trauma and the Archive in Indonesia." *Indonesia* 83 (April 2007): 17–40.

——. "Modernity and Decadence in *Fin-de-Siècle* Fiction of the Dutch Empire." *Indonesia* 90 (November 2010): 97–124.

——. *Situated Testimonies: Dread and Enchantment in an Indonesian Literary Archive*. Honolulu: University of Hawaii Press, 2013.

Siegel, James. *Naming the Witch*. Stanford, CA: Stanford University Press, 2005.

Spivak, Gayatri. *Death of a Discipline*. New York NY: Columbia University Press, 2003.

Strachey, James, with Anna Freud et al. *The Standard Edition of the Complete Psychological Works of Sigmund Freud*. Trans. James Strachey. Vintage: The Hogarth Press, 1959

Toer, Pramoedya Ananta. *Sang Pemula*. Jakarta: Hasta Mitra, 1985.

——. *Jejak Langkah*. Kuala Lumpur: Wira Karya, 1986.

——. *Rumah Kaca: Sebuah roman sejarah*. Jakarta: Hasta Mitra, 1988.

——. "Ma'af, Atas Nama Pengalaman." *Kabar Seberang* 23 (1992): 1–9.

Utami, Ayu. *Saman*. Jakarta: Kapustakaan Populer Gramedia, 1998.

——. *Larung*. Jakarta: Kapustakaan Populer Gramedia, 2001.

——. *Bilangan Fu* [*The Fu Numeral*]. Jakarta: Kapustakaan Populer Gramedia, 2008.

——. *Manjali dan Cakrabirawa*. Jakarta: Kepustakaan Populer Gramedia, 2010.

Wertheim, W. F. "Pramoedya as Historian." *Pramoedya Ananta Toer 70 Tahun: Essays to Honour Pramoedya Ananta's Toer's 70th Year*. Ed. B. B. Hering. Stein: Yayasan Kabar Seberang, 1995: 81–90.

Zurbuchen, Mary. "Historical Memory in Contemporary Indonesia." *Beginning to Remember: The Past in the Indonesian Present*. Ed. Mary Zurbuchen. Seattle, WA: University of Washington Press, 2005: 3–32.

A HISTORY OF
INDONESIAN HISTORY

Jean Gelman Taylor

History is lived and experienced by every one of us. Schools, governments, and the media sustain national myths that include some citizens, maybe many, but not all; they produce a partial consensus, and can stimulate feelings of belonging or outsider status. The writing of history by professional historians is the product of institutions—libraries, archives, academic positions, and research granting bodies. There are also histories written outside of academe by journalists, activists, and enthusiasts. The writing of history by professional and popular authors alike is conditioned by, and reflective of, the individual's own historical time period, class, gender, ethnicity, religion, and other circumstances. The writer's own times throw up the questions asked, and the theories, causes, and opportunities explored.

The state of Indonesian history—in the United States and abroad—is closely bound up with the history of Cornell's Modern Indonesia Project, and so I start here with the CMIP's own history. It was born in January 1954 into a society whose government judged it important to obtain, and quickly, knowledge of the independent states in Asia that had emerged following World War II. The Cornell Modern Indonesia Project was brought into being, then, for American purposes. The research generated was not to be knowledge conditioned by colonial scholarship, but knowledge developed by a new generation of young scholars employing new methods in research, notably fieldwork. These were some of the expectations: contemporary conditions in Indonesia should drive research questions; projects should be devised that were of practical relevance to Indonesia and Indonesians; the methodologies applied should come from the new social sciences; and the new studies would not be buttressed by knowledge of the Dutch language and colonial archives, but founded on knowledge of Indonesian and possibly regional languages as well. The Ford Foundation lent its substantial support to this endeavor, financing the CMIP from 1954 through 1974.

CMIP's first director was the late Professor George Kahin.[1] He had been a postgraduate student engaged in fieldwork in Indonesia in 1948, an eyewitness to

---

[1] Elsewhere in this volume, fellow panel member Rudolf Mrázek also acknowledges Kahin's scholarly impact and his socially committed sense of the academic's role.

the birth of Indonesia itself. His *Nationalism and Revolution in Indonesia* (1952) established conceptualization of Indonesia's modern history as the product of Western, secularized, Dutch-speaking Indonesians who, from a background of politicking in study groups and parties in the 1920s and 1930s, had harnessed popular aspirations for independence to support self-government in the form of a republic. Historian William O'Malley challenged this interpretation in a 1980 essay. He drew attention to pre-war parties championing special rights for their religion, ethnicity, or home region, and to parties opposing republicanism in favor of monarchy. The numbers of these politically active individuals far exceeded membership figures for nationalist parties. So, O'Malley concluded, pre-war politics was not a linear movement from particular to nationalist identity and goals, but a politics of competing claims by many stakeholders. Little notice was taken of O'Malley's assessment almost until the chaotic years following President Suharto's resignation, when it seemed as if Indonesia were breaking apart.

Kahin's sympathy for Indonesia gave him access to the highest levels of its government—access that now seems extraordinary for an academic. In setting up the research agenda of the Cornell Modern Indonesia Project, he consulted with Indonesia's President Sukarno, Vice-President Muhammad Hatta, and former Prime Minister Sutan Sjahrir, as well as with senior Indonesian academics. He persuaded Ford Foundation authorities that funds should be used to support not only Cornell academics and postgraduate students, but Indonesian academics and advanced students from the University of Indonesia, too, for joint and separate research projects in the fields of government and economics. Kahin's vision resulted in studies of villages, family, and household, of regional economies, of Indonesia's citizens of Chinese ancestry, and of urban and legal-administrative histories. In the 1960s, the scope expanded to histories of the revolution and Indonesia's international relations. Indonesians also studied at Cornell University.

THE CMIP INFLUENCE

In April 1966, the first issue of Cornell's journal *Indonesia* appeared. It became an essential, indeed, prestigious journal for scholars of Indonesia in the United States and elsewhere. The first issue announced the journal's mission: it would be open to all disciplines and to multi-disciplinary research; it would cater to specialists and non-specialists alike; it would be informal, exploratory, and spur discussion; it would translate documents and literary pieces from Indonesian into English; and it would publish open letters from scholars in the field.

In that same year, the "Cornell Paper" circulated, a preliminary analysis of the 1965 coup in Indonesia, later published in 1971 (Anderson and McVey). Its conclusions, at variance with the official line already developed within Indonesia by the New Order, brought an end to the fieldwork and academic collaboration that had been so productive. Now research visas were denied or restricted, and fewer Indonesians ventured to enroll at Cornell. This rift did not stop CMIP's impetus for study of Indonesia. The journal continued. It attracted contributions from scholars from outside Cornell. By 1976, *Indonesia* was including book reviews, while it retained an original feature, regular analysis of Indonesia's military in terms of the political careers of officers. As journal and scholars aged, "In Memoriam" notices also appeared in its pages.

The CMIP influence was felt outside the United States and Indonesia. It had a particular impact on Australia. Australia's north had been bombed by the Japanese in February 1942 to forestall Allied counterattacks into eastern Indonesia. A generation of Australians died in Indonesia fighting the Japanese or in Japanese forced labor camps. In the 1950s, and especially after 1959, the fondness Australia's governments had professed for Indonesia evaporated with the Free Irian and Crush Malaysia campaigns. Australia clearly needed Indonesian Studies. Instruction in Indonesian language began at the University of Melbourne in 1956, followed by the addition of history courses in 1959. Australia's first Indonesia specialists were young men who, like Kahin, had experienced Southeast Asia at its birth, often as members of the Allied forces. They were elated by the overthrow of colonial rule and establishment of the Republic of Indonesia.

Jamie Mackie, Herbert Feith, and John Legge, with their Cornell connections, brought a focus on contemporary Indonesia and its economy, labor, government, and regional administration. Theirs was a blend of social activism with a high regard for Sukarno. Reading lists were short. Their students read Furnivall, Vlekke, Wertheim, and Benda, authors whose conceptions had been formed in the Netherlands Indies. For Wertheim and Benda, there was the harsh school of learning in a Japanese prison camp, which they endured as their families in Europe were perishing in the Holocaust. From Feith there was the determination that Australian students should also read political science theorists and anthropology, and a general sense that we should turn our backs on Indonesia's older past. A generation of Australian journalists enrolled in these courses, and there were connections to mobile Americans such as Willard Hanna and Harrison Parker, as well as to Cornell. Australia's founding Indonesianists sent their students to Indonesia and America, not to the Netherlands. By the time I enrolled at the University of Wisconsin, publications were flowing from Cornell, and we read McVey, Anderson, Maryanov, Weinstein, Bunnell, Dewey, and Wilmott.

Australia's Indonesia scholars reflect "traditions" developed at Cornell, Yale, SOAS (School of Oriental and African Studies), and, subsequently, in home-grown centers, such as the Australian National University and Monash. They are more likely to be formed through political science, anthropology, and ethnomusicology than through history. The near universal decline in interest in history and the emergence of new fields of research in the study of Asian societies and cultures, such as globalization studies, diaspora studies, postcolonial studies, sexuality studies, and media and cultural studies, are reflected in appointments made in Australian universities over the past decade. But scholars who have made a major impact on Indonesian Studies outside Australia are historians. Anthony Reid and Cornell-trained Barbara Watson Andaya pioneered "early modern" studies and the integration of Chinese and women into the grand narrative. Heather Sutherland focused attention on Makassar within the larger history of the archipelago. Cornell graduate Merle Ricklefs has dominated the study of Javanese Islam and the interaction of royal Java with the Dutch. Robert Cribb has fostered study of Indonesia's historical geography; Robert Elson has challenged scholarship on the colonial economy.

DUTCH SCHOLARSHIP ON INDONESIA

In 1989, Kahin surveyed the scholarship of twenty-five years flowing from Cornell's Modern Indonesia Project. To grasp what was essentially Cornell, it is useful to turn to the Dutch tradition and an assessment undertaken in 1994. Dutch scholarship on Indonesia was shaped by history, institutions, and a journal. That history was the creation of a colony, which, from around 1850, was spreading into what the Javanese and Dutch characterized as "Outer Islands." In 1851, the Royal Institute of Linguistic, Geographic, and Ethnographic Studies (Koninklijk Instituut voor Taal-, Land- en Volkenkunde, KITLV; now the Royal Netherlands Institute of Southeast Asian and Caribbean Studies) was formed on the initiative of former Governor-General J. C. Baud, former Minister of Colonies G. Simons, and Taco Roorda, professor of Javanese at the Delft Academy (established 1842), which trained candidates for the colonial civil service. The KITLV brought out the first volume of the *Bijdragen* in 1852 as part of this enterprise to educate aspirants for a career in the colonies, and also to bring to a Dutch reading public articles on languages, literatures, arts, law, archaeology, history, and public administration of the colony. Contributors in pre-war years were a mix of colonial officers, missionaries, interpreter–translators, and scholars. The first contribution by an Indonesian was published in 1878. Indonesians—read Javanese—wrote on ethnological and archaeological subjects. Their articles were few in number, around one percent of all articles published during the colonial period.

The *Bijdragen* is the world's oldest journal devoted to study of things Indonesian. The Delft Academy is no more. Instruction in Javanese and Malay Language and Literature, inaugurated at Leiden University in 1877, survives, as do the KITLV and *Bijdragen* in the post-colonial era. The context of Dutch scholarship in the 1950s and 1960s was not new men and new methodologies for the study of Indonesia. For Dutch students, fieldwork was out of the question in the tense years following transfer of sovereignty, leading up to Sukarno's expulsion of Dutch nationals from Indonesia in 1957 and the nationalization of Dutch businesses. Journal articles did not give preference to contemporary Indonesia, its problems, or needs. Historical studies were of the distant past.

In the 1970s, the KITLV and its journal began a process of reorienting. The study of Indonesia was no longer a Dutch preserve. Old colonial hands were succeeded in the journal's pages by professional contributors, and increasingly the journal published in English as it became the international language of scholarship (and the foreign language taught in Indonesia's education system). Since the 1970s, over half the contributing authors are non-Dutch nationals. Indonesian contributors remain few. In the *Bijdragen*'s pages, articles on archaeology, literature, and language studies have given way to cultural anthropology and the arts. Historical studies have centered on the period 1500 to 1800. Publications in the post-war years were dominated by survivors' memoirs of prison camps and the *bersiap* period.[2] In place of interest in contemporary Indonesia, there was a nostalgia fostered by elegant images in books for a time dubbed *Tempo Doeloe* (times past).

---

[2] *Bersiap* ("watch out, be alert") was a warning cry of Indonesian militias in the months following the surrender of the Japanese in August 1945. Dutch people emerging from prison camps were targets of the militias, and gave this term to a period they experienced as targets of Indonesians opposing return of the Dutch colonial state.

The *Bijdragen* now focuses on Southeast Asia, rather than specifically on Indonesia, and extends its coverage to Oceania. The KITLV has built up its impressive library collections on Indonesia, Southeast Asia, and the Caribbean. Despite the ups and downs in Indonesian–Dutch relations, there is now a new era. Indonesians flock to the KITLV. The Dutch open their archives to the whole world through digitalization. This innovation is of especial importance for Indonesians. From their own computers in Indonesia, they can study documents, scanned books, maps, images, and manuscripts with an ease of access not yet afforded by Indonesia's own research libraries. The KITLV opened a Jakarta office in 1969, in conjunction with the Indonesian Institute for Sciences (Lembaga Ilmu Pengetahuan Indonesia, LIPI), to facilitate the collection of Indonesia publications and translation of Dutch works into Indonesian. It has also become an important supporter in Indonesia of new scholarship published by Indonesians.

In her contribution to the stocktaking occasioned by the 150th year of the *Bijdragen*, historian Heather Sutherland linked historiography to relationships between the Netherlands and Indonesia at any one time, to prevailing attitudes, and to the cultural context of institutions and ideas that shape academic research agendas. If scholars primarily mined Dutch archives, their topics and fundamental conceptions were likely to be aligned with those of the old colonial administration, and their periodization would continue to reflect colonial organizing principles, as, indeed, much of Indonesian historiography still does. Sutherland argued that research primarily derived from the contents of colonial archives bound all Indonesian histories within periods such as the British Interregnum and Cultivation System, so that it was not possible to discern fundamental shifts of significance in Indonesian societies themselves.

Histories of Indonesians and Indonesia written in Holland have moved on from these gloomy considerations. A generation of Dutch historians, raised in a world where Indonesia's separate existence is an accepted fact, influenced by the corpus of research from centers like Cornell, informed by fieldwork in Indonesia, conditioned by the resumption of more cordial relations with Indonesia, and the return of Indonesians to Holland seeking their own histories in Dutch archives—this new generation has been producing works of importance in recent decades. They are works of anthropology, and political and economic analysis, but also history, especially social history grounded in the belief that ordinary people need to be written into it.

Mention can be made here of Henk Schulte Nordholt's historical studies, his reflections on historiography, and his driving vision of the necessity, for future generations of Indonesians, to create a permanent record of life as it is lived by Indonesians, rich and poor, great and unknown, across the archipelago. This vision is being realized in the audiovisual archive "Recording the Future," a joint venture of the KITLV and LIPI. Filming, interviewing, and subtitling are the work of the Indonesian team members. They demonstrate how sound and sight can furnish data for the historian and enrich textbook studies. "Virtual Indonesia" (http://rtf.kitlv.nl), launched in Indonesia and the Netherlands in 2011, gives access to more than five hundred hours of recording.

INDONESIAN SCHOLARS AND INDONESIAN HISTORY

What of Indonesian history writing in Indonesia? Indonesian historiography had numerous traditions: from Indonesia's regions in the form of *hikayat* and *babad* (epic tales, chronicles); from Dutch scholarship, especially its tradition of establishing "standard" editions of Indonesian manuscripts; and from academic trends evolving in Western universities. But in Indonesia, as elsewhere, history is shaped by institutions and publishing. And first we can note that not all the new universities in the new country of Indonesia had history departments.

Historians were called by political leaders into service to the nation. Attention must be drawn to the National History Seminar held in 1957 in Yogyakarta. Its findings were written up by the late Soedjatmoko and published in English in 1960 in the CMIP's translation series. A year as guest lecturer in Southeast Asian history and politics at Cornell University followed. Then, in 1965, that fateful year for Indonesians, this preliminary reporting found fuller expression in *An Introduction to Indonesian Historiography*, in which papers from the 1957 seminar were published in full by Cornell. An Indonesian language version was also published.

In the introductory chapter, Soedjatmoko characterized the development of Indonesian historiography as "haphazard," full of gaps, and uneven in its coverage of various eras and regions. He then got to the essential issue:

> There is no continuous historical narrative nor is there any central point of vision [...] Although for some periods there is a more or less continuous historical narrative, the material is organized according to a viewpoint that was not, and in all fairness could not have been, an Indonesia-centric viewpoint—e.g., the Hindu–Javanese, East India Company, and the Netherlands Indies Government periods. (1965, xii)

He called for "a rational plan for the systematic study of Indonesian history" that would encompass a "vigorous examination of material already known, a search for new data, especially of indigenous and general Asian material," and training of historians in "critical method and a thorough familiarity with its use." These new historians would place Indonesian history within Southeast Asian history and draw on the social sciences for concepts, methodologies, and insights (1965, xxvi).

On the threshold of Indonesia's second decade as a nation, Soedjatmoko wrote of the dilemma facing Indonesian historians. They were not just concerned with collecting data and sifting evidence: they were a part of society, expected to produce national history textbooks and national myths that would speak to the temper of the times, the crisis years of early nationhood. For Soedjatmoko, the study of history and history writing is intimately bound up with citizenship and with the freedoms to think and make choices. He characterized societies making up the new nation-state as having an ahistorical view of the world. Indonesia's historians had to educate them to understand "the historical process" as "essentially indeterminate and open to man's deliberate participation in it." History would only be important when Indonesians realized they could make history, that they had choices among alternative courses of action and policies that would affect the course of events.

> Then history ceases to be mere fulfillment of man's curiosity, a mirror for his moral enlightenment or a fountain for narcissistic admiration, but becomes

essential for man's orientation and meaningful participation in the modern world. (1965, 415)

Here is a conviction, formulated in the last years of Sukarno's Guided Democracy, of the "emancipating force of history."[3]

The first generation of modern Indonesian historians were products of Dutch scholarly traditions, the next of training in Indonesia. Some were graduates of overseas institutions. I think here of the late Onghokham, who studied under Professor Harry Benda at Yale University. In the new historical production, centrality was given to Indonesians and Indonesia. But questions of perspective, periodization, and terminology were unresolved. Indonesia was the geographic zone in which Indonesian history took place. That zone was projected backwards in time, a space coterminous with the republic proclaimed in 1945, and seemingly inhabited by people calling themselves Indonesians in centuries before the very term was born in the early twentieth. Important concerns were to produce histories that engendered a loyalty to Indonesia, a personal identification and attachment to it. Sukarno, Suharto, and the times demanded it.

General Suharto took office in 1966, forcing President Sukarno to transfer the mandate of governance to him, the evocatively named, but misplaced, *Supersemar*. Suharto began his administration by crushing all opposition on a national scale, through killings, imprisonment of opponents, and by devising a national credo on what had happened in 1965. In Suharto's judgment, people who were fed, clothed, schooled, and employed would not fall prey to the seductions of communism; they would be quiet, orderly, industrious, and not get in the way of rapid economic development, but, rather, contribute to it. This kind of people needed a narrative that projected into the past a history of unity against colonialism, one that downplayed or obliterated histories of conflicts, whether of class, religion, or ethnicity, that emphasized unities between government and its people, and that portrayed his government as establishing order out of the chaos of the Sukarno years.

Such New Order histories were studied by the Australian historian Katherine McGregor (2007). She argues that Indonesian historiography took a militaristic turn and castigates the late brigadier-general and professor Nugroho Notosusanto for obliterating entire sectors of Indonesia's population from the histories he personally wrote or oversaw as head of the Armed Forces History Center. McGregor also studied museums for which Nugroho was the inspiration, such as the Museum of Communist Treachery and the Museum of Eternal Vigilance, and their collections, dioramas, captions, and guidebooks. She labeled Nugroho's analysis of the coup and its aftermath "hypocritical." His life's work was to place history in service to the Armed Forces to justify its dominating presence in politics and business and in the daily life of Indonesians.

McGregor does not take a stand on which groups in Indonesian society actually planned and launched the 1965 coup. This is not the purpose of her study. Neither does she examine the years leading up to the coup. This is a significant issue, for the reader is left unable to judge why and how the policy of exterminating communism and communists acquired legitimacy. Did Indonesia's communists plan a mass

---

[3] Elsewhere in this volume, fellow panel member Laurie Sears discusses the late Pramoedya Ananta Toer's historical writing through his historical fiction, which was conceptualized in his long years in the *gulag* on Buru Island.

extermination of classes, ethnic groups, and religious groups, as did communist Cambodia's Pol Pot? Did they plan forced collectivization of land and imprisonment of political opponents in labor camps, as in communist-led Vietnam?

McGregor's *History in Uniform* found a receptive Indonesian readership among *Reformasi*-era activists. It was published in an Indonesian translation in 2008. In McGregor's scholarship we can see the long reach of Cornell. Her *isnad* (chain of authorities) would include McVey, Anderson, Feith, and Charles Coppel.

Forty years after Soedjatmoko's *Introduction to Indonesian Historiography*, SOAS-trained Bambang Purwanto published a critique of histories written by Indonesian scholars with the provocative title *Gagalnya Historiografi Indonesiasentris?!* (The Failure of Indonesia-centric Historiography?!). He judges that Indonesian history writing has become disoriented. Its founding principle was to be the antithesis of colonial-centric historiography, but instead history writing in Indonesia became a tool for hurling abuse at others. Purwanto argues that it has shrunk the past by allotting 350 years to Dutch history and colonial culture rather than understanding the Dutch era as part of Indonesia's history and Indonesians' past.

Purwanto argues that, although Indonesia-centric history has succeeded in bringing Indonesian actors to the forefront of historical narrative, it is basically political history. Indonesian historiography does not research and construct a history for the "people without history"—peasants, women, children—so that a sizable proportion of Indonesia's population has no past. Indonesia-centric history, as conceived by Indonesia's scholars, is elitist, formal, and admits only a national or nationalist spirit as the prevailing ethos at any point in time. It has produced the kind of fuzzy thinking that calls Gajah Mada, Diponegoro, and Cut Nya Din Indonesian, as Soedjatmoko also observed long ago.

With *Reformasi*, the term *pelurusan sejarah* (straightening out history) entered general discourse, and it was used to call for an alternative to the New Order's doctrinaire version of Indonesia's history. But instead, Purwanto argues, it became similarly dogmatic. To counteract the single interpretation, Purwanto introduces the concept of empathy. Empathy, he says, is necessary to the historian. It leads the historian to bring into the narrative groups hitherto overlooked, as Indian historians aimed to do in subaltern studies. Along with empathy and critical analysis, Purwanto calls for historical imagination to infuse the history written for its principal consumers, the living and future generations of Indonesians. His new conceptualization of Indonesia's history is not cast as a special and extraordinary narrative, but one brimming with the ordinary life of ordinary people. He calls for Indonesia's historians to supplement documentary evidence with non-textual sources such as paintings, names of people and streets, types of music, symbols, caricatures, and the like. A rich variety of sources, guided by a commitment to the human, should produce new themes as well as new methodologies in the study of Indonesian history.

Most professional historians in Indonesia have considered themselves empiricists, concerned with facts and structure. Purwanto describes his kind of history as deconstruction, and he notes the threats that have reared up in Indonesian circles. Critics have charged that social historians deny the religious sense of humankind and the very existence of God. We are reminded of Soedjatmoko's insistence that history teach Indonesians they are the ones who determine their destiny. Purwanto counters denunciation with the argument that history and fiction arise from the same bedrock of language, that language is embedded in its culture, that language cannot directly represent absolute facts about the past. And he makes the argument that histories are products of the now, that is, of their authors' own historical time period, context, language, and experience as individuals. So history imparts a relative truth, and there is no absolute and single truth about the past. In an Indonesia today, which oscillates between a fondness for the certainties of the New Order and the radicalism of the Salafis, this is a statement tantamount to heresy.

Recognizing and describing the daily life of the masses, Purwanto argues, grants history its humanity; micro-history is history imbued with humanness, a study of institutions and doings of people who are sometimes irrational. The pitfalls of this kind of approach, which Purwanto sees, is that it can be reduced to a kind of antiquarianism, an anecdotal romanticizing of the past, approaches that are unable to explain the contemporary world where change is very rapid. Purwanto refers to the 1957 Yogyakarta history seminar and the perceived need of the times for history to help develop a national identity. The late Sartono Kartodirdjo shifted the focus from straight anticolonialism to other social factors, such as millenarianism, in his study of the Banten peasants' revolt of 1888, but, critiquing from the stance dubbed by Adrian Vickers the "loyal opposition" (2007), Purwanto still finds Sartono's main explanation for the revolt is economic exploitation by the Dutch. He says Sartono failed to examine the internal dynamics of peasant life, such as growing conflicts between *hajis* and other social groups in Banten in an era of economic growth.

Muhammad Ali and Onghokham were social historians who struck out on different paths relative to the rest of their fellow practitioners, but, says Purwanto, they had no followers. Colonial power is only one element among many in the history of Indonesia's past. He gives several examples. Regarding the Cultivation System, Indonesian writers' focus has been on foreign private capital and exploitation, rather than on peasant agriculture and smallholder trade in coffee, off-farm employment, non-formal employment, and the growth of Indonesian hostels and food stalls, signs of what Purwanto terms the horizontal mobility of the indigenous population. He takes as another example the phenomenon of bandits, or *jagos*. They enter history as anticolonial nationalists, but, in political, economic, and social terms, they were criminals. In avoiding analysis of this dimension, Indonesian historiography avoids internal conflicts and tensions. *Max Havelaar* is read only as an anticolonial novel of exploitation by the Dutch, but it actually portrays the reality of repression of the population by indigenous elites.[4] (And here we may note that the Suharto government concurred in this historical interpretation and *therefore* banned screening of the 1976 film in Indonesia.) Sartono, Purwanto says, saw Java's villages as peaceful and orderly; he described the labor of their inhabitants for the *bupati* as part of a patron–client relationship, but termed their labor for the Dutch as exploitation. In Purwanto's judgment, this anticolonial point of view prevented Indonesia's major historian from studying the internal dynamics of villages. Subaltern or underbelly history still does not get attention from Indonesians writing history; that is left to foreign historians.

Heather Sutherland, in the article previously mentioned, noted the decline in history as a discipline. Social scientists sometimes turn to historians for a few facts,

---

[4] *Max Havelaar* is an 1860 novel by Eduard Douwes Dekker (pen name Multatuli) that served as an indictment of Dutch colonialism. It was adapted into a Dutch-language feature film in 1976, directed by Fons Rademakers.

she says; historians turn to the social sciences for ideas. Why have historians of Indonesia—Indonesian and Western—had so little influence on international history debates and historiography? Indonesian historiography *should* have left a major imprint on the historiography of Asia, Africa, and the Middle East. We had J. C. van Leur and John Smail making breakthroughs, commanding us to consider the angle of vision in history writing, beckoning us to come ashore, or to look beyond the car's headlights into the dark places along the highway.

Van Leur died defending Indonesia in the battle of the Java Sea in 1942. His 1934 thesis was published in English in 1955. Smail's landmark essay, "On the Possibility of an Autonomous History of Southeast Asia," was published in 1961. But all this was overturned by the publication in 1976 of Edward Said's *Orientalism*. He turned the clock back for Asian historiographies. By focusing on what Europeans said, did, wrote, and painted, and taking scant interest in what the colonized said, did, wrote, and painted, Said effectively obliterated them from their own histories. Now students wanted to study Europeans in colonies, dissect the kind of material they collected, sneer at the photographs and sketches they made, study representations. Said's book had an extraordinary appeal, perhaps because, in the case of Western scholars, it satisfied a need to study ourselves.[5] Foucault's analyses of power also encouraged concentrated interest on Europeans, rather than on Asians as the subject of their own histories. The great possibilities opened up by Van Leur and Smail for an Indonesia-centric history were lost. The human majority receded again into the background, just as it had been in colonial historiography, to become Van Leur's grey, undifferentiated mass.

In all the words written in the works noted above, surprisingly little was said about the Islamic historiographical tradition. Soedjatmoko characterized Indonesians as having an ahistorical view of life. And yet history writing can be said to have developed inside Indonesian societies as part of the process of conversion to Islam. There was a felt need to connect past to present, to give new Muslim rulers a royal genealogy, and to incorporate royals claiming descent from Hindu gods into an Islamic present. Histories, therefore, narrated how the existing king became Muslim.

But what exactly could be characterized as Muslim historiography? Arabic terms for history are story, anecdote, period, and time. Indonesia's noun for history, *sejarah*, derives from the Arabic, not Greek. Arab historiography began with narratives of single events, told in poetic forms whose meters and patterns facilitated memorization and were entertaining when recited or sung to an audience. At the heart of Islamic historiographical tradition are biography and genealogy. They served as sources of authentication of transmitted information. Islamic historiography evolved in the context of Jewish and Christian historiography. Jews and Christians had laid down their versions and forms of history in the Tanach and Bible; they had a concept of a history of the future, that is, a known end of time by which present actions could be evaluated.

Islamic history was narrated within a succession of years, with emphasis on transmission of received facts and views. The moral purpose of history was to cultivate loyalty to the established order and foster regard for Islamic cultural heritage. History, in the hands of Islamic geographers, preserved mundane knowledge and accumulation of new knowledge. For while historian–geographers

---

[5] Sears also cites the impact of Said, but in relation to the perceived intellectual foundations of area studies.

incorporated passages from previous writings, both acknowledged and unacknowledged, they also sought out new information, traveled extensively, interviewed people, took notes, gave information on the natural world, and referred to documents, letters, and speeches. Popular histories were rhymed romances involving heroes of Islam. One may argue that through them audiences got a sense of Islam and of Muslims as historical phenomena. History was a means of cultivating ideals and aspirations of Islam in the minds of Muslims, more than an intellectual evolution toward evaluating the facts being transmitted.

The demands in Indonesia in the early *Reformasi* years for "straightening out history" have not yet led to a wholesale rethinking of the past, how to write about the pre-Islamic past, or how to understand that colonial history was also Indonesians' history. Instead, historians now wanted to write "correct" versions of history that made Suharto the villain and focused on 1965 and brought justice to victims of the coup, of its aftermath of massacre and imprisonment. Asvi Warman Adam wanted to sue the Dutch for history; GAM (Gerakan Aceh Merdeka, Free Aceh Movement) supporters in Aceh produced a historiography in which Javanese colonialism succeeded the Dutch; and writers of popular Islamic histories argued that Islam had been the religion of indigenous Indonesians already in the seventh century.

* * *

I am a product of Cornell as mediated through Australian academics, Nugroho Notosusanto's history seminars at the University of Indonesia, and John Smail's lectures at the University of Wisconsin; influenced by colleagues in the Netherlands, such as Schulte Nordholt, and colleagues in Indonesia, such as Onghokham and Bambang Purwanto. In *Indonesia: Peoples and Histories* (2003), I tried to implement Smail's call for autonomous history, to tell parallel histories of communities, to narrate histories through byways and minor characters, as well as through big events, and to bring in ordinary lives, problems, and encounters. In discussions, John contended that putting Indonesians at the center of their history could probably not be sustained for the nineteenth and twentieth centuries. His illness prevented him from assessing whether I had managed to continue to construct those centuries within that perspective. Eric Tagliacozzo understood this. In his perceptive review (2004), he suggested I had gone too far in accentuating indigenous agency and had almost written the Dutch out of Indonesia's history.

A new generation of scholars established in US and other universities have learned Arabic. I think of Michael Laffan, Julian Millie, Peter Riddell, Nico Kaptein, and Martin Bruinessen. New riches come from new scholarship based on new sources. We are a long way from Clifford Geertz's confident assumption that Indonesians only got a "scriptural Islam" late in the nineteenth century. In Indonesia, there are scholars of Indonesian Islam, such as Azyumardi Azra, whose research has pushed back the establishment of continuous networks of travel, contact, and study between archipelago scholars and scholars in Mecca to the sixteenth century. There are activists such as Hilmar Farid who study history to respond to the demands of their time, and groups such as Komunitas Bambu at the University of Indonesia and new publishing houses such as Masup and Ombak bringing new histories to a wide reading public. There is great interest in history. Every bookstore in Indonesia has popular histories alongside the self-help books. Soedjatmoko reminds us that historical consciousness is bound up with a sense of individual liberties and active citizenship.

Now, here we are considering Indonesian history in a US context, in the context of 9/11 and of an American president with connections of a personal kind to Indonesia. Indonesians, post-Suharto, have lost their fear of Cornell University. It seems time to build on Cornell's strengths of the past. Taking the liberty offered, I make two recommendations, and they are that the CMIP foster projects championed by Kahin. First, I recommend financial support for a six-month period of residence at Cornell for outstanding Indonesian scholars to rewrite their dissertations for publication. English-language publication ensures an Indonesian scholar access to positions in Western universities, the chance to use great libraries, to attend seminars, and to engage with colleagues worldwide. Such publication helps build a scholar's international academic reputation. Ideally, there should be support also for producing an Indonesian-language translation of such work. The Indonesian publication will bring to academics and the reading public in Indonesia the fruits of first-class research. It will be an inspiration for new postgraduate students, and make a strong contribution to Indonesian historiography.

The second plank of Kahin's platform was Cornell's translation series, whereby Indonesian scholarship was brought, through the medium of the international language of English, to the widest audience. Publication in English puts the results of Indonesian research into academe, and makes it available to be reviewed in international academic journals and presses. Reestablishing Indonesian-to-English translations will provide our students with the results of new research and histories through the different perspectives of our Indonesian colleagues. I would start with Bambang Purwanto's *Gagalnya Historiografi Indonesiasentris?!*

Works Cited

Anderson, Benedict, and Ruth McVey, *A Preliminary Analysis of the October 1, 1965, Coup in Indonesia*. Ithaca, NY: Cornell Southeast Asia Program Publications, 1971.

Boomgaard, Peter, "Historical Studies in 150 Volumes of *Bijdragen*." *Bijdragen tot de Taal-, Land- en Volkenkunde* 150.4 (1994): 685–702.

"Don't Forget to Remember Me: A Day in the Life of Indonesia." Based on "Recording the Future," an audiovisual archive. Leiden: KITLV Press, 2008. CD-Rom.

Kahin, George McTurnan. *Nationalism and Revolution in Indonesia*. Ithaca, NY: Cornell University Press, 1952.

——. "Cornell's Modern Indonesia Project." *Indonesia* 48 (October 1989): 1–25.

Knaap, Gerrit. "One Hundred and Fifty Volumes of *Bijdragen*." *Bijdragen tot de Taal-, Land- en Volkenkunde* 150.4 (1994): 637–52.

Leur, Jacob C. van. *Indonesian Trade and Society: Essays in Asian Social and Economic History*. The Hague: W. van Hoeve, 1955.

McGregor, Katharine E. *History in Uniform: Military Ideology and the Construction of Indonesia's Past*. Singapore: Singapore University Press, 2007.

O'Malley, William. "Second Thoughts on Indonesian Nationalism." *Indonesia: Australian Perspectives.* Ed. J. J. Fox et al. Canberra: Australian National University Press, 1980: 601–13.

Purwanto, Bambang. *Gagalnya Historiografi Indonesiasentris?!* Yogyakarta: Ombak, 2006.

"Recording the Future." http://www.kitlv.nl/home/Projects?Id=20

Rosenthal, Franz. *A History of Muslim Historiography.* 2nd ed. Leiden: Brill, 1968.

Said, Edward. *Orientalism.* New York, NY: Vintage Books, 1979.

Schulte Nordholt, Henk. "De-Colonising Indonesian Historiography." *Politik Kebudayaan dan Identitas Etnik.* Ed. I Wayan Ardika and I Nyoman Darma Putra. Udayana University, Bali: Balimangsi Press, 2004: 65–87.

Schulte Nordholt, Henk, Bambang Purwanto, and Ratna Saptari, eds. *Perspektif Baru Penuslisan Sejarah Indonesia.* Jakarta: Obor/KITLV, 2008.

Smail, John R. W. "On the Possibility of an Autonomous History of Indonesia." *Journal of Southeast Asian History* 2.2 (1961): 72–102.

Soedjatmoko et al., eds. *An Introduction to Indonesian Historiography.* Ithaca, NY: Cornell Southeast Asia Program Publications, 1965.

Sutherland, Heather. "Writing Indonesian History in the Netherlands: Rethinking the Past." *Bijdragen tot de Taal-, Land- en Volkenkunde* 150.4 (1994): 785–804.

Tagliacozzo, Eric. "Review of *Indonesia: Peoples and Histories.*" *Journal of Southeast Asian Studies* 35.2 (June 2004): 366–68.

Taylor, Jean Gelman, *Indonesia: Peoples and Histories.* New Haven, CT: Yale University Press, 2003.

Tibbets, G. R. *A Study of the Arabic Texts containing Material on South-East Asia.* Leiden: Brill, 1979.

Vickers, Adrian. "Sartono Kartodirdjo, 1921–2007, Indonesia's Premier Historian." *Inside Indonesia* 90 (October–December 2007); http://www.insideindonesia.org/edition-90/sartono-kartodirdjo-1921-2007, March 7, 2011.

LANGUAGE, LITERATURE

INDONESIAN: LANGUAGE, LINGUISTICS, AND LITERATURE

Abigail C. Cohn and Jolanda Pandin

Our approach in this section of the volume is rather different from the others. We are not focusing on a particular discipline per se, but rather on the Indonesian language (Bahasa Indonesia, or BI) and Indonesian languages as objects of study from the perspectives of language, linguistics, and literature. The magnitude of this domain of language highlights both the theoretical and practical problems that we face in thinking about language in the Indonesian context. The linguistic situation in Indonesia is fascinating in its own right, because of the incredible linguistic diversity, complex multilingualism, and the interesting history of Indonesian as the national language. Indonesian and its literature also have played a critical role both organically (as the voice of a new nation) and as a political tool as a unifying factor in nation building.[1] At the same time, language is foundational to all disciplines of Indonesian studies serving as the primary vehicle for studying and understanding Indonesia through various disciplinary and interdisciplinary lenses.

Each of the chapters in this section addresses one important dimension of the fundamental question: "What is Indonesian?" Joseph Errington, in his paper "Indonesian among Indonesia's Languages," addresses the socio-political context of the rich and complex linguistic situation in Indonesia, or what within linguistics would be considered to be issues of language choice and use. Bambang Kaswanti Purwo, in his paper "Constructing a New Grammar of Indonesian: From Expectation to Reality," addresses issues of language structure, tackling the myth of Indonesian as "easy" by considering the balance of grammatical and pragmatic demands of Indonesian. Tineke Hellwig, in her paper "Indonesian Literature and Literary Criticism," investigates the development of Indonesian as a medium of literary expression. Both Errington and Purwo focus primarily on the nature of spoken language, while Hellwig turns to the question of written language. This highlights another dimension of linguistic complexity at play. Each of these papers has important implications for language pedagogy—how and why we teach Indonesian—which, in turn, connects with all the other rubrics addressed in this

---

[1] Benedict Anderson, *Imagined Communities: Reflections on the Origin and Spread of Nationalism* (London: Verso, 1983).

volume on the state of Indonesian studies, since Indonesian is one of the central tools or vehicles for investigation used within these other domains.

We first introduce each of the papers, considering their implications for the study of language (whether through its social aspects, its linguistics structures, or its literature) and connections to Indonesian studies, and then briefly consider implications for language pedagogy.

Errington's essay considers Indonesia's post-New Order narrative, which describes Bahasa Indonesia as a national language used to unify the country. First he develops the idea of Indonesian as "un-native," in juxtaposition to the usual native–nonnative dichotomy. This formulation provides the space for the Indonesian state to have used language as a means to a political end, and has led to the perception of language planning in Indonesia as one of the state's great success stories. Errington raises the important question of whether, in post-New Order Indonesia, the image of linguistic homogeneity is not both oversimplified and premature.

Errington considers the question of "what is Indonesian" and what is its relationship with the regional and ethnic languages of Indonesia. One of the consequences of Indonesian being "un-native" is that both the state and individuals can play with its definition. For the state, Indonesian served as an official medium "for information and instruction," not as the voice of the people. For individuals, "In the absence of native-speaking exemplars, then, 'interference phenomena' can easily be used and evaluated as normal, not different or deficient." It is not really clear what it means when someone says that he or she "can speak Indonesian." Errington observes, "Un-nativeness helped not just to make Indonesian a successful part of the national project, but also made it difficult, even under the New Order, to fully regiment that language's form. Now, in an age of decentralization, it seems reasonable to expect the dynamics of local language contact will create more diversity in the national language at the same time it affects native languages."

This observation sets the stage for the issues addressed in the second half of the paper, considering the impact of Indonesian on the regional languages. There is clearly not a uniform outcome, as among other things, the size of the speaking population is critical to the outcome. The impact on languages with very large speaking communities (such as Javanese), where newcomers to central Java still strive to learn (colloquial) Javanese, is very different from that on languages with very small speaking populations, especially in eastern Indonesia where the issues of language endangerment and loss are very real. Concerns about language endangerment highlight the need for integrated and collaborative approaches to documentation of endangered languages between foreign linguistics and Indonesian scholars and students.

In addition to these two extremes, Errington discusses the very interesting linguistic changes and developments going on in Indonesia's two hundred or so mid-size regional towns, which he argues are the loci of change, especially as "zones of linguistic contact between Indonesian and the regional languages spoken by immigrants to these growing, plural communities." On the whole, the linguistic situation in Indonesia is a complex, rich, and dynamic one greatly in need of study and documentation.

Purwo's paper, "Constructing a New Grammar of Indonesian: From Expectation to Reality," tackles the myth of Indonesian as an "easy" language. As Purwo explains, part of this attitude comes from the absence of obligatory grammatical marking of tense and agreement compared to widely studied European languages.

However, this prevailing view does not take note of the complementary complexities in terms of aspect, context, and other effects of pragmatics, notably "expectation." Pedagogically, the risk is that students choose to study Indonesian for the wrong reasons and are surprised when faced with the complexities that learning Indonesian presents.

Analytically, the difficulties stem largely from the inadequacies of the approaches applied to the linguistic analysis of Indonesian. If we start from a vantage point that assumes obligatory tense marking on verbs and agreement marking on nouns, Indonesian will be seen as "deficient." The deficiency, however, rests with the analytic methods, not the language. Purwo argues compellingly that we need a new, pragmatically based analytic framework. Discussing a series of interesting examples of the use of *sudah* (roughly translated as "completed") and other aspect markers, Purwo explains the critical role of expectation underlying the structure of discourse in Indonesian. From this vantage point, it is English that is deficient, for example, for not allowing speakers to convey in their answer to a question like "How many children do you have?" whether they find "two" to be too many, too few, or just the right number.

This analysis highlights broader issues in linguistic research, the first being the need to integrate grammatical and pragmatic analysis; the second being the consequence of analyzing language through either a too narrow or an inappropriate analytic lens. In turn, both of these issues have important implications for how we teach Indonesian, especially to students who are speakers of languages with different dominant frameworks.

Hellwig, in "Indonesian Literature and Literary Criticism," provides a concise and informative historical overview of Indonesian literature and critical studies of Indonesian literature. She addresses the question of who both the practitioners and the audiences are and, in turn, the foci of the scholars engaged in literary criticism of Indonesian literature.

In terms of the literature itself, Hellwig introduces both what is taken to be the inception of modern Indonesian literature, as well as recent post-New Order trends where the literary effects of new-found freedoms are seen. Of particular interest in this regard is the increased visibility of female authors and Hellwig's observation that "Female authors seem to be willing to venture into new linguistic explorations." This highlights the linguistic choices faced by authors in terms of whether to use more formal or more informal varieties of the language, and to what degree to integrate a local flavor, for example, with the use of kinship terms from regional languages. In turn, this leads to the issue of what counts as "literature" and how that determination fits together with popular culture and media in the post-Suharto era.

In terms of the study of literature, Hellwig considers both developments within Indonesia (e.g., the establishment of university programs on literature and literary studies and the founding of literary journals as outlets for the publication of both prose and poetry) as well as internationally. As Hellwig discusses, the study of Indonesian literature outside of Indonesia starts with the earlier philological traditions within the colonial context. More recent approaches include, on one hand, the application of modern literary theories and, on the other hand, increasingly interdisciplinary approaches, drawing together literary studies, anthropology, history, and so forth. Hellwig examines "how Indonesian literary studies positions itself vis-à-vis interdisciplinarity." This is a key question as we grapple with implicit and sometime explicit boundaries drawn between the literary study of English and

European literatures and those of the rest of the world. At the same time, we struggle with the issue of the role of area studies and its relationship with more disciplinarily defined domains of investigation. Hellwig notes, "It is my experience that within the marginality of our area studies the interdisciplinary nature of Indonesian literary criticism renders our field even more invisible." In terms of the potential audience for the literature itself and the study and literary criticism of Indonesian literature, a crucial factor is an increasing body of good high quality translations.

Thus, all three papers have profound implications for the question "What is Indonesian" as a socio-cultural vehicle, as a cognitive frame for communication, and as the medium of literary expression. In the context of Indonesian studies as practiced outside of Indonesia, these complex facets of Indonesian have serious implications for language pedagogy in the classroom and beyond.

Errington's paper leads us to consider the following questions: What styles or registers should be taught? What regional variant(s) should be taught? Is there such a thing as Indonesian outside of a specific social and regional context? What teaching methods are most effective? Purwo's paper critiques the myth of Indonesian as "easy" and highlights the issue of pedagogical tradition and how this might impose a restrictive lens on how we teach a language. How can one teach in a comparative way, building on one's students' prior experiences, while not taking that experience as defining a linguistic reality through which Indonesian is learned? Hellwig's paper points out the importance of translations but also reminds us of the role of style, register, and time-bound works in how we teach Indonesian. Such questions need to be kept in mind both in our day-to-day language instruction and as the community of Indonesian studies instructors works to develop more effective and comprehensive teaching materials.

In closing the introduction to these three very engaging papers, we are reminded that there is no simple answer to the question "What is Indonesian?"

INDONESIAN AMONG INDONESIA'S LANGUAGES

Joseph Errington

With an eye to the past, I try here to situate the Indonesian language in an era defined by both decentralization (*pemekaran*) and diminishing linguistic diversity. For three generations Indonesian has been regarded as the country's dominant language, and so I need to frame the current situation with an eye to its ideological and institutional primacy under the New Order, diverse ways that it has been situated and used by Indonesians, and collateral effects of its entry into diverse ethnic groups, speechways, and communities. A bit of hindsight helps particularly to read against the grain of received versions of the New Order's language project, and in this way better consider newer, pressing questions about ethnic languages in Indonesia that have been increasingly marginalized and are threatened with extinction.

The ideological and institutional distinctiveness of Indonesian, *bahasa Indonesia yang baik dan benar,* cannot be ignored because it is the language of the nation-state but not of any native speakers. The consequences and effects of this unusual condition are not all obvious or trivial, ranging from the practical (for instance, the challenges it presents for teaching the language to foreigners) to the political and cultural (Indonesian's un-nativeness, though never identified as such, is a leitmotif in accounts of Indonesian nationalism and political culture). When considering scenes of Indonesian contact with diverse native languages, it is important to avoid the habits of thought that come into play too easily when it is described as a language spoken "non-natively." This is because qualifiers like "non-native" or "nonethnic," though not entirely incorrect, imply a contrast between the kind of Indonesian in question and some other, "native" kind that, in fact, does not exist. To describe someone's English as "non-native," for instance, is to compare it with that of "native speakers" of the language. Since the category of "native" or "ethnic" Indonesian speaker does not exist, no such comparison can be made. So it less misleading, if also a bit awkward, to describe Indonesian as a language that is spoken "un-natively." Using the prefix *un-* signals that we are speaking of a condition of absence that is not defined in contrast with some independent reference point.

From the earliest days, when it was first dubbed "Indonesian," the language's un-ethnic character was important for the nationalist movement. Later, during the

New Order, the language's un-nativeness facilitated the establishment of a kind of custodial relation between the state and the national language. As primary propagator and definer of "good and true" Indonesian, the New Order could likewise indirectly assert oversight over public genres of discourse that were recognized to be legitimate for disseminating information and propaganda to the citizenry. So the Indonesian language's social history helped blur lines between the kinds of discourse that counted as official (from and for the state) and as public (in and for civil society). Since the fall of the New Order, non-codified, colloquial styles of Indonesian have gained enough purchase in "public" venues to make strikingly clear how circumscribed and limited public discourse used to be.

More important here, though, are issues of contact between Indonesian and ethnic languages, during and since the New Order program of language development. Then, as now, there are firm ideological lines between un-native Indonesian and native languages, including some that resemble Indonesian closely enough to be regarded as related dialects. This became evident, for instance, during a 2000 conference sponsored by the quasi-official Pusat Bahasa on regional and linguistic autonomy. One participant, Ediruslan Pe Amarinza, reminded his colleagues that the Malay spoken in his native region, Riau, is universally acknowledged to be the source (*cikal-bakal*) for Indonesian (2001, 153). But, he also acknowledged, Riau Malay (itself spoken in several dialects) now counts as one among the nation's many regional language (*bahasa daerah*). By forgoing any claim that the native Malay of Riau has some kind of exemplary privilege, he bolstered his alternate argument that, because of its distinctiveness, Riau Malay should be taken as a reference point for defending Indonesian against the "attack" of foreign words that threaten to alienate the Indonesian language from its people (2001, 159).

Overt, ideological assertions of Indonesian's special status do not offer answers to more complex questions about the shaping effects of its un-nativeness among native speakers of hundreds of languages living in thousands of communities. Any effort to deal with this issue will involve what Jan van der Putten (2010) calls in a recent paper to *"bongkar bahasa,"* roughly, "deconstruct the concept of language." Like him, I recognize here the need for a critical review of the full range of meanings and functions of *bahasa* (language) in the Indonesian context. This would explicitly link a critical question about language—"What kind of national language is Indonesian?"—to another: "What kind of nation is Indonesian the language of?" Thinking about language and nationality together presents new challenges in social and linguistic milieux of post-New Order Indonesia.

BAHASA NASIONAL VS. BAHASA DAERAH

Semi-official views of the national and ethnic languages carry over from the New Order era a geographic framing that contrasts the singular language of the nation (*bahasa nasional*) to the many languages of its regions (*bahasa daerah*). As a report from the Pusat Bahasa (2007, 3) puts it: "the Indonesian people should locate *bahasa Indonesia, bahasa daerah,* and *bahasa asing* in their respective positions, each in accordance with its place and function, as determined by national politics." This terminology resonates with the program of language development that was carried out to spread linguistic knowledge across national territory, a program that by 1990, census data suggest, had been largely accomplished.

Reconsidered in light of Indonesian's un-nativeness, though, it seems oversimple to view this program as an unqualified success.

First, consider the difficulty of comparing this program of "language development," centered on an un-native language, with others undertaken in ethnolinguistically plural nation-states. In "the Indonesian case," unlike others, language development occurred in zones of contact between different languages but not necessarily members of different social groups: majority and minority, dominant and subordinate, native and non-native, and so forth. As Indonesian has been learned from or with un-native speaking Indonesians, it has spread through a different kind of contact. This is one reason, the linguist Akio Shiohara has recently argued, that speakers of ethnic languages she has worked with on Sumbawa have developed no movements aimed at "restoring the mother language" (2010, 204). Such situations (and others in Eastern Indonesia, touched on below) suggest that Indonesian's un-nativeness is now an important factor in its continuing spread because resistance to that language is muted by the absence of a native speaking "target" group.

Indonesian's un-nativeness raises two other important questions about the roles and shaping effects it can have in particular locales and communities.

One has to do with Indonesian's structural diversity, which is indirectly shaped as the language is acquired in the absence of native speakers. Obviously, but not trivially, a "second language" is spoken in ways that reflect primary or "native" habits of speech, these "interference phenomena" (accentual, grammatical, etc.) reflecting the shaping effects of that prior language competence. For Indonesians to learn their national language without active interactional engagement with native speakers means that they do not have direct, experiential contact with a kind of embodied reference point: someone with the ability to monitor, evaluate, and perhaps correct their usage. In the absence of native-speaking exemplars, then, "interference phenomena" can easily be used and evaluated as normal, not different or deficient. A Javanese who speaks Indonesian predominantly with other Javanese, for instance, need have little sense that he or she is speaking "a dialect" of Indonesian, or even speaking with "a Javanese accent."

The resulting variation in spoken Indonesian presents an enormous task to those who might want to document a wide range of accents, dialects, and styles of speech. From this point of view, "Indonesian" is really a kind of cover term for what Michael Ewing (2005, 228) describes as a social style or register that is identifiable by ethnically and locally distinctive lexical, morphological, syntactic, and discourse features.

That Indonesian is spoken in quasi-nativized ways, and is "naturally" assimilated to local habits of speech, can have important effects on peoples' senses of difference between local and national identities. This can be seen clearly in communities of native speakers of Malay dialects not just in Riau but the straits of Malakka more widely, coastal Kalimantan, and Eastern Indonesia. Research I have conducted in Pontianak, West Kalimantan, for instance, demonstrates that ethnic Malays need not have much sense that their native idiom differs from Indonesian, even if the two varieties are not entirely mutually intelligible. Members of these communities can maintain a sense of their linguistic autonomy at the same time they use (the local version of) the language without fundamentally altering the ways they speak. At the same time, structural similarities between native dialect and national language make it easy to borrow extensively from the standard Indonesian lexicon, albeit for speaking in a way outsiders would otherwise regard as a distinct, not fully intelligible vernacular.

The second complication has to do with kinds of competences speakers can acquire in un-native Indonesian. James Sneddon (2003, 200), Simon Musgrave (n.d.), and Hein Steinhauer (1994, 759) have rightly raised questions about data gathered regarding language for the 1990 census (and its predecessors). Some people with a passive competence in Indonesian—who consume it in the media but have little need to speak it—might truthfully report that they "can speak Indonesian" (*bisa berbahasa Indonesia*). In the absence of opportunities or obligations to deal with native speakers of the language, it can be unclear whether they have active competencies. In 1990, a cynic might have linked the propagation of this passive knowledge to the New Order's political agenda to create a "floating mass" of citizens, one that needed Indonesian as a conduit for information and instruction, not to develop public voices of their own.

I do not mean to criticize received versions of the Indonesian success story, but to point to an aspect of it that is easily overlooked from the vantage point of architects, implementers, or statisticians who judged its success. Un-nativeness helped not just to make Indonesian a successful part of the national project, but also made it difficult, even under the New Order, to fully regiment that language's forms. Now, in an age of decentralization, it seems reasonable to expect that dynamics of local language contact will create more diversity in the national language at the same time that it affects native languages.

LARGE BUT ENDANGERED(?) LANGUAGES

I turn now to another story about language change in Indonesia, one that began to circulate towards the end of the New Order era in tacit opposition to this developmental "success story." It tells instead of scenes of language endangerment, as Indonesian marginalizes and threatens to "kill" regional languages. I consider this possibility here first with an eye to large or "strong" languages like Javanese, and then more immediately threatened, smaller languages spoken mostly in Eastern Indonesia.

The New Order neither aimed to do away with regional languages nor really made enough concrete efforts to honor fully constitutional guarantees that "the state will respect and maintain regional languages as assets of the national culture" (Chapter 13, Article 32). Despite lip service for ethnolinguistic diversity, and some sporadic efforts to study and document *bahasa daerah* by the Pusat Bahasa, George Quinn (2010, 207) is correct to observe, discussing Javanese, that ethnic languages were generally perceived by the New Order as a "hidden threat to the unity of the nation and the strength of central power."

In the last five or ten years, popular commentary and academic work have drawn attention to Indonesian's worrisome inroads into everyday life among young people in urban Java and Bali. Similar patterns of change might well be found among speakers of Sundanese, Madurese, and, perhaps, other "large" regional languages. Academics like Yacinta Kurniasih (2005) and Smith-Hefner (2007) have documented a preference for Indonesian among younger Javanese in informal interaction, with women leading the way. Such gender-linked patterns of language shift have parallels elsewhere in the world, and so could be understood as marking women's preference for Indonesian as the language they perceive as most likely to expand their opportunities for autonomy vis-à-vis their families and communities.

But many worries expressed about the resulting "endangerment" of Javanese have a particular focus, and reflect particular interests: not all of the language's roughly 75 million speakers of Javanese, but just those participating in a distinctive urban youth culture. When anxieties about knowledge of Javanese are expressed more specifically, moreover, they often focus on polite *basa* styles of Javanese that have never been widely used outside south-central Java, or outside fairly small traditional elite circles.

For reasons noted above, many complaints about the speech of "kids these days" likely have for their targets syncretic mixtures of Javanese and Indonesian. Structural similarities between the two languages, like those between native Malay and Indonesian touched on earlier, make it easy for Javanese morphosyntax and discourse particles to come together with lexical material from Indonesian. So what some foresee as evidence of the demise of Javanese might be seen otherwise as a new kind of syncretic usage, distinctive of and limited to Java, that neutralizes felt differences between languages of an ethnic and national community. Such "mixed usage" could become a key linguistic vehicle for the interplay of different senses of identity, serving as the linguistic ground for what Anderson (1991) called the modularity of a postcolonial sense of Indonesian national community.

Comments on Javanese as a threatened language generally pass over other complicating factors. For instance, Javanese has now gained purchase in mass media that once were the exclusive province of Indonesian; in this *jaman pemekaran*, Indonesians can watch distinctly Surabayan dialect TV news broadcasts. So, too, what was once counted as a marginal dialect of Javanese, *bahasa Using*, has achieved the quasi-distinct status of a regional language, thanks in part to its use in immensely popular radio broadcasts (Arps 2010). Also worth mentioning, though it has not yet been fully documented by scholars, are urban, modern, yet distinctively Javanese genres of verbal art: rap styles that indicate the language is not being spurned by all young urbanites.[1] Finally, there is now evidence (Goebel 2002, 2010) that non-Javanese who move to cities like Yogyakarta and Semarang take pains to learn Javanese there so as to better fit into their new neighborhoods, rather than relying solely on the national language of wider communication. This strongly suggests that in other communities Indonesian's use is also restricted, even as a language of wider communication across ethnolinguistic lines.

Space permits nothing more than this brief catalogue of reasons to reconsider stories about the endangerment of languages like Javanese in light of broader social concerns they reflect. With that caveat and a sense of how these contact situations differ from others in the country, I turn now to the challenges presented by numerous scenes of imminent language death in eastern Indonesia.

DESCRIBING AND DOCUMENTING ENDANGERED LANGUAGES

As of June 1, 2011, according to the UNESCO Atlas of the World's Languages in Danger,[2] at least 146 of 730 ethnic languages in Indonesia are at some level of

---

[1] For more in the popular press, go to http://killtheblog.com/2011/01/02/hiphop-van-yogyakarta/. Several examples of Hip Hop Jowo by RotrA, among others, can be found at http://www.youtube.com.

[2] http://www.unesco.org/culture/languages-atlas/, accessed June 2013.

endangerment, or have become extinct. By far the majority are found in Eastern Indonesia. Of these, by Florey and Himmelman's estimate (2010), just 5 to 10 percent have been documented in any way, and 637 have fewer than 100,000 native speakers. As concern over the global future of human languages has widened, this regional condition is attracting attention from outside the field of Indonesian studies. This "hot spot" of threatened linguistic diversity may now become an arena for linguists seeking new methods and goals of research, and new strategies of cooperation with dwindling communities of speakers.

Until recently, linguists' typological and comparative interests led them to exclude the full complexity of language use in communities. They could *describe* languages' sound systems, grammars, and lexicons by relying on elicitation techniques in one-on-one interviews with native speakers (Errington 2003). From this point of view, the challenge presented by endangered languages is to determine their most basic properties before they cease to have native speakers.

But over the last twenty years, a new generation of linguists has recognized that endangered languages require broader kinds of engagement so as not just to be described but *documented* in and with speakers' lives. This is true at least because the issue of language survival cannot be addressed without considering social conditions needed for linguistic knowledge to be reproduced. This new stance and documentary approach recalls a style of linguistics practiced before the Chomskyan revolution, forty years ago, and requires research techniques that extend well beyond elicitation strategies. Nikolaus Himmelmann, a documenter of endangered languages spoken on Sulawesi, has observed in this regard that the old "structuralist conception of linguistic structures lacks adequate grounding in the social realities of the speech community, a problem that has accompanied linguistic structuralism since its inception" (2008, 337). In other words, language documentation requires linguists to broaden their discipline's purview, and engage in more ethnographically and sociolinguistically grounded approaches.

This widened intellectual agenda brings with it a broader moral and intellectual challenge, as Florey and Himmelman (2010) learned from their work in Indonesia. Language documentation needs to prioritize leadership and the involvement of community members, work that requires nothing less than an effort, as Florey and Himmelman describe it, to "indigenize the academy." And beyond academic goals, methods, and ethics lie the practical challenges of finding support for and coordinating this work. At present, there are few signs that the Pusat Bahasa[3] or any other governmental institution is actively working to coordinate or fund work among academic linguists in this field. It may be that increased communication and cooperation across lines of national and institutional difference will produce more coherent and efficient approaches to the formidable challenge of documenting, and perhaps revitalizing, Eastern Indonesian languages.

Foreign linguists who find ways of sharing new methods of fieldwork, data formats, and databases should also be able to leverage modest resources in stronger networks of cooperation with their Indonesian counterparts. The right initiatives might attract young members of local communities to this kind of work without requiring that they undergo a full course of training in formal linguistics. Their participation could have a multiplier effect for professional linguists who could then

---

[3] Specifically, Pusat Bahasa's Proyek Penelitian dan Pengkajian Kebudayaan Nusantara, or "project for the study and assessment of ethnic cultures."

involve themselves more as consultants in multiple projects, rather than primary actors in just one or two.

In this way, then, Eastern Indonesia could become an important arena for developments in a linguistics that engages the moral, institutional, and practical challenges of doing fieldwork. What once was old may become new again if the study of language contact in this part of the country stimulates new concern for languages as fundamentally social phenomena.

CLOSING REMARKS: CITIES, REGIONS, AND THE FUTURE

For brevity's sake, I have allowed a blind spot in these comments by not critically considering the hierarchical distinction between un-native Indonesian as the national language (*bahasa nasional*), and others as native, regional languages (*bahasa daerah*). In two ways, though, this geopolitical division simplifies important features of the linguistic landscape in Indonesia.

First, as just indirectly noted, this division invokes a simple geographical contrast that effectively equates languages that may, in fact, differ enormously, not least in numbers of speakers and potential influence. Javanese is a regional language like Ndhao, spoken by five thousand or so people on the island of Rote, yet both stand in the same contrast with Indonesian. By the same token, this distinction makes it easy to envision un-native Indonesian as having unitary roles and uses, if not forms, in all regions of the country.

A second, more concrete implication of the geographical distinction is that no particular locales need be recognized as particularly important as scenes of contact between national and regional languages. But there are distinctly important scenes of language change, as of social change: two hundred or so regional towns where perhaps 40 percent of Indonesian people live, what Gerry van Klinken (in press) has dubbed "Middle Indonesia."[4]

In this era of decentralization, regional cities have become more visible in increasingly regionalized political dynamics. But they were important zones of sociolinguistic contact long before 1998 because, as points of institutional contact between the state and regions, they were also zones of linguistic contact between Indonesian and the regional languages spoken by immigrants to these growing, plural communities. The multiplicity of languages, as well as Indonesian, has made for highly entangled zones of linguistic "contact."

Cities have always been important for far-reaching dynamics of language contact in Indonesia, producing distinctively urban patterns of usage that cumulatively affect surrounding communities. The dynamic tension between national center and region is now being augmented by tension between regional urban centers and their surrounds. Such dynamics may, for instance, now be allowing the creation of regional versions of the urban youth vernacular called *bahasa gaul* (Smith-Hefner 2007). Like the standard language from which it so conspicuously deviates, *bahasa gaul* may vary in meanings and uses from place to place, allowing for diversity within unity among a young urban generation.

At the same time, regional urban vernaculars that incorporate elements of standard Indonesian may have different social trajectories in their respective regions.

---

[4] More information on Middle Indonesia as a concept and research project can be found at http://www.kitlv.nl/home/Projects?id=14, accessed June 2013.

My current research provides some evidence that some of these urban vernaculars may be spreading to surrounding areas as what linguists call koinés. This seems to be happening with the Kupang dialect of Indonesian in Nusa Tenggara Timur, for instance, and the Ternate dialect in Maluku Utara. It may be that these urban vernaculars will spread and more directly affect local patterns of language shift than will standard Indonesian itself. Increased mobility is allowing younger migrants to cities to hear and learn those vernaculars as nativized versions of Indonesian, and as travelers between city and country they may introduce them as regional versions of the national language.

For this quick tour of too many questions and possibilities I have taken a cue from Manneke Budiman's (2010) recent observation that Indonesian nationalism is too often taken for granted, along with what is authentic about the Indonesian "national character." My parallel—if more prosaic—line of argument has centered on what might be taken for granted about what is authentic about "the Indonesian language." I have foregrounded assumptions that are now more visible and so more questionable than they were during the New Order era, arguing that *"bahasa Indonesia yang baik dan benar"* can no longer be taken as the primary reference point for understanding language dynamics in the country. If we are now able to bring into view the wider speechways and social life in which Indonesian figures, along with other regional languages, we will be better positioned to hear the political and cultural resonances of what happens when Indonesians speak to each other.

Works Cited

Anderson, Benedict R. O'G. *Imagined Communities: Reflections on the Origin and Spread of Nationalism.* London: Verso, 1991.

Arps, B. "Terwujudnya bahasa Using di Banyuwangi dan peranan media elektronik di dalamnya (Selayang Pandang, 1970–2009)." *Geliat bahasa selaras zaman: perubahan bahasa-bahasa di Indonesia pasca-Orde Baru.* Ed. Mikihiro Moriyama and Manneke Budiman. Jakarta: Kepustakaan populer Gramedia, 2010: 225–47.

Ediruslan Pe Amarinza. "Sumbangan bahasa daerah terhadap Bahasa Indonesia: sebuah tinjauan." *Bahasa daerah dan otonomi daerah: risalah konferensi bahasa daerah.* Ed. Dendy Sugono and Abdul Rozak Zaidan. Jakarta: Pusat Bahasa, Departemen Pendidikan Nasional Jakarta, 2001: 153–64.

Manneke Budiman: "Bahasa Asing dan Kosmopolitanisme dalam fiksi kontemporer Indonesia sebagai strategi redefinisi keindonesiaan pasca-order baru." *Geliat bahasa selaras zaman: perubahan bahasa-bahasa di Indonesia pasca-Orde Baru.* Ed. Mikihiro Moriyama and Manneke Budiman. Jakarta: Kepustakaan populer Gramedia, 2010: 88–122.

Errington, Joseph. "Getting Language Rights." *American Anthropologist* 105.4 (2003): 723–32.

Ewing, Michael C. "Colloquial Indonesian." *The Austronesian Languages of Asia and Madagascar.* Ed. Alexander Adelaar and Nikolaus P. Himmelmann. New York, NY: Routledge, 2005: 227–58.

Florey, Margaret, and Nikolaus P. Himmelmann. "New Directions in Field Linguistics: Training Strategies for Language Documentation in Indonesia." *Endangered Languages of Austronesia*. Ed. Margaret Florey. New York, NY: Oxford University Press, 2009: 121–40.

Goebel, Zane. *Language, Migration, and Identity: Neighborhood Talk in Indonesia*. Cambridge: Cambridge University Press, 2010.

——. "Code Choice in Interethnic Interactions in Two Urban Neighborhoods of Central Java, Indonesia." *International Journal of the Sociology of Language* 158 (2002): 69–87.

Himmelmann, Nikolaus P. "Reproduction and Preservation of Linguistic Knowledge: Linguistics' Response to Language Endangerment." *Annual Review of Anthropology* 37 (2008): 337–50.

Klinken, Gerry Van, ed. *In Search of Middle Indonesia: Middle Classes in Provincial Towns*. Leiden: Brill, in press.

Musgrave, Simon. "Language Shift and Language Maintenance in Indonesia." http://users.monash.edu.au/~smusgrav/publications/LMLS_Indoneisa_Musgrave.pdf. n.d. Accessed June 1, 2011.

Pusat Bahasa. *Laporan Adibahasa*. Unpublished paper, 2007.

Putten, John van der. "Bongkar bahasa: meninjau kembali konsep yang beraneka makna dan beragam fungsi." *Geliat bahasa selaras zaman: perubahan bahasa-bahasa di Indonesia pasca-Orde Baru*. Ed. Mikihiro Moriyama and Manneke Budiman. Jakarta Kepustakaan populer Gramedia, 2010: 1–31.

Quinn, George. "Kesempatan dalam kesempitan? Bahasa dan sastra Jawa sepuluh tahun Pasca-Ambruknya Orde Baru." *Geliat bahasa selaras zaman: perubahan bahasa-bahasa di Indonesia pasca-Orde Baru*. Ed. Mikihiro Moriyama and Manneke Budiman. Jakarta Kepustakaan populer Gramedia, 2010: 207–24.

Shiohara, Asako. "Penutur bahasa minoritas di Indonesia bagian timur: mempertanyakan keuniversalan konsep multibahasa." *Geliat bahasa selaras zaman: perubahan bahasa-bahasa di Indonesia pasca-Orde Baru*. Ed. Mikihiro Moriyama and Manneke Budiman. Jakarta: Kepustakaan populer Gramedia. 2010. 168–206.

Smith-Hefner, Nancy. "Youth Language, *Gaul* Sociability, and the New Indonesian Middle Class." *Journal of Linguistic Anthropology* 17.2 (2007): 184–203.

Sneddon, James Neil. *The Indonesian Language: Its History and Role in Modern Society*. Sydney: University of New South Wales Press, 2003.

Steinhauer, Hein. "The Indonesian Language Situation and Linguistics: Prospects and Possibilities. *Bijdragen tot de Taal-, Land- en Volkenkunde* 150.4 (1994): 755–84.

Yacinta K. Kurniasih. "Gender, Class, and Language Preference: A Case Study in Yogyakarta. *Selected Papers from the 2005 Conference of the Australian Linguistic Society*. Ed. K. Allen. http://als.asn.au/proceedings/als2005/kurniasih-gender.pdf. 2006. Accessed April 11, 2011.

Constructing a New Grammar of Indonesian: From Expectation to Reality

Bambang Kaswanti Purwo

Introduction

Indonesian has been characterized in almost every Indonesian language textbook (e.g., Singgih 1977; Oetomo et al. 1986) as a language lacking the grammatical categories common in a language like English, such as tense, number, gender, articles, and a copular verb.[1] These absences have created a perception of Indonesian as a relatively simple language, especially for students at the initial stage of study. While such an image may be a good advertisement to attract students wanting to learn Indonesian, for example, in Australia, where they may choose to enroll in an Indonesian language course rather than studying Chinese or Japanese, Sneddon (2003) notes that the general impression created by this characterization is false, and that the false image of Indonesian as "easy" may backfire.

> Students who choose Indonesian because it is easy are soon disabused, failing to become fluent "in three weeks" and rarely even after three years of university study. Much of the "drop-out" after a brief period studying Indonesian in Australian universities is a result of frustration that expectations of an easy ride were not fulfilled.[2]

---

[1] The present paper is a revised version of the one presented at the conference on "The State of Indonesian Studies" at Cornell University, April 29–30, 2011, and has been expanded to incorporate the two works, an outcome of my ongoing research on *sudah* (Kaswanti, June and December 2011). I am indebted to the participants of the conference for their enthusiastic support of and response to my presentation. I would like to thank Faizah Sari for very useful discussions of the issues involved during the course of this research. I am very grateful to the anonymous reader for the insightful comments and suggestions on the version I presented for the conference. I am solely responsible for any errors that might remain.

[2] James Sneddon, *The Indonesian Language: Its History and Role in Modern Society* (Sydney: UNSW Press, 2003).

These learners are *kecelé*, an Indonesian way of describing those whose expectation is not met. Indonesian appears to be a simple language to learn for students in the earliest stage of study, as illustrated in (1) and (2), but it turns out not to be the case when they come across cases like those in (3)–(5) in their later studies. For example, a novice learner may assume that constructing a sentence in Indonesian merely entails the sequencing of words from left to right without worrying about the change of word forms. The syntax is simple, as though there were no "grammar"; thus, the student assumes that (s)he can learn Indonesian simply by learning the words.

(1) a. Ia pergi.
        [s/he-go]
        '(S)he went out.'
     b. Mereka di perpustakaan.
        [they-in-library]
        'They are/were in the library.'
     c. Mereka berangkat besok.
        [they-leave-tomorrow]
        'They are leaving tomorrow.'
     d. Mereka berangkat kemarin.
        [they-leave-yesterday]
        'They left yesterday.'

As illustrated in (2), the word *sudah* is translatable into the English *already*, or is comparable to the English perfect aspect.

(2) a. Anak-anak **sudah** tidur ketika kami sampai rumah.
        [child-child-*sudah*-sleep-when-we-arrive-home]
        'The children were already asleep when we got home.'
        'The children had gone to bed when we got home.'
     b. Saya **sudah** melihat lukisannya.
        [I-*sudah*-see-paintings-her]
        'I have seen her paintings.'

The following sentences may illustrate the assumption that the syntax is simple:

(3) A: Saya tunggu suratnya.
        [I-wait-letter-the]
        'I'm looking forward to the letter.'
        Kirimkan segera.
        [send-soon]
        'Send it to me soon.'
     B: **Sudah**, kemarin.
        [*sudah*-yesterday]
        'I did, yesterday.'
        Belum terima?
        [*belum*-receive]
        'You haven't got it?'

When arriving at the later stage in their course of study, however, students may begin to get frustrated when, for example, they encounter constructions with temporal expressions, such as these five: *sudah* 'already'; *jadi* 'end up doing something'; *baru* 'just'; *masih* 'still'; and *tinggal* 'still,' illustrated below. Such constructions are a possible source of frustration not only for language students, but also for textbook writers who must attempt to provide an explanation for the usage of those words. Consider Oetomo's et al. (1986, 71) attempt to help learners understand the use of such words:

> They offer difficulty because it is mandatory to use them in many contexts where they would not be translated into English. Thus, it is best to learn the rule now: whenever these words *could* be used, they *should* be used [emphasis in the original].[3]

The following sentence, which includes *sudah*, is quoted to illustrate such a difficulty. *She's married* is translatable into Indonesian not as *Ia kawin but *Ia sudah kawin*, in which *sudah* must be used [see (5) for the context of use]. Oetomo et al. proposed an explanation for such a difficulty using the framework of the tense-aspect system:

> Its use [*sudah*] is mandatory whenever we are discussing something which is true at a particular point in time, but was not true in the past.[4]

Such an explanation may work not only for the mandatory use of *sudah* in the sentence quoted, *ia sudah kawin*, but also for the mandatory non-use of *sudah* in sentences such as those exemplified in (4) and the last utterance in (5).

(4) Finally she married a third John who works at the magazine company.[5]
    'Akhirnya **ia kawin** dengan John ketiga yang bekerja [...]'
    [finally-she-married-with-John-third-who-work-...]

(5) A: You seem to fall in love with her.
    B: Uh-uh.
    A: But she's married. 'Tetapi ia **sudah kawin**.'
    B: Oh, yeah?
    A: She married her classmate. '**Ia kawin** dengan teman sekelasnya.'

When the presence and absence of *sudah* in (4) and (5) are compared to cases of *sudah* in (2) and (3), the following two questions pop up. Why is *sudah* equivalent not only to the English perfective in (2), but also to the simple past in (3) and to the simple present in (5)? Why is *sudah* absent from the Indonesian translation of *she married* in (4) and in the last utterance in (5), both of which are in simple past? Does this indicate that the tense-aspect framework fails to account for the use of *sudah*?

---

[3] Dédé Oetomo, Daniel Fietkiewicz, and John U. Wolff, *Beginning Indonesian through Self-Instruction*, Second Revised Edition (Ithaca, NY: Cornell Southeast Asia Program, 1986), p. 71.

[4] Ibid.

[5] Example from http://www.sparknotes.com/lit/brooklyn/section3.rhtml, *A Tree Grows in Brooklyn*, chapter seven.

The present paper is an attempt to propose an explanation for *sudah* and the other four temporal expressions using a framework other than the tense-aspect system, a framework that requires that the context of use—the pragmatic factors—be taken into account. It starts with the presentation of constructions that are likely to be frustrating for Indonesian learners, followed by a section on the application of the pragmatic analysis to such construction.

THE POTENTIALLY FRUSTRATING CONSTRUCTIONS

The sample constructions below are likely to frustrate learners of Indonesian, and trigger tough questions. Those questions and answers will be dealt with in the next section.

As a language with no tense marker, the Indonesian verb form remains the same regardless of tense, be it in the present [as in (6a)] or in the past [as in (6b)].

(6) a. I hear and **I forget**. I see and I remember. I do and I understand.[6]
'Saya mendengar dan **saya lupa** [...]'
[I-hear-and-I-forget]
b. **I forgot** to tell you that [...]
'**Saya lupa** memberi tahu kamu bahwa [...]'
[I-forget-tell-you-that] ...
c. Maaf, saya **sudah lupa** itu.
[sorry-I-*sudah*-forget-that]
'I'm sorry, I **forgot**.'

But, as noted in the previous section, several questions come up about the presence and absence of *sudah* in (2)–(5). One of them is why *sudah* turns out to be not always as it is commonly assumed, i.e., marking the past tense, either translatable into the English perfective [as in (2b)] or simple past [as in (6c)], but also into the present tense, as exemplified in (5): *Ia sudah kawin* is the equivalent of *she's married*. *Ia kawin* cannot be used in that sense.

A possible explanation as to why *sudah* is used in the translation of *she's married* (5), but not for *she married* (4) is because *kawin*—lexical semantically—is ambiguous: *kawin* in *she's married* is a state verb, while *kawin* in (4) and in the last utterance in (5) is an action verb. The lexical semantic explanation, however, is not helpful for the cases of the verbs illustrated below.

Relative to the presence and absence of *sudah*, the following two state verbs—*tahu* 'to know' and *lupa* 'to forget'—have different distributions. *Sudah* seems to have no role as a temporal marker when used with *tahu*. That is, regardless of whether *sudah* is used, *tahu* is translatable into English either as simple present or past tense.

(7) a. A: Tak seorang pun tahu ini.
[nobody-EMPH-know-this]
'Nobody knows this.'
B: Saya **tahu**.
[I-know]
'I do **know**.'

---

[6] Confucius.

    b. Ya, saya **tahu** itu, tapi tidak ingat lagi sekarang.
       [yes-I-know-that-but-not-remember-again-now]
       'Yes, I **knew** that, but I don't remember now.'

(8) a. A: Ia ke Yogya tadi pagi.
          [(s)he-to-Yogya-awhile-ago-morning]
          'She left for Yogya this morning.'
      B: Saya **sudah tahu**.
          [I-*sudah*-know]
          'I **know**.'
    b. Saya **sudah tahu** dinosaurus ketika di taman kanak-kanak.
      [I-sudah-know-dinosaurus-when-in-kindergarten]
      'I **knew** dinosaurus when I was at kindergarten.'

With the state verb *lupa* that is equivalent to the English past, *sudah* is optional in (9a) and (9b), but is not appropriate in (9c).

(9) a. Sekarang kamu ingat ... tetapi **saya (sudah) lupa**.
      [now-you-remember ... but-I-(*sudah*)-forget]
      'Now you remember ... but **I forgot**.'
    b. Saya **(sudah) lupa** rasanya jatuh cinta.
      [I-(sudah)-forget-feeling-the-fall-love]
      'I **forgot** how it feels to fall in love.'
    c. Saya tahu itu, tapi saya **lupa** ketika di ujian.
      [I-know-that-but-I-forget-when-in-exam]
      'I knew that, but I **forgot** (it) when I was in the exam.'

Just as taking into account the lexical semantics of the verb does not work with the two state verbs (*tahu* and *lupa*), it does not work either with the following action verbs.

With action verbs, the verb marked with *sudah* may either be translatable into the English perfective [as in (2b)] or into the simple past [as in (10) and (11)]. The presence of *sudah* is obligatory in those three constructions, and also in (12b), but *sudah* is optional in (12a). In order to understand what triggers the use of *sudah*, see the pragmatic analysis below.

(10) Saya **sudah** bilang tadi.
     [I-*sudah*-tell-awhile-ago]
     'I told you a few moments ago.'

(11) A: Did you get my letter?
     B: Yeah, I got it.
    a. Ya, *saya terima.
      [yes-I-receive]
    b. Ya, **sudah** saya terima.
      [yes-*sudah*-I-receive]

(12) a. Ia **(sudah)** berangkat satu jam yang lalu.
      [(s)he-(*sudah*)-leave-one-hour-past]
      '(S)he left an hour ago.

b. Ia **sudah** berangkat.
   [(s)he-*sudah*-leave]
   '(S)he has left.'

Sudah, as a temporal expression, tolerates any time words. It is not bound to any restrictions with respect to the setting up of time in terms of, for example, specificity. Unlike the English perfective, *sudah* may be used for an event or action that occurs at a specific time in the past,[7] as exemplified in (12a) and in the response utterances in (3a) and (11). Like the English perfective, *sudah* may also be used when time is not specified, as in (12b).

Not only is Indonesian accommodating with respect to the choice of temporal markers—e.g., for the use of *sudah.* It also does not offer restrictive rules in syntax. While English syntax requires verb arguments to be explicitly mentioned in a sentence, Indonesian sentences allow verb argument(s) to remain implicit when understood in context. Sentences with deleted arguments are exemplified in (3) and (11). The arguments that *must* be explicitly stated in English are left unstated in Indonesian. Note that it is not only the verb arguments, as in (11), but also the whole clause, as in (3), that may be left unstated, and *sudah* serves as a pro-form of the understood clause.

For other samples of the use of *sudah* as a pro-form in response utterance, see (13) and (14).

(13) A: Pintunya tidak dikunci?
        [door-the-not-be-locked]
        'You didn't lock the door?'
     B: **Sudah**.
        'I did.'

(14) [in the elevator]
     A: Lantai lima.
        [floor-five]
        'Number five, please.'
     B: **Sudah**.
        'It's on.'

Indonesian abounds with constructions with deleted arguments, not only constructions with *sudah* but also, among others, with *jadi.* As the English translation indicates, a one-word equivalent for *jadi* is not available in English.

(15) a. Saya **jadi** (pergi) ke Yogya.
        [I-*jadi*-(go)-to-Yogya]
        'I ended up going to Yogya.'
     b. Rapatnya **jadi**.
        [meeting-the-*jadi*]
        'The meeting is not cancelled.'

---

[7] Or, to use Larson's term, "overt temporal adverb." See Richard Larson, "Time Event Measure," *Philosophical Perspective* 17, *Language and Philosophical Linguistics,* 2003 (http://semlab5.sbs.sunysb.edu/~rlarson/philp_010.pdf, accessed October 27, 2013), p. 248.

c. Rapatnya tidak **jadi**.
[meeting-the-not-*jadi*]
'The meeting is cancelled.'

The core argument is not only deleted, as in (13) and (14), but it is also context-bound. Out of context, the deleted argument may be ambiguous, as (16) illustrates you or we? Furthermore, in (16b) the (main) verb may be left unstated, the interpretation of which depends on the context of use: it may be *go, swim, conduct a meeting*, or any other activity.

(16) a. **Jadi** pergi?
[*jadi*-go]
'Are you/we going?'
b. **Jadi**, nggak?
[*jadi*-not]
'Will you/Shall we go/swim/conduct a meeting/_____
as you/we plan to do?'

The questions posed thus far about *sudah* center around the kinds of verb that may accompany *sudah*, the presence and absence of *sudah*, the comparability of *sudah* with the English perfective, and the function of *sudah* in verbal constructions. In short, I've portrayed *sudah*'s verbal aspect. *Sudah*, however, does not only go with verbs, portraying a completive aspect. It may also go with "durative temporal adverbs" (Larson 2003, 248), as exemplified in (17b).

(17) For many years I have eaten an egg for breakfast.
a. Selama bertahun-tahun saya **sudah makan** telur saat makan pagi.
[for-years-I-*sudah*-eat-egg-when-breakfast]
b. **Sudah bertahun-tahun** saya makan telur saat makan pagi.
[*sudah*-years-I-eat-egg-when-breakfast]

Treating *sudah* as "verbal aspect" by translating the English sentence in (17) into Indonesian (as in 17a) yields an awkward construction. In order to make it sound Indonesian, *sudah* must go with the durative adverbs (17b), not with the verb (17a).

To illustrate these two types of *sudah*, the following two dialogues provide a more obvious contrast. A question with *sudah* in (18) may have a negative answer *belum* 'not yet,' but in response to a question with *sudah* in (19), *belum* sounds odd and *baru* 'just' sounds natural. I will attempt to provide an explanation for the distinction between the first and second type of *sudah* after the section on pragmatic-based analysis.

(18) A: **Sudah makan**?
[*sudah*-eat]
'Have you had lunch?'
B: Belum.
'No.'

(19) A: **Sudah lama** menunggu saya?
[*sudah*-long-wait-me]
'Have you been waiting me for long?'
B$_1$: *Belum. 'No.'
B$_2$: Nggak apa-apa.
[no-what-what]
'It's ok.'
B$_3$: Nggak, baru saja.
'No, just awhile.'

Sudah as verbal aspect (i.e., the first type), as exemplified in (20a), (20b), and (21a), belongs to the same group as *jadi* 'end up doing something,' while the second type of *sudah*—which refers to durative adverbs—belongs to the same group as *baru* 'just'; *masih* 'still'; and *tinggal* 'still'; see (22). These three temporal expressions, just like *sudah*, may either go with verbs (the first type) or with durative adverbs (the second type).

(20) a. Ia **sudah** berangkat satu jam yang lalu.
[(s)he-*sudah*-leave-one-hour-past]
'(S)he left an hour ago.
b. Ia **sudah** berangkat.
[(s)he-*sudah*-leave]
'(S)he has left.'
c. Ia **baru** (saja) berangkat.
[(s)he-*baru*-(just)-leave]
'(S)he has just left.'

(21) a. Itu saya **sudah** tahu [sudah lama saya tahu itu]
that-I-*sudah*-know [*sudah*-long-I-know-that]
'That I knew (already)' [I have known that for long]
b. Itu saya **masih** tahu [kamu tidak perlu khawatir saya lupa]
that-I-*masih*-know [you-not-need-worry-I-forget]
'That I know of' [don't worry, I still remember]

(22) [she-*sudah* / *baru* / *masih* / *tinggal*-one-year-stay-in-Indonesia]

a.		**sudah**
b.	Ia	**baru**
c.		**masih**
d.		**tinggal**

satu tahun berada di Indonesia.

The description of the five temporal expressions thus far leads to the following two questions, which I will discuss after I summarize the present section:

(a) How can *sudah* and *jadi,* as in (15) and (16), be explained using a single framework?
(b) How do *sudah, baru, masih,* and *tinggal* differ from one another, when each may be used with durative adverbs in an utterance like *She has been staying in Indonesia for a year* (22a–d)?

INTERIM RECAPITULATION

The tense-aspect system seems to fail to account for *sudah* (nor for *jadi*). Taking into account the lexical semantics of verbs in the interaction with the verbal aspects—which work nicely with English (Celce-Murcia and Larsen-Freeman 1999, 119–22)—is not helpful, either, as illustrated above in the discussion of various uses of *sudah*.

It is plausible to analyze *sudah* as a verbal aspect, but that will not reveal the whole story of *sudah*. One may also analyze *sudah* as indicating a completive aspect, but only with the understanding that it is *not* completive in the sense of the English perfective. Usages of *sudah* are translatable into the English perfective as well as the simple present and past.

Furthermore, the following piece of data provides another argument that the comparability of *sudah* to English perfective does not work. It illustrates an instance of present perfect in English that does not call for the use of *sudah* in Indonesian.

(23) —Siapa itu?
[who-that]
'Who knocks?' [meaning 'who is it?']
—Lelakimu pulang, perempuan budiman.
[man-your-come-home, woman-faithful]
'Your man has come home, faithful woman.'[8]

The challenge ahead, then, is how to explain the sense of "completive" when applied to the case of *sudah* and *jadi*. The various instances of use of *sudah* and *jadi*, and the other three temporal expressions illustrated above, trigger the need to have two sets of explanations, already formulated into the two questions posed at the end of the previous section. The next section addresses those questions and shows that:

(a) *sudah* and *jadi* are used when an endpoint in a time span is shared by the speaker and hearer; and
(b) *sudah*, *baru*, *masih*, and *tinggal* have to do with the speaker's perspective with regard to a particular temporal line or "durative temporal adverbs" (Larson 2003, 248) that the speaker wishes to share with the hearer.

Such an account requires an independent new framework for a language like Indonesian.

PRAGMATIC-BASED ANALYSIS

In the course of unraveling the intricacies of the various instances of the use of *sudah* (in comparison to *jadi* as well as to *baru*, *masih*, and *tinggal*, such as is presented here, in an earlier section), Kaswanti's (1978, 1979, 1984) study of *telah* and *sudah*, two temporal lexical items, which are presented as being synonymous in Indonesian dictionaries, resulted in a new grammar.

That *telah* and *sudah* may be synonymous is exemplified in (24) and (25).

---

[8] *Rendra Ballads and Blues: Poems Translated from Indonesian*, trans. Burton Raffel, Harry Aveling, and Derwent May (Kuala Lumpur and New York, NY: Oxford University Press, 1977), pp. 10–11.

(24) Kita bergembira *karena **telah** lulus* dari ujian yang sangat berat, yaitu [...]
[we-happy-because-*telah*-pass-from-exam-which-very-hard, that is [...]]
'We were happy because we passed the very hard exam, that is [...]'

(25) seluruh siswa terlihat bahagia *karena **sudah** lulus*
[whole-pupils-look-happy-because-*sudah*-pass]
'All the pupils looked happy because they passed.'

But, as the following contrast between (26) and (27) indicates, *telah* is used in the context of an "objective report," while *sudah* indicates the speaker's subjectivity (Kaswanti Purwo 1979, 1984). It portrays the speaker's emotional involvement. On uttering (27), the speaker verbalized his disappointment in failing to see the grandma before she died. Such a feeling is not there in (26), as *telah* is textual or "non-contextual" in the sense that it is not in an utterance that is speaker–hearer context-bound.

(26) [obituary]
telah meninggal dengan tenang nenek kami Natasusanta
[*telah*-die-with-peaceful-grandma-our-Natasusanta]
'died peacefully our grandma Natasusanta'

(27) ketika kami sampai rumah sakit, nenek *sudah* meninggal
[when-we-arrive-hospital, grandma-*sudah*-die]
'when we arrived at the hospital, grandma had passed away'

The speaker's involvement with regard to the utterance of *sudah* may be negative or positive, depending on what was previously expected (Kaswanti Purwo 1979, 1984). In the case of (28), when the speaker expects to see Prof. Anton, but upon arriving on campus he finds out that Prof. Anton is no longer there, he is disappointed. He is *kecelé*, his expectation does not come true. But, when he does not expect to see Prof. Anton on campus, he feels relieved to learn that Prof. Anton is out.

(28) Prof. Anton **sudah** pulang?
[prof. Anton-*sudah*-go home]
'Has Prof. Anton left the office?'

Such a pragmatic account is what the present paper attempts to deal with under the name of new grammar. This is in line with similar approaches outlined in the work of, among others, Rafferty (1982) and Grangé (2006). The new grammar will deal, first, with what is completive in the sense of *sudah* and *jadi*, followed by a consideration of the speaker's perspective when using *sudah*, *baru*, *masih*, or *tinggal*.

COMPLETIVE IN THE SENSE OF *SUDAH* AND *JADI*

In what follows, the tense-based analysis (TBA) is applied first before the application of the new framework—the "pragmatic-based analysis" (PBA)—is proposed. The PBA takes into account what motivates a speaker to decide to use a particular utterance and not another. PBA, when used to analyze *sudah* across different contexts, may clarify the core meaning of *sudah*, which can be rendered as a timeline that maps the movement from expectation to reality.

Consider the use of *sudah* in the three contexts below (29a–c)—*sudah* in a two-clause sentence (29a,c) and *sudah* in a single clause sentence (29b)—and note which of the three constructions would be clarified by a TBA. The TBA is not applicable in (29b–c), but it might be in (29a), where *sudah* is comparable to the perfective aspect.

(29) a. Pertunjukan **sudah** mulai ketika kami sampai.
   [show-*sudah*-begin-when-we-arrive]
   'The performance had started when we arrived.'
   b. Ia **sudah** kawin.
   [s/he-*sudah*-married]
   '(S)he is married.'
   c. Kalau **sudah** sampai, akan saya telepon.
   [when-*sudah*-arrive, will-I-telephone]
   'When I get there, I'll call you.'

In (29a), of the two sequential actions, *mulai* 'begin,' occurs before *sampai* 'arrive, get,' and it is the prior action or event that is marked with *sudah* in the English perfective aspect.

The meaning of *sudah* in a sentence such as (29a) is more than what the English translation superficially indicates. The basic or core meaning of *sudah* can only be unveiled by the pragmatic-based analysis. To apply the PBA, one must take into account the context of the utterance. A possible context for (29a) is as follows: The speaker (S) drove to the theater and was caught in a traffic jam. He was worried he would not arrive on time to see the performance. Although he did his best to arrive on time, he did not make it and so utters (29a).

Compare the tense-based analysis of (29a), as summarized in (30), and the pragmatic-based analysis of (29a) in (31). The former is represented by a timeline between two explicit actions, while the latter is represented by a timeline linking an (implied) expectation to a real event.

(30) TBA: timeline of two explicit actions
   action/event-1 [prior]   action/event-2
   (*mulai/started*)   (*sampai/arrived*)
   • —————————————————————————>•

(31) PBA: timeline from (implied) expectation to reality
   S expectation   reality (event, fact)
   [worried **he will** be late]   (*sudah mulai*)
   • —————————————————————————>•

The timelines in the two analyses differ in that the two dots in the TBA mark two (explicit) actions (i.e., prior and later action), while in the PBA, the first dot marks the speaker's expectation (he was worried that he would not make it), which is implied from the context, and the second dot is the (explicit) action marked with *sudah*.

The timeline leading from expectation to reality, which serves to illustrate the use of *sudah*, requires a number of comments. The two dots in the PBA (31) constitute a "timeline" in the following sense. In (29a), *sudah* should be interpreted as a time marker that is not associated with a particular point in time but with a stretch of time, i.e., the duration of an event that has a (possibly vague) beginning, middle, and ending. The locus of *sudah* is at the terminal point, marking the end of the event. *Sudah*, then, indicates that the event-in-progress has been accomplished, that it is completed. The starting point is not explicitly stated in the sentence; it is context-bound, the knowledge of which is shared by the speaker and hearer. The beginning may have nothing to do with an event or an action. It could be an expectation, an anticipation, or a plan (of action)—with regard to the (expected or anticipated) event or action.

When the expectation in the context of (31) is not met, the speaker utters (32), with *belum*.

(32) Syukurlah, pertunjukan **belum** mulai ketika kami sampai.
    'What a relief, the performance **had not started** yet when we arrived.'

As the PBA indicates, in the Indonesian utterance (29a), it is not the sequencing of the two (explicit) actions (*mulai* 'start'; and *sampai* 'arrive') that determines the use of *sudah*. What matters is the timeline from prior expectation to the action marked with *sudah*, despite the fact that, as appears in the English translation, the use of *sudah* seems to be explainable with the frame in (30).

An utterance may have more than one prior expectation, as illustrated by (33): whether or not one expects the action (eating dinner) to be completed. When expecting dinner to be through at the time he or she arrives at the location, the speaker is relieved (35). When expecting the dinner not to be completed, the speaker is disappointed (36).

(33) Mereka **sudah** selesai makan ketika kami sampai sana.
    [they-*sudah*-finish-eat-when-we-arrive-there]
    'They **had finished** eating when I got there.'

(34) [S relieved]
    expectation-1   reality (event, fact)
    [expecting eating done]   (it's done)
        • ————————————————————> •

(35) [S disappointed]
    expectation-2   reality (event, fact)
    [expecting eating not done]   (it's done)
        • ————————————————————> •

As for *sudah* in the second context, (29b), which was initially and partly discussed in the previous section under (5) and is repeated in (36), below, the use of *sudah* is mandatory. Notice the presence of *sudah* in the Indonesian equivalence of *she's married* and the absence of *sudah* in the Indonesian translation of *she married her classmate*.

(36) A: You seem to fall in love with her.
    B: Uh-uh.
    A: But she's married.
        'Tetapi **ia sudah kawin**.' [but-she-sudah-married]
    B: Oh, yeah?

A: She married her classmate.
  '**Ia kawin** dengan teman sekelasnya.'
  [she-married-with-friend-one-school]

The PBA reveals the meaning of *sudah* in (29b) and (36), as this phrase is graphed with a timeline spanning expectation to reality, just as *sudah* would be in (29a). The timeline in the case of *kawin*—with respect to the starting point—goes beyond the conventional area of linguistics, however. The kind of expectation involved here takes into account Indonesian culture, as demonstrated in the two quotations below. In Indonesian society, getting married marks a change of status, that is, an achievement in an individual's evolution. It is collectively assumed that any member of society is expected to reach the state (or the terminal point) of getting married. In other words, getting married is a societal expectation.

People in Indonesia gain the status of full adults through marriage and parenthood. In Indonesia, one does not ask, "Is he (or she) married?" but, rather, "Is he (or she) married yet?," to which the correct response is, "Yes" or "Not yet." Even homosexuals are under great family pressure to marry.[9]

Marriage is a very crucial aspect in one's life cycle in the Javanese society since it shows one's development to a higher status.[10]

Thus, the type of expectation expressed when *sudah* is paired with *kawin* is a societal expectation. The kind of expectation relevant for instances of *sudah*, then, requires refinement. There are two types of expectation: "individual," as in (29a), and "societal," as in (38). See the two types of expectations summarized in (37).

(37) individual expectation [*sudah* (30a)]
      societal expectation [*sudah* (30b, 37)]   event, fact

      •——————————————————————————————————> •

The mandatory use of *sudah* also goes with other words of progression, like *besar* 'grown up' and *mandiri* 'independent.'

(38) Ia **sudah** besar sekarang, tetapi …
      [he-already-big-now, but]
      'He is grown up now, almost an adult, but … '
(39) Ia **sudah** mandiri …
      [he-already-independent]
      'He is on his own!' [I already gave my "don't" list!]

For the use of *sudah* in the third context, (29c), consider the tense-based analysis in the following sense. Although the two verbs in the sentence are not eventive (they are conditional) and have the same tense marker (both are in simple present), they are in sequential order, and the prior action is the one marked with *sudah*. The prior

---

[9] http://www.everyculture.com/Ge-It/Indonesia.html
[10] Hildred Geertz, *The Javanese Family: A Study of Kinship and Socialization* (Glencoe, IL: The Free Press of Glencoe, 1961).

action, i.e., the action verb marked with *sudah* in (29c), unlike the one in (29a), is not in the perfective aspect when translated into English.

If analyzed and graphed with PBA, the two verbs marked with *sudah* in (29a) and (29c) share the same timeline from expectation to reality. They differ in that the progression of the timeline in (29a) is from the speaker's expectation to reality, while the one in (29c) is from the hearer's expectation to reality.

To illustrate the case of (29c) in another construction, consider (40), which maps the timeline from the hearer's anticipation to reality.

(40) Sebentar. Aku belum siap. Nah, sekarang **sudah** siap.
    'Just a second, I'm not ready. Now I'm ready.'[11]

Now that all of the three instances of the use of *sudah* have gone through the PBA, consider the types of expectation represented in (41).

(41) [timeline from expectation to reality]
    S expectation [*sudah* (29a)]
    H anticipation [*sudah* (29c)]   event, fact
    societal expectation [*sudah* (29b)]
    •————————————————————————>•

Is the PBA applicable to words other than *sudah*? Consider *jadi*, which was initially and partially discussed in the previous section under (15) and (16), in the following examples. As the English translation indicates, the one-word equivalence is not available in English. It may be helpful to refer to *jadi* as a completive (or, more accurately, resultative) aspect.

(42) a. Saya **jadi** (pergi) ke Yogya.
        [I-*jadi*-(go)-to-Yogya]
        'I ended up going to Yogya.'
     b. Saya tidak **jadi** (pergi) ke Yogya.
        [I-not-*jadi*-(go)-to-Yogya]
        'I didn't get to go to Yogya.'

The same framework that was applied to the instances of the use of *sudah* may also be applicable to explain instances of *jadi* in (42). Utterances (42a, b), for example, make sense given the condition that the interlocutor knows the speaker's plan to go to Yogya. The plan to travel to Yogya is the starting point of the timeline from expectation (or plan) to reality. The speaker's plan to travel to Yogya is old information. The cancellation (42b) or non-cancellation (42a)—i.e., the end point—for the interlocutor is an event that constitutes new information; thus, it is necessary for the speaker to utter (42a) or (42b). Like *sudah*, *jadi* marks the terminal point.

(43) starting point   end point
    S–H shared knowledge of the plan   event, fact
    •————————————————————————>•

All utterances with *jadi* in (42) imply that both the speaker and the interlocutor share a particular plan that they anticipate will be executed by the speaker in the

---

[11] Oetomo et al., *Beginning Indonesian through Self-Instruction*, p. 549.

(near) future. The plan that this shared information concerns may or may not be carried out, may or may not be acted upon. Either way, *jadi* is used to mark the plan executed by the speaker, the knowledge of which is shared by the speaker and the interlocutor. With *jadi* added to the PBA, the summary appears as in (44).

(44) [timeline from expectation to reality]
    S expectation [*sudah* (29a)]
    H anticipation [*sudah* (29c)]   event, fact
    S–H shared knowledge of the plan [*jadi* (42)]
    societal expectation [*sudah* (29b)]
    •——————————————————————>•

SPEAKER'S PERSPECTIVE IN THE USE OF *SUDAH, BARU, MASIH,* OR *TINGGAL*

The words *sudah* and *jadi* under discussion thus far modify either the verb or (predicative) adjective. The predicate to which *sudah* or *jadi* is attached may be deleted if the predicate is understood from the context. In other words, *sudah* as in (13), and *jadi* as in (16), may serve as the pro-form of the verb.

The word *sudah*, however, may not only go with the verb, but also with time periods or durative adverbs, as exemplified in (46), below. Interestingly, *sudah* is not the only marker for such a construction, and in order to unveil the full meaning of *sudah*, one must cross-examine the other markers: *baru, masih, tinggal*. The discussion of these four temporal markers follows this order: when they go with time periods or durative adverbs, state verbs, and action verbs.

Compare the use of time periods in English with no temporal markers (45) and the ones in Indonesian that require the speaker choose which temporal marker to use. Basically, (46) is the translation of the English utterances in (45), but Indonesian provides the speaker with a choice in terms of what perspective to take with respect to the period of time.

(45) A: How long have you been in Ithaca
    B: A week.

(46) A: Berapa lama di Ithaca? [how-long-in-Ithaca]
    B_1:   **Baru**
    B_2:   **Sudah**
    B_3:   **Masih**   satu minggu [one-week]
    B_4:   **Tinggal**

    'I've been staying in Ithaca for a week' [for *baru* and *sudah*]
    'I'll be staying in Ithaca for another week' [for *masih* and *tinggal*]

The speaker's perspective in (46) is within the context of the frame of a "timeline from expectation to reality." The perspective under question here may have to do with either the parameter (a) closed vs. open, or (b) long vs. short.

The two sentences that include *tidak* and *belum* in (47) illustrate the difference between closed and open. In (47a), *tidak* is "closed" in the sense that no meal will be taken on that day, but in (47b), *belum* is "open" in that the speaker is likely to have a meal on that day.

(47) a. Saya **tidak** makan hari ini. [I-not-eat-day-this]
　　　'I don't/won't eat today.'
　　b. Saya **belum** makan hari ini. [I-not yet-eat-day-this]
　　　'I haven't had any meal today.'

(48) A: How many children do you have?
　　　B₁: Two.
　　　B₂: Just two.
　　　B₃: **Baru** dua.
　　　B₄: **Sudah** dua.

There can be two possible answers to the question in (48) in English, where in Indonesian, no fewer than to possible answer may be used: with *baru* or *sudah*. If *baru* is used, it is open: the speaker is expecting to have more children. If *sudah* is used, it is closed: the speaker does not expect to have more children.

To illustrate a perspective in terms of long and short, consider (49).

(49) [when presenting a paper at a conference]
　　　A: How much time do I have left?
　　　B: Ten minutes.
　　　B₁: **Masih** sepuluh menit.
　　　B₂: **Tinggal** sepuluh menit.

If the speaker chooses to say *masih sepuluh menit* —'masih ten minutes'—then, from the speaker's perspective, ten minutes is long enough to go through the rest of the materials. If she says *tinggal sepuluh menit*—'tinggal ten minutes'—then she is indicating that she thinks ten minutes is too short to cover the rest of the materials. The former is similar to "take your time," while the latter means "you'd better hurry up."

A possible piece of evidence for this is to test out which of these two go with: *lama* 'long' (of duration) or *sebentar* 'for a moment.' *Masih* opts for the former, while *tinggal* for the latter: *masih lama* vs. *tinggal sebentar*. Such a test may also be used to reveal the difference between *sudah* and *baru*: *sudah lama* vs. *baru sebentar*.

The question remains: within the PBA frame of "timeline from expectation to reality," what is the difference between *baru* and *sudah*, on the one hand, and *masih* and *tinggal*, on the other hand, taking into account the parameter "open–closed" and "long–short"? Before the discussion of their differences, the syntactic features of the four words that goes with durative verbs and the one that goes with verbs require a word of comment.

With durative adverbs, the four temporal expressions are in phrase level. With verbs, they are in clause or sentence level. They are verbal aspect in the latter, but not in the former.

Sudah, however, as elaborated in the present section—which is in phrase level or which goes with durative adverbs—shares a common locus with *baru*. In sentence level, *sudah* as verbal aspect is at the terminal point, marking the end of an event. In phrase level, however, together with *baru*, *sudah* is in the initial stage within the context of the time period of the sentence to which the durative adverb is attached.

The difference between *baru*/*sudah* and *masih*/*tinggal* lies in the locus in terms of the timeline. The locus of *baru*/*sudah* is in the *initial* stage, while *masih*/*tinggal* are situated at the *final* stage of the timeline. In (46), for B₁ and B₂ one week is the initial stage of their stay in Ithaca, while it is one more week to go for B$_3$ and B$_4$; one week is the final stage of their stay in Ithaca. Consider the summary in the graph below.

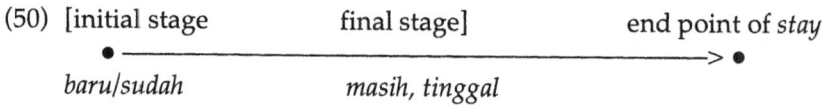

(50) [initial stage   final stage]   end point of *stay*

    ● ————————————————————————————————> ●

    baru/sudah   *masih, tinggal*

Some of the senses as graphed in (50) may be explainable using tense-aspect framework. The initial stage pinpoints a context referring to past time, while the final stage references a context heading for the future, as reflected in the English translation of (46) and (51). Using the pragmatic-based analysis, one may say that *baru* and *sudah* (in phrase level)—within the time line of the larger context of the whole sentence in (46)—are in the initial stage, while *masih* and *tinggal* are in the final stage. The four possible utterances in (46) have in common in that when uttering each of the four, the speaker is in Ithaca—the staying at Ithaca has not reached an end point.

    To sum up, the difference between each of the four, in the phrase level, is most obviously apparent in (51). *Baru* and *sudah* are in the initial stage of the timeline within the context of sentence level: *baru* is open and short, while *sudah* is closed and long. *Masih* and *tinggal* are in the final stage of the timeline within the context of sentence level: *masih* is open and long, while *tinggal* is closed and short.

    (51) a. **Baru** satu minggu, tenang-tenang sajalah.   [open, short]
        [*baru*-one-week, calm-calm-EMPHATIC PARTICLE]
        'It's only been a week, just relax.'
      b. Nggak terasa **sudah** satu minggu.   [closed, long]
        [not-feel-*sudah*-one-week]
        'It doesn't seem like I have been here for a week.'
        'I can't believe I've been here for a week.'
      c. **Masih** satu minggu.   [open, long]
        'You still have a week left.'
      d. **Tinggal** satu minggu.   [closed, short]
        'You only have a week left.'

Sudah with durative adverbs, temporal expressions in phrase level, as elaborated from (46) to (51), is in the initial stage of the timeline. *Sudah* with verbs, temporal expressions in sentence level, as graphed in (31), the locus of which is at the terminal point, marks the end of an event—— *sudah* as a verbal aspect, a completive aspect.

    In a construction with state verbs, as exemplified in (52), of the four temporal adverbs, *tinggal* may not be used, for reasons that I have not yet explained. The use of the three utterances in (52) have in common that each asserts something that is contrary to the hearer's state of knowledge or expectation.

    (52) a. Itu saya **baru** tahu [tadi pagi ada yang kasih tahu]
        that-I-*baru*-know [last-morning-exist-give-knowledge]
        'That I just knew' [(just) this morning someone told me]
      b. Itu saya **sudah** tahu [sudah lama saya tahu itu]
        that-I-*sudah*-know [*sudah*-long-I-know-that]
        'That I knew (already)' [I have known that for long]

c. Itu saya **masih** tahu [kamu tidak perlu khawatir saya lupa]
   that-I-*masih*-know [you-not-need-worry-I-forget]
   'That I know of' [don't worry, I still remember]

With *baru* (52a), the information has just entered into the beginning stage of my state of knowledge. With *sudah* (52b), the information has been there for a long time. The use of *masih* in (52c) indicates that the information is still there; I am not at the stage of losing the information (my knowledge is not fading or coming to an end yet).

In a construction with action verbs, however, as exemplified in (53), the four of them may be used in the context of paying for the bill at the cashier. With *baru* and *sudah*, the payment has been accomplished. With *baru*, the action took place awhile ago, while with *sudah* it was even longer ago. The use of *masih* indicates that the action of paying for the bill has not come to an end, with no clue as to when it will be accomplished. With *tinggal*, the speaker has done all the prerequisites necessary before paying for the bill and what (53d) implies is that paying for the bill is the only thing left to do.

(53) [she-*sudah* / *baru* / *masih* / *tinggal*-pay-at-cashier]

a.   ⎧ **baru**[12] ⎫
b.   Ia ⎨ **sudah**   ⎬ bayar di kasir.
c.   ⎪ **masih**   ⎪
d.   ⎩ **tinggal** ⎭

a. [*baru*] 'She has just finished paying for the bill at the cashier.'
b. [*sudah*] 'She has just finished paying for the bill at the cashier.'
c. [*masih*] 'She is still [e.g., in a long line] waiting for her turn to pay the bill at the cashier.'
d. [*tinggal*] 'Paying for the bill at the cashier is the only (last) thing she is going to do' [as she has finished doing her other obligations, e.g., checking whether transportation back to the hotel for all the guests (invited to the dinner) has been arranged].

RECAPITULATION

To recapitulate, what this paper has attempted to portray is that, unlike English sentences, in which generally syntax requires verbal arguments to be explicitly stated in a sentence, Indonesian sentences allow verb argument(s) to remain implicit when understood from context. The TBA that works well with a language like English is not helpful to unravel the intricacies of the various instances of use of *sudah* and the other temporal expressions in Indonesian. For such an analysis, one needs a new framework.

At present, grammatical analyses of Indonesian are comparable to the earlier English grammar books written in the sixteenth to eighteenth century, when Latin

---

[12] *Baru* may be synonymous with *sedang* to mark action in progress: *Ia baru / sedang mandi* 'She is taking a shower.' *Saja* 'just' may only optionally go with *baru* in (53), not with *baru* to mark action in progress: *Ia baru (saja) bayar di kasir* 'She has just finished paying for the bill at the cashier.' The presence of *saja* makes the utterance emphatic.

terms and some Latin rules were imposed upon English. It is high time to construct a new grammar that provides an alternative framework for describing Indonesian. For a much more accurate description of languages like Indonesian, one must abandon "external devices"—such as an analysis modeled on the grammar for a language structured like English—and make use of "internal devices"—qualities specific in the language under study.

Indonesian is a language that registers duration of time and anticipation—the timeline from expectation to reality. An attempt to understand Indonesian sentences requires that the context of usage be taken into account. The explanation as to why, for example, *ia kawin* [she-married] is out in (54) but is fine in (55) and why *sudah* is mandatory in (54) but not allowed in (55) works with PBA but not with TBA.

(54)   A: Kamu jatuh cinta, ya, ama dia?
         [you-fall (in)-love, yes, with-her]
         'You seem to fall in love with her.'
       B: Iya.
         'Uh-uh.'
       A: Tetapi **ia sudah kawin**/*ia kawin.
         [but-she-*sudah*-married / she-married]
         'But she's married.'
       B: O ya?
         'Oh, yeah?'

(55)   [Context: Anita parents forbid her to marry Budi.]
       A: Kamu udah denger belum tentang Anita?
         [you-sudah-hear, not, about-Anita]
         'Did you hear any news about Anita?'
         Aku nggak ngira.
         [I-not-think]
         'I never thought that would happen.'
       B: Apa?
         'What?'
       A: **Ia kawin.**
         [she-married]
         'She's married. /She got married.'
       B: Dengan Budi? [with-Budi]
         'She married Budi?'

It is not only in the sentence *ia sudah kawin* (54) that—to quote Oetomo et al. (1986, 71)—"we are discussing something which is true at a particular point in time, but was not true in the past," but also in the sentence *ia kawin* (55), which rejects the use of *sudah*. The tense-based explanation, then, fails to account for the presence and absence of *sudah* in the sentence.

An explanation as to what makes *sudah* mandatory to go with *kawin* in (54) but not permissible with *kawin* in (55) requires a pragmatic analysis. No expectation is involved in the context of *kawin* (55) but there is one in *kawin* (54)—a societal expectation—see the discussion of (36). As for individual expectation, see the discussion of (31) through (35), which involve the speaker's (31) or hearer's expectation [(29c) and (40)] to justify the use of *sudah* and the speaker-hearer's shared anticipation (42) to justify the use of *jadi*.

Within the context of the frame of a "timeline from expectation to reality," a choice is open for the speaker in terms of what perspective to take with respect to the period of time—see (45) through (53). The parameter for such a choice is either (a) closed vs. open or (b) long vs. short. The use of *baru* and *sudah* has to do with (a), the use of *masih* and *tinggal* with (b).

Students of Indonesian, thus, should be supplied with information not from an (external) viewpoint or framework, relative to their own language, but from a model based on an internal perspective, relative to the language they are trying to learn, informed by a recognition of the special qualities that decorate and enrich Indonesian.

For language teachers, the challenge ahead is to present in classroom practice the model suggested in the present paper and, for textbook writers, it is to model their books appropriately for learners of Indonesian. For linguistic researchers, the path is open for a scrutiny of words and phrases other than the five temporal expressions discussed in the present paper and other than the spatial expressions of *tiba* and *sampai*—both of which lexically mean 'to arrive at'—the difference of which is accounted for in Kaswanti (2011).

Works Cited

Celce-Murcia, Marianne and Diane Larsen-Freeman. *The Grammar Book: An ESL/EFL Teacher's Course*. Second Edition. Heinle and Heinle Publishers, 1999.

Geertz, Hildred. *The Javanese Family: A Study of Kinship and Socialization*. Glencoe, IL: The Free Press of Glencoe, 1961.

Grangé, Philippe. Temps et Aspect en Indonésien. PhD Dissertation. Poitiers: Université de Poitiers, 2006.

Kaswanti Purwo, Bambang. "On the Indonesian *Telah* and *Sudah*: Two Perspectives of Looking at the Past Time." Unpublished paper, University of Michigan, Ann Arbor, MI. 1978.

——. "Menelusuri Perbedaan Antara *Telah* dan *Sudah*," Makalah Seminar Masyarakat Linguistik Indonesia. Yogyakarta, Maret 22–24, 1979. Published in *Dewan Bahasa*, November 1981.

——. "Deiksis Dalam Bahasa Indonesia." PhD dissertation. Jakarta: Universitas Indonesia, 1982.

——. *Deiksis Dalam Bahasa Indonesia*. Jakarta: Balai Pustaka, 1984.

——. "*Sudah* in Contemporary Indonesian." Fifteenth International Seminar on Malay/Indonesian Linguistics (ISMIL 15), Universitas Islam Negeri Malang, June 24–26, 2011.

——. "The Indonesian *Sampai*: From Space to the Deictics (of Time and Person) and to the Pragmatics (of Precipitation)." International Workshop on Deixis and Spatial Expressions in Indonesian Languages. Osaka, July 2–23, 2011.

——. "The English Perfective and the Indonesian *Sudah*: Temporal-Ideational vs. Interpersonal Functions." The Second INASYSCON "Systemic Functional

Linguistics: Applied and Multiculturalism." Universitas Brawijaya, Malang, December 17-18, 2011.

Larson, Richard. "Time Event Measure." *Philosophical Perspective* 17, *Language and Philosophical Linguistics*, 2003. http://semlab5.sbs.sunysb.edu/~rlarson/philp_010.pdf (October 27, 2013).

McDonald, R. Ross, and Soenjono Dardjowidjojo. *Indonesian Reference Grammar.* Washington, DC: Georgetown University Press, 1967.

Oetomo, Dédé, Daniel Fietkiewicz, and John U. Wolff, *Beginning Indonesian through Self-Instruction.* Second Revised Edition. Ithaca, NY: Cornell Southeast Asia Program, 1986.

Rafferty, Ellen. "Aspect in Conversational Indonesian." *Tense-Aspect: Between Semantics and Pragmatics.* Ed. Paul Hopper. Amsterdam: John Benjamins Publishing Company, 1982: 65–90.

Raffel, Burton, Harry Aveling, and Derwent May, trans. *Ballads and Blues* [by W. S. Rendra], *Translated from Indonesian.* Kuala Lumpur: Oxford University Press, 1977.

Singgih, Amin. *Belajar Bahasa Indonesia.* Jakarta: Erlangga, 1977.

Sneddon, James. *The Indonesian Language: Its History and Role in Modern Society.* Sydney: UNSW Press, 2003.

Van den Berg, J. D. Inleiding to de bahasa Indonesia door Dr. M.G. Emeis (vierde druk), bewerkt door ... Pro manuscripto, 1967.

INDONESIAN LITERATURES AND LITERARY CRITICISM

Tineke Hellwig[1]

1. CONTEMPORARY INDONESIAN LITERATURE AND LITERARY CRITICISM IN INDONESIA

Much has changed in Indonesia's literary world since the fall of Suharto's New Order. Instead of living in fear of government control and censorship, writers, artists, journalists, scholars, and the public at large have been able to exercise their freedom of expression from 1998 onwards. Creative writing and cultural production turned a corner and broke out of a slumber of apathy and inertia. Women emerged prominently on the scene. They published novels and short stories, and engaged in filmmaking and various other art forms. Ayu Utami's novel *Saman* (1998) came to signify the new freedom of speech. *Saman*, as well as works by other women, broke through taboos regarding governance, politics, gender and female sexuality. In 2002, this led to the labeling of *sastrawangi*, "fragrant literature/literati." The term focused on the female authors' "young attractive bodies" while their literary works were condescendingly referred to as "chick lit." The *sastrawangi* controversy became known outside of Indonesia through a BBC News World Edition web article (September 10, 2003).[2] While women have become significantly visible in Indonesian literature in the past fifteen years, the following overview of the state of Indonesian literatures and literary criticism makes it blatantly clear that from its inception the field was, in fact, dominated by male authors and scholars and their unavoidably masculine gender biases.

When we examine Indonesian literatures and literary criticism, it is obvious that we find the primary audiences of literary texts and studies *inside* Indonesia; the most lively discussions and debates take place in Indonesian newspapers, magazines, and journals, and on campuses. A critical mass of Indonesian intellectuals and scholars can be found on campuses and at cultural centers, first and foremost in Jakarta (Universitas Indonesia, Komunitas Utan Kayu/Salihara, Dewan Kesenian

---

[1] I would like to thank Manneke Budiman and Willem van der Molen for their assistance, suggestions, and feedback.

[2] Becky Lipscombe, "Chick-lit Becomes Hip Lit in Indonesia. In the West It's Known as Chick-Lit; Here, It's 'Sastrawangi' or 'Fragrant Literature.'" http://news/bbc/co/uk/2/hi/asia-pacific/3093038.stm, accessed June 2007.

Jakarta/Taman Ismail Marzuki, Pusat Bahasa), but also in Yogyakarta, Bandung, and Surabaya. In the post-Suharto period, some outspoken Yogya-based cultural critics, such as Saut Situmorang and Katrin Bandel, have taken a strong oppositional stance vis-à-vis those in Jakarta and the Komunitas Utan Kayu (Utan Kayu Community) because they perceived the focus on and explicit portrayal of female sexuality and sexual relationships as offensive and provocative. Literary journals such as *Horison* (Jakarta, founded 1966), *Jurnal Kalam* (founded 1994), *Jurnal Sastra Hiski* (founded 2004) and *K@ta* (Surabaya, founded 1999) publish commentaries and interpretations as well as creative writing. The literary columns in the weekly *Tempo* and Sunday edition of *Kompas* daily inform wider audiences of literary publications and provide critical opinions. Veterans such as Taufiq Ismail (b. 1935), Budi Darma (b. 1937), Ajip Rosidi (b. 1938), Sapardi Djoko Damono (b. 1940), and Goenawan Mohamad (b. 1941) have taken on multiple roles as fiction writers, poets, essayists, critics, journalists, and university lecturers. They paved the way for literary criticism and scholarship and still actively contribute through publications, participation at events, and by serving on boards or committees for literary awards. A younger generation of intelligentsia has joined their ranks, including, for example, Melani Budianta, Manneke Budiman, Nirwan Dewanto, Sitok Srengenge, and Eko Endarmoko. Even more junior are Ugoran Prasad, Eka Kurniawan, and Alia Swastika, who do not belong to any community or academic institution.

Universities with strong programs in Indonesian literature, literary criticism, critical theory, and cultural studies are Universitas Indonesia, Gadjah Mada, Sanata Dharma, Negeri Surabaya, Kristen Petra, Airlangga, Pajajaran, and Pendidikan Indonesia. Their faculty members organize and attend conferences and participate in literary debates.[3] Understandably, these scholars publish their work mostly in Indonesian. Only the journal *K@ta* publishes articles in English, while *Tempo* has been available in English since 2000. Indonesian is therefore not only a medium of literary expression, but it is also used in the academy. This has implications for language teaching to non-native speakers. They need an advanced level of Indonesian to have access to this artistic community's fiction, poetry, and theater, as well as critical discussions and polemics.

In his essay "The Changing Ecology of Southeast Asian Studies in the United States, 1950–1990" (1992), Benedict Anderson emphasizes how important it is "for American Southeast Asianists to have a more thorough acquaintance with the written languages of the region [...] and to understand at least their modern literatures." He observes that, unfortunately, "language study in the United States has been damagingly skewed in a narrowly utilitarian–oral direction" (1992, 36–37). In 1975, a number of American scholars founded what came to be known as the Consortium for the Teaching of Indonesian (COTI). Its goals were to provide intensive in-country instruction in advanced Indonesian and to foster mutual cross-cultural understanding. Twelve American universities are COTI members: Arizona

---

[3] Jakarta, Universitas Indonesia: Melani Budianta, Riris K. Toha-Sarumpaet, Sapardi Djoko Damono, Manneke Budiman, Ibnu Wahyudi, Maman S. Mahayana, Apsanti Djokosujatno, Intan Paramaditha; Yogyakarta, Universitas Gadjah Mada: Faruk H. T., Bakdi Sumanto; Sanata Dharma: Katrin Bandel, St. Sunardi; Surabaya, Universitas Negeri Surabaya: Budi Darma, Fabiola Kurnia; Universitas Kristen Petra: Nani Indrajani Tiono, Jenny Mochtar Djundjung; Universitas Airlangga: Diah Ariani Arimbi; Bandung, Universitas Pajajaran: Ari Jogaiswara Adipurwawijana, Lestari Manggong, Aquarini Prabasmoro; Universitas Pendidikan Indonesia: Safrina Noorman.

State University, University of California–Berkeley, University of California–Los Angeles, University of Colorado at Boulder, Cornell University, University of Hawaii, University of Michigan, Northern Illinois University, Ohio University, University of Washington, University of Wisconsin at Madison, and Yale University. In addition, the University of California–Riverside and the Canadian universities of British Columbia and Victoria offer Indonesian language courses. Below I note those faculty members whose primary research focus is literature. While language training is of crucial importance, translations of literary works and essays are essential, too, to reach a broader, international readership. Only translations allow larger international audiences to gain access to Indonesian texts and the ideas conveyed through them, and to join the discussions. For those of us who teach (undergraduate) literature courses in English, translations are an absolute necessity.

2. THE STUDY OF TEXTS: HISTORICAL PERSPECTIVE

The study of Indonesian literature(s) *outside* the archipelago finds its roots in colonial interests, old-style area studies, and orientalist practices. The Dutch and other Europeans were captivated by oral traditions and performances that they tried to understand. They searched for, collected, and appropriated manuscripts, as Abdullah bin Abdul Kadir observes in his chapter "Mr. Raffles in Malacca":

> There were also people who brought Malay manuscripts and books [to Mr. Raffles], I do not remember how many hundreds of these texts there were. Almost, it seemed, the whole of Malay literature of the ages, the property of our forefathers, was sold and taken away from all over the country [...] these were all written in longhand and now copies of them are no longer available. (1969, 76)

Philology—the study of texts, manuscript variants, and their history—developed as a discipline in "oriental studies," and European philologists transliterated and translated manuscripts from the archipelago and produced annotated editions. The first critical editions in Dutch not only produced knowledge about the various Indonesian cultures, but also helped to prepare colonial civil servants (*taalambtenaren*) to understand the languages and cultures of the region in preparation for their deployment in the colony.[4] In the 1950s, philology continued to remain strong at Leiden University, as it was practiced by scholars such as A. Teeuw, R. Roolvink, J. Noorduyn, and J. J. Ras, whose research focused on the Malay, Javanese, Buginese, and Sundanese classics. They trained students to appreciate textual traditions and classical writings, and supervised PhD students, guiding them to decipher manuscripts and become philologists in their own right. Stuart Robson, Willem van der Molen, and Roger Tol, to name a few, made unpublished manuscripts available through annotated printed editions and translations.

Meanwhile, colonial ties between Great Britain and Malaya had resulted in studies of Malay literary traditions written in English. After R. O. Winstedt and R. J. Wilkinson had laid the groundwork for research on Malay literary and cultural

---

[4] C. C. Berg (Java), G. W. J. Drewes (Malay, Aceh, Java), C. Hooykaas (Bali), P. Voorhoeve (Batak), and N. Adriani (Bare'e Toraja) were among those who published text editions in the early 1900s.

production, others followed in their footsteps. At the London School for Oriental and African Studies (SOAS), Russell Jones became the most distinguished expert of Malay manuscripts, while Nigel Phillips studied Minangkabau narratives and focused on the interrelationship between orality and literacy. Vladimir Braginsky (PhD Moscow) continued to emphasize the importance of classical Malay genres. His book *The Heritage of Traditional Malay Literature: A Historical Survey of Genres, Writings, and Literary Views* (2004) is a comprehensive survey of literary history that approaches Malay literature "as the development of integral literary systems [...] subject especially to the process of Islamization."[5] Working from the British Library, Annabel Gallop has published her studies about seals, epistolary styles, and illuminations in Malay and Acehnese manuscripts.

Expertise in Indonesian philology can also be found in France, Germany, Australia, and Singapore. From its start in 1938, the École Française d'Extrême Orient (EFEO) branch in Jakarta (Batavia), with its first representative Louis-Charles Damais, focused its attention on epigraphy and archeology. Its current director, Henri Chambert-Loir, is renowned for his *hikayat* and *syair* text editions—for example, his editions of Malay writings about the Bima sultanate—and his scholarly contributions to modern Indonesian literature. At the University of Cologne, Edwin Wieringa's research and teaching include Indonesian philology and Islamic studies, while Jan van der Putten, who succeeded Liaw Yock Fang at the National University of Singapore, focuses on the Buginese–Malay heritage in Riau writing traditions. Wieringa and Van der Putten are 1990s Leiden PhD graduates. Liaw Yock Fang received his doctorate in Leiden (1976) based on his textual study of the laws of Malacca, and so did Peter Worsley (1972), who dedicated his career at the University of Sydney to Old Javanese and Balinese *babad* and *kakawin*. Worsley supervised S. Supomo, Helen Creese, and Raechelle Rubinstein as they studied to become area specialists in the same field. While Supomo and Creese's PhD research resulted in *kakawin* text editions, Adrian Vickers "began [his study] as a philologist looking for his text and ended it as a historian" (2005, 1). His 1986 dissertation shook the Leiden philological tradition as he "adopted a provocative approach" (2005, vii) and examined the *Malat* text in the wider context of Balinese literary traditions, i.e., performances and visual representations. Subsequently, Rubinstein and Creese no longer published annotated editions but rather explored Balinese religious literacy and *kakawin* composition (Rubinstein) and the roles of women—as daughters, wives, and mothers—in courtship, marriage, and death, as portrayed textually in *kakawin* and visually in temple reliefs and Balinese illustrations (Creese 2004). Virginia Matheson Hooker (Australian National University) collaborated with Barbara Watson Andaya on an annotated translation of Raja Ali Haji's *Tuhfat Al-Nafis*. She subsequently published her research on classical Malay, modern Malaysian, and modern Indonesian literature.

When Henk Maier defended his 1985 Leiden thesis exploring the oral–aural origins of a nineteenth-century Malay text from Kedah and its historical developments, he dismissed philology and applied modern literary theories and the concept of intertextuality for his analysis instead. Gijs Koster used Western critical theories and anthropology in his doctoral study eight years later to understand traditional Malay poetics and interpret heroic epics and Panji romances, while Will Derks examined oral Malay traditions and singers of tales in Riau (1994). In tandem,

---

[5] *IIAS Newsletter* 21, http://www.iias.nl/iiasn/21/regions/21SEA14.html, accessed July 2013.

these Leiden students of classical genres, traditional writing, and orality no longer adhered to philology but followed an interdisciplinary approach to understand the texts, taking the cultural-historical context, politics, and prevailing ideologies into consideration.

Philology never took root in North America. At the University of California–Berkeley, Amin Sweeney's interest in Malay literary traditions resulted in *A Full Hearing* (1987), a groundbreaking work in the way it addressed oral creativity, story telling, performance (Malay *wayang*), and musical traditions. He published his text editions of Abdullah bin Abdul Kadir's prose and poetry between 2005 and 2008 after he had moved to Jakarta. Nancy Florida (University of Michigan) transliterated numerous Javanese *kraton* manuscripts from Surakarta. Her 1995 book, *Writing the Past, Inscribing the Future*, provides a translation and meticulous analysis of the *Babad Jaka Tingkir* and examines reading practices in Java. At this point, it is worthwhile to note that Indonesian literary studies has always been characterized by a strong interdisciplinary dimension. Historians, anthropologists, and political and other social scientists have reached out to Indonesian literary texts from within their own disciplinary fields. Merle Ricklefs, Jean Taylor, Rudolf Mrázek, James Siegel, Benedict Anderson, Peter Carey, Charles Coppel, and many others have studied and made scholarly contributions about literature—traditional and modern genres—without necessarily self-identifying as, or claiming to be, literary critics.

3. THE STUDY OF MODERN INDONESIAN LITERATURE *OUTSIDE* INDONESIA

A. Teeuw and H. B. Jassin

This section discusses studies of modern Indonesian literature and theater outside Indonesia.[6] Literatures in other languages (Javanese, Sundanese, and others) lie beyond the scope of this paper. In 1967, A. Teeuw published *Modern Indonesian Literature,* volume 1, an English reworking of his 1952 *Pokok dan tokoh dalam kesusasteraan Indonesia baru.* Volume 2 came out in 1979, and these two books became influential as the standard reference works for literature written in Indonesian. According to Teeuw, modern Indonesian literature started in the 1920s with Balai Pustaka authors and Pudjangga Baru poets who wrote in what was to become "standard Indonesian," or *Bahasa Indonesia yang baik dan benar,* a language that Joseph Errington has called "un-native" (2007, 55; also in this volume). Teeuw's point of view and definition of "what makes Malay/Indonesian literature modern" would later be contested. In 1954, Teeuw's colleague and friend H. B. Jassin published *Gema tanah air: Prosa dan puisi,* followed by *Pudjangga Baru: Prosa dan puisi* (1963). Based in Leiden and Jakarta, respectively, Teeuw and Jassin gained authority as the founders of modern Indonesian literary criticism. They taught generations of students and their publications were seminal for many others who wanted to understand and appreciate Indonesian literature.

It was scholars who examined so-called "Low" (*Pasar*) Malay writings, such as Nio Joe Lan, John B. Kwee, and Bill Watson, who critiqued Teeuw's date marking the

---

[6] I have not been able to include a summary of Indonesian literary studies in Japan, Korea, China, or other Asian countries.

start of modern Indonesian literature and emphasized the importance of this undercurrent in literary production. Claudine Salmon's 1981 *Literature in Malay by the Chinese of Indonesia* opened up a treasure trove of narratives written in non-standard, *lingua franca* Malay that had never received the attention that they deserved. Her bibliography has resulted in several studies regarding early colonial modernity.

Australia

Outside of Indonesia, the strongest Indonesian literature programs can be found in Australia. Harry Aveling (Melbourne) is a prolific scholar who surveyed the developments in the field in "A Checklist on Indonesian Literary Criticism" (1968). His publications not only critically discuss a wide range of· topics, but also include many English translations of fiction and poetry. These materials were (and are) desperately needed for teaching Indonesian literature to students who did (and do) not have the proficiency to read the original texts and for opening up Indonesian works to a broader readership. Keith Foulcher's research (Adelaide, Sydney) started interrogating issues related to clashes of ideologies surrounding the 1963 *Manifes Kebudayaan* (Cultural Manifesto). His study of LEKRA (Lembaga Kebudayaan Rakyat, Institute of People's Culture) describes the leftist cultural organization and its social realism, and addresses the political conflicts that affected the arts in 1950–1965. In 2002, Foulcher and Tony Day co-edited *Clearing a Space*, which included thirteen postcolonial readings of Indonesian texts, a collection that made "an important contribution to the critical study of literature and society in Indonesia" (2002, 2). This volume is often cited and quoted in contemporary research, and contains essays by Melani Budianta, Michael Bodden, Marshall Clark, Will Derks, Barbara Hatley, Thomas Hunter, Doris Jedamski, Ward Keeler, Henk Maier, Goenawan Mohamad, Paul Tickell, and the two editors. Based in Indonesia, Australia, the United States, Canada, and the Netherlands, the contributors represent an important cross-section of contemporary scholarship regarding modern Indonesian literature.

In the early 2000s, the University of Tasmania housed three modern Indonesian literature specialists: Barbara Hatley, Pam Allen, and Marshall Clark. Hatley's main research foci have been on theater, women's writing, literary representations of women, and gender ideologies. Allen's critical approach to literary works explores broader issues of cultural identity, social and religious values, and morality. Her translation of *Saman* has been included in course materials and exposed the novel to English audiences. Clark (currently in Melbourne) studies fiction, cinema, and popular culture, and scrutinizes gender (in)equality by problematizing masculinity. At Murdoch University, David Hill is another eminent scholar whose early work examined novels and authors from the post-independent period (Ashadi Siregar, Mochtar Lubis). His focus shifted to broader issues concerning freedom of speech, the press and journalism, modern media, and popular music in his collaborative projects with Krishna Sen (University of Western Australia). Currently, Hill serves as the director of the Australian Consortium for In-Country Indonesian Studies (ACICIS). He has been an advocate for more Indonesian language teaching at school and university levels within Australia,[7] while at the same time continuing his

---

[7] See "Bid to Rejuvenate Indonesian Language Training," http://media.murdoch.edu.au/bid-to-rejuvenate-indonesian-language-learning, accessed July 2013.

research on contemporary media and culture. Australian PhD graduates worth mentioning are Soe-Tjen Marching, Diah Ariani Arimbi, and Andy Fuller.

The Lontar Foundation

While Aveling, Allen, Hill, and others have published English translations of Indonesian works, there is no denying that the Lontar Foundation, and John McGlynn, one of its most prominent founders, have played, and continue to play, the most crucial role in promoting Indonesian literature through English translations. Founded in 1987, this non-profit organization sets as its goals to "stimulate the further development of Indonesian literature; make Indonesian literature accessible to an international audience; [and] preserve Indonesia's literary record for future generations."[8] The first *Menagerie* volume (1992) contained short stories, poetry, essays, and photographs. Volume 7 (2010), entitled "People Like Us," which included stories about gay men, lesbians, bisexuals, and transgendered persons, is proof of the openness (*keterbukaan*) that has come into place since 1998. Besides numerous translations of prose and poetry, Lontar started a modern drama project in 2001. Lontar collected and scanned playscripts and published those in volumes of anthologies, four in Indonesian and three in English.

Europe: The Netherlands, Great Britain, and Germany

Until recently, Leiden University continued to teach a rigorous undergraduate program that included Indonesian and Javanese language and literature. Boen Oemarjati was among the first PhD graduates (1972) to scrutinize modern literature and the language use of 1940s poet Chairil Anwar. She returned to Jakarta to teach at the University of Indonesia. Henk Maier translated many modern works into Dutch and was particularly interested in Pramoedya Ananta Toer's oeuvre. In *We Are Playing Relatives*, he focuses on the concept of Malay-ness and modernity. Maier moved to the University of California–Riverside in 2003. My own research on representations of women and gender ideologies in fiction began in Leiden and continued at the University of British Columbia, concentrating on early twentieth-century Chinese-Malay writings and contemporary, post-1998 female authors.

Ben Arps's expertise is Javanese language, *wayang* theater, and the impact of media on the forms and functions of language. He developed his scholarly interests on new information technology in projects such as "Verbal Art in the Audio-visual Media" and "Indonesian Mediations." He currently investigates Osing language use, performance, and popular culture in Banyuwangi (East Java). Edwin Jurriëns's Leiden dissertation analyzes how artists in West Java use local media, language, and culture to renegotiate the impact of national and global sociopolitical forces. Jurriëns teaches at the University of Melbourne, where his ongoing research interests are radio journalism and "media ecology, or the study of complex interactions between people and their information and communication environments."[9]

At SOAS, Ulrich Kratz (PhD Frankfurt) taught for many years in the Indonesian program alongside Jones, Philips, and Braginsky. His research interests straddle

---

[8] http://www.lontar.org/

[9] http://asiainstitute.unimelb.edu.au/about/staff/academic/edwin_jurriens, accessed July 2013.

Malay philology, traditional genres, and modern Indonesian literature. His bibliography of literature in journals and his *Sumber Terpilih Sejarah Sastra Indonesia* (2000) are important works of reference. Kratz and his colleagues have retired as SOAS research associates. At present, Ben Murtagh is responsible for teaching Indonesian language and literature courses. He publishes on gender identity and gay/queer sexualities as represented in literary texts and film. In the Department of Drama and Theatre Studies, University of London, Matthew Isaac Cohen scrutinizes performance traditions in modern societies such as *komedie stamboel*, Javanese and Balinese *wayang*, and popular theater (*ketoprak, ludruk, sandiwara*).

In Germany, in addition to the University of Cologne, mentioned above, Indonesian studies are offered at the University of Hamburg with faculty members Rainer Carle, Martina Heinschke, and Monika Arnez, and the University of Frankfurt, with Arndt Graf. Research interests and publications on twentieth-century Indonesian literature include Rendra's poetry and Batak "opera" (Carle), the Angkatan 45 (Heinschke), and contemporary post-1998 women writers, such as Helvy Tiana Rosa and Oka Rusmini (Arnez). Doris Jedamski (PhD Hamburg) has published on Balai Pustaka, colonial policies, and modern Malay/Indonesian genres and their origins. Graf's interests focus on rhetoric and the media. Noteworthy, too, is Stefan Danerek's 2005 dissertation at Lund University, Sweden, presenting literary developments from the revolutionary era until *Reformasi*.

North America

Above I have already mentioned the research interests of Nancy Florida (Michigan), the late Amin Sweeney (UC–Berkeley), Henk Maier (UC–Riverside), and myself (UBC). At the University of Wisconsin–Madison, Ellen Rafferty is the driving force behind Indonesian Studies, which is part of the larger Southeast Asia Program. The university hosted SEASSI (South East Asian Studies Summer Institute) in 1994–95 and has continued to do so every year since 2000. Rafferty's 1979 dissertation studied the structure of discourse of Chinese Indonesians in conversations and their socio-cultural context. She edited a collection of essays on Putu Wijaya's play *Gerr!* and of translations of his short stories. Patricia Henry, at Northern Illinois, is a linguist by training but published the text and annotated translation of the Old Javanese *Arjuna Wiwaha* and translated Indonesian short stories. Over the past decades, she has put much effort into computer-aided language instruction of the less commonly taught languages (Indonesian, Thai, Tagalog) and developed web-based learning and translation sites. Her *Learning Bahasa Indonesia on the Internet* website[10] is an excellent comprehensive site with innumerable links, including computerized dictionaries. At UC–Berkeley, Sylvia Tiwon teaches and researches literature, gender, oral, and cultural studies. Her 1999 book explores poetic influence and the beginnings of modern literature from Malay to Indonesian. Her interests in women, postcolonialism, national imaginary, and cultural resistance have directed her professional attention toward activist work, community-based and non-governmental organizations, and the roles of women in the production of discourse.

At the University of Victoria, Michael Bodden's research foci are modern Indonesian theater, fiction, and social and political discourses. He has translated poetry, short stories, plays, and essays. His 2010 book analyzes how theater

---

[10] http://www.seasite.niu.edu/Indonesian/, accessed July 2013.

contributed to resistance movements and social protest against the New Order between 1985 and 1998. Within performing arts studies, we find Bodden and Hatley, who examine modern drama and contemporary stage plays, while Arps and Cohen study performances of tradition-based *wayang kulit* plays and also occasionally perform as *dalang* (shadow puppeteers). Interdisciplinarity is particularly noticeable in the wide range of *wayang* studies: scholars from various disciplines have published on its practice, discourses, socio-religious contexts, socio-political roles, and so on (e.g., Ward Keeler, Andrew Weintraub, Laurie Sears, and Jan Mrázek).

4. WHAT HAS CHANGED AND FUTURE DIRECTIONS

Reflecting on the pedagogical challenges within Southeast Asian studies, Frank Reynolds contends that "the kind of peripherality that we suffer is inevitable" (1992, 70). It is my own experience that within the marginality of our *area* studies, the interdisciplinary nature of Indonesian literary criticism renders this particular field even more invisible. In course offerings, we often teach literature under "culture" or "history" headings. As literary critics, we are limited in numbers and habitually mistaken for anthropologists or historians. We are frequently told that Indonesian literary criticism is not as well developed or recognized as other Asian literary studies (Chinese, Japanese, or Indian), that it is not as "prestigious" or intellectually relevant, and that our publications reach merely restricted audiences. It is not an easy task to amend these kinds of perceptions as they most likely depend on larger forces, e.g., economic power and market-driven influences. It will be a challenge for Indonesian language and literature to be taken seriously in the Western academy.

In the 1980s, Indonesian literary studies shifted its focus from philology to New Historicist and interdisciplinary approaches, and from classical texts to modern genres. Research referred increasingly to deconstructionist, feminist, gender-based, and postcolonial critical theories. Nowadays, academic scrutiny concentrates on the context of the literary work, its production and reception, the "politics of culture," and studies of representation, identity, and social and political discourses. Inside Indonesia, interest in literature is ongoing as expressed in blogs and on Facebook, Twitter, and mailing lists. However, students and scholars pay progressively more attention to popular culture, television, and cinema and less to printed literature.

Outside Indonesia, interest in literary texts—novels, poetry—seems to have waned as well and been replaced by studies of popular culture, modern electronic media, the internet, media arts, film, and journalism as framed within the nation and political processes. Karl Heider and Krishna Sen studied cinema in the 1990s; the latter's work has morphed into media studies projects with David Hill. David Hanan, Ben Murtagh, and Intan Paramaditha scrutinize feature films, Ariel Heryanto publishes on popular culture, and Philip Kitley on television, while Arps and Jurriëns, as mentioned, focus on audio-visual media, video art, radio, and televisual metadiscourse. As printed matter and hard copies gradually make way for electronic versions in everyday life, academic interest is following this trend and moves further away from printed textual materials in the direction of audio-visuals and digital media.

5. LANGUAGE USED IN LITERATURE

As a final point, I will address how Indonesian, as a rapidly developing language, is reflected in literature and how gender plays a role in the language, in literature, and as reflected by authors' choices of themes and language. The following relates mostly to the use of language in literary prose. It leaves language use in poetry, popular culture, film, and modern media out of the discussion.

Fiction is commonly written in the standard *Bahasa Indonesia yang baik dan benar*. In literary prose, we see a growing trend, however, of using (kinship) terms from regional languages alongside Indonesian, especially when depicting *adat* in novels/stories that are set in the "outer islands." Oka Rusmini's works—*Tarian Bumi* (2000), *Sagra* (2001), *Kenanga* (2003)—contain Balinese words related to the concept of *varna* (caste system), and Nukila Amal's *Cala Ibi* (2003) includes expressions and passages in the vernacular language of Ternate. Novia Syahidah's novel *Di Selubung Malam* (2004) contains Sasak words referring to Lombok's customary laws and traditions. Another trend is to incorporate expressions and dialogues in foreign languages into Indonesian fiction. This is evident in Dewi Lestari's novels (the *Supernova* trilogy), where the characters speak in many different Western and Asian languages (Spanish, English, French, Thai, Cambodian), and also in the works of Islamic writers (Abidah El Khalieqy, Helvy Tiana Rosa), where Arabic words and expressions frequently appear.

Male writers such as Sitok Srengenge, Seno Gumira Ajidarma, Eka Kurniawan, Kurnia Efendi, and Nur Zen Hai frequently use local or regional settings, but they use standard Indonesian as their medium rather than integrating vernacular languages into their writing. Female authors seem to be willing to venture into new linguistic explorations, whereas male writers tend to reinforce what Afrizal Malna (2000) refers to as a "linguistic alienation" among modern Indonesian writers, which results from using Bahasa Indonesia as a medium of expression while most Indonesians feel more at home with their regional languages than with the "national" language.

Jakarta-born urban middle-class writers such as Ayu Utami, Djenar Maesa Ayu, and Fira Basuki write in standard Indonesian even though their works are cosmopolitan in terms of themes and characterization. Djenar and Fira occasionally slip in spoken Jakartan in conversations, using, for example, *gue* (I, me) and *lu* (you). Many other Jakarta-produced works, especially chick lit and teen lit written by Raditya Dika, Moemoe Rizal, Stephanie Zen, and Mya Ye, contain generous amounts of so-called *bahasa gaul* that is popular amongst teenagers (ABG, *anak baru gede*). These popular works, as well as Literature with a capital "L," along with television series, movies, and creative modern media will continue to be fertile ground for future research and interdisciplinary studies. They will serve as sources to better understand artistic expression, linguistic explorations, social dynamics, or cultural developments in Indonesia.

Works Cited

Abdullah bin Abdul Kadir. *The Hikayat Abdullah: An Annotated Translation by A. H. Hill*. Kuala Lumpur: Oxford University Press, 1969.

Afrizal Malna. *Sesuatu Indonesia: Personifikasi pembaca-yang-tak-bersih*. Yogyakarta: Yayasan Bentang Budaya, 2000.

Allen, Pamela. *Membaca dan pembaca lagi: [Re]interpretasi fiksi Indonesia 1980–1995*. Magelang: IndonesiaTera, 2004.

Anderson, Benedict R. "The Changing Ecology of Southeast Asian Studies in the United States, 1950–1990." *Southeast Asian Studies in the Balance: Reflections from America*. Ed. Charles Hirschman, Charles F. Keyes, and Karl Hutterer. Ann Arbor, MI: Association for Asian Studies, 1992: 25–40.

Arimbi, Diah Ariani. *Reading Contemporary Indonesian Muslim Women Writers: Representation, Identity, and Religion of Muslim Women in Indonesian Fiction*. Amsterdam: Amsterdam University Press, 2009.

Arps, Bernard. *Tembang in Two Traditions: Performance and Interpretation of Javanese Literature*. London: School of Oriental and African Studies, 1992.

Aveling, Harry. "A Checklist on Indonesian Literary Criticism." *Review of Indonesian and Malay(si)an Affairs* 2 (1968): 19–22.

Bodden, Michael. *Resistance on the National Stage: Theater and Politics in Late New Order Indonesia*. Athens, OH: Ohio University Press, 2010.

Braginsky, Vladimir. *The Heritage of Traditional Malay Literature: A Historical Survey of Genres, Writings, and Literary Views*. Leiden: KITLV Press, 2004.

Carey, Peter. *Babad Dipanagara: An Account of the Outbreak of the Java War (1825–30): The Surakarta Court Version of the Babad Dipanagara with Translations into English and Indonesian Malay*. Kuala Lumpur: Council of the MBRAS, 1981.

——. *The British in Java, 1811–1816: A Javanese Account: A Text Edition, English Synopsis and Commentary on British Library Additional Manuscript 12330 (Babad Bedhah ing Ngayogyakarta)*. Oxford: Oxford University Press, 1992.

Carle, Rainer. *Gedichtsammlungen (1957–1972); ein Beitrag zur Kenntnis der zeitgenössischem indonesischen Literatur*. Berlin: Reimer, 1977.

——. *Opera Batak: das Wandertheater der Toba-Batak in Nord Sumatra. Schauspiele zur Wahrung Kultureller Identität im nationalen indonesischen Kontext*. Berlin: Reimer, 1990.

Chambert-Loir, Henri. *Hikayat Dewa Mandu. Epopée malaise. I. Texte et presentation*. Paris: EFEO, 1980.

——. *Syair Kerajaan Bima (Le Poème du royaume de Bima)*. Jakarta: EFEO, 1982.

——. *Sadur: Sejarah terjemahan di Indonesia dan Malaysia*. Jakarta: Kepustakaan Populer Gramedia, EFEO, 2009.

Clark, Marshall. *Maskulinitas: Culture, Gender and Politics in Indonesia*. Caulfield: Monash University Press, 2010.

Cohen, Matthew Isaac. *The Komedie Stamboel: Popular Theater in Colonial Indonesia, 1891–1903*. Athens, OH: Ohio University Press, 2006.

——. *Performing Otherness: Java and Bali on International Stages, 1905–1952*. Basingstoke: Palgrave Macmillan, 2010.

Creese, Helen. "Subhadrawiwaha: An Old Javanese Kakawin; Vol. 1: Introduction and Text. Vol. 2: Translation and Notes." PhD dissertation, Australian National University, Canberra, 1981.

——. *Women of the Kakawin World: Marriage and Sexuality in the Indic Courts of Java and Bali*. Armonk, NY: M. E. Sharpe, 2004.

Danerek, Stefan. *The Short Story Genre in Indonesia: Post New Order Literature*. Lund: Lund University Press, 2005.

Derks, Will. "The Feast of Storytelling on Malay Oral Tradition." PhD dissertation, Leiden University, 1994.

Errington, Joseph. "Going 'Un-Native' in Indonesia(n)." *Identifying With Freedom: Indonesia after Suharto*. Ed. Tony Day. New York, NY: Berghahn Books, 2007: 49–57.

Foulcher, Keith. *Social Commitment in Literature and the Arts: The Indonesian "Institute of People's Culture" 1950–1965*. Clayton: Monash University Press, 1986.

Foulcher, Keith, and Tony Day, eds. *Clearing a Space: Postcolonial Readings of Modern Indonesian Literature*. Leiden: KITLV Press, 2002.

Florida, Nancy. *Writing the Past, Inscribing the Future: History as Prophecy in Colonial Indonesia*. Durham, NC: Duke University Press, 1995.

Gallop, Annabel Teh. *The Legacy of the Malay Letter* [Warisan Warkah Melayu]. Trans. Matheson Hooker. London: British Library, 1994.

Graf, Arndt. *Indonesische Medienrhetorik: eine methodologische Fallstudie anhand der Kommentarkolumne "Catatan Pinggir" von Goenawan Mohamad*. Berlin: Reimer, 1998.

Hanan, David, and Basoeki Koesasi. "*Betawi Moderen*: Songs and Films of Benyamin S from Jakarta in the 1970s—Further Dimensions of Indonesian Popular Culture." *Indonesia* 91 (April 2011): 35–76.

Hasanudin, W. S., Mursal Esten, and Maizar Karim. *Ensiklopedi sastra Indonesia*. Bandung: Titian Ilmu, 2009.

Hatley, Barbara. "New Directions in Indonesian Women's Writing? The Novel *Saman*." *Asian Studies Review* 23.4 (1999): 449–60.

——. *Javanese Performances on an Indonesian Stage: Contesting Culture, Embracing Change*. Singapore: National University of Singapore Press, 2008.

Heider, Karl. *Indonesian Cinema: National Culture on Screen*. Honolulu, HI: University of Hawaii Press, 1991.

Heinschke, Martina. *Angkatan 45: Literaturkonzeptionen im gesellschaftspolitischen Kontext: zur Funktionsbestimmung von Literatur im postkolonialen Indonesien*. Berlin: Reimer, 1993.

Hellwig, Tineke. *In the Shadow of Change: Images of Women in Indonesian Literature*. Berkeley, CA: Center for South and Southeast Asian Studies, 1994.

——. *Women and Malay Voices: Undercurrent Murmurings in Indonesia's Colonial Past*. New York, NY: Peter Lang, 2012.

Hellwig, Tineke, and Michael Bodden. "Post-Soeharto Women's Writing and Cultural Production." *Review of Indonesian and Malaysian Affairs* 41.2 (2007): 1–204.

Henry, Patricia. "Mapu Kanwa's Arjuna Wiwaha, Sargas I–XIII, Text Translation and Commentary." *The South East Asian Review* 10.1–2 (1986), published by The Center for South East Asian Studies, Gaya (India).

Heryanto, Ariel. *Popular Culture in Indonesia: Fluid Identities in Post-Authoritarian Politics*. New York, NY: Routledge, 2008.

Hill, David. *The Press in New Order Indonesia*. Nedlands: University of Western Australia Press, 1995.

Hill, David, and Krishna Sen. *Media, Culture, and Politics in Indonesia*. Melbourne: Oxford University Press, 2000.

——. "Global Industry, National Politics: Popular Music in New Order Indonesia." *Refashioning Pop Music in Asia: Cosmopolitan Flows, Political Tempos, and Aesthetic Industries*. Ed Allen Chun, Ned Rossiter, and Brian Shoesmith. London: Routledge Curzon, 2004.

——. *Politics and the Media in Twenty-first Century Indonesia. Decade of Democracy*. London: Routledge, 2011.

Jassin, H. B. *Gema tanah air: Prosa dan puisi*. Djakarta: Perpustakaan Perguruan Kementerian PP dan K, 1954.

——. *Pudjangga Baru. Prosa dan puisi*. Djakarta: Gunung Agung, 1963.

Jedamski, Doris. *Die Institution Literatur und der Prozess ihrer Kolonisation: Entstehung, Entwicklung und Arbeitsweise des Kantoor voor de Volkslectuur "Balai Poestaka" in Niederländisch-Indiën zu Beginn dieses Jahrhunderts*. Münster: Lit, 1992.

Jones, Russell. "An Essay at Dating and Description of a Malay Manuscript." *Kajian Malaysia* 1.2 (1983): 1–13.

——. "Crescent and Eagle Watermarks." *Persembahan: Studi in Onore di Luigi Santa Maria*. Ed. Sitti Faizah Soenoto Rivai. Napoli: Istituto Universitario Orientale, 1998.

Jurriëns, Edwin. *Cultural Travel and Migrancy: The Artistic Representation of Globalization in the Electronic Media of West Java*. Leiden: KITLV Press, 2004.

Keeler, Ward. *Javanese Shadow Plays, Javanese Selves*. Princeton, NJ: Princeton University Press, 1987.

Kitley, Philip. *Television, Nation, and Culture in Indonesia*. Athens, OH: Ohio University Press, 2000.

Koster, Gijs. *Roaming through Seductive Gardens: Readings in Malay Narrative*. Leiden: KITLV Press, 1997.

Kratz, E. U. *A Bibliography of Indonesian Literature in Journals: Drama, Prose Poetry*. Yogyakarta: Universitas Gadjah Mada; London: School of Oriental and African Studies, 1988.

——. *Sumber terpilih sejarah sastra Indonesia abad XX*. Jakarta: Kepustakaan Populer Gramedia, 2000.

Kwee, John B. "Chinese Malay Literature of the *Peranakan* in Indonesia, 1888–1942. PhD dissertation, University of Auckland, 1977.

Liaw Yock Fang. *Undang-undang Melaka* [The Laws of Melaka]. Den Haag: Nijhoff, 1976.

Liem, Maya H. T. and Tony Day, eds. *Cultures at War: The Cold War and Cultural Expression in Southeast Asia*. Ithaca, NY: Cornell Southeast Asia Program Publications, 2010.

Maier, H. M. J. *In the Center of Authority: The Hikayat Merong Mahawangsa*. Ithaca, NY: Cornell Southeast Asia Program Publications, 1988.

——. *We Are Playing Relatives: A Survey of Malay Writing*. Leiden: KITLV Press, 2004.

Matheson Hooker, Virginia, and Barbara Watson Andaya. *The Precious Gift* [Tuhfat Al-Nafis]. Oxford: Oxford University Press, 1982.

Molen, Willem van der. *Javaanse tekstkritiek. Een overzicht en een nieuwe benadering geïllustreerd aan de Kunjarakarna*. Dordrecht: Foris, 1983.

Mrázek, Jan. *Phenomenology of a Puppet Theatre: Contemplations on the Art of Javanese Wayang Kulit*. Leiden: KITLV Press, 2005.

Mrázek, Jan, and Morgan Pitelka, eds. *What's the Use of Art? Asian Visual and Material Culture in Context*. Honolulu, HI: University of Hawaii Press, 2008.

Murtagh, Ben. "Istana Kecantikan: The First Indonesian Gay Movie." *South East Asia Research* 14.2 (2006): 211–30.

——. 2007. "Beautiful Men in Jakarta and Bangkok," *South East Asia Research* 15.2 (2007): 281–99.

Nio Joe Lan. *Sastera Indonesia-Tionghoa*. Djakarta: Gunung Agung, 1962.

Noorduyn, J. *Een achttiende-eeuwse kroniek of Wadjo: Buginese historiografie*. Den Haag: Smits, 1955.

Oemarjati, Boen. *Chairil Anwar: The Poet and His Language*. Den Haag: Nijhoff, 1972.

Phillips, Nigel. *Sijobang: Sung Narrative Poetry of West Sumatra*. Cambridge: Cornell University Press, 1981.

Putten, Jan van der. *Di dalam berkekalan persahabatan: "In Everlasting Friendship": Letters from Raja Ali Haji*. Leiden: Department of Languages and Cultures of Southeast Asia and Oceania, 1995.

Rafferty, Ellen. *Putu Wijaya in Performance. A Script and Study of Indonesian Theatre*. Madison, WI: University of Wisconsin Press, 1989.

Rafferty, Ellen, and Laurie Sears. *Bomb: Indonesian Short Stories*. Madison, WI: University of Wisconsin Press, 1988.

Ras, J. J. *Hikajat Bandjar: A Study in Malay Historiography*. Den Haag: Martinus Nijhoff, 1968.

Reynolds, Frank E. "Southeast Asian Studies in America: Reflections on the Humanities." *Southeast Asian Studies in the Balance: Reflections from America*. Ed. Charles Hirschman, Charles F. Keyes, and Karl Hutterer. Ann Arbor, MI: Association for Asian Studies, 1992: 57–73.

Robson, S. O. *Wangbang Wideya. A Javanese Panji Romance*. Den Haag: Martinus Nijhoff, 1971.

Roolvink, R. *The Variant Versions of the Malay Annals*. Jogjakarta: Jajasan Penerbit FKSS-IKIP, 1968.

Rubinstein, Raechelle. *Beyond the Realm of Senses: The Balinese Ritual of Kekawin Composition*. Leiden: KITLV Press, 2000.

Salmon, Claudine. *Literature in Malay by the Chinese of Indonesia: A Provisional Annotated Bibliography*. Paris: Association Archipel, 1981.

Sears, Laurie. *Shadows of Empire: Colonial Discourse and Javanese Tales*. Durham, NC: Duke University Press, 1996.

——. "Reading Ayu Utami: Notes toward a Study of Trauma as the Archive in Indonesian." *Indonesia* 83 (April 2007): 17–39.

Sen, Krishna. *Indonesian Cinema: Framing the New Order*. London: ZED Books, 1994.

Supomo, S. *Arjunawijaya. A Kakawin of Mpu Tantular*. Den Haag: Martinus Nijhoff, 1977.

Sweeney, Amin. *A Full Hearing. Orality and Literacy in the Malay World*. Berkeley, CA: University of California Press, 1987.

Teeuw, A. *Het Bhomakawya: Een Oudjavaans gedicht*. Groningen: Wolters, 1946.

——. *Shair Ken Tambuhan*. Kualal Lumpur: Oxford University Press, 1966.

——. *Modern Indonesian Literature*. Vol. 1. Den Haag: Martinus Nijhoff, 1967.

——. *Modern Indonesian Literature*. Vol. 2. Den Haag: Martinus Nijhoff, 1979.

Tiwon, Sylvia. *Breaking the Spell: Colonialism and Literary Renaissance in Indonesia*. Leiden: Department of Languages and Cultures of Southeast Asia and Oceania, 1999.

Tol, Roger. *Een haan in oorlog: Toloqno Arung Labuaja, Een twintigste-eeuws Buginees heldendicht van de hand van I Mallaq Daéng Arung Manajéng*. Dordrecht: Foris, 1990.

Vickers, Adrian. *Journeys of Desire: A Study of the Balinese Text Malat*. Leiden: KITLV Press, 2005.

Watson, C. W. "Some Preliminary Remarks on the Antecedents of Modern Indonesian Literature." *Bijdragen tot de taal-, land- en volkenkunde* 127.4 (1971): 417–33.

Weintraub, Andrew. *Power Plays: Wayang Golek Puppet Theater of West Java*. Athens, OH: Ohio University Press, 2004.

Wieringa, Edwin. *Carita Bangka: Het verhaal van Bangka: Tekstuitgave met introductie en addenda*. Leiden: Vakgroep Talen en Culturen van Zuidoost-Azië en Oceanië, 1990.

——. "Babad Bangun Tapa: De ballingschap van Pakubuwana VI op Ambon 1830–1849." PhD dissertation, Leiden University, 1994.

Winstedt, R. J., and R. O. Wilkinson, eds. *Malay Literature*. 3 vols. Kuala Lumpur: Oxford University Press, 1907.

Worsley, Peter. *Babad Buleleng: A Balinese Dynastic Genealogy*. Den Haag: Martinus Nijhoff, 1972.

GOVERNMENT, POLITICAL SCIENCE

Introduction: State of Indonesian Political Studies

Thomas B. Pepinsky[1]

The field of Indonesian political studies was born alongside Indonesia itself. The great early works of Indonesian politics—*Nationalism and Revolution in Indonesia* (Kahin 1952), *The Decline of Constitutional Democracy in Indonesia* (Feith 1962), and *The Transition to Guided Democracy: Indonesian Politics, 1957-1959* (Lev 1966)—analyzed the landmark changes in Indonesian politics almost as they happened. These early works are distinctive in their historical detail and comprehensive scope, and they are the foundations upon which the field of Indonesian political studies was built. They are conspicuously not works of political science in the contemporary academic sense, but they are deeply political, and widely read among Indonesianists across disciplines.

The academic study of Indonesian politics has weathered two important sea changes since the early 1960s. The first came from Indonesia itself, with the collapse of Guided Democracy and the rise of the New Order. Suharto's regime depoliticized the study of Indonesia at the same time that it depoliticized Indonesian society. After 1966, it was no longer possible to study Indonesian politics with anything close to the detail and personal knowledge of current events that George Kahin, Herbert Feith, and others had. The first academic study of the September 30th movement—the so-called Cornell White Paper (Anderson and McVey 1971)—resulted in one of its authors (Anderson) being banished from Indonesia until 1999. Subsequently, scholars of Indonesian politics were by necessity more careful. Many focused on topics (such as the state, or development policy) that could be studied in less overtly political ways than before, others gravitated towards historical topics, and still others adopted a heavily theoretical approach to Indonesian politics that did not require the collection of detailed empirical evidence. A few abandoned the study of Indonesia entirely.

The second change came from the discipline of political science, as scholars of Indonesian politics employed in US colleges' political science departments faced both the behavioral revolution of the 1950s–60s and the rational-choice revolution of

[1] I benefited greatly from conversations with Ed Aspinall, Bill Liddle, Don Emmerson, and other conference participants. The usual disclaimer applies.

the 1970s–80s. What both revolutions shared was a commitment to a science of comparative politics that could identify patterns in political outcomes and explain spatial and temporal variation across political units (individuals, classes, states, and so forth). Deep, country-specific knowledge and familiarity with the particulars of individual country cases were relatively less important to these endeavors than they were to scholars like Kahin. It is no accident that the three great early works identified above came from the government department at Cornell, where the behavioral and rational choice revolutions were late to arrive (and where scholars of Indonesian politics had a second home in the multidisciplinary Southeast Asia Program).

After three decades in which the study of Indonesian politics was made difficult by both a hostile political environment and a discipline uninterested in specific knowledge of faraway and geopolitically uninteresting countries, one might expect the field of Indonesian political studies to be in trouble. Yet in three comprehensive surveys, Edward Aspinall, Donald Emmerson, and R. William Liddle describe Indonesian political studies today as vibrant and diverse. However, reflecting the changes in the academy and the developments in Indonesian politics identified above, contemporary Indonesian political studies is also very different from Indonesian political studies of the 1950s–60s in terms of its geographical center, its theoretical concerns, and its conceptual and methodological toolkit.

Aspinall observes that the center of gravity for knowledge production about Indonesian politics has moved from the United States to Australia. Similarly, Liddle notes that all major recent contributions to Indonesian studies by US political scientists have been multi-country studies, comparing Indonesia to at least one other country in order to make causal claims about some political phenomenon. In the United States, the study of Indonesian politics for its own sake has been subsumed by use of Indonesian data to make general statements about politics everywhere (or, at least, in countries that are somehow comparable to Indonesia). In Australia, as in Europe and Asia, understanding the specific content of Indonesian politics remains more a priority, and scholars working in these regions tend to focus on contributions to knowledge about Indonesia rather than to mainstream comparative politics. The debate that Emmerson recalls between Feith (1964, 1965) and Harry Benda (1964)—"why did democracy fail in Indonesia?" versus "how could democracy ever succeed in Indonesia?"—no longer animates Indonesianists. Those inclined to area studies explore what Emmerson terms "the quirk and the murk" of Indonesian politics. The generalists study the parts that they think can be exported.

For a global discipline like Indonesian political studies, a division of labor like that is probably unavoidable, and might even be healthy. The Feith–Benda debate reminds us that choosing between specificity versus generality in Indonesian studies is a matter of taste, not of principle (dissenting views from some in the mainstream of US political science notwithstanding). The generalists cannot ever know if their generalizations are valid unless they know all of the details of Indonesian politics. The "specifists" cannot ever know if cross-national generalizations should be rejected unless they are willing to examine all other countries and cases. Either way, to demonstrate (rather than assert) that Indonesia is special, or that it is *not* special, requires complete knowledge of both the Indonesian case and every other plausible comparison. Since this is impossible, scholars gravitate to the ideographic or the nomothetic approach to Indonesian politics, depending on what suits their tastes. And as Aspinall and Liddle both observe, many of the in-depth studies of

Indonesian politics produced in Australia and elsewhere borrow theories and concepts from mainstream comparative politics, while US-based political scientists working in the mainstream tradition are increasingly eager to get their hands on the rich micro-data that Indonesia has to offer.

But if Aspinall, Emmerson, and Liddle are all fairly comfortable with the state of Indonesian political studies, their chapters each convey some worries about various ways that disciplinary thinking will limit the scope of inquiry by political scientists studying Indonesia in years to come. The return to multiparty democracy in Indonesia has, by and large, removed the political impediments to studying Indonesian politics, but disciplinary constraints remain, especially in the United States. Broadly, the authors worry that scholars working to satisfy the demands of mainstream comparative politics will produce research that is superficial, irrelevant, or both.

Aspinall notes that throughout the past half century, scholars have tended to privilege the center—high-level, relatively formal, Jakarta-focused "national" politics—in Indonesian studies. Especially in the era of decentralization, conventional Jakarta politics simply is not relevant for the daily lives of most Indonesians (even among Jakartans). For Indonesianists seeking to study any topic other than macroeconomic policymaking or Indonesia's foreign relations, scholars must be conversant with the informal sources of power and authority in the *kampung* (village, community) and the unique regional concerns that motivate political actors at the *kabupaten* (district), or provincial, level. Ignoring local politics during the New Order was excusable, both because political research in the regions was highly restricted and because the Suharto regime was organized around principles of political centralization, hierarchy, and control. Today, Aspinall implies, talking to Jakarta elites or following the national press will tell us relatively little about the issues relevant to the political lives of most Indonesians.

Fortunately, studying local or regional politics in Indonesia could, in principle, be done using the standard template of mainstream comparative politics. Not so with agency, as Liddle argues. Agency is a slippery concept that has bedeviled scholars working across the social sciences, but the variable-centered approach of mainstream comparative politics lends itself more to structural explanations for political outcomes than to explanations that rely on agency or process. Yet it seems impossible to understand Indonesia's political trajectory after the collapse of the New Order without taking into account the personal motivations, decision-making capabilities, and political choices made by individual leaders such as Abdurrahman Wahid and Megawati Sukarnoputri. The course of democratic consolidation in Indonesia is not reducible to the interaction of structural pressures. Still, both mainstream comparative politics and critical political economy approach Indonesian politics with a bias towards structural variables such as religious cleavages, economic performance, class, or the nature of the global economy. These explanations are helpful because they can easily be deployed to study any country, not just Indonesia. Liddle illustrates the ways that public opinion surveys and careful field research can be used to think rigorously about how agency matters for understanding Indonesian politics, but it is hard to publish such work in the most prestigious outlets for mainstream comparative politics.

Emmerson, too, laments the way that mainstream comparative politics favors structural explanations for the nature of contemporary Indonesian politics. But his essay concentrates less on structure and more on interpretation, and turns the focus away from mainstream political science to address internal debates among Indonesianists. His concern is whether scholars of Indonesia's political history have been too bound to their favored interpretive frameworks to be able to grasp the momentous upheavals—the revolution, Gestapu, Trisakti, and the like—that have proven so decisive in Indonesia's political history. These events represent sudden shifts in the very basis of political order in Indonesia, and they demand explanation and interpretation. They also challenge scholars' interpretive frameworks for understanding Indonesian politics. Emmerson cautions scholars not to cling to frameworks (or "formats") in the face of dramatic political change, and praises a new, contrarian strand of Indonesian political history that both borrows from and challenges existing narratives. He also hopes for a new addition to the "Ithacan Trilogy" that will interpret contemporary political developments with the detail and nuance found in works by Kahin, Feith, and Daniel Lev, but it is safe to say that Emmerson does not see mainstream comparative politics in the United States as compatible with such an enterprise.

A field of Indonesian political studies that privileges national politics, favors structure over agency, and is incapable of analyzing contemporary political change will never have the same grand ambitions as did the early works of Feith, Benda, Kahin, Lev, and others. Still, as the following three chapters make clear, the study of Indonesian politics is thriving, not least as a result of the new intellectual openness of post-Suharto Indonesia. And, happily, the new focus on subnational comparative research in mainstream comparative politics promises to bring renewed attention to Indonesia precisely because it is such a large and diverse country. This renewed focus on Indonesia may yet give scholars of Indonesian politics the space that they need to pursue the ambitious intellectual projects that created the field of Indonesian political studies itself.

Works Cited

Anderson, Benedict R., and Ruth T. McVey. *A Preliminary Analysis of the October 1, 1965, Coup in Indonesia*. Ithaca, NY: Cornell Modern Indonesia Project, 1971.

Benda, Harry J. "Democracy in Indonesia." *Journal of Asian Studies* 23.3 (May 1964): 449–56.

Feith, Herb. *The Decline of Constitutional Democracy in Indonesia*. Ithaca, NY: Cornell University Press, 1962.

——. "History, Theory, and Indonesian Politics: A Reply to Harry J. Benda," *Journal of Asian Studies* 24.2 (February 1965): 305–12.

Kahin, George McTurnan. *Nationalism and Revolution in Indonesia*. Ithaca, NY: Cornell University Press, 1952.

Lev, Daniel S. *The Transition to Guided Democracy: Indonesian Politics, 1957–59*. Ithaca, NY: Cornell Modern Indonesia Project, 1966.

RESEARCHING INDONESIAN POLITICS: THREE GENERATIONS, THREE APPROACHES, AND THREE CONTEXTS

Edward Aspinall[1]

I will begin with what might seem like a truism: the study of politics, arguably more so than any other field of scholarly research, is greatly influenced by politics. Most obviously, it is influenced by changes in the object of its attention: political events, actors, and systems. For present purposes, this means that the study of Indonesian politics has been affected above all by changes in Indonesia's political system. But the study of politics is also particularly sensitive to other forms of political influence, notably in the host countries where the research takes place. Developments that are at first sight internal to the discipline are often linked to the broader institutional, structural, and political context in which the research occurs.

Later in this paper I sketch out three main approaches that I believe dominate the study of Indonesian politics today, and I offer some thoughts on how different country contexts and geopolitical imperatives have shaped these approaches. But I begin by looking at how changes in Indonesian politics have driven changes in the field over time, giving rise to three main temporal and thematic waves in political science research on Indonesia. Over the last sixty years, the broad agenda of the field has always been driven more by a struggle to understand the macropolitical changes that have transformed the country rather than by a concern with the micropolitics or deeper structures of Indonesian political life. This focus is largely because Indonesia has experienced a relatively tumultuous political history, and analysts have struggled to keep up with it.

THREE GENERATIONS OF INDONESIAN POLITICS AND SCHOLARSHIP

We may thus, roughly and schematically, divide analysis of Indonesian politics over the last six decades into three broad and overlapping phases. First, in the 1950s, 1960s, and into the early 1970s, the first generation of political specialists analyzed

[1] In addition to the participants in the workshop that gave rise to this volume, I would like to thank Marcus Mietzner, Michael Buehler, and Robert Cribb for their comments on this chapter, though none can be held responsible for its contents.

the formative dramas of independent Indonesia: the revolution (Kahin 1952; Anderson 1972a), the dynamics and downfall of parliamentary democracy (Feith 1962), the rise of Guided Democracy (Lev 1966; Feith 1963), and the politics of the communist party and of the peasantry (McVey 1965; Mortimer 1974). Their works were based on a deeply immersive fieldwork-based method and marked by breadth and ambition that have often eluded subsequent generations. The classic works of this era were written on a relatively blank slate, with their authors eager and qualified to explain the totality of Indonesian politics.

That breadth was also a product of the area studies approach then developing with much government support in the United States, as that country strove to develop regional expertise in keeping with its greatly expanded global role. Area studies, with its emphasis on language skills, country knowledge, and inter-disciplinary breadth, underpinned these early authors' attempts to embed their analysis of Indonesian politics in historical context and in sociological or anthropological insights about the nature of Indonesian society (even if some of them, notably Herbert Feith,[2] also responded to political science debates of the day). Particularly important in this generation and beyond was the seepage from anthropology, especially the influence of Clifford Geertz (1959, 1960) and his *aliran* (stream) framework for characterizing major socio-political currents in Javanese society, and Benedict Anderson's (1972b) efforts to link Indonesian political dynamics to a deep understanding of Javanese culture. This culturally embedded approach was also, of course, partly a product of the nature of Indonesian politics in those decades, when key political actors themselves included mass-based political movements rooted in various Indonesian communities. Understanding politics required an understanding of society.

Subsequent generations have been marked by growing thematic specialization and increasing engagement with political science theory. A second generation roughly coincides with the New Order period (1966–98), while naturally overlapping with both the generation that preceded it and the one that followed. Early on, in the late 1960s, 1970s, and early 1980s, there was a burst of inventive scholarship concerning the rise of military power and the New Order regime (e.g. Crouch 1978; Emmerson 1976; Raillon 1984). However, the later consolidation of the regime ushered in what was in some respects a period of relative sterility in the study of Indonesian politics.

This is not to say that fine works were not generated in the 1970s–1990s; many were. Key book-length studies focused on describing the nature of the New Order regime, its developmentalist orientation, its relations with the capitalist class, and the reasons for its resilience (e.g., Crouch 1978; Robison 1986; MacIntyre 1991; Winters 1996). A focus on the state and its relations with the private economy was the theme par excellence of political science research on Indonesia in this period, with a dominant view portraying the state as largely autonomous and all-powerful vis-à-vis society.[3] For comparative purposes, scholars drew on the literature regarding

---

[2] Herbert Feith, *The Decline of Constitutional Democracy in Indonesia* (Ithaca, NY: Cornell University Press, 1962).

[3] See, for example, on the continuity between the colonial-era *beamtenstaat* and the New Order, Ruth McVey, "The Beamtenstaat in Indonesia," in *Interpreting Indonesian Politics: Thirteen Contributions to the Debate*, ed. Benedict R. O'G. Anderson and Audrey Kahin (Ithaca, NY: Cornell Southeast Asia Program Publications, 1982), pp. 84–91; or Benedict Anderson's influential 1983 essay on the dominance of the "state qua state": Benedict Anderson, "Old

bureaucratic authoritarianism in Latin America and developmentalism in East Asia. Major debates in the field focused on how best to characterize the authoritarian regime (see various articles in Anderson and Kahin 1982). There were also normative disagreements about the proper attitude scholars should take toward the New Order, given its repressive character.[4]

Overall, however, a number of factors colluded to dampen the vigor that had earlier characterized the field, and to narrow the range of topics that were the subject of analysis. The main reason was that the pace of Indonesian political change had stagnated and the diversity that had previously characterized Indonesian political society was greatly constrained. Thus, though the period saw the production of a major study of Golkar (Reeve 1985), major book-length studies focused on pre-New Order topics, such other political parties or the politics of Islam (e.g., Boland 1971; Dijk 1981). Moreover, intellectual life on Indonesia's own campuses and at research institutions was moribund. Foreign scholars faced difficulties in conducting fieldwork-based research and accessing information about crucial political issues, ranging from the inner workings of the upper bureaucracy to political dynamics at the local level. Partly arising out of these practical limitations, but also stemming from an analytical framework that saw the state as an island "cut off from the social sea" surrounding it (Jackson 1978, 4), research during this period tended to be grounded less in fieldwork and the study of Indonesian societies than earlier scholarship. Several leading scholars of Indonesian politics moved on to other countries or topics, with the result that some of the most influential books on Indonesian politics in this period were written by journalists, perhaps because they had local and "inside" access that political scientists lacked (e.g., McDonald 1980; Jenkins 1984).

This situation began to change in the early 1990s, when the ripples of the global "third wave" of democratization began to lap on Indonesian shores. Burgeoning scholarship on democratization internationally posed questions about whether Indonesia would also experience democratic change, or, at least, about how it was that the country was such an obdurate hold-out (e.g., Emmerson 1995). This shift coincided with the beginning of my own research and was for me personally signaled by a 1992 Monash University conference held to mark the retirement of Herbert Feith that linked pressures for democratic change in the 1990s to the country's earlier experiences of democracy in the 1950s (Bourchier and Legge 1994). As the politics of succession and social protest became more contentious through the 1990s, the possibility of democratization became a major underlying concern in scholarship on Indonesia (e.g., Ramage 1995). To be sure, most scholars of Indonesian politics continued to be skeptical of the likelihood of democratic political

---

State, New Society: Indonesia's New Order in Comparative Historical Perspective," *Journal of Asian Studies* 42,3 (1983): 477–96. For an exception to the structuralism of this period of scholarship, see R. William Liddle, *Leadership and Culture in Indonesian Politics* (Sydney: Asian Studies Association of Australia in association with Allen & Unwin, 1996), which emphasizes the agency of political actors.

[4] For example, in Australia in the 1970s, there was a much-mythologized division between Indonesianists at Monash University, where a more critical stance was defined by scholars like Rex Mortimer, and those at the Australian National University, where economists such as Heinz Arndt were close to Indonesia's technocrats and broadly supportive of their efforts to pursue economic development. For one articulation of this division, see Rex Mortimer, *Showcase State: The Illusion of Indonesia's "Accelerated Modernisation"* (Sydney: Angus and Robertson, 1973).

change, an attitude that meant that very few predicted that the Suharto regime would end in such a spectacular fashion, let alone be superseded by democracy.[5] Debate on the possibilities of democratization had hardly started when events took over and the regime collapsed.

With the transition to a more democratic government beginning in 1998, a third generation of Indonesian political scholarship arose, in which democratization, its causes, and implications have been the overarching focus, but in which there has been an explosion of studies of various sub-themes. Significant books focused on the regime change and democratic consolidation (e.g., Aspinall 2005; Mietzner 2009; Crouch 2009). With the hurried pace of change, an equally important form of scholarly production was edited volumes, with several focusing on the major political change early in the period (e.g., Emmerson 1999; Budiman, Hatley, and Kingsbury 1999). The general interest in democratization gave rise to several sub-fields, including on the closely related topics of political corruption, voter behavior, and political parties (e.g., Tomsa 2008).

With Indonesian politics becoming far more diverse, so, too, inevitably, has Indonesian political-science scholarship. By the mid-2000s, arguably the major research foci for theses and publications were three overlapping topics: political violence, especially communal and separatist conflict (e.g. Aspinall 2009; Bertrand 2004; Davidson 2008; Purdey 2006; Sidel 2006; van Klinken 2007; Wilson 2008); decentralization and local politics (e.g., Aspinall and Fealy 2002; Erb and Sulistiyanto 2009; Hadiz 2010; Schulte Nordholt and van Klinken 2007); and political Islam (e.g., Platzdasch 2009). Another less prominent but still important field involves the various sectors of Indonesian civil society, and the struggle for progressive political and social change (e.g., Blackburn 2004; Priyono et al. 2007; Ford 2009). These thematic concerns have required Indonesianist scholars to engage with new sets of literature derived from geographic areas with which we were formerly less familiar (e.g., Eastern Europe, the Middle East, and South Asia). Democratization has remained the overarching analytical framework, however, with many authors framing their studies in terms of how democratic transformation has given rise to or been affected by the various other phenomena.

Major Approaches to the Study of Indonesian Politics

Having described the major thematic concerns of Indonesian politics scholarship over time, let me now sketch, equally schematically, three general approaches to the study of Indonesian politics that I believe dominate the field. It should be noted, however, that performing this mapping is not an easy task. Rather than dividing into readily discernible streams, the field of Indonesian political studies is instead characterized by a large, messy center, cross-hatched with multiple little traditions and what Robert Cribb (2005) has described as "circles of esteem"—small groups of scholars who read, promote, and cite one another's work. In addition to this center, however, it is possible to identify two discrete tendencies on the margins, which require separate consideration: critical political economy approaches and positivist political science.

---

[5] For one critique of this failure, see Gerry van Klinken, "The Coming Crisis in Indonesian Area Studies," *Journal of Southeast Asian Studies* 32,2 (2001): 263–68.

1. Mainstream Eclecticism

The origins of Indonesian political studies, exemplified in the work of George Kahin and his students, including Herbert Feith, Benedict Anderson, and Daniel Lev, were grounded in the use of historical method, immersive fieldwork in Indonesia, and direct access to primary sources and political actors, especially by way of elite interviews. Using such methods, these scholars built up careful portrayals of particular episodes in modern Indonesian political history, or of particular institutions in the political landscape, emphasizing careful collation and cross-checking of facts as they did so. They also viewed Indonesia's politics as growing out of its past, especially the colonial past, and placed great importance on fieldwork and language competence for the same empirical reasons as historians do: one really needs to know one's material in order to make a solid claim about it.[6] Nevertheless, as Benedict Anderson put it, this work was founded on an underlying American "cultural paradigm" that "assumes a natural and inextricable interconnection between private enterprise and property (capitalism), constitutional democracy, personal liberty, and progress"(Anderson 1982, 70). Harry Benda put it even more bluntly, in his famous critique of Herbert Feith's 1962 book, when he wrote that Feith, and many of his peers, began by asking the mistaken question: "What's wrong with Indonesia?" (Benda 1964, 450).[7]

This question—What's wrong with Indonesia?—remains central to much political science research on Indonesia. Over time, the particular version of the question has varied: Why did constitutional democracy fail? Why did the army come to power? Why did authoritarianism survive? Why hasn't democracy taken root more deeply? But the unstated standard against which Indonesia is measured remains an idealized vision of stable, liberal democracy. Benda wrote that the answer most often offered to the question in the 1950s and 1960s was: "It was the Dutch" (1964, 450). A set of answers that became popular in the 1960s and 1970s pointed toward Indonesian—or Javanese—culture as a catch-all explanation for Indonesian authoritarianism, but this approach was subsequently discredited by Marxist critiques (Robison 1981), constructivist views of culture (Pemberton 1994), and analyses that systematically demolished the New Order regime's own claims to cultural authenticity (Simanjuntak 1994; Bourchier 1997). In any case, the mainstream approach has always been to build thickly descriptive explanations of Indonesian political developments based on nuanced accounts of interactions between structure, institutions, and actors, with a strong emphasis on agency (an emphasis that was given an added fillip by democratization literature from the late 1980s onward). As a result, scholars have typically identified one or another political actor (the army, Suharto, the elite, etc.) as the *diabolus ex machina*, to again borrow from Benda, of alleged Indonesian political failure.

Most political science research on Indonesia continues to stem from this broad tradition, and is founded in fieldwork, sensitivity to and understanding of local political actors' views and actions, and an analysis of interactions between actors and structures. Theoretically, much of this research is located in what Peter Evans once described as the "eclectic messy center" of comparative politics (1995, 2). Many

---

[6] My thanks to Robert Cribb for this point.

[7] See the chapter by Donald Emmerson in this volume for a more extended discussion of this debate.

leading scholars of Indonesian politics thus borrow promiscuously from different theoretical paradigms to explain whatever it is that happens to be the focus of their research at a particular moment, without necessarily developing a distinctive style or approach.

In the current era of democratization, as in the past, most such research by foreign scholars has been founded on a strong normative commitment to democracy, and—very often—strong sympathy with various sectors of Indonesian civil society and (especially lately) the liberal end of the Islamic political spectrum. This sympathy is sometimes overt, usually unstated, but typically strongly informs scholarship. Indeed, most foreign researchers—especially PhD students but also more established scholars—are typically dependent on a select group of interlocutors in Indonesia, usually liberal intellectuals or NGO activists, who are the investigator's first port of call and sometimes primary source of information, especially in the formative stages of a research project. Even if each foreign researcher has his or her favorite institutions and individuals, this is a consistent but rarely remarked upon pattern. (It is also a tradition that dates back at least to the years of George Kahin, who was close to leaders of the Republic in Yogyakarta, and to the experiences of Herbert Feith, who was sympathetic to the intellectuals of the Indonesian Socialist Party as sources). Thus, if the unstated starting point for much research continues to be "What's wrong with Indonesia?," it is not surprising that today the answer is almost always "the elite," because this echoes the refrain of liberal Indonesian political opinion.

Much of this research, in taking specifically Indonesian developments as its starting point, tends to be driven by context-specific questions and puzzles, and to be broadly descriptive, empirical, and interpretivist in style. To be sure, most such research is located within the broad comparative politics tradition, and most authors treat Indonesian problems within a comparative framework, even if the comparisons are often implicit and arise more through the foregrounding of certain kinds of questions and approaches than from sustained inquiry. As a consequence, mainstream scholarship on Indonesia can readily be subject to the accusations of methodological and theoretical weakness usually leveled at area studies scholarship. Indeed, it is arguably true that Indonesian political-science scholars have contributed relatively little to the major debates that have shaped political science as a field. On the other hand, they still produce brilliantly researched, detailed, and nuanced studies, even if most studies now focus on just one particular aspect or sector of Indonesian life, lacking the ambition that was possible in the age of Kahin and Feith.

2. Political Economy Approaches

Amidst the theoretical eclecticism of much Indonesian politics research, there is one small group of scholars that has developed a distinctive approach: the Marxist-influenced political economists. Special attention here must be paid to the Australian scholar, Richard Robison, whose 1986 book, *Indonesia: The Rise of Capital,* was one of the most influential books on Indonesian politics published during the New Order years. In it, Robison charted the rise of an Indonesian capitalist class from within the shelter of the bureaucratic state, arguing that capitalism should thus be seen as inextricably linked to authoritarianism rather than as the harbinger of its doom (even if he also reversed the lens of Marxist class analysis, viewing the state as giving rise to the capitalist class, rather than vice versa). Robison also trained a group of graduate students who researched various countries of Southeast Asia. Known for their critical political economy approach that places capitalism and class relations at its center, some of their number (e.g., Garry Rodan, Kevin Hewison) have gone on to become leading scholars of the region. One of Robison's graduate students, Vedi R. Hadiz, a former participant in leftist Jakarta student study groups in the 1980s, has emerged as one of the most productive and influential scholars of contemporary Indonesian politics. Other scholars, such as the American Jeffrey Winters, though not part of the group founded by Robison, also draw on class analysis to come to broadly similar conclusions (Winters 1996, 2011).

In a series of books and widely cited articles over the last decade or so, Robison and Hadiz (see especially Robison and Hadiz 2004) have argued that Indonesia's democratic transition is characterized above all by the reconstitution of the same class forces that dominated Indonesia during the New Order period. As Hadiz puts it, Indonesian democracy has been captured by "coalitions of predatory power rooted in the now demised New Order" (2010, 172). This has been a powerful and influential analysis, even if its analytical thrust is not far from the mainstream, which has also been marked by a generally critical interpretation of the depth of Indonesian democracy. What above all distinguishes Robison and Hadiz's recent work is their framing of it as a relentless critique of neo-liberal analysis, their insistence on placing class at the center, and, above all, a pessimistic tone and assessment. Particularly striking is the absence of the revolutionary optimism in the transformative powers of the lower classes and social movements that was once the hallmark of Marxist scholars in the Cold War years (virtually the only international author who writes in that original vein is Max Lane [2008], though his work lies outside mainstream political science). Instead, positive identification with Indonesian political actors tends to be expressed more forcefully within the eclectic center of Indonesian political analysis, where scholars are often transparently sympathetic to the efforts of Indonesian reformers.

3. Positivist Political Science

A trend over the last decade or so has been the growing importance of Indonesia as an object of study in mainstream positivist political science, especially in the United States. Put crudely, there is an increasing tendency for scholars to treat Indonesia, or Indonesian materials, not as interesting for their own sake, but primarily as case study ingredients for building a broader theory.[8] There are at least three reasons for this trend. First, and most obvious, Indonesia has become a major case of successful democratization, putting the country firmly on the map of global political currents and therefore of comparative political studies. Accordingly, senior comparativists and scholars of democratization have now turned their attention to Indonesia (e.g., Diamond 2010; Horowitz 2013; Künkler and Stepan 2013). Second, Indonesia has also become an easier place in which to conduct research. It is a far more open society than in the New Order years, with the result that media reporting is far more detailed and revealing of underlying political trends. It is also much

---

[8] Of course, this formulation is a simplification for the purpose of argument. It is not my intention to set up a false dichotomy between theory-driven comparative literature and Indonesia-focused and theoretically derivative literature. Clearly, there is great overlap and much of the best material written in the "eclectic center" is deeply concerned with both theory and comparison.

easier for visiting scholars to forge networks and conduct field interviews even in relatively short periods of time. This greater openness also means that Indonesia (as one graduate student at the 2011 Association for Asian Studies meeting in Honolulu put it to me) has become a "data-producing country," ready to be mined for the purposes of quantitative analysis.

Third, and most importantly, the changing place of Indonesia in political science research is related to broader trends in (especially) American political science, with its turning away from country expertise and area studies approaches, and its emphasis on cross-country skills and method-driven research agendas. Scholars who might in the past have been attracted to empirical minutiae are under increasing pressure to present their findings in terms of broad theoretical propositions and comparisons across a large number of cases. In particular, the longstanding positivist emphasis on devising and testing hypotheses has been combined with a new emphasis on counterfactual reasoning that requires scholars to compare Indonesia to other countries if they wish to draw meaningful conclusions about national-level phenomena.[9]

If in what I have termed the eclectic center of Indonesian political studies it is hard to generalize about distinctive approaches because scholars borrow so widely, it is equally difficult to summarize the impact of Indonesia's shift to the mainstream of political science literature, because it is increasingly possible for specialists in this or that sub-field of political science theory to draw on Indonesian material for their theory-building. One striking development (at least for an outsider to American political science) is the early signs of the growing influence of quantitative approaches to measuring and analyzing Indonesian political phenomena. Such approaches are especially evident among recent or current (mostly North American) graduate students researching Indonesia, and will surely leave a mark on the field in coming years, as will other methods such as field experiments (Olken 2007). Another important development is that some of the strongest work on Indonesia over the last decade has occurred in the context of broader comparative books that place Indonesia in a wider Southeast Asia perspective (e.g., Boudreau 2009; Pepinsky 2009; Slater 2010; Vu 2010), reflecting the survival of at least a Southeast Asia area studies impulse in US political science, even if Indonesia specialization is problematic, as we shall see in a moment. Though this scholarship also produces important empirical research about Indonesia, its primary intended audience is readers from the broad political science discipline and persons with wide concerns about theory, comparative issues, and global trends, rather than readers with a particular interest in Indonesia and its problems.

NORMATIVE FOUNDATIONS, INSTITUTIONAL LOCATIONS, AND COUNTRY TRADITIONS

What have been the influences of country and institutional location and imperatives on the trends so far summarized? Scholarship on Indonesian politics does not, after all, arise merely from the interaction between Indonesian political developments and the curiosity of the individual scholar. It is also influenced by the institutional context in which such scholarship is produced, and the incentives that shape it. Space prohibits detailed exploration of this theme. Such an exploration

---

[9] Regarding the emphasis on devising and testing hypotheses, see R. William Liddle's contribution to this volume.

would require, at least, discussion of Indonesian political-science scholarship in The Netherlands, Singapore, and Germany, as well as the influence of other factors, such as the growing impact of democracy assistance, political consultancy, and international agencies (such as the World Bank) in shaping research agendas. Nevertheless, it is worth considering briefly the two countries where most research on Indonesian politics takes place outside Indonesia, and then to consider Indonesia itself.

For a long time, the United States was the major site for the study of Indonesian politics, with the field originating at Cornell University in the 1950s and spreading outwards from that center. Though the relative importance of US-based scholarship on Indonesian politics has declined significantly, scholarship in the United States remains important because that country is the home of the modern discipline of political science, and largely continues to define it. It should already be obvious from what I have written that I see certain trends in the political science discipline in the United States as having significant impacts on the study of Indonesian politics globally. The decline of area studies in the United States after the end of the Cold War has been well canvassed elsewhere (e.g., Fukuyama 2004); one result is that it has become increasingly difficult for younger scholars to find employment in US political science departments by defining themselves as Indonesia specialists.[10] The rise of quantitative methods, economic modeling, and the related rational choice sensibility has especially strongly influenced younger scholars and graduate students working on Indonesia in the United States. Accordingly, American political scientists working on Indonesia (and Southeast Asia more broadly) often seem to exhibit greater anxiety to justify their geographical focus to the discipline than do their colleagues elsewhere (e.g., Kuhonta, Slater, and Vu 2008), and there are greater pressures on them to produce work that is self-consciously methodologically rigorous and theoretically parsimonious. At the same time, given the very recent resurgence of interest in Indonesia in mainstream positivist political science mentioned above, more PhDs on Indonesian politics are now being earned and conferred in the United States, but often now in political science departments without traditions of Indonesia or even Southeast Asia expertise.

These changes, and the broader evolution of the political science discipline in the United States, are surely connected to wider political and cultural changes in the country and its changing global role in the post-Cold War period: since the US figures as the remaining global superpower, it is perhaps not surprising that there emerged in the United States a belief in universally applicable theories and methods that can be applied to any part of the globe, and a concomitant turn against the particularism of area studies.

By contrast, Australia arguably has become the major center of Indonesian politics scholarship over the last two to three decades. In Australia, Indonesian

---

[10] One striking fact is that since the late 1990s very few single-author books focusing mainly on Indonesian politics have been published by political scientists located at US universities; indeed, I can think of only one: Ehito Kimura, *Political Change and Territoriality in Indonesia: Provincial Proliferation* (Abingdon: Routledge, 2012). In contrast, more than a dozen such books have been written by Australia-based scholars, and several by American scholars employed outside the United States (see, for example, Jamie S. Davidson, *From Rebellion to Riots: Collective Violence on Indonesian Borneo* [Madison, WI: University of Wisconsin Press, 2008]; and John Sidel, *Riots, Pogroms, Jihad: Religious Violence in Indonesia* [Ithaca, NY: Cornell University Press, 2006].

political studies remain strongly regionalist and particularlist in focus. Australian scholars studying Indonesia do not encounter institutional pressure to treat Indonesia as a case study, and instead are encouraged to see it as an important field of scholarship in its own right. (For more detailed discussion, see Aspinall 2013.) The broader political context is again key: Indonesia looms larger on the horizon of the Australian political landscape, for better and for worse, than it does in the United States, and, as a result, specialist knowledge of Indonesia is relatively highly valued by the media, policy makers, and, consequently, among Australian academics.[11] Many specialists of Indonesian politics working in Australian universities are thus located in Asian Studies rather than political science departments, and many have not received advanced political science training as part of their graduate education. Accordingly, rather than valuing political science method or theoretical innovation, they tend to place great value on deep fieldwork knowledge, language skills, direct interaction with informants, and being up to date on the latest political developments in-country. (It is no coincidence that one of the major Indonesian Studies institutions in Australia is the annual "Indonesia Update" conference at the Australian National University.) Accordingly, Australian research on Indonesian politics tends to fall squarely within the eclectic center summarized above.

Where do Indonesian scholars and scholarship fit in all of this? Over the last two decades, perhaps hundreds of Indonesians have attained graduate training in political science overseas, and numerous Indonesian universities run political science programs. There is also a massive market in Indonesia for public media commentary on Indonesian political affairs, and a concomitantly important role for media savvy "public intellectuals." Are these Indonesians significantly transforming the shape of the international field of Indonesian political studies? The answer is less unequivocal than it would have been a generation ago, but still largely negative. With some exceptions, Indonesian scholars continue to have limited direct impact on the international, English-language scholarship on Indonesia. Again, the explanation can be found in the academic political economy and surrounding context. Thus, many Indonesian political scientists, upon returning home from attaining their PhDs in the United States, Australia, or elsewhere, have gone on to achieve public recognition and fame as media commentators and pundits—to a degree that would be unimaginable for their mentors and colleagues overseas—and some have become important as political consultants or policy makers. These career paths have opened up widely in the post-Suharto period and can promise comfortable incomes. But relatively few of these graduates have continued to produce high quality publications based on systematic primary research or to publish in international scholarly outlets. Indonesian universities have not to date provided sufficient research support or salaries to sustain such activities, and promising researchers therefore find themselves readily diverted into administrative work, or find themselves doing most of their research for external projects and consultancies.

This political economy of academic production is reflected in the data showing that the Indonesian contribution to international scholarly publication is very low, even when compared to other Southeast Asian countries. Thus, according to one recent study, "When measured through the number of published articles in

---

[11] To be sure, Indonesianists in Australian universities are also under pressure from the marketization of higher education and declining enrollments in Indonesian language courses, but the long-term effects of these developments remain to be seen.

international peer-reviewed journals indexed by Social Sciences Citation Index (SSCI), only about 12 percent of social science research publications on Indonesia [are produced] by authors based in the country" (Suryadarma et al. 2011, 1). To be sure, much original research continues to be conducted and published in Indonesia, in the Indonesian language, but little of it engages with international political science debates or has much impact on that broader field.[12] On the other hand, a small but growing number of Indonesians are among the most innovative and influential scholars writing on Indonesian politics internationally, but they are often employed in overseas universities (for example, Vedi Hadiz, now located at Murdoch University in Western Australia, and Ariel Heryanto, now at the Australian National University). On the other hand, the debt that the field as a whole owes to Indonesian scholars is largely unacknowledged, given that international researchers typically rely on their Indonesian partners for building up and updating their own knowledge of Indonesian political events.

THE FUTURE

Regarding possible future trends, much will be obvious from what is written above. The most important point is that the field will continue to be shaped, above all, by political changes in Indonesia itself. Already, work is being written on the theme of "democratic recession" in Indonesia (e.g., Mietzner 2011), and we can expect more if the current stagnation in democratic reform continues. Decentralization has also been a crucial influence, and under its influence a fourth generation of scholarship is already visible, defined above all by an interest in local politics and regional variation within Indonesia. Broader changes in the discipline will also have an impact, and we can expect more rigorous quantitative research on Indonesian politics, especially from the United States. This is a welcome development, though I believe the eclectic center of Indonesian politics research will hold. Even if over time contextual and interpretivist research is increasingly marginalized within the United States academy, it will remain strong in Australia, Singapore, and, increasingly, Indonesia itself.

A final thought on which to end, offered in the inter-disciplinary spirit in which this volume is conceived, regards exchange with other disciplines, especially anthropology. One feature that still distinguishes most Indonesian political studies research is its concern with formal organizations and its orientation to the elite as the *diabolus ex machina* of Indonesian politics. Even the proliferation of local case studies since the demise of decentralization has found expression, above all, in a proliferation of studies of local elites. Meanwhile, major trends in the social sciences more broadly, such as the influence of Foucauldian approaches and the analysis of governmentality, have largely bypassed the writings on Indonesian politics. To the extent to which they have been taken up, it has largely been by anthropologists, who have produced some of the more important and interesting work on Indonesian politics, understood broadly (e.g., Pemberton 1994; Li 2007). Indeed, the colonization by anthropologists of the study of the micropolitics of Indonesian society is one of

---

[12] Well-researched and information-packed books are often published by Indonesian authors on particular topics long before equivalent books appear in English, for example, on Islamic political movements. See Aay Muhammad Furkon, *Partai Keadilan Sejahtera: Ideologi dan Praksis Politik Kaum Muda Muslim Indonesia Kontemporer* (Jakarta: Teraju, 2004); and Solahudin, *NII Sampai JI: Salafy Jihadisme di Indonesia* (Jakarta: Gramedia, 2011).

the defining features of the study of Indonesian politics over the last decade or two, and one that political scientists should take note of and learn from. There is surely room for political scientists to take the political activities and experiences of ordinary people more seriously.

Works Cited

Anderson, Benedict R. O'G. *Java in a Time of Revolution: Occupation and Resistance, 1944–1946*. Ithaca, NY: Cornell University Press, 1972a.

——. "The Idea of Power in Javanese Culture." *Culture and Politics in Indonesia*. Ed. Claire Holt. Ithaca, NY: Cornell University Press, 1972b: 1–69.

——. "Perspective and Method in American Research on Indonesia." *Interpreting Indonesian Politics: Thirteen Contributions to the Debate*. Ed. Benedict R. O'G. Anderson and Audrey Kahin. Ithaca, NY: Cornell Southeast Asia Program Publications, 1982: 69–83.

——. "Old State, New Society: Indonesia's New Order in Comparative Historical Perspective." *Journal of Asian Studies*, 42.3 (1983): 477–96.

Anderson, Benedict R. O'G., and Audrey Kahin, eds. *Interpreting Indonesian Politics: Thirteen Contributions to the Debate*. Ithaca, NY: Cornell Southeast Asia Program Publications, 1982.

Aspinall, Edward. *Opposing Suharto: Compromise, Resistance, and Regime Change in Indonesia*. Stanford, CA: Stanford University Press, 2005.

——. *Islam and Nation: Separatist Rebellion in Aceh, Indonesia*. Stanford, CA: Stanford University Press, 2009.

——. "The Politics of the Study of Indonesian Politics: Intellectuals, Political Research, and Public Debate in Australia." *Ways of Knowing Indonesia*. Ed. Jemma Purdey. Clayton, Victoria: Monash Asia Institute Press, 2012.

Aspinall, Edward, and Greg Fealy, eds. *Local Power and Politics in Indonesia: Democratisation and Decentralisation*. Singapore: Institute of Southeast Asian Studies, 2002.

Benda, Harry J. "Democracy in Indonesia." *Journal of Asian Studies*, 23.3 (1964): 449–56.

Boland, B. J. *The Struggle of Islam in Modern Indonesia*. The Hague: Martinus Nijhoff, 1971.

Boudreau, Vincent. *Resisting Dictatorship: Repression and Protest in Southeast Asia*. Cambridge: Cambridge University Press, 2009.

Bourchier, David. "Totalitarianism and the 'National Personality': Recent Controversy about the Philosophical Basis of the Indonesian State." *Imagining Indonesia: Cultural Politics and Political Culture*. Ed. James Schiller and Barbara Martin-Schiller. Athens, OH: Ohio University Center for International Studies, 1997: 157–85.

Bourchier, David, and John Legge, eds. *Democracy in Indonesia, 1950s and 1990s*. Clayton, Victoria: Monash University, Centre of Southeast Asian Studies, 1994.

Bertrand, Jacques. *Nationalism and Ethnic Conflict in Indonesia*. Cambridge: Cambridge University Press, 2004.

Blackburn, Susan. *Women and the State in Modern Indonesia*. Cambridge: Cambridge University Press, 2004.

Budiman, Arief, Barbara Hatley, and Damien Kingsbury, eds. *Reformasi: Crisis and Change in Indonesia*. Clayton, Victoria: Monash Asia Institute, 1999.

Cribb, Robert. "Circles of Esteem, Standard Works, and Euphoric Couplets: Dynamics of Academic Life in Indonesian Studies." *Critical Asian Studies* 37.2 (2005): 289–304.

Crouch, Harold. *The Army and Politics in Indonesia*. Ithaca, NY: Cornell University Press, 1978.

——. *Political Reform in Indonesia after Soeharto*. Singapore: Institute of Southeast Asian Studies, 2010.

Davidson, Jamie S. *From Rebellion to Riots: Collective Violence on Indonesian Borneo*. Madison, WI: University of Wisconsin Press, 2008.

Diamond, Larry. "Indonesia's Place in Global Democracy." *Problems of Democratisation in Indonesia: Elections, Institutions, and Society*. Ed. Edward Aspinall and Marcus Mietzner. Singapore: Institute of Southeast Asian Studies, 2010: 21–49.

Dijk, Cornelis van. *Rebellion under the Banner of Islam: The Darul Islam in Indonesia*. The Hague: Martinus Nijhoff, 1981.

Emmerson, Donald K. *Indonesia's Elite: Political Culture and Cultural Politics*. Ithaca, NY: Cornell University Press, 1976.

——. "Region and Recalcitrance: Rethinking Democracy in Southeast Asia." *Pacific Review* 8.2 (1995): 223–48.

Emmerson, Donald K., ed. *Indonesia beyond Suharto: Polity, Economy, Society, Transition*. Armonk, NY: M. E. Sharpe, 1999.

Erb, Maribeth, and Priyambudi Sulistiyanto, eds. *Deepening Democracy in Indonesia? Direct Elections for Local Leaders (Pilkada)*. Singapore: Institute of Southeast Asian Studies, 2009.

Evans, Peter. "The Role of Theory in Comparative Politics: A Symposium." *World Politics* 48.1 (1995): 2–10.

Feith, Herbert. *The Decline of Constitutional Democracy in Indonesia*. Ithaca, NY: Cornell University Press, 1962.

——. "The Dynamics of Guided Democracy." *Indonesia*. Ed. Ruth T. McVey. New Haven, CT: Yale University Southeast Asia Studies, 1963: 309–409.

Ford, Michele. *Workers and Intellectuals: NGOs, Trade Unions, and the Indonesian Labour Movement*. Singapore: Singapore University Press, 2009.

Fukuyama, Francis. "How Academia Failed the Nation: The Decline of Regional Studies." *Saisphere*. Winter 2004. At http://www.campus-watch.org/article/id/1507.

Furkon, Aay Muhammad. *Partai Keadilan Sejahtera: Ideologi dan Praksis Politik Kaum Muda Muslim Indonesia Kontemporer.* Jakarta: Teraju, 2004.

Geertz, Clifford. "The Javanese Village." *Local, Ethnic, and National Loyalties in Village Indonesia.* Ed. G. William Skinner. New Haven, CT: Yale University Cultural Report Series, 1959: 34–41.

——. *The Religion of Java.* New York, NY: Free Press of Glencoe, 1960.

Hadiz, Vedi R. *Localising Power in Post-Authoritarian Indonesia: A Southeast Asia Perspective.* Stanford, CA: Stanford University Press, 2010.

Horowitz, Donald L. *Constitutional Change and Democracy in Indonesia.* Cambridge: Cambridge University Press, 2013.

Jackson, Karl. "Bureaucratic Polity: A Theoretical Framework for the Analysis of Power and Communications in Indonesia." *Political Power and Communications in Indonesia.* Ed. Karl D. Jackson and Lucian W. Pye. Berkeley, CA: University of California Press, 1978: 3–22.

Jenkins, David. *Suharto and His Generals: Indonesian Military Politics, 1975–1983.* Ithaca, NY: Cornell Southeast Asia Program Publications, 1984.

Kahin, George McT. *Nationalism and Revolution in Indonesia.* Ithaca, NY: Cornell University Press, 1952.

——. *Communal Violence and Democratization in Indonesia: Small Town Wars.* London: Routledge, 2007.

Kimura, Ehito. *Political Change and Territoriality in Indonesia: Provincial Proliferation.* Abdingdon: Routledge, 2012.

Klinken, Gerry Van. "The Coming Crisis in Indonesian Area Studies." *Journal of Southeast Asian Studies* 32.2 (2001): 263–68.

Kuhonta, Erik Martinez, Dan Slater, and Tuong Vu, eds. *Southeast Asia in Political Science: Theory, Region, and Qualitative Analysis.* Stanford, CA: Stanford University Press, 2008.

Künkler, Mirjam, and Alfred Stepan, eds. *Democracy and Islam in Indonesia.* New York, NY: Columbia University Press, 2013.

Lane, Max. *Unfinished Nation: Indonesia Before and After Suharto.* London: Verso, 2008.

Lev, Daniel. *The Transition to Guided Democracy: Indonesian Politics, 1957–59.* Ithaca, NY: Cornell Modern Indonesia Project, 1966.

Liddle, R. William. *Leadership and Culture in Indonesian Politics.* Sydney: Asian Studies Association of Australia in association with Allen & Unwin, 1996.

Li, Tania Murray. *The Will to Improve: Governmentality, Development, and the Practice of Politics.* Durham, NC: Duke University Press, 2007.

MacIntyre, Andrew. *Business and Politics in Indonesia.* Sydney: Allen & Unwin, 1991.

McDonald, Hamish. *Suharto's Indonesia.* Blackburn: Fontana–Collins, 1980.

McVey, Ruth. *The Rise of Indonesian Communism.* Ithaca, NY: Cornell University Press, 1965.

——. "The Beamtenstaat in Indonesia." *Interpreting Indonesian Politics: Thirteen Contributions to the Debate.* Ed. Benedict R. O'G. Anderson and Audrey Kahin. Ithaca, NY: Cornell Southeast Asia Program Publications, 1982: 84–91.

Mietzner, Marcus. *Military Politics, Islam, and the State in Indonesia: From Turbulent Transition to Democratic Consolidation.* Singapore: Institute of Southeast Asian Studies, 2009.

——. "Indonesia's Democratic Stagnation: Anti-reformist Elites and Resilient Civil Society." *Democratization* 19.2 (2012): 209–29.

Mortimer, Rex, ed. *Showcase State: The Illusion of Indonesia's "Accelerated Modernisation."* Sydney: Angus and Robertson, 1973.

——. *Indonesian Communism under Sukarno: Ideology and Politics, 1959–1965.* Ithaca, NY: Cornell University Press, 1974.

Olken, Benjamin A. "Monitoring Corruption: Evidence from a Field Experiment in Indonesia." *Journal of Political Economy* 115.2 (2007): 200–249.

Pemberton, John. *On the Subject of "Java."* Ithaca, NY: Cornell University Press, 1994.

Pepinsky, Thomas B. *Economic Crises and the Breakdown of Authoritarian Regimes: Indonesia and Malaysia in Comparative Perspective.* Cambridge: Cambridge University Press, 2009.

Platzdasch, Bernhard. *Islamism in Indonesia: Politics in the Emerging Democracy.* Singapore: Institute of Southeast Asian Studies, 2009.

Priyono, A. E., Willy Purna Samadhi, and Olle Törnquist. *Making Democracy Meaningful: Problems and Options in Indonesia.* Jakarta: Demos, 2007.

Purdey, Jemma. *Anti-Chinese Violence in Indonesia, 1996–99.* Singapore: Singapore University Press, 2006.

Raillon, François. *Les etudiants indonesiens et l' Orde nouveau: Politique et ideologie du Mahasiswa Indonesia (1966–1974).* Paris: Editions de la Maison des Sciences de l'Homme, 1984.

Ramage, Douglas E. *Politics in Indonesia: Democracy, Islam, and the Ideology of Tolerance.* New York, NY: Routledge, 1995.

Reeve, David. *Golkar of Indonesia: An Alternative to the Party System.* Singapore: Oxford University Press, 1985.

Robison, Richard. "Culture, Politics, and Economy in the Political History of the New Order." *Indonesia* 31 (April 1981): 1–29.

——. *Indonesia: The Rise of Capital.* Sydney: Allen & Unwin, 1986.

Robison, Richard, and Vedi R. Hadiz. *Reorganising Power in Indonesia: The Politics of Oligarchy in an Age of Markets.* London: RoutledgeCurzon, 2004.

Schulte Nordholt, Henk, and Gerry van Klinken, eds. *Renegotiating Boundaries: Local Politics in Post-Suharto Indonesia.* Leiden: KITLV Press, 2007.

Sidel, John. *Riots, Pogroms, Jihad: Religious Violence in Indonesia.* Ithaca, NY: Cornell University Press, 2006.

Simanjuntak, Marsillam. *Pandangan Negara Integralistik: Sumber, Unsur dan Riwayatnya dalam Persiapan UUD 1945*. Jakarta: Grafiti, 1994.

Slater, Dan. *Ordering Power: Contentious Politics and Authoritarian Leviathans in Southeast Asia*. Cambridge: Cambridge University Press, 2010.

Solahudin. *NII Sampai JI: Salafy Jihadisme di Indonesia*. Jakarta: Gramedia, 2011.

Suryadarma, Daniel, Jacqueline Pomeroy, and Sunny Tanuwidjaja. "Economic Factors Underpinning Constraints in Indonesia's Knowledge Sector." Australian National University, unpublished monograph, 2011.

Tomsa, Dirk. *Party Politics and Democratization in Indonesia: Golkar in the Post-Suharto Era*. New York, NY: Routledge, 2008.

Vu, Tuong. *Paths to Development in Asia: South Korea, Vietnam, China, and Indonesia*. Cambridge: Cambridge University Press, 2010.

Wilson, Chris. *Ethno-Religious Violence in Indonesia: From Soil to God*. London: Routledge, 2008.

Winters, Jeffrey A. *Power in Motion: Capital Mobility and the Indonesian State*. Ithaca, NY: Cornell University Press, 1996.

——. *Oligarchy*. Cambridge: Cambridge University Press, 2011.

POLITICAL SCIENCE SCHOLARSHIP ON INDONESIA: REVIVED BUT CONSTRAINED

R. William Liddle[1]

Political science scholarship on Indonesia has revived in the twenty-first century. This revival is most apparent in the United States, but is also evident in Australia, Europe, and—less strongly—in Indonesia itself. In the United States, mainstream positivist approaches predominate, while most scholars elsewhere focus directly on Indonesia, "area studies" style, or adopt an interpretivist approach. Marxism-based critical scholarship has become increasingly popular, especially in Australia, Europe, and Indonesia.

On the plus side, the new mainstream scholarship has succeeded in joining Indonesian studies more closely to the political science discipline as a whole, particularly in its use of direct multi-country comparison to build comparative theories of nation-state politics. But it has also been constrained by a Procrustean temptation, counter impulses to theory destruction, excessive determinism, and America-centrism. Each of these criticisms is elaborated below. Area studies and interpretive scholarship, valuable in their own right, serve as a useful corrective to the weaknesses of mainstream political science.

Less valuable is the contribution of critical scholars, whose reliance on a materialist interpretation of history obscures more than it clarifies our understanding of Indonesian politics. Most disturbing, a seemingly unbridgeable gap continues to divide mainstream and critical political science, powerfully constraining our ability to address democratic Indonesia's most pressing problems.

THE NEW AMERICAN POLITICAL SCIENCE RESEARCH

In American political science scholarship on Indonesia, the twenty-first century has begun strong. Four exemplary books—in order of publication, Benjamin Smith (2007), Thomas Pepinsky (2009), Tuong Vu (2010), and Dan Slater (2010)—provide but do not exhaust the evidence for a trend. These and other recent books and

[1] I thank Jay Hanan for his valuable research assistance and comments.

articles grapple with large theoretical issues, of normative and empirical significance for understanding present and future Indonesia as well as other modern states, developed and developing. The authors are also driven by ambition to be at the cutting edge of contemporary American political science. Accordingly, they are mainstream or positivist political scientists, positivist in the sense that they formulate empirically testable propositions, then test those propositions as rigorously as possible with data carefully specified to operationalize theoretically relevant variables.

Amazingly, for a Southeast Asianist of my generation, all four studies are explicitly comparative, analyzing more than one country in detail. At the same time they are all based on substantial fieldwork in Indonesia and deep knowledge of the Indonesian case, arguably the principal hallmark of Indonesia-focused political scientists since the 1950s. Smith compares Indonesia (where Suharto's New Order was not fundamentally destabilized by the oil export boom of the mid-1970s) with Iran (where the Shah's monarchy was overthrown in 1979). This comparison produces the insight, which Smith subsequently tests with quantitative data for many countries, that the pre-boom origins of the New Order constrained Suharto to build a broadly based and thus durable support coalition. Pepinsky compares the impact of different economic interest coalitions in Indonesia (divided) and Malaysia (united) on authoritarian stability (the New Order fell, but Malaysia remains authoritarian) when both were hit hard by the 1997–98 Southeast Asian financial crisis.

Within political science, Smith's and Pepinsky's studies belong to a subfield called political economy. Vu and Slater, on the other hand, while also political scientists, adopt the approach and methods of comparative historical sociology. Vu argues, based on in-depth comparisons of South Korea, Vietnam, Republican and Maoist China, and Sukarno's and Suharto's Indonesia, that patterns of inter-elite and mass-elite relations at the time of state formation determined both subsequent state cohesion and the state's commitment to developmental policies. Slater claims that patterns of contentious politics in the immediate post-World War II period are most responsible for differences in authoritarian durability. Among these authors, Slater wins the prize for most countries directly compared: Burma, Indonesia, Malaysia, the Philippines, Singapore, South Vietnam, and Thailand.

What these four studies do not share is a commitment to quantitative analysis as the highest form of positivist political science. The point is important because of the recent publication of *Southeast Asia in Political Science: Theory, Region, and Qualitative Analysis* (Kuhonta, Slater, and Vu 2008), whose authors (including two of the scholars mentioned above) believe, mistakenly in my view, that the current methodological pluralism of political science is threatened by monomaniacal quantifiers. It is true that a group of quantitatively oriented political scientists, with rational choice scholars the vanguard of this group, are today committed to the development of political science as science. These scholars do, indeed, define science, beyond the positivist consensus outlined above, as primarily or even exclusively relying on quantitative data.

Fortunately for the pluralists, however, it is also true that the qualitative versus quantitative methodological debate has existed in the discipline for many decades, without a final resolution. As I read the history, the intensely committed quantifiers and the intensely committed qualitative scholars have long been balanced by a pluralist center consisting of a much larger number of political scientists who believe that choice of method should follow, not precede, choice of analytical problem or puzzle to be studied (King, Keohane, and Verba 1994). It is worth noting that of my four authors, the quondam quantifiers Smith and Pepinsky are also methodological pluralists, both in principle (as they aver in their respective books) and by example. While they make extensive use of the latest quantitative data and statistical techniques, they also rely on time-honored techniques of conducting elite interviews and reading documents and mass media accounts.

The standard, in my view still unequaled, for this kind of modern political science research, though without the direct comparisons to other nation-states, was set by Herbert Feith (1962). Feith's valuable distinctions between political elite and political public, and, more famously (and controversially), between "administrators" and "solidarity makers," were grounded explicitly in the political science of Harold Lasswell (1958) and the political development theories of Gabriel Almond (Almond and Coleman 1960) and Edward Shils (1960), among others. Perhaps setting another as-yet unequaled standard, Feith conducted field research in Indonesia for four years before heading to Cornell to write his master work.

While not stated explicitly, a deep normative commitment to democracy was apparent in Feith's book. That commitment extended to "constitutional democracy," the rules and procedures of Western-style democracy, which Feith identified as the institutional foundation for the realization of other values desired by citizens of the newly independent Indonesian republic, including individual civil liberties; economic, political, and social equality; and national power on the international stage.

Other political scientists publishing their first books in this period included, by date of publication, me (1970), a study of national integration viewed through an East Sumatran lens; Donald Emmerson (1976), an examination of the political impact of elite cultural division in Parliament and the bureaucracy during the early New Order; and Karl Jackson (1980), an exploration of the causes of peasant rebellion as seen in the case of Dar'ul Islam in West Java. Like Feith's work and the twenty-first century studies, these three books are all theoretically and methodologically self-conscious and ambitious. Interestingly, unlike Feith, they are all responses to Clifford Geertz's powerful argument (Geertz 1960) about the impact of intra-Islamic religious cleavages in modern Indonesian political life. (Feith mentions some of Geertz's work, but his own study was probably conceived too early to have been significantly affected by Geertz's ideas.) All are based on extensive fieldwork in Indonesia. Finally, all have a strong normative component, a sense that part of the job of a political scientist is to contribute to resolving the great national and global challenges of one's time.

Let me now shift my focus back to the present, without claiming a vast wasteland or dark ages between 1980 and 2007, but, more modestly, attesting that no work in this period threatened to topple Feith's *The Decline of Constitutional Democracy in Indonesia* from its pedestal. What accounts for the relative paucity of comparative political science research in the late twentieth century, followed by the twenty-first-century surge?

Democracy is probably the major suspect. Comparative political scientists were captivated for decades with the phenomenon identified by Samuel Huntington (1993) as a historic "third wave" of nation-state democratization sweeping the world since the early 1970s. Few scholars riding this wave were attracted to the study of Indonesian politics, which remained thoroughly authoritarian until 1998. Democratic (and, more broadly, humanist) values probably also help to explain Feith's apostasy, why he abandoned the study of Indonesian politics shortly after the bloody beginning of the New Order. In 1963 he published what is still the best analysis of Guided Democracy ("Dynamics of Guided Democracy"), and in 1968 an insightful article on Suharto's strategy and tactics after assuming power in 1965 ("Suharto's Search for a Political Format"). His final, incomplete manuscript (Feith 1982) on Indonesian political developments deftly pinned the New Order as a "repressive-developmental" regime, a label subsequently adopted by many other scholars. Regrettably, this was the last of his writings to shape political scientists' contemporary understanding of Indonesian politics.

After democratization, perhaps the second most important driver of research in the late-twentieth century was political economy, the interaction between economic and political variables. In scholarship on the developing world, one prominent hypothesis claimed a causal relationship between authoritarian politics (the "developmental state") and national economic growth. South Korea, Taiwan, Thailand, and Singapore received major scholarly attention in this literature, but, inexplicably, there was no book-length political science study of Indonesia. A partial exception is an excellent descriptive study by the Columbia University Indonesian studies scholar John Bresnan (1993). See also Liddle (1991) and Mallarangeng (2008).

In the twenty-first century, theories about durable authoritarianism have finally emerged, in part in response to backsliding in "third wave" democracies, most notably in the former Soviet Union and its satellites. Of our four twenty-first century authors, Slater is most clearly writing within this new literature. Smith's and Pepinsky's main dependent variable is also stable authoritarianism, while Vu is writing within the developmental-state literature.

Though generally positive for both political science and Indonesian studies, the new mainstream approach suffers from several weaknesses or limitations. One weakness is the Procrustean temptation to fit one's facts to the theory or hypothesis rather than the other way around. As someone who studied the New Order up close and personal from beginning to end, I often see (what are to me, anyway) clear examples of facts exaggerated or misconnected to support one's theoretical point.

Second, theory-building in political science seems driven in part by the need of some members of successor generations to demolish predecessors' edifices. Few political scientists of my generation wanted to be seen as mere data collectors or box fillers for the structural-functionalism of Gabriel Almond. The result is that the project of constructing cumulative knowledge so beloved of positivist theorists is continually undermined by some of the discipline's most creative younger scholars.

A third weakness is the unwillingness of positivist political scientists to accept the significance of the fact that the actors we study are conscious human beings whose choices are not fully predictable (Lukes 1977). Political scientists mostly look for causes or, in the jargon, independent variables that will explain as much as possible of the variance in the dependent variables or effects. In my experience, however, these variables are never more than (strong or weak) constraints on behavior, factors that push individual actors in one direction or another but rarely, if ever, determine their behavior.

This weakness leads to debilitating empirical and normative problems. We have great difficulty incorporating the role that strong individuals play in producing political or social change. Obvious modern Indonesian examples are Sukarno, Suharto, Mohammad Natsir, D. N. Aidit, Nurcholish Madjid, and Abdurrahman

Wahid. But the argument applies to all actors at all levels, including, for example, district and municipality executive heads and legislators in today's democratic and decentralized Indonesia. Normatively, democratic theory (certainly Feith's "constitutional democracy") requires an assumption that political leaders are responsible for their actions and can therefore be held accountable at regular intervals in the polling booth. Most positivist political science, unfortunately, is designed to demonstrate just how much of human behavior is governed by factors beyond an individual leader's control.

Finally, mainstream American political science is poorly attuned to the concerns of others, including Indonesians. In itself there is nothing wrong with an American academic discipline responsive to Americans. It is, indeed, the normal condition of a world in which both values and interests (as well as reason) shape behavior, including the behavior of scholars. My point is rather that there is as yet no comparable Indonesian political science. Further, that not enough has been done over the past half-century to create a political science in Indonesia as responsive to Indonesian concerns and interests as American political science is to American concerns and interests. I will return to this issue in my third and fourth main points below.

THE REVIVAL IN AUSTRALIA AND EUROPE

The revival of research on Indonesian politics in the twenty-first century is not an exclusively American phenomenon. Important books and articles have been written recently by scholars in Australia and Europe. Notable younger Australian scholars include but are not limited to Edward Aspinall (2005; 2009), the displaced German Marcus Mietzner (2008), Stephen Sherlock (2010), and Greg Fealy (Fealy and Barton 1996; Fealy and White 2008). Notable Europe-based scholars include the displaced American John Sidel (2006), now at the London School of Economics, Christian von Luebke (2010), trained at the Australian National University but recently returned to Freiburg University in Germany, and Gerry van Klinken (2007; van Klinken and Barker 2009), an Australian now resident at the KITLV in the Netherlands.

These scholars are, in general, much less oriented to positivist science than are the US-based political scientists discussed above (von Luebke is an exception, to be discussed in the last section, below). Their work is directly focused on Indonesia, "area studies"-style, and intended to explain Indonesian phenomena in their own terms. There is little concern for exploring how Indonesian cases might illuminate similar phenomena elsewhere. These scholars' findings are typically published in area studies journals, often in the Southeast Asian region, or in edited books following conferences, rather than in mainstream political science journals.

Many of the Australian scholars studied under or were influenced by Feith and Feith's student Harold Crouch (Aspinall and Fealy 2010). Crouch's *The Army and Politics in Indonesia* (1988) is by far the most important book published by a political scientist on Indonesia during the last two decades of the twentieth century, but it has mainly influenced fellow Indonesia specialists. Andrew MacIntyre has been the Australian political scientist most attracted to positivist approaches, evidenced first in his book on business and politics in the New Order (MacIntyre 1991), then most fully developed in his application (MacIntyre 2002) of Tsbelis's (2000) "veto player" model to explain rigidity versus volatility in patterns of policy management in Thailand, the Philippines, Malaysia, and Indonesia.

The positivist versus area studies distinction among Australia-based scholars should not be overdrawn, however. Aspinall's *Opposing Suharto* (2005), for example, adopts the mainstream political scientist Juan Linz's (1973) categorization of authoritarian and totalitarian regime types. Aspinall finds the concept of "sultanism" a useful way to characterize the late New Order. Mietzner's *Military Politics, Islam, and the State in Indonesia* (2008) deploys the "two-generation model" of Cottey, Edmunds, and Forster (2001) to explain the causes and consequences of the Indonesian armed forces' partial and tardy withdrawal from political power. Sherlock (2010) directly attacks, in the Indonesian case, the conventional wisdom of the mainstream democratic theorist Larry Diamond (2009) about the negative effects of grand coalitions on presidential democracies.

We also need to be careful to avoid the trap of conflating area studies with non-positivist, specifically interpretivist, approaches. Aspinall's second book, on Aceh (2009), makes effective use of the constructivist Rogers Brubaker's (1996) conception of nation as a "category of practice" rather than an objective reality. If these works are read together with Sidel's "structuralist—and in some ways poststructuralist" (2006, xii) analysis of the pattern of religious violence in Indonesia from 1995 to 2005, I am reminded of the extent to which the area studies label, meaning atheoretical or purely descriptive, is often misapplied by positivists to interpretivist studies of both the left and right.

What explains the difference in approaches among these national scholarly communities? Australians, as a society, pay far more attention to Indonesia than do Americans. Geographical proximity means that there are many groups (e.g., business, religious, even holiday-seeking) with connections to Indonesia. The long, common sea border, combined with differences in levels of economic development and degrees of political stability, means that the Australian government and foreign policy community (including non-governmental think tanks, universities, and public intellectuals) have a strong interest in following events and assessing causes. Indonesia-specific studies are bound to have a wider and more devoted readership in Australia than anywhere else.

In the United States, by contrast, political science scholarship regarding Indonesia has never been driven by a single public interest, multiple interest groups, or even a government with a strongly felt need. American inattention has a long history. American politicians and scholars began to take notice early in the Cold War, when Indonesia's position in the global competition between the West and the communist world was contested. After the destruction of the communist party in 1965–66, however, Indonesia was regarded as being firmly in the Western camp and no longer the object of serious concern. Despite these trying circumstances, Donald Emmerson (Emmerson and Pitsuwan 2009) deserves the not-giving-up prize for publishing many first-quality analyses of US-Indonesia relations.

The pattern of neglect began to change after the September 11, 2001, attack on the US's World Trade Center and the Pentagon. At least one prominent Indonesian Islamic terrorist appears to have been linked to Al Qaeda. More generally, as the world's largest country with a majority Muslim population, Indonesia has increasingly been seen as a source of valuable comparative information and analysis. This concern has in turn prompted a broader literature on the causes and characteristics of Islamic radicalism. Young American political scientists conducting research on this topic include Robin Bush (2008), Pepinsky (Pepinsky, Liddle and Mujani 2012), Julie Chernov Hwang (2009), and the Japan-born Kikue Hamayotsu (2011).

STIRRINGS IN INDONESIA

Like most academic disciplines, political science is a global scholarly activity with "branches" (that is, an array of university departments plus a national professional association) in sovereign nation-states. In many of those branches, especially in industrialized economies (where universities, like most other modern institutions, have had resources to develop), study of the politics of one's own country is central to the discipline. Regrettably, this is not yet the case in Indonesia.

In the United States, American politics is one of four main fields into which the discipline is organized. The others are comparative politics, international relations, and political theory or philosophy. American politics specialists are divided by subfield or topic (e.g., the presidency, political parties, electoral behavior) and by theoretical and methodological persuasion. Yet they are united by their desire to improve the quality of the nation's political life by providing citizens with the best information and analyses possible. A large part of the mission of the other three fields is also to inform and educate the American public.

In Indonesia, the academic study of Indonesian politics is at best just beginning to make a significant contribution to public understanding. Political scientists have not yet cohered into a self-conscious community with its own internal standards and external sense of purpose. Local political science journals are not highly rated or widely read. Indonesian political scientists as individuals address political and mass audiences, but without the ballast that comes from having tested one's ideas and arguments before a community of peers.

Few Indonesians are publishing at an international-quality level, either in English or Indonesian, although the number appears to be growing. The prolific Vedi Hadiz (Robison and Hadiz 2004; Hadiz 2010) is the most prominent, followed by Ariel Heryanto (2007; 2008). Other political scientists who have published at least one book with a major international publisher include Salim Said (1991), Dewi Fortuna Anwar (1994), Bahtiar Effendy (2003), Yudi Latif (2008), and Rizal Sukma (2008). Luthfi Assyaukanie, though not a political scientist, has published a significant scholarly book on Islamic politics, *Islam and the Secular State in Indonesia* (2009). If we include English-language professional journal articles and Indonesian-language scholarly books, the list lengthens but remains well below the needs of Indonesian society.

Although they have not yet published a book internationally, Saiful Mujani (Liddle and Mujani 2007; Mujani and Liddle 2010) and Anies Baswedan (2004; 2007) are making an impact on the public discourse. In their writings, Mujani and Baswedan have made effective use of the public opinion survey, simultaneously a powerful new instrument of analysis and a political resource that is shaping the careers of individual politicians, the fortunes of political parties, and the quality of Indonesian democratic life (Mietzner 2009). It is worth noting that survey research is one area in which the most up-to-date methods of Western and comparative political science are being brought to Indonesia by Indonesians themselves.

What accounts for the paucity of Indonesian scholarship? One likely suspect is the combination of carrots and sticks deployed by senior professors and administrators. Hadiz and Heryanto have spent their whole careers in publish-or-perish foreign universities. Indonesian universities have historically not made scholarly publication a seriously implemented criterion of advancement, although this pattern is now beginning to change. Low salaries have worsened the problem, forcing faculty to teach on several campuses simultaneously or to find non-academic *proyek* (projects). More fundamentally, Indonesia's low GDP and tax base (and resultant paucity of economic resources in the society as a whole) have been reflected in the quality of its academic as well as other institutions.

Not all barriers to scholarship are related to the nation's weak economy and lack of incentives. Political repression has been a major impediment, especially during the New Order, when political scientists were among the most closely watched university faculty. The prospects for political science scholars in democratic Indonesia are much brighter now than ever before. Moreover, state universities today are under intense pressure to reform. They charge higher fees, making possible higher faculty salaries and increased funds for faculty research, and compete among themselves to attract the best students. They also face a challenge from both old and new private universities, which compete in the markets for new faculty and students.

Finally, the Yudhoyono administration (Susilo Bambang Yudhoyono, 2004–present) has made higher education reform a top priority, always an important legitimating step in a democratic country. It is now possible for Indonesians to study abroad for degrees and to conduct research as faculty members with funds provided by the ministry of national education. Improving the quality of higher education is a primary element in the new US-Indonesia "comprehensive partnership" agreement signed during US President Obama's visit to Indonesia in 2010.

The Role of Critical Scholarship

To an outside observer such as myself, the defining characteristic of critical scholarship is the Marxian commitment to a materialist interpretation of history. The scholarship is "critical" because it is hostile to the capitalists who allegedly exploit working and other lower classes. While there are differences of emphasis and internal battles between structural and cultural Marxists, and among scholars in each group, it is the prior and untested belief in the materialist basis of social development that distinguishes them from the mainstream. Critical scholars also disdain the institutions of Feith's constitutional (a.k.a. "bourgeois") democracy, seen as a façade for capitalist control.

The epistemological gap between mainstream and critical scholars is wide. As described above, the former are open to investigation of a wide range of potential variables, both as cause and effect. They focus on developing methodologies and research techniques that will enable them to discover whether and how particular variables cause particular effects. Critical scholars, already convinced of the determining force of capitalist wealth, typically disdain this methodology.

In Indonesian studies, the post-World War II roots of the mainstream–critical scholarship cleavage are visible in the first generation of scholars affiliated with the Cornell Modern Indonesia Project: George Kahin (1952) and Herbert Feith (1962) on the one side, Benedict Anderson (1972; 1983) and Ruth McVey (1965) on the other. Today, most critical political science research is conducted in Europe and Australia, although its products are widely appreciated and applauded by many Indonesians.

In the United States, Jeffrey Winters (1996; 2011) is the principal representative of the genre.

Two of the most prolific and widely cited critical scholars writing today are the Australia-based Richard Robison and Vedi Hadiz (Robison 1986; Robison and Hadiz 2004; Hadiz 2010). In their main work to date, *Reorganising Power in Indonesia: The Politics of Oligarchy in an Age of Markets* (2004), they trace the emergence during the Suharto period of a complex oligarchy, a "system of government in which virtually all political power is held by a very small number of wealthy ... people who shape public policy primarily to benefit themselves financially ... while displaying little or no concern for the broader interests of the rest of the citizenry" (16–17). The members of the oligarchy are state officials, "politico-business families," and corporate conglomerates.

Predictably, Robison and Hadiz argue that post-Suharto democratization has not made a difference in oligarchic control. At the national and local levels (where there has been extensive decentralization of governmental authority as well as democratization), the members of the oligarchy nonetheless still call the shots behind the scenes. The authors' forecast is pessimistic:

> In reality, the possibility that cohesive reformist parties might emerge from the wreckage, driven by a coherent agenda of market liberalism rather than being swallowed in a system of power relations embedded in the pursuit of rents, appears even more remote than ever ... [This means] a system of democratic rule where the state apparatus will provide some form of order in which oligarchies rather than markets will prevail. (265)

There are many problems with this argument. It is a one-sided analysis of the economic legacy of the Suharto period, neglecting entirely the broad distributional effects of New Order macro-economic policies and also of the many specific government infrastructural programs that provided economic (and ultimately political) resources to most Indonesians. It exaggerates the expectations of economists (derided as "neo-liberals"), in the Suharto period and since, for the immediate economic, social, and political consequences of their policies. It claims but does not provide persuasive evidence for the existence of a politico-economic elite unified across regimes. The elite was indeed unified during the New Order, but has since become fragmented and internally competitive.

Robison and Hadiz thereby miss the powerful causal impact of Suharto's leadership (deploying mixed resources of coercion, exchange, and persuasion for more than thirty years) as explanation for elite unity during the New Order. More importantly, they miss an opportunity to assess the causes and consequences of elite disunity and patterns of conflict today, not only at the center but in several hundred provinces, districts, and municipalities. Perhaps most consequentially, theirs is a counsel of despair for Indonesians who want to elect governments responsive to their interests as individuals and interest groups. The oligarchy, in Robison and Hadiz's view, just has too much wealth (in their critical scholarship view, the only really valuable political resource), is too unified internally, and is too well-connected internationally to be opposed by any group or coalition in existence or on the horizon.

An example of the kind of analysis that does offer a way, *contra* critical scholarship, to test the existence of an oligarchy or other power structure at the local level and its consequences for policy outcomes that directly impact ordinary Indonesians is Christian von Luebke's (2009) "The Political Economy of Local Governance: Findings from an Indonesian Field Study." Von Luebke's dependent variable is good governance, operationalized as variations in district-level government taxation, licensing, and corruption practices. His independent variables are demands on government from local businesses and other groups and the autonomous leadership exerted by district heads whose main incentives are to win reelection and to avoid criticism in the local media.

From analysis of eight controlled district comparisons, von Luebke's primary finding is that "district heads with strong managerial skills and long-term career aspirations have successfully used their official powers to initiate broad-based reform and supervise bureaucratic performance" (202). For Indonesian voters and political scientists, he concludes with two important implications—that strong district leadership can make a positive difference in the lives of ordinary people in an underdeveloped economy and society (but democratic polity) like Indonesia, but that this leadership is also increasingly influenced by public awareness and rising demands for governmental transparency.

In conclusion, while I have taken issue with mainstream scholars on several grounds, I frankly believe that solutions to Indonesia's current economic, political, and social problems will be found mostly by mainstream researchers like von Luebke and others discussed in this essay. Area studies and interpretivist scholars will also continue to enrich our understanding of Indonesian society and culture. Critical scholars are unlikely to do so until they escape their self-imposed materialist analytical bonds. For the future, I place my hopes on today's young Indonesian scholars, of whatever current analytical persuasion. Especially in the present democratic era, the stakes and also the opportunities are greatest for them.

Works Cited

Almond, Gabriel, and James Coleman. *The Politics of the Developing Areas*. Princeton, NJ: Princeton University Press, 1960.

Anderson, Benedict R. O'G. *Java in a Time of Revolution*. Ithaca, NY: Cornell University Press, 1972.

——. *Imagined Communities: Reflections on the Origin and Spread of Nationalism*. London: Verso, 1983.

Anwar, Dewi Fortuna. *Indonesia in ASEAN: Foreign Policy and Realism*. London: Palgrave MacMillan, 1994.

Aspinall, Edward. *Opposing Suharto: Compromise, Resistance, and Regime Change in Indonesia*. Stanford, CA: Stanford University Press, 2005.

——. *Islam and Nation: Separatist Rebellion in Aceh, Indonesia*. Stanford, CA: Stanford University Press, 2009.

Aspinall, Edward, and Greg Fealy. *The Legacy of Soeharto's New Order: Essays in Honour of Harold Crouch*. Canberra: ANU E-Press, 2010.

Assyaukanie, Luthfi. *Islam and the Secular State in Indonesia*. Singapore: Institute of Southeast Asian Studies, 2009.

Baswedan, Anies. "Political Islam: Present and Future Trajectory." *Asian Survey* 44.5 (2004): 669–69.

——. "Indonesian Politics in 2007: The Presidency, Local Elections, and the Future of Democracy." *Bulletin of Indonesian Economic Studies* 43.2 (2007): 323–40.

Bresnan, John. *Managing Indonesia: The Modern Political Economy*. New York, NY: Columbia University Press, 1993.

Brubaker, Rogers. *Nationalism Reframed: Nationhood and the National Question in the New Europe*. Cambridge: Cambridge University Press, 1996.

Bush, Robin. "Regional Sharia Regulations in Indonesia: Anomaly or Symptom?" *Expressing Islam: Islamic Life and Politics in Indonesia*. Ed. Greg Fealy and Sally White. Singapore: Institute of Southeast Asian Studies, 2008.

Cottey, Andrew, Timothy Edmunds, and Anthony Forster. "Soldiers, Politics, and Defence: Some Initial Conclusions on the Democratisation of Civil-Military Relations in Post-Communist Central and Eastern Europe." Civil-Military Relations in Central and Eastern Europe Project, unpublished paper, 2001.

Crouch, Harold. *The Army and Politics in Indonesia*. Ithaca, NY: Cornell University Press, revised edition, 1988.

Diamond, Larry. "Is a 'Rainbow Coalition' a Good Way to Govern?" *Bulletin of Indonesian Economic Studies* 45.3 (2009): 333–36.

Effendy, Bahtiar. *Islam and the State in Indonesia*. Singapore: Institute of Southeast Asian Studies, 2003.

Emmerson, Donald K. *Indonesia's Elite: Political Culture and Cultural Politics*. Ithaca, NY: Cornell University Press, 1976.

Emmerson, Donald K., and Surin Pitsuwan. *Hard Choices: Security, Democracy, and Regionalism in Southeast Asia*. Stanford, CA: Walter H. Shorenstein Asia-Pacific Research Center, 2009.

Fealy, Greg, and Greg Barton, eds. *Nahdlatul Ulama. Traditional Islam and Modernity in Indonesia*. Clayton, Victoria: Monash Asia Institute, Monash University, 1996.

Fealy, Greg, and Sally White, eds. *Expressing Islam: Islamic Life and Politics in Indonesia*. Singapore: Institute of Southeast Asian Studies, 2008.

Feith, Herbert. *The Decline of Constitutional Democracy in Indonesia*. Ithaca, NY: Cornell University Press, 1962.

——. "Dynamics of Guided Democracy." *Indonesia*. Ed. Ruth T. McVey. New Haven, CT: Yale University Southeast Asia Studies, 1963: 309–409.

——. "Suharto's Search for a Political Format." *Indonesia* 6 (1968): 88–105.

——. "Repressive-Development Regimes in Asia." *Alternatives* 7.4 (1982): 491–506.

Geertz, Clifford. *The Religion of Java*. Glencoe, IL: The Free Press, 1960.

Hadiz, Vedi R. *Localising Power in Post-Authoritarian Indonesia: A Southeast Asian Perspective*. Stanford, CA: Stanford University Press, 2010.

Hamayotsu, Kikue. "Islam for All? Electoral Changes and Religious Party Mobilization in Democratic Indonesia." Paper presented at the Annual Meeting of the Association for Asian Studies. Honolulu, HI, 2011.

Heryanto, Ariel. *State Terrorism and Political Identity in Indonesia: Fatally Belonging*. London: Routledge, 2007.

——., ed. *Popular Culture in Indonesia: Fluid Identities in Post-Authoritarian Politics*. London: Routledge, 2008.

Jackson, Karl D. *Traditional Authority, Islam, and Rebellion: A Study of Indonesian Political Behavior*. Berkeley, CA: University of California Press, 1980.

Huntington, Samuel P. *The Third Wave: Democratization in the Late Twentieth Century*. Norman, OK: University of Oklahoma Press, 1993.

Hwang, Julie Chernov. *Peaceful Islamist Mobilization in the Muslim World: What Went Right*. London: Palgrave Macmillan, 2009.

Kahin, George McT. *Nationalism and Revolution in Indonesia*. Ithaca, NY: Cornell University Press, 1952.

King, Gary, Robert O. Keohane, and Sidney Verba. *Designing Social Inquiry: Scientific Inference in Qualitative Research*. Princeton, NJ: Princeton University Press, 1994.

Klinken, Gerry Van. *Communal Violence and Democratization in Indonesia: Small Town Wars*. London: Routledge, 2007.

Klinken, Gerry Van, and Joshua Barker. *State of Authority: The State in Society in Indonesia*. Ithaca, NY: Cornell Southeast Asia Program Publications, 2009.

Kuhonta, Erik, Dan Slater, and Tuong Vu. *Southeast Asia in Political Science: Theory, Region, and Qualitative Analysis*. Stanford, CA: Stanford University Press, 2008.

Lasswell, Harold. *Politics: Who Gets What, When, How*. New York, NY: Meridian Books, 1958.

Latif, Yudi. *Indonesian Muslim Intelligensia and Power*. Singapore: Institute of Southeast Asian Studies, 2008.

Liddle, R. William. *Ethnicity, Party, and National Integration: An Indonesian Case Study*. New Haven, CT: Yale University Press, 1970.

——. "The Relative Autonomy of the Third World Politician: Soeharto and Indonesian Economic Development in Comparative Perspective." *International Studies Quarterly* 35.4 (1991): 403–27.

Liddle, R. William, and Saiful Mujani. "Leadership, Party, and Religion: Explaining Voting Behavior in Indonesia." *Comparative Political Studies* 40.7 (2007): 832–57.

Linz, Juan. "Opposition in and under an Authoritarian Regime: The Case of Spain." *Regimes and Oppositions*. Ed. Robert A. Dahl. New Haven, CT: Yale University Press, 1973: 171–259.

Luebke, Christian von. "The Political Economy of Local Governance: Findings from an Indonesian Field Study." *Bulletin of Indonesian Economic Studies* 39.2 (2010): 201–30.

Lukes, Steven. "Power and Structure." *Essays in Social Theory*. New York, NY: Columbia University Press, 1977.

Mallarangeng, Rizal. *Mendobrak Sentralisme Ekonomi Indonesia 1986–1992*. Jakarta: Gramedia, 2008 (third printing).

MacIntyre, Andrew. *Business and Politics in Indonesia*. North Sydney: Allen and Unwin, 1991.

——. *The Power of Institutions: Political Architecture and Governance*. Ithaca, NY: Cornell University Press, 2002.

McVey, Ruth. *The Rise of Indonesian Communism*. Ithaca, NY: Cornell University Press, 1965.

Mietzner, Marcus. *Military Politics, Islam, and the State in Indonesia: From Turbulent Transition to Democratic Consolidation*. Singapore: Institute of Southeast Asian Studies, 2008.

——. "Political Opinion Polling in Post-Authoritarian Indonesia: Catalyst or Obstacle to Democratic Consolidation?" *Bijdragen tot de Taal-, Land- en Volkenkunde* 165.1 (2009): 95–126.

Mujani, Saiful, and R. William Liddle. "Voters and the New Indonesian Democracy." *Problems of Democratisation in Indonesia*. Ed. Edward Aspinall and Marcus Mietzner. Singapore: Institute of Southeast Asian Studies, 2010: 75–99.

Pepinsky, Thomas. *Economic Crisis and the Breakdown of Authoritarian Regimes*. Cambridge: Cambridge University Press, 2009.

Pepinsky, Thomas, R. William Liddle, and Saiful Mujani. "Testing Islam's Political Advantage: Experimental Evidence from Indonesia." *American Journal of Political Science* 56.3 (2012): 584–600.

Robison, Richard. *Indonesia: The Rise of Capital*. Sydney: Allen and Unwin, 1986.

Robison, Richard, and Vedi R. Hadiz. *Reorganizing Power in Indonesia: The Politics of Oligarchy in an Age of Markets*. London: RoutledgeCurzon, 2004.

Said, Salim. *Genesis of Power: General Sudirman and the Indonesian Military in Politics, 1945–49*. Singapore: Institute of Southeast Asian Studies, 1991.

Sherlock, Stephen. "The Parliament in Indonesia's Decade of Democracy: People's Forum or Chamber of Cronies?" *Problems of Democratisation in Indonesia*. Ed. Edward Aspinall and Marcus Mietzner. Singapore: Institute of Southeast Asian Studies, 2010: 160–78.

Shils, Edward. "Political Development in the New States." *Comparative Studies in Society and History* 2.3 (1960): 379–411.

Sidel, John. *Riots, Pogroms, Jihad: Religious Violence in Indonesia*. Ithaca, NY: Cornell University Press, 2006.

Slater, Dan. *Ordering Power: Contentious Politics and Authoritarian Leviathans in Southeast Asia*. Cambridge: Cambridge University Press, 2010.

Smith, Benjamin. *Hard Times in the Lands of Plenty: Oil Politics in Iran and Indonesia*. Ithaca, NY: Cornell University Press, 2007.

Sukma, Rizal. *Islam in Indonesian Foreign Policy*. London: Routledge, 2008.

Tsebelis, George. "Veto Players and Institutional Analysis." *Governance* 13.4 (2000): 441–74.

Vu, Tuong. *Paths to Development in Asia: South Korea, Vietnam, China, and Indonesia.* Cambridge: Cambridge University Press, 2010.

Winters, Jeffrey A. *Power in Motion: Capital Mobility and the Indonesian State.* Ithaca, NY: Cornell University Press, 1996.

——. *Oligarchy.* Cambridge: Cambridge University Press, 2011.

FACTS, MINDS, AND FORMATS: SCHOLARSHIP AND POLITICAL CHANGE IN INDONESIA

Donald K. Emmerson

"When the facts change, I change my mind. What do you do, sir?"
—John Maynard Keynes[1]

"I didn't change. The world changed."

—Dick Cheney[2]

This chapter does not comprehensively review the literature on Indonesian politics. My hope is to offer something usefully different: an homage to the Ithacan—Cornellian—origins of Indonesian political studies in the United States, and a review of some twentieth-century disagreements whose epistemological implications remain relevant for the study of Indonesian politics today. The disagreements arose over how to interpret two consequential changes of regime inside Indonesia. At stake were perspectival commitments developed inside the minds, disciplines, and careers of professional analysts of Indonesia.

The choice posed by dissonance between an outlook and the events it is supposed to explain is not unique to Indonesian studies. The question is whether to replace or revise the outlook (Keynes), to reaffirm it (Cheney), or to say nothing at all, judging the dissonance to be too weak to justify the first choice yet too strong to justify the warrant. None of these decisions is intrinsically superior to the others. They cannot be fairly judged in the abstract. That can be done only for the fit

---

[1] Keynes was defending himself against an accusation of inconsistency by pointing to the Great Depression of the 1930s as the massive new fact that had led him to abandon his earlier faith in monetary policy and acknowledge the value of fiscal stimulation as a tool of economy recovery. Alfred L. Malabre, Jr., *Lost Prophets: An Insider's History of the Modern Economists* (Boston, MA: Harvard Business School Press, 1994), p. 220.

[2] Cheney was responding to a remark that the events of September 11, 2001, had somehow changed him. Daniel Henninger, "I Didn't Change. The World Changed," *The Wall Street Journal*, August 30, 2011, p. A15.

between a particular outlook and the specific available evidence that is relevant to it, compared with the explanatory leverage afforded by other points of view.

That said, evaluating outlooks by how well they fit the facts is beyond my purpose here. I wish merely to review the use of some facts on behalf of some arguments involving the interpretation of two changes of regime in Indonesia: the demise of liberal democracy and the rise of President Sukarno's leftward "Guided Democracy" in 1959, and the latter's replacement by General Suharto's anti-leftist "New Order" starting in 1965. A closing section will draw some implications for students of Indonesian politics today.

First, however, I want to recall the distinctive role of Cornell in the incubation of Indonesian studies in the United States.

THE CENTRALITY OF CORNELL

Ithaca was the Mecca of Indonesian political studies in the United States for much of the second half of the twentieth century. The tenor of US-based scholarship on Indonesian politics in the decades after World War II owed more to what was thought, taught, and written at Cornell University than to scholarship at any other institution of higher education in the world.

Cornell's renowned Modern Indonesia Project promoted a scholarly style that ignored—indeed, refused to entertain—the increasingly positivistic inclinations of disciplinary political science. No graduate student hoping to work on Indonesian politics could ignore the epistemological and methodological gulf between these approaches. At Cornell, a distinctively ideographic style of Indonesian political studies—qualitative, detailed, descriptive—became *de rigueur* in the tellingly named Department of Government. In contrast, at other universities, graduate students planning disciplinary careers were being socialized into an increasingly nomothetic—number-crunching, variable-regressing, generality-seeking—enterprise bent on implementing the "science" in Political Science.[3]

In 1932, Cornell's Department of Government had physically joined the Department of History in the same building. Their new proximity had been welcomed at the time as "particularly fortunate" in light of "the natural affinity between History and Government" ("History Courses Get New Home" 1932). This "natural affinity" would inspire and shape the sort of Indonesian studies that George Kahin, Benedict Anderson, and Ruth McVey later practiced and promoted at Cornell, where Anderson and McVey received their PhDs.

Indonesian political studies benefited from Cornell's fine-combed historical approach. Consider what might be called, admiringly, the "Ithacan Trilogy": George Kahin (1952) on Indonesia from 1945 to 1949; Herbert Feith (1962) on Indonesia from

---

[3] In a conversation I had with one Cornell-credentialed Southeast Asianist, he recalled that, as a graduate student, he had worried that he would not be competitive for a university position in political science. He had asked a local expert on Indonesia what he should read to close that gap. "Nothing," the scholar had replied—political science theories and methods were not worth knowing about. For my views of the simultaneously vexed and creative relations between Southeast Asian studies and political science, see Donald K. Emmerson, "Southeast Asia in Political Science: Terms of Enlistment," in *Southeast Asia in Political Science: Theory, Region, and Qualitative Analysis,* ed. Erik Martinez Kuhonta et al. (Stanford, CA: Stanford University Press, 2008), pp. 302–24.

1949 to 1957; and Daniel Lev (1966) on Indonesia from 1957 to 1959.[4] As a graduate student in the late 1960s, reading these milestone works, I only regretted—I still do—that the series did not include a fourth volume on "Guided Democracy" from 1959 to 1965. A granular, historical, Cornell-style account of that regime would have helped scholars to assess the extent to which the ensuing "New Order" (1965–67 in transition, 1968–98 in place) was an authoritarian continuation of, a militarized variation on, a developmental corrective to, or a brutal negation of its predecessor.

Such a volume might also have helped to clarify and evaluate the differing accounts of the pivotal murders of seven army officers in Jakarta on October 1, 1965, that were used to justify the replacement of Guided Democracy by the New Order—accounts still in contention nearly half a century later. Should the killings be construed as an attempted coup and blamed on the Indonesian Communist Party (PKI, Partai Komunis Indonesia)? Should the conspiracy be understood as the outcome of prior rivalry, as the Indonesian army and the PKI headed toward an unavoidable showdown? As a mutiny inside the army in which the PKI played no proactive role? As a conspiracy of junior officers acting in concert with individual schemers high up in the PKI? As a putsch instigated, abetted, or tolerated by the prior knowledge and/or intervention of General Suharto, President Sukarno, and/or the governments of the United States and the United Kingdom?

If the facts of such a momentous change in Indonesian history could be so variously interpreted, how scholars had been inclined to arrive at those interpretations—their different habits of mind, or "formats"—could be interpreted as well.

FORMATS I AND II

No one contributed more to Cornell's prominence in Indonesian political studies in the twentieth century than Benedict Anderson. In an essay written in 1971, he identified two roughly sequential ways of studying Indonesian politics. Each of these approaches combined an ideological orientation with a methodological preference: If scholars in what Anderson called "Format I" valued "anticolonial [anti-Dutch] liberalism and the historical method," those working within the subsequent "Format II" preferred "imperial [pro-American] liberalism and the comparative method." Although he criticized both approaches, he objected far more to the second than to the first (1982 [1973], 71–73).

Format I's *locus classicus* was Kahin's influential political history of the Indonesian revolution (1952). In Anderson's view, the Kahinians had rightly acknowledged "the historic authenticity and autonomy of Indonesian nationalism." But they had been led by their "liberal-democratic concerns" to focus on "Westernized political leaders" and Western-style "parliamentary institutions." Anderson also criticized what he saw as a tendency of Format I authors to privilege the Jakarta elite as the true custodians of Indonesian nationalism and to stress the

---

[4] Comparably fine-grained historical works also published at Cornell University included those by Feith (Herbert Feith, *The Wilopo Cabinet, 1952–1953: A Turning Point in Post-Revolutionary Indonesia* [Ithaca, NY: Cornell Southeast Asia Program Publications and Department of Far Eastern Studies, 1958]; McVey (Ruth T. McVey, *The Rise of Indonesian Communism* [Ithaca, NY: Cornell University Press, 1965]; and Anderson (Benedict R. O'G. Anderson, *Java in a Time of Revolution: Occupation and Resistance, 1944–1946* [Ithaca, NY: Cornell University Press, 1972]). All of these authors save Kahin earned Cornell PhDs.

sense in which low-status Indonesians made life difficult for that elite rather than the other way around (1982, 72–73).

In Anderson's account, the "hegemony" of Westernist Kahinian elitism had become a casualty of the advent of authoritarian rule—Guided Democracy—in the mid-to-late 1950s. That lurch toward autocracy had disrupted two key instances of "natural congruence" assumed by Format I's exponents: felicitous harmony between "the best [liberal-democratic] interests of America and Indonesia" and between Indonesian "nationalism and constitutional democracy" (1982, 73). In Keynes's terms, the facts had changed; it was time to lose one's illusions.

In the meantime, the burgeoning global power of the United States had gestated, in Anderson's terms, a new and toxic paradigm: Format II. American imperialism needed a universal pattern on whose basis it could proceed. Format II-type theories of "modernization" fit the bill; they served the global primacy of the United States by ignoring non-capitalist (including, notably, communist) roads to modernity. In countries such as Indonesia, "the autonomist choice" had become "difficult and dangerous." Faced with preeminent American power, it had been easier to choose "compliance, cooperation, and subordination." If the generals in charge of the New Order were "fully committed to cooperationism," so also had Format II scholars taken that path of least resistance to the United States (Anderson 1982, 75–76).

Figuring in this indictment was a fellow Cornellian, Herbert Feith. In *The Decline of Constitutional Democracy in Indonesia* (1962), whose very title overlooked the corresponding "rise of radical autonomism" that loomed so large on Anderson's horizon (1982, 78), Feith located liberalism's failure in the richly detailed context of a struggle between two elite groups inside Indonesia: the "administrators," who might have rescued liberalism, had they won, versus the "solidarity-makers," including Sukarno, who did win, thereby causing its demise. In Anderson's narrative, Feith had been a Kahinian in Format I but had fallen under the influence of Format II scholars whose neglect of nationalism, silence on imperialism, and faith in modernization Anderson decried.

In that 1950s "era of American hegemony," wrote Anderson, "most of the 'administrators' were cooperationists, and most of the 'solidarity-makers' [were] autonomists." Yet this crucial difference had somehow "escaped [Feith's] attention." The omission had allowed others to dismiss the "solidarity-makers," whom Anderson admired for their pro-nationalist, anti-imperialist standing, "as mere trouble-makers and vacuous ideologues." However unintended, Feith's assignment of responsibility for democracy's decline to "solidarity-makers" such as Sukarno had amounted to an "attack" on Indonesian autonomism. Thus Feith had "used elements from both formats [I and II] to undermine the credentials of nationalism" (1982, 78).

Rereading Feith's book, it is hard to agree that the international context had escaped Feith's attention. Feith acknowledged the administrators' role in seeking Western cooperation with Indonesia to further Indonesian ends. Administrators and solidarity-makers were neither idolized nor demonized; the skills of both were acknowledged as having been "equally necessary" to Indonesian success (1962, 24–25). Feith's complex and nuanced account did not simplify Indonesian history ino a morality play between good and evil.

For Anderson, the "logic of nationalism" and the "drive for autonomy" from American hegemony were one and the same (1982, 75). What mattered to him about Guided Democracy was its courageously nationalist willingness, prompted by the PKI, to stand up to the United States. For him, the purpose of Format II-style research was to discredit Indonesian nationalism as anti-capitalist, anti-democratic, and culturally regressive. Scholars working in Format II had pointed to Sukarno's close relations with the PKI as evidence that communism had degraded nationalism (Anderson 1982, 77–78). The reverse possibility—that nationalism had enhanced communism—was not entertained.

What Anderson himself did not entertain, but Feith did, was a third possibility: that the repertoires of nationalism were not limited to a single autonomist theme, but could include serving Indonesia's interest through non-craven, realistic, pragmatic, and even nationalist cooperation with an outside world that was mainly capitalist in orientation.

FEITH OR BENDA?

In the mid-1960s, Feith and another scholar with a Cornell PhD, the historian Harry J. Benda, debated democracy's decline. Their exchange was not mentioned by Anderson in his essay on formats. But Anderson followed Benda in faulting Feith for having written *Decline* in answer to a wrong question, namely, "Why did liberal democracy decline?" In Benda's opinion, the right question to ask was "Why should it have survived?" Anderson, in effect, preferred a third query: "Why did radical autonomism rise?" (Compare Feith 1962; Benda 1982 [1964], 18; Feith 1982 [1965]; and Anderson 1982, 78.)

Unsurprisingly for a historian, Benda took the long view: "From the very outset" of the contest between the administrators and solidarity-makers, the odds were "far more heavily weighted against constitutional democracy" than Feith had been willing to admit. History, in effect, had doomed the fatally incongruous Western-style liberal system. Dutch colonial rule had been a mere "deviation" from Indonesia's Hindu–Javanese past, or had even reinforced that authoritarian legacy. In this context, "Indonesian (especially Javanese) history" had returned "to its own moorings" (Benda 1982, 17–18). In sharp contrast, Feith's *Decline* had charted a struggle among leaders and parties with its own dynamics, contingencies, and turning points—a contest whose outcome was not associated with Javanism's weight, autonomism's strength, or any other overriding condition.

These three ways of interpreting democracy's decline—Benda's historicism, Feith's possibilism, Anderson's nationalism—have enriched the study of Indonesian politics. But they hardly exhaust the repertoire of guiding assumptions that can inspire and shape explanations of change and continuity in Indonesia. Consider four sets of gradations—continua—along which an analyst may select a stance that cognitively features, or normatively favors, either of two contrasting phenomena: continuity or change, structure or agency, revolution or reform, and autocracy or democracy.

Contemplating democracy's decline in Indonesia, different authors saw different things along all of these lines. Benda's historicism contextualized democracy's demise within a larger and determining *continuity*, while Feith's possibilism sustained an open-ended chronicle of *change*. If Benda's historicism and Anderson's nationalism invoked the constraining *structure* of historical precedent and American dominance, respectively, Feith's possibilism highlighted the *agency* of clashing elites. If Anderson's nationalism foregrounded autonomist *revolution*, Feith's possibilism detailed efforts and failures of developmental *reform*. Of these authors, none approved of *autocracy*. But Feith's possibilism made him more likely than Benda and

Anderson to believe that, had events gone differently, *democracy* might have survived. (These continua could also be applied to scholarly views of Suharto's New Order and its successor, *Reformasi* Democracy.)

The Feith–Benda debate did not validate a simplistically Keynesian faith in the power of factual change to change minds. Benda the historian and Feith the political scientist were already inclined by their disciplines to acknowledge, respectively, the influence of an authoritarian past and the struggle for a democratic future. Feith was less skeptical of modernization theory and more taken with its attention to political change, including democratization—an approach that Benda was inclined to criticize as overly hopeful and naively Western. The two men interpreted the durability of Indonesia's liberal experiment in the light of what they already knew and believed.

Comparable evidence of the influence of consistency on interpretation would soon surface in the divergent understandings of another instance of demise-and-rise: the replacement of Guided Democracy by the New Order in the 1960s.

ANGER AND ANALYSIS

Early on October 1, 1965, in Jakarta, a self-styled 30th of September Movement kidnapped and killed six generals and a first lieutenant in the Indonesian army in circumstances that appeared to implicate the PKI. A surviving general, Suharto, used the conspiracy to demonize and destroy the PKI and replace Sukarno's left-leaning Guided Democracy with his own fiercely anticommunist arrangement. Contemplating the physical elimination of the Indonesian left in 1965–66, no reasonable observer could deny that continuity had been severed and change had occurred.

Nowhere in American academe was the impact of these events felt more deeply than at Cornell. Anderson and McVey had personal reasons to be horrified by the slaughter of the PKI. They had come to appreciate the nationalist autonomism of the PKI. McVey had become an expert on the party itself. Her detailed history of the party's early years (1914–27), planned as the first volume in a general history of Indonesian communism, had appeared in 1965, scant months before the PKI's destruction began.

In late 1965, Anderson and McVey, with the help of a third Cornell scholar, Frederick Bunnell, researched and wrote *A Preliminary Analysis of the October 1, 1965, Coup in Indonesia*. First circulated early in 1966, but not published until 1971, it argued that the PKI had not been responsible for the army officers' deaths (Anderson and McVey 1971 [1966], 1). The party "had no demonstrable cause to plan or join the September 30th Movement" (115). It had become involved only "after the coup plans were well under way" (1). What had happened was likely "a power play of some sort" inside the army, a "colonels' revolt" (147), "essentially an internal Army affair" (63)—a description that happened to match the designation of the Movement's actions as "an internal Army affair" (131) in the October 2, 1965, edition of the PKI's own newspaper.

The Feith–Benda debate was a gentlemanly skirmish compared with the controversy—indeed, the enmity—stirred by Anderson and McVey's "Cornell paper," as it came to be called. In a letter to Kahin, Feith was simultaneously critical, impressed, and ambivalent. "Strongly as I disagree with quite a bit of it," he wrote, "it is certainly tremendous stuff and opens a new page in the study of Indonesian politics" (Purdey 2011, 5, quoting Feith). As to "his own thinking on the facts of the events," Feith confessed in his letter to being "massively confused" (Purdey 2011, 5).

Feith's ambivalence had already been expressed in a little-known dialogue that would appear in a local journal on February 19, 1966, the day after he wrote Kahin. The essay is an imagined conversation about the killings between two speakers, "A" and "B." Feith gave the humanitarian side of the dialogue to Speaker A, and the realist response to B. For A, the slaughter was horrific; for B, it was merely tragic.

The piece was printed under the title "Killings in Indonesia: To Moralize or Analyze: A Dialogue" (Feith 1966). Although the whiff of self-righteousness in the word "moralize" in the phrase "moralize or analyze" did not convey impartiality between A's *moralpolitik* and B's *realpolitik*, Feith was careful not to turn either protagonist into a straw man for the other to knock down. A does not use emotionally wrought language to condemn the army or praise the PKI, and B does not actually say that the party deserved its fate. But in linking the killings to a choice by the army to destroy the party, A highlights contingency and agency. B, in contrast, sees what happened as the inevitable result of longstanding structural conflict between the army and the party. In this particular respect, the dialogue parallels the Feith–Benda debate, with A reprising Feith's desire not to overdetermine change and B voicing Benda's fatalistic "what did you expect?"

Feith mailed a copy of the piece to Anderson and McVey, who were not impressed by its dialogic character. They viewed it as an attack on the Cornell paper. Not only that, according to Purdey, "they read it as an apologia for the anti-Communist purge [then] still taking place in Indonesia." In her reply, McVey wrote, in verse, an "intentionally cruel critique of what she depict[ed] as amoral detached scholarship that dismisses the mass killing in favor of 'higher' science." Anderson's letter to Feith was less "acute" in its tone, but it did alter parts of the dialogue by replacing certain pronouns with inflammatory alternatives: "'Berlin' for 'Jakarta,' 'Jews' for 'Communists,' and 'Third Reich' and 'Nazis' for the 'Indonesian Army'" (Purdey 2011, 7, including quotes from McVey 1966 and Anderson 1966).

Although Feith's relations with his colleagues at Cornell were not permanently strained, a lasting mutual disregard developed between the authors of the Cornell paper and the RAND Corporation's Indonesianist Guy Pauker. Pauker rejected Anderson and McVey's exoneration of the PKI, and they believed he had circulated the Cornell paper in violation of their explicit request not to do so. In 1973, two years after the paper's publication, when Anderson landed in Jakarta to attend an academic conference, he learned that the New Order authorities had blacklisted him. His visa was cancelled at the airport, and he was forced to depart. He did not return until 1999, following Suharto's resignation and the inception of *Reformasi* Democracy the year before.

Two Kinds of Consistency

Feith died in 2001, Pauker a year later. Among Pauker's papers is a letter to him sent from Jakarta in March 1966 by B. Hugh Tovar, whose time in Indonesia as the CIA's chief of station included October 1, 1965. In a spirit radically different from Feith's dialogue, Tovar's letter invoked two of the clashing interpretations to which the officers' murders had given rise—the case for communist collusion notably favored by Western officials versus the Cornell authors' explanatory focus on populist resentments against the army's high command held by junior officers in the army's Diponegoro division in Central Java:

> I have thought of you particularly in connection with the PKI, and with your views ... on that subject as they had evolved many months ago. You must take considerable satisfaction in having contended, against the prophecies of the school of McVey et al., that the Party did *indeed* present a threat. ... I suppose that if one were back in the US, drawing solely upon published press accounts of events during the Gestapu episode[5] and its sequel, it would be quite possible to develop the Diponegoro theory of the coup attempt. On the other hand, it strikes me simply as an effort to justify or rationalize an earlier position which had proved to be fallacious [Tovar 1966].

The relevance of Tovar's point to Keynes's rhetorical question is clear. Certainly the facts had changed on October 1, 1965. But the implications of Tovar's critique undermined Keynes's straightforward admonition to learn from reality. Whose reality? Whose facts? Note also the implicit downgrading of the value of surprise. What seemed to matter more in Tovar's letter was internal consistency—the validation of what one already believed. Perhaps the satisfaction of having one's old opinion ostensibly confirmed by new facts was a way of subordinating change to a need for continuity inside one's own mind. In this context, Feith's admission to being "massively confused" about the facts of October 1, 1965, seems an honest admission by a scholar doing his best to consider Keynes's advice.

As to external consistency—a persisting or recursive pattern in Indonesia's past—the historical strength of Indonesian studies at Cornell made this a natural interest of analysts there. In his 1971 introduction to the published edition of the Cornell paper, Anderson cited eight consecutive instances of division, subversion, and rebellion involving the Indonesian army to show that its history had evinced "intermittent turmoil from the moment of its formation in 1945." That continuity rendered more plausible the Cornell paper's description of the conspiracy on October 1, 1965, as an intra-army affair (vi–viii).

Pauker explicitly rationalized his own recourse to external consistency over time in the service of an exactly contrary claim: The party, he wrote (1969, 1), "has been led by several generations of political activists, all of whom made fatal mistakes and were consequently destroyed by antagonistic forces"—including the leaders who, in his view, had in 1965 driven the PKI to yet another rendezvous with disaster. Despite the clear differences in topic and outlook, Pauker's use of historical continuity to reduce surprise echoed the "what-did-you-expect?" determinism of the responses made a few years earlier by Speaker B to Speaker A and by Benda to Feith.

How Many Died?

Partisans of any theory in circulation could at least agree that seven army officers had been killed on October 1, 1965. No such consensus has restrained speculation on

---

[5] The new regime's propagandists had coined the acronym "Gestapu" for the 30th of September Movement (Gerakan Tigapuluh September, or G30S) in order to demonize it by association with the Gestapo in Nazi Germany.

the numbers massacred in the conspiracy's "sequel," as Tovar called it in his letter to Pauker. Estimates of the number of leftists, real or accused, who died in that mass politicide have ranged from 78,500 to at least three million.

Of these polar figures, the first and lowest is obviously defective, having been reported by Sukarno's fact-finding team while blood was still being shed (Cribb 1990, 7–8). The second and maximal guess—"not less than 3,000,000" (Yayasan 2001)—is implausibly high, relying as it does on a remark purportedly made to a prominent psychic by a former army general and special forces commander, Sarwo Edhie, before he died in 1989.[6] Other guesses have filled the gradations between these extremes. Cribb (1990, 12) located twenty-five unique estimates published from 1966 to 1987 alone.

It would be unfair to attribute these differences in "the facts" merely to wishfully consistent thinking in the minds of observers already inclined to exaggerate or underestimate the toll. There were real obstacles to knowing how many had died. The killers did not document what they did, and independent observers feared the risk of doing so.

The US government had little interest in helping American scholars investigate the carnage. In Washington and other Western capitals, with the Cold War in full swing and a hot war escalating in Vietnam, Indonesia's political U-turn tended to sideline humanitarian concerns—or even to elicit relief verging on *schadenfreude* at the destruction of the PKI. *Realpolitik* trumped *moralpolitik*. In contrast, among international activists on the revolutionary left, *ideopolitik* tended to enlarge the toll.

The moral implications of high numbers were obvious; they made what happened that much more repugnant. But the more numerous the dead were thought to have been, the harder it was to limit responsibility for the killing to Suharto and the army alone, ignoring the willing assent of civilians who could have had their own scores to settle with the PKI. The army was deeply and directly complicit in the killings. But the party had civilian enemies as well, notably in Islamist circles. Years later, the liberal head of Nahdlatul Ulama, some of whose members had joined the bloodshed, said that Muslim Indonesians had massacred half a million people (Wahid 1993).

To varying degrees, scholars have incorporated this horizontal—inter-group—aspect of the violence into their accounts (cf., Friend 2003, 99, 108–116; Sulistyo 1997, iii, 259–60). Most scholarly analysts, however, would probably not disagree with John Roosa (2006, 28–31) that Suharto and the anticommunist generals on whom he relied bore vertical responsibility for what occurred—that instigation and facilitation by the state were necessary (if insufficient) conditions for the ideocide's having taken place.

Roosa's scholarship is instructive in another sense as well. Recall Anderson's idea that the ideological orientation of an analyst operating within any scholarly "format" influences his or her interpretation of the world. Insofar as scholars also require that their beliefs be ideologically constrained—consistently interlinked to form a single coherent system—they may have more than normal difficulty shifting interpretive gears in the mind to accommodate factual change on the ground.

In the case of the October 1 assassinations and the massacres that followed, Suharto's regime tied the two sets of corpses into a single series of causal moves: by

---

[6] Edhie had played a key role in overseeing and instigating the killings of leftists on Java and Bali nearly a quarter century before.

lauding the murdered officers; blaming their deaths on the PKI; avenging the officers by demonizing the party; disavowing and downplaying but actually licensing and abetting the massacres of PKI members; and using the resulting emergency to warrant the New Order's installation. Internal consistency—a mix of phobia and self-interest—required a hermetically anticommunist narrative of external events.

Could an unconscious desire for consistency have influenced scholars, too, including those who viscerally hated the New Order for what it had done to a segment of its own population? Apart from the killings, the regime engaged in a ludicrously broad campaign of guilt by association, effectively blaming the murders of the seven officers in Jakarta on "all the millions of people associated with the PKI, even illiterate peasants in remote villages" (Roosa 2006, 22). Many of the accused were imprisoned without trial and stigmatized for life on lists of persons "directly or indirectly involved" in the G30S. How could a regime with so much blood and injustice on its hands and with so blatantly mendacious and self-serving a record be credited with getting *anything* right? By this logic, the more one despised Suharto, the easier it was to minimize what he had maximized, namely, the role of the PKI in the G30S cabal, and even to believe that Suharto himself, or the CIA, or anyone but someone in the PKI had been responsible for the officers' deaths.

BETWEEN TWO INDUCEMENTS

Roosa's book is contrarian and "Keynesian" in this context. Starting in early 2000, Roosa took advantage of *Reformasi* Democracy's new openness to do fieldwork on the killings—consulting documents and interviewing survivors. He based his conclusions on a range of sources. Most important among them were, first, an accounting of what had transpired from September 30 through October 2, 1965, apparently written in 1966 by then-Brigadier General Supardjo, a participant in the conspiracy; and, second, a series of interviews with "Hasan," an apparently knowledgeable insider and member of the PKI at the time.

In relation to the scholarly literature that had basically exonerated the PKI from the G30S, Roosa's findings were strikingly revisionist: A clandestine "Special Bureau" inside the PKI, the unit cited by New Order propagandists as having planned the conspiracy, really did exist. It had been chaired by the party's own chair, D. N. Aidit. A man known as Sjam, who appeared to have played a key role in the G30S, was not an army agent working covertly to frame the PKI. He was a loyal subordinate of Aidit, who had given him operational responsibility for the Special Bureau. As for Aidit, he had not opposed the conspiracy, nor had he been tricked into supporting it. It had been his own project.

The import of Roosa's conclusions should not be overdrawn. Roosa's book is a serious work of scholarship, based on "new facts" and new interpretations of old ones, but he readily acknowledges uncertainty; his narrative is only what "*probably* happened" (2006, 202). His evidence and reasoning do not vindicate the New Order's propaganda. He pointed to "the culpability only of Aidit and Sjam, not the entire party leadership" (203). He did not cast Suharto in the role of a naïve bystander. What Suharto and his colleagues in army intelligence had known and done, or chosen not to do, remains "the largest gray zone remaining in our understanding of the movement" to seize the generals (214). Roosa is a man of the left who is unstinting in his condemnation of Suharto's regime.

It is natural to hope that fresh facts and inferences will sustain one's prior perspectives, especially on emotionally and politically loaded subjects. Yet Roosa allowed his research to convince him that the head of the PKI had overseen a secret unit pivotally implicated in the G30S conspiracy. For Roosa, the moral and political cost of appearing to "blame the victim" would have been especially acute in the case of Aidit, who was executed without trial in November 1965 shortly after being captured by Suharto's troops.

By stressing that among PKI figures "only Aidit and Sjam" were involved in the plot, Roosa protected his revisionist finding from being used to warrant the New Order's vilification of the PKI itself. It was Suharto and his regime who had blamed the victim (31) in order to destroy it—by falsely claiming that the party, not just two leading figures within it, had masterminded the October 1 assassinations, and by using that false claim as a *Pretext for Mass Murder*, as Roosa entitled his book.

Interviewed a decade before *Pretext* appeared, Anderson (1996) acknowledged that individuals from the PKI might have gone along with the G30S's plans or been fooled by "this or that" group. But he continued to believe that the PKI had not been the chief architect of the conspiracy, a role he still reserved for officers from the Diponegoro division. Interviewed after *Pretext*'s publication, Anderson (2010) said that over-reliance on Supardjo's account had made Roosa's argument "too simplistic,"[7] and hoped that "a smart PKI member" would someday "produce a logical analysis." Or perhaps, if and when still secret British and American files were opened, they would contain "new information"—mind-changing facts, in the terms used here—on what had actually transpired.

FORMAT ANTI-II?

The epigraphs that began this chapter illustrate very different responses to discontinuity. The Great Depression led Keynes to change his mind about policy. Cheney believes that 9/11 changed the world but he stayed the same. In between these categorical claims lies Feith's reaction when he first read the Cornell paper in February 1966. His admission of ambivalence and uncertainty made him hard to classify as Format I or Format II. As for the "new page" in Indonesian political studies that he felt the Cornell paper had opened, did it herald the beginning of a new format?

Arguably, yes, it did. Over the four decades from its circulation in 1966 to the publication of Roosa's revision in 2006, *A Preliminary Analysis* achieved permanence as a foundational expression of what might be termed "Format Anti-II." If Format I had been characterized by "anticolonial liberalism and the historical method," and Format II by "imperial liberalism and the comparative method," Format Anti-II combined anti-imperial autonomism with a conjunctural method.

Anti-imperial autonomism favored descriptions of the New Order as a creation of, or at least beholden to, American imperialism; a corrupt and predatory political economy penetrated by global capitalism; and a brutal betrayal of the Indonesian revolution and its promise of national autonomy and social justice. As for conjunctural dependence, that method preserved the causal primacy and interpretive salience of the New Order's formative initial condition—the massacres of 1965–66—

---

[7] Ruth McVey expressed a similarly demurring view during a conversation I had with her in Singapore on January 13, 2009.

as a birthmark from which the regime, and Suharto, neither could nor should escape.

Kuhonta (2008) and Slater (2010), among other students of Southeast Asian politics, have been attracted to the focus on "critical junctures" in comparative political history. In contrast, the conjunctural approach to Suharto's regime associated with Format Anti-II assumed rather than investigated the inability of the New Order to overcome its origin. That impeccably ethical standpoint did not encourage research into the actual dynamics, performance, and durability of Suharto's regime. Nor was such empirical work facilitated by the regime's willingness to ban Indonesianists such as Anderson from visiting the country to find out for themselves what was and was not going on.

The question posed by Feith's dialogue recurs: How much should morality be allowed to affect analysis? Were the rapid growth of the economy, the slowing of population growth, and the attendant reduction in poverty achieved on Suharto's watch worth acknowledging? Or were those "new facts" merely a façade for political repression, endemic corruption, and environmental ruin?

Feith's compound description of the regime as "repressive–developmentalist" (1980) took both of those two attributes of the New Order into account—certainly not excusing Suharto's regime, but also not reducing it to the blood on its hands. Such a recognition of difference was not a "format" in the sense of a school of consistently negative or positive thought. But if the idea of a format were opened to normative diversity, composite assessments entailing both censure and credit might instantiate a Mixed-Picture Format—a Format Minus-Plus, or Plus-Minus, depending on the tilt of an author's focus and judgment in a particular text.

LOOKING BACK—AND AHEAD

This chapter has focused on how some American-trained scholars responded to, and differed regarding, two major political changes in Indonesia in the latter part of the twentieth century. Are there larger inferences to be drawn from the results? A few, perhaps, though as much in the form of questions and speculations as conclusions.

First, the Ithacan Mecca: It is hard to exaggerate the debt owed to Cornell University by Indonesianists around the world—Feith, Benda, Anderson, and McVey, whatever their disagreements, all held Cornell PhDs. One can nevertheless wonder how different the study of Indonesian politics would have been if no single institution had loomed as large over the field as Cornell did. Cornell's concentration of resources allowed it to gain and sustain critical mass, but the cultivation of other academic centers might have complemented the ideographic style and historical penchant of the Kahinians in Format I with other approaches, including, say, a "Berkeley mafia" of West Coast scholars focusing on Indonesia's political *economy*. In any event, whether Cornell regains its centrality to the *American* study of Indonesian politics, the days of the Ithacan Mecca are over. Scholarship on Indonesian politics has been irrevocably dispersed, not only in the United States but across the world, and insofar as this will encourage scholarly diversity, it is to be welcomed.

Second, the unformattable Feith: If scholarship is to advance, it requires both competition and introspection—the collision of interpretive formats *and* the willingness of scholars to acknowledge the ambiguities that formats elide. Feith stands out in this context as a scholar who straddled the difference. *Decline* was distinctively Kahinian in its chronicling of events, and possibilist in its refusal to consider that outcome foreordained. Yet, as discussed above, Feith accommodated seeming inconsistency. Certainly he shared the ethics of Speaker A. But he felt obliged to compose and convey as well B's contention that Indonesians were likely better off for having been rescued from impoverishment in a wildly inflationary economy whose reform in 1963 the PKI had refused to allow (Feith 1966, 11).

The relevant choice for Indonesianists today as they debate continuity and change, including the nature and future of *Reformasi* Democracy, is not which side or format one should join, but whether there are facts and ideas that no side presently or sufficiently represents that can improve or replace a given interpretation. Roosa's interpretation of what happened on October 1 is instructive in this regard. Although he did not cite and may not have read Feith's dialogue, *Pretext to Mass Murder* (224) rejects the position taken by Speaker B. Yet the consonance between Roosa's perspective and Format Anti-II did not stop him from concluding, contra the Cornell paper, that the G30S was likely Aidit's own project. His scholarship, alongside Feith's, illustrates another alternative to ideological constraint.

Third, and finally, consider the uses of constraint. Anderson introduced Formats I and II to colleagues and students at the 1971 convention of the Association for Asian Studies convention in Washington, DC. Naturally, the question arose: What did he advise Indonesianists to do next? Could he preview Format III? He declined to predict the future. But he did recommend that "at the present juncture"—the early-to-mid-1970s, which he defined "as a period of political and economic subordination" of Indonesia to the United States—scholars should focus on "those aspects of Indonesian life where autonomy is likely to prove strongest, i.e., the realm of culture and experience." In addition to his case for cultural autonomism, he recommended class analysis and comparative history (Anderson 1982, 82–83).

The Indonesianist historian (and Cornell PhD) John Smail was in the audience for Anderson's presentation. Anderson had chosen not to categorize himself, but the specialists present knew that autonomism and culture were already among Anderson's most favored concerns. When the session was opened to the floor, Smail remarked that listening to Anderson's advice reminded him of George Bernard Shaw's description of H. G. Wells as "a man who could project his own ego and call it the future." The audience burst into laughter.[8]

A lesson to be drawn from this chapter is that students of contemporary Indonesian politics should diversify but not abandon political science. Despite the knowledge to be gained from carefully chronicling events, the one-case, intra-country priorities of Format I should not be—and will not be—the only way of studying political change in Indonesia. One can hope, nevertheless, that the scholarly quality and utility of the Ithacan Trilogy will someday reappear in a comparably fine-combed study of *Reformasi* Democracy.

If Format I has legs, however, II and Anti-II do not; their applicability to Indonesia today is too limited by their coinage as responses to the New Order and its interpretation. Too many new facts have intervened: The Cold War's end, Indonesia's democratization, China's rise, the Internet's spread, and the prospect of America's decline all come to mind. Interdependence fostered by globalization has not consigned imperialism and nationalism to history's dustbin. But trends toward complex interconnection have diversified what these phenomena mean. In this new

---

[8] Smail meant to be taken in good humor, and was. The audience enjoyed the joke, and Anderson showed no umbrage.

context, to equate nationalism with the autonomism of the PKI is even less tenable today than it was in the 1960s.

But Anderson's patterns are more than four decades old. He never said they would accommodate a post-Cold War world, either inside or outside Indonesia. As for swearing off formats altogether, no one can specialize—research, teach, publish—on a place or a topic without developing a point of view. Assumptions, preferences, and priorities are not infectious diseases, and no vaccine can keep them at bay.

What a scholar can and should do is to be and remain aware that *any* format, however cherished, both clarifies *and* distorts reality. Introspective awareness of these contrary effects is critical to a scholar's ability to learn from Keynes's deceptively simple question: "When the facts change, I change my mind. What do you do, sir?"

Works Cited

Anderson, Benedict R. O'G. Letter to Herb Feith. February 24, 1966. MON 78 1991/09, Folder 181. Melbourne: Monash University Records and Archives.

——. "Introduction." *A Preliminary Analysis of the October 1, 1965, Coup in Indonesia.* Ed. Benedict R. O'G. Anderson and Ruth T. McVey. Ithaca, NY: Cornell Southeast Asia Program Publications, 1971 [1966]: v–viii.

——. *Java in a Time of Revolution: Occupation and Resistance, 1944–1946.* Ithaca, NY: Cornell University Press, 1972.

——. "Perspective and Method in American Research on Indonesia." *Interpreting Indonesian Politics: Thirteen Contributions to the Debate.* Ed. Benedict R. O'G Anderson and Audrey Kahin. Ithaca, NY: Cornell Southeast Asia Program Publications, 1982: 69–83.

Anderson, Benedict R. O'G., and Audrey Kahin, eds. *Interpreting Indonesian Politics: Thirteen Contributions to the Debate.* Ithaca, NY: Cornell Southeast Asia Program Publications, 1982.

Anderson, Benedict R. O'G., and Ruth T. McVey. *A Preliminary Analysis of the October 1, 1965, Coup in Indonesia.* Ithaca, NY: Cornell Southeast Asia Program Publications, 1971 [1966].

Benda, Harry J. "Democracy in Indonesia." *Interpreting Indonesian Politics: Thirteen Contributions to the Debate.* Ed. Benedict R. O'G Anderson and Audrey Kahin. Ithaca, NY: Cornell Southeast Asia Program Publications, 1982: 13–21.

Cribb, Robert. "Problems in the Historiography of the Killings in Indonesia." *The Indonesian Killings of 1965–1966: Studies from Java and Bali.* Ed. Robert Cribb. Clayton, Australia: Centre of Southeast Asian Studies, Monash University, 1990: 1–43.

Emmerson, Donald K. "Southeast Asia in Political Science: Terms of Enlistment." *Southeast Asia in Political Science: Theory, Region, and Qualitative Analysis.* Ed. Kuhonta et al. Stanford, CA: Stanford University Press, 2008: 302–24.

Feith, Herbert. *The Wilopo Cabinet, 1952–1953: A Turning Point in Post-Revolutionary Indonesia.* Ithaca, NY: Cornell Southeast Asia Program Publications and Department of Far Eastern Studies, 1958.

——. *The Decline of Constitutional Democracy in Indonesia.* Ithaca, NY: Cornell University Press, 1962.

——. "Killings in Indonesia—To Moralise or Analyse: A Dialogue." *Nation* 9.11 (February 19, 1966).

——. "Repressive-Developmentalist Regimes in Asia: Old Strengths, New Vulnerabilities." *Prisma* [Jakarta] 19 (December 1980): 39–55.

——. "History, Theory, and Indonesian Politics: A Reply to Harry Benda." *Interpreting Indonesian Politics: Thirteen Contributions to the Debate.* Ed. Benedict R. O'G Anderson and Audrey Kahin. Ithaca, NY: Cornell Southeast Asia Program Publications, 1982: 22–29.

Friend, Theodore. *Indonesian Destinies.* Cambridge, MA: Harvard University Press, 2003.

"History Courses Get New Home: Boardman to be Rearranged to House Departments of History, Government." *The Cornell Daily Sun.* June 17, 1932: 6.

Henninger, Daniel. "I Didn't Change. The World Changed." *The Wall Street Journal,* August 30, 2011: A15.

Kahin, George McTurnan. *Nationalism and Revolution in Indonesia.* Ithaca, NY: Cornell University Press, 1952.

Karim DP, A. "Tiga Faktor Penyebab G30S." Paper read to Seminar Satu Hari PAKORBA (Paguyuban Korban Orde Baru) on October 25, 1999, posted December 21, 1999, http://www.minihub.org/siarlist/msg04198.html

Kuhonta, Erik Martinez. "Studying States in Southeast Asia." *Southeast Asia in Political Science: Theory, Region, and Qualitative Analysis.* Ed Kuhonta et al. Stanford, CA: Stanford University Press, 2008: 30–54.

Kuhonta, Erik Martinez, Dan Slater, and Tuong Vu, eds. *Southeast Asia in Political Science: Theory, Region, and Qualitative Analysis.* Stanford, CA: Stanford University Press, 2008.

Lev, Daniel S. *The Transition to Guided Democracy: Indonesian Politics, 1957–1959.* Ithaca, NY: Southeast Asia Program Publications and Department of Asian Studies, 1966.

Malabre, Alfred L., Jr. *Lost Prophets: An Insider's History of the Modern Economists.* Boston, MA: Harvard Business School Press, 1994.

McVey, Ruth T. *The Rise of Indonesian Communism.* Ithaca, NY: Cornell University Press, 1965.

——. Letter to Herb Feith. February 25, 1966. MON 78 1991/05, Folder 203. Melbourne: Monash University Records and Archives.

Pauker, Guy J. *The Rise and Fall of the Communist Party of Indonesia.* Santa Monica, CA: The RAND Corporation, 1969.

Purdey, Jemma. "Being an Apologist? The Cornell Paper and a Debate between Friends." *Transmission of Academic Values in Asian Studies: Workshop Proceedings.* Ed. Robert Cribb. Canberra: Australian National University, June 25–36, 2009. http://www.aust-neth.net/transmission_proceedings, 2011.

Roosa, John. *Pretext for Mass Murder: The September 30th Movement and Suharto's Coup d'État in Indonesia.* Madison, WI: University of Wisconsin Press, 2006.

Slater, Dan. *Ordering Power: Contentious Politics and Authoritarian Leviathans in Southeast Asia.* Cambridge: Cambridge University Press, 2010.

Sulistyo, Hermawan. "The Forgotten Years: The Missing History of Indonesia's Mass Slaughter (Jombang–Kediri 1965–1966)." Doctoral dissertation, Arizona State University, Tempe, AZ, 1997.

Tovar, B. Hugh. Letter to Guy Pauker, March 28, 1966. Guy Jean Pauker Papers, 1928–1996, Box 1, File 69. Stanford, CA: Hoover Institution Archives, Stanford University.

Wahid, Abdurrahman. Interview. *Editor* [Jakarta] 6.49 (September 4, 1993). Quoted in Karim 1999.

Yayasan Penelitian Korban Pembunun 65/66 (YPKP, Institute for the Study of 1965/1966 Massacre). "The Death Toll of the Massacre 1965/1966." Jakarta. http://www.wirantaprawira.de/ypkp/ypkp.htm, March 4, 2001.

ETHNOMUSICOLOGY

OF ARCS AND DE-/RE-CENTERINGS: CHARTING INDONESIAN MUSIC STUDIES

Christopher J. Miller

The three participants in the panel on Indonesian music studies have taken up the invitation to describe the arc in our field from distinct perspectives. The metaphor of the arc fits two of the three presenters quite well. Marc Perlman's ambitious overview of the field as a whole does not quite achieve exhaustive comprehensiveness,[1] but nonetheless summarizes succinctly the major shifts in the field's intellectual orientation and its objects of study. Perlman surveys the different ways in which the field has broadened from an initial emphasis on the musical particulars of the gamelan traditions of Java and Bali: geographically, beyond the "inner islands"; methodologically, away from "natural history" type description towards anthropological interpretation; topically, to explore the interface of music and other socio-cultural realms, forces, and dimensions; and, in terms of genre, to embrace rather than reject as "impure" the syncretic and the popular. This last direction is closely scrutinized by Andrew Weintraub in his focused and critical review of Indonesian popular music studies. Weintraub explicitly frames the arc of his survey in terms of a move from center to periphery, referring not to the shift in focus from "inner" to "outer islands," but instead to developments in the related but distinct "cultures" of Indonesian music studies and the discipline of ethnomusicology. He celebrates the beginnings, and calls for the continuation of a "decentering" of Indonesianist ethnomusicology that allows, among other things, for

---

[1] Perlman's bibliography overlooks, for example, the work of two important contributors to the scholarship on gender roles, Susan Walton and Nancy Cooper. For Susan Pratt Walton, see: "Aesthetic and Spiritual Correlations in Javanese Gamelan Music," *Journal of Aesthetics and Art Criticism* 65,1 (2007): 31–41; "Singing against the Grain: A Javanese Composer Challenges Gender Ideologies," *Women & Music* 2 (1998): 110–122; "Heavenly Nymphs and Earthly Delights: Javanese Female Singers, their Music and their Lives" (PhD dissertation, University of Michigan, 1996); and *Mode in Javanese Music* (Athens, OH: Ohio University Center for International Studies, 1987). For Nancy I. Cooper, see: "Singing and Silences: Transformations of Power Through Javanese Seduction Scenarios," *American Ethnologist* 27,3 (2000): 609–44; and "The Sirens of Java: Gender Ideologies, Mythologies, and Practice in Central Java" (PhD dissertation, University of Hawaii, 1994).

popular Indonesian music to be taken seriously. Where Perlman and Weintraub trace and project trajectories up and away from the former center of Indonesian music studies, Sumarsam bores down into the historiography of Javanese gamelan. As Sumarsam notes, this area has been pursued by a number of notable scholars from the field's beginnings. It has not, however, become a central pursuit, and Sumarsam stands out for having explored gamelan's historiography most deeply. He summarizes how others have dealt with the key problem of a lack of written sources, and then presents an original case study—one that, in piecing together disparate sources of evidence, enacts its own decentering, positing that much of the celebrated gamelan traditions of the Central Javanese courts derives from once formidable states in East Java.

Of the three contributors, Weintraub has the most to say about the future of Indonesian music studies. He not only observes where it seems to be going, but advocates where it ought to go, and what it needs to do to get there. It is hard to argue with the proposition that Indonesian popular music, as the music that the majority of Indonesians listen to and identify with, not only deserves to be taken seriously, but must be an important or even a central part of Indonesian music studies if the field is to represent the actual state of music in Indonesia, and if it is to contribute to a broader understanding of Indonesian society. In the version of his paper that Weintraub delivered at the conference from which this publication derives, he recounted the bemused response he has received to describing himself as "an ethnomusicologist of *dangdut*." That there are still those who laugh at the idea of taking *dangdut* seriously indicates that arguments like those made by Weintraub are still necessary. It seems to me, however, that the dismissive attitudes he encountered are mostly residual, and that the tide is very definitely changing. In the field of ethnomusicology overall, the study of popular music is very much on the rise, and has been for some time.[2]

The study of popular music, in Indonesia as elsewhere, will, I believe, take care of itself—which is to say a critical mass of scholars are now committed to taking care of it, evidenced most recently by the dedication of a special issue of Asian Music to Indonesian pop (Wallach and Clinton 2013). But what of other aspects of Indonesia's musicscape? I would not want to see the arguments for why we should take popular music seriously turn into reasons to not study music other than popular music. I would not want a project such as Sumarsam's dismissed as passé, or research on *musik kontemporer*, my own focus, to be deemed irrelevant because hardly anyone listens to it. I was, in fact, once so challenged by another notable scholar of popular Indonesian music. Taking his challenge then as more provocative than completely earnest, I see it now also as a manifestation of a tension that has long existed within ethnomusicology—between, on one side, the enthusiasm of some for particular "art" or "classical" traditions, and, on the other, a commitment in principle to the cultural expressions of ordinary people and an aversion to that which smacks of elitism.

---

[2] Charles Keil's *Urban Blues* (1966) is a pioneering example. Charles Keil, *Urban Blues* (Chicago, IL: University of Chicago Press, 1966). Another is Christopher Waterman's study of Nigerian Juju (1990), the first monograph in the centrally important Chicago Studies in Ethnomusicology series. See Christopher Alan Waterman, *Jùjú: A Social History and Ethnography of an African Popular Music* (Chicago, IL: University of Chicago Press, 1990). It is also worth noting that here at Cornell, Marty Hatch's line has been filled by Catherine Appert, who researches hip hop in Senegal.

Indonesianist ethnomusicology, as Perlman notes, remains something of a "stronghold of 'musicological' study," as the "obvious technical sophistication" of Javanese and Balinese gamelan invites a focus on musical nuts and bolts. This tendency follows also from the fact that the performance of this music outside Indonesia has grown from a facet of ethnomusicological training to an endeavor pursued for its own sake, whether on college campuses or in community groups. It has become an end in itself for some, amplifying its gravitational pull on those scholars for whom it was a point of entry to the broader field. But it is no longer the singular center. There has, indeed, been a decentering, or perhaps more precisely a number of recenterings, effected by all manner of shifts from all sides. On the ground there is the increasing dominance throughout Indonesia of commercialized popular musics that lies behind the increased attention to such musics by scholars. In the academy, on an intellectual level, there is the increasing concern with theoretical sophistication, but also, as Perlman acknowledges, career practicalities, such as the "race against the tenure clock," which combine to draw scholars toward certain kinds of topics and approaches and push them away from others. So while the field has broadened, there is still much music that most likely will continue to be overlooked. Yampolsky's monumental *Music of Indonesia* twenty-volume CD series went a long way towards documenting traditional musics found both far from the historical center and, in the case of "Music from the Outskirts of Jakarta" on Volume 3, in the new center's backyard. In the version of his paper delivered at the conference, Perlman pointed to Yampolsky's undertaking as the "afterlife" of an "encyclopedic survey tradition" that has all but disappeared from print publications. Yampolsky's notes are as thorough and extensive as one could hope for within the limitations of the form, but his repeated qualifications mark the work of the series as admittedly preliminary. Some follow-up work is being conducted by Indonesian scholars, but the relationship of the field of European-language Indonesian music studies—the focus of all three papers here—to the current constellation of large bodies, academic and otherwise, has curved its arcs in different directions.

These arcs have not, however, diverged so widely as to result in a splintering of the field. We continue to be bound together by "an area studies logic" that is "hard-wired in our disciplinary practice" (Stokes 2008), evident in the Indonesia panels that continue to grace the Society for Ethnomusicology's annual meetings even while some call for greater priority to be given to thematic and theoretical connections. Neither the small amount of offhand sparring nor more considered critiques, such as Weintraub's here, reflect an unbridgeable divide. For the most part, Indonesianist ethnomusicologists and those in other fields who study Indonesian music believe that all the work being done contributes in its own way to a broader understanding of music in Indonesia, and take a healthy interest in each others' work. In that respect, at least, the field is in a pretty good state.

Works Cited

Cooper, Nancy I. "Singing and Silences: Transformations of Power Through Javanese Seduction Scenarios." *American Ethnologist* 27.3 (2000): 609–44.

——. "The Sirens of Java: Gender Ideologies, Mythologies, and Practice in Central Java." PhD dissertation, University of Hawaii, 1994.

Keil, Charles. *Urban Blues*. Chicago, IL: University of Chicago Press, 1966.

Stokes, Martin. "Afterword." *The New (Ethno)Musicologies*. Ed. Henry Stobart. Lanham, MD: Scarecrow Press, 2008.

Wallach, Jeremy and Esther Clinton, eds. "Constructing Genre in Indonesian Popular Music: From Colonized Archipelago to Contemporary World Stage." Special issue, *Asian Music* 44.2 (2013).

Walton, Susan Pratt. "Aesthetic and Spiritual Correlations in Javanese Gamelan Music." *The Journal of Aesthetics and Art Criticism* 65.1 (2007): 31–41.

——. "Singing against the Grain: A Javanese Composer Challenges Gender Ideologies." *Women & Music* 2 (1998): 110–122.

——. "Heavenly Nymphs and Earthly Delights: Javanese Female Singers, their Music and their Lives." PhD dissertation, University of Michigan, 1996.

——. *Mode in Javanese Music*. Athens, OH: Ohio University Center for International Studies, 1987.

Waterman, Christopher Alan. *Jùjú: A Social History and Ethnography of an African Popular Music*. Chicago, IL: University of Chicago Press, 1990.

Yampolsky, Philip, ed. *Music of Indonesia,* a series of twenty audio CDs. Washington, DC: Smithsonian/Folkways, 1991–99.

(Ke)maju(an) ke Belakang[1]: Some Thoughts about the Future of Indonesianist Ethnomusicology

Martin Hatch

Because the ethnomusicology panel was the last in the symposium, I took the opportunity to comment mostly about where the presentations by professors Andrew Weintraub, Marc Perlman, and Sumarsam fit in the general flow and drift of the entire two-day event. Since Chris Miller had already done a fine job of identifying the central points of Andrew's, Mas Marsam's, and Marc's presentations, and placed them in the context of the field of ethnomusicology, I said a few words about how Indonesianist ethnomusicology fit into the even broader picture of global issues and needs. Below is a summary of what I said, with a few added comments on the three panelists' presentations.

During the first day of the symposium, Rudolf Mrázek told us that prospects are bleak for non-Indonesian students studying Indonesian history—that, now and in the future, Europeans and Americans should study their own history, beginning with introspection: defining who they are culturally and socially, and locating their place in the historical and present-day state of humankind. As a student of the history and current practice of music in Indonesia, I took Rudolf's advice to heart and in my comments reflected on my reading and introspection about American history and contemporary life and my place in it. In doing so, something was quite obvious to me—the "elephant in the room" at the symposium on the state of Indonesian studies was America's position and role in the world today.

Over the past fifty years that I have studied the history and practice of Indonesian music, most Americans have become increasingly dependent on exploitative associations with places and environments all around the world, including Indonesia, to the extent that they consume an inordinate proportion of the world's finite resources. Over that same period of time, "America" has become more and more a dominating presence in the lives of Indonesians and the structure of Indonesian society. I put "America" in quotes because it means not just the effects of

---

[1] Progress (moving) backward (toward the back of the bus)

the American government and business policies and activities; more than that, it means the patterns of consumption and use of resources that the "American Way of Life" exemplifies and its exponents and cultural/economic institutions promote around the world.

Those of us in research and education have the challenge of structuring our research and teaching to stimulate knowledge of these conditions and, in the contexts of the scholarship and teaching in our respective fields, correct the imbalances that these conditions have produced. America is the most powerful nation militarily (and economically, for the time being). For the past fifty years, Americans have exercised that military power disproportionately to the size of our population, usually in defense of our economic interests, or in wars to protect them. We have exercised it either in profligate disregard for the consequences or in ignorance of them, and with distorted and deceptive justifications for our actions.

Here I'm stuck in Format 2 of Don Emmerson's characterization of Benedict Anderson's 1971 presentation (see the political science contributions in this volume). And, in that position, I'm asking: when did imperialism end? Certainly not yet, if we allow ourselves to recognize gluttonous resource exploitation and consumption as the exercising of American imperial power. Missing from our discussion of the role of Indonesian studies in America was our responsibility to advocate for—to assist in—putting the breaks on American misuse of the world's resources (human and natural), and our need to make contacts and alliances with Indonesians who are working on a similar tooling (and in certain sectors, a re-tooling) of Indonesian society toward a sustainable future (someone had to use the word "sustainable" at least once in the symposium).

Also missing from our symposium was a discussion of changes in demography (population growth) and the relationship of these changes to areas of scientific inquiry like biology, forestry, agricultural economics, and, in general, consumption and conservation of natural resources—perhaps first and foremost ameliorating and slowing the effects of climate change. Earlier in the symposium the term "biodiversity" came up in connection with endangered languages. But the complex of sustainability issues, of which biodiversity is one, was missing in all of the topics we considered—from political science to art history, to languages, to music. We can begin with unpacking the effects of the language of ideologies of and commitments to models of "growth," "development," and "modernization" on material infrastructure and on education. We can also jettison our commitment to measuring the economic and social health of a country, its communities, and its peoples solely by the growth of its gross national product.

More than seven billion people are alive in the world today. When I started playing gamelan in the mid-1960s, the world population was less than half of what it is now. Indonesia's population was 104 million; it is 245 million now. Don Emmerson has said we are entering a multi-polar world. But we know that, if Americans are consuming 40 percent of the world's resources, we have a way to go before we are multi-polar in that regard. Even if China increases its consumption to 40 percent and the US share declines to 20 percent, there is still a disproportionality in national and individual use. Even if it turns out that China does not use resources in a more "democratic" way than the US does (though China is developing sustainable energy-use policies, practices, and technologies at a much faster rate than America is), perhaps the US can shift the paradigm implicit in the "American Way of Life" so that other places in the world will find it more "hip" to be sensible than to be oblivious of the implications of greed and gluttony on the future of the ecosystem. Use of finite natural resources cannot continue at the rate that unregulated-capitalism-based (this includes corporate welfare as a characteristic of unbridled free-market capitalism) countries are consuming them; we need a better distribution of use, a righting of the skewed use of resources where far too few use much too much.

So, in the short term at least, we American Indonesianists need to direct our teaching, research, and writing to developing ways of integrating our studies with those that propose and advocate solutions—to set a new course, a Plan B, for living in the world today. And American Indonesianist ethnomusicologists need to avoid the temptation to fiddle while the environment burns. How can American Indonesianist ethnomusicologists do this? At one time I thought that it might be in taking lots more time to play and teach the values of old-style community-based gamelan. Gamelan performance is a renewable resource and a sustainable practice. It promotes community solidarity in an activity that takes time away from consumption of finite resources. Why not teach the budding leaders of finance, law, and business an alternative to structuring the tone of their future around credit swaps, the protection of special interests, and the maximization of profit? While it may have had some possibilities then, that seems to be a rather naïve approach now, given the size of the environmental crises, the economic imbalances, and the imbalances in the world's social configurations.

Seventy years ago, Tan Malaka proposed that gamelan music was perhaps "*terlalu halus untuk perjuangan,*" that is, too refined/courteous for (revolutionary) struggle. (In his 1995 *Gamelan: Cultural Interaction and Musical Development in Central Java*, Mas Marsam [Sumarsam 1995] has a section on Tan Malaka's comments in which he quotes sections of Rudolf Mrázek's 1972 work on Sjahrir and Tan Malaka.) When Tan Malaka was writing, various styles of gamelan were dominant forms of musical expression in the cultural–social lives of a large number of Indonesians. At the time in the 1970s that I read about Tan Malaka's misgivings, I was writing my thesis for a degree in musicology that would make me competitive for a job teaching music (with a specialty in Southeast Asian musical cultures). I assumed that I would be directing a gamelan ensemble in whatever job I got, and I wondered how teaching that music in the 1970s would be helpful, not in the struggle that Tan Malaka was referring to, against the imperialism of his time, but against the reconfigured and much larger version of imperialism embedded in systems of power and commerce of my own time, in the sense that gamelan could provide a sustainable, alternative engagement with another place, another people, on their own terms. I turned to the writing of other Indonesian "revolutionary" intellectuals for an image of the gamelan community as a model for social–political organization in Indonesia, and, perhaps, as a model for how countries might get along with each other in the world—without dominance, but contributing to the growth of the human family by example, by transfer of skills, by play together for the common goods of spiritual and intellectual satisfaction. There was a residue of the idealistic quotient of the 1960s alternative politics in this, and it kept me going in my teaching of Indonesian ethnomusicology even through the 1990s.

Was this enough to expect that an Indonesian ethnomusicologist might do? Was there something more? Perhaps the scholarship on Indonesian music that was documented and demonstrated in this panel was another way to effect the necessary changes. Mas Marsam's presentation is a fine study of a particular set of scholarly issues as they work themselves out in a particular time period in Indonesian history.

It is hard to say whether his study will lead scholars of the future to solutions for the problems I've noted above. Perhaps it will, if, in his contributions to de-centering the focus in history of Indonesian music away from Central Javanese and southern and central Balinese gamelan traditions, he further inspires scholars, in their work and play, to concentrate on other areas of Indonesia, or, if, in his focus on the importance of the vitality of local traditions of expression and community interaction, he helps to diffuse the concentrations of nation-state power that promote excesses in resource consumption, and to advance the more sustainable local uses.

Marc's masterful and detailed description of scholarship on Indonesian music from mainly the past thirty years gives us a picture of the crescendo of scholarly activities and products since the end of the American war in Southeast Asia. But, looking at this abundance of articles covering a wide geographic and stylistic range in Indonesia from the perspective of the current problems of sustainability of resources, the environmental crises, the economic imbalances, and the imbalances in social configurations of the world, I wonder how much of this has been simply "rearranging the deck chairs on the Titanic." (This makes an analogy with trivial pursuits oblivious to natural forces. In keeping with the dominance of the military component in international relations, the analogy might be "dancing in the ballroom of the RMS Lusitania.") Perhaps the most deceptively encouraging area of scholarship that Marc notes is at the end of his presentation: "the arts have consistently been recognized by the wielders of power as useful agents or emblems of social order." This doesn't really give us confidence that Indonesian music can be an agent for social mobilization, for protest to correct economic, social, and environmental exploitation and imbalances. Indeed, it focuses our attention on arts that are, more often than not, "marketed" by, manipulated by, or in the hands of the .1 percent, not the 99.9 percent, or arts that provide entertaining diversions from the need to "struggle." What about music "of the people"? While Marc acknowledges that studies of Indonesian "popular music" have been a major area of growth in the past thirty years, he focused his survey on scholarship that has dealt with the more "traditional" genres of the Indonesian archipelago, probably because he knows that "popular music" is the subject of Andy's presentation. Which brings us to Andy's paper on "popular music."

Andy gives us as sweeping and comprehensive a study of scholarship on various kinds of Indonesian "popular" music from the twentieth and twenty-first centuries as Marc did for scholarship on "traditional" Indonesian music. Among the five definitions that Andy gives us for the term "popular music," the one that comes closest to speaking to the struggle to redress the misuse of human and natural resources is "a *representation* of the aspirations and desires of the *rakyat*, 'the people,' an abstract grouping together of people in terms of social class and political representation (or lack thereof)." But there are contradictions between this definition and aspects of the other four: for example, "commodified music emanating from the dominant cultural industry ..." can be mass-mediated music that once represented the aspirations and desires of the *rakyat*, but once it was commodified—in Indonesia especially in the period since the 1990s—it lost a sizable portion or all of its power to mobilize. In Indonesia, the tradition of socially embedded or engaged arts was strong in the eighteenth and nineteenth and early twentieth centuries. This was in large part a consequence of the close integration of the arts with daily life processes, rites, and rituals. As they developed in the twentieth century, social relevance certainly gained traction in the "popular" arts, in Andy's *rakyat* sense, even while it lost many of its associations in the older, "traditional" art forms that are examined in the scholarship that Marc surveys. Those traditional arts, perhaps through being "recognized by the wielders of power as useful agents or emblems of social order," became more and more symbols of a past social order or "classical" forms to be maintained as displays for locals and outsiders and high culture goals for the *rakyat*. But it seems clear from what Andy surveys that, except for a few types of music, practiced by small numbers of people in a few regions of Indonesia, Indonesian popular music has become largely disengaged from the current environmental crises, economic imbalances, and imbalances in social configurations in Indonesia and elsewhere. Perhaps we now have to say that Indonesian music is *"tidak lagi relevan* (or *lagi tidak relevan*) *untuk perjuangan"* (no longer [or once again not] relevant for struggle).

Works Cited

Mrázek, Rudolf. *Sjahrir: Politics and Exile in Indonesia.* Ithaca, NY: Cornell Southeast Asia Program Publications, 1972.

Sumarsam. *Gamelan: Cultural Interaction and Musical Development in Central Java.* Chicago, IL: The University of Chicago Press, 1995.

THE ETHNOMUSICOLOGY OF INDONESIAN PERFORMING ARTS: THE LAST THIRTY YEARS

Marc Perlman

Reduced to its barest outline, the story of ethnomusicology (particularly in North America) has been a journey from natural history to theory, "sound" to "context," and "authenticity" to "hybridity." For much of its history, North American ethnomusicology maintained its identity by counterposing itself to musicology (the study of the history of Western art music). On one hand, it was distinguished by its object (non-Western traditions). On this dimension of contrast, ethnomusicology's identity was assured by the styles and repertoires it analyzed; hence, it could adapt the topics and methods already familiar in the Western academy for the study of music: scales, modes, meters, formal structures, and so forth. But on the other hand, ethnomusicology also distinguished itself along a methodological dimension: it regarded music not simply as an aesthetic object but as a social and cultural medium inextricably bound to its context. On this understanding, it could focus on any music whatsoever—including European art music—but it was set apart by its embrace of an anthropological (or later, cultural studies) approach. Broadly speaking, the history of ethnomusicology is one of the increasing dominance of this anthropological orientation.

In its early days, ethnomusicology, like other nascent disciplines, took somewhat of a "natural history" approach to its object: the goal was to describe a tradition as completely as possible, and no explicit theoretical framework was necessary. This approach suited the "salvage" orientation of many early researchers. They were haunted by a pressing deadline—what they considered to be the imminent and inevitable disappearance of traditional music in the face of Western popular music— and hence struggled first of all to document as much of it as possible. Naturally, this worldview did not bring them to look kindly on popular music, especially not the local hybrid forms that were sprouting up everywhere under Western influence.

As it became more established, ethnomusicology developed more highly theorized approaches, often inspired by neighboring disciplines (e.g., cultural–historical, functionalist, semiotic, structuralist). Under these influences, and the widespread social changes engulfing the globe, ethnomusicology expanded its vision to include a wider range of topics (among them gender, identity, media, technology, power, violence, diaspora, globalization, and tourism). And as it became apparent that traditional musics, though changing, were not facing wholesale extinction (or assimilation into Western pop music without remainder), ethnomusicologists became less obsessed with "authenticity" and more interested in hybrid traditions.

This, in the broadest strokes, is the story of ethnomusicology. Indonesia has been an object of ethnomusicological scrutiny since the founding of the discipline, hence to some extent the record of scholarship on Indonesia tracks the general drift of the field's changing preoccupations. In what follows I will illustrate this by presenting a broad summary of the scholarship of the last three decades, sacrificing detail in reaching toward comprehensiveness.[1] (Even so I had to set some limits, so I have chosen to restrict my survey to publications in European languages. This very regrettable limitation acknowledges my own lack of access to scholarship in Japanese, and sets aside the rich body of work in Indonesian, which deserves its own survey.)

A STARTING POINT

While the earliest researchers were interested in several Indonesian music-cultures (there were, for example, Dutch investigations of Sundanese music, and the music of Madura), the first ones to receive the most intensive study were the court music of Central Java, and the gamelan of Bali. The early classics on these subjects—Jaap Kunst's *Music in Java, Its History, Its Theory, and Its Technique* (1934/1973), and Colin McPhee's *Music in Bali: A Study in Form and Instrumental Organization in Balinese Orchestral Music* (1966)—display features of the natural-history type survey, as their titles suggest. They aim to document these traditions little known in the West, not to establish a thesis or verify a hypothesis. (Kunst indulges in a few theoretical excursions, but these have been the least influential aspect of his work. Few now read him for his speculations on intercontinental musical affinities; his application of Hornbostel's now-defunct culture-historical theory of "blown fifths" has been more or less completely ignored.) But as the titles also suggest, both books are strongly oriented to the technicalities of sound organization, and exhibit a fascination with scales, time-cycles, formal structures, and other so-called "musicological" topics.

The study of these two traditions has had a broad influence on North American ethnomusicology, though it has not contributed much to the discourse of the field. Unlike Indonesianist anthropology—the source of concepts ranging from "deep play" to "dubbing culture"—the study of gamelan, aside from a few technical concepts (stratified polyphony, colotomic structure), has produced little of general theoretical interest to ethnomusicologists. Rather, Javanese and Balinese gamelan became exemplary markers of a certain tradition of pedagogy. Mantle Hood was a student of Jaap Kunst's (one of the founders of ethnomusicology), and wrote his dissertation on Javanese music; he returned to the United States to found UCLA's Institute of Ethnomusicology, and over more than a decade he built on that campus

---

[1] I owe an enormous debt of gratitude to Philip Yampolsky for his bibliographic help and his challenging comments. While the debt I owe Dana Rappoport may be less evident, it is equally real. Neither one is to blame for whatever errors, omissions, or misinterpretations remain in the text.

what remains the largest ethnomusicology program in the country. He also had the university purchase several sets of Indonesian gamelan, and he made learning to perform on them part of ethnomusicological training. This pedagogical emphasis, which Hood called bi-musicality, has retained an important role in many programs. And while gamelan was by no means the only vehicle for bi-musicality (performance ensembles at ethnomusicology programs have also encompassed the musics of India, Japan, West Africa, Latin America, the Caribbean, and many more) the gamelan occupies a "canonic" position in this roster (Solís 2004, 7). It has been jokingly attributed a totemic significance as the proudest emblem an ethnomusicology program can display (Trimillos 2004, 52).[2]

BEYOND THE "INNER ISLANDS"

In some ways the history of the ethnomusicology of Indonesia is the story of its gradual expansion beyond these founding areas. I have tried to represent its growth beyond Bali and Central Java graphically in Figure 1, where I have listed the authors of all the European-language publications known to me from 1976 to 2011 dealing with music outside these two regions.[3] (The columns do not represent geographical areas of equal size. Thus West and East Java have their own columns, while the far larger and more heterogeneous regions of Sumatra, Kalimantan, Sulawesi, and the rest of eastern Indonesia receive only one column each.)

It should not be surprising that among the first traditions to become (and remain) objects of interest were those geographically close and/or musically similar to the two "founding" exempla. In the case of Java, this meant the music of Sunda, Cirebon, and Banyumas, on the one hand; and of Banyuwangi, Madura, and Malang, on the other. Similarly, scholars familiar with Bali found the music of Lombok to be a rewarding study.

There had been ethnomusicological research on areas outside of these two so-called "inner islands," but before the 1980s it was scattered and desultory. Consistent with the growing Indonesian interest in documenting local cultures, experts and government agencies throughout the country had been issuing a steady stream of studies, but most of the early publications in European languages seem to have been side projects by anthropologists or students of oral literature, or sometimes by-products of missionary activity.[4]

Margaret Kartomi was one of the first to drive concentrated ethnomusicological attention beyond the inner islands. Her own travels ranged far and wide throughout

---

[2] The triumph of campus gamelan ensembles is perhaps best signified by the fact that they have been considered worth attacking. For example, Averill criticizes the enthusiasm over gamelan performance for "reproducing … an Euro-American fetish for sophistication" in ethnomusicology programs. See: Gage Averill, "Where's 'One'?": Musical Encounters of the Ensemble Kind," in *Performing Ethnomusicology: Teaching and Representation in World Music Ensembles* ed. Ted Solís (Berkeley, CA: University of California Press, 2004), p. 97.

[3] I would not have dared draw up such a chart (which, despite an author's vociferous disclaimers, always projects an air of comprehensiveness) had Philip Yampolsky not generously allowed me to consult his formidable bibliography. He is, however, not responsible for whatever gaps remain. I'd like to express my gratitude to Philip, and my apologies to any scholars whose publications I have inadvertently omitted.

[4] It is worth noting that the earliest publications documenting these traditions to become available outside Indonesia often took the form of scholarly recordings (a point I owe to Philip Yampolsky).

Figure 1
Published Authors and Their Region(s) of Interest, 1976–2011

	Sunda	Cirebon	Banyumas	Sumatra	Banyuwangi
1976					
1977	DeVale, Heins				
1978		Wright		Goldsworthy	
1979	Foley			Goldsworthy	
1980				Jansen, Phillips	
1981	Grijns	Suanda		M. Kartomi, Moore, Thomsen	
1982	Falk, Hugh-Jones			Simon, Turner	
1983					
1984	van Zanten			Moore, Simon	
1985	Foley, Weintraub	Suanda		Moore, Simon	
1986	Baier, van Zanten	Foley, Rogers	Sutton	Goldsworthy, Nor, K. Kartomi, M. Kartomi,	Wolbers
1987	van Zanten			M. Kartomi, Patton, Simon	Wolbers
1988		North, Suanda, Wright		Phillips, Purba, Schefold, Simon	
1989	Fryer, DeVale, van Zanten, Williams				Wolbers
1990	Foley, M. Kartomi, Weintraub, Williams		Lysloff	Carle	
1991	M. Kartomi		Sutton	M. Kartomi, Simon, Turner	
1992	Koesasi			Phillips, M. Kartomi	Arps, Wolbers
1993	Hellwig, Spiller, Weintraub, Williams, van Zanten		Lysloff	M. Kartomi, Nor, Simon	Sutton, Wolbers
1994	Weintraub, van Zanten			Junus, Okazaki	
1995	van Zanten			Hutajulu, Pauka	
1996	Spilller				
1997	M. Kartomi, van Zanten, Weintraub	Cohen		M. Kartomi, Turner, Wieringa	
1998	Simon, Weintraub, Williams		Sukarno	M. Kartomi, Pauka	
1999	Hellman, Jurriens, Williams				Wessing
2000				Barendregt, Salisbury	
2001	Weintraub, Williams				
2002	Herbert, Weintraub		Lysloff	Purba	
2003	Williams			Cohen, Suryadi	
2004	Jurriens, Weintraub			Manhart, M. Kartomi	
2005				Amir, M. Kartomi, Purba	
2006	Hellman			Byl, Hodges, M. Kartomi	
2007				Fraser	
2008					
2009		Ross		Hodges, Raseuki	
2010	Andrieu, Spiller			M. Kartomi	
2011				Nor	

Figure 1 (continued)
Published Authors and Their Region(s) of Interest, 1976–2011

	East Java & Madura	Lombok	Kalimantan	Sulawesi	Eastern Indonesia
1976		Seebass			
1977					
1978					
1979					
1980				Hamonic, Watuseke	
1981				M. Kartomi	Adams, Oguri, Peckham
1982					
1983					Oguri
1984					Gieben
1985	Bouvier	Harnish		Acciaioli	Soedarsono
1986		Harnish			
1987	Hefner				
1988		Harnish	Gorlinski		
1989			Gorlinski	George	Messner
1990		Harnish		George	Barraud
1991	Schreiber, Sutton	Harnish			Simon
1992		Harnish	Gorlinski, M. Kartomi	Hamonic, Koubi	M. Kartomi, Royl
1993		Harnish	Skog	George	M. Kartomi, Myers
1994	Bouvier, Marah, Peacock		Gorlinski	Flaes	M. Kartomi
1995	Burman-Hall, Oetomo, Widodo		Gorlinski	Rappoport, Sutton	
1996	Suyanto			Aragon	Rutherford
1997		Harnish		Rappoport	Suwardi
1998				Rappoport, Sutton	
1999	Wilson			Rappoport	
2000					Spyer
2001	Oetomo				M. Kartomi
2002			M. Kartomi	Sutton	
2003		Harnish			
2004				Rappoport	
2005		Harnish			Bos
2006		Harnish		Sutton	
2007	Sunardi	Harnish	Simeda		
2008					
2009	Sunardi			Hicken, Munger, Rappoport	
2010	Sunardi				Rappoport
2011	Sunardi				Rappoport

the archipelago, and her influence was instrumental in fostering an Australian tradition of study of the music-cultures of Sumatra. Meanwhile, Gorlinski was documenting the Dayak music of East Kalimantan, and Rappoport was doing the same in Sulawesi (followed by Sutton and his students).[5]

---

[5] In one recent development, scholars have pushed this expansion beyond national borders by studying widely dispersed groups, such as the Bajau (Bajo/Sama Dilaut) whose communities

NEW TOPICS

Along with this geographical expansion, ethnomusicology also explored new subject matter (Figure 2). As disciplinary attitudes toward syncretic or "impure" music began to soften, Indonesianist ethnomusicology welcomed a wider range of genres. Thus, concomitant with the geographical broadening described above came a new interest in *dangdut* and other forms of popular music.

These developments were fueled in part by the inherent expansionary dynamic of the discipline: those who came later found some of the ground already cultivated, and went elsewhere to find their own niche. (The option of producing an encyclopedic treatment of some music—in the spirit of Kunst and McPhee—was increasingly unavailable to young academics, who had to race against the tenure clock.) But these developments were also driven by ongoing changes in Indonesian society. The increasing prominence of Islam in both personal and political life, for example, has musical ramifications that are reflected in a growing ethnomusicological literature. The presence of Arabic music and musical influences (which while by no means synonymous with Islamic influence yet intersects with it in interesting ways) is also now attracting attention. The growing interest of traditional musicians in creative "experimentation" with their art now has its chroniclers as well. But the two main areas of growth (outside of popular music) focus on changes attendant on globalization, and on shifting gender roles.

The first aspect of globalization to be studied was the effect of tourism on the traditional arts. Here the lion's share of attention was given to Bali, which became the focus of a long-running debate on the influence of tourism. But there was also another aspect of globalization that was slower to come into focus, though, ironically, it was stimulated by the actions of ethnomusicologists like Mantle Hood (as described above). The introduction of gamelan instruments and instruction in European countries, North America, and Japan—soon followed by Latin America, the Middle East, and continental Asia—has produced gamelan-based subcultures around the world. Some of them were taught by traditionally trained musicians, but many were not. Moreover, a few enterprising instrument builders constructed their own gamelan-like ensembles. Both the imported instruments and the newly made ones attracted the attention of composers, who wrote pieces more or less indebted to Indonesian models. These musical enclaves incubated many future ethno-musicologists—some of whom eventually turned their scholarly attention on the transcultural presence of Indonesian music.

An even more transformative change that has affected both Indonesian musical life and scholarship concerns the role of women. Here the long-term global trends in social life and in academic work are ultimately inseparable, since we may assume that the influence of women's studies and gender studies on ethnomusicology—clearly felt by the 1980s—was a response to the same social forces that have slowly molded the status and relationships of men and women throughout the twentieth century.

---

are also found in Sabah and the Philippines (Abels 2011, 2012, 2013). These publications can not be easily located in my Figure 1, since they transcend the regional boundaries it presupposes.

Figure 2
Published Authors by Subject Areas, 1976–2011
(continued on next page)

	Pop	Tourism	Dangdut	Women
1976				
1977				
1978	Kornhauser			·
1979		McKean		
1980				
1981				
1982	Lohanda		Frederick	Pausacker
1983				
1984				
1985				
1986	Manuel & Baier	Kam		
1987	Möller			
1988		Sanger		
1989	Hatch, Yampolsky	McKean		
1990		Picard		
1991	Murray			
1992				
1993		Connell, Hughes-Freeland, Picard		Weiss
1994		McCarthy		
1995			Pioquinto	
1996	Baulch	Picard	Simatupang	Scott-Maxwell, Weiss
1997		Jenkins & Catra, Picard		Bakan, Willner
1998				Perlman, Williams, Weiss
1999				
2000	Pickles	Minca	Browne	
2001		Dunbar-Hall		
2002	Barendregt & van Zanten, Baulch, Sutton, Wallach			Pausacker, Weiss
2003	Baulch, Sutton, Supanggah, Wallach			Susilo
2004				McGraw
2005	Bodden, Wallach	Harnish	Van Wichelen	Ballinger
2006			Weintraub	Weiss
2007	Baulch, Farram, Pickles, Spiller			
2008	Coutas, Keppy, Richter, Laronga, Wallach		Weintraub	Diamond, Downing, Weiss
2009	Luvaas			Palermo
2010	McIntosh, Yampolsky		Weintraub	Downing, Rasmussen
2011				

Figure 2 (continued)
Published Authors by Subject Areas, 1976–2011

	Transnationalism	Islam, Arab	New Composition	Pop
1976				
1977				
1978				Kornhauser
1979	·			
1980				
1981				
1982				Lohanda
1983	Perlman			
1984				
1985				
1986		Pacholczyk	McDermott, Roth	Manuel & Baier
1987				Möller
1988				
1989	Heins			Hatch, Yampolsky
1990				
1991				Murray
1992				
1993	Hadley			
1994	Perlman			
1995		Capwell		
1996			Wenten	Baulch
1997				
1998			McGraw	
1999			McGraw	
2000				Pickles
2001	Diamond	Rasmussen	Notosudirdjo	
2002	Catra, Mendonca	Gade	Vitale, Warde	Barendregt & van Zanten, Baulch, Sutton, Wallach
2003		Notosudirdjo		Baulch, Sutton, Supanggah, Wallach
2004	Harnish, Sumarsam, Susilo, Vetter, Witzleben	Gade		
2005	Susilo	Rasmussen	McGraw	Bodden, Wallach
2006	Lindsay	Barendregt	Miller	
2007	Lindsay	Berg		Baulch, Farram, Pickles, Spiller
2008	Weiss	Barendregt	Miller	Coutas, Keppy, Laronga, Richter, Wallach
2009	Emigh, McIntosh, Spiller	Raseuki	McGraw	Luvaas
2010	Hughes-Freeland, McGraw, Mendonca	Rasmussen		McIntosh, Yampolsky
2011		Harnish & Rasmussen		

This new perspective expressed itself in Indonesianist ethnomusicology in two ways. First, it was necessitated by new developments such as the rise of all-female gamelan and dance groups. But it also directed attention at long-established phenomena, such as representations of women (e.g., in the Javanese *wayang*), women as performers, and the so-called "female style" of Central Javanese gendèr-playing.

This taxonomy is by no means exhaustive. There are also scattered studies on hybridity (Sutton 2010; Weiss 2008a), on Chinese–Indonesians as patrons and tradition-bearers (Clara van Groenendael 1993; Brakel-Papenhuyzen 1995; Kartomi 2000; Pausacker 2005; Collier 2007), on gender identity (Sunardi 2009), on the effects of internal migration (Redding 2002), and religious conversion (Poplawska 2004, 2008; Rappoport 2004), and many other topics.

There were also occasional echoes of academic upheavals in North American ethnomusicology. Following the anthropological "crisis of representation" of the 1980s, some ethnomusicologists came to feel that the usual mode of ethnographic writing (in which the researcher's presence is more or less effaced) was illegitimate. They called for a reflexive approach, in which the ethnomusicologist acknowledges his or her contribution to the knowledge-producing process. While this position was always controversial, and has perhaps passed its period of peak influence, it did strongly affect at least one ethnography of Balinese music (Bakan 1999).

PARTICULARITIES OF INDONESIANIST ETHNOMUSICOLOGY

In its widening geographic scope, in its embrace of popular music, and in the increasing prominence of topics like globalization and gender, Indonesianist ethnomusicology reflects the broad development of ethnomusicology as a whole. Still, it is not simply a microcosm of the larger field; it bears its own particularities of emphasis and nuance. Without pretending to offer a comprehensive list of these particularities, I may mention two characteristic features.

First, the gradual shift from the study of "sound" to "context" has perhaps not pervaded Indonesianist ethnomusicology to the degree that it has in the larger universe of ethnomusicological research. The obvious technical sophistication of some Indonesian traditions—especially Javanese and Balinese gamelan—and the musicians' own concern with technical matters, invite a focus on "music sound." Hence the ethnomusicology of Indonesia has remained to some extent a stronghold of "musicological" study.[6] Yet the current approach to "music sound" is not simply a relic of an earlier methodology, but has been rejuvenated by new interdisciplinary influences (such as cognitive psychology; for example, Brinner 1995; Perlman 2004).

On the other hand, the cultural effects of state power have been a continually recurring theme in Indonesianist ethnomusicology. Scholars have been fascinated by the various ways in which the performing arts have been used as both object and instrument of social control—whether the controlling agent is the colonial state or native rulers (Sumarsam 1995), the New Order regime (Pemberton 1987; Yampolsky 1995), state educational institutions (Hough 1999, 2000; Fraser 2007), or state-

---

[6] Of the books given the Society for Ethnomusicology's highest honor, the only two to focus on Indonesian traditions pay a great deal of attention to the details of musical structures and processes. See Michael Tenzer, *Gamelan Gong Kebyar: The Art of Twentieth-Century Balinese Music* (Chicago, IL: University of Chicago Press, 2000); and Marc Perlman, *Unplayed Melodies: Javanese Gamelan and the Genesis of Music Theory* (Berkeley, CA: University of California Press, 2004).

sponsored festivals (Noszlopy 2002). Perhaps this focus, too, is attributable to certain historical constants in Indonesian societies; perhaps the arts have consistently been recognized by the wielders of power as useful agents or emblems of social order. And while the passing of the Suharto regime has ushered in an era of political decentralization and local autonomy, some of the New Order's top-down cultural policies seem to linger on in official attitudes and institutions—suggesting that this topic will remain a staple of ethnomusicological research.

I would not, however, want to overly emphasize these centripetal forces. As I mentioned above, ethnomusicology today is receptive to theoretical developments in a variety of disciplines. Recent work in Indonesianist ethnomusicology shows a wide range of influences, from topos theory (Tenzer 2000) to media theory (Weintraub 2004b) to philosophical aesthetics (Benamou 2010) to Lacanian psychoanalysis (Spiller 2010a). It is probably too soon to say which, if any, of these approaches will prove inspiring to the next generation of scholars. But observing the centrifugal force of so many intellectual currents, we can be confident that scholars will seek inspiration in an ever-growing array of interdisciplinary perspectives.

Abbreviations Used in Works Cited

AM	Asian Music
AR	Archipel
ATJ	Asian Theatre Journal
BKI	Bijdragen tot de Taal-, Land- en Volkenkunde
EM	Ethnomusicology
IC	Indonesia Circle
MQ	Musical Quarterly
RIMA	Review of Indonesian and Malaysian Affairs
SRE	Selected Reports in Ethnomusicology
WM	World of Music
YTM	Yearbook for Traditional Music

Works Cited

Abels, Birgit. "Music, Metamorphoses, Movement: The Traditional Music of the Sama Dilaut, Musical Change, and Spatiality." *Proceedings of the First Symposium of the ICTM Study Group on Performing Arts of Southeast Asia.* Ed. Mohd. Anis Md. Nor, Tan Sooi Beng, Patricia Matusky, et al. Kuala Lumpur: Nusantara Performing Arts Research Center (NusPARC) and the Department of Southeast Asian Studies of the University of Malaya, 2011: 165–69.

——. "Songs of Belonging: Vocal Music among the 'Sea Nomads' of the Sulu and Celebes Seas." *Sama Celebrations: Ritual, Music, and Dance in Southern Philippines and North Borneo.* Ed. Hanafi Bin Hussin and M. C. M. Santamaria. Kuala Lumpur: University of Malaya Press, 2013: 37–56.

Abels, Birgit, with Hanafi Hussin and M. C. M. Santamaria, eds. *Oceans of Sound: Sama Dilaut Performings Arts.* Hildesheim: Olms, 2012.

Acciaioli, Gregory L. "Culture As Art: From Practice to Spectacle in Indonesia." *Canberra Anthropology* 8.1,2 (1985): 148–72.

Adams, Marie Jeanne (Monni). "Instruments and Songs of Sumba, Indonesia: A Preliminary Survey." *AM* 13 (1981): 73–83.

Amir, Iwan Dzulvan. "Sing, Adapt, Persevere: Dynamics of Traditional Vocal Performances in the Islamic Region of Aceh from the Late 19th to the Early 21st Century." PhD dissertation. Clayton, Victoria: Monash University, 2005.

Andrieu, Sarah. "Performances et Patrimonialisations du Wayang Golek Sundanais (Java Ouest, Indonésie)." PhD dissertation. Paris: École Des Haute Études En Sciences Sociales, 2010.

Aragon, Lorraine V. "Suppressed and Revised Performances: Raego' Songs of Central Sulawesi." *EM* 40.3 (1996): 413–39.

Arps, Bernard. "Tembang in Two Traditions: Performance and Interpretation of Javanese Literature." PhD dissertation. Leiden: Leiden University, 1992.

Arps, Bernard, ed. *Performance in Java and Bali: Studies of Narrative, Theatre, Music, and Dance.* London: School of Oriental and African Studies, University of London, 1993.

Averill, Gage. "Where's 'One'?: Musical Encounters of the Ensemble Kind." *Performing Ethnomusicology: Teaching and Representation in World Music Ensembles.* Ed. Ted Solís. Berkeley, CA: University of California Press, 2004: 93–114.

Baier, Randal. "Si Duriat Keueung: The Sundanese Angklung Ensemble of West Java, Indonesia." MA thesis. Middletown, CT: Wesleyan University, 1986.

Bakan, Michael. "From Oxymoron to Reality: Agendas of Gender and the Rise of Balinese Women's Gamelan Beleganjur in Bali, Indonesia." *AM* 29.1 (1997/1998): 37–85.

——. *Music of Death and New Creation: Experiences in the World of Balinese Gamelan Beleganjur.* Chicago, IL: University of Chicago Press, 1999.

Ballinger, Rucina. "Woman Power." *Inside Indonesia* 83 (2005).

Barendregt, Bart. "Told in Heaven to become Stories on Earth: A Study of Change in Randai Theatre of the Minangkabau in West Sumatra Using Visual Documentation from the 30s." Leiden: Institute of Social and Cultural Studies and International Institute for Asian Studies, 2000.

——. "Cyber-Nasyid: Transnational Soundscapes in Muslim Southeast Asia." *Medi@asia: Communication, Culture, Context.* Ed. T. Holden and T. Scrase. London: Routledge, 2006a: 171–87.

——. "Hoe een Islamitische toekomst klinkt: Zuidoost Aziatische popmuziek en het gebruik van de nieuwe media." *ZemZem: Tijdschrift over het Midden-Oosten, Noord-Afrika en Islam* 4 (2006b): 89–93.

——. "The Sound of Islam: Southeast Asian Boybands." *ISIM Review* 22 (2008): 24–25.

Barendregt, Bart, and Wim van Zanten. "Popular Music in Indonesia since 1998, in Particular Fusion, Indie, and Islamic Music on Video Compact Discs and the Internet." *YTM* 34 (2002): 67–113.

Barraud, Cecile. "A Turtle Turned on the Sand in the Kei Islands: Society's Shares and Values." *BKI* 146 (1990): 35–55.

Baulch, Emma. "Punks, Rastas, and Headbangers: Bali's Generation X." *Inside Indonesia* (1996) 48: 23–25.

——. "Alternative Music and Mediation in Indonesia." *Inter-Asia Cultural Studies* 3.2 (2002a): 119–234.

——. "Creating a Scene: Balinese Punk's Beginnings." *International Journal of Cultural Studies* 5.2 (2002b).

——. "Gesturing Elsewhere: The Identity Politics of the Balinese Death/Thrash Metal Scene." *Popular Music* 22 (2003): 195–215.

——. *Making Scenes: Reggae, Punk, and Death Metal in 1990s Bali.* Durham, NC: Duke University Press, 2007.

Benamou, Marc. Rasa: *Affect and Intuition in Javanese Musical Aesthetics.* New York, NY: Oxford University Press, 2010.

Berg, Birgit. "The Music of Arabs, the Sound of Islam: Hadrami Ethnic and Religious Presence in Indonesia." PhD dissertation. Providence, RI: Brown University, 2007.

Bodden, Michael. "Rap in Indonesian Youth Music of the 1990s: 'Globalization,' 'Outlaw Genres,' and Social Protest." *AM* 36.2 (2005): 1–26.

Bos, Paula. "Nagi Music and Community: Belonging and Displacement in Larantuka, Eastern Indonesia." *Diasporas and Interculturalism in Asian Performing Arts: Translating Traditions.* Ed. Hae-kyung Um. London: RoutledgeCurzon, 2005: 144–58.

Bouvier, Hélène. "Le topeng dalang de Madura." *ASEMI* [Asie du Sud-Est et Monde Insulindien] 16.1–4 (1985): 249–77.

——. *La matière des émotions: les arts du temps et du spectacle dans la société madouraise (Indonésie).* Publications de l'Ecole Française d'Extrême-Orient 172. Paris: Ecole Française d'Extrême-Orient, 1994.

Brakel-Papenhuyzen, Clara. "Javanese Talèdhèk and Chinese Tayuban." *BKI* 151 (1995): 545–69.

Brinner, Ben. *Knowing Music, Making Music: Javanese Gamelan and the Theory of Musical Competence and Interaction.* Chicago, IL: University of Chicago Press, 1995.

Browne, Susan. *The Gender Implications of Dangdut Kampungan: Indonesian "Low-Class" Popular Music.* Clayton, Victoria: Monash Asia Institute, 2000.

Burman-Hall, Linda. "The Fahnestock South Sea Expeditions: Excursions in Madurese Music." *Across Madura Strait: The Dynamics of an Insular Society.* Ed. Kees van Dijk, Huub de Jonge, and Elly Touwen-Bouwsma. *Koninklijk Instituut voor Taal-, land- en Volkenkunde, Proceedings, No. 2.* Leiden: KITLV Press, 1995: 135–56.

Byl, Julia. "Antiphonal Histories: Performing Toba Batak Past and Present." PhD dissertation. Ann Arbor, MI: University of Michigan, 2006.

Capwell, Charles. "Contemporary Manifestations of Yemeni-Derived Song and Dance in Indonesia." *YTM* 27 (1995): 76–89.

Carle, Rainer. *Opera Batak: das Wandertheater der Toba-Batak in Nord-Sumatra: Schauspiele zur Wahrung kultureller Identität im nationalen indonesischen Kontext.* Veröffentlichungen des Seminars für Indonesische und Südseesprachen der Universität Hamburg, Band 15. Berlin: Dietrich Reimer Verlag, 1990.

Catra, I Nyoman, and Ron Jenkins. "Finding Equilibrium in Disequilibrium: The Impact of ISTA on Its Balinese Participants." *Negotiating Cultures: Eugenio Barba and the Intercultural Debate.* Ed. Ian Watson. Manchester: Manchester University Press, 2002: 59–66.

Clara van Groenendael, Victoria. "Po-te-hi: The Chinese Glove-puppet Theatre in East Java." *Performance in Java and Bali: Studies of Narrative, Theatre, Music, and Dance.* Ed. Bernard Arps. London: School of Oriental and African Studies, University of London, 1993: 11–32.

Cohen, Matthew Isaac. "An Inheritance from the Friends of God: The Southern Shadow Puppet Theater of West Java, Indonesia." PhD dissertation. New Haven, CT: Yale University, 1997.

——. "Look at the Clouds: Migration and West Sumatran 'Popular' Theatre." *New Theatre Quarterly* 19.75 (2003): 214–29.

Collier, Bethany. "The 'Chinese' in Contemporary Balinese Performing Arts: Stories, Objects, and Representations." PhD dissertation. Ithaca, NY: Cornell University, 2007.

Connell, John. "Bali Revisited: Death, Rejuvenation, and the Tourist Cycle." *Environment and Planning D: Society and Space* 11 (1993): 641–61.

DeVale, Sue Carole. "A Sundanese Gamelan—A Gestalt Approach to Organology." PhD dissertation. Chicago, IL: Northwestern University, 1977.

Diamond, Catherine. "Wayang Listrik: Dalang Larry Reed's Shadow Bridge between Bali and San Francisco." *Theatre Research International* 26 (2001): 257–76.

——. "Fire in the Banana's Belly: Bali's Female Performers Essay the Masculine Arts." *ATJ* 25.2 (2008): 231–71

Downing, Sonja L. "Arjuna's Angels: Girls Learning Gamelan Music in Bali." PhD dissertation. Santa Barbara, CA: University of California–Santa Barbara, 2008.

——. "Agency, Leadership, and Gender Negotiation in Balinese Girls' Gamelans." *EM* 54.1 (2010): 54–80.

Dunbar-Hall, Peter. "Culture, Tourism, and Cultural Tourism: Boundaries and Frontiers in Performances of Balinese Music and Dance." *Journal of Intercultural Studies* 22. 2 (2001): 173–87.

Emigh, John. "'Living in a Different House': A Gambuh Macbeth in Bali." *Re-playing Shakespeare in Asia.* Poonam Trivedi and Minami Ryuta, eds. London: Routledge, 2009: 291–307.

Falk, Catherine A. "The Tarawangsa Tradition in West Java." PhD dissertation. Clayton, Victoria: Monash University, 1982.

Farram, Steven. "Wage War against Beatle Music!: Censorship and Music in Soekarno's Indonesia." *RIMA* 41.2 (2007): 247–77.

Flaes, Boonzajer. "Bamboo Brass in Minahasa." *Experimental Musical Instruments* 9.4 (1994): 10–15.

Foley, Kathy M. "The Sundanese Wayang Golek: The Rod Puppet Theatre of West Java." PhD dissertation. Honolulu, HI: University of Hawaii, Honolulu, 1979.

——. "The Dancer and the Danced: Trance Dance and Theatrical Performance in West Java." *ATJ* 2 (1985): 28–49.

——. "At the Graves of the Ancestors: Chronicle Plays in the Wayang Cepak Puppet Theatre of Cirebon, Indonesia." *Historical Drama.* Ed. James Redmond. Cambridge: Cambridge University Press, 1986: 31–49.

——. "My Bodies: The Performer in West Java." *The Drama Review* 34.2 (1990): 62–80.

Fraser, Jennifer. "Packaging Ethnicity: State Institutions, Cultural Entrepreneurs, and the Professionalization of Minangkabau Music in Indonesia." PhD dissertation. Champaign, IL: University of Illinois at Urbana–Champaign, 2007.

Frederick, William. "Rhoma Irama and the Dangdut Style: Aspects of Contemporary Indonesian Popular Culture." *Indonesia* 34 (October 1982): 103–40.

Gade, Anna. "Taste, Talent, and the Problem of Internalization: A Qur'anic Study in Religious Musicality from Southeast Asia." *History of Religions* 41.4 (2002): 328–68.

——. *Perfection Makes Practice: Learning, Emotion, and the Recited Qur'an in Indonesia.* Honolulu, HI: University of Hawaii Press, 2004.

George, Kenneth. "The Singing from the Headwaters: Song and Tradition in the Headhunting Rituals of an Upland Sulawesi Community." PhD dissertation. Ann Arbor, MI: University of Michigan, 1989.

——. "Felling a Song with a New Ax: Writing and the Reshaping of Ritual Song Performance in Upland Sulawesi." *Journal of American Folklore* 103.407 (1990): 3–23.

——. "Music-making, Ritual, and Gender in a Southeast Asian Hill Society." *EM* 37.1 (1993): 1–27.

Gieben, Claartje, Renee Heijnen, and Anneke Sapuletej. *Muziek en Dans Spelletjes en Kinderliedjes van de Molukken.* Hoevelaken: Christelijk Pedagogisch Studiecentrum, 1984.

Goldsworthy, David. "Honey-Collecting Ceremonies on the East Coast of North Sumatra." *Studies in Indonesian Music.* Ed. M. J. Kartomi. Clayton, Victoria: Monash University Centre of Southeast Asian Studies, 1978: 1–44.

——. "Melayu Music of North Sumatra." PhD dissertation. Clayton, Victoria: Monash University, 1979.

——. "The Dancing Fish Trap (lukah menari): A Spirit Invocation Song and a Spirit-Possession Dance from North Sumatra." *Musicology Australia* 9 (1986): 12–28.

Gorlinski, Virginia K. "Some Insights into the Art of Sape Playing." *Sarawak Museum Journal* 39.60 (1988).

——. "Pangpagaq: Religious and Social Significance of a Traditional Kenyah Music-dance Form." *Sarawak Museum Journal* 40.61 n.s., Part 3 (December 1989): 279–301.

——. "Why Women Do Not Play Sampé": Some Comments on Gender Relations and the Plucked Lute of the Kenyah and Kayan." Paper presented at "Music in Southeast Asia: A Workshop on Music Research in Southeast Asia." Universiti Kebangsaan Malaysia, July 16–17, 1992, Bangi, Selangor, Malaysia.

——. "Gongs among the Kenyah Uma' Jalan: Past and Present Position of an Instrumental Tradition." *YTM* 26 (1994): 81–99.

——. "Songs of Honor, Words of Respect: Social Contours of Kenyah Lepo' Tau Versification, Sarawak, Malaysia." PhD dissertation. Madison, WI: University of Wisconsin–Madison, 1995.

Grijns, C. D. "Distributional Aspects of Folk Performances in the Jakarta Malay Area." *Masyarakat Indonesia* 8.2 (1981): 187–226.

Hadley, Peter. "New Music for Gamelan by North American Composers." MA thesis. Middletown, CT: Wesleyan University, 1993.

Hamonic, Gilbert. "Mallawolo: Chants Bugis pour la sacralisation des anciens princes de Célèbes-Sud." *AR* 19 (1980): 43–79.

Hamonic, Gilbert. "Dérouler les mots, tresser la vie: chants de rencontre entre princes bugis." *Chants alternés: Asie du Sud-Est—à Jacques Dournes—Dam Bo.* Ed. Nicole Revel. Paris: Sudestasie, 1992: 250–65.

Harnish, David. "Musical Traditions of the Lombok Balinese: Antecedents from Bali and Lombok." MA thesis. Manoa, HI: University of Hawaii at Manoa, 1985.

——. "Sasak Music in Lombok." *Balungan* 2.3 (1986): 17–22.

——. "Music and Religion: Syncretism, Orthodox Islam, and Musical Change in Lombok." *SRE* 7 (1988): 123–37.

——. "The Preret of the Lombok Balinese: Transformation and Continuity within a Sacred Tradition." *SRE* 8 (1990): 201–20.

——. "Music at the Lingsar Temple Festival: The Encapsulation of Meaning in the Balinese/Sasak Interface in Lombok, Indonesia." PhD dissertation. Los Angeles, CA: University of California–Los Angeles, 1991a.

——. "The Performance, Context, and Meaning of Balinese Music in Lombok." *Balinese Music in Context: A Sixty-fifth Birthday Tribute to Hans Oesch.* Ed. Danker Schaareman. Forum Ethnomusicologicum: Basler Studien zur Ethnomusikologie. Winterthur: Amadeus Verlag (Bernhard Päuler), 1992: 29–58.

——. "The Future Meets the Past in the Present: Music and Buddhism in Lombok." *AM* 25.1/2 (1993/1994): 29–50.

——. "Music, Myth, and Liturgy at the Lingsar Temple Festival in Lombok, Indonesia." *YTM* 29 (1997): 80–106.

——. "The World of Music Composition in Bali." *Journal of Musicological Research* 20 (2000): 1–40.

——. "Worlds of Wayang Sasak: Music, Performance, and Negotiations of Religion and Modernity." *AM* 34.2 (2003): 91–120.

——. "'No, Not "Bali Hai"!': Challenges of Adaptation and Orientalism in Performing and Teaching Balinese Gamelan." *Performing Ethnomusicology: Teaching and Representation in World Music Ensembles*. Ed. Ted Solís. Berkeley, CA: University of California Press, 2004: 126–137.

——. "Teletubbies in Paradise: Tourism, Indonesianisation, and Modernisation in Balinese Music." *YTM* 37 (2005a): 103–123

——. "'Isn't this nice? It's just like being in Bali': Constructing Balinese Music Culture in Lombok." *EM* Forum 14.1 (2005b): 3–24.

——. "New Lines, Shifting Identities: Interpreting Change at the Lingsar Festival in Lombok, Indonesia." *EM* 49.1 (2005c): 1–24.

——. *Bridges to the Ancestors: Music, Myth, and Cultural Politics at an Indonesian Festival.* Honolulu, HI: University of Hawaii Press, 2006.

——. "'Digging' and 'Upgrading': Government Efforts to 'Develop' Music and Dance in Lombok, Indonesia." *AM* 38.1 (2007): 61–87.

Harnish, David, and Anne Rasmussen, eds. *Divine Inspirations: Music and Islam in Indonesia.* Oxford: Oxford University Press, 2011.

Hatch, Martin. "Popular Music in Indonesia." *World Music, Politics, and Social Change: Papers from the International Association for the Study of Popular Music.* Ed. Simon Frith. Manchester: Manchester University Press, 1989: 47–67.

Hefner, Robert W. "The Politics of Popular Art: Tayuban Dance and Culture Change in East Java." *Indonesia* 43 (April 1987): 75–95.

Heins, E. "Goong Renteng: Aspects of Orchestral Music in a Sundanese Village." PhD dissertation. Amsterdam: University of Amsterdam, 1977.

——. "132 jaar gamelan in Nederland." *Wereldmuziek* 1.2 (1989): 4–7.

Hellman, Jörgen. *Longser Antar Pulau: Indonesian Cultural Politics and the Revitalisation of Traditional Theatre.* Göteborg: Department of Social Anthropology, University of Göteborg, 1999.

——. *Performing the Nation: Cultural Politics in New Order Indonesia.* Copenhagen: Nordic Institute of Asian Studies, Monograph Series No. 89, 2003.

——. "Entertainment and Circumcisions: Sisingaan Dancing in West Java." *Anpere: Anthropological Perspectives on Religion*, 2006.

Herbert, Mimi, with Nur S. Rahardjo. *Voices of the Puppet Masters: The Wayang Golek Theater of Indonesia.* Jakarta/Honolulu: Lontar Foundation/University of Hawaii Press, 2002.

Heryanto, Ariel. *Popular Culture in Indonesia: Fluid Identities in Post-authoritarian Politics.* London: Routledge, 2008

Hicken, Andy. "Slankers Tongkonan Blues: Toraja (South Sulawesi, Indonesia) Songs in a Disjunctive Mediascape." PhD dissertation. Madison, WI: University of Wisconsin, Madison, 2009.

Hodges, William Robert, Jr. "Referencing, Reframing, and (Re)presenting Grief through Pop Laments in Toba Batak (North Sumatra, Indonesia)." *Etnomusikologi* [Departemen Etnomusikologi, Universitas Sumatera Utara] 1.3 (2006): 310–18.

——. "Ganti Andung, Gabe Ende (Replacing Laments, Becoming Hymns): The Changing Voice of Grief in the Pre-funeral Wakes of Protestant Toba Batak." PhD dissertation. Santa Barbara, CA: University of California, Santa Barbara, 2009.

Hough, Brett. "Education for the Performing Arts: Contesting and Mediating Identity in Contemporary Bali." *Staying Local in the Global Village: Bali in the Twentieth Century.* Ed. Raechelle Rubinstein and Linda Connor. Honolulu, HI: University of Hawaii Press, 1999: 231–63.

——. "The College of Indonesian Arts, Denpasar: Nation, State, and the Performing Arts in Bali." PhD dissertation. Clayton, Victoria: Monash University, 2000.

——. "'Ancestral Shades': The Arti Foundation and the Practice of Pelestarian in Contemporary Bali." *ATJ* 28.1 (2011): 67–103.

Hughes-Freeland, Felicia. "Packaging Dreams: Javanese Perceptions of Tourism and Performance." *Tourism in South-East Asia.* Ed. Michael Hitchcock, Victor T King, and Michael J. G. Parnwell. London: Routledge, 1993: 138–154.

——. "Creativity and Cross-Cultural Collaboration: The Case of Didik Nini Thowok's Bedhaya Hagoromo." *Contemporary Southeast Asian Performance: Transnational Perspectives.* Ed. Laura Noszlopy and Matthew Isaac Cohen. Newcastle upon Tyne: Cambridge Scholars Publishing, 2010: 25–46.

Hugh-Jones, J. "Karawitan Sunda: Tradition Newly Writ: A Survey of Sundanese Music since Independence." *Recorded Sound* [Journal of the British Institute of Recorded Sound] 82 (1982): 19–34.

Hutajulu, Rithaony. "Tourism's Impact on Toba Batak Ceremony." *BKI* 151.4 (1995): 639–55.

Jansen, Arlin. "Gonrang Music: Its Structure and Function in Simalungun Batak Society in Sumatra." PhD dissertation. Seattle, WA: University of Washington, 1980.

Jenkins, Ron, and Nyoman Catra. "Taming the Tourists." *Performance Research* 2.2 (1997): 22–26.

Junus, Umar. "Kaba: An Unfinished (His-)story." *Tonan Ajia Kenkyu* 32.3 (1994a): 399–415.

——. "Kaba as a Text." *Masyarakat Indonesia* 21.1 (1994b): 95–110.

Jurriëns, Edwin. "Postcolonialism and the Space-clearing Gestures of Sundanese Pop Songs." *RIMA* 33.2 (1999): 59–85.

——. *Cultural Travel and Migrancy: The Artistic Representation of Globalization in the Electronic Media of West Java.* (Verhandelingen van het Koninklijk Instituut voor de Taal-, Land- en Volkenkunde, 216.) Leiden: KITLV Press, 2004.

Kam, Garrett. "Javanese Court Dance and Tourism: Behind the Scene Dynamics in a Modern Performance Group." *UCLA Journal of Dance Ethnology* 10 (1986): 39–47.

Kartomi, Karen S. "Mendu Theatre on the Island of Bunguran, Sumatra." Honors thesis. Clayton, Victoria: Monash University, 1986.

Kartomi, Margaret. *Studies in Indonesian Music*. Cheltenham: Monash University, 1978.

——. "Dualism in Unity: The Ceremonial Music of the Mandailing Raja Tradition." *AM* 12.2 (1981a): 74–108.

——. "Randai Theatre in West Sumatra: Components, Origins, Music, and Recent Change." *RIMA* 15.1 (1981b): 1–44.

——. "His Skyward Path the Rainbow Is: Funeral Music of the Sa'dan Toraja in South Sulawesi." *Hemisphere* 25.5 (March/April 1981c): 303–9.

——. "'Lovely When Heard from Afar': Mandailing Ideas of Musical Beauty." *Five Essays on the Indonesian Arts: Music, Theatre, Textiles, Painting, and Literature*. Ed. Margaret J. Kartomi. Clayton, Victoria: Monash University, 1981d: 1–16.

——. "Music and Dance in Aceh: A Preliminary Survey." *IC* 24 (March 1981e): 15–28.

——. "Tabut—A Shi'a Ritual Transplanted from India to Sumatra." *Nineteenth and Twentieth Century Indonesia: Essays in Honour of Professor J. D. Legge*. Ed. David P. Chandler and M. C. Ricklefs. Monash Papers on Southeast Asia, 14. Clayton, Victoria: Centre of Southeast Asian Studies, Monash University, 1986a: 141–62.

——. "Muslim Music in West Sumatra Culture." *WM* 28.3 (1986b): 12–32.

——. "Kapri: A Synthesis of Malay and Portuguese Music on the West Coast of North Sumatra." *Cultures and Societies of North Sumatra*. Ed. Rainer Carle. Veröffentlichungen des Seminars für Indonesische und Sudseesprachen der Universität Hamburg, Band 19. Berlin: Dietrich Reimer, 1987: 351–93.

——. "Taxonomical Models of the Instrumentation and Regional Ensembles in Minangkabau." *On Concepts and Classifications of Musical Instruments*. Ed. Margaret J. Kartomi. Chicago, IL: University of Chicago Press, 1990a: 225–34.

——. "Dabuih in West Sumatra: A Synthesis of Muslim and Pre-Muslim Ceremony and Musical Style." *AR* 41 (1991): 33–52.

——. "Experience-Near and Experience-Distant Perceptions of the *Daboih* Ritual in Aceh, Sumatra." *Von der Vielfalt musikalischer Kultur: Festschrift für Josef Kuckertz zur Vollendung des 60, Lebensjahre*. Ed. Rüdiger Schumacher. Anif/Salzburg: Verlag Ursula Müller-Speiser, 1992a: 247–60.

——. "Appropriation of Music and Dance in Contemporary Ternate and Tidore." *Studies in Music* 26 (1992b): 85–94.

——. "The Nurturing, Revival, and Abandonment of the Banjarese Performing Arts in South Kalimantan, with Special Reference to Mamanda and Wayang Kulit Theatre." Paper presented at the international seminar "Southeast Asian Traditional Performing Arts: The State of the Art." Universiti Sains Malaysia, Penang, Malaysia, 1992c.

——. "The Paradoxical and Nostalgic History of Gending Sriwijaya." *AR* 45 (1993a): 37–50.

——. "Revival of Feudal Music, Dance, and Ritual in the Former 'Spice Islands' of Ternate and Tidore." *Culture and Society in New Order Indonesia.* Ed. Virginia Hooker. New York, NY: Oxford University Press, 1993b: 185–220.

——. "Is Maluku Still Musicological Terra Incognita? An Overview of the Music-Cultures of the Province of Maluku." *Journal of Southeast Asian Studies* 25.1 (1994): 141–71.

——. "The Royal Nobat Ensemble of Indragiri in Riau, Sumatra, in Colonial and Post-Colonial Times." *Galpin Society Journal* (March 1997): 3–15.

——. "A Malay–Portuguese Synthesis on the West Coast of North Sumatra." *Portugal e o mundo: o encontro de culturas na música* (Portugal and the World: The Encounter of Cultures in Music). Ed. Salwa El-Shawan Castelo-Branco. Nova Enciclopédia, 54. Lisbon: Publicações Dom Quixote, 1997b: 289–321.

——. "The Music-Culture of South-Coast West Sumatra: Backwater of the Minangkabau 'Heartland' or Home of the Sacred Mermaid and the Earth Goddess?" *AM* 30.1 (1998/99): 133–82.

——. "Indonesian–Chinese Oppression and the Musical Outcomes in the Netherlands East Indies." *Music and the Racial Imagination.* Ed. Ronald M. Radano and Philip V. Bohlman. Chicago, IL: University of Chicago Press, 2000: 271–317.

——. "Music and Ritual of Pre-Twentieth Century Origins in Manggarai, West Flores." *RIMA* 35.1 (2001a): 79–136.

——. "Change in Manggarai Music and Ritual in the Twentieth Century." *RIMA* 35.2 (2001b): 61–98.

——. "Meaning, Style, and Change in Gamalan and Wayang Kulit Banjar since Their Transplantation from Hindu–Buddhist Java to South Kalimantan." *WM* 44.2 (2002b): 17–55.

——. "'If a Man Can Kill a Buffalo with One Blow He Can Play a Rapa'i Pasè': How the Frame Drum Expresses Facets of Acehnese Identity." *Journal of Chinese Ritual, Theatre and Folklore* 144 (2004): 39–88.

——. "Some Implications of Local Concepts of Space in the Dance, Music, and Visual Arts of Aceh." *YTM* 36 (2004): 1–42.

——. "On Metaphor and Analogy in the Concepts and Classifications of Musical Instruments in Aceh." *YTM* 37 (2005): 25–57.

——. "Aceh's Body Percussion: From Ritual Devotionals to Global Niveau." *Musiké: International Journal of Ethnomusicological Studies* 1 (2006): 85–108.

——. "The Development of the Acehnese Sitting Song-Dances and Frame-Drum Genres as Part of Religious Conversion and Continuing Piety." *BKI* 166.1 (2010a): 83–106.

——. "Toward a Methodology of War and Peace Studies in Ethnomusicology: The Case of Aceh, 1976–2009 Conflict." *EM* 54.3 (2010b): 452–83.

Keppy, Peter. "Keroncong, Concours, and Crooners: Home Grown Entertainment in Twentieth-century Batavia." *Linking Destinies: Trade, Towns, and Kin in Asian History*. Ed. P. Boomgaard, D. Kooiman, and Henk Schulte Nordholt. Verhandelingen van de Koninklijk Instituut voor de Taal-, Land- en Volkenkunde, 256. Leiden: KITLV Press, 2008: 141–57.

Koesasi, B. *Lenong and Si Pitung*. Working paper. Clayton, Victoria: Centre of Southeast Asian Studies, Monash University, 1992.

Kornhauser, Bronia. "In Defense of Kroncong." *Studies in Indonesian Music*. Ed. M. J. Kartomi. Papers on Southeast Asia No. 7. Cheltenham: Monash University, 1978: 104–83.

Koubi, Jeannine. "Telle biche en liberté: couplets toradja." *Chants alternés: Asie du Sud-Est—à Jacques Dournes—Dam Bo*. Ed. Nicole Revel. Paris: Sudestasie, 1992: 209–30.

Kunst, Jaap. *Music in Java: Its History, Its Theory, and Its Technique*. 2 vols. Ed. Ernst Heins. The Hague: Martinus Nijhoff, 1934/1973.

Laronga, Steve. "Campursari Music, 1958–Present: Tracing a Javanese Fusion Aesthetic." MA thesis. Madison, WI: University of Wisconsin–Madison, 2008.

Lindsay, Jennifer. "Performing Translation: Hardja Susilo's Translation of Javanese Wayang Performance." *Between Tongues: Translation and/of/in Performance in Asia*. Ed. Jennifer Lindsay. Singapore: Singapore University Press, 2006: 138–69.

——. "Intercultural Expectations: I La Galigo in Singapore." *TDR: The Drama Review* 51.2 (2007): 60–75.

Lohanda, Mona. "Majoor Jantje and the Indisch Element in Betawi Folkmusic." Papers of the Dutch–Indonesian historical conference held at Lage Vuursche, The Netherlands, June 1980. Ed. Gerrit Schutte and Heather Sutherland. Leiden/Jakarta: Bureau of Indonesian Studies, 1982: 378–92.

Luvaas, Brent. "Dislocating Sounds: The Deterritorialization of Indonesian Indie Pop." *Cultural Anthropology* 24.2 (2009a): 246–79.

——. "Generation DIY: Youth, Class, and the Culture of Indie Production in Digital-Age Indonesia." PhD dissertation. Los Angeles, CA: University of California–Los Angeles, 2009b.

Lysloff, René T. A. "Non-Puppets and Non-Gamelan: Wayang Parody in Banyumas." *EM* 34 (1990a): 19–36.

——. "Srikandi Dances Lengger: A Performance of Shadow Puppet Theatre in Banyumas." PhD dissertation. Ann Arbor, MI: University of Michigan, 1990b.

——. "A Wrinkle in Time: The Shadow Puppet Theatre of Banyumas (West Central Java)." *ATJ* 10.1 (1993): 49–80.

——. "Rural Javanese 'Tradition' and Erotic Subversion: Female Dance Performance in Banyumas." *AM* 33.1 (2002a): 1–24.

——. "A Tale of Two Artists: Tradition and Innovation in the Shadow Theater of Banyumas (West Central Java)." *Puppet Theater in Contemporary Indonesia: New Approaches to Performance-Events*. Ed. Jan Mrázek. Ann Arbor, MI: University of Michigan, 2002b: 169–78.

McCarthy, John. *Are Sweet Dreams Made of This? Tourism in Bali and Eastern Indonesia.* Northcote: Indonesia Resources and Information Program, 1994.

McDermott, Vincent. "Gamelans and New Music." *MQ* 72.1 (1986): 16–27.

McGraw, Andrew. "The Gamelan Semara Dana of Banjar Kaliungu Kaja, Denpasar, Bali, Indonesia." MA thesis. Medford, MA: Tufts University, 1998.

——. "The Development of the Gamelan Semara Dana and the Expansion of the Modal System in Bali, Indonesia." *AM* 31.1 (1999): 63–93.

——. "'Playing like Men': The Cultural Politics of Women's Gamelan." *Latitudes* 47 (2004): 12–17.

——. "Musik Kontemporer: Experimental Music by Balinese Composers." PhD dissertation. Middletown, CT: Wesleyan University, 2005.

——. "Radical Tradition: Balinese Musik Kontemporer." *EM* 53.1 (2009).

——. "Transnational Aesthetics and Balinese Music." *Contemporary Southeast Asian Performance: Transnational Perspectives.* Ed. Laura Noszlopy and Matthew Isaac Cohen. Newcastle upon Tyne: Cambridge Scholars Publishing, 2010: 47–78.

McIntosh, Jonathan. "Indonesians and Australians Playing Javanese Gamelan in Perth, Western Australia: Community and the Negotiation of Musical Identities." *Asia Pacific Journal of Anthropology* 10.2 (2009): 80–97.

——. "Dancing to a Disco Beat? Children, Teenagers, and the Localizing of Popular Music in Bali." *AM* 41.1 (2010): 1–35.

McKean, Philip Frick. "From Purity to Pollution? The Balinese *Ketjak* (Monkey Dance) as Symbolic Form in Transition." *The Imagination of Reality: Essays in Southeast Asian Coherence Systems.* Ed. A. Becker and A. Yengoyan. Norwood, NJ: Ablex, 1979.

——. "Towards a Theoretical Analysis of Tourism: Economic Dualism and Cultural Involution in Bali." *Hosts and Guests: The Anthropology of Tourism.* Second Edition. Ed. Valene L Smith. Philadelphia, PA: University of Pennsylvania Press, 1989: 119–38.

Manhart, Thomas Markus. "A Song for Lowalangi: The Interculturation of Catholic Mission and Nias Traditional Arts with Special Respect to Music." PhD dissertation. National University of Singapore, 2004.

Manuel, Peter, and Randal Baier. "Jaipongan: Indigenous Popular Music of West Java." *AM* 18 (1986): 91–110.

Marah, Risman, and Supriyadi. *Topeng Jabung: A Traditional Theater in East Java.* Jakarta: Project for the Development of Cultural Media, Directorate General for Culture, Department of Education and Culture, 1994.

McPhee, Colin. *Music In Bali: A Study in Form and Instrumental Organization in Balinese Orchestral Music.* New Haven, CT: Yale University Press, 1966.

Mendonça, Maria. "Javanese Gamelan in Britain: Communitas, Affinity, and Other Stories." PhD dissertation. Middletown, CT: Wesleyan University, 2002.

——. "Gamelan in Prisons in England and Scotland: Narratives of Transformation and the 'Good Vibrations' of Educational Rhetoric." *EM* 54.3 (2010a): 369–94.

——. "Prison, Music, and the 'Rehabilitation Revolution': The Case of Good Vibrations." *Journal of Applied Arts & Health* 1.3 (2010b): 295–307.

Messner, Gerald. "Jaap Kunst Revisited: Multipart Singing in Three East Florinese Villages Fifty Years Later, a Preliminary Investigation." *WM* 21.2 (1989): 3–50.

Miller, Christopher J. "Indonesian Musik Kontemporer and the Question of 'Western Influence.'" Paper presented at the annual meeting of the Society for Ethnomusicology, Honolulu, Hawaii, November 19, 2006.

——. "In the Face of *Industri*: Alternative Populisms in Indonesian *Musik Kontemporer*." Paper presented to the Musicology Colloquium at Cornell University, Ithaca, NY, September 18, 2008.

Minca, Claudio, "'The Bali Syndrome': The Explosion and Implosion of 'Exotic' Tourist Spaces," *Tourism Geographies* 2.4 (2000): 389–403.

Möller, Allard. *Batavia, A Swinging Town: Dansorkesten en Jazzbands in Batavia, 1922–1949*. The Hague: Moesson, 1987.

Moore, Lynette M. "An Introduction to the Music of the Pakpak Dairi of North Sumatra." *IC* 24 (March 1981): 39–45.

——. "Music of the Pakpak Dairi." *Journal of the Australian Indonesian Association*, July 1984: 9–11.

——. "Songs of the Pakpak of North Sumatra." PhD dissertation. Clayton, Victoria: Monash University, 1985.

Mrázek, Jan, ed. *Puppet Theater in Contemporary Indonesia: New Approaches to Performance-Events*. Ann Arbor, MI: Centers for South and Southeast Asian Studies, University of Michigan (Michigan Papers on South and Southeast Asia, no. 50), 2002.

Munger, Jennifer. "Nostalgia for Modernity: Brass Bands and the Making of Minahasa, Indonesia." PhD dissertation. Madison, WI: University of Wisconsin, Madison, 2009.

Murray, Alison. "Kampung Culture and Radical Chic in Jakarta." *RIMA* 25.1 (1991): 1–16.

Myers, Douglas. "Outside Influences on the Music of Nusa Tenggara Timur." *Culture and Society in New Order Indonesia*. Ed. Virginia Matheson Hooker. Southeast Asian Social Science Monographs. Kuala Lumpur: Oxford University Press, 1993. 211–27.

Nor, Mohd Anis Md. *Randai Dance of Minangkabau Sumatra with Labanotation Scores*. Kuala Lumpur: University of Malaya, 1986.

——. 1993. Zapin: Folk Dance of the Malay World. Oxford: Oxford University Press.

——. 2011. "Malay-Islamic Zapin: Dance and Soundscapes from the Straits of Malacca." *Austronesian Soundscapes: Performing Arts in Oceania and Southeast Asia*. Ed. Birgit Abels. IIAS [International Institute for Asian Studies] Publications Series, Edited Volumes, vol. 4. Amsterdam: Amsterdam University Press, 2011: 71–84.

North, Richard. "An Introduction to the Musical Traditions of Cirebon." *Balungan* 3.3 (December 1988a): 2–6.

——. "An Introduction to Wayang Kulit Cirebon." *Balungan* 3.3 (Dec 1988b): 16–20.

Noszlopy, Laura. "The Bali Arts Festival—Pesta Kesenian Bali: Culture, Politics and the Arts in Contemporary Indonesia." PhD dissertation. Norwich: University of East Anglia, 2002.

Notosudirdjo, R. Franki S. "Music, Politics, and the Problems of National Identity in Indonesia." PhD dissertation. Madison, WI: University of Wisconsin, Madison, 2001.

——. "*Kyai Kanjeng*: Islam and the Search for National Music in Indonesia." WM 45.2 (2003): 39–52.

Oetomo, Dédé. "Gender and Sexuality in and around Ludruk: Implications for Sexual Health." *Kumpulan Makalah Temu Ilmiah MSPI '95, Mataram, Lombok NTB, 24–25 Oktober 1995.* Kerja sama Masyarakat Seni Pertunjukan Indonesia (MSPI) Taman Budaya Nusa Tenggara Barat. Surakarta: Masyarakat Seni Pertunjukan Indonesia, c.1995: 85–92.

——. "East Java's Ludruk Theater: Survival in Transformation." *Latitudes* [Denpasar] 8 (September 2001): 16–21.

Oguri, Hiroko. "The Music of the Isirawa." *Irian: Bulletin of Irian Jaya* 9.3 (1981): 1–33.

——. "The Music of the Isirawa." *Gods, Heroes, Kinsmen: Ethnographic Studies from Irian Jaya, Indonesia.* Ed. William R. Merrifield, Marilyn Gregerson, and Daniel Ajamiseba. International Museum of Cultures Publication 17. Duncanville, TX: Universitas Cenderawasih dan the International Museum of Cultures, 1983: 42–67.

Okazaki, Yoshiko. "Music Identity and Religious Change among the Toba Batak People of North Sumatra." PhD dissertation. Los Angeles, CA: University of California–Los Angeles, 1994.

Pacholczyk, Jozef. "Music and Islam in Indonesia." *WM* 28.3 (1986): 3–12.

Palermo, Carmencita. "*Anak mula keto*, 'It Was Always Thus': Women Making Progress, Encountering Limits in Characterising the Masks in Balinese Masked Dance–Drama." *Intersections: Gender and Sexuality in Asia and the Pacific* 19 (February 2009), http://intersections.anu.edu.au/issue19/palermo.htm, accessed August 2013.

Patton, Marlene Meyer. "Traditional Music in South Nias, Indonesia, with Emphasis upon 'Hoho': Voices of the Ancestors." MA thesis. Honolulu, HI: University of Hawaii, 1987.

Pauka, Kirstin. "Conflict and Combat in Performance: An Analysis of the *Randai* Folk Theatre of the Minangkabau in West Sumatra." PhD dissertation. Honolulu, HI: University of Hawaii, 1995.

——. *Theater and Martial Arts in West Sumatra:* Randai *and* Silek *of the Minangkabau.* Athens, OH: Ohio University Center for International Studies, 1998.

Pausacker, Helen. "Nyi Suharni Sabdawati: A Portrait of a Woman *Dhalang*." *AIA* [Australian Indonesian Association] *Journal* (June 1982): 8–9.

——. "Dalangs and Family Planning Propaganda in Indonesia." *Love, Sex, and Power: Women in Southeast Asia.* Ed. Susan Blackburn. Melbourne: Monash University Press, 2001.

——. "Limbuk Breaks Out: Changes in the Portrayal of Women Clown Servants and the Inner Court Scene over the Twentieth Century." *Puppet Theater in Contemporary Indonesia: New Approaches to Performance-Events.* Ed. Jan Mrázek. Ann Arbor, MI: University of Michigan, 2002: 284–95.

——. "Presidents as Punakawan: Portrayal of National Leaders as Clown-Servants in Central Javanese Wayang." *Journal of Southeast Asian Studies* 35 (2004): 213–33

——. "Peranakan Chinese and Wayang in Java." *Chinese Indonesians: Remembering, Distorting, Forgetting—A Festschrift for Charles A Coppel.* Ed. Tim Lindsey and Helen Pausacker. Singapore: ISEAS, with Clayton, Victoria: Monash Asia Institute, 2005: 165–84.

Peacock, James L., and Hélène Bouvier. "Ludruk Revisited: An Epistolary Interview with James L. Peacock." *Theatre Research International* 19.1 (Spring 1994): 9–16.

Peckham, Nancy. "Day and Night Songs in Mairasi Festival Music." *Irian: Bulletin of Irian Jaya* 9.1 (1981): 55–65.

Pemberton, John. "Musical Politics in Central Java (or How Not to Listen to a Javanese Gamelan)." *Indonesia* 44 (October 1987): 16–30.

Perlman, Marc. "Reflections on the New American Gamelan Music." *Ear Magazine* 8.4 (1983): 4–5.

——. "American Gamelan in the Garden of Eden: Intonation in a Cross-Cultural Encounter." *MQ* 78.3 (1994): 484–529.

——. "The Social Meanings of Modal Practices: Status, Gender, History, and Pathet in Central Javanese Music." *EM* 42.1 (1998): 45–80.

——. *Unplayed Melodies: Javanese Gamelan and the Genesis of Music Theory.* Berkeley, CA: University of California Press, 2004.

Perlman, Marc, and Carol Krumhansl. "An Experimental Study of Internal Interval Standards in Javanese and Western Musicians." *Music Perception* 14.2 (1996): 95–116.

Phillips, Nigel. *Sijobang.* Cambridge: Cambridge University Press, 1980.

——. "Further Thoughts on the Metre of Sijobang." Papers from the third European colloquium on Malay and Indonesian studies, Naples, June 2–4, 1981. Ed. Luigi Santa Maria, Faizah Soenoto Rivai, and Antonio Sorrentino. Naples: Dipartimento di Studi Asiatici, Istituto Universitario Orientale, 1988: 195–214.

——. "A Note on the Relationship between Singer and Audience in West Sumatran Story-telling." *IC* 58 (June 1992): 67–70.

Picard, Michel. "'Cultural Tourism' in Bali: Cultural Performances as Tourist Attraction." *Indonesia* 49 (April 1990): 37–74.

——. "'Cultural Tourism' in Bali: National Integration and Regional Differentiation." *Tourism in South-East Asia.* Ed. Michael Hitchcock, Victor T. King, and Michael J. G. Parnwel. London: Routledge, 1993: 71–98.

——. *Bali: Cultural Tourism and Touristic Culture*. Singapore: Archipelago Press, 1996.

——. "Cultural Tourism, Nation-building, and Regional Culture: The Making of a Balinese Identity." *Tourism, Ethnicity, and the State in Asian and Pacific Societies*. Ed. M. Picard and R. Wood. Honolulu, HI: University of Hawaii Press, 1997.

Pickles, Joanna. "Punks for Peace: Underground Music Gives Young People Back Their Voice." *Inside Indonesia* 64 (2000): 9–10.

——. "Punk, Pop, and Protest: The Birth and Decline of Political Punk in Bandung." *RIMA* 41.2 (2007): 223–46

Pioquinto, Ceres. "Dangdut at Sekaten." *RIMA* 29 (1995): 59–90.

Poplawska, Marzanna. "Wayang Wahyu as an Example of Christian Forms of Shadow Theatre." *Asian Theatre Journal* 21.2 (2004): 194–202.

——. "Christian Music and Inculturation in Indonesia." PhD dissertation. Middletown, CT: Wesleyan University, 2008.

Purba, Mauly. "Gordang Sembilan: Social Function and Rhythmic Structure." MA Thesis. Middletown, CT: Wesleyan University, 1988.

——. "*Adat ni Gondang*: Rules and Structure of the *Gondang* Performance in Pre-Christian Toba Batak *Adat* Practice." *AM* 34.1 (Fall/Winter 2002/2003): 67–109.

——. "From Conflict to Reconciliation: The Case of the *Gondang Sabangunan* in the Order of Discipline of the Toba Batak Protestant Church." *Journal of Southeast Asian Studies* [National University of Singapore] 36.2 (June 2005a): 207–33.

——. "Results of Contact between the Toba Batak People, German Missionaries, and Dutch Colonial Officials: Musical and Social Change." *Etnomusikologi* [Departemen Etnomusikologi, Universitas Sumatera Utara] 1.2 (September 2005b): 118–48.

——. "Review of Research into the *Gondang Sabangunan* Musical Genre in Batak Toba Society of North Sumatra." *Etnomusikologi* [Departemen Etnomusikologi, Universitas Sumatera Utara] 1.1 (May 2005c): 38–64.

Rappoport, Dana. "Du Repérage Musical au Travail de Terrain Ethnomusicologique en Indonésie." *Cahiers de Musiques Traditionnelles* 8 (1995): 13–32.

——. *Musiques rituelles des Toraja Sa'dan: Musiques du couchant, musiques du levant (Celebes-sud, Indonesie)*. Villeneuve d'Asq: Presses Universitaires du Septentrion, 1997.

——. "Percussions des Taman." *Percussions* 9.59 (1998): 3–9.

——. "Chanter sans Être Ensemble: Des Musiques Juxtaposées pour un Public Invisible." *L'Homme* 152 (1999) :143–62.

——. "Ritual Music and Christianization in the Toraja Highlands, Sulawesi." *EM* 48.3 (2004): 378–404.

——. *Songs from the Thrice-blooded Land: Ritual Music of the Toraja (Sulawesi, Indonesia)*. Two volumes and DVD–ROM. Paris: Editions de la Maison des Sciences de l'Homme. 2009.

——. "L'énigme des Duos Alternés à Flores et Solor (Lamaholot, Indonésie)." *AR* 79 (2010): 215–56.

——. "To Sing the Rice in Tanjung Bunga (Eastern Flores) Indonesia." *Austronesian Soundscapes: Performing Arts in Oceania and Southeast Asia.* Ed. Birgit Abels. IIAS [International Institute for Asian Studies] Publications Series, Edited Volumes, vol. 4. Amsterdam: Amsterdam University Press, 2011: 103–31.

Raseuki, Nyak Ina. "Being Islamic in Music: Two Contemporary Genres from Sumatra." PhD dissertation. Madison, WI: University of Wisconsin, Madison, 2009.

Rasmussen, Anne. "The Qur'an in Indonesian Daily Life: The Public Project of Musical Oratory." *EM* 45.1 (2001): 30–57.

——. "The Arab Musical Aesthetic in Indonesian Islam." *WM* 47.1 (2005): 65–90.

——. *Women, the Recited Qur'an, and Islamic Music in Indonesia.* Berkeley, CA: University of California Press, 2010.

Redding, Danni. "Performing Arts, Identity, and the Construction of Place in Three Balinese Transmigration Settlements." MA Thesis. Honolulu, HI: University of Hawaii, 2002.

Richter, Max. "Other Worlds in Yogyakarta: From Jatilan to Electronic Music." *Popular Culture in Indonesia: Fluid Identities in Post-authoritarian Politics.* Ed. Ariel Heryanto. London: Routledge, 2008: 164–81.

Rogers-Aguiniga, Pamela. "Topeng Cirebon: The Masked Dance of West Java as Performed in the Village of Slangit." MA thesis. Los Angeles, CA: University of California, Los Angeles, 1986.

Ross, Laurie M. "Journeying, Adaptation, and Translation: Topeng Cirebon at the Margins." PhD dissertation. Berkeley, CA: University of California, Berkeley, 2009.

Roth, Alec. "New Compositions for Javanese Gamelan." PhD dissertation. Durham: Durham University, 1986.

Royl, Ekkehart. *Untersuchungen zur Mehrstimmigkeit in den Gesängen der Hochlandbewohner von Irian Jaya (West-Neuguinea).* Berlin: Freie Universität Berlin, 1992.

Rutherford, Danilyn. "Of Birds and Gifts: Reviving Tradition on an Indonesian Frontier." *Cultural Anthropology* 11.4 (1996): 577–616.

——. *Raiding the Land of the Foreigners: The Limits of the Nation on an Indonesian Frontier.* Princeton, NJ: Princeton University Press, 2003.

Salisbury, David. "Aspects of Musical and Social Identity in the Talempong Musical Tradition of the Payakumbuh Region, West Sumatra, Indonesia." PhD dissertation. Biddeford, ME: University of New England, 2000.

Sanger, Annette. "Blessing or Blight? The Effects of Touristic Dance-Drama on Village-Life in Singapadu, Bali." *Come Mek Me Hol' Yu Han': The Impact of Tourism on Traditional Music.* International Council for Traditional Music (ICTM) Colloquium, 1986. Kingston: Jamaica Memory Bank, 1988: 89–104.

Schefold, Reimar. *Lia: Das Grosse Ritual auf den Mentawai-Inseln (Indonesien).* Berlin: Dietrich Reimer, 1988.

Schreiber, Karen Elizabeth. "Power in the East Javanese Jaranan and Wayang Topeng." MA thesis. Richmond, VA: University of Virginia, 1991.

Scott-Maxwell, Aline. "Women's Gamelan Groups in Central Java: Some Issues of Gender, Status, and Change." *Aflame with Music: One Hundred Years of Music at the University of Melbourne.* Melbourne: Centre for Studies in Australian Music, University of Melbourne, 1996: 223–30.

Seebass, Tilman, I Gusti Bagus Nyoman Pandji, I Nyoman Rembang, and Poedijono. *The Music of Lombok: A First Survey.* Bern: Francke Verlag, 1976.

Simatupang, G. R. Lono Lastoro. "The Development and Meanings of Dangdut: A Study of Indonesian Popular Music." MA thesis. Clayton, Victoria: Monash University, 1996.

Simeda, Takasi. "Identity Manipulation and Improvisatory Singing in Central Borneo." *Authenticity and Cultural Identity: Performing Arts in Southeast Asia.* Ed. Yoshitaka Terada. Senri Ethnological Reports, 65. Osaka: National Museum of Ethnology, 2007: 79–89.

Simon, Artur. "Altreligiöse und soziale Zeremonien der Batak." *Zeitschrift für Ethnologie* 107.2 (1982): 177–206.

——. "Functional Changes in Batak Traditional Music and its Role in Modern Indonesian Society." *AM* 15.2 (1984): 58–66.

——. "The Terminology of Batak Instrumental Music in Northern Sumatra." *YTM* 17 (1985): 113–145.

——. "Social and Religious Functions of Batak Ceremonial Music." *Cultures and Societies of North Sumatra.* Ed. Rainer Carle. Veröffentlichungen des Seminars für Indonesische und Sudseesprachen der Universität Hamburg. Berlin: Dietrich Reimer, 1987: 337–49.

——. "A Film Documentation of Social and Religious Ceremonies and Ceremonial Music of the Batak in Northern Sumatra, Indonesia." *Visual Anthropology* 1 (1988): 349–56.

——. "Synkretismus und Kulturelle Identität in den Musikkulturen Indonesie." *Musikkulturgeschichte: Festschrift Constantin Floros.* Ed. Peter Peterson and Constantin Floros. Wiesbaden: Breitkopf & Härtel, 1990. 527–42.

——. "Ethnomusicological Research in the Central Highlands of Irian Jaya (West New Guinea)." *Music and Dance of Aboriginal Australia and the South Pacific.* Ed. Alice M. Moyle. Oceania Monographs Series, 41. Sydney: University of Sydney, 1991a: 40–57.

——. "Musik und Besessenheitstänze bei einem altreligiösen Fest der Karo-Batak in Indonesien." *Musik als Droge? Parlando 1: Schriften aus der Villa Musica.* Ed. Helmut Rösing. Mainz: Villa Musica, 1991b: 48–60.

——. "Gondang, Gods and Ancestors, Religious Implications of Batak Ceremonial Music." *YTM* 25 (1993): 81–88.

——. "Von Calung Tarawangsa bis Goong Ajeng: eine Aufnahmereise durch Westjava mit einem Abstecher nach Yogyakarta." *Ethnologische, historische, und systematische Musikwissenschaft: Oskar Elschek zum 65. Geburtstag.* Ed. Franz Födermayr and L. Burlas. Bratislava: ASCO Art & Science, 1998: 167–92.

Skog, Inge. *North Borneo Gongs and the Javanese Gamelan: Studies in Southeast Asian Gong Traditions.* Studier i Musikvetenskap/Studies in Musicology, 2. Stockholm: Stockholms Universitet, 1993.

Soedarsono, R. M. "Dance in Irian Jaya: A Preliminary Report." *Dance as Cultural Heritage, II.* Ed. Betty True Jones. New York, NY: CORD [Committee on Research in Dance], 1985: 62–66.

Solís, Ted. "Teaching What Cannot Be Taught: An Optimistic Overview." *Performing Ethnomusicology: Teaching and Representation in World Music Ensembles.* Ed. Ted Solís. Berkeley, CA: University of California Press, 2004: 1–22.

Spiller, Henry. "Sundanese Dance Accompaniment: The Career of Pa Kayat." *Balungan* 5.2 (Summer/Fall 1993): 15–18.

——. "Continuity in Sundanese Dance Drumming: Clues from the 1893 Chicago Exposition." *WM* 38.2 (1996): 23–40.

——. "Negotiating Masculinity in an Indonesian Pop Song: Doel Sumbang's 'Ronggeng.'" *Oh Boy! Masculinities and Pop Music.* Ed. Freya Jarman-Ivens. London: Routledge, 2007: 39–57.

——. "University Gamelan Ensembles as Research." *Mapping Landscapes for Performance as Research: Scholarly Acts and Creative Cartographies.* Ed. Shannon Rose Riley and Lynette Hunter. Hampshire: Palgrave Macmillan, 2009: 171–78.

——. "Tunes that Bind: Paul J. Seelig, Eva Gauthier, Charles T. Griffes, and the Indonesian Other." *Journal of the Society for American Music* 3.2 (2009a): 129–54.

——. "Lou Harrison's Music for Western Instruments and Gamelan: Even More Western than It Sounds." *AM* 39.2 (2009b): 31–52.

——. *Erotic Triangles: Sundanese Dance and Masculinity in West Java.* Chicago, IL: University of Chicago, 2010a.

——. "Sundanese Dance as Practice and as Spectacle: It's All Happening at the Zoo." *Austronesian Soundscapes: Performing Arts in Oceania and Southeast Asia.* Ed. Birgit Abels. IIAS (International Institute for Asian Studies) Publications Series, Edited Volumes, vol. 4. Amsterdam: University of Amsterdam Press, 2010b.

Spyer, Patricia. "'Zaman Belanda': Song and the Shattering of Speech in Aru, Eastern Indonesia." *Indonesia* 70 (October 2000): 53–70.

Suanda, Endo. "The Social Context of Cirebonese Performing Artists." *AM* 13 (1981): 27–42.

——. "Cirebonese Topeng and Wayang of the Present Day." *AM* 16 (1985): 84–120.

——. "Topeng Cirebon in Its Social Context." MA thesis. Middletown, CT: Wesleyan University, 1988a.

——. "Dancing in Cirebonese Topèng." *Balungan* 3.3 (1988b): 7–15.

Sukarno, Yono. "Singing 'round the Table: Vocalized Wayang and Gamelan in Jemblung/Purwacarita." *Balungan* 6.1/2 (1998): 3–11.

Sumarsam. *Gamelan: Cultural Interaction and Musical Development in Central Java.* Chicago, IL: University of Chicago Press, 1995.

Sunardi, Christina. "Gendered Dance Modes in Malang, East Java: Music, Movement, and the Production of Local Senses of Identity." PhD dissertation. Berkely, CA: University of California, Berkeley, 2007.

——. "Pushing at the Boundaries of the Body: Cultural Politics and Cross-Gender Dance in East Java." *BKI* 165.4 (2009): 459–92.

——. "Making Sense and Senses of Locale through Perceptions of Music and Dance in Malang, East Java." *AM* 41.1 (2010): 89–126.

——. "Negotiating Authority and Articulating Gender: Performer Interaction in Malang, East Java." *EM* 55.1 (2011): 31–54.

Susilo, Emiko Saraswati. *Gamelan Wanita: A Study of Women's Gamelan in Bali.* Southeast Asia Paper No. 43. Manoa, HI: School for Hawaiian, Asian, and Pacific Studies, University of Hawaii–Manoa, 2003.

Susilo, Hardja. "The Logogenesis of Gendhing Lampah." *Progress Reports in Ethnomusicology* 2.5 (1989).

——. "'A Bridge to Java': Four Decades Teaching Gamelan in America." *Performing Ethnomusicology: Teaching and Representation in World Music Ensembles.* Ed. Ted Solís. Berkeley, CA: University of California Press, 2004: 53–68.

——. *Enculturation and Cross-Cultural Experiences in Teaching Indonesian Gamelan.* Wellington, New Zealand: Asian Studies Institute, 2005.

Sutton, R. Anderson. "The Crystallization of a Marginal Tradition: Music in Banyumas, West Central Java." *YTM* 18 (1986a): 115–32.

——. "New Theory for Traditional Music in Banyumas, West Central Java." *Pacific Review of Ethnomusicology* 3 (1986b): 79–101.

——. "Identity and Individuality in an Ensemble Tradition: The Female Vocalist in Java." *Women and Music in Cross-Cultural Perspective.* Ed. Ellen Koskoff. Westport, CT: Greenwood, 1987: 111–30.

——. *Traditions of Gamelan Music in Java.* Cambridge: Cambridge University Press, 1991.

——. "Semang and Seblang: Thoughts on Music, Dance, and the Sacred in Central and East Java." *Performance in Java and Bali: Studies of Narrative, Theatre, Music, and Dance.* Ed. Bernard Arps. London: School of Oriental and African Studies, University of London, 1993: 121–43.

——. "Performing Arts and Cultural Politics in South Sulawesi." *BKI* 151.4 (1995): 672–99.

——. "From Ritual Enactment to Stage Entertainment: Andi Nurhani Sapada and the Aestheticization of South Sulawesi's Music and Dance, 1940s–1970s." *AM* 29.2 (1998): 1–30.

——. "Drumming in Java and Makassar, Indonesia: Structure, Process, and Experience." *Asian Music Research Journal* 23 (2002a): 123–42.

——. *Calling Back the Spirit: Music, Dance, and Cultural Politics in Lowland South Sulawesi.* New York, NY: Oxford University Press, 2002b.

——. "Popularizing the Indigenous or Indigenizing the Popular? Television, Video, and New Music in Indonesia." *Wacana seni/Journal of Arts Discourse* 1 (2002): 13–31.

——. "Local, Global, or National? Popular Music on Indonesian Television." *Planet TV: A Global Television Reader.* Ed. Lisa Parks and Shanti Kumar. New York, NY: New York University Press, 2003: 320–40.

——. "'Reform Arts'? Performance Live and Mediated in Post-Soeharto Indonesia." *EM* 48.2 (2004): 203–28.

——. "Tradition Serving Modernity? The Musical Lives of a Makassarese Drummer." *AM* 37.1 (Winter/Spring 2006): 1–23.

——. "Gamelan Encounters with Western Music in Indonesia: Hybridity/Hybridism." *Journal of Popular Music Studies* 22.2 (2010): 180–97.

Suwardi, Aloysius. "The Music of Flores: A Study of Vocal Music in Gua Mézé Festival." MA thesis. Middletown, CT: Wesleyan University, 1997.

Suyanto. "Wayang Malangan: Background, Performers, and Performance." MA thesis. Sydney: School of Asian Studies, University of Sydney, 1996.

Tenzer, Michael. *Gamelan Gong Kebyar: The Art of Twentieth-Century Balinese Music.* Chicago, IL: University of Chicago Press, 2000.

Thomsen, Martin. "Ein Totengesang von der Insel Nias." *BKI* 137.4 (1981): 443–55.

Trimillos, Ricardo. "Subject, Object, and the Ethnomusicology Ensemble: The Ethnomusicological 'We' and 'Them.'" *Performing Ethnomusicology: Teaching and Representation in World Music Ensembles.* Ed. Ted Solís. Berkeley, CA: University of California Press, 2004: 23–52.

Turner, Ashley. "Duri-Dana Music and Hoho Songs in South Nias." BA thesis. Clayton, Victoria: Monash University, 1982.

——. "Belian As a Symbol of Cosmic Reunification." *Metaphor: A Musical Dimension.* Ed. Jamie Kassler. Sydney: Currency Press, 1991: 125–45.

——. "Cultural Survival, Identity, and the Performing Arts of Kampar's Suku Petalangan." *BKI* 153.4 (1997): 648–71.

Van Wichelen, Sonja. "'My Dance Immoral? Alhamdulillah No!' Dangdut Music and Gender Politics in Contemporary Indonesia." *Resounding International Relations: On Music, Culture, and Politics.* Ed. M. I. Franklin. New York, NY: Palgrave, 2005: 161–77.

Vetter, Roger. "A Retrospect on a Century of Gamelan Tone Measurements." *EM* 33 (1989): 217–27.

——. "A Square Peg in a Round Hole: Teaching Javanese Gamelan in the Ensemble Paradigm of the Academy." *Performing Ethnomusicology: Teaching and Representation in World Music Ensembles*. Ed. Ted Solís. Berkeley, CA: University of California Press, 2004: 115–25.

Vitale, Wayne. "Balinese Kebyar Music Breaks the Five-Tone Barrier: New Composition for Seven-Tone Gamelan." *Perspectives of New Music* 40.1 (2002): 5–69.

Wallach, Jeremy. "Exploring Class, Nation, and Xenocentrism in Indonesian Cassette Retail Outlets." *Indonesia* 74 (October 2002a): 79–102.

——. "Modern Noise and Ethnic Accents: Indonesian Popular Music in the Era of Reformasi." PhD dissertation. Philadelphia, PA: University of Pennsylvania, 2002b.

——. "'Goodbye My Blind Majesty': Music, Language, and Politics in the Indonesian Underground." *Global Pop, Local Languages*. Ed. Harris M. Berger and M. T. Carrol. Jackson, MI: University of Mississippi Press, 2003: 53–86.

——. "Engineering Techno-Hybrid Grooves in Two Indonesian Sound Studios." *Wired for Sound: Engineering and Technologies in Sonic Cultures*. Ed. Paul D. Greene and T. Porcello. Middletown, CT: Wesleyan University Press, 2005: 138–155.

——. "Living the Punk Lifestyle in Jakarta." *EM* 52.1 (2008a): 98–116

——. *Modern Noise, Fluid Genres: Popular Music in Indonesia, 1997–2001*. Madison, WI: University of Wisconsin Press, 2008b.

Warde, Ann. "Contemporary Indonesian Composition: Elastic-edged Experimentalism." *AM* 34.1 (2002/2003): 111–53.

Watuseke, F. S. "Minahasische liederen uit Tonséa." *BKI* 136.2/3 (1980): 353–71.

Weintraub, Andrew. "A Manual for Learning Sundanese Gamelan." Senior thesis in music. Santa Cruz, CA: University of California at Santa Cruz, 1985.

——. "The Music of Pantun Sunda, an Epic Narrative Tradition of West Java, Indonesia." MA thesis. Manoa, HI: University of Hawaii–Manoa, 1990.

——. "Theory in Institutional Pedagogy and 'Theory in Practice' for Sundanese Gamelan Music." *EM* 37 (1993): 29–40.

——. "Creative Musical Practices in the Performance of Pantun Sunda." *Balungan* 5.2 (Summer/Fall 1993): 2–7.

——. "Tune, Text, and the Function of Lagu in Pantun Sunda, a Sundanese Oral Narrative Tradition." *AM* 26.1 (Fall/Winter 1994/1995): 175–211. *

——. "Constructing the Popular: Superstars, Performance, and Cultural Authority in Sundanese Wayang Golek Purwa of West Java, Indonesia." PhD dissertation. Berkeley, CA: University of California, Berkeley, 1997.

——. *The Birth of Gatotkaca: A Sundanese Wayang Golek Purwa Performance from West Java* (translation and introduction). Jakarta: Lontar Publications, 1998.

——. "Contest-ing Culture: Sundanese Wayang Golek Purwa Competitions in New Order Indonesia." *ATJ* 18.1 (2001a): 87–104.

——. "Instruments of Power: Sundanese 'Multi-Laras' Gamelan in New Order Indonesia." *EM* 45.2 (2001b): 197–227.

——. "New Order Politics and Popular Entertainment in Sundanese Wayang Golek Purwa." *Puppet Theater in Contemporary Indonesia: New Approaches to Performance-Events*. Ed. Jan Mrázek. Ann Arbor, MI: University of Michigan, 2002: 124–35.

——. "The Crisis of the Sinden: Gender, Politics, and Memory in the Performing Arts of West Java, 1959–1964." *Indonesia* 77 (April 2004a): 1–21.

——. *Power Plays: Wayang Golek Puppet Theater of West Java*. Athens, OH: Ohio University Press, 2004b.

——. "Dangdut Soul: Who Are "The People" in Indonesian Popular Music?" *Asian Journal of Communication* 16.4 (2006): 411–31.

——. "Dance Drills, Faith Spills: Islam, Body Politics, and Popular Music in Indonesia." *Popular Music* 27.3 (2008): 365–90.

——. "Music and Malayness: Orkes Melayu in Indonesia, 1950–1965." *AR* 79 (2010a): 57–78.

——. *Dangdut Stories: A Social and Musical History of Indonesia's Most Popular Music*. Oxford: Oxford University Press, 2010b.

Weiss, Sarah. "Gender and Gendèr: Gender Ideology and the Female Gendèr Player in Central Java." *Rediscovering the Muses: Women's Musical Traditions*. Ed. Kimberly Marshall. Boston, MA: Northeastern University Press, 1993: 21–48.

——. "Rules or Rasa: Aesthetics and Gender in the Performance of Central Javanese *Wayang*." *About Performance* 2 (1996): 91–99.

——. "Paradigms and Anomalies: Female-style Genderan and the Aesthetics of Central Javanese *Wayang*." PhD dissertation. New York, NY: New York University, 1998.

——. "Gender(ed) Aesthetics: Domains of Knowledge and 'Inherent' Dichotomies in Central Javanese *Wayang* Accompaniment." *Puppet Theater in Contemporary Indonesia: New Approaches to Performance-Events*. Ed. Jan Mrázek. Ann Arbor, MI: University of Michigan, 2002: 296–314.

——. *Listening to an Earlier Java: Aesthetics, Gender, and the Music of Wayang in Central Java*. Leiden: KITLV Press, 2006.

——. "Permeable Boundaries: Hybridity, Music, and the Reception of Robert Wilson's 'I La Galigo.'" *EM* 52.2 (2008a): 203–38.

——. "Gender and Gendèr Redux: Rethinking Binaries and the Aesthetics of Old-Style Javanese Wayang." *Women & Music* 12 (2008b): 22–39.

Wenten, I Nyoman. "The Creative World of Ki Wasitodipuro: The Life and Work of a Javanese Gamelan Composer." PhD dissertation. Los Angeles, CA: University of California–Los Angeles, 1996.

Wessing, Robert. "A Dance of Life: The Seblang of Banyuwangi, Indonesia." *BKI* 155.4 (1999): 644–82.

Widodo, Amrih. "The Stages of the State: Arts of the People and Rites of Hegemonization." *RIMA* 29 (1995): 1–36.

Wieringa, Edwin. "The Kaba Zamzami jo Marlaini: Continuity, Adaptation, and Change in Minangkabau Oral Storytelling." *Indonesia and the Malay World* 73 (1997): 235–51.

Williams, Sean. "Current Developments in Sundanese Popular Music." *AM* 21.1 (1989): 105–36.

——. "The Urbanization of Tembang Sunda, an Aristocratic Musical Genre of West Java, Indonesia." PhD dissertation. Seattle, WA: University of Washington–Seattle, 1990.

——. "'Our Laughter Balances Our Tears': Humor in Sundanese Arts." *Balungan* 5.2 (Summer/Fall 1993): 11–14.

——. "Constructing Gender in Sundanese Music." *YTM* 30 (199): 74–84.

——. "Competition in the Sundanese Performing Arts of West Java, Indonesia." *Current Musicology* 63 (1999): 27–45.

——. *The Sound of the Ancestral Ship: Highland Music of West Java.* Oxford: Oxford University Press, 2001.

——. "Competing against 'Tradition' in the Sundanese Performing Arts." *WM* 45.1 (2003): 79–96.

Willner, Sarah. "Kebyar Wanita: A Look at Women's Gamelan Groups in Bali." Unpublished manuscript. 1997.

Wilson, Ian Douglas. "*Reog* Ponorogo: Spirituality, Sexuality, and Power in a Javanese Performance Tradition." *Intersections: Gender and Sexuality in Asia and the Pacific* 2 (May 1999), http://intersections.anu.edu.au/issue2/Warok.html, accessed August 2013.

Witzleben, J. Lawrence. "Cultural Interactions in an Asian Context: Chinese and Javanese Ensembles in Hong Kong." *Performing Ethnomusicology: Teaching and Representation in World Music Ensembles.* Ed. Ted Solís. Berkeley, CA: University of California Press, 2004: 138–51.

Wolbers, Paul. "Gandrung and Angklung from Banyuwangi: Elements of a Past Shared with Bali." *AM* 18 (1986): 71–98.

——. "Account of an Angklung Caruk, July 28, 1985." *Indonesia* 43 (April 1987): 67–75.

——. "Transvestism, Eroticism, and Religion; In Search of a Contextual Background for the Gandrung and Seblang Traditions of Banyuwangi, East Java." *Progress Reports in Ethnomusicology* 2.4–7 (1989): 1–22.

——. "Maintaining and Using Identity through Musical Performance: Seblang and Gandrung of Banyuwangi, East Java (Indonesia)." PhD dissertation. Urbana, IL: University of Illinois at Urbana-Champaign, 1992.

——. "The Seblang and Its Music: Aspects of an East Javanese Fertility Rite." *Performance in Java and Bali: Studies of Narrative, Theatre, Music, and Dance.* Ed. Bernard Arps. London: School of Oriental and African Studies, University of London, 1993: 34–46.

Wright, Michael R. "The Music Culture of Cirebon." PhD dissertation. Los Angeles, CA: University of California, Los Angeles, 1978.

——. "Tarling: Modern Music from Cirebon." *Balungan* 3.3 (December 1988): 21–25.

Yampolsky, Philip. "Hati Yang Luka, an Indonesian Hit." *Indonesia* 47 (April 1989): 1–18.

——. "Forces for Change in the Regional Performing Arts of Indonesia." *BKI* 151.4 (1995): 700–25.

——. "Kroncong Revisited: New Evidence from Old Sources." *AR* 79 (2010): 7–56.

——. "The Record Industry in Indonesia / Malaysia / Singapore: The Mechanics of an Estimate of Quantity. Part 1: 1903–1920; Part 2: 1920–1942." *The Lindström Project: Contributions to the History of the Record Industry,* vol. 3. Ed. Pekka Gronow and Christiane Hofer. Vienna: Gesellschaft für Historische Tonträger, 2011: 181–212.

Zanten, Wim van. "The Poetry of Tembang Sunda." *BKI* 140 (1984): 289–316.

——. "Structure in the Panambih Pelog Songs of Tembang Sunda in West Java." *Teken van Leven: Studies in Etnocommunicatie. Liber amicorum bij het afscheid van Professor Dr. A. A. Gerbrands.* Ed. Ad Boeren, Fransje Brinkgreve, and Sandy Roels. Leiden: [Rijksuniversiteit Leiden], Instituut voor Culturele Antropologie en Sociologie der Niet-Westerse Volken, 1985: 187–98.

——. "The Tone Material of the Kacapi in Tembang Sunda in West-Java." *EM* 30 (1986b): 84–112.

——. "Tembang Sunda: An Ethnomusicological Study of the Cianjuran Music of West-Java." PhD dissertation. Leiden: University of Leiden, 1987.

——. *Sundanese Music in the Cianjuran Style: Anthropological and Musicological Aspects of Tembang Sunda.* Dordrecht: Foris Publications 1989.

——. "Sung Epic Narrative and Lyrical Songs: Carita Pantun and Tembang Sunda." *Performance in Java and Bali: Studies of Narrative, Theatre, Music, and Dance.* Ed. Bernard Arps. London: School of Oriental and African Studies, University of London, 1993: 144–61.

——. "L'esthétique musicale de Sunda (Java-Ouest)." Trans. Isabelle Schulte-Tenckhoff. *Cahiers de Musiques Traditionnelles* 7 (1994): 75–93.

——. "Notation of Music: Theory and Practice in West Java." *Oideion* 2 (1995a): 209–33.

——. "Aspects of Baduy Music in Its Sociocultural Context, with Special Reference to Singing and Angklung." *BKI* 151.4 (1995b): 516–44.

——. "Inner and Outer Voices: Listening and Hearing in West Java." *WM* 39.2 (1997): 41–49.

Javanese Music Historiography: The Lost Gamelan of Gresik

Sumarsam[1]

"Ethnomusicology is often represented as a discipline concerned mainly, or even exclusively, with the performances of living musicians and the roles of such performances in the present-day societies" (Widdess 1993b, 219), implying a field lacking interest in historical perspective. This understanding of the field is reinforced by the practice of participant observation, one of the standard practices in ethnomusicology, especially since the 1960s. This practice requires a student or researcher to study music in its local context, intimately observing the life of musicians and others in that community. More importantly, learning to play or sing the music being studied is almost obligatory.[2] This approach has produced many ethnomusicologists who are adept at performing the music they study; some of them even become accomplished teacher/musicians. Although they never completely lose sight of their historical interests and orientation, their focus is clearly on contemporary musical life.

The present study emphasizes the importance of historical construction for comprehending the formative process of musical phenomena. "Analyzing musical data in its cultural setting has always been a central tenet of ethnomusicological inquiry" (Shelemay 1989, 3). On this point, Kay Shelemay is inspired by Clifford Geertz, "who writes that cultural forms and their creators 'are brought into actual existence by the experience of living in the midst of certain sorts of things to look at, listen to, handle, think about, cope with, and react to ... Art and the equipment to grasp it are made in the same shop'" (Geertz, quoted in Shelemay 1989, 3). Shelemay contends that rituals and art forms "are both reflections and repositories of a

---

[1] I would like to thank Professor Margaret Sarkissian of Smith College, who read a draft of this essay. She made invaluable suggestions and made my English prose clearer.

[2] Requiring students to learn to play non-Western music that he or she is studying began in the UCLA ethnomusicology program led by Mantle Hood. This requirement was meant to implement his concept of bi-musicality, a concept that recognizes the importance of Western students acquiring some practical experience of non-Western music. The original term used for the ensemble in which students learn to play the music was "performance-study group," in line with the context in which the ensemble was established: to learn to play the music as a requisite for understanding it in academic discourse.

people's sensibilities and history." Furthermore, drawing on a notion proposed by art historian Robert Goldwater, she goes on to say: "the arts are 'primary documents' within cultures that both convey and embody meaning." And, by "contextualizing these 'documents' in a broader cultural field we can gain insight into the history that gave them shape and meaning" (1989, 3).

In the study of Western music, this historical approach falls into the domain of music historiography or historical musicology. Ethnomusicologists studying Indonesian music generally do not refer to the works of historical musicologists, since the focus of their work is on Western music. Instead, because of the burgeoning social science discipline (especially in the United States), scholars of Indonesian music ally themselves with Indonesianists, especially anthropologists and historians, but also linguists (Becker 1993, 382). The names and the works of towering figures in these fields, such as Clifford Geertz and Benedict Anderson, are no strangers to ethnomusicologists. In fact, in his "Toward the Re-modeling of Ethnomusicology," Timothy Rice, a prominent ethnomusicologist, invoked Geertz's definition of music as "historically constructed, socially maintained and individually applied" (1987, 473). The responders to his proposal also supported the importance of a historical approach. For example, Shelemay (1987, 490) has suggested that the study of manuscript and archival sources, which requires source-critical and text-critical skills, should be included in the training of ethnomusicologists. Thus, as in the historical study of the arts more generally, "critical examination of sources, chronological narrative, periodization, change and causality, and biography" are among the subject areas that should be critically examined by music scholars committed to gaining a historical perspective (Stanley 2001, 547). The aesthetic views of the art historian cannot be avoided by those dealing with music and art history generally (Stanley 2001, 547).

Like most studies of non-Western music that attempt historical inquiry, the study of gamelan history is hampered by the lack of written sources. There are only a handful of historical studies from which to draw any meaningful discussion of sources, methods of study, and theoretical questions. Furthermore, there has been much discussion questioning the validity of using Javanese historiography as a historical source. Javanese sources (in both literary and aural forms) are not conventional historical records. Soedjatmoko has acknowledged that these sources "do not seem to yield to the conventional methods of historical examination" (1965, xviii), yet he went on to argue that, in fact, Javanese historiography "does yield to conventional critical examination and does, with the necessary checks against non-Javanese sources, constitute a treasure house of historical information" (xix). The qualities and the value of these sources will become clearer in the discussion below and in the case study that I will present as the main part of this paper. Regardless of the lack of evidence, existing gamelan studies with historical perspectives have given us much to ponder as we pursue our historical investigations.

One of the major historical works of Javanese music is Jaap Kunst's *Hindu-Javanese Musical Instruments* (1968).[3] Kunst's book is filled with the names of hundreds of musical instruments gathered from old Javanese manuscripts, and

---

[3] A colonial official with a law degree, Jaap Kunst spent more than fifteen years living in Indonesia, primarily Java. He was also a violinist, specializing in European folk music. While in Indonesia, he spent much of his time studying gamelan and music from other islands. When he returned to the Netherlands, he promoted the study of non-Western music; he is known as one of the founders of ethnomusicology.

suggestions about the periods in which they may have existed. Kunst studied depictions of instruments on the walls of ancient temples, such as the ninth-century Buddhist monument Borobudur in Central Java and the fourteenth-century Panataran temple in East Java.

In spite of the hundreds of named musical instruments listed by Kunst, no evidence of any large ensemble similar to today's gamelan can be found in the early history of Java. In regard to pictorial evidence, while there are many musical instruments depicted on the walls of Borobudur, only a few of them are similar to modern gamelan instruments. It is true that many drums of different types are depicted there, but they might just as well be Indian as Javanese. In fact, drawings of Indian musical instruments seem to be more conspicuously present than Javanese instruments on Borobudur's walls; we find, for example, plucked stringed instruments, vertical flutes, and the earthenware drum known as *ghatam*. An Indian plucked stringed musical instrument, *bin*, is clearly depicted on the walls of the fourteenth-century Pananggungan temple. Interestingly, some of the instruments depicted on the wall of Borobudur cannot be found in Java, but can still be found in other parts of Indonesia and Southeast Asia. For example, mouth organs and certain types of plucked stringed instruments, pictured on the monument, can still be found in Kalimantan and mainland Southeast Asia.

The minimal pictorial evidence of Javanese gamelan instruments on the walls of Borobudur has made it difficult to support the Javanese belief in the antiquity of the gamelan ensemble. Defending gamelan's antiquity, a prominent American ethnomusicologist, Mantle Hood, speculated that because Java was colonized by Indian rulers at the time, the lack of gamelan representation on the walls of Borobudur is "simply an Indian way of showing that the autochthonous musical culture was aesthetically inferior to that of the ruling [Indian] Çailendras" (Hood 1984, 28). However, such speculation is clearly false, since Java was never colonized by Indian rulers. The spread of Indian culture in Southeast Asia happened not by conquest but by trade; traders brought with them Brahman priests to introduce Javanese people—starting with the elite circle of the court—to Indian religion and literature (Hall 1981, 16–22).

Speculation is inevitable when working with insufficient data. But how far can one speculate based only on limited data? I can think of a very interesting historical speculation on the origin of a gamelan instrument called *gendèr* (a metallophone) proposed by Purbatjaraka (1987 [1957]). As a linguist, he proposed that the name *gendèr* derives from Gendhara (a region in India) by way of wordplay. He argued that (1) a number of words ending in the syllables *èk, èl, èt,* and *èr* originally ended in *ak, al, at,* and *ar* (e.g., *suwèk – suwak; dhèdèl – dhadhal; sèrèt – sarat; cèrèt – carat*); and (2) the final *a* of many Indian words has disappeared: *Singapura – Singapur; daca – das.* Therefore, *gendèr* must have derived from *gendara* by way of *gendar* (which happen to be the name of cracker, *karak gendar*, shaped like *gender*). Purbatjaraka strengthens his argument by pointing out that (1) *gendara* in Javanese *wayang* refers to a land of the birthplace of Dewi Gendari (the mother of Kurawa brothers); and (2) in Old Javanese literature (*Wiratha Parwa*), the word *gandhara* means a musical instrument.

It is not my intention here to validate Purbatjaraka's fascinating speculation. The fact remains, however, that there was a musical link between India and Java, as evidenced by the presence of Indian musical instruments depicted on the walls of Javanese temples. Yet, while these drawings of Indian musical instruments present tantalizing evidence of India–Java musical interaction, we do not know the extent of this interaction. Had Indian music ever been performed in Java at that time? No evidence can be found to support or contradict such an assumption. We might also ask what impact Indian music had on the development of gamelan. In light of the fact that many musical aspects of gamelan are so very different from aspects of Indian music—the emphasis on percussion in gamelan versus strings and singing in Indian music; limited scales and modes in gamelan versus a large repertoire of scales, tuning, and modes in Indian music—there seems to be little possibility for the two musical systems to have had any close connection with each other, at least viewed from the perspective of contemporary musical practice. However, Richard Widdess (1993), an ethnomusicologist specializing in Indian music, suggests that if we examine the practice of Indian music as described in the *Natyasastra* treatise written c. 500 CE, then we find that the melodic and rhythmic organization of Indian music at that time was actually similar to today's gamelan. So, speculation on the possible link between Javanese and Indian music continues.

The mention of Indian names of musical instruments and terms in old Javanese literature compared to Javanese names and terms supports this Java–India link. For example, the fourteenth-century *kakawin* poem *Negarakertagama* not only uses Indian terms such as *mredangga* (ceremonial drum), *samahepa* (stringed instrument?), and *gitada* (singers), but also Javanese terms such as *salukat*, *gendèr*, and *salonding*. And yet, despite *Negarakertagama*'s rather long chapter on the court festival, with descriptions of all sorts of music and dance, there is no description of any large ensembles. It does seem that performing arts were well maintained during the period described in the poem: a certain division of the court led by a *rakyan demung* was responsible for supervising "the Seven Musics, singing, dancing, things of beauty, and especially excursions, and the organization of the delights, entertainments, to make designs for luxury and clothing, to make various arrangements for voluptuous displays of art, the charm of amorous poetry, the making of *kawyas* (high poetry), [the making] of all kinds of musical instruments ... the loveliness of the *ringgitan* (dances and female dancers)..." (Pigeaud 1960, 122). Nevertheless, a clue suggesting the presence of any types of large orchestras cannot be found.

During this period, pictorial evidence of gamelan instruments appears on the walls of temples in East Java. For example, on the wall of the fourteenth-century Panataran, one finds different sizes of gongs; an ensemble of *gambang* (a xylophone played with a pair of Y-shaped sticks—an ensemble that still can be found in Bali today); and an ensemble consisting of *reyong* (a pair of gongs attached to the two ends of a pole—which also still exists in Bali, although it is almost extinct). References to music can also be found in literary works such the fourteenth-century poem *Wangbang Wideya*. In this poem, Javanese terms such as *luwarak*, *cantung*, *gendhing*, *gong*, and *raket* are frequently used (Robson 1971, 72, 73, 117, 198).

In the seventeenth century, Europeans entered the archipelago, and travelers and traders occasionally provided reports on and drawings of gamelan. One such report, written by the sailors of the *Golden Hind*, describes an exchange of music between one of the Javanese local chiefs and Francis Drake, the captain of the expedition. Responding to the performance of some English consort music on board the ship, the chieftain presented Drake with a performance of Javanese "country musick," which he described thus: "though it were of a strange kind; yet the sound was pleasant and delightful" (Woodfield 1995, 275). Woodfield (277) also includes drawings of an ensemble consisting of various sizes of gongs that were engraved by members of the

Dutch expedition of 1595–97. The function of the ensemble was described in the engraving's caption: "to sound the hours, and play all their music ... and also when they want to summon people in the king's name, as they did when we first arrived there, to show that anyone might buy and sell with us" (Lodewycksz 1598, in Reid 1988, 213). Purchas, quoted by Woodfield (1995, 276), describes a similar gong ensemble from the same place that consisted of

> ... ten or twelve pannes of Tombaga, carried upon a coulstaffe between two; these were tunable, and every one of note above another, alwayes two went by them which were skillfull in their Country musique, and played on them having this in their hands of purpose to strike them.

As can be seen in an illustration from "Tweede Boeck," an account of De Houtman's voyage to Asia in the late sixteenth century, a similar ensemble was used in Tuban, East Java, in 1599 to accompany a horse tournament (Reid 1988, 188). This tradition was still practiced in the nineteenth-century Central Javanese courts,[4] along with a tiger-baiting (*rampogan*) spectacle.

It seems that, in the early development of Javanese music, gong-type instruments became the dominant instruments in the ensemble. In fact, in the past, the term "gong" might even refer to the ensemble itself: "*gong-gongan*" meant to play gamelan. In Bali, "gong" still refers to an ensemble: consider, for example, Gong Kebyar and Gong Gede. The gong also became an invaluable instrument and symbol of power throughout the Indonesian archipelago from the seventeenth century. The contemporary Indonesian practice of naming a large gong, and adopting that same name for the whole ensemble, is a further indication of the symbolic power that resides in the gong. Gamelan *monggang*, an honoring ensemble consisting of mostly gongs of different sizes, is still considered the most sacred and archaic gamelan in the courts of Central Java.

Among the early European accounts, one written by Ryklof van Goens, the VOC (Vereenigde Oostindische Compagnie, Dutch East India Company) ambassador to the seventeenth-century kingdom of Mataram, seems to indicate vaguely the existence of a rather large ensemble; the ambassador reports having seen several ensembles, each consisting of from twenty to thirty or fifty small and large gongs (Goens 1856 [1656], 322–23). However, he does not mention the metallophone-type instruments (such as *gendèr* or *saron*) that are indispensable to contemporary gamelan ensemble. He also mentions an ensemble consisting of many small gongs with a soft melody provided by a few flutes and viols accompanying a type of courtship dance, and a dance contest between two men accompanied by great gongs (Goens 1856, 327–28).

At this juncture, a question lingers regarding the period during which contemporary gamelan and other performing arts developed. In my case study below, I suggest that the development of today's gamelan performance tradition can be traced to the period of the efflorescence of Javanese performing arts in the north coast (*pesisir*) of Java in the sixteenth century; this was the time when this area

---

[4] See a drawing from an early nineteenth-century Javanese court in Anthony Reid, *Southeast Asia in the Age of Commerce, 1450–1680*, vol. 1. (New Haven, CT, and London: Yale University Press, 1988), p. 186.

became the locus of economic and cultural activity.[5] Jaap Kunst also suggests this time frame. He asserts that during the early history of Javanese music, two chief instrumental groupings can be identified: soft sounding instruments to be played indoors and loud-sounding instruments for outdoor performance. At the end of the Hindu–Javanese period, a marriage between these two instrumental groupings was arranged; hence, the development of a grander contemporary gamelan ensemble (Kunst (1973 [1949], 113–14). Yet other reports suggest alternative theories of gamelan's development. According to an oral account and a few contemporary references, the development of today's gamelan and performing art generally should be attributed to Sultan Agung, the ruler of the court of Mataram (r. 1613–45).

Evidence of a full gamelan ensemble surfaced in the mid-eighteenth century. This was the period after the permanent division of the Mataram kingdom into two major courts in 1755; later, other courts were established. As order and peace were restored, literature flourished, so much so that scholars describe this period as a "renaissance" of classical literature. Much evidence about the performing arts can be found in the court literary works from this period. For example, the late eighteenth-century *Serat Babad Nitik* (1929 [1791], 488) mentions the names of three gamelan sets at the Mangkunegaran court: Kanyut, Mèsem, and Udan Riris. These three sets of full gamelan still exist and are playable today. The author of *Serat Babad Nitik* refers to Kanyut (Carried Away) and Mèsem (Smile) as the names of two separate gamelan sets. However, we know today that the two names were combined (Kanyutmèsem), referring to a single, full set of *sléndro-pélog* gamelan. What is relevant to our discussant is that the year of A.J. 1700 (1770 CE) was carved in one of the keys of a *saron* instrument, presumably indicating the year of the construction of the gamelan. An oral account also supports the antiquity of this gamelan, and describing its existence within the context of the history of the founding of the court of Mangkunegaran under the leadership of Mas Said.[6]

As the story goes, the king of Kartasura, Paku Buwana II, gave gamelan Kanyutmèsem to his son-in-low, the regent of Ponorogo. In 1740, the Chinese population rose against the Dutch and their ally, Paku Buwana II. Consequently, the kingdom of Kartasura was destroyed, and Paku Buwana II retreated to East Java. Eventually, he regained his capital in 1743 with the help of the Dutch. But before returning to the court city, his nephew, Mas Said, joined by Paku Buwana II's younger brother, prince Mangkubumi, rose against the Dutch and Paku Buwana II and his successor. While this struggle was going on, Mas Said married Mangkubumi's daughter. But in 1754 the two princes, Mas Said and Mangkubumi, turned against each other. Legend has it that the beautiful sound of gamelan Kanyutmèsem was the major cause of the dispute. The gamelan instruments were seized by Mas Said from Paku Buwana II's son-in-law, along with some beautiful *bedaya/srimpi* dancers. Prince Mangkubumi demanded the return of the gamelan and two of the dancers, but Mas Said refused; hence, their alliance splintered. We learn

---

[5] According to Javanese tradition, *gamelan sekatèn*, a full ensemble consisting of gong type instruments, *saron* metallophones, and a large drum (*bedhug*), arose in this period of the early Islamization of Java. Believed to have been used as a tool to promote the spread of Islam, this gamelan was performed once each year in front of the mosque, during the week of the *garebeg* religious festival, to celebrate the life of the Prophet Muhammad.

[6] The story below is drawn from Robert Brown and Nancy Pemberton, "Java: Court Gamelan Volume II" (Liner Notes), Nonesuch Explorer Series, H-72074, a recording of gamelan Kanyutmesèm and Udan Arum at the court of Mangkunegaran.

from history that after a long war between the princes' forces, a solution was found: to divide the Mataram kingdom permanently into the two major courts, with Kasunanan of Surakarta ruled by Paku Buwana II and Kasultanan of Yogyakarta reigned by Mangkubumi (Hamengku Buwana I). Later, two minor courts were established: Mangkunegaran in Surakarta, ruled by Mangkunegara I (Mas Said), and Paku Alaman in Yogyakarta, governed by Paku Alam.

As I mentioned earlier, *Serat Babad Nitik* is one of the literary works that describes cultural activities in the court of Mangkunegaran. All sorts of celebratory events, often with splendid displays of the performing arts that included dances, dance drama, gamelan, and processional music, can be found in this literary work. Although it lacks detailed descriptions of these performances, we get a sense of the presence of a large *sléndro-pélog* gamelan ensemble. *Ramé* (a boisterous/ complex/busy atmosphere) was a feature of many court occasions, produced by a combination of Javanese and European soundscapes. During the *tingalan ageng* (an important birthday according to Javanese calendrical reckoning) of Mangkunegara I, two sets of gamelan were sounded outdoors ... then in the morning, the sound of gamelan *monggang* and cannons was thunderous ... *Wayang wong* dance drama was staged in the *pandhapi* hall with an interlude by a male *badhaya* dance (*Serat Babad Nitik* I, 45).

Another important literary work, the early nineteenth-century *Serat Tjentini*, also offers us a wealth of information about Javanese performing arts within and outside the Javanese courts. The theme of this classic narrative—the story of wanderers and their recollections of experiences about diverse subjects: religious knowledge, topography, medicine, performing arts, and so forth—has cemented its reputation as a great Javanese encyclopedic work. The *Serat Tjentini*'s encyclopedic form also encompasses coverage of music and performing arts. All sorts of musical performances, accompanying dance performances, and theatrical productions appear throughout the multi-volume poetic work. We learn about various gamelan ensembles, Islamic music (*terbangan*), *terbangan*-gamelan hybrid music, and vocal music. We learn that gamelan practice in the time of *Serat Tjentini* was as elaborate as today's practice. For example, the narrative describes large *sléndro-pélog* ensembles, notes the names of various gamelan ensembles (such as Alun Jeladri and Samodra), identifies gamelan compositions such as *gendhing rebab* and *gendhing bonang*, and lists hundreds of compositions.

The eighteenth- and nineteenth-court literary works also often inform us of the conspicuous presence of European sounds. Cannon, salvos, and even fireworks were often sounded together with gamelan. In addition, European marching bands were often an integral part of many splendid celebratory events in the Javanese courts. In examining the soundscape of colonial Java, I have suggested that the competition between Javanese and European sounds in both musical and non-musical court rituals provided a basis for developing a musical style that emphasized the production of the loudest sounds, a contest that led to a gradual increase in the size and number of instruments in the gamelan ensemble (Sumarsam 1995, 62). This led to the construction of many new gamelan ensembles that included relatively larger and more numerous instruments in the nineteenth-century courts of Surakarta and Yogyakarta.

By the early nineteenth century, evidence provided by Europeans such as Sir Thomas Stamford Raffles, the British governor of Java, confirm definitively the existence of full ensembles similar to the modern gamelan. His *History of Java* (1817) contains lavish illustrations, including photographs and drawings of large gamelan ensembles. Moreover, Raffles himself brought two sets of gamelan instruments to England (see Raffles 1817; William Fagg 1970; Sam Quigley 1996). Another valuable description of such ensembles comes from the Dutch Resident of Gresik, Cornets de Groot (1852). As I will discuss in detail in my study case below, de Groot mentions various types of gamelan ensembles, including a number of large ensembles similar to the modern gamelan, a list of many gamelan compositions, and the use of gamelan for dance and theatrical accompaniment.

If we wish to look at gamelan history from a different angle, Judith Becker's work should be mentioned. In *Gamelan Stories* (1993), she offers us a historical perspective that clarifies not only gamelan musical development, but the meaning of music more generally. Departing from a number of contemporary definitions of the term "gamelan," she reconstructs a musical meaning, the root of which can be traced to the Hindu/Buddhist–Javanese period. One of her discussions revolves around a parallel between a contemporary interpretation of the five pitch names of gamelan with the concept of "the five senses, the six perceptions, and the convergence of consciousness at the heart [of Buddhist] *cakra* and medieval Javanese and Indian Tantric formulations" (74). Reading contemporary interpretations of the meaning of "gamelan," such as Sastrapustaka's and other interpretations similar to it (including the interpretation of *bedhaya*, a ceremonial dance of the Javanese court), Becker suggests that

> ... one must read on more than one level, finding the secondary, suggested meanings (*laksanā, vyañjanā*) or the abstract, concealed meanings (*surasa*) ... The Tantric past, the Sufi past, colonialism and modern independence are all keys with which to unlock and release *surasa*, the hidden meanings that may be only partially intended by the teller or the writer. (168)

Let me summarize my particular approach to historical inquiry regarding gamelan. Throughout history, the states in Southeast Asia, whether "traditional" or "modern," have been and remain important patrons of the arts (Lindsay 1995). In light of this fact, I venture to suggest that nation-state, culture, and performing arts are inextricably linked in the region. Perhaps it is useful to know something about the formation and nature of the state in Southeast Asia, a subject that has been rigorously reviewed by Tony Day (2002). The regions of Southeast Asia have gone through interrelated chains of historical events, revolving around religious conversion, trading, colonialism, and transitions from revolution to independent states. If we place an emphasis on historical events as a product of human cultural practice (not as elements arranged by simple temporal periodicity), it is inaccurate to define the state "as a finished product or structure that has existed in 'traditional,' 'colonial,' or 'modern' forms" (Day 2002, 2). Rather, the state is the result of temporally interrelated human, social, and institutional practices. Given this concept, then the history of Southeast Asia from early times to the present should be understood as "an overlapping series of localizing, transcultural processes differently distributed over the whole region and occurring over many centuries at different rates in different places" (Day 2002, 32).

I mentioned earlier Geertz's notion that performing arts are historically constructed, socially maintained, and individually applied. This notion, combined with Day's notion of state formation as an overlapping series of localizing transcultural processes, is the key to understanding the complex relationship and interdependency between the nation-state, culture, and performing arts. The history of gamelan is inextricably linked to the formation of state. Thus, the writing of the history of gamelan is a complex undertaking, as it depends on how much evidence can be accumulated, in what ways these evidentiary sources (Javanese and non-Javanese; facts and myth) relate or talk to each other, how musical meaning and context can be discovered, and how to acknowledge the inextricable link between state, culture, and performing arts as the basis to examine musical development. I hope the perspectives I have enumerated above will become transparent in my case study below.

GRESIK AND GIRI[7]

My case study concerns a historical account of a lost gamelan and the disappearance of a lively performing arts tradition in early nineteenth-century Gresik, a town on the north coast of East Java. The main source for my study is an archival document written by Cornets de Groot, a Dutch official who later became the Resident of Gresik in 1825. It is an ethnographic report that includes sections on various kinds of performing arts, including *wayang*, dance, dance drama, and gamelan.

According to this archival document, the Gresik Regency owned several gamelan ensembles. The document lists the name of each gamelan and its particular repertoire. Upon closer examination, it appears that the kinds of gamelans and the pieces each played are not far different from the gamelans and musical repertoire in the courts of Surakarta and Yogyakarta. Other sources inform us that Gresik was one of the towns well known for its gamelan foundry. In short, in the early nineteenth century, the Gresik Regency seems to have been a lively home for the performing arts.

Armed with these references, in the summer and fall of 2008 I went to Gresik to determine whether I could find gamelans and any trace of the gamelan foundry mentioned in my reference. The result was a disappointment. After searching thoroughly, meeting cultural experts, musicians, and government officials, I could not find any trace of the several gamelans in question. Gresikians had forgotten about the lively performing arts and the well-known gamelan foundry in their city. The pertinent questions are: what happened to these gamelans? Where are they? What is the state of performing arts in contemporary Gresik?

The content of the archival document that I am interested in consists of (1) drawings of five sets of gamelan ensembles presented side-by-side with all kinds of ceremonial paraphernalia and weaponry; and (2) a list of gamelans, their performance contexts, and the pieces performed by each. One can learn facts about the music of the region from these drawings, such as the existence of various kinds of gamelan sets, specific numbers of instruments for each set, decorative styles of the wooden frames of the instruments, the sizes of the instruments, and so forth. A closer

---

[7] The case study presented here is based on a keynote lecture that I delivered at the Society for Asian Music's annual membership meeting, held in conjunction with the Society for Ethnomusicology annual conference at Wesleyan University (October 25–28, 2008). I would like to acknowledge Peter Carey's and Amrit Gomperts's studies, which have dealt intensively with this topic and with the dynamic of the relationships between the "center" and the "periphery" in Javanese society. I have drawn many points in my case study from their works.

inspection of these drawings leads to a number of other questions: Why are non-gamelan items, including all sorts of ceremonial paraphernalia and traditional weapons, drawn in juxtaposition with the gamelans? Is the artist trying to tell us that these non-gamelan objects have something to do with the performance context and/or the development of the gamelan? The fact that the list of gamelans and their repertoire suggests a practice similar to the gamelan tradition in the courts of Surakarta and Yogyakarta leads me to a further question: can we deduce a political and cultural relationship between the central sovereignty and its periphery from these documents?

Let me began with some historical background about Gresik and its neighboring town Giri. Giri was one of the earliest historic Islamic states. It was founded in the mid-sixteenth century by Sunan Giri, one of the nine Islamic saints (*walisongo*) responsible for the spread of Islam in Indonesia. Politically, religiously, and in terms of trade, Giri, with Gresik as its harbor, was one of the most influential states at the time, extending its influence outside Java into Lombok, Sulawesi, Kalimantan, and Maluku. In their journal, the Portuguese adventurers Tomé Pires and Duarte Barbosa, who visited Java in the early sixteenth century, testified to this highly influential state and other states in the north coast area, the *pesisir*. The rise of these states happened as a result of the fall of Majapahit (the last Hindu–Javanese kingdom) and the rise of elite Islamic commercialism in the fifteenth and sixteenth century in the *pesisir*.

These two major events brought about economic development and the emergence of political centers throughout the area, resulting in an intensive development of performing arts in the area. "There are great musicians and sempstresses who are very cunning in work of every kind, and are given to love-enchantments," says Barbosa (translated by Dames 1921, 194). Javanese gongs of different sizes from the north coast area were transported to other islands, reaching as far as North Borneo and the Southern Philippines (Skog 1993, 168–74). Barbosa also reports that gongs from Java were valuable commodities and important instruments in the royal music ensemble of Maluku (Dames 1921, 202–3). Traders spread news about the exuberant life of performing arts in Giri, and this news reached as far as South Kalimantan. As told in *Hikayat Lembu Mangkurat*, the traders noted that in the kingdom of Giri people very noisily entertain themselves day and night with all kinds of *wayang* and mask-dance performances, *gambus* (short-necked lutes), and dancing, because the king is very intelligent (Ras 1985, vii). This artistic fame compelled the king to summon his minister to go to Giri, near the town-harbor of Gresik, to borrow people who were skillful in all sorts of theatrical performances and music, including *wayang*, mask dance, and the playing of *gambus* (Ras 1985, vii).

Sultan Agung

During this early period of Islamized Java, competitions arose among several states in the *pesisir* area. Demak, the first state to rise and gain power after the fall of Majapahit, launched a campaign to control other *pesisir* states. The history of Java became more complex when another influential center of power emerged in inland central Java, namely the Mataram kingdom. It is a commonly held opinion that in the seventeenth century, the ruler of Mataram, Sultan Agung, and his heirs developed a genre of court, "classical," style performing arts that would last for centuries to come. After the emergence of this new power in the seventeenth century, there were many conflicts and betrayals among the royal families, encroachments of one center against another, and brutal campaigns to expand sovereignty and gain economic benefits. In this regard, Sultan Agung was known as a king with an iron will. In his early years, he launched a series of brutal campaigns to rule all of Java. Year after year, he ordered his armies to war, conquering his rival states and bringing back to Mataram treasures from the defeated kingdoms, presumably including musical instruments and artisans, and queens and princesses, as the booty of war.

In his campaign to expand his power, Sultan Agung confronted the mighty state of Surabaya, a powerful and rich state because of its intensive trading. Gresik was the harbor for Surabaya. It took Sultan Agung five years (1620–25) to defeat Surabaya. As with other assaults of the time, the treasures and royal princesses became the booty of war. Realizing the importance of Surabaya, however, Sultan Agung brought the king's son, Pangeran Pekik, to Mataram, married him to his sister, and reinstalled him as ruler of Surabaya. This marriage diplomacy established an alliance between Surabaya and Mataram that lasted for a long time. But it did not insure the safety of all the towns in the region. Pursuing his wish to rule all of Java, Sultan Agung, in collaboration with Sunan Pekik, destroyed Giri in 1636.

Evidently, in the seventeenth century, Surabaya was at the peak of its power, an influential state controlling all of East Java and Sukadana of Kalimantan. With the downfall of Giri, Surabaya became even more powerful. Surabaya's political prestige and economic advantage brought about a cultural efflorescence. In light of the relationship between Mataram and Surabaya (in war, and later as close allies), it is safe to suggest, as has Carey (1997, 717), that the Mataram kingdom emulated the cultural attainments of Surabaya. This is a plausible hypothesis, although direct evidence of the nature of this emulation is hard to find. One can strengthen this thesis only by citing contemporary perspectives and evidence.

We know that stories based on East Javanese historical events became important sources for certain *wayang* and dance dramas in central Java. The Panji story, a story about a prince in the twelfth-century East Javanese kingdom, is performed in *wayang gedhog* and *wayang topèng* (mask dance). *Wayang krucil* (wooden-puppet shows) and *langendriyan* dance opera perform the Damarwulan story, a narrative based on the conflict between the ruler of Majapahit and the king of Blambangan.

During the heyday of the state of Surabaya, these stories spread along the northeast coast of Java and were subsequently introduced to inland central Java when Pangeran Pekik became a close ally of Mataram (Carey 1997, 717–18). According to Kusumadilaga (a learned courtier and *wayang* expert in the mid- to late nineteenth-century court of Surakarta), it was during Pangeran Pekik's rule of Surabaya that the story of Damarwulan was performed in Mataram, using a newly created shadow puppet play especially created to perform this story. The accompaniment for this *wayang* was provided by an East Javanese gamelan ensemble otherwise used to accompany East Javanese *wayang krucil* (a puppet show using two-dimensional wooden puppets to tell the story of Damarwulan).[8] Kusumadilaga (1930 [1870], 159–76) also attributes the origin of Central Javanese *wayang* and dance to East Javanese rulers.[9]

---

[8] This gamelan consisted of *kethuk, saron, kenong, rebab, kecèr,* and *kempul*. A performance of *wayang krucil* from Klatèn that I saw in the 1960s used a similar instrumentation.

[9] He says that certain kings of Jenggala in East Java drew *wayang* figures on palm leaves (later transferred to paper), created *pakem* (synopses of *wayang* stories), and established the use of *sléndro* gamelan to accompany *wayang* and the use of the Kawi language for *sulukan* songs. All sorts of gamelan (including *monggang, carabalèn,* and *kodhokngorèk*) and court dances (*serimpi,*

Kusumadilaga wrote his manuscript in the mid-nineteenth century without offering any evidence to prove his theory. To support his point, we can cite the following passages from *Serat Tjentini* (I/II, 248–49), a literary work written between the late eighteenth century and the early nineteenth century. The passages describe a gamelan in the *pélog* tuning system named Alun Jeladri (Ocean Waves) that performed the opening of an instrumental piece (*bonangan*) in a musical mode (*pathet*) called *lima*. This work states that no one can fail to recognize the unmatched and lively sound of this gamelan; it can awaken the feelings of happiness and of longing for the incredibly sweet tuning of Alun Jeladri. More is said about the beauty of this gamelan. The author notes that the original owner of the main instruments in this gamelan set was the Regent of Wirasaba of East Java. Originally, the gamelan was inherited from his ancestor, the Regent of Bintara (Demak), who obtained it from the kingdom of Giri.[10] Here, the supremacy of East Javanese art is revealed.

Let me provide you with another piece of evidence regarding the contribution of East Java to the development of Central Javanese music. This concerns the origin of a particular instrument: *kenong Japan*, a very distinctive *kenong* (a large, cradled gong) found in the court gamelan of Yogyakarta and defined by its prominent, robust, strong, low pitch, and reverberating sound. History informs us that in the eighteenth century and earlier, a town in East Java now known as Majakerta was called "Japan." Is *kenong Japan* derived from or modeled after the style of *kenong* that came from Japan (Majakerta)? The probability is there. We know not only that an intimate relationship linked East Javanese and Central Javanese states in general, but also that at one time the court of Yogyakarta appointed a member of the royal family from Japan (Majakerta) named Sumadipura as minister (*patih*) of the court from 1813–47 (Carey 1997, 725). We do not know for sure if Sumadipura brought *kenong Japan* to Yogyakarta; it is possible his father did, since he was the minister of the Sultan when he was still Crown Prince (Carey 1992, 498). Kunst (1973/1, 161) says that supposedly Sumadipura introduced the *kenong* to Yogyakarta. In any event, this kind of circumstantial evidence, and other kinds of events involving the presence of East Javanese people or officials in the court of Yogyakarta at that time,[11] suggest that the transfer probably did take place.

Now I would like to present another piece of evidence supporting the theory that musical styles and instruments were probably transferred from East Java to Central Java. This concerns the origin of gamelan *carabalèn*, which the Javanese believe is one of the ancient ensembles, together with *monggang* and *kodhok ngorèk*. It has been suggested that the word *carabalèn* means "in the manner of" (*cara*), or à la Bali (*balèn*)

---

dhadhap, lawung, et cetera) were created by a certain king during the Jenggala period. *Wayang bèbèr* was created during the Majapahit era. Subsequently, it was used by the Sultan of Demak as the basis for creating *wayang purwa* puppets. Kusumadilaga also says that Sunan Giri added more figures to *wayang purwa* puppets and created *wayang gedhog*.

[10] The story is set in Wonomarto, a village in East Java. The point here is that the authors, the learned courtiers of Central Java, testify to the beauty of East Javanese gamelan.

[11] Carey notes that a large number of east Javanese workers and officials were transferred to central Javanese courts as part of a building project that obliged the *bupati* from the outlying areas to provide corvée labor to the courts of Central Java. Gamelan belonging to *bupati* from East Java were played during the construction project in order to boost the moral of the east Javanese workers, and a dance based on east Javanese dance was one of the dance repertoires performed to entertain the east Javanese officials who were overseeing the project. See: Peter Carey, "Civilization on Loan: The Making of an Upstart Polity: Mataram and its Successors, 1600–1830," *Modern Asian Studies* 31,3 (1997): 725.

(Kunst 1973, 265); hence, it refers to a Balinese style of gamelan. In fact, older literature employs the term *cara bali*, a clearer reference to Bali, instead of its derivative, *balèn*. Certainly, the fast tempo and interlocking style of the *bonang* and two-drums in *carabalèn* remind us of the Balinese gamelan. I suggest that the creation of *carabalèn* was inspired by Balinese gamelan *bebonangan* or *beleganjur*. During the heyday of the Balinese courts, this ensemble was used to accompany armies in battle.

Here is a piece of history suggesting that it is possible a Balinese gamelan was transferred and transformed to become Javanese *carabalèn*. Throughout the seventeenth century, Blambangan was under the sway of the Balinese rulers of Gelgel, Buleleng, and Mengwi. These Balinese courts assisted Blambangan against Sultan Agung and/or the Dutch and also against the rebel Surapati when he established his headquarters in East Java. It was in this context that the Balinese gamelan *bebonangan* was introduced to Blambangan. Subsequently, the Javanese created an ensemble that was inspired by *bebonangan*, leading to the development of gamelan *cara bali* (gamelan in Balinese style). The most likely scenario of the transfer is that *bebonangan* was brought to the eastern part of Java by Balinese armies fighting in the service of the rulers of Blambangan during the period when Blambangan was under the sway of Balinese rulers (Carey 1997). In fact, some of the Blambangan rulers and members of the aristocracy were of Balinese descent. The East Javanese *carabalèn* gamelan was then introduced to and subsequently adapted by the courts in central Java. In the past century, *carabalèn* in the court of Surakarta was used to accompany *wirèng* (a fighting dance) and a soldiers' drill using lances (Kusumadilaga 1930, 182); hence, we find a military connection with the original context of *carabalèn* and *beleganjur* in Bali. At the present time, the ensemble can be heard in festivities to honor the arrival of guests and to accompany certain ritual processions.

GRESIK IN THE EIGHTEENTH AND NINETEENTH CENTURY

After Giri was destroyed, the cultural center was fully taken over by Surabaya, which came to control the territory associated with Gresik. As I mentioned earlier, during the period before it became the vassal of Mataram, Surabaya was at the peak of its cultural development. It seems that after Surabaya became the vassal and close ally of Mataram, from the mid-seventeenth century to the early part of the nineteenth century, both Surabaya and Gresik were able to sustain their cultural attainments. Two references from the early nineteenth century testify to the dynamic cultural life of Gresikians. British Lieutenant Governor Raffles (1982 [1816], 473) mentions the importance of Gresik as the principal manufacturer of gamelan instruments. He remarks: "the gongs in particular furnish a valuable article of export. Every native chief in authority has one or more gamelans, and there are more or less perfect sets in all the populous towns of the eastern provinces" (473).

Rather comprehensive information about gamelan and performing arts in Gresik was written by Dutch official Cornets de Groot (1852)—this is the archival document I mentioned earlier.[12] In his long ethnographic report, he included sections on

---

[12] The drawings appear in Ann Kumar's book, *Java and Modern Europe: Ambiguous Encounters* (Richmond, Surrey: Curzon, 1997). (Much of Kumar's chapter is drawn from de Groot's manuscript.) The list of gamelans and their repertoire is from the Groot article published in the journal *Tijdschrift voor Nederlandsch Indie* (1852/53). See Cornets A. D. de Groot, "Bijdrage tot de kennis van de zeden en gewoonten der Javanen," *Tijdschrift voor Nederlandsch-Indie* 2 (1852):

various kinds of performing arts, including *wayang*, dance, dance drama, and gamelan. His report includes the descriptions and instrumentation of each of the ensembles, descriptions of each of the instruments and their playing techniques, and a list of the pieces performed by each ensemble. In addition, he provides drawings of the instruments of six different gamelans. He makes a chart, showing nine ensembles with a list of pieces and their usage in performance.[13] Examining the pieces and the kinds of gamelans reported by de Groot, I find a strong similarity between gamelan tradition in central Javanese courts and the Gresik gamelan tradition.[14] Many pieces in his list are classical pieces associated with Central Javanese court gamelan.[15]

Based on de Groot's and Raffles's reports, it seems apparent that the heyday of the gamelan tradition in Gresik lasted from the mid-eighteenth century to the 1830s (Gomperts and Carey 1994). Jaap Kunst notes that Gresik was "the ancient centre of forging gongs." But by the time he arrived in Java in the 1930s, gamelan and gong making in Gresik had completely disappeared (Kunst 1973, 137).[16]

What is more relevant to our inquiry is the fact that Gresik continued to maintain its strong economic development because of its harbor and the presence of the elite community of Islamic traders there. Confirming this point, additional gamelan manufacturers in the early nineteenth century can also be found in other north coast trading centers, including Banyuwangi, Semarang, Cirebon (Cirebon had six gamelan manufacturers) (Fernando 1996, 82), Blora (Kunst 1973), and Jepara (according to a passage from *Serat Tjentini*).[17]

419–21. In the summer of 2010, I had the opportunity to see the original drawings and documents at the KITLV library in Leiden.

[13] For example, thirty-three *gendhing* are listed in the *saléndro* gamelan used for accompanying *wayang*. The nine ensembles in the list are gamelan *senèn, kodok ngorèk, tjara bali, bonang rèntèng, saléndro, mentaraman, pélog, soerabayan,* and *salomprèt*. Elsewhere in his report, he also mentions *gamelan sekatèn*: a large gamelan tuned to *pélog*, used for the Islamic festival to commemorate the life of the Prophet Muhammad.

[14] It is true that the name gamelan *surapringgan* (another name for the city of Surabaya) points us to the East Javanese identity, but other gamelans and many of the pieces listed by Groot are also known in the courts of Central Java.

[15] I should mention that although he wrote his report in 1822–23, de Groot makes reference to the situation as it existed quite some time earlier, and Raffles used some of his material on music (Kumar 1997, 111). I do not yet have access to Groot's original manuscript. Instead, I examined the published version of it, which appears in *Tijdschrift voor Nederlandsch-Indie* with the title "Bijdrage tot de kennis van de zeden en gewoonten der Javanen." According to Kumar, this version is a somewhat abbreviated version of the original. I should mention that Kumar freely translates some parts of Groot's manuscript into English with commentary in her book entitled *Java and Modern Europe*, in the chapter on "The Socialization of the People: 'Becoming Javanese.'" See Ann Kumar, *Java and Modern Europe: Ambiguous Encounters* (Surrey: Curzon, 1997).

[16] Jaap Kunst also mentions that Gresik was producing kettledrums to be exported to Alor for a purchase-price of a bride even until the late nineteenth century. See Jaap Kunst, *Hindu-Javanese Musical Instruments*, 2nd. ed. (The Hague: Martinus Nijhoff, 1968), p. 47; and Jaap Kunst, *Music in Java: Its History, Its Theory, and Its Techniques*, vol. 1 (The Hague: Martinus Nijhoff, 1973), p. 106.

[17] In their work, originally published in 1907, Edward Jacobson and J. H. van Hasselt inform us of a detailed process of gamelan making in Semarang, where gongs were manusfactured since early times. See Edward Jacobson and J. H. van Hasselt, "The Manufacturer of Gongs in Semarang," trans. Andrew Toth, *Indonesia* 19 (April 1975): 127–52. The Semarang gongs were particularly well known; they were sold not only within Java, but a large number of gongs also went to Bali and Lombok. Smaller size gongs of low quality were exported to islands

In the mid-eighteenth to early nineteenth centuries, Gresik produced many fine gamelans, sending them to the courts of Surakarta and Yogyakarta, and the courts in Madura (Bangkalan) and Kalimantan (Banjarmasin, Kutai, Pasir) (Gomperts and Carey 1994, 25).[18] Adding to its fame, Gresik also made cannons, guns, and bells (*loncèng*). Joint manufacturing between gong smithies and gun foundries was common throughout Javanese history (Gomperts and Carey 1994, 25). Raffles (1817, 1, 44–45) notes that, besides gong making, Gresik exported "brass guns of considerable caliber."

Gresik Gamelan, the Mataram Kingdom, and the Dutch

After the permanent division of Mataram, the courts of Yogyakarta and Surakarta continued to subjugate and influence outlying areas, including Gresik and Surabaya; they were a microcosm of Mataram. I would suggest that this is the reason why the Regent of Gresik had the same kinds of gamelan as in Mataram. In other words, the relationship between East Java and the Central Javanese state remained strong after the permanent partition. Perhaps this explains why Gresik musicians played gamelan compositions associated with the courts of Surakarta and Yogyakarta.

What is also worth noting is that although the economy of the East Javanese states in the eighteenth century had declined as a consequence of constant warfare, Dutch economic control, and taxes owed to Mataram, Gresik was able to maintain its performing arts. In addition to de Groot's report, a French traveler also testified to the lively cultural life in Gresik in the early nineteenth century (Stockdale 1811, 388–89). John Joseph Stockdale said that as his group entered the palace, "noisy music and a Malay play" welcomed them.

---

outside of Java, and also to Singapore, the Malay peninsula, and Brunei. Ibid., pp. 150–51. The best quality of large gong was usually made for the courts of Surakarta and Yogyakarta.

So far I haven't found any references to the existence of an old gamelan smithy in inland Central Java. From aural information, we are told that the oldest and best-known gamelan smith in Surakarta was born in the mid-nineteenth century, giving us an idea that gamelan instruments were manufactured in this town in the late nineteenth century. Sam Quigley, "Gong Smithing in Twentieth Century Surakarta," *Asian Arts and Culture* 8,3 (1995): 12–31. However, this does not rule out the possibility of gamelan-making before the nineteenth century. We know from Bemmelen (quoted in Reid) that in the seventeenth century, a significant source of copper was found in a village southeast of Surakarta (Tegalombo), implying the possibility of important bronze work in the area. Nevertheless, no evidence can be found of gamelan manufacture there at the time or afterward. See Anthony Reid, *Southeast Asia in the Age of Commerce 1450–1680*, vol. 1 (New Haven, CT, and London: Yale University Press, 1998), p. 118.

[18] Gomperts and Carey report that the remnants of Gresik gamelan with their distinct carved frames and stands and fine sound quality can be found scattered in many places, in the courts of Central Java, Jakarta, Madura, and Kalimantan. See Amrit Gomperts and Peter Carey, "Campanalogical Conundrums: A History of Three Javanese Bells," *Archipel* 48 (1994): 25, fn. 25. It is worth mentioning that, according to Kunst, in the 1930s in Gresik there were sixteen complete bronze *sléndro* gamelan, three complete bronze *pélog* gamelan, thirty-one sets of *wayang kulit purwa*, two sets of *wayang gedhog*, and fourteen sets of *wayang kerucil* (*klithik*). See Jaap Kunst, *Music in Java: Its History, Its Theory, and Its Techniques*, 2 vols. (The Hague: Martinus Nijhoff, 1973). I have not had an opportunity to conduct thorough research into gamelan activity in Gresik today, but from information I gathered over the summer of 2008, there isn't much gamelan activity going on there now.

The Malay director (the puppeteer) at the same time sung of the different fights and victories of the ancestors of the emperor and other princes of the country, to the sound of a number of kettle-drums and gomgoms (*gongs*) of different sizes. The two-stringed fiddle ... was the principal instrument, and played by the leader of the band.

Stockdale also witnessed a dancing event (perhaps a *tayuban*?): "In the long square ... were thirty rouguins (*ronggeng*), fourteen to sixteen years old, ornamented with garlands of flowers." While dancing, the performers were also

> ... singing, [in] a languishing tone, the victories and praises of the emperors. They now and then sate down in a groupe on the ground to rest. In one of the angles outside the shed were two tables set out with Bourdeaux wine, gin, liquors, and pipes, and it is customary to drink ever instant.

This description reminds us of a similar report by a trade ambassador to the kingdom of Mataram in the seventeenth century about a dancing event he saw there.[19]

The end of the Java War in the mid-nineteenth century marked the full colonization of Indonesia by the Dutch. The whole of Java suffered as the Dutch stepped up their exploitation. Consequently, regents in different part of Java, including Gresik, had limited resources to maintain their cultural lives. This most likely led to the loss of Gresik gamelans and the decline of its traditional performing arts.

Another factor could also help explain the loss of Gresik's gamelan tradition, namely, the changing perspective of the Javanese toward Islam. By the nineteenth century, the strength of Islamic orthodoxy had brought about the marginalization of an older Java–Islam syncretistic tradition. This development caused the decline of traditional performing arts and gamelan-making in the central and northeastern coastal areas of Java, including Gresik. Several gamelan belonging to the nineteenth-century regent of Gresik vanished, and Gresikians' memories of their town having an exuberant cultural life and a first-rate gamelan-making tradition gradually faded away.

CONCLUSION

In conclusion, let us return to the sketches of Gresik's gamelan. Gamelan instruments are presented in juxtaposition with all kinds of paraphernalia, including flags, flowers, pikes, and weaponry. I think that this juxtaposition captures well the context in which music was performed and developed. The artist of these sketches tells us not only that gamelan was an integral part of ritual and celebration, but also that its development and survival were linked to warfare.

---

[19] Rijklof van Goens, "Rejsbeschijving van den weg uijt Samarang nae De Konincklijke Hoofdplaets Mataram Mitsgaders de Zeede, Gewoonten ende Regeringe van den Sousouhounan Groot Machtichste Koningk van 't Eijlant Java." *Bijdragen tot de Taal-, Land-en Volkenkunde van Nederlands-Indie* 4 (1856): 307–67. Original work, 1656.

The present study also reveals a highly dynamic interaction between the center and the periphery, between Mataram and the *pesisir*. Having experienced an economic boom resulting from the work of the Islamic commercial elite, the *pesisir* became a hotbed of performing arts, gamelan-making, and the creation of myths about the past. Subsequently, Mataram found sources from the *pesisir* to explain the development of their performing arts. After the permanent partition of Mataram, the dynamic interaction between the center and the *pesisir* continued, as the *pesisir* became the vassal of Mataram; this explains the existence of a court-like gamelan tradition in Gresik and other outlying regions.

As Europeans interfered more and more in Javanese life and consolidated their power, the relationship between the *pesisir* and Mataram became even more dynamic. Blessed by Mataram, the Dutch exploited the wealth of the *pesisir*, causing a strange relationship between the *pesisir*'s regents and Mataram. Eventually, by the mid-nineteenth century, the *pesisir*'s wealth dried up, consumed by the Dutch and by Mataram. The situation became worse when the Dutch launched more economic exploitation after the end of the Java War in 1930. Together, these factors caused the loss of the lively performing arts tradition of the *pesisir*.

The final nail in the coffin of the region's performing arts was the changing perspective of the Javanese towards Islam. The syncretistic Java–Islam tradition that had been fostered and developed since the early Islamization of Java in the sixteenth century was gradually marginalized because of the rise of Islamic orthodoxy in the nineteenth century. The *pesisir* gradually embraced an orthodox, *syariah*-minded view that saw the local performing arts as obstacles in its attempt to purify Islam, thus completing the marginalization of Javanese performing arts in the area.

Works Cited

Becker, Judith. *Gamelan Stories: Tantrism, Islam, and Aesthetics in Central Java*. Tempe, AZ: Arizona State University, Program for Southeast Asian Studies, 1993.

Brown, Robert, and Nancy Pemberton. Liner Notes. "Java: Court Gamelan Volume II." Nonesuch Explorer Series, H-72074, 1977.

Carey, Peter. "Civilization on Loan: The Making of an Upstart Polity: Mataram and its Successors, 1600–1830." *Modern Asian Studies* 31.3 (1997): 711–34.

——. *The British in Java 1811–1816: A Javanese Account*. New York, NY: Oxford University Press, 1992.

Dames, Mansel Longworth. *The Book of Duarte Barbosa*, vol. 2. London: The Hakluyt Society, 1921.

Day, Anthony. *Fluid Iron: State Formation in Southeast Asia*. Honolulu, HI: University of Hawaii Press, 2002.

De Groot, Cornets A. D. "Bijdrage tot de kennis van de zeden en gewoonten der Javanen." *Tijdschrift voor Nederlandsch-Indie* 14.2 (1852): 257–80; 346–67; 393–424.

Fernando, M. R. "Growth of Non-agricultural Economic Activities in Java in the Middle Decades of the Nineteenth Century." *Modern Asian Studies* 30.1 (1996): 77–119.

Goens, Rijklof van. "Rejsbeschijving van den weg uijt Samarang nae De Konincklijke Hoofdplaets Mataram Mitsgaders de Zeede, Gewoonten ende Regeringe van den

Sousouhounan Groot Machtichste Koningk van 't Eijlant Java." *Bijdragen tot de Taal-, Land-en Volkenkunde van Nederlands-Indie* 4 (1856 [1656]): 307–67.

Gomperts, Amrit, and Peter Carey. "Campanalogical Conundrums: A History of Three Javanese Bells. *Archipel* 48 (1994): 13–31.

Hall, D. G. E. *A History of South-East Asia.* 4th. ed. New York, NY: St Martin's Press, 1981.

Hood, Mantle. *The Evolution of Javanese Gamelan Book II: The Legacy of the Roaring Sea.* New York, NY: C. F. Peters Corporation, 1984.

Jacobson, Edward, and J. H. Van Hasselt. "The Manufacture of Gongs in Semarang [1907]." Trans. Andrew Toth. *Indonesia* 19 (April 1975): 127–52.

Kumar, Ann. *Java and Modern Europe: Ambiguous Encounters.* Surrey: Curzon Press, 1997.

Kunst, Jaap. *Music in Java: Its History, Its Theory, and Its Techniques.* 2 vols. The Hague: Martinus Nijhoff, 1973.

——. *Hindu-Javanese Musical Instruments,* 2nd. revised edition. The Hague: Martinus Nijhoff, 1968.

Kusumadilaga, Kangjeng Pangeran Harya. *Serat Sastramiruda* [The Book of Sastramiruda]. Solo: De Bliksem, 1930 [1879].

Lindsay, Jennifer. "Cultural Policy and the Performing Arts in Southeast Asia." *Bijdragen to de Taal-, Land- en Volkenkunde* 151 (1995): 656–71.

Pigeaud, Theodore G. *Java in the Fourteenth Century,* vol. 3. The Hague: Nijhoff, 1960.

Poerbatjaraka, Prof. Dr. "Raden Inu Main Gamelan: Bahan Untuk Menerangkan Kata Pathet" [Raden Inu Plays Gamelan: Sources for the Explanation of the Word Pathet]. *Karawitan: Sources Readings in Javanese Gamelan and Vocal Music.* Ed. Judith Becker. Ann Arbor, MI: Center for South and Southeast Asian Studies, The University of Michigan, 1987 [1957].

Quigley, Sam. "Gong Smithing in Twentieth Century Surakarta." *Asian Arts and Culture* 8.3 (1995): 12–31.

Raffles, T. Stanford. *The History of Java.* 2 vols. Kuala Lumpur: Oxford University Press, 1982 [1817].

Ras, J. J. "Kata Pengantar" [Preface]. *Serat Kandhaning Ringgit Purwa,* Vol. 1. Transliterated by R. S. Subalidinata. Jakarta: Djambatan and KITLV–Jakarta, 1985.

Reid, Anthony. *Southeast Asia in the Age of Commerce, 1450–1680,* vol. 1. New Haven, CT: Yale University Press, 1988.

Rice, Timothy. "Toward the Remodeling of Ethnomusicology." *Ethnomusicology* 31.3 (1987): 469–88.

Robson, S. O. *Wangbang Wideya.* The Hague: Nijhoff, 1971.

Serat Babad Nitik Mangkunegaran wiwit tahun Alip 1707 ngantos dumugi Je 1718. 1929 [1791]. Ms. SMP MN 193/6 (typed transliteration of Koninklijk Instituut ms. KITLV Or. 231).

Serat Tjentini: Babon Asli Saking Kita LEIDEN in Negara Nederland, vol. 4. Transcribed and ed. R. Wirawangsa, with assistance of M. Ardjawidjaja. Batavia: Ruygrok, 1912–15 [1814].

Shelemay, Kay. "Response to Rice." *Ethnomusicology* 31.3 (1987): 489–90.

——. *Music, Ritual, and Falasha History*. East Lansing, MI: Michigan State University Press, 1989.

Skog, Inge. *North Borneo Gongs and the Javanese Gamelan: Studies in Southeast Asian Gong Traditions*. Stockholm: Stockholms Universitet, 1993.

Soedjatmoko, et al. *An Introduction to Indonesian Historiography*. Ithaca, NY: Cornell University Press, 1965.

Stanley, Glenn. "Historiography." *The New Grove Dictionary of Music and Musicians*. 2nd. ed. Ed. Stanley Sadie and John Tyrrell. Vol. 11. London: Macmillan Publishers, 2001: 547.

Stockdale, John Joseph. *Island of Java*. Singapore: Periplus, 1995 [1811].

Sumarsam. *Gamelan: Cultural Interaction and Musical Development in Central Java*. Chicago, IL: University of Chicago Press, 1995.

Widess, Richard. "Sléndro and Pélog in India." *Performance in Java and Bali: Studies of Narrative, Theatre, Music, and Dance*. Ed. Ben Arps. London: University of London, School of African and Oriental Studies, 1993a: 186–96.

——. "Historical Ethnomusicology." *Ethnomusicology: An Introduction*. Ed. Helen Myers. New York, NY: W. W. Norton and Company, 1993b.

Woodfield, Ian. *English Musicians in the Age of Exploration*. Stuyvesant, NY: Pendragon Press, 1995.

Zoetmulder, P. J. *Kalangwan: A Survey of Javanese Literature*. The Hague: Nijhoff, 1974.

DECENTERING ETHNOMUSICOLOGY: INDONESIAN POPULAR MUSIC STUDIES

Andrew N. Weintraub

One would expect to find a rich and extended engagement with Indonesian popular music in ethnomusicology, the study of music "in the context of human life" (Titon 2002, xiii). Indonesian popular music (*musik populer*) is "of the people," the music that the vast majority of Indonesian citizens listen to, dance to, and identify with. Despite the centrality of popular music to human life and the development of individual subjectivities, it was excluded from the scope of ethnomusicology during the field's formative period (circa 1950) through the mid-1970s. Mass-mediated, made-for-profit, and mixed, popular music was viewed by ethnomusicologists as standardized, Westernized, and inauthentic. Fast-forward forty years, and the study of popular music is now one of the richest and most active areas of growth in the field of ethnomusicology. In this essay, I show how the field of ethnomusicology, particularly the study of Indonesian music, has changed over time, such that popular music is now central to its purview.[1]

This essay presents a critical review of published research on popular music of Indonesia chronologically and in terms of various center–periphery models within the field of ethnomusicology. Indonesianists are quite familiar with the notion of center and periphery, developed during the Dutch colonial era, in which Java occupies the center and the "outer" islands constitute the periphery (Anderson 1972; Errington 1989; Andaya 1993; Dove 1996). During the 1970s and 1980s, the spatial metaphor of center and periphery was fundamental to studies of politics and culture in Indonesia (e.g., Benedict Anderson's ideal form of the traditional polity in Java in the person of a ruler [1972] and Clifford Geertz's "exemplary center" of the theater state in Bali, 1980). Politically, according to Benedict Anderson, the ideal form of the traditional polity in Java is "that of a cone of light cast downward by a reflector lamp" (1972). Power and authority are symbolized by a focused source of light in the person of a ruler who personifies unity of society. Power diminishes as the distance increases between the light source and the periphery, leading Anderson to postulate

[1] I thank R. Anderson Sutton, Ricardo Trimillos, and Philip Yampolsky for valuable feedback on the content of this article.

that "oneness is Power and multiplicity is diffusion and weakness" (1972.). As the light source became diffuse, the peripheries faded and eventually became hidden from view and unrecognizable. These ideas about power formed the basis of Anderson's analysis of politics and culture in the New Order.[2]

In this essay, I have something disciplinary in mind, namely, how center–periphery models shape fields of intellectual production. By "center," I am referring to the dominant ideas, values, and practices of a "field of cultural production" (Bourdieu 1983). This field of cultural production is a social space where people engage in struggles over symbolic as well as material resources (capital). Bourdieu uses the concept of field to analyze the activities of intellectuals, who engage in similar struggles over resources to define the very terms of the field itself.

The object of my critique will be the field of ethnomusicology, specifically studies of the music of Indonesia. In this sense, one can speak about a dominant "culture" of Indonesian music studies that privileges certain types of music, methods of analysis, and styles of representing music, while marginalizing others. As forms of representation, fields of knowledge "structure" the limits of a field and constrain the possibilities for shaping meanings about people, culture, and society in Indonesia.[3]

The ethnomusicological study of Indonesian music has historically aligned with four centers and peripheries: (a) area (Java vs. the "outer islands"); (b) genres of music (traditional vs. popular); (c) religious (Hindu–Buddhist vs. Islamic); and (d) ensemble type (gamelan[4] vs. non-gamelan). I will describe these center–periphery structures, trace their shifting boundaries over time, and offer some explanations for why such shifts have occurred. Further, in tandem with trends in the field of ethnomusicology, new theoretical paradigms, research methods, and analytical tools have accompanied new disciplinary approaches. Interdisciplinary approaches and the emergence of new topics—for example, studies of gender, electronic mass mediations, and Islam—point to increasingly stronger links between popular music studies and the broader field of Indonesian studies in the future.

My review is representative but not comprehensive. First, I focus on English-language sources.[5] Ethnomusicology in Indonesia does not generally encompass the study of popular music, although there are some notable exceptions.[6] Indonesian

---

[2] This framework of center and periphery has been the subject of recent post-colonial critique in Indonesian studies. See Eriko Aoki, "'Center' and 'Periphery' in Oral Historiography in a Peripheral Area in Southeast Asia," in *Globalization in Southeast Asia*, ed. Shinji Yamashita and J. S. Eades (New York, NY: Berghahn Books, 2003), p. 145; Jacqueline Aquino Siapno, *Gender, Islam, Nationalism, and the State in Aceh: The Paradox of Power, Co-optation, and Resistance* (New York, NY: RoutledgeCurzon, 2002), p. 24; and William Cummings, "Would-be Centers: The Texture of Historical Discourse in Makassar," *Centering the Margin: Agency and Narrative in Southeast Asian Borderlands*, ed. Alexander Horstmann and Reed L. Wadley (New York, NY: Berghahn Books, 2006), p. 53.

[3] The otherwise impressive *Indonesia Reader: History, Culture, Politics* (Tineke Hellwig and Eric Tagliocozzo, eds. [Durham, NC: Duke University Press, 2009]), with not a single article about the music of Indonesia, belies the substantial amount of scholarship about music in Indonesia.

[4] In ethnomusicology, gamelan, the large ensemble characterized by a variety of gong-chime instruments (bossed gongs), is a theoretical metonym for Indonesian music.

[5] This is not to discount the relatively few but important studies in other languages. I will cite some of them herein.

[6] These include studies conducted by STSI Padang Panjang (on *kroncong* and *pop Minang*), STSI Bandung (on *pop Sunda*), ISI Yogyakarta (on *kroncong*), and ISI Surakarta (on *campursari*). Additional sources of information about popular music include popular print media,

institutions that publish scholarly materials include the government-sponsored college-level conservatories of performing arts (Sekolah Tinggi Seni Indonesia, STSI) in Bandung, Denpasar, Padang Panjang, and Surakarta (now called Institut Seni Surakarta, ISI); and the Performing Arts Society of Indonesia (Masyarakat Seni Pertunjukan Indonesia, MSPI, originally called Masyarakat Musicologi Indonesia, MMI), founded in 1989 in Surakarta, Central Java. Journals published by these institutions tend to be short-lived or irregular (e.g., *Seni Pertunjukan Indonesia*, published by MSPI, and *Panggung*, published by STSI Bandung). There is a rich storehouse of knowledge about popular music in popular print media that has yet to be explored by scholars.

POPULAR MUSIC AND ETHNOMUSICOLOGY IN INDONESIA

Indonesia has long been an object of study for Europeans in the field of comparative musicology (*vergleichende Musikwissenschaft*), the precursor to ethnomusicology, which emerged in the late-nineteenth and early twentieth centuries and focused, initially, particularly on instrument tunings (e.g., Ellis 1885), description of musical characteristics (Stumpf 1886), and the classification of instruments (e.g., Hornbostel and Sachs 1914) of "non-European" music. Scholars associated with the "Berlin school" of comparative musicology in the late-nineteenth and early twentieth century were trained in a variety of fields including psychology and philosophy (Carl Stumpf), medicine (Otto Abraham), and chemistry (Erich von Hornbostel). Early studies of music in Indonesia were conducted by the Swedish natural scientist Walter Kaudern (1927).

Popular music of all kinds was excluded in early ethnomusicology. During the post-World War II formative years of the field, only certain kinds of music were acceptable as objects of study. Jaap Kunst (1891–1960), a Dutch musicologist and colonial administrator for the Dutch colonial education system, was the first scholar to use the term "ethno-musicology" in print, in 1950 (Nettl 2005, 11). Kunst, who made the music of Indonesia the focus of his prolific career, stated that popular music was not part of the purview of ethnomusicology:

> The study-object of ethnomusicology … is the traditional music and musical instruments of all cultural strata of mankind, from the so-called primitive peoples to the civilized nations … Western art- and popular (entertainment-) music do not belong to its field. (1959, 1)

The important point is not Kunst's evolutionist ideas ("from the so-called primitive peoples to the civilized nations"); the study-object of ethnomusicology included music from all cultural strata. Rather, what is significant is that this pioneer viewed music as a tonal product from a cultural group that could be objectified, analyzed, and compared with tonal products of other groups. Grouping and ordering of music was based on differences in characteristics and a concern with

---

biographies of artists and composers (e.g., Hawe Setiawan, ed. *Sang Komponis: Nano S. 60 Tahun* [Jakarta: Pustaka Jaya, 2004]), conference proceedings (e.g., Gunawan Subagio, ed., *Apa Itu Lagu Pop Daerah* [Bandung: Citra Aditya Bakti, 1989]), and teaching materials (e.g., Mauly Purba and Ben Pasaribu, *Musik Populer: Buku Pelajaran Kesenian Nusantara Untuk Kelas VIII* [Jakarta: Lembaga Pendidikan Seni Nusantara, 2005]).

authenticity. Tonal products born out of blending and assimilation (e.g., Western art music and popular music) were excluded from consideration.

Kunst's monumental *Music in Java* (1973; revised and enlarged third edition of the original 1934 publication in Dutch entitled *De Toonkunst van Java*) focused on court gamelan traditions of Surakarta and Yogyakarta. Gamelan fascinated European listeners, including composer Claude Debussy, at the 1889 Exposition Universelle in Paris.[7] But Kunst's life-long research agenda was not dominated by a geographic center; he conducted fieldwork in Nias (1939), Flores (1942), the Kei islands (1994 [1945]), Papua (1967 and 1994 [1946]), as well as Sumatra, Borneo, Sulawesi, Nusa Tenggara, Timor, and the Moluccas (1994 [1946]). The center of his research agenda was "traditional" music of various peoples, countries, and territories. All other kinds of music ("non-traditional") were placed on the periphery. Traditional music originated from or was defined in terms of a geographical region, ethnicity, culture, descent, and language of a group of people. For Kunst, and other scholars of the period, traditional music was static, uncontaminated, and self-contained.

In contrast, popular music in Indonesia tends to reflect a high level of interaction among Malay, Middle Eastern, Indian, European, Chinese, and American music. Transcultural border-crossing was common in the music of *bangsawan* in the 1890s; *orkes harmonium* and *orkes gambus* in the 1930s; *orkes Melayu* in the 1940s and 50s; and early forms of *pop Indonesia* (called *hiburan*, or band) in the 1950s and 60s. The center was defined by traditionality, and the periphery was defined by its absence (non-traditionality). Kunst's ideas about the purity of gamelan were later disproved by Sumarsam (1995), who showed how gamelan music in central Java, the study-object par excellence, has been shaped by Javanese ethno-cultural interactions with Hindu, Islamic, European, Chinese, and Malay cultural forces.

Ethnomusicologists of Indonesian music through the 1960s were concerned primarily with documenting, preserving, and classifying types of instruments; and with their construction, their distribution, and their scales and tuning systems. After Kunst, the majority of sources on Indonesian music related to the islands of Java and Bali, and within those areas, to gamelan. Here we have two center–peripheries, one based on instruments (gamelan and non-gamelan) and one based on geography (Java/Bali and everywhere else). The Java/Bali grouping reflected another Indonesianist bias centering on the study of ancient Hindu–Javanese culture, in which gamelan-type instruments in Java and Bali played a large role. Notable research about gamelan before 1970 includes the pioneering work of McPhee in Bali (1966); Kunst 1973 [1934]; Kunst's student Mantle Hood on *pathet* (1954) and *laras* (1966); and Ernst Heins on cueing in gamelan music (1970). Thus, the established ethnomusicology on Indonesia did not engage the dynamic and omnipresent developments in popular music.

Scholarship on Indonesian music since the 1970s opened the field to larger questions, including the relationship between music and theater (and dance to a lesser extent); music theory; performance structure and practice; and the relationship between music, culture, and society (e.g., relating to ethnicity, politics, religion, and gender). These trends reflected broader issues in ethnomusicology about the shift in emphasis from musical products (music as an object) to musical processes ("music as

---

[7] Gamelan music has influenced well-known composers, including Debussy (France), Colin McPhee (Canada), Benjamin Britten (Great Britain), and Lou Harrison (United States), to name a few.

culture," à la Merriam 1964). Research on traditional music of Indonesia during the 1970s addressed musical change (Kartomi 1979); electronic technologies and mass mediations (Toth 1980); and new institutional apparatuses and corresponding changes in music production, circulation, and meaning (Hatch 1979; Becker 1980).

Twenty-five years after Kunst's dismissal, ethnomusicologists Judith Becker, Ernst Heins, and Bronia Kornhauser all wrote articles about *kroncong*, Indonesian string band popular music that fused Western and non-Western musical elements (Becker 1975; Heins 1975; Kornhauser 1978). A serious ethnomusicological engagement ensued, encompassing social contexts of music-making (in the Portuguese settlements of Tugu in Batavia), the historical spread and development of *kroncong* in the nineteenth century, and musicological questions pertaining to song repertoire, vocal style, and variant styles of *kroncong*.

Changes within Indonesia itself propelled a more serious engagement with popular music in the 1970s. What accounts for the change in topic and orientation? New socioeconomic and political realities stimulated the rise of American and British popular music after Suharto came to power in 1966–67. The coup that ushered in the New Order opened Indonesia to sustained industrial expansion, Western-style capitalism, intensified commodification, and a culture of consumerism. New electronic technologies enabled music to travel in the form of cassette recordings to regions far from the urban centers of production. Innovative forms of promotion—films, billboards, and magazines—generated interest in the social lives of entertainers and celebrities. New ways of presenting music in public concerts, festivals, and outdoor fairs in big cities promoted emerging forms of rock and pop. And a new ethos of consumerism in Indonesia gave more people the motivation, as well as the resources, to buy commercial products associated with popular music.

In a seminal article published in the journal *Indonesia*, historian William Frederick wrote this about *dangdut*, a genre of Indonesian popular music: "In a recent collection of studies on modern Indonesian culture [Davis 1979] … *dangdut* receives not a single mention" (Frederick 1982, 104). The dearth of research about *dangdut* was remarkable to Frederick given that it was Indonesia's most popular music during the late 1970s. Circulated via the new medium of cassettes, *dangdut* could be heard in streets and homes, public parks and narrow alleyways, stores and restaurants, and all forms of public transportation. In addition to its dominant economic role in the music industry, *dangdut* was socially significant for religious and political reasons. *Dangdut*'s fan base was made up of primarily underclass urban male youths, and it became a platform from which to proselytize about Islam during the mid-1970s period of Islamization. As the most popular music in Indonesia, *dangdut* had been used in political campaigns to gather crowds since at least 1977. Yet ethnomusicologists did not pay serious attention to *dangdut* until the early 2000s (Wallach 2008; Weintraub 2010).

One of the main trends in the ethnomusicology of Indonesian music during the 1970s and 1980s was structuralist. A rich body of literature aimed to show how various forms of music in Indonesia were constructed (Kartomi 1976; Vetter 1984; van Zanten 1989). Attention to repertoire, piece structures, and formal playing techniques in gamelan music of Java and Bali grew out of a deeper engagement with the music, often in conjunction with gamelan performance classes in university music departments (Hood and Susilo 1967; Becker 1979). Based on extensive fieldwork and knowledge gained from studying how to play gamelan music, scholars developed new modes of analysis based on structural linguistics (Becker and Becker 1983 [1979)]; "inner melody" (Sumarsam 1975); variation and flexibility within constraints of performance practice (Susilo 1987; Sutton 1978 and 1993; Vetter 1981; Sutton and Vetter 2006); and competence and interaction (Brinner 1995).

Concurrently with these structuralist approaches, Kartomi (1980; 1985) characterized the history of musical development in Sumatra, Java, and Bali as a series of four musical "strata," or layers, defined in terms of "predominant religious and cultural characteristics that color the musical styles of each layer" (1980, 111): animist pre-Hindu; Hindu–Buddhist (c. fourth century CE to c. fourteenth century); Islamic (thirteenth century CE); and European (sixteenth century). The latter three strata emerged due to contact with external cultural influences. In practice, all of these strata mix together into syncretic forms (see also Kartomi 1998/1999).[8]

During the 1980s, Indonesian music research reflected a broader engagement with the culture and politics of the 1980s in Indonesian studies (Acciaoli 1985; Hefner 1987; Pemberton 1987). In these studies, traditional music was a site where contemporary cultural (ideological) and social (political and economic) values and meanings were debated (Becker 1980; Sutton 1991; Kartomi 1992). For example, Sutton was especially good at showing how gamelan was being adapted to new media in modern Indonesia: government programs (formal education, contests, festivals); regional practices of print, broadcast, and recording; and regional pluralism of modern (post-independence) composers and musicians.

In the 1980s, ethnomusicologists branched out further from traditional music to popular music, including regional forms.[9] The research reflected an awareness of the remarkable musical diversity of the archipelago, as well as dominant–subordinate relations in the arena of cultural representation at the national level. A new center–periphery model for popular music studies emerged in the 1980s to describe the relationship between national culture and ethnic and regional identity and affiliation (Yampolsky 1989, 13; Hatch 1985; Yampolsky 1991). In the "national–popular" model of Indonesian music, music genres are analyzed as signifiers of either local (also called regional or ethnic) identity *or* national identity. Indonesian national–popular music genres are characterized by the following criteria: (1) they are sung in the national language; (2) musical elements (instruments, timbres, melodic, rhythmic, and formal organization) are based on Western models, or, at the very least, not associated with one ethnic group or another; and (3) recordings of the music are produced (overwhelmingly in Jakarta) by a centralized group of producers and circulate within a nationwide media network.

Local popular musics, by comparison, are characterized by the following criteria: (1) they are sung in local languages, (2) they may have indigenous musical elements, and (3) they are produced in local recording studios or in Jakarta studios for a local

---

[8] Similarly, Miller and Williams characterize the history of music in Southeast Asia in terms of "waves of cultural influence, from both nearby and distant societies." Terry E. Miller and Sean Williams, eds., *Southeast Asia* (New York, NY: Routledge, 1998), p. 55. In contrast, Yampolsky identifies various traits and complexes (e.g., "the gamelan-*wayang* complex" and "the Melayu complex") across the archipelago that may be considered alone or in combination with others. See Philip Yampolsky, "Indonesia," Grove Music Online [www.oxfordmusiconline.com, July 9, 2013], parts I and III (New York, NY: Oxford University Press, 2007–10).

[9] Yampolsky's monumental twenty-volume "Music of Indonesia" series of recordings (1991–99) showed that music of Indonesia was far more extensive and varied than the "great" gamelan traditions of Java and Bali. See: Philip Yampolsky, *Music of Indonesia*. vol. 1–20 (Washington, DC: Smithsonian/Folkways, 1991–99).

market. "Local" refers to musical practices of an ethnic or regional group in contradistinction to the national level (for example, Minang, Javanese, Acehnese), representing local interests in the realm of culture. Local popular musics rarely cross ethnolinguistic borders.[10] The basic premise of this model is that local music is defined by local content, whereas national music is constituted by supra-local elements.

National forms not only stand for national affiliations, but they help to produce these affiliations, and these affiliations become symbolic markers of national cultural identity. Yampolsky writes:

> In Indonesia, the distinction between national and regional is extremely important: what is national—Indonesian language, mass media, government, the educational system—unites the country, and what is regional—local loyalties, languages, customs, music—has the potential to fragment it. (1991, 1)

The national–popular model describes the way in which the production of Indonesian national culture emanates from the center (Jakarta) and works its way out to the peripheries (everywhere else). For example, national–popular forms were produced in Jakarta and circulated throughout the provinces. Furthermore, due to their hegemonic force in media, national–popular forms maneuvered in such a way as to threaten and displace local music, exerting a homogenizing force in the realm of culture. The national center threatened to "grey-out" the peripheries.[11] As with the national language (Bahasa Indonesia), people began speaking the same musical "language." This approach reflects historical shifts in the ethnomusicology of Indonesia, from an emphasis on gamelan in Java and Bali to so-called regional music (including non-gamelan genres). Regional studies of popular music include Gieben, Heijnen, and Sapuletej on *pop Maluku* (1984); Manuel and Baier on *jaipongan* (1986); and Williams on *pop Sunda* (1990).

Hatch (1985) provided an overview of popular music in Indonesia that raised awareness of artists, genres, repertoire, form, performance practice, and the music industry. Manuel and Baier (1986) examined *jaipongan*, a local Sundanese genre of dance music mass mediated through cassettes in the late 1970s. Inspired by communication studies, the study showed that mass mediations did not always produce the same cultural effects (à la Adorno) but, rather, that new technologies could support the diverse interests of people in local decentralized environments. Yampolsky's (1989) close and careful analysis of a 1988 popular song, "Hati Yang Luka" (A Wounded Heart), showed how national–popular music produced in Jakarta had become the subject of government appropriation, regulation, monitoring,

---

[10] Jaipongan is an exception. See Peter Manuel and Randal E. Baier, "Jaipongan: Indigenous Popular Music of West Java," *Asian Music* 18,1 (1986): 91–110.

[11] Ethnomusicologist Alan Lomax used the term "cultural grey-out" to describe the harmful effects of an "over-centralized electronic communication system" that encouraged "standardized, mass-produced, and cheapened cultures everywhere." ("An Appeal for Cultural Equity," first published in 1972, http://www.culturalequity.org/ace/ce_ace_appeal.php, accessed September 18, 2013). This process would eventually lead to destruction of local cultures, or cultural "grey-out." We should be careful about Lomax's reductive reasoning because media networks alone did not determine the social uses or meanings of those media forms. In fact, the spread of electronic communication stimulated musical innovations and creativity in many places. Further, it is important to remember that a cultural text may have multiple meanings, and these meanings may change over time.

and censorship. Yampolsky dedicated volume 2 ("Indonesian Popular Music") of his magisterial twenty-volume CD set to three genres of popular music (*kroncong, dangdut,* and *langgam jawa*).[12]

Previous to the 1980s, scholars of music tended to ignore the influence of Islam on music, particularly various kinds of Islamic music (*musik Islami*). In the Dutch colonial era, Islam was described as a "thin veneer" spread over the surface of Javanese culture (Hefner 1997, 11). Scholarship on music and Islam came rather late, as the influence of Hindu–Buddhist religion and philosophy (and gamelan) were viewed as more central to Indonesia's core culture and history. Kartomi (1986) was the first to take the music of Indonesian Muslims seriously, followed by Capwell (1995), Arps (1996), and Rasmussen (2001). Capwell and Arps focused on mass-mediations of Islam-related popular music (*qasidah* and *gambus,* respectively).

In the 1990s, knowledge about popular music was produced by scholars in a wide variety of disciplines. The first and only thesis on *dangdut* by an Indonesian student was completed (Simatupang 1996, in anthropology at Monash University). Following the work of Frederick, studies of *dangdut* blossomed in Asian studies (Pioquinto 1995 and 1998) and women's studies (Browne 2000). Popular music studies in West Java were produced by scholars trained in anthropology (Hellwig 1993, on *jaipongan*) and Indonesian studies (Jurriëns 1999, on *pop Sunda*).

New approaches to research on Indonesian performance characterized the field of scholarship in post-New Order Indonesia. For example, Jan Mrázek's edited volume on *wayang* puppet theater (2002) emphasized social and cultural change rather than continuities. It also incorporated *wayang* studies from the "outer islands" of Lombok, Kalimantan, and southern Sumatra (Palembang). Following Becker (1980) and Sutton (1991), scholars of traditional music began to focus on how music adapted to changing social conditions in *tembang Sunda* (Williams 2001), *wayang golek* (Weintraub 2004), and *gamelan degung* (Swindells 2004).

The mass mediation of music intensified after the fall of Suharto in 1998. Recordings of new genres proliferated—including fusion and indie, as well as Islamic music (Barendregt and van Zanten 2002). Anthropologist Bart Barendregt (2002) noted that post-Suharto calls for regional autonomy, and new electronic technologies for circulating popular music, contributed to a "renaissance" of regional popular music, including *pop Minang*. New technologies, including the pervasive Video Compact Disc (VCD), engendered new forms of production, circulation, and listening/viewing (Barendregt and van Zanten 2002; Sutton 2003; Weintraub 2006). The rise of private television in the 1990s encouraged diversity of programming and entertainment (Kitley 2000, 249). Looking back to trends beginning in the 1970s, we can see that the center of musicological research was shifting from Java and Bali to other cultural–geographic areas, from traditional music to popular music, and from ethnomusicology to other fields of knowledge production.

In the 2000s, three ethnographic monographs focused on Indonesian popular music. Emma Baulch's richly textured ethnography of popular music in Bali during

---

[12] Paradoxically, *pop Indonesia* was excluded from the volume on Indonesian popular music. Yampolsky states: "I chose not to include the national popular music known as *pop Indonesia*. While the lyrics of *pop Indonesia* are in Indonesian and the genre is significant in Indonesia both economically and socially, it was (at least at that time) musically indistinguishable from European and American pop." See Philip Yampolsky, "Making the Music of Indonesia Series: a Memoir," in *Ethnomusicological Encounters with Music and Musicians: Essays in Honor of Robert Garfias,* ed. Timothy Rice (Farnham, Surrey, UK: Ashgate, 2011), p. 171.

the late 1990s analyzed how transnational music (reggae, punk, and death metal) helped define what it meant to be Balinese during a period of globalization and turbulent political change (2007). Jeremy Wallach's multi-sited ethnography showed how artistic and creative efforts blossomed in *dangdut*, pop, rock, and underground during the politically tumultuous post-authoritarian period (2008). And my own *Dangdut Stories* (2010) placed *dangdut* within a range of broader narratives about class, gender, ethnicity, and nation in post-independence Indonesia (1945–2010). Interestingly, Baulch and Wallach obtained doctoral degrees in politics and anthropology, respectively. (See also Luvaas 2009 and Jurriëns 2010.)

During the mid-2000s, a cohort of young ethnomusicology students focusing on the islands of Indonesia other than Java and Bali have included popular music in their dissertations. Julia Byl (2006) addressed a variety of popular musical genres to discuss Toba Batak history (North Sumatra) as a site of centuries-old global trade routes and influences from India, the Middle East, and the West. Birgit Berg (2007) examined *orkes gambus* as part of Arab–Indonesian communities in eastern Indonesia (North Sulawesi). The study documents the centrality of Arab-derived music within a long history of cultural historical connections among Arab communities in Yemen and Indonesia. Andy Hicken (2007) focused on the production, circulation, and reproduction of regional pop among the Toraja people of South Sulawesi to show "how regional pop's use of lowly 'market language' and valorization of romantic love poses a threat to arranged marriage and the traditional caste system" (abstract). Jennifer Fraser (2007) examined the ways in which the commercialization of indigenous arts through a process she calls "packaging ethnicity for display" has encouraged the creation of new musical styles and modes of production. In a study of laments in pre-funeral wakes among Protestant Toba Batak, Hodges (2009) noted the historical basis of *pop Batak* in Western music (including church music). These studies have not only addressed popular music genres, but they have helped to re-contextualize historical and traditional music forms that were the purview of establishment ethnomusicology. The growth of regional popular music studies by ethnomusicologists of Indonesian music points to a decentering of the field.

Gamelan is no longer the privileged center of research, although it is still dominant in university music department ensemble offerings and in the teaching of world music. The main textbooks for teaching world music include Indonesia's music both as chapters in larger books (Sutton 2008; Capwell 2007; Bakan 2007) and as individual volumes in a larger series (Gold 2004; Brinner 2007; Spiller 2008 [2004]). Gamelan ensembles continue to enjoy popularity in university music departments in many countries. The scholarship on gamelan has changed, however, shifting from an emphasis on static tradition-based repertoires to gamelan traditions in flux (Weintraub 2001; Vitale 2002; Supanggah 2003). Ethnomusicologists recognize that musical "mixing" is a condition of modernity. Musical mixing is a continual, open-ended process, a circular stirring up of things, movement, and also a process of adding to without necessarily needing to take away (Moehn 2008, 167).

New topics have enriched the field of music studies. The field has expanded to include gender as a focus of attention. Rasmussen, for example, has published an ethnographic study about Islamic music in Indonesia, and the prominent role that women play in religious ritual and expressive culture (2010; see also Sutton 1984; Weiss 2006; Spiller 2010). In popular music, a flurry of scholarship grew around Inul Daratista, a *dangdut* singer whose eroticized performance style stimulated conservative Muslim authorities to call for monitoring and censorship (Wichelen 2005; Heryanto 2008; Weintraub 2008).

In the early twenty-first century, greater attention to Islam and music reflects the heightened presence of Islam in the public sphere. Although certain kinds of music have raised the ire of some vocal orthodox groups, the articles in Harnish and Rasmussen (2011) show that music is a privileged medium for expressing Islam rather than a harmful influence. Following Capwell (1995) and Arps (1996), recent articles examine contemporary manifestations of Islam in popular music and culture (Barendregt 2011; Berg 2011; Irama 2011). Identified as an important marker of post-Suharto popular culture, popular music is central to youth identification and Islamization (see Barendregt and van Zanten 2002; Weintraub, ed. 2011; Harnish and Rasmussen, eds. 2011).

THE FUTURE OF INDONESIAN POPULAR MUSIC STUDIES

The field of ethnomusicology has changed since the 1950s. Kunst's exclusion of popular music, and Western-influenced art music, is no longer viable. Multiple musical practices previously relegated to the margins of ethnomusicology have come increasingly into sharper focus. A "de-centered" ethnomusicology challenges a prescribed set of ideas about the nature of music and the methodologies used to study it. Popular music challenges the "music/culture-concept" that was dominant in ethnomusicology through the 1980s (Stokes 2001). Popular music represents "traveling cultures" that move across regional and national boundaries, as opposed to the "music/culture" paradigm that binds cultural expression to ethnicity, region, language, descent, and tradition. The shift from traditional to popular is one example of the decentering of ethnomusicology.

Scholars of popular music can learn a great deal from ethnomusicology. Popular music studies could be more attentive to regional traditions, as ethnomusicologists have been. For example, there are no studies of popular music in Kalimantan and popular music studies in Bali are limited. Ethnographic methods could be used more extensively in the study of popular music (Pruett 2011).

Ethnomusicologists can agree that it is important to listen seriously to (popular) music. Our training gives us the tools to analyze music as sound organized in time. Popular music studies could benefit from ethnomusicology's attention to formal musical characteristics: compositional forms, melodic and rhythmic elements, repertoire, relationships between parts, and playing techniques, among others. If we are going to take popular music seriously, we need to know how it is structured and theorized. Why can't popular music be treated as extensively as gamelan music in Bali (McPhee 1966; Tenzer 2000), or vocal music in Java (van Zanten 1989; Arps 1992)?

Histories of popular music genres are few, and this is where ethnomusicology of traditional music does a bit better (Kartomi 1980; Becker 1993; Sumarsam 1995; Weiss 2006). Scholars have only scratched the surface of a rich history of music and cultural contact, despite the fact that cultural blending was integral to a vast range of music, including gamelan. Future research will address the relationship between Indonesia and the popular music of India, the Middle East, the United States, Malaysia, and Singapore. For example, the study of film music, which has still not been adequately addressed (except for Sumarsam 2008), is important because film is the medium that brought Indonesians into contact with a wide variety of music. Radio is another area for future research, although there are some good studies available (Lindsay 1997; Jurriëns 2010).

In order to do this work, we need different kinds of resources. Several projects have begun to address the lack of accurate information about recordings and recording companies in Indonesia. Toth's discography of Balinese recordings (1980) and Yampolsky's discography of recordings produced by the national recording company Lokananta (1987) provide useful information, especially for dates of recordings.[13] The KITLV project on music and modernity is a key intervention.[14] We need more studies like Yampolsky's (2010), which uses information from 78-rpm recordings of *kroncong* as well as newspaper accounts of and advertisements for *kroncong* performances in the late colonial era. This "new evidence" clarifies the history of *kroncong*, especially during the years 1900 to 1942, the heyday of *kroncong*. Studying the popular press is especially useful for topics that have received little or no attention in ethnomusicology. Popular music histories are important, and the popular press is arguably the only place where these histories have been written.

During the last forty years, research on the popular music of Indonesia has been conducted by scholars in a variety of fields, including ethnomusicology, anthropology, sociology, communication and media studies, history, and literature. My review of the field reveals a wide range of scholars who are asking similar questions and engaging in similar scholarly debates. But their theoretical approaches and research methodologies for addressing these questions are widely divergent. I contend that this diversity has enriched the field of Indonesian studies.

The current state of the field suggests that the peripheries of the past have begun to displace the traditional centers. The focus on popular music need not exclude research on "traditional" musics. The locus of studies of "traditional music" has shifted to monograph recordings (for example, Rappoport on Toraja, 2009; Schefold and Persoon on Mentawai in West Sumatra, 2009; and Yampolsky on Biboki in western Timor, 2011b). Although the islands of Java and Bali continue to receive attention, recent scholarship sheds light on regional music, popular music, fusion music, Islam, and non-gamelan traditions. Indonesian music research today reflects a broad engagement with the shifting geopolitical and cultural terrain of Indonesia, as well as a greater focus on Indonesia in the world.

Works Cited

Acciaioli, Greg. "Culture as Art: From Practice to Spectacle in Indonesia." *Canberra Anthropology* 8.1–2 (1985): 148–72.

Andaya, Leonard. *The World of Maluku: Eastern Indonesia in the Early Modern Period.* Honolulu, HI: University of Hawaii Press, 1993.

Anderson, Benedict R. O'G. "The Idea of Power in Javanese Culture." *Culture and Politics in Indonesia.* Ed. Claire Holt et al. Ithaca, NY: Cornell University Press, 1972: 1–69.

---

[13] Suryadi discusses the arrival of sound recording technology (the Edison phonograph) in West Sumatra in the early 1880s, and the first recordings of Minangkabau music in the 1930s. See Suryadi, "Minangkabau Commercial Cassettes and the Cultural Impact of the Recording Industry in West Sumatra," *Asian Music* 34,2 (Spring/Summer 2003): 51–89.

[14] KITLV, "The Making of Popular Music in Twentieth Century Southeast Asia and the Rise of New Audienes," http://www.kitlv.nl/home/Projects?id=22, accessed August 20, 2013.

Aoki, Eriko. "'Center' and 'Periphery' in Oral Historiography in a Peripheral Area in Southeast Asia." *Globalization in Southeast Asia.* Ed. Shinji Yamashita and J. S. Eades. New York, NY: Berghahn Books, 2003: 145–64.

Arps, Bernard. *Tembang in Two Traditions: Performance and Interpretation of Javanese Literature.* London: School of Oriental and African Studies, 1992.

——. "To Propagate Morals through Popular Music: The Indonesian Qasida Moderen." *Qasida Poetry in Islamic Asia and Africa.* Ed. Stefan Sperl and Christopher Shackle. Leiden: Brill, 1996: 389–409.

Bakan, Michael. "Interlocking Rhythms and Interlocking Worlds in Balinese Gamelan Music." *World Music: Traditions and Transformations.* Ed. Michael Bakan. Boston, MA: McGraw Hill, 2007: 87–116.

Barendregt, Bart. "The Sound of 'Longing for Home': Redefining a Sense of Community through Minang Popular Music." *Bijdragen tot de Taal-, Land- en Volkenkunde* 158.3 (2002): 411–50.

——."Pop, Politics, and Piety: Nasyid Boy Band Music in Muslim Southeast Asia." *Islam and Popular Culture in Indonesia and Malaysia.* Ed. Andrew N. Weintraub. London: Routledge, 2011: 235–56.

Barendregt, Bart, and Wim van Zanten. "Popular Music in Indonesia since 1998, in Particular Fusion, Indie, and Islamic Music on Video Compact Discs and the Internet." *Yearbook for Traditional Music* 34 (2002): 67–113.

Baulch, Emma. *Making Scenes: Reggae, Punk, and Death Metal in 1990s Bali.* Durham, NC: Duke University Press, 2007.

Becker, Judith. "Kroncong, Indonesian Popular Music." *Asian Music* 7.1 (1975): 14–19.

——. "Time and Tune in Java." *The Imagination of Reality: Essays in Southeast Asian Coherence Systems.* Ed. A. L. Becker and Aram Yengoyan. Norwood, NJ: Ablex Publishing, 1979: 197–210.

——. *Traditional Music in Modern Java: Gamelan in a Changing Society.* Honolulu, HI: University of Hawaii Press, 1980.

——. *Gamelan Stories: Tantrism, Islam, and Aesthetics in Central Java.* Tempe, AZ: Program for Southeast Asian Studies, Arizona State University, 1993.

Becker, Judith, and Alton Becker. "A Grammar of the Musical Genre Srepegan." *Asian Music* 14 (1983 [1979]): 30–72. (Originally published in *Journal of Music Theory* 23 [1979]: 1–43.)

Berg, Birgit. "The Music of Arabs, the Sound of Islam: Hadrami Ethnic and Religious Presence in Indonesia." PhD dissertation. Providence, RI: Brown University, 2007.

——. "Musical Modernity, Islamic Identity, and Arab Aesthetics in Arab-Indonesian Orkes Gambus." *Islam and Popular Culture in Indonesia and Malaysia.* Ed. Andrew N. Weintraub. London: Routledge, 2011: 166–84.

Bourdieu, Pierre. "The Field of Cultural Production, or The Economic World Reversed." Trans. Richard Nice. *Poetics* 12.4–5 (1983): 311–56.

Brinner, Benjamin. *Knowing Music, Making Music: Javanese Gamelan and the Theory of Musical Competence and Interaction*. Chicago, IL: University of Chicago Press, 1995.

——. *Music in Central Java: Experiencing Music, Expressing Culture*. Oxford: Oxford University Press, 2007.

Browne, Susan. "The Gender Implications of Dangdut Kampungan: Indonesian 'Low-Class' Popular Music." Working paper no. 109. Victoria: Center of Southeast Asian Studies, Monash University, 2000.

Byl, Julia. "Antiphonal Histories: Performing *Toba Batak* Past and Present." PhD dissertation. Ann Arbor, MI: University of Michigan, 2006.

Capwell, Charles. "Contemporary Manifestations of Yemeni-derived Song and Dance in Indonesia." *Yearbook for Traditional Music* 27 (1995): 76–89.

——. "The Music of Indonesia." *Excursions in World Music*. Fourth ed. Ed. Bruno Nettl. Upper Saddle River, NJ: Pearson Prentice Hall, 2007: 141–70.

Cummings, William. "Would-be Centers: The Texture of Historical Discourse in Makassar." *Centering the Margin: Agency and Narrative in Southeast Asian Borderlands*. Ed. Alexander Horstmann and Reed L. Wadley. New York, NY: Berghahn Books, 2006: 53–66.

Davis, Gloria. Ed. *What is Modern Indonesian Culture?* Papers in International Studies, Southeast Asia series. Athens, OH: Southeast Asia Program, Ohio University Center for International Studies, 1979.

Dove, Michael. "Center, Periphery, and Biodiversity: A Paradox of Governance and a Developmental Challenge." *Valuing Local Knowledge: Indigenous People and Intellectual Property Rights*. Ed. Stephen B. Brush and Doreen Stabinsky. Washington, DC: Island Press, 1996: 41–67.

Ellis, Alexander John. "On the Musical Scales of Various Nations." *Journal of the Royal Society of Arts* 33 (1995): 485–527.

Errington, Joseph. *Exemplary Centers, Urban Centers and Language Change in Java*. Chicago, IL: Center for Psychosocial Studies, 1989.

Fraser, Jennifer. "Packaging Ethnicity: State Institutions, Cultural Entrepreneurs, and the Professionalization of Minangkabau Music in Indonesia." PhD dissertation. Urbana–Champaign, IL: University of Illinois, 2007.

Frederick, William H. "Rhoma Irama and the Dangdut Style: Aspects of Contemporary Indonesian Culture." *Indonesia* 34 (October 1982): 103–30.

Geertz, Clifford. *Negara: The Theatre State in Nineteenth Century Bali*. Princeton, NJ: Princeton University Press, 1980.

Gieben, Claartje, Renee Heijnen, and Anneke Sapuletej. *Muziek en dans, spelletjes en kinderliedjes van de Molukken*. Hoevelaken: CPS pg OOM [Christelijk Pedagogisch Studiecentrum for the Projektgroep Ondersteuning Onderwijs Molukkers], 1984.

Gold, Lisa. *Music in Bali: Experiencing Music, Expressing Culture*. New York, NY: Oxford University Press, 2004.

Harnish, David D., and Anne K. Rasmussen, eds. *Divine Inspirations: Music and Islam in Indonesia*. Oxford: Oxford University Press, 2011.

Hatch, Martin. "Theory and Notation in an Oral Tradition: Some Notes on ASKI, Surakarta." *What is Modern Indonesian Culture?* Ed. Gloria Davis. Papers in International Studies, Southeast Asia series. Athens, OH: Southeast Asia Program, Ohio University Center for International Studies, 1979: 11–18.

——. "Popular Music in Indonesia." *Popular Music Perspectives 2; Papers from the Second International Conference on Popular Music Studies, Reggio Emilia, September 19–24, 1983*. Ed. D. Horn. Göteborg: International Association for the Study of Popular Music, 1985: 210–27.

Hefner, Robert W. "The Politics of Popular Art: Tayuban Dance and Culture Change in East Java." *Indonesia* 43 (1987): 75–95.

——. "Islam in an Era of Nation-States: Politics and Religious Renewal in Muslim Southeast Asia." *Islam in an Era of Nation-States*. Ed. R. W. Hefner and P. Horvatich. Honolulu, HI: University of Hawaii Press, 1997: 3–42.

Heins, Ernst L. "Cueing the Gamelan in Javanese Wayang Performance." *Indonesia* 9 (April 1970): 101–27.

——. "Kroncong and Tanjidor: Two Cases of Urban Folk Music in Jakarta." *Asian Music* 7.1 (1975): 20–32.

Hellwig, Jean. "Jaipongan: The Making of a New Tradition." *Performance in Java and Bali: Studies of Narrative, Theatre, Music, and Dance*. Ed. Bernard Arps. London: School of Oriental and African Studies, University of London, 1993: 47–58.

Hellwig, Tineke, and Eric Tagliocozzo, eds. *The Indonesia Reader: History, Culture, Politics*. Durham, NC: Duke University Press, 2009.

Heryanto, Ariel. "Pop Culture and Competing Identities." *Popular Culture in Indonesia*. Ed. Ariel Heryanto. London: Routledge, 2008: 1–36.

Hicken, Andy. "Slankers Tongkonan Blues: Toraja (South Sulawesi, Indonesia) Songs in a Disjunctive Mediascape." PhD dissertation. Madison, WI: University of Wisconsin–Madison, 2007.

Hodges, Robert. "Ganti Andung, Gabe Ende (Replacing Laments, Becoming Hymns): The Changing Voice of Grief in the Pre-funeral Wakes of Protestant Toba Batak (North Sumatra, Indonesia)." PhD dissertation. Santa Barbara, CA: University of California–Santa Barbara, 2009.

Hood, Mantle. *The Nuclear Theme as a Determinant of Patet in Javanese Music*. Groningen: J. B. Wolters, 1954.

——. "Slendro and Pelog Redefined." *Selected Reports in Ethnomusicology* 1.1 (1966): 36–48.

Hood, Mantle, and Hardja Susilo. Liner notes to *Music of the Venerable Dark Cloud*. IER 7501, 1967.

Hornbostel, Erich M. von, and Curt Sachs. "Systematik der Musikinstrumente: Ein Versuch." *Zeitschrift für Ethnologie* 46 (1914): 553–98.

Irama, Rhoma. "Music as a Medium for Communication, Unity, Education, and Dakwah." *Islam and Popular Culture in Indonesia and Malaysia*. Ed. Andrew N. Weintraub. London: Routledge, 2011: 235–56.

Jurriëns, Edwin. "Postcolonialism and the Space-clearing Gestures of Sundanese Pop Songs." *Review of Indonesian and Malay Affairs* 33.2 (1999): 87–114.

——. *From Monologue to Dialogue: Radio and Reform in Indonesia*. Honolulu, HI: University of Hawaii Press, 2010.

Kartomi, Margaret J. "Performance, Music, and Meaning of Reog Ponorogo." *Indonesia* 22 (1976): 85–130.

——. "Minangkabau Musical Culture: The Contemporary Scene and Recent Attempts at its Modernization." *What is Modern Indonesian Culture?* Ed. Gloria Davis. Papers in International Studies, Southeast Asia Series 52. Athens, Ohio: Southeast Asia Program, Ohio University, 1979: 19–36.

——. "Musical Strata in Sumatra, Java, and Bali." *Musics of Many Cultures*. Ed. Elizabeth May. Berkeley, CA: University of California Press, 1980: 111–33.

——. *Musical Instruments of Indonesia: An Introductory Handbook*. Melbourne: Indonesian Arts Society, 1985.

——. "Muslim Music in West Sumatran Culture." *World of Music* 28.3 (1986): 13–30.

——. "Appropriation of Music and Dance in Contemporary Ternate and Tidore." *Studies in Music* 26 (1992): 85–95.

——. "The Music-culture of South-coast West Sumatra: Backwater of the Minangkabau 'Heartland' or Home of The Sacred Mermaid and the Earth Goddess?" *Asian Music* 30.1 (Fall/Winter, 1998/1999): 133–81.

Kaudern, Walter. *Ethnographical Studies in Celebes: Results of the Author's Expedition to Celebes, 1917–1920*. [*Musical Instruments in Celebes*, vol. 3.] Göteborg: Elanders Boktryckeri, 1927.

Kitley, Philip. *Television, Nation, and Culture in Indonesia*. Athens, OH: Ohio University Press, 2000.

Kornhauser, Bronia. "In Defence of Kroncong." *Studies in Indonesian Music*. Ed. Margaret J. Kartomi. Monash Papers on Southeast Asia 7. Clayton: Monash University, 1978: 104–83.

Kunst, Jaap. *Music in Nias*. Translated by J. S. A. Carrière-Lagaay. Leiden: Brill, 1939.

——. *Music in Flores: A Study of the Vocal and Instrumental Music among the Tribes Living in Flores*. Leiden: E. J. Brill, 1942.

——. *Ethnomusicology: A Study of its Nature, Methods, and Representatives to which is added a Bibliography*. The Hague: Martinus Nijhoff, 1959. First published as *Musicologica*, 1950.

——. *Music in New Guinea: Three Studies*. Trans. (and correction) Jeune Scott-Kemball. *Verhandelingenvan het Koninklijk Instituut voor Taal, Land-en Volkenkunde*, no. 53. 's-Gravenhage: Nijhoff, 1967.

——. *Hindu–Javanese Musical Instruments*. Second revised and enlarged ed. The Hague: Martinus Nijhoff, 1968. First published in Dutch as *Hindoe-Javaansche Muziek-Instrumenten*, 1927.

——. *Musicologica: A Study of the Nature of Ethno-musicology, Its Problems, Methods, and Representative Personalities*. Amsterdam: Uitgave van het Indisch Instituut, 1950.

——. *Music in Java: Its History, Its Theory, and Its Technique*. Third ed., two vols. Ed. Ernest L. Heins. The Hague: Nijhoff, 1973. First published in Dutch as *De Toonkunst van Java*, 1934.

——. "Music and Dance on the Kai Islands [1945]." Tran. Sandra Reijnhart. *Indonesian Music and Dance: Traditional Music and Its Interaction with the West*. Amsterdam: Royal Tropical Institute, Tropenmuseum and University of Amsterdam, and the Jaap Kunst Ethnomusicology Centre, 1994: 205–31.

——. "Indigenous Music and the Christian Mission: Lecture Presented to the Missionary School in Oegstgeest, the Netherlands, 1946." Tran. Maya Frijn. *Indonesian Music and Dance: Traditional Music and Its Interaction with the West*. Amsterdam: Royal Tropical Institute, Tropenmuseum and University of Amsterdam, and the Jaap Kunst Ethnomusicology Centre, 1994: 57–87.

Lindsay, Jennifer. "Making Waves: Private Radio and Local Identities in Indonesia." *Indonesia* 64 (October 1997): 105–23.

Lomax, Alan. "An Appeal for Cultural Equity." From the Program of the Festival of American Folklife. Ed. Thomas Vennum, Jr., Smithsonian Institution, 1985. First published in *World of Music* 14.2 (1972): 3–17.

Luvaas, Brent. "Generation DIY: Youth, Class, and the Culture of Indie Production in Digital-age Indonesia." PhD dissertation. Los Angeles, CA: University of California–Los Angeles, 2009.

Manuel, Peter, and Randal E. Baier. "Jaipongan: Indigenous Popular Music of West Java." *Asian Music* 18.1 (1986): 91–110.

McPhee, Colin. *Music in Bali: A Study in Form and Instrumental Organization in Balinese Orchestral Music*. New Haven, CT: Yale University Press, 1966.

Merriam, Alan. *The Anthropology of Music*. Evanston, IL: Northwestern University Press, 1964.

Miller, Terry E., and Sean Williams, eds. *Southeast Asia* (*Garland Encyclopedia of World Music*, Vol. 4.). With CD. New York, NY: Routledge, 1998.

Moehn, Frederick. "Music, Mixing, and Modernity in Rio de Janiero." *Ethnomusicology Forum* 17.2 (2008): 165–202.

Mrázek, Jan. *Puppet Theater in Contemporary Indonesia: New Approaches to Performance Events*. Michigan Papers on South and Southeast Asia Number 50. Ann Arbor, MI: University of Michigan Centers for South and Southeast Asian Studies, 2002.

Nettl, Bruno. *The Study of Ethnomusicology: Thirty-one Issues and Concepts*. Champaign, IL: University of Illinois Press, 2005.

Pemberton, John. "Musical Politics in Central Java (or How Not to Listen to a Javanese Gamelan)." *Indonesia* 44 (October 1987): 17–29.

Pioquinto, Ceres. "Dangdut at Sekaten: Female Representations in Live Performance." *Review of Indonesian and Malaysian Affairs* 29 (1995): 59–90.

——. "A Musical Hierarchy Reordered: Dangdut and the Rise of a Popular Music." *Asian Cultural Studies* 24 (1998): 73–125.

Pruett, David. "When the Tribe Goes Triple Platinum: A Case Study toward an Ethnomusicology of Mainstream Popular Music in the US." *Ethnomusicology* 55.1 (2011): 1–30.

Purba, Mauly, and Ben Pasaribu. *Musik Populer: Buku Pelajaran Kesenian Nusantara Untuk Kelas VIII.* Jakarta: Lembaga Pendidikan Seni Nusantara, 2005.

Rappoport, Dana. *Songs from the Thrice-blooded Land: Ritual Music of the Toraja (Sulawesi, Indonesia).* Two vols. plus DVD–ROM. Référentiels–Patrimoines Immatériels. Paris: Éditions Épistèmes/Éditions de la Maison des Sciences de l'Homme, 2009.

Rasmussen, Anne. "The Qur'an in Daily Life: The Public Project of Musical Oratory." *Ethnomusicology* 45.1 (2001): 30–57.

——. *Women, the Recited Qur'an, and Islamic Music in Indonesia.* Berkeley and Los Angeles, CA: University of California Press, 2010.

Schefold, Reimar, and Gerard A. Persoon. Liner notes for *Songs from the* Uma: *Music from Siberut Island (Mentawai Archipelago), Indonesia.* Two CDs. Leiden: Pan Records, 2111–12, 2009.

Setiawan, Hawe, ed. *Sang Komponis: Nano S. 60 Tahun.* Jakarta: Pustaka Jaya, 2004.

Siapno, Jacqueline Aquino. *Gender, Islam, Nationalism, and the State in Aceh: The Paradox of Power, Co-optation, and Resistance.* New York, NY: RoutledgeCurzon, 2002.

Simatupang, G. R. L. L. "The Development of Dangdut and Its Meanings: A Study of Popular Music in Indonesia." PhD dissertation. Clayton: Monash University, 1996.

Spiller, Henry. *Focus: Gamelan Music of Indonesia.* New York, NY, and London: Routledge, 2008 (first published in 2004).

——. *Erotic Triangles: Sundanese Dance and Masculinity in West Java.* Chicago, IL: University of Chicago Press, 2010.

Stokes, Martin. "Ethnomusicology (IV): Contemporary Theoretical Issues." *New Grove Dictionary of Music and Musicians.* Ed. Stanley Sadie. Oxford: Oxford University Press, 2001.

Stumpf, Carl. "Lieder der Bellakula Indianer." *Vierteljahrschrift für Musikwissenschaft* 2 (1886): 405–26.

Subagio, Gunawan, ed. *Apa Itu Lagu Pop Daerah.* Bandung: Citra Aditya Bakti, 1989.

Sumarsam. "Inner Melody in Javanese Gamelan Music." *Asian Music* 7.1 (1975): 3–13.

——. *Gamelan: Cultural Interaction and Musical Development in Central Java.* Chicago, IL: University of Chicago Press, 1995.

——. "Music in Indonesian 'Historical' Films: Reading *Nopember 1828*." *Global Soundtracks: Worlds of Film Music*. Ed. Marc Slobin. Middletown, CT: Wesleyan University Press, 2008: 217–40.

Supanggah, Rahayu. "Campur Sari: A Reflection." *Asian Music* 34.2 (2003): 1–20.

Suryadi. "Minangkabau Commercial Cassettes and the Cultural Impact of the Recording Industry in West Sumatra." *Asian Music* 34.2 (Spring/Summer 2003): 51–89.

Susilo, Hardja. "Improvisation in Wayang Wong Panggung: Creativity within Cultural Constraints." *Yearbook for Traditional Music* 19 (1987): 1–11.

Sutton, R. Anderson. "Notes toward a Grammar of Variation in Javanese Gender Playing." *Ethnomusicology* 22.2 (1978): 275–96.

——. "Who is the Pesindhèn? Notes on the Female Singing Tradition in Java." *Indonesia* 37 (April 1984): 118–31.

——. *Traditions of Gamelan Music in Java: Musical Pluralism and Regional Identity*. Cambridge: Cambridge University Press, 1991.

——. *Variation in Central Javanese Gamelan Music: Dynamics of a Steady State*. Special Report No. 28. De Kalb, IL: Northern Illinois University Center for Southeast Asian Studies, 1993.

——. "Local, Global, or National? Popular Music on Indonesian Television." *Planet TV: A World Television Reader*. Ed. S. Kumar and L. Parks. New York, NY: New York University Press, 2003.

——. "Asia/Indonesia." *Worlds of Music: An Introduction to the Music of the World's Peoples*. Fifth ed. Ed. Jeff Todd Titon. New York, NY: Schirmer, 2008: 279–330.

Sutton, R. Anderson, and Roger R. Vetter. "Flexing the Frame in Javanese Gamelan Music." *Analytical Studies in World Music*. Ed. Michael Tenzer. New York, NY: Oxford University Press, 2006: 237–72.

Swindells, Rachel. "Klasik, Kawih, Kreasi: Musical Transformation and the Gamelan Degung of Bandung, West Java, Indonesia." PhD dissertation. London: City University, 2004.

Tenzer, Michael. *Gamelan Gong Kebyar: The Art of Twentieth Century Balinese Gamelan Music*. Chicago, IL: University of Chicago Press, 2000.

Titon, Jeff Todd. *Worlds of Music: An Introduction to the Music of the World's Peoples*. Fourth ed. Belmont, CA: Wadsworth/Thomson Learning, 2002.

Toth, Andrew. "Recordings of the Traditional Music of Bali and Lombok." Society for Ethnomusicology. Special Series no. 4, 1980.

Vetter, Roger. "Flexibility in the Performance Practice of Central Javanese Music." *Ethnomusicology* 25.2 (1981): 199–214.

——. "Poetic, Musical, and Dramatic Structures in a Langen Mandra Wanara Performance." *Aesthetic Tradition and Cultural Transition in Java and Bali*. Ed. Stephanie Morgan and Laurie Jo Sears. Madison, WI: University of Wisconsin Center for Southeast Asian Studies, 1984: 163–208.

Vitale, Wayne. "Balinese Kebyar Music Breaks the Five-Tone Barrier: New Composition for Seven-Tone Gamelan." *Perspectives of New Music* 40.1 (2002): 5–69.

Wallach, Jeremy. *Modern Noise, Fluid Genres: Popular Music in Indonesia, 1997–2001.* Madison, WI: University of Wisconsin Press, 2008.

Weintraub, Andrew N. "Instruments of Power: 'Multi-Laras' Gamelan in New Order Indonesia." *Ethnomusicology* 45.2 (2001): 197–227.

——. *Power Plays: Wayang Golek Puppet Theater of West Java.* Athens, OH: Ohio University, 2004.

——. "Dangdut Soul: Who Are 'the People' in Indonesian Popular Music?" *Asian Journal of Communication* 16.4 (2006): 411–31.

——. "'Dance Drills, Faith Spills': Islam, Body Politics, and Popular Music in Post-Suharto Indonesia." *Popular Music* 27.3 (2008): 367–92.

——. *Dangdut Stories: A Social and Musical History of Indonesia's Most Popular Music.* New York, NY: Oxford University Press, 2010.

Weintraub, Andrew N., ed. *Islam and Popular Culture in Indonesia and Malaysia.* London: Routledge, 2011

Weiss, Sarah. *Listening to an Earlier Java.* Verhandelingen 237. Leiden: KITLV Press, 2006.

Wichelen, Sonja van. "'My Dance Immoral? Alhamdulillah No!' Dangdut Music and Gender Politics in Contemporary Indonesia." *Resounding International Relations: On Music, Culture, and Politics.* Ed. M. I. Franklin. New York, NY: Palgrave Macmillan, 2005.

Williams, Sean. "Current Developments in Sundanese Popular Music." *Asian Music* 21.2 (1990): 105–36.

——. *The Sound of the Ancestral Ship: Highland Music of West Java.* New York, NY: Oxford University Press, 2001.

Yampolsky, Philip. *Lokananta: A Discography of the National Recording Company of Indonesia, 1957–1985.* Madison, WI: University of Wisconsin Center for Southeast Asian Studies, 1987.

——. "Hati Yang Luka: An Indonesian Hit." *Indonesia* 47 (April 1989): 1–17.

——. *Music of Indonesia.* Vol. 1–20. Washington, DC: Smithsonian/Folkways, 1991–99. SF 40055-7; SF 40420-9; SF 40441-7. Liner notes.

——. "Indonesian Popular Music: Kroncong, Dangdut, and Langgam Jawa." Liner Notes to Smithsonian/Folkways SF 40056, vol. 2. *Music of Indonesia* series. Ed. P. Yampolsky. Washington, DC: Smithsonian Folkways, 1991.

——. "Indonesia." Grove Music Online [www.oxfordmusiconline.com, July 9, 2013]. Parts I and III. New York, NY: Oxford University Press, 2007–10.

——. "Kroncong Revisited: New Evidence from Old Sources." *Archipel* 79 (2010): 7–56.

——. "Making the Music of Indonesia Series: a Memoir." *Ethnomusicological Encounters with Music and Musicians: Essays in Honor of Robert Garfias.* Ed. Timothy Rice. SOAS Musicology Series. Farnham, Surrey: Ashgate, 2011a: 155–79.

——. *Indonesia: Songs of Biboki (Western Timor)*. CD. VDE Gallo CD 1351. Recordings and commentary by Philip Yampolsky. (Archives Internationales de Musique Populaire, 102.) Geneva, Switzerland: Musée d'Ethnographie, 2011b.

Zanten, Wim van. *Sundanese Music in the Cianjuran Style: Anthropological and Musicological Aspects of Tembang Sunda*. Dordrecht: Foris, 1989.

CONTRIBUTORS

Edward Aspinall is a Professor in the Department of Political and Social Change, School of International, Political and Strategic Studies, College of Asia and the Pacific, Australian National University. He is the author of *Opposing Suharto: Compromise, Resistance, and Regime Change in Indonesia* (2005), and *Islam and Nation: Separatist Rebellion in Aceh, Indonesia* (2009).

Abigail C. Cohn is Professor in the Department of Linguistics and member of the Southeast Asia Program at Cornell University. Her research interests include the documentation of regional languages of Indonesia, supported most recently by a Fulbright Senior Research Fellowship to study the impact of the increased use of Indonesian as a factor in language shift.

Donald K. Emmerson heads the Southeast Asia Forum at Stanford University. His recent writings include "The Spectrum of Comparisons" for a proposed special issue of *Pacific Affairs* on Southeast Asian studies; "Kishore's World" (2013) and "Southeast Asia: Minding the Gap between Democracy and Governance" (2012) in the *Journal of Democracy*; and "Is Indonesia Rising?" in Anthony Reid, ed., *Indonesia Rising* (2012).

Joseph Errington is a professor in the Department of Anthropology at Yale University. He is the author of *Linguistics in a Colonial World: A Story of Language, Meaning, and Power* (2008), and "In Search of Middle Indonesian: Linguistic Dynamics in a Provincial Town." His current project is a book tentatively titled *Other Indonesians: Nationalism in an Un-Native Language*.

Kenneth M. George is Professor of Anthropology and Director of the School of Culture, History, and Language in the Australian National University's College of Asia and the Pacific. He is the author of *Picturing Islam: Art and Ethics in a Muslim Lifeworld* (2010) and past editor of the *Journal of Asian Studies* (2005–08).

Marty Hatch is Graduate School Professor at Cornell University, having retired from the Department of Music and Department of Asian Studies there in 2011. He is a member of the executive committee of the American Institute for Indonesian Studies (AIFIS) and the vice president of the board of Cornell Cooperative Extension of Tompkins County.

Tineke Hellwig is Associate Professor Emerita of Asian Studies at the University of British Columbia. Her research interests include Indonesian literature and culture, representations of women, and gender and sexuality studies. She is the author of *In the Shadow of Change* (1994), and *Women and Malay Voices: Undercurrent Murmurings in Indonesia's Colonial Past* (2012), and co-editor of *Asian Women: Interconnections* (2005) and *The Indonesia Reader: History, Culture Politics* (2009).

Bambang Kaswanti Purwo is professor in linguistics at Atma Jaya Catholic University, Jakarta, Indonesia. His research interests are syntax, pragmatics, and discourse. He is the author of *Kekhasan Bahasa Indonesia: Hasil Penelitian 1978–2012* [Indonesian Language Specifics] (2013).

R. William Liddle is emeritus professor of political science, Ohio State University. His current research includes book projects on Indonesian voting behavior and presidential leadership.

Kaja M. McGowan is Associate Professor in the History of Art at Cornell University, a social historian of South and Southeast Asian Art with emphasis on Indonesia, particularly Java and Bali. Her work is governed by the complex ways in which the History of Art and Visual Studies intersect with Anthropology, Material Culture, Colonial and Postcolonial Theory, Performance, Gender, and Religious Studies. Currently, in collaboration with Puri Lukisan Museum in Ubud, Bali, Indonesia, she is writing a biography on the Balinese artist and architect, I Gusti Nyoman Lempad, a founding member of Pita Maha, an artist cooperative established in the 1930s.

Christopher J. Miller is a Lecturer at Cornell University, where he directs the Cornell Gamelan Ensemble, and a PhD candidate in ethnomusicology at Wesleyan University, completing a dissertation on Indonesian *musik kontemporer*. In addition to his scholarship, he has composed numerous pieces for Javanese gamelan, and is active as a performer of traditional Javanese and experimental improvised musics.

E. Edwards McKinnon is retired after a career in development work and currently living in Java. He is a research associate with the Institute of Southeast Asian Studies, Nalanda-Srivijaya Project Archaeology Unit. He is the co-author with Abu Ridho of *The Pulau Buaya Wreck: Finds from the Song Period* (1998). His research interests include the pre-sultanate archaeology and history of Aceh, archaeological ceramics, and inter-regional mediaeval trade.

Rudolf Mrázek is Professor in the History Department of the University of Michigan. He is the author of *Sjahrir: Politics and Exile in Indonesia* (1994), *Engineers of Happy Land: Technology and Nationalism in a Colony* (2002), and *A Certain Age: Colonial Jakarta through the Memories of its Intellectuals* (2010).

Jolanda Pandin is a Senior Lecturer in Indonesian Language in the Department of Asian Studies at Cornell University. As an active member of the Consortium for the Teaching of Indonesian, she has worked as its oral proficiency assessment evaluator for its summer programs and developed an Indonesian standardized curriculum and Web-based reading materials. She collaboratively promotes Indonesian language through the bilingual annual Northeast Conference on Indonesia sponsored by Cornell and Yale.

Thomas Pepinsky is Associate Professor of Government and Associate Director of the Modern Indonesia Project at Cornell University. He is the author of *Economic Crises and the Breakdown of Authoritarian Regimes: Indonesia and Malaysia in Comparative Perspective* (2009).

Marc Perlman is Associate Professor of Music at Brown University. His scholarly writings have appeared in the journals *Ethnomusicology, Asian Music, Musical Quarterly, Postmodern Culture, Music Perception, Indonesia, Social Studies of Science*, and the revised edition of the *New Grove Dictionary of Music and Musicians*.

Bambang Kaswanti Purwo is professor in linguistics at Atma Jaya Catholic University, Jakarta, Indonesia. His research interests are syntax, pragmatics, and discourse. His latest book is *Kekhasan Bahasa Indonesia: Hasil Penelitian 1978–2012* (2013).

Natasha Reichle is Associate Curator of Southeast Asian Art at the Asian Art Museum in San Francisco. Her publications include *Bali: Art, Ritual, Performance* (2011) and *Violence and Serenity: Late Buddhist Sculpture from Indonesia* (2007).

Danilyn Rutherford is a Professor in the Anthropology Department of the University of California, Santa Cruz. She is the author of *Raiding the Land of the Foreigners: The Limits of the Nation on an Indonesian Frontier* (2002) and *Laughing at Leviathan: Sovereignty and Audience in West Papua* (2012). She's currently completing a book on sympathy, technology, and colonial state-building in the highlands of Dutch New Guinea.

Laurie J. Sears is Professor of History at the University of Washington in Seattle. Her most recent book is *Situated Testimonies: Dread and Enchantment in an Indonesian Literary Archive* (2013), and her most recent edited volume is *Knowing Southeast Asian Subjects* (2007). She teaches Indonesian histories and literatures as well as feminist and postcolonial theories.

Patricia Spyer is Chair of Cultural Anthropology of Contemporary Indonesia at Leiden University and was Global Distinguished Professor at New York University's Center for Religion and Media and Department of Anthropology from 2009–12. She is the author of *The Memory of Trade: Modernity's Entanglements on an Eastern Indonesian Island* (2000), editor of *Border Fetishisms: Material Objects in Unstable Spaces* (1997), co-editor of the *Handbook of Material Culture* (2006), and of *Images That Move* (2013). Her current book project, *Orphaned Landscapes: Violence, Visuality, and the Work of Appearances in Post-Suharto Indonesia*, focuses on the mediations of violence and postviolence in the religiously inflected conflict in the Moluccas, Indonesia.

Sumarsam is a Professor of Music at Wesleyan University. He is the author of *Gamelan: Cultural Interaction and Musical Development in Central Java* (1995), and *Javanese Music and the West* (2013). As a gamelan musician and a keen amateur puppeteer (*dhalang*), he performs, conducts workshops, and lectures throughout the world.

Eric Tagliacozzo is Professor of History at Cornell University. He is the author of *The Longest Journey: Southeast Asians and the Pilgrimage to Mecca* (2013) and *Secret Trades, Porous Borders: Smuggling and States Along a Southeast Asian Frontier* (2005). He is also editor of four other books, and has served as Director of the Cornell Modern

Indonesia Project, of the Comparative Muslim Societies Program, and as editor of the journal *Indonesia*.

Jean Gelman Taylor taught Southeast Asian History at the University of New South Wales between 1992 and 2011. She is the author of *The Social World of Batavia: European and Eurasian in Colonial Indonesia* (1983, second ed. 2009), *Indonesia: Peoples and Histories* (2003), *Global Indonesia* (2013), co-author of *The Emergence of Modern Southeast Asia* (2005), and co-editor of *Culture and Cleanliness: Histories from Indonesia* (2011).

Andrew N. Weintraub is Professor of Music at the University of Pittsburgh, where he teaches graduate and undergraduate courses in ethnomusicology and popular music and directs the University Gamelan program. He is the author of *Power Plays* (2004) and *Dangdut Stories* (2010), editor of *Islam and Popular Culture in Indonesia and Malaysia* (2011), and co-editor of *Music and Cultural Rights* (2008).

Marina Welker is an Assistant Professor in the Anthropology Department at Cornell University. She has published articles in *American Ethnologist, Cultural Anthropology,* and *Current Anthropology,* and is the author of *Enacting the Corporation: An American Mining Firm in Post-Authoritarian Indonesia* (University of California Press, 2014).

Astri Wright is Professor of Southeast Asian Art History in the Department of History in Art at the University of Victoria, Canada. Her book, *Soul, Spirit and Mountain: Preoccupations of Contemporary Indonesian Painters* (1994) offered the first full-length analytical survey of Indonesian art since Claire Holt's important work (1967). The survey was based on case studies of the multiple locally and globally informed modern streams of Indonesian art. Besides English-language academic essays, Wright has published extensively in bilingual (Bahasa and English) publications.

SOUTHEAST ASIA PROGRAM PUBLICATIONS
Cornell University

Studies on Southeast Asia

Number 62   *Ties that Bind: Cultural Identity, Class, and Law in Vietnam's Labor Resistance,* Trần Ngọc Angie. 2013. ISBN 978-0-87727-762-0 (pb.)

Number 61   *A Mountain of Difference: The Lumad in Early Colonial Mindanao,* Oona Paredes. 2013. ISBN 978-0-87727-761-3 (pb.)

Number 60   *The* Kim Vân Kieu *of Nguyen Du (1765–1820),* trans. Vladislav Zhukov. 2013. ISBN 978-0-87727-760-6 (pb.)

Number 59   *The Politics of Timor-Leste: Democratic Consolidation after Intervention,* ed. Michael Leach and Damien Kingsbury. 2013. ISBN 978-0-87727-759-0 (pb.)

Number 58   *The Spirit of Things: Materiality and Religious Diversity in Southeast Asia,* ed. Julius Bautista. 2012. ISBN 970-0-87727-758-3 (pb.)

Number 57   *Demographic Change in Southeast Asia: Recent Histories and Future Directions,* ed. Lindy Williams and Michael Philip Guest. 2012. ISBN 978-0-87727-757-6 (pb.)

Number 56   *Modern and Contemporary Southeast Asian Art: An Anthology,* ed. Nora A. Taylor and Boreth Ly. 2012. ISBN 978-0-87727-756-9 (pb.)

Number 55   *Glimpses of Freedom: Independent Cinema in Southeast Asia,* ed. May Adadol Ingawanij and Benjamin McKay. 2012. ISBN 978-0-87727-755-2 (pb.)

Number 54   *Student Activism in Malaysia: Crucible, Mirror, Sideshow,* Meredith L. Weiss. 2011. ISBN 978-0-87727-754-5 (pb.)

Number 53   *Political Authority and Provincial Identity in Thailand: The Making of Banharn-buri,* Yoshinori Nishizaki. 2011. ISBN 978-0-87727-753-8 (pb.)

Number 52   *Vietnam and the West: New Approaches,* ed. Wynn Wilcox. 2010. ISBN 978-0-87727-752-1 (pb.)

Number 51   *Cultures at War: The Cold War and Cultural Expression in Southeast Asia,* ed. Tony Day and Maya H. T. Liem. 2010. ISBN 978-0-87727-751-4 (pb.)

Number 50   *State of Authority: The State in Society in Indonesia,* ed. Gerry van Klinken and Joshua Barker. 2009. ISBN 978-0-87727-750-7 (pb.)

Number 49   *Phan Châu Trinh and His Political Writings,* Phan Châu Trinh, ed. and trans. Vinh Sinh. 2009. ISBN 978-0-87727-749-1 (pb.)

Number 48   *Dependent Communities: Aid and Politics in Cambodia and East Timor,* Caroline Hughes. 2009. ISBN 978-0-87727-748-4 (pb.)

Number 47   *A Man Like Him: Portrait of the Burmese Journalist, Journal Kyaw U Chit Maung,* Journal Kyaw Ma Ma Lay, trans. Ma Thanegi, 2008. ISBN 978-0-87727-747-7 (pb.)

Number 46   *At the Edge of the Forest: Essays on Cambodia, History, and Narrative in Honor of David Chandler,* ed. Anne Ruth Hansen and Judy Ledgerwood. 2008. ISBN 978-0-87727-746-0 (pb).

Number 45   *Conflict, Violence, and Displacement in Indonesia,* ed. Eva-Lotta E. Hedman. 2008. ISBN 978-0-87727-745-3 (pb).

Number 44 *Friends and Exiles: A Memoir of the Nutmeg Isles and the Indonesian Nationalist Movement*, Des Alwi, ed. Barbara S. Harvey. 2008. ISBN 978-0-877277-44-6 (pb).

Number 43 *Early Southeast Asia: Selected Essays*, O. W. Wolters, ed. Craig J. Reynolds. 2008. 255 pp. ISBN 978-0-877277-43-9 (pb).

Number 42 *Thailand: The Politics of Despotic Paternalism* (revised edition), Thak Chaloemtiarana. 2007. 284 pp. ISBN 0-8772-7742-7 (pb).

Number 41 *Views of Seventeenth-Century Vietnam: Christoforo Borri on Cochinchina and Samuel Baron on Tonkin*, ed. Olga Dror and K. W. Taylor. 2006. 290 pp. ISBN 0-8772-7741-9 (pb).

Number 40 *Laskar Jihad: Islam, Militancy, and the Quest for Identity in Post-New Order Indonesia*, Noorhaidi Hasan. 2006. 266 pp. ISBN 0-877277-40-0 (pb).

Number 39 *The Indonesian Supreme Court: A Study of Institutional Collapse*, Sebastiaan Pompe. 2005. 494 pp. ISBN 0-877277-38-9 (pb).

Number 38 *Spirited Politics: Religion and Public Life in Contemporary Southeast Asia*, ed. Andrew C. Willford and Kenneth M. George. 2005. 210 pp. ISBN 0-87727-737-0.

Number 37 *Sumatran Sultanate and Colonial State: Jambi and the Rise of Dutch Imperialism, 1830-1907*, Elsbeth Locher-Scholten, trans. Beverley Jackson. 2004. 332 pp. ISBN 0-87727-736-2.

Number 36 *Southeast Asia over Three Generations: Essays Presented to Benedict R. O'G. Anderson*, ed. James T. Siegel and Audrey R. Kahin. 2003. 398 pp. ISBN 0-87727-735-4.

Number 35 *Nationalism and Revolution in Indonesia*, George McTurnan Kahin, intro. Benedict R. O'G. Anderson (reprinted from 1952 edition, Cornell University Press, with permission). 2003. 530 pp. ISBN 0-87727-734-6.

Number 34 *Golddiggers, Farmers, and Traders in the "Chinese Districts" of West Kalimantan, Indonesia*, Mary Somers Heidhues. 2003. 316 pp. ISBN 0-87727-733-8.

Number 33 *Opusculum de Sectis apud Sinenses et Tunkinenses (A Small Treatise on the Sects among the Chinese and Tonkinese): A Study of Religion in China and North Vietnam in the Eighteenth Century*, Father Adriano de St. Thecla, trans. Olga Dror, with Mariya Berezovska. 2002. 363 pp. ISBN 0-87727-732-X.

Number 32 *Fear and Sanctuary: Burmese Refugees in Thailand*, Hazel J. Lang. 2002. 204 pp. ISBN 0-87727-731-1.

Number 31 *Modern Dreams: An Inquiry into Power, Cultural Production, and the Cityscape in Contemporary Urban Penang, Malaysia*, Beng-Lan Goh. 2002. 225 pp. ISBN 0-87727-730-3.

Number 30 *Violence and the State in Suharto's Indonesia*, ed. Benedict R. O'G. Anderson. 2001. Second printing, 2002. 247 pp. ISBN 0-87727-729-X.

Number 29 *Studies in Southeast Asian Art: Essays in Honor of Stanley J. O'Connor*, ed. Nora A. Taylor. 2000. 243 pp. Illustrations. ISBN 0-87727-728-1.

Number 28 *The Hadrami Awakening: Community and Identity in the Netherlands East Indies, 1900-1942*, Natalie Mobini-Kesheh. 1999. 174 pp. ISBN 0-87727-727-3.

Number 7   *A Malay Frontier: Unity and Duality in a Sumatran Kingdom,* Jane
            Drakard. 1990. 2nd printing 2003. 215 pp. ISBN 0-87727-706-0.

Number 6   *Trends in Khmer Art,* Jean Boisselier, ed. Natasha Eilenberg, trans.
            Natasha Eilenberg, Melvin Elliott. 1989. 124 pp., 24 plates.
            ISBN 0-87727-705-2.

Number 5   *Southeast Asian Ephemeris: Solar and Planetary Positions, A.D. 638–2000,*
            J. C. Eade. 1989. 175 pp. ISBN 0-87727-704-4.

Number 3   *Thai Radical Discourse: The Real Face of Thai Feudalism Today,* Craig J.
            Reynolds. 1987. 2nd printing 1994. 186 pp. ISBN 0-87727-702-8.

Number 1   *The Symbolism of the Stupa,* Adrian Snodgrass. 1985. Revised with
            index, 1988. 3rd printing 1998. 469 pp. ISBN 0-87727-700-1.

SEAP Series

Number 23   *Possessed by the Spirits: Mediumship in Contemporary Vietnamese
            Communities.* 2006. 186 pp. ISBN 0-877271-41-0 (pb).

Number 22   *The Industry of Marrying Europeans,* Vũ Trọng Phụng, trans. Thúy
            Tranviet. 2006. 66 pp. ISBN 0-877271-40-2 (pb).

Number 21   *Securing a Place: Small-Scale Artisans in Modern Indonesia,* Elizabeth
            Morrell. 2005. 220 pp. ISBN 0-877271-39-9.

Number 20   *Southern Vietnam under the Reign of Minh Mạng (1820-1841): Central
            Policies and Local Response,* Choi Byung Wook. 2004. 226pp. ISBN 0-0-
            877271-40-2.

Number 19   *Gender, Household, State: Đổi Mới in Việt Nam,* ed. Jayne Werner and
            Danièle Bélanger. 2002. 151 pp. ISBN 0-87727-137-2.

Number 18   *Culture and Power in Traditional Siamese Government,* Neil A. Englehart.
            2001. 130 pp. ISBN 0-87727-135-6.

Number 17   *Gangsters, Democracy, and the State,* ed. Carl A. Trocki. 1998. Second
            printing, 2002. 94 pp. ISBN 0-87727-134-8.

Number 16   *Cutting across the Lands: An Annotated Bibliography on Natural Resource
            Management and Community Development in Indonesia, the Philippines,
            and Malaysia,* ed. Eveline Ferretti. 1997. 329 pp. ISBN 0-87727-133-X.

Number 15   *The Revolution Falters: The Left in Philippine Politics after 1986,* ed.
            Patricio N. Abinales. 1996. Second printing, 2002. 182 pp. ISBN 0-
            87727-132-1.

Number 14   *Being Kammu: My Village, My Life,* Damrong Tayanin. 1994. 138 pp., 22
            tables, illus., maps. ISBN 0-87727-130-5.

Number 13   *The American War in Vietnam,* ed. Jayne Werner, David Hunt. 1993.
            132 pp. ISBN 0-87727-131-3.

Number 12   *The Voice of Young Burma,* Aye Kyaw. 1993. 92 pp. ISBN 0-87727-129-1.

Number 11   *The Political Legacy of Aung San,* ed. Josef Silverstein. Revised edition
            1993. 169 pp. ISBN 0-87727-128-3.

Number 10   *Studies on Vietnamese Language and Literature: A Preliminary
            Bibliography,* Nguyen Dinh Tham. 1992. 227 pp. ISBN 0-87727-127-5.

Number 8   *From PKI to the Comintern, 1924–1941: The Apprenticeship of the Malayan
            Communist Party,* Cheah Boon Kheng. 1992. 147 pp. ISBN 0-87727-125-9.

Number 7   *Intellectual Property and US Relations with Indonesia, Malaysia, Singapore, and Thailand*, Elisabeth Uphoff. 1991. 67 pp. ISBN 0-87727-124-0.

Number 6   *The Rise and Fall of the Communist Party of Burma (CPB)*, Bertil Lintner. 1990. 124 pp. 26 illus., 14 maps. ISBN 0-87727-123-2.

Number 5   *Japanese Relations with Vietnam: 1951–1987*, Masaya Shiraishi. 1990. 174 pp. ISBN 0-87727-122-4.

Number 3   *Postwar Vietnam: Dilemmas in Socialist Development*, ed. Christine White, David Marr. 1988. 2nd printing 1993. 260 pp. ISBN 0-87727-120-8.

Number 2   *The Dobama Movement in Burma (1930–1938)*, Khin Yi. 1988. 160 pp. ISBN 0-87727-118-6.

Cornell Modern Indonesia Project Publications

Number 76   *Producing Indonesia: The State of the Field of Indonesian Studies*, ed. Eric Tagliacozzo. 2014. ISBN 978-0-87727-302-8 (pb.)

All Following CMIP titles available at http://cmip.library.cornell.edu

Number 75   *A Tour of Duty: Changing Patterns of Military Politics in Indonesia in the 1990s.* Douglas Kammen and Siddharth Chandra. 1999. 99 pp. ISBN 0-87763-049-6.

Number 74   *The Roots of Acehnese Rebellion 1989–1992*, Tim Kell. 1995. 103 pp. ISBN 0-87763-040-2.

Number 72   *Popular Indonesian Literature of the Qur'an*, Howard M. Federspiel. 1994. 170 pp. ISBN 0-87763-038-0.

Number 71   *A Javanese Memoir of Sumatra, 1945–1946: Love and Hatred in the Liberation War*, Takao Fusayama. 1993. 150 pp. ISBN 0-87763-037-2.

Number 69   *The Road to Madiun: The Indonesian Communist Uprising of 1948*, Elizabeth Ann Swift. 1989. 120 pp. ISBN 0-87763-035-6.

Number 68   *Intellectuals and Nationalism in Indonesia: A Study of the Following Recruited by Sutan Sjahrir in Occupation Jakarta*, J. D. Legge. 1988. 159 pp. ISBN 0-87763-034-8.

Number 67   *Indonesia Free: A Biography of Mohammad Hatta*, Mavis Rose. 1987. 252 pp. ISBN 0-87763-033-X.

Number 66   *Prisoners at Kota Cane*, Leon Salim, trans. Audrey Kahin. 1986. 112 pp. ISBN 0-87763-032-1.

Number 64   *Suharto and His Generals: Indonesia's Military Politics, 1975–1983*, David Jenkins. 1984. 4th printing 1997. 300 pp. ISBN 0-87763-030-5.

Number 62   *Interpreting Indonesian Politics: Thirteen Contributions to the Debate, 1964–1981*, ed. Benedict Anderson, Audrey Kahin, intro. Daniel S. Lev. 1982. 3rd printing 1991. 172 pp. ISBN 0-87763-028-3.

Number 60   *The Minangkabau Response to Dutch Colonial Rule in the Nineteenth Century*, Elizabeth E. Graves. 1981. 157 pp. ISBN 0-87763-000-3.

Number 57   *Permesta: Half a Rebellion*, Barbara S. Harvey. 1977. 174 pp. ISBN 0-87763-003-8.

Number 52 *A Preliminary Analysis of the October 1 1965, Coup in Indonesia (Prepared in January 1966)*, Benedict R. Anderson, Ruth T. McVey, assist. Frederick P. Bunnell. 1971. 3rd printing 1990. 174 pp. ISBN 0-87763-008-9.

Number 48 *Nationalism, Islam and Marxism*, Soekarno, intro. Ruth T. McVey. 1970.

Number 37 *Mythology and the Tolerance of the Javanese*, Benedict R. O'G. Anderson. 2nd edition, 1996. Reprinted 2004. 104 pp., 65 illus. ISBN 0-87763-041-0.

Copublished Titles

The Ambiguous Allure of the West: Traces of the Colonial in Thailand, ed. Rachel V. Harrison and Peter A. Jackson. Copublished with Hong Kong University Press. 2010. ISBN 978-0-87727-608-1 (pb.)

The Many Ways of Being Muslim: Fiction by Muslim Filipinos, ed. Coeli Barry. Copublished with Anvil Publishing, Inc., the Philippines. 2008. ISBN 978-0-87727-605-0 (pb.)

Language Texts

INDONESIAN

Beginning Indonesian through Self-Instruction, John U. Wolff, Dédé Oetomo, Daniel Fietkiewicz. 3rd revised edition 1992. Vol. 1. 115 pp. ISBN 0-87727-529-7. Vol. 2. 434 pp. ISBN 0-87727-530-0. Vol. 3. 473 pp. ISBN 0-87727-531-9.

Indonesian Readings, John U. Wolff. 1978. 4th printing 1992. 480 pp. ISBN 0-87727-517-3

Indonesian Conversations, John U. Wolff. 1978. 3rd printing 1991. 297 pp. ISBN 0-87727-516-5

Formal Indonesian, John U. Wolff. 2nd revised edition 1986. 446 pp. ISBN 0-87727-515-7

TAGALOG

Pilipino through Self-Instruction, John U. Wolff, Maria Theresa C. Centeno, Der-Hwa V. Rau. 1991. Vol. 1. 342 pp. ISBN 0-87727—525-4. Vol. 2., revised 2005, 378 pp. ISBN 0-87727-526-2. Vol 3., revised 2005, 431 pp. ISBN 0-87727-527-0. Vol. 4. 306 pp. ISBN 0-87727-528-9.

THAI

A. U. A. Language Center Thai Course, J. Marvin Brown. Originally published by the American University Alumni Association Language Center, 1974. Reissued by Cornell Southeast Asia Program, 1991, 1992. Book 1. 267 pp. ISBN 0-87727-506-8. Book 2. 288 pp. ISBN 0-87727-507-6. Book 3. 247 pp. ISBN 0-87727-508-4.

A. U. A. Language Center Thai Course, Reading and Writing Text (mostly reading), 1979. Reissued 1997. 164 pp. ISBN 0-87727-511-4.

A. U. A. Language Center Thai Course, Reading and Writing Workbook (mostly writing), 1979. Reissued 1997. 99 pp. ISBN 0-87727-512-2.

KHMER

Cambodian System of Writing and Beginning Reader, Franklin E. Huffman. Originally published by Yale University Press, 1970. Reissued by Cornell Southeast Asia Program, 4th printing 2002. 365 pp. ISBN 0-300-01314-0.

Modern Spoken Cambodian, Franklin E. Huffman, assist. Charan Promchan, Chhom-Rak Thong Lambert. Originally published by Yale University Press, 1970. Reissued by Cornell Southeast Asia Program, 3rd printing 1991. 451 pp. ISBN 0-300-01316-7.

Intermediate Cambodian Reader, ed. Franklin E. Huffman, assist. Im Proum. Originally published by Yale University Press, 1972. Reissued by Cornell Southeast Asia Program, 1988. 499 pp. ISBN 0-300-01552-6.

Cambodian Literary Reader and Glossary, Franklin E. Huffman, Im Proum. Originally published by Yale University Press, 1977. Reissued by Cornell Southeast Asia Program, 1988. 494 pp. ISBN 0-300-02069-4.

HMONG

White Hmong-English Dictionary, Ernest E. Heimbach. 1969. 8th printing, 2002. 523 pp. ISBN 0-87727-075-9.

VIETNAMESE

Intermediate Spoken Vietnamese, Franklin E. Huffman, Tran Trong Hai. 1980. 3rd printing 1994. ISBN 0-87727-500-9.

Proto-Austronesian Phonology with Glossary, John U. Wolff, 2 volumes, 2011. ISBN vol. I, 978-0-87727-532-9. ISBN vol. II, 978-0-87727-533-6.

To order, please contact:
Mail:
Cornell University Press Services
750 Cascadilla Street
PO Box 6525
Ithaca, NY 14851 USA

E-mail: orderbook@cupserv.org

Phone/Fax, Monday–Friday, 8 am – 5 pm (Eastern US):
Phone: 607 277 2211 or 800 666 2211 (US, Canada)
Fax: 607 277 6292 or 800 688 2877 (US, Canada)

Order through our online bookstore at:
www.einaudi.cornell.edu/southeastasia/publications/

www.ingramcontent.com/pod-product-compliance
Lightning Source LLC
Chambersburg PA
CBHW081734270326
41932CB00020B/3271